INTRODUCTION TO COMPUTERS AND INFORMATION SYSTEMS

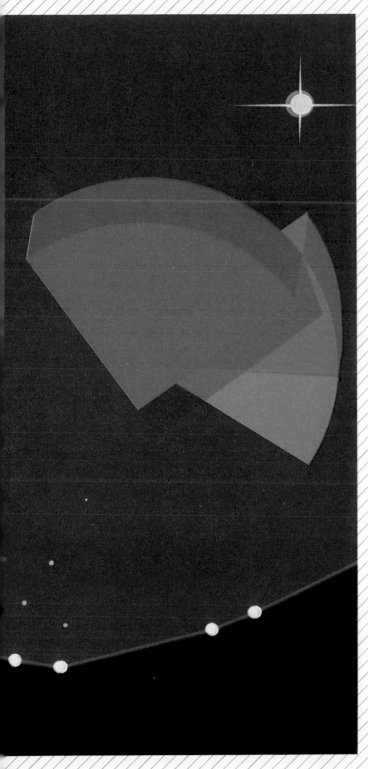

INTRODUCTION TO COMPUTERS AND INFORMATION SYSTEMS

ROBERT A. SZYMANSKI

DONALD P. SZYMANSKI

NORMA A. MORRIS

DONNA M. PULSCHEN

Merrill Publishing Company
A Bell & Howell Information Company
Columbus Toronto London Melbourne

Cover Art: Design by Cathy Watterson; computer-generated art by ICOM, Inc., Columbus, Ohio

Published by
Merrill Publishing Company
A Bell & Howell Information Company
Columbus, Ohio 43216

This book was set in Meridien and Univers.

Administrative Editor: Vernon R. Anthony
Developmental Editors: Pamela Kusma,
William Lindsey, Dwayne Martin,
and Penelope Semrau
Production Editor: Constantina Geldis
Art Coordinator: Peter Robison
Cover Designer: Cathy Watterson
Text Designer: Cynthia Brunk

Library of Congress Catalog Card Number: 87-61715
International Standard Book Number: 0-675-20768-1
Printed in the United States of America
1 2 3 4 5 6 7 8 9 — 92 91 90 89 88

All photographs without specific credits following their
captions are by Merrill Publishing/Cobalt Productions.

Part opening quotations: Part One (p. 1), Asimov,
Isaac. "Asimov Ponders PCs." *PC World.* (September
1985): 190. Part Two (p. 139), Diebold, John.
"Rethinking Automation." *Computerworld.* (3
November 1986): 124. Part Three (p. 227), Ritchie,
David. *The Binary Brain: Artificial Intelligence in the Age
of Electronics.* (Boston: Little, Brown, & Co., 1984):
196. Part Four (p. 345), Case, John. *Digital Future:
The Personal Computer Explosion—Why It's Happening
and What It Means.* (New York: William Morrow &
Co., 1985): 177. Part Five (p. 491), Kurzweil,
Raymond. "The Second Industrial Revolution."
Computerworld. (3 November 1986): 58.

All screen representations of software are used with
permission of their respective copyright owners:
MultiMate®, MultiMate Advantage™, and MultiMate
Advantage II™ are copyright © Ashton-Tate
Corporation, 1987. MultiMate Advantage and
MultiMate Advantage II are trademarks, and
MultiMate is a registered trademark of Ashton-Tate
Corporation, Torrance, California; SideKick by Borland
International, Inc., Scotts Valley, California; PC-TALK
III by The Headlands Press, Tiburon, California; The
Twin Spreadsheet by Mosaic Software, Inc.,
Cambridge, Massachusetts; Open Access II by
Software Products International, Inc., San Diego,
California; PFS:First Choice by Software Publishers
Corporation, Mt. View, California; WordPerfect by
WordPerfect Corporation, Orem, Utah; Commodore
Educational by Commodore Computer Systems
Division, West Chester, Pennsylvania; MultiPlan by
Microsoft Corporation, Redmond, Washington; and
Apple Desktop Publishing by Apple Computer, Inc.,
Coopertino, California. Apple, McIntosh, and
LaserWriter are trademarks of Apple Computer, Inc.

Part opening credits: pp. xxxii–1, Courtesy of Roman
Kuchkuda, Megatek Corp.; pp. 138–139, Copyright ©
Robert L. Bowers, Jr., Advanced Computing Center
for Art and Design, The Ohio State University; pp.
226–227, Copyright © Merrill Publishing/Graphic
generated by ICOM, Inc.; pp. 344–345, Courtesy BTS,
Ms. Susan Crouse-Kemp; and pp. 490–491, Courtesy
of David Kurlander, Columbia University.

Chapter opening credits (left to right across chapter
opening spread): Chapter 1, Courtesy of Inmos 1986,
Image produced by an Array of Inmos transputers
programmed in OCCAM. OCCAM and IMS are
trademarks of the Inmos group of companies;
Courtesy of BTS, Mr. Kelly Daniels; and Courtesy of
George Tsakas, Intelligent Light, Inc. Chapter 2,
Courtesy of Jerry Weil, AT&T Bell Laboratories;
"Depth of Feel" by Jim Dixon, Pacific Data Images,
1986; and "Enchanted Mesa," courtesy of Peter
Watterberg, Savannah River Lab. A ray traced image
of a stochastically generated terrain model. Chapter 3,
Courtesy of G. D. Searle and Co.; Copyright © David
Laidlaw, Barb Meier; and Mapped by Dr. Michael
Rossmann and team at Purdue University/Evans and
Sutherland. Model of one unit from surface of cold
virus Rhinovirus-14. Chapter 4, Courtesy of Intergraph
Corp.; Merrill Publishing/Image generated by ICOM,
Inc.; and Merrill Publishing/Image generated by
ICOM, Inc. Chapter 5, Courtesy of Michael F. Cohen
and Philip J. Brock, Cornell University Program of

Computer Graphics; Visual provided Courtesy of Cromatics, Inc.; and Courtesy of Xerox Corp., Palo Alto Research Center. Chapter 6, Courtesy of Evans and Sutherland; Courtesy of Megatek Corp.; and Reprinted with permission from Calma Co., a wholly owned subsidiary of the General Electric Co., U.S.A. Chapter 7, Filene #2, courtesy of David Breen, RPI CICG Animation Group, Software: The Clockworks. Hardware: DG MV/10000, E & S PS300, RTI Model 1/20, Dunn Instruments Camera 635; Courtesy of BTS— Ms. Carol Moy and Mr. Kelly Daniels; and Visual provided courtesy of Cromatics, Inc. Chapter 8, Courtesy of Los Alamos National Laboratory, Melvin L. Prueitt; Courtesy Matrix Instruments, Sara Darroch; and Courtesy of Los Alamos National Laboratory, Melvin L. Prueitt. Chapter 9, Courtesy ICOM, Inc.; Courtesy of Apollo Computer, Inc.; and Courtesy of David Laidlaw, Husane Kogak. Chapter 10, Courtesy Megatek Corp.; Courtesy ICOM, Inc.; and Courtesy of Los Alamos National Laboratory. Chapter 11, Courtesy of Scholastic Software, a Division of Scholastic, Inc.; Courtesy of Caltec University and Evans & Sutherland; and Courtesy of David Breen, RPI CICG Animation Group, modeled by Randy Bradley on a Data General MV 10000 using raster technology/Evans & Sutherland and Dunn Instruments, Software: The Clockworks. Chapter 12, Courtesy of G. D. Searle & Co.; Courtesy of Jeanne Mara, Intelligent Light, Inc.; and Courtesy of Hansen Disease Center, Louisiana State University, Kinematics Study/Evans & Sutherland. Chapter 13, Copyright Vibeke Sorensen; Courtesy of Micro Control Systems; and Courtesy of Jerry Weil, AT&T Bell Laboratories. Chapter 14, IC layout courtesy of Calma Co., a wholly owned subsidiary of General Electric Co., U.S.A.; Perspective at the McDonnell Douglas ISG Campus in the Building Design Systems, courtesy McDonnell Douglas Information Systems Group; and Electronic design using CADD, courtesy of Calma Co., a wholly owned subsidiary of General Electric Co., U.S.A. Chapter 15, Merrill Publishing/Image generated by ICOM, Inc.; Melvin L. Prueitt, Los Alamos National Laboratory; and Merrill Publishing/Image generated by ICOM, Inc. Chapter 16, Courtesy of Cromatics CX; R. G. Belie—Rockwell International, copyright 1986; and Courtesy of Los Alamos National Laboratory. Chapter 17, Courtesy of Roman Kuchkuda, Megatek Corp.; Copyright Robert L. Bowers, Jr., Advanced Computing Center for Art and Design, The Ohio State University; and Courtesy of Cromatics, Inc. Chapter 18, Copyright Robert L. Bowers, Jr., Advanced Computing Center for Art and Design, The Ohio State University.

To Laura for her love and support, and to my loving parents

R. A. S.

To Sue, Paul, Stacy, and Michael for being patient and for being there

D. P. S.

To Edward, Erin, Jason, and Rachel who lovingly encouraged and supported me throughout the project

N. A. M.

To family and friends for their love, encouragement, and understanding— especially Chip

D. M. P.

- **Glossary,** at the end of the book, contains all the alphabetized and defined key terms and serves as a handy reference.
- **Index** supplies a detailed guide to text and InfoModule topics. The number of the page on which a key term is defined is boldfaced.

Finally, full-color, functional illustrations and over 300 photographs clarify concepts, depict applications, and show equipment. Sixty-five of these full-color photographs are interspersed throughout the book to illustrate some fascinating ways computers and microprocessors are used, such as scuba diving safety (p. 49), offshore oil exploration (p. 147), tracking drifting icebergs (p. 273), choreographing dancers' moves (p. 351), pooling data about zoo animals (p. 403), and designing the hull of the 1987 America's Cup winner Stars and Stripes (p. 469).

Coverage

Comprehensive coverage of topics in the text includes several chapters on hardware, software, information systems, application software, and social concerns and trends. Basic concepts and how those concepts are integrated into work situations, personal business, school activities, and leisure-time activities are also discussed.

Because microcomputers are the ones that are the easiest to use and because most people (many of whom never become involved with larger systems) will encounter them in their daily lives, we have included significant coverage of microcomputers throughout the text. In addition, Chapter 6 is completely devoted to the topic.

Expandability/Flexibility

Perhaps the most unique feature of this text is the inclusion of the subchapters called InfoModules. These subchapters enable instructors to modify their courses by expanding or deleting according to time constraints and individual preference. The InfoModules include succinct, but significant, coverage of additional topics, such as computer evolution, number systems, computers in design and manufacturing, computers in business, expert systems, legislation, and electronic networks. Key terms, if any, and review questions are also included so the material can be treated as separate chapters. If preferred, the material can be assigned as outside reading.

Organization

The text is divided into five logical parts. Part One (Chapters 1 through 4) provides an overview of computers and computing. Part Two (Chapters 5 through 7) describes computer systems, and Part Three (Chapters 8 through 11) explains information systems and programming concepts. Part Four (Chapters 12 through 16) describes popular application packages, while Part Five (Chapters 17 and 18) discusses social concerns and trends. Here is a quick look at the topics discussed in each chapter and InfoModule:

Preface

B ased on the premise that information is essential to survival and that computers are essential to the best use of information, this book explains how computers and information systems work, where they work, and how they affect society's physical, political, and ethical environment. It is a reflection of our commitment to students and their need to prepare for the demands of the Information Age. Whether a student wishes simply to understand the use of computers and the role they play in today's world, to work with computers to manage information in his or her own life, or to design information systems, this text offers a comprehensive, up-to-date look at computers and their considerable impact.

Computers in Preparation of This Text

The existence of this textbook confirms the relevance and importance of the new technologies of the Information Age. From the contract negotiation stage when the publishing company ran computer budgeting and production analyses, to the drafting, revising, and typesetting of the manuscript, the computer was a team member in creating the finished product and presenting it in a way that is pleasing to the reader.

The image on the cover was created using state-of-the-art computer graphics equipment, and computer-generated graphics appear on all of the part and chapter openings. Computers even enhanced the color in many photographs and slides.

The manuscript was prepared using microcomputer and word processing software. It was then sent on floppy diskette to the editor for the copyediting stage. After the necessary changes were made, the manuscript was transmitted electronically through telephone lines to a compositor's larger computers and typesetting equipment located in another state. There, exact margins were set and text lines were justified; then the text was retransmitted electronically to the publisher for further corrections. Final composition of the pages was executed on computer; then pages were printed out for editorial review. Final film was sent to the printer, and computer-controlled presses produced the finished book.

While computers played an important role in the preparation of this text, so did a talented group of publishing professionals. Computers and people working together—they made this book possible.

Note to the Student

Computers *will* be an important part of your future, whether in your personal life or at your workplace. Some experts think that, eventually, the person who does not know how to use a computer will be just as handicapped in performing his or her job as the person today who cannot read.

To be computer literate, you should not only know who uses computers, but also how and where they can be used, the kinds of tasks they perform, how they affect our society and economy, and how to use them to benefit your own life and career. If you are taking this course to familiarize yourself with the world of computers, *Introduction to Computers and Information Systems* serves as an interesting and informative guide on your journey to computer literacy. If you intend to become a computer professional, this book will give you the broad-based background you will need to pursue more advanced coursework in the area.

Long after you have completed this course, this book will remain a handy reference. When you select and purchase your own personal computer system, you can use the consumer information and checklists in the InfoModule "A Buyer's Guide" on page 189. The chapters on popular application packages will provide additional information when you are ready to evaluate and select your own software. After you have purchased your computer system, the InfoModule on page 134, "The Care and Handling of Microcomputers," will provide numerous tips. The Glossary at the end of the book contains standard definitions of common computer-related terms that you may encounter later. The consumer information found in the InfoModule "Electronic Networks" on page 484 describes networks, commercial data bases, and information services that you may want to use in your academic research, in your work, or for your personal interests.

Key Features of the Text

In an effort to present thorough coverage of concepts, hardware and software, computer systems, information systems, and other related topics that educators have indicated they feel are important, these key features have been incorporated:

- **Unique organization,** through the use of subchapters called InfoModules, that allows for flexibility and expandability in structuring a course
- **Readability** at the appropriate reading level, and a conversational writing style that holds the student's interest
- **Sound and effective pedagogy** designed to facilitate student understanding and interest in the subject matter
- **Current examples** of computer applications that relate concepts to actual situations

- **Comprehensive coverage** which, beyond the usual core coverage, includes discussions of contemporary issues such as:
  - Artificial intelligence
  - Expert systems
  - Work monitoring
  - Robotics
  - Legal issues and computer-related legislation
  - Trends in new chip technologies, optoelectronics, parallel processing, and communication
  - Popular types of application packages
  - Increasing use of communication technology
  - Increasing use of networks, commercial information services, and data-base services by professionals, organizations, businesses, and the home user
  - Increasing home use of computers and helpful microcomputer software buyers' tips
  - Career information about computer professions and about noncomputer professions that use computers
- **Written for everyone**—not only for introductory level students who may be interested in continuing their study of computers and information systems as a career, but also for students who plan to enter noncomputer fields

Pedagogy

These pedagogical devices were chosen with both student and instructor in mind:

- **Chapter objectives** alert students and instructor to the major points and concepts to be gleaned from the chapter.
- **Chapter outlines** preview chapter topics and organization so students can see the relationship between the topics covered.
- **Profiles** acquaint students with people who made major contributions to the Information Age.
- **Highlight boxes** focus on interesting articles illustrating current computer uses and issues.
- **Sidelines,** placed in the margin near relevant text discussion, review key points and serve as memory joggers.
- **Summaries** review major concepts in the chapter.
- **Key terms** spotlight words that are important to understanding the material. They are boldfaced in the text for easy reference. At the end of the chapter, key terms are listed alphabetically with appropriate page numbers for reference and review.
- **Review questions** check the student's understanding of the main topics in the chapter. They appear at the end of each chapter as a set comprised of twenty-five questions.
- **InfoModules** provide significant coverage of special-interest topics. These subchapters (one per chapter) offer flexibility in structuring course content. Key terms, if any, are boldfaced, and five review questions are included with each InfoModule.

Chapter 1, "A World with Computers," introduces the student to the computer and describes examples of where computers are used, briefly explains how they work, what they can and cannot do, and explains the need to become computer literate. **InfoModule, "A History of Computers,"** provides the student with a summary of events and significant people and their contributions throughout the history of computers and computing.

Chapter 2, "The Central Processing Unit," is an overview of the internal design and operations of the central processing unit. Data representation is also explained. **InfoModule, "Number Systems,"** describes various number systems that are used to represent data, including the binary system used in the computer.

Chapter 3, "Input and Output Devices," describes input and output concepts and devices for both large and small computer systems. **InfoModule, "Computers in Design and Manufacturing,"** focuses on computers as an integral part of the design and manufacturing processes. It includes coverage of CAD/CAM, CIM, computer-numerical control, robotics, and programmable controllers.

Chapter 4, "Storage Devices and File Organization," describes various secondary storage media and ways to organize and access data on the media. **InfoModule, "The Care and Handling of Microcomputers,"** offers microcomputer owners many helpful tips on maintaining and protecting their computer systems and data.

Chapter 5, "Large Computer Systems," describes the three large computer systems—supercomputers, mainframes, and minicomputers. The chapter also distinguishes between general-purpose and special-purpose computers. **InfoModule, "The Value of Information and Computer Technology,"** discusses the importance of information in our world and how its value is determined. It describes how some organizations and individuals make the most of computer technology.

Chapter 6, "Microcomputers," describes microcomputer systems and discusses their popularity. It gives a brief history of the microcomputer industry and describes current microcomputer applications. **InfoModule, "A Buyer's Guide,"** offers suggestions for selecting and purchasing the hardware and software for a microcomputer system.

Chapter 7, "Communication and the Computer," explains how data are transferred from one computer to another and describes applications of data communication. **InfoModule, "Networks and Distributed Data Processing,"** explains local-area networks, wide-area networks, topologies, and distributed data processing.

Chapter 8, "Information System Life Cycle," describes steps in a system life cycle. **InfoModule, "Case Study: The System Life Cycle in a Small Business,"** shows how these steps might be implemented in a small business.

Chapter 9, "Management Information Systems and Data-base Design Concepts," describes management information systems, details data-base design concepts, and describes how the data base is related to an MIS. The role and information needs of managers and the use of decision support systems and microcomputers by managers are also discussed. **InfoModule, "Case Study: Overview of a Manufacturing MIS System,"** shows a simplified model of how an MIS might be applied in a manufacturing firm.

Chapter 10, "Structured Programming and the Program Development Process," differentiates between system and application software, describes why it is important to learn about programming, presents structured programming concepts, and sets forth the steps in the program development process. **InfoModule, "Expert Systems,"** describes the evolution, the components, and the operation of expert systems.

Chapter 11, "Programming Languages and Operating Systems," introduces the basic programming instructions that are found in any programming language, describes the major categories of programming language, and discusses operating systems for both large and small computer systems. **InfoModule, "Careers in an Information Age,"** describes major computer-related professions and discusses how computers affect other jobs and professions.

Chapter 12, "Introduction to Application Packages," introduces the five major application packages and distinguishes between the various types of integrated packages. **InfoModule, "The Expanding World of Computers,"** describes how computers are used for personal use, in education, in the arts, and in health care.

Chapter 13, "Word Processors," describes the uses and features of a typical word processor. **InfoModule, "The Automated Office,"** discusses the use of computers and information technology within the office environment. Discussions on desktop publishing and ergonomics are also included.

Chapter 14, "Data Managers," describes the uses and features of a typical data manager. **InfoModule, "Computers in Government,"** sets forth examples of the various government agencies that use computers in their operations and to manage large data bases.

Chapter 15, "Spreadsheets," describes the uses and features of a typical electronic spreadsheet. **InfoModule, "Computers in Business,"** describes the variety of computer applications in the business environment.

Chapter 16, "Graphics and Communication Packages," describes the uses for and features of typical graphics packages and communication packages. **InfoModule, "Electronic Networks,"** describes the available networks that the computer can access with communication software. The networks discussed include bulletin boards, electronic mail, information services, commercial data-base services, and videotext services.

Chapter 17, "Social Concerns," discusses major social concerns including privacy of data, computer crimes, electronic work monitoring, health and safety, and computer ethics. **InfoModule, "Legal Issues and Legislation,"** discusses responsibility and liability for computer errors and incorrect information. Software reliability and copyright infringement are also presented. A table of some of the computer-related federal legislation passed during the 1970s and 1980s is included.

Chapter 18, "A Future with Computers," describes some technological trends—new chip technology, natural-language processing, parallel processing, and optoelectronics. Some societal trends and progress and competition at the international level are also discussed. **InfoModule, "Artificial Intelligence,"** presents some scientists' views on the progress made in AI thus far and the direction and role of AI in the future.

The Instructional Package

- **Instructor's Resource Manual** contains chapter-by-chapter lecture outlines, answers to all questions in the text and worktexts, suggestions for using alternative instructional material, and a list of sources for additional reading.
- **Computerized Test Bank** includes true/false, short answer, multiple choice, and fill-in questions. All questions are coded with the chapter or InfoModule number and organized by subject. This versatile test bank program allows the instructor to generate tests, edit existing questions, and add new questions.
- **Printed Test Bank** is a hard copy version of all questions in the computerized test bank.
- **BASIC/Pascal Worktext** starts each chapter with a section on proper program design. Following this are two sections, one on BASIC and the other on Pascal, that teach syntax and reinforce design concepts. The instructor is free to choose BASIC or Pascal, or compare the two languages.
- **Transparency Package** consists of fifty full-color and seventy black-only overhead transparencies that illustrate concepts presented in the text.
- **Tutorial Diskette** is the award-winning PC Instructor, a study aid diskette that enables the user to have interactive, hands-on experience at the computer.
- **Worktext for Open Access II Software** is a hands-on tutorial guide to help students learn basic functions of an integrated application package. The Open Access software accompanies the worktext.
- **Worktext for VP-Planner, WordPerfect, and dBASE III PLUS Software** is a hands-on tutorial guide to help students learn basic functions of the various application packages. Software accompanies the worktext.
- **Data Diskettes to Accompany Worktexts** are files that save keyboarding time for instructors and eliminate the possibility of introducing incorrect data during rekeyboarding.
  - ☐ Open Access II data disk contains files necessary to run Open Access II worktext examples and complete the exercises.

□ VP-Planner data disk has files necessary to run VP-Planner, WordPerfect, dBASE III worktext examples and complete the exercises.

□ BASIC/Pascal disk consists of example problems and material needed to complete the exercises in the BASIC/Pascal worktext.

■ **Videotapes**—Adopters of *Introduction to Computers and Information Systems* can purchase instructional tapes directly from the following companies at a discounted rate.

□ International Business Machines Corporation (IBM)—Using Your IBM PC, Merrill version
A ninety-minute tape divided into seven lessons on how to use the IBM PC.

Lesson 1—Assembling Your System

Lesson 2—Using Your Keyboard

Lesson 3—About Disks

Lesson 4—The Disk Directory

Lesson 5—Programming Languages

Lesson 6—Installing DOS

Lesson 7—Programming in BASIC

□ American Micro Media—A series of ten videotapes, each running approximately thirty minutes. New terms are explained as they are introduced and a review of concepts appears approximately every ten minutes.

Electronic Words—explains key concepts related to word processors

Keeping Track—explains key concepts related to data management packages

Computer Calc—explains key concepts of electronic spreadsheets

Computer Talk—explains key communication concepts

Computer Images—explains key graphics concepts

Computer Crime—focuses on crime awareness, prevention, and ethics

Computer Careers—describes how computers affect the workplace

Computer Peripherals—explains differences between computer systems

Computer Music—shows how computer sounds are generated

Computer Business—explores microcomputers and office automation

ACKNOWLEDGMENTS

So many people were involved in the development, production, and creative aspects of this project that the list of names would go on and on. All of the professionals we worked with at Merrill Publishing provided support, enthusiasm, and helpful suggestions. Special acknowledgment, however, goes to our administrative editor and friend, Vernon Anthony, who steadfastly led us through every phase of the publication process. The developmental editorial support of Pamela Kusma, William Lindsey, Penelope Semrau, and Dwayne Martin is unrivaled. Everyone in Merrill's production, art, and design departments is to be commended for their creativity, patience, and hard work. In particular, we thank Connie Geldis, production editor; Pete Robison, art coordinator; Cindy Brunk, text designer; and Cathy Watterson, cover designer. Additionally, we are grateful to the organizations and businesses that provided photographs and technical material for use in this book. We also appreciate the work of Jerry Houston, who wrote and developed the BASIC and Pascal worktext.

Robert A. Szymanski
Donald P. Szymanski
Norma A. Morris
Donna M. Pulschen

REVIEWERS

We would like to thank the following people who reviewed the manuscript and provided thoughtful and helpful suggestions for *Introduction to Computers and Information Systems*.

Gertrude Abrahamson	Baruch College
John Anderson	University of South Carolina
Robert A. Barrett	Indiana University at Fort Wayne
Harvey Blessing	H. R. Blessing and Associates
Ronald Bush	Austin Community College
Cathy Fitch	Educational Design Consultant
Paulette Gannette	Broome County College
Joseph Greenwald	DeVry Institute of Technology at Atlanta
George Grill	University of North Carolina at Greensboro
Donald Gruver	Santa Monica College
Thomas Harris	Ball State University
Richard Hatch	San Diego State University
Seth Hock	Columbus State Community College
Ava Honan	Auburn University
Brian Honess	University of South Carolina
George Jacobsen	California State University at Los Angeles
Wesley Jones	Educational Consultant
David Kay	Moorpark College
Barry Kolb	Ocean County College
P. J. Lamont	Western Illinois University
William Lepenski	Tarrant County Junior College
Chang-Yang Lin	Eastern Kentucky University
Anthony Malone	Raymond Walters College
Bruce McLaren	Indiana State University
Michael Michaelson	Palomar College
Michael Nakoff	Cincinnati Technical College
Thomas W. Osgood	Indiana University at Richmond
James Phillips	University of Kentucky Community College System
Walter E. Poplarchek	University of Cincinnati
Waldo Roth	Taylor University
William Sailer	Saint Phillip's College
Gregory Scott	Richland College
Kathy Short	Modesto Junior College
Edward Solinski	Purdue University
Ralph Szweda	Monroe Community College
Julia Tinsley	Indiana University at Kokomo
Janet Truscott	San Joaquin Delta College
Dennis L. Varin	University of Southern Oregon
Lauren Whittaker	Educational Consultant
Wayne Zage	Purdue University

Brief Contents

Contents

PART THREE

INFORMATION SYSTEMS AND PROGRAMMING CONCEPTS   227

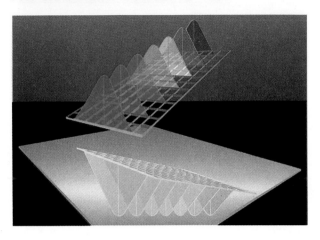

PART FOUR

APPLICATION PACKAGES 345

CHAPTER 12

Introduction to Application Packages 347

PART FIVE

IMPLICATIONS OF THE INFORMATION AGE   491

CHAPTER 17

Social Concerns   493

PART ONE

Information Age: An Overview of Computing and Computers

In my opinion, the future will see computers and humans, each representing totally different forms of intelligence, working in cooperation rather than in competition and accomplishing more together than either could possibly achieve alone.

Isaac Asimov, science fiction writer

OBJECTIVES

- ☐ Explain what a computer is and give examples of where computers are used
- ☐ Describe the different types of computers
- ☐ Give examples of how the different sizes of computers are used
- ☐ Describe how the computer processes data and converts those facts into useful information
- ☐ Discuss why you should study computers

1

A World With Computers

PROFILE: Raymond Kurzweil

Raymond Kurzweil is an impatient man—and a hopeful one. So when he gets an idea for a computer application, his first thought seems to be, "How quickly can we get it on the market?"

It is no wonder, then, that the native New Yorker didn't bother with a lot of formal schooling before plunging into the infant computer world of the late '50s and early '60s. In fact, he was only twelve years old when he developed a software package so useful and well-constructed that IBM agreed to distribute it.

In 1964, when he was sixteen, Kurzweil won seven national awards, including first prize at the International Science Fair in Electronics and Communications, for his pioneering work in artificial intelligence. By the mature age of eighteen, he had sold a software package for $100,000 to a New York publishing company. Clearly, the bright young man had a bright future before him.

As the child of a music professor who was a refugee from Nazi Germany, Kurzweil spent his early years in a working-class neighborhood in New York City. His two passions as a youngster were the piano and computer technology, and Kurzweil found ways to exploit both enthusiasms.

Blind singer and composer, Stevie Wonder, first encountered Kurzweil after the young computer whiz began marketing a machine that could scan books and then read them aloud by translating the signals it picked up visually into a synthesized voice. Wonder bought one of the first reading machines.

In talking to Kurzweil about the exotic work being performed by computers, Wonder complained that the music synthesizers available, while useful in their own right, could not simulate the richly varied sounds of traditional acoustic instruments. Out of this conversation grew the idea for the Kurzweil Model 250 keyboard.

Although some professional musicians say the Model 250 lacks the depth and range of a grand piano, others are enthusiastic, praising both its "natural" sound and its portability. Prince, Herbie Hancock, the Pat Metheny Group, Lynn Stanford of the American Ballet Theater, and other top musicians also have used the Kurzweil 250. These days, Kurzweil's name and inventions are as well-known to performers as they are to the U.S. Patent Office.

Another Kurzweil enthusiasm is the VoiceWriter, a system that "hears" the spoken word and instantly prints it onto paper.

A great deal of the inventor's success is attributable to his zeal for self-promotion. He is remarkably agile in both the laboratory and the boardroom. Kurzweil founded and presently directs several companies; and he personally raised the money to get them started.

In 1982, at the age of thirty-four, Kurzweil was inducted into the Computer Industry Hall of Fame.

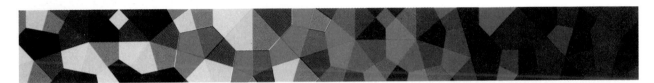

Welcome to the world of computers and data processing. Although this may be the beginning of your formal introduction to computers, you probably already use them—perhaps without realizing it. Do you ever make a withdrawal from your bank account using an automated teller machine? Or do you use a shopping service that allows you to preview thousands of products, make a purchase, and pay for the selection by inserting a credit card into the machine? Well then, you are using a computer. For example, automated teller machines are part of a large computer system at the bank (Figure 1–1). After you enter your bank account number, individual identification number, and the amount of money you require into the machine, the withdrawal is made automatically from your account, and the cash is delivered to you.

Many of today's computers are easy to use because of software, such as word processing, spreadsheet, data management, communications, and graphics packages, that is geared to specific applications. These special programs allow you, with very little experience, to use a computer. You can create term papers with a word-processing package, manage personal finances with a spreadsheet package, keep records of addresses, birthdays, and other vital statistics of family and friends with a data management package, communicate with other users on an electronic bulletin board, and perhaps design unique greeting cards with a graphics package.

As you read further in this chapter, you'll learn what a computer is, where it can be found, what it can do and how it does it, and what it can't do and why, as well as familiarize yourself with the various components that make up a computer system. More importantly, you'll understand why you need to know about computers at all. In the process, you will also discover new terminology and new meanings for familiar words.

WHAT COMPUTERS ARE

A **computer** is simply a tool for people to use; it is a machine that can solve problems by accepting data, performing certain operations on that data, and presenting the results of those operations. It is generally thought

FIGURE 1–1
This automated teller machine is conveniently located in the lobby of an office building. (Photo courtesy of Diebold, Inc.)

Classes of Computers

- Analog
  - ☐ Measures physical properties
- Digital
  - ☐ Counts discrete signals (units)

of as one of two classifications—analog or digital—depending on the logic it uses.

Analog computers recognize data as a continuous measurement of a physical property. Their output is usually in the form of readings on dials or graphs. Voltage, pressure, speed, and temperature are some physical properties that can be measured in this way. Analog computers include an automobile speedometer (Figure 1–2) and a furnace thermostat.

Digital computers are high-speed, programmable, electronic devices that perform mathematical calculations, compare values, and store the results. They recognize data by counting discrete signals representing either a high ("on") or low ("off") voltage state of electricity. Numbers and special symbols can all be reduced to representation by 1s ("on") and 0s ("off"). Figure 1–3 shows how the capital letters A, B, and C can be reduced to representation by a number system of 1s and 0s. This and other number systems used for data representation are discussed in the InfoModule in Chapter 2.

To illustrate the differences between analog and digital devices, think of an electrical switch that has a dimmer dial. There are many gradations in the amount of light that can be turned on in the room. The dimmer switch allows you to increase from full dark to full light, and vice versa, moving in a continuous line through the various gradations. That process constitutes an analog measurement of light. Analog measurement is not particularly accurate, because, from one day to the next, it is difficult to set the lights to exactly halfway.

FIGURE 1–2
An automobile speedometer is an example of an analog computer.

Drive shaft

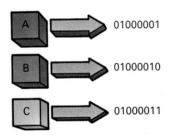

FIGURE 1–3
A computer can recognize only characters that are coded as a series of 1s and 0s. Here, the letters A, B, and C are shown with this numeric representation.

With a regular light switch, which exemplifies a digital measurement of light, the lights are either on or off. There is no in-between or smooth continuous change between full dark and full light.

Sometimes both types of computers are used in one application. For example, the radical body design of the supersonic X–29 fighter developed in the early 1980s by Grumman Aerospace Corporation, caused the plane to fly so erratically that it could tear itself apart in one-fifth of a second. As many as forty in-flight adjustments per second were required to keep that from happening—more than even the best human pilot could make. To stabilize the plane and avoid scrapping the project, Grumman placed three analog and three digital computers on board that made the necessary measurements within the required time.

The focus of this text, however, will be on digital computers because they are the most widely used and will probably be the classification of computers you are most apt to find.

WHERE COMPUTERS ARE USED

Even when you don't see them, computers are usually working behind the scenes—where you go to school, shop, work, or transact business. Some computers are responsible for your leisure enjoyment and entertainment; others are found in government operations and professions such as medicine and law.

HIGHLIGHT

IS THAT A BUG ON THE MENU?

The most enduring importance of an invention is neither the amount of money it makes for its developers nor the number of jobs that result from its manufacture. Rather, it is the impact the invention has on our language. Computers have changed our language a great deal already, and the changes continue.

To begin with, words such as *byte, microchip, bubble memory, bar code, floppy disk, microprocessor,* and *artificial intelligence* were coined as names for devices and processes that didn't exist (or which had limited uses) until the computer came into its own. Then, some commonly-used terms began to have specific computer-related meanings: *boot, address, BASIC, bit, bug, bus, disk, dump, execute, file, flag, input, interpreter, list, load, loop, menu, monitor, mouse, network, output, plotter, program, PROM, prompt, RAM, swapping, terminal,* and *track.* While some of these words will no doubt become obsolete, the perseverance of our computer-based society will assure the others a long, active life.

In 1987, when the Merriam-Webster Company published a supplement to its 1961 *Third International Dictionary,* the list of new terms contained 12,000 words, many of them originating from their use in the computer field. *A Supplement to the Oxford English Dictionary* (the final volume of the dictionary's update) also contains some new American computer terminology, including *update* and *user-friendly.*

Perhaps it is poetic justice that the machine that brought so many new words into the language is now the main tool for helping dictionary makers keep track of the changing language.

Business and Industry

Computers are used in business for many tasks that can be grouped into a category called data processing. Data processing includes tasks such as word processing, filing, and assembling numbers and facts associated with general office functions, such as accounting, payroll processing, personnel record keeping, and compliance with federal regulations.

In addition to all the standard data processing activities, let's see how computers are used outside corporate headquarters. The people at Allen-Bradley have been building industrial devices since 1903. During the late 1970s, management realized that manufacturing changes had to be made if the company was to remain competitive. Some parts they manufactured were competing against substantially lower priced parts made in West Germany and Australia. To address the problem, management established a new department (Department 260), designed a line of 600 products, and created an automated and computerized assembly process to build them.

Today, a mainframe computer, one of the large computer systems, oversees the plant operations in Milwaukee, accumulating orders from all over the world, preparing the plant for daily operations, and networking with twenty-nine smaller computers in Department 260. Although it was expensive to set up this computer-integrated manufacturing plant, increased production is expected to cover start-up costs and produce a profit as well.

Small businesses and growing businesses use computers, too. In Dallas, owners of I Can't Believe It's Yogurt stores installed computerized cash registers to monitor inventory. Even though fresh ingredients assure a tasty treat and cheerful employees improve business, owners are convinced that the addition of computerized inventory control enabled the business to grow to nine stores in 1987 with expected revenues of $22 million.

Grumman Aerospace Corporation's A–6F fighter plane is equipped with the most advanced sensors, processors, and displays. The pilot's controls in the cockpit provide ready access to information generated by onboard computers. Among other capabilities, the computers can process radar data, improve night maneuverability, and display digitized mapping data. (Courtesy of Grumman Aerospace Corp.)

FIGURE 1–4
The computers in General Motors' Corvette monitor vital engine functions and display digital readings from devices such as odometers and speedometers. (Courtesy of General Motors Technical Center)

People who are in charge of making large investments in the stock market rely heavily on computer-generated information. But they also know that computers can neither predict the future nor make assumptions about market trends. Anyone who uses computer-generated information knows not to rely totally on the computer; human intuition often enters the decision-making process, too.

Products We Use

Some businesses put computers inside many of the items they produce (Figure 1–4); others use computers to design the item itself.

Automobile manufacturers place computers in many of their models. Computers control climate inside the car, adjust power seats and steering wheel settings, monitor electronic sensors that turn the headlights on when sunlight is inadequate, and convert instrument panel readings into metric and Celsius measurements. Other computers control gasoline flow, ignition spark, and coolant sensors; signals even warn the driver of road hazards.

In the future, computer chip "watchdogs" may be able to protect cars or their parts from being stolen. The Pontiac 6000 STE's radio already contains computer chips that prevent it from being played if the radio is removed from the car. Other automobile manufacturers are using similar techniques.

Science and Technology

If all this talk of computers has your head in a spin, go to the emergency room of a major hospital and you will find that information about your admission will be entered into a computer. Indeed, your entire hospitalization stay will be recorded—all prescribed medications, doctor visits, and other hospital services (Figure 1–5). In fact, your itemized bill most likely will be ready when you are released.

In 1985, physicians at Humana Hospital Audubon in Louisville, Kentucky, used computer-controlled equipment to monitor pulse rate, blood pressure, and other vital signs after William Schroeder received the Jarvik-7 artificial heart implant. Alarms not only warned nurses of emergency situations, but also told the staff what particular problem to expect. A portable computer even allowed Schroeder more mobility than the computer that the first mechanical heart recipient, Barney Clark, used. Clark had been hampered by monitoring wires and tubes, as well as an entire microcomputer consisting of an Apple IIe, a hard disk, a monitor, and a printer.

Although neither of these artificial heart recipients is alive now, reams of data were collected and sorted by a computer system so future implant patients can benefit from the information generated.

Dental Health By placing a magnetic square containing three sensors between the front teeth and lip, dentists use small computer systems to help diagnose jaw misalignments. The sensors are attached to a computer;

FIGURE 1–5
Nurses refer to patients' charts when entering data into the main computer. (Courtesy of Travenol Laboratories, Inc.)

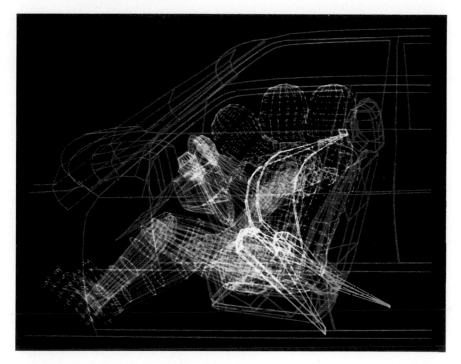

This body model is designed to show mass and other characteristics that simulate an actual human body so that a proposed seat belt design can be tested. Computer simulation aids engineers in identifying the most effective seat belt design that eliminates shoulder belt slack on impact. (Courtesy of Daimler Benz and Evans & Sutherland)

they follow the magnet's movement by tracing a line on the screen as the patient's mouth opens. If the jaw moves improperly, the line will bend, and corrective action is indicated. On the other hand, if the line is straight, the patient just needs to keep flossing; the computer is programmed to send a reminder for a check-up in six months.

Simulation Because supercomputers have huge memories, fast processing speeds, and the capability of processing vast amounts of data, they are used widely in simulation tests. Simulation of automobile crashes or airplane emergency landings involves a variety of factors that must all be evaluated and compared so potential weaknesses in new designs are located without risking human lives. NASA astronauts train by studying computer-simulated problems that could be encountered during launch, in space, or upon return to Earth. In addition, supercomputers help design aircraft models and simulate the effects that winds and other environmental forces might have on those designs.

Geology At Stanford University, civil engineers use a computer system, called SEISMIC, containing expert architectural information that evaluates the effects of an earthquake on structures in the Palo Alto, California, area. Buildings are assessed on their age, proximity to the San Andreas fault, soil

A General Motors technician makes appropriate adjustments on a robotic testing device that simulates a body's reaction during crash testing. The robot helps to identify potential problem areas in new automobile designs. (Courtesy of General Motors Technical Center)

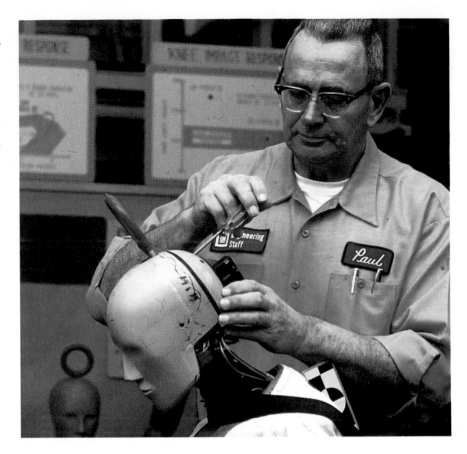

type, size, shape, and construction material. Even though SEISMIC contains enough information about earthquakes to be labeled an "expert," an engineer is still needed to interpret and evaluate the information provided and then draw conclusions.

Flying Even legendary test pilot Chuck Yeager, known for his ability to see at night, could use Northrop Corporation's miniature chip that computer-enhances a pilot's vision. This innovation is called a focal plane array and contains 16,348 sensors that absorb heat radiated from objects on the ground. When the heat energy is processed, it is converted into a picture on a monitor that shows the pilot exactly what's down below.

Education

Ninety-seven percent of the public schools in the U.S. have computers, located in scientific laboratories, classrooms, and the registration office. In many cases, however, they are not used to their full potential because teachers are not totally aware of computers' capabilities.

As educators learn to use computers more effectively, they will find them to be valuable aids for instruction and tutoring. Computers are tireless and nonjudgmental when drilling students on mathematical facts or offering specialized lessons on particular subjects. Because many science laboratory experiments can be simulated by a computer, young students become interested and excited by the interaction. Students get the feeling of accomplishment for right answers, and the graphics that are part of many educational packages hold their interest (Figure 1–6).

Government

Computers used in government keep tabs on national security matters, on legislative actions, and on private citizens through Social Security and Internal Revenue Service records.

Military Schools But computers are also an important addition at the U.S. Air Force Academy at Colorado Springs, Colorado, where microcomputers are issued to all incoming cadets. Cadets have reported saving an hour each day on academic studies. A unique $6.5 million network links cadets, faculty, staff, and buildings—6,000 users. Not to be outdone, cadets at both the West Point Military Academy and the U.S. Naval Academy in Annapolis have microcomputers, too.

Traffic Control State and local governments use computers for city planning and traffic control. For example, New York City's bureau of traffic operations enlisted a computer's expertise to eliminate the dreaded grid-

FIGURE 1–6
Many elementary schools use computers as tools to teach a variety of subjects.

lock (Figure 1–7). A real-life traffic jam becomes a gridlock when traffic is at a total standstill in an area of eight or more blocks for fifteen minutes. Beyond being an annoyance, gridlock is a threat to public safety because emergency vehicles cannot get through.

To alleviate the problem, traffic engineers designed a system that includes induction loops of wire embedded in the asphalt at many intersections across the city. As cars drive over the wires, electrical pulses are counted by a central computer that translates the pulses into a number of cars, converts the number to a rate of flow, and tells the traffic lights when to change. The computer also saves the information, so predictions can be made of potential gridlock areas or days. If necessary, the chief of operations can send additional traffic patrols to problem areas.

Legal System

By using computers to search through huge data banks such as LEXIS or Shepard's Citations, lawyers have shortened the time required to conduct legal precedent and case research (Figure 1–8). Subscribers to Shepard's Citations use an electronic retrieval system to: look through millions of individual cases; find whether similar or parallel cases were approved, denied, criticized, or overruled; and decide whether to use them in their arguments for the current case. Lawyers then formulate strategies based on past case decisions.

FIGURE 1–7
The New York City Department of Transportation prepared charts of streets and intersections of the various boroughs before implementing their computerized traffic-control system. (Courtesy of New York City Department of Transportation)

FIGURE 1-8
Computers using data banks such as LEXIS have made conducting legal research faster and more efficient. (Courtesy of Mead Data Central)

FIGURE 1-9
Computers are used in restaurants to record purchases and keep track of inventory.

Attorneys also use computers to keep track of their appointments, case dockets, time journals, and clients' bills. Luckily for many legal secretaries, the word processor helps them quickly prepare legal documents and briefs in time for filings, because their bosses are notorious for rewriting drafts so that just the right words and tone of voice are set.

Many courts docket cases and trials using computers. Kurzweil's VoiceWriter may become as much an asset to the court reporter as the transcription machine. Records could be dictated directly into the voice-activated typewriter instead of first being spoken into one machine and later transcribed by a typist.

Recreation and Entertainment

Our entertainment and most leisure-time pursuits have been affected by computerization.

Dining Almost everyone has eaten at a fast-food restaurant where the clerk enters an order by indicating choices on a rather unusual looking cash register. In fact, the device actually enters data directly into a computer that, in turn, lists your order, calculates the cost, and prints a receipt (Figure 1-9).

Computers are found in haute cuisine restaurants, too. With the aid of these computers, master chefs can store their recipes, plan menus, and perhaps consult a data base that offers suggestions of complimentary wine selections for each course.

Sports In most sports, computers compile statistics, sell tickets, create training programs and diets for athletes, and suggest game plan strategies based on the competitor's past performance. Much of the graphic art displays flashed on scoreboards are generated by computers.

Scouts for the Dallas Cowboys football team have been using computers for almost twenty-five years to rate both strong and weak players. During the recruitment process for new players, Gil Brandt plans to use portable computers to conduct on-the-spot evaluations of college athletes. Getting ratings information sooner enables him to make knowledgeable decisions and to expedite offers.

But, what if you're a sports fan watching in an armchair? Computers don't affect you—or do they? Well, television networks use computers in the control room to bring you play-by-play action. With the help of a computer, a technician inserts the commercial breaks on schedule. If that's not enough, the sport shoes you wear were probably designed using computers that checked stress points and then created the style and shape that offer maximum support for the foot. Nike and other athletic shoe manufacturers use computers to produce as well as design footwear.

FIGURE 1–10
A musical instrument digital interface (MIDI) links computers to musical instruments to control and create sounds. (Courtesy of Apple Computer, Inc.)

FIGURE 1–11
Computers can generate three-dimensional, special-effect scenes for television and movies. (Created by Greg Anderson and Dave Novak/Advanced Computing Center for the Arts and Sciences)

Music Electronic pianos contain digital computers. The Kurzweil Ensemble Grande creates the sounds of the piano and thirty-two other instruments, plays pre-set rhythms, and stores and replays 4,000 notes. The Kurzweil 250 synthesizer is another example (see page 3).

More recent is the introduction of the musical instrument digital interface (MIDI) which links musical instruments to a personal computer, thereby creating a variety of sounds (Figure 1–10). Often, the background music in movies, television shows, and commercials is electronically generated.

Even when you buy concert tickets, the ticket agency is probably part of a computerized network that registers the number of seats sold.

Movies Computer-generated art gives freedom to designers so that sets, special effects, and even imaginary characters can play a part in making movies, videos, and commercials (Figure 1–11). Creatures, spaceships, and entire galaxies are created and manipulated by computers, then photographed by computer-driven cameras. When computer-controlled lighting systems are used on sound stages or in theaters, a dramatic range of atmospheres can be produced. Not all special effects are computer creations,

17

FIGURE 1–12
With help from a computer, a travel agent can quickly identify availability and the price that suits a client's needs when booking airline flights, hotel rooms, and car rentals.

though. The mine walls seen in *Indiana Jones and the Temple of Doom* were created by the not-so-high-tech scrunching and painting of aluminum foil.

Digital Productions developed the battling starships in *The Last Starfighter* for $4 million. Although these computer-generated effects were expensive, scale models of the starships would have cost three times that amount.

Travel and Tourism Want to "get away from it all?" Computers will help prepare the ticket, monitor the train's route, or guide the plane to a safe landing. They will even confirm hotel room and rental car reservations (Figure 1–12). Tulsa, Oklahoma, is the hub for American Airlines' reservation system, SABRE, the world's largest network of computers not used for military purposes. The system processes data at the rate of 1,400 messages per second. With the aid of over 700,000 miles of wires and circuits connecting the five large computers, reservations can be confirmed while you wait.

As you visit the theme parks throughout the United States, including Walt Disney World and Disneyland, you will find many displays brought to life by computer animation. Computers monitor the voices, lights, music, and speed of many attractions.

A few of you may still think that computers do not affect your lives. But, remember those pieces of mail you receive that say things like "Return this immediately to claim your million-dollar winnings!" Mail sent to your "personal" attention is generated by computers that merge a list of names into typeset copy to create a personalized touch.

Anyone else who thinks they have not been affected by computers now faces the fact that the manuscript for this textbook was drafted and revised on microcomputers using word-processing software. Some of the slides were computer-enhanced to give the final photographs the best clarity and color. Not only that, but the cover art and other chapter opening art designs were created with computer graphics. Without any doubt, computers are a part of your world.

COMPUTER SYSTEMS

A Computer System

- Hardware
  - ☐ Computer
  - ☐ Primary storage
  - ☐ Secondary storage
  - ☐ Input devices
  - ☐ Output devices
- Software
- User

What components make up a computer system? First, the **hardware,** or equipment, includes: the computer, where the processing occurs; memory, which includes **primary** and **secondary storage; input devices,** such as the keyboard and the mouse; and **output devices,** such as printers and monitors. Next, the **software,** or instructions, tells the computer what to do. Finally, a person, or user, is required to activate the system.

Computer sizes are available for every situation. The size and configuration of a system depend on the processing requirements, necessary functions, and budget constraints. Large computers are grouped into three categories: supercomputers; mainframes; and minicomputers.

Supercomputers (Figure 1–13) are the most expensive and most powerful computers; they are used where vast quantities of data must be manipulated, primarily by government agencies, scientists, and large corporations.

FIGURE 1–13
Used primarily by government and large corporations, supercomputers are the most high-powered computers made. (Courtesy of Los Alamos National Laboratory)

FIGURE 1–14
Mainframes are most often used for business processing in medium-sized to large corporations. (Courtesy of AccuRay Corp.)

Mainframe computers are smaller, cheaper, and not as powerful as supercomputers. They are used as the "traditional" computer for a company where many users at separate workstations share the same computer. Figure 1–14 shows a mainframe computer in a workplace setting.

FIGURE 1–15
Minicomputers are smaller and have less power than mainframes. They are used in many small and medium-sized organizations. (Photo courtesy of Hewlett-Packard Co.)

FIGURE 1–16
Microcomputers are used not only in the office, but also at home, for a wide variety of tasks.

Sizes of Computers

- Large systems
  □ Supercomputers
  □ Mainframe computers
  □ Minicomputers
- Small systems
  □ Microcomputers

Minicomputers are the next step down, being smaller and less expensive, and containing somewhat less memory and processing capabilities. They are usually used in small and medium-sized businesses, and they can serve several users simultaneously (Figure 1–15).

These categorical distinctions in size, memory, and speed of operation are becoming blurred because of innovations in memory and storage capacities. New technology and faster processing speeds allow greater amounts of data to be stored in smaller areas; therefore, many of the new smaller machines have characteristics and capabilities of the larger ones.

Computers that are cheaper, smaller, and contain less memory than minicomputers are called **microcomputers** (Figure 1–16). Unlike the larger computers, a single microcomputer is generally used by only one person at a time.

HOW COMPUTERS ARE USED AND WHAT THEY CAN DO

There are three basic ways in which computers are used: data processing; control; and design and development.

Data Processing This processing includes statistics, mathematical calculations for payrolls, filing tasks, and even word processing—all traditional business applications. The automated teller machine records your banking transactions, retail stores and factories have computerized inventory control, and federal and state governments use computers to organize their many files.

Control Computers control many mechanical devices and processes (Figure 1–17). They direct robots in factories and monitor traffic lights at intersections throughout many cities. At the heart of many of these computer-controllers are sensors that activate a device or system of devices. For example, sensors are embedded in New York City streets to control traffic at

FIGURE 1–17
Computerized robot, Jason, Jr., leaves its "garage" aboard the manned submersible Alvin and sets out for a day's work photographing the remains of the luxury liner Titanic, located 13,000 feet below the surface of the North Atlantic. (Courtesy of Woods Hole Oceanographic Institution)

busy intersections. Often, computers direct factory operations, assembly lines, and machinery for large manufacturers.

Design and Development Engineers can design a product and test it by computer before manufacturing it. For example, a new type of airplane wing can be designed by engineers using a computer, then tested by computer simulation to see how it will function under certain conditions.

Computers used in the medical field design and produce artificial joints and limbs. Not only do the prostheses fit the users better, but most of these devices are developed in one-third the time and at only one-third the cost of hand-drafted designs. Raw data in the forms of computerized tomography scans (CTs) and X rays are fed into the computer. Surgeons and design engineers collaborate and enter variables, such as the patient's age, body size, and amount of activity that the new "part" must be capable of sustaining, into the computer. The computer then analyzes the input to create the best fit.

Functions

Although computers have many applications with their three basic uses, they can perform only three basic tasks:

1. Arithmetic functions on numeric data (adding, subtracting, multiplying, and dividing)
2. Test relationships between data items (by comparing values)
3. Store and retrieve data

These skills are really no more than people can do, but the computer can accomplish the tasks

- ☐ Faster
- ☐ More accurately
- ☐ More reliably

A computer can solve complex mathematical problems in fractions of a second; it can work with the greatest accuracy imaginable; and it can store great volumes of data. A disparity of performance between a computer and a person would be readily evident if the task, for example, involved the multiplication of two 32-digit numbers.

But, before the computer can begin any solution, the data must be presented. Let's discover how this happens.

How They Operate

Converting the **data** (raw facts) into **information** (an organized, usable form) is called **data processing.** Some sources refer to data processing as information processing; however, it is the data that are processed. But, before data processing can occur, the data must get into the system by means of an input device. Then the computer performs the necessary calculations or manipulations on the data; finally, the organized information

---

Basic Uses

- ■ Data processing
- ■ Control
- ■ Design and development
  - ☐ Products
  - ☐ Ideas

Computer Functions

- ■ Arithmetic
- ■ Comparisons
- ■ Storage and retrieval

HIGHLIGHT

LET J.J. DO IT! Some of us are interested in a life of risk and adventure; others prefer the safety of the known. Consider the novice photographer who draws the assignment of taking pictures of the promenade deck of a luxury liner. Sounds as if it could be a terrific job, unless of course, the luxury liner has been resting on the bottom of the Atlantic Ocean since 1912, and this particular ship's log is for the Titanic.

You might say this assignment warrants hazardous duty pay—but not the new guy on the block. He goes where he's commanded with no threat of walking out on an assignment or thought of quitting his job. He's small—only about the size of a lawnmower—but mighty. Just who is this adventuresome person? It's not a person at all; it's a creation. This specially designed robot—Jason, Jr.—can travel underwater, complete with cameras and lights. Explicit instructions and guidance come from humans in a nearby submarine.

The photographs that this robot took were breathtaking, although one tense moment did occur. Jason, Jr.'s control line got tangled on some jagged metal near the wheelhouse, but through clever maneuvering, it was freed. When scientists tried to get a closer look at the wheelhouse by sending the robot through a porthole, however, they discovered it didn't fit. Isn't it ironic that even robots have to watch their weight?

Flow of Data

- Input
- Processing
- Output

---

is displayed by output devices. Therefore, data flow through the system according to the following steps: input; processing; and output.

Input involves collecting, verifying, and encoding data into a machine-readable form for the computer. **Processing** means the computer creates useful information from that data by classifying, sorting, calculating, summarizing, and storing the results. **Output** includes retrieving the data, converting them into a human-readable form, and displaying the information to the user. Figure 1–18 illustrates the basic flow of data through a computer system.

Data processing requires careful planning and appropriate instructions. Accurate data must be input or the information delivered as output is useless. This phenomenon is called "garbage-in, garbage-out," meaning that the output is only as accurate as the input and the program that processes the data. If you simply enter a meaningless series of numbers and letters, the computer will not automatically process that data into a list of names and addresses. Correct data have to be entered. By the same token, the accuracy of a program has to be verified so that subsequent processes can be performed correctly.

FIGURE 1–18
The basic flow of data through a computer system involves three steps: input; processing; and output. A user enters data at an input device, and the computer converts the data to machine-readable form. In this example, the computer's instructions specify that the data should be alphabetized. After the computer completes that procedure, the output, in human-readable form, prints out on the output device.

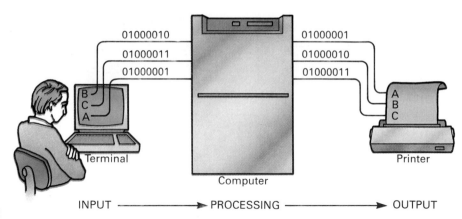

INPUT ⟶ PROCESSING ⟶ OUTPUT

WHAT COMPUTERS CANNOT DO

Computer Incapabilities

- Decide how to be programmed
- Provide its own input
- Interpret data
- Implement decisions
- "Think"

Computers are very good at what they do, but there are many tasks that they can't do. They can't do anything unless they are first programmed with specific instructions. Computers can't decide how they are to be programmed or provide their own input; they can't interpret the data they generate; they can't implement any decisions that they suggest; and they can't "think."

Computers can be programmed to store recipes, but they can't decide to fix dinner. They can keep track of scientific data, but they can't conceive or express the ideas for continued research. Their memories can contain the contents of encyclopedias, but only humans can decide what to do with that knowledge.

THE NEED FOR COMPUTER LITERACY

Computers are found nearly everywhere in our personal lives and work world. Unless you intend to be a hermit, computers will affect you. What is computer literacy, and why would you want or need it? Well, **computer literacy** means having a general knowledge about computers, knowing who uses them, what kinds of functions they perform, how they are used by others, where they are, how they are affecting society, and learning how to use them to benefit your own life or work. Some experts think that, eventually, the person who does not know how to use a computer will be just as handicapped in performing his or her job as the person today who cannot read.

This formal introduction to the computer leads to further exploration in your quest for computer literacy. In subsequent chapters, you will learn more about the operation of the computer and its specific parts, find out what devices are used in conjunction with the computer, and discover how those devices are related. Later, chapters are devoted to both large and small systems, where you will study the differences between each system and the types of jobs that each performs. You will learn how computers communicate with each other and the rules that govern that communication. You'll see how managers at various levels use computers in different ways and understand why those managers who use computers wisely end up with a powerful business partner.

Several microcomputer application packages, such as word processor, data manager, spreadsheet, and graphics and communication, will be introduced. These programs give people who are not mathematical wizards or computer programmers the opportunities to use computers and the advantages that go along with them.

Although the courses you choose in school may not demand a technical knowledge of computers and programming, you likely will be directly or indirectly involved with them in your work. Many jobs and careers depend on some familiarity with the use of computers. For those who are interested in careers or jobs directly involved with information or computer technology, all kinds of possibilities exist—keying in data, defining the way data are processed, managing the computer system, or managing the information system.

Other chapters will address the latest computer trends and some of the concerns people have about the effects of computers on our society. Because innovations are occurring so rapidly, it is impossible to predict the future with any degree of accuracy; however, some observations and a general forecast are provided.

SUMMARY

A computer is a machine that can solve problems by accepting data, performing certain operations, and presenting the results of those operations. Analog computers recognize data as continuous measurement of a physical property. Digital computers are high speed, programmable, electronic devices that perform mathematical calculations, compare values, and store results.

Computers are found in a diversity of areas—from business, science, education, government, and law to recreation and leisure.

A computer system includes hardware, input and output devices, software, and a user. Large computers are categorized as supercomputers, mainframe computers, and minicomputers. Small computers are called microcomputers.

Computers are used three basic ways: data processing; control; and design and development. Computers can perform only three basic tasks—arithmetic functions, comparisons, and storage and retrieval—but they can do these tasks faster, more accurately, and more reliably than people.

Data processing is converting data into information. This procedure occurs as a flow of data through the computer: input; processing; and output.

Input involves collecting, verifying, and encoding data so the machine can read them. Processing means the computer classifies, sorts, calculates, summarizes, and stores the results; output means the data are retrieved and converted so a person can read the results.

Computers cannot decide how to be programmed, provide input, interpret data, implement decisions, or "think." Computer literacy means having a general knowledge about computers, knowing who uses them, what functions they perform, how they are used, where they are, how they affect society, and learning to use them yourself.

Key Terms

analog computer (p. 5)

computer (p. 4)

computer literacy (p. 24)

data (p. 22)

data processing (p. 22)

digital computer (p. 5)

hardware (p. 18)

information (p. 22)

input (p. 23)

input device (p. 18)

mainframe computer (p. 19)

microcomputer (p. 21)

minicomputer (p. 21)

output (p. 23)

output device (p. 18)

primary storage (p. 18)

processing (p. 23)

secondary storage (p. 18)

software (p. 18)

supercomputer (p. 18)

Review Questions

1. List several kinds of software packages that make today's computers easy to use.
2. Describe an analog computer.
3. How does a digital computer recognize data?
4. List several data processing tasks for which businesses use computers.
5. What functions do computers perform in automobiles?
6. Give examples telling how the medical profession might use computers.
7. Give examples of computer simulation. What advantages do you see to simulations?
8. How are computers used in the field of education?
9. Give examples of how computers are applied in the legal system.
10. Computers are used in sports. Explain what they can do.
11. How can computers be used in making movies?
12. Give examples of how computers might affect your vacation.
13. What are some of the ways computers are used in the production of books?
14. List the components of a computer system.
15. Large computer systems are grouped into which three categories?

16. What are the characteristics of a microcomputer?

17. Computers are used in basically three ways. Name them.

18. What are the three functions of a computer?

19. Computers have three advantages over people when it comes to solving problems. What are they?

20. Explain the difference between data and information.

21. List the steps in the flow of data through a computer?

22. Explain what is involved during each step in the flow of data through a computer.

23. List three things that computers cannot do.

24. Explain why computer literacy is important to today's student.

25. What is the most interesting fact that you learned about computers in Chapter 1? Explain.

INFOMODULE
A History of Computers

As soon as humans domesticated animals and started to carry on trade with other people, they needed a system to keep track of numbers. First, people counted on their fingers; then, they cut notches on sticks, counted stones, and even tied knots in ropes. The abacus—a rudimentary, first computing device—is generally thought to be of Chinese origin, but it actually evolved in different cultures at about the same time. This simple device, which uses beads to represent digits and wires to hold places, is still used today.

PEOPLE AND THEIR CONTRIBUTIONS

What Might Have Been

Early in the 17th century, Wilhelm Schickard, a professor of astronomy, mathematics, and Hebrew at Turbingen, Germany, designed an ingenious machine to add, subtract, and, to some degree, multiply and divide numbers into the hundreds. Unfortunately, before the device was half completed, the factory where it was housed burned. Schickard and his entire family died of the plague before he could construct another model. Much later, a master mechanic recreated the instrument from Schickard's old letters and rough models. Had this invention been available to subsequent innovators, it could have changed the history of computers entirely.

The Way It Was!

The evolution of computing devices did proceed, although slowly, even without Schickard's clever machine as a prototype. But first, an interesting thing was happening with numbers.

In the 1600s, John Napier, a Scotsman, discovered a way to manipulate numbers so that multiplication and division could be reduced to addition and subtraction of other numbers. The series of numbers and their relationships were called logarithms. By placing the numbers on ivory rods (called Napier's bones), solutions to complex problems could be found relatively quickly by matching logarithms and then adding or subtracting the appropriate numbers. Robert Bissaker's invention of the slide rule around 1650 replaced Napier's ivory rods.

FIGURE 1
Pascaline (Courtesy of International Business Machines Corp.)

Blaise Pascal, a French mathematician and philosopher interested in the branch of mathematics known as probability theory, invented the first mechanical digital calculator that could perform addition and subtraction on whole numbers. Although this machine was an improvement over time-consuming manual calculations, it was not as technically advanced as Schickard's computing device. The Pascaline (Figure 1), developed around 1642, was a dismal financial failure. First, Pascal was the only person who could repair it. Second, it was cheaper to have people complete the calculations; and, third, workers feared being replaced by the Pascaline, thereby losing their jobs. Regardless, Pascal's gear-driven, decimal counting wheel was used until the electronic calculator made it obsolete. A programming language, Pascal, was later named to honor his contributions.

Later, Gottfried Wilhelm von Leibniz, a German mathematician who along with Sir Isaac Newton co-invented calculus, produced the stepped-wheel calculator. This device, created in 1673, resembled a combination slide rule and meat grinder and could perform all four arithmetic functions—addition, subtraction, multiplication, and division. The Leibniz wheel (Figure 2) was an improvement on Pascal's calculator; however, it was not particularly reliable and never became widely used. It did impress Peter the Great, however, who sent one to the Emperor of China to convince him of Germany's technology and to increase trade between the East and West.

In 1804, Frenchman Joseph Marie Jacquard built an automated punched-card machine that was used to operate weaving looms (Figure 3). Jacquard's invention showed that data could be coded on cards; the cards could be joined to create a series of instructions, and these instructions could automate the weaving. Programmable instructions proved to be a concept of great importance for modern computers.

FIGURE 3
Jacquard's loom (Courtesy of International Business Machines Corp.)

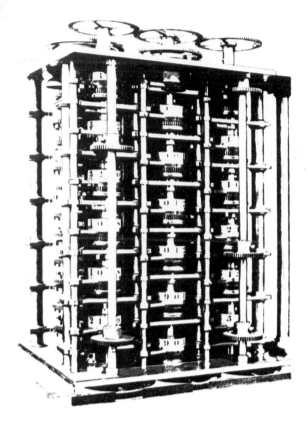

FIGURE 4
Babbage's difference engine (Courtesy of International Business Machines Corp.)

In 1822, a British inventor and mathematician, Charles P. Babbage, designed an all-purpose problem-solving machine, the difference engine (Figure 4), that had a mechanical memory to store results. The Royal Astronomical Society encouraged Babbage with government grants, and his design grew more complex as revisions occurred to him. The grants ceased in 1834, but undaunted, Babbage proposed a more elaborate computing machine, the analytical engine. Although the power from six steam engines would have been required to run the analytical engine and it would have occupied the length of a football field, Babbage's steam-powered machine would have computed mathematical tables and logarithms automatically. Data would have been entered by using punched cards, and the machine could have been programmed to change operating procedures. Regrettably, the analytical engine was never built; however, this concept was a mechanical predecessor of the modern-day computer.

For his contributions, Babbage earned the title, "father of the computer;" however, he also invented the speedometer, locomotive cow catcher, and the first reliable life-expectancy (actuarial) tables for the insurance profession.

Babbage had a confidante and partner, Augusta Ada, Countess of Lovelace and daughter of poet Lord Byron. Lady Lovelace understood Babbage's ideas, recognized their great value, and in the 1840s, wrote scientific papers explaining his ideas to others. She even suggested using a binary rather than decimal system for storage. Lady Lovelace is sometimes thought of as "the first programmer" because she refined the design of the analytical engine by including the automatic repetition of a series of calculations. This looping procedure is extremely valuable to today's programmers.

In the 1850s, George Boole, a self-taught English mathematician, realized that complex mathematical problems could be solved by reducing them to a series of affirmatively- or negatively-answered questions. The binary system of 1s for positive answers and 0s for negative could thus be implemented. This theory of Boolean logic became fundamental to the design of computer circuitry.

In the 1880s, Dr. Herman Hollerith built the first electromechanical, punched-card, data-processing machine (Figure 5). Hollerith, whose father-in-law was a census official, suggested that his machine could tabulate and sort census information by using the 80-column punched cards that he also invented.

Using his tabulating equipment, Hollerith processed the 1890 United States census information pertaining to 63,056,000 people in one-third the time required to count 50,262,000 people in 1880. He then founded the Tabulating Machine Company, one of many companies that eventually merged to become IBM.

After Hollerith's discoveries, there was a lag in creativity in the computer field. Progress was being made, but nothing spectacular was reported.

Then, in 1927 at Massachusetts Institute of Technology (MIT), Vannevar Bush and his col-

FIGURE 5
Hollerith's punched-card machine (Courtesy of International Business Machines Corp.)

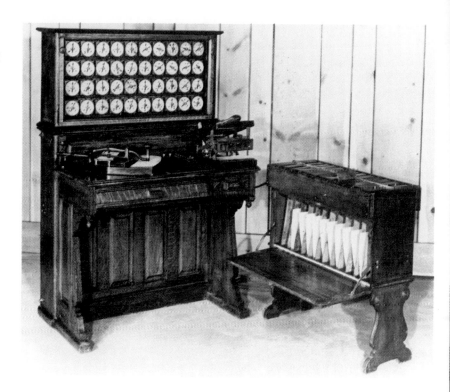

leagues created an electromechanical machine that solved simple differential equations. By 1931, the machine had been modified and perfected to solve more complex equations. The differential analyzer carried out calculations by the rotation of various shafts. Although it resembled a giant dishpan with steel rods sticking out, it was a good analog computing device.

George Stibitz, a research mathematician at Bell Telephone Laboratory, tinkered with the idea that Boolean logic provided a natural language for electromechanical circuits. His device, created in 1937 from batteries, flashlight bulbs, wire, and tobacco-can strips of metal, controlled the on and off flow of electricity. Called the Complex Number Calculator, the machine added binary numbers—a basic requirement for all future digital computers. In 1940, Stibitz and his colleague, Samuel Williams, demonstrated how using this device with teletype machines could send calculations over a distance of 250 miles.

In Iowa in 1939, John Atanasoff and Clifford Berry collaborated to build the Atanasoff-Berry Computer (the ABC). The ABC (Figure 6) was the world's first general-purpose, electronic, digi-

tal computer; but even though its purpose was to solve simultaneous linear algebraic equations, it did not generate a lot of interest in the scientific community. When Dr. Atanasoff contacted IBM about his machine, the company said that they would never be interested in an electronic computing machine.

FIGURE 6
Atanasoff-Berry Computer (ABC) (Courtesy of Iowa State University)

In 1941, in the midst of World War II, Konrad Zuse built the first operational general-purpose computer for Germany. His machine used binary logic even though Zuse had not heard of George Boole. To assist the German war effort, Zuse proposed an updated model using vacuum tubes instead of electromechanical relays to increase operational speed a thousandfold. He suggested to Adolph Hitler that the new machine could be used by the military to compare and evaluate aircraft designs and to break wartime codes. Hitler refused funding saying that the war would be over before the two years Zuse needed to finish the machine.

Fortunately for the Allies, the Polish secret service smuggled a replica of the Enigma, a German message-scrambling device, to the British. Alan Turing, an eccentric English genius, began to work at unraveling the mysteries of the Enigma. In 1943, Turing and his colleagues capitalized on the vacuum-tube technology that Zuse had wanted to pursue. The British machine built to counteract Enigma was called Colossus; it could process 25,000 characters per second. In 1950, Turing also constructed the Automatic Computing Engine (ACE), which some touted as the first programmable, digital computer. Because of the secrecy involved with most of Turing's projects, his contributions were not acknowledged until after his death.

Most industries in the United States rallied to support the war effort. Thomas J. Watson, president of IBM, offered to supply thousands of punch-card sorting machines. His plans also included Howard Aiken, a Harvard mathematician. Aiken wanted to build a general-purpose, programmable computer similar to the one Babbage had proposed.

Aiken completed the first automatic, sequence-controlled calculator, Mark I (Figure 7), in 1944. It calculated by using electromechanical relays (i.e., electricity rather than muscles), effectively replacing Hollerith's gear mechanism.

The Mark I was not a small machine. At 51 feet long and 8 feet high, it contained over 750,000 parts and was strung with 500 miles of wires. It used paper tape input and required 3,000 telephone relays that made loud clicking noises when operating. Output was on punched cards; calculations of 23-digit numbers took only three seconds. Six months of manual calculations could be completed in one day. With these calculation capabilities, the Mark I and its successors aided the military in computing ballistics data.

Technology now was advancing rapidly, and many people worked on similar ideas simultaneously. John Mauchly, a physicist on the staff at the University of Pennsylvania's Moore School of Engineering, visited Atanasoff in Iowa in

FIGURE 7
Mark I (Courtesy of International Business Machines Corp.)

FIGURE 8
ENIAC (Courtesy of International Business Machines Corp.)

1941, when the ABC computer was still in its prototype stages of construction. The possible applications of the machine interested and impressed Mauchly.

In 1942, Mauchly and another Moore School colleague, J. Presper Eckert, submitted a proposal to the government to build a machine that would compute artillery firing tables. On April 9, 1943, the government granted the Moore School a $400,000 contract to build the Electronic Numerical Integrator and Computer (ENIAC) (Figure 8).

At 80 feet long by 18 feet high, ENIAC was twice as big as the Mark I. Instead of gears or mechanical relays, the 30-ton ENIAC contained over 100,000 electronic components, including 17,468 vacuum tubes. Although the vacuum tubes took up a lot of space, their use increased the speed of calculations by a thousandfold. The ENIAC operated on the decimal system which allowed the punched-card output to be read easily by humans. A major drawback, however, was the extreme difficulty in changing programs or operations because instructions had to be manually wired into the circuitry.

The ENIAC was put into operation at Aberdeen Proving Ground, Maryland, in 1947. Although too late for service in wartime, it was used for calculations in weather forecasting, wind tunnel designs, ballistics tables, and cosmic-ray study. Since it took the operators as long as two days to manually replug the wires involved in changing instructions, the ENIAC was not an efficient general-purpose computer.

Mauchly and Eckert claimed the ENIAC was the first general purpose, electronic, digital computer, but on October 19, 1973, a court settlement declared that the Atanasoff-Berry Computer was entitled to that honor.

The ENIAC was obsolete almost before it was completed, and Mauchly and Eckert planned a successor called the Electronic Discrete Variable Automatic Computer (EDVAC). Completed in 1949, EDVAC stored its instructions electronically and used the binary system of coding instructions and input.

The EDVAC was one of the first two stored-program computers. It consisted of five units: arithmetical; central control; memory; input; and output. The improvements over the ENIAC included reduction of the number of tubes, increased memory, easier use, and a simpler, faster way to set up additional problems.

The development of the stored-program concept used in EDVAC has been claimed by many; however, the definitive paper outlining this and other differences in the computer's design features has been credited to John von Neumann, the special consultant hired by the Moore School for the EDVAC project. John von Neumann was a mathematical genius with a photographic memory. His paper "First Draft of a Report on the EDVAC" presented in the mid-1940s served as a blueprint for future stored-program computers.

Also in 1949, Englishman Maurice V. Wilkes of Cambridge incorporated the von Neumann stored-program concept into the Electronic Delay Storage Automatic Computer (EDSAC). The EDSAC was available a few months before the EDVAC and was, therefore, awarded the title of the first stored-program computer.

At Harvard around 1949, An Wang, founder of Wang Laboratories developed magnetic-core memories. Subsequently, Jay Forrester at MIT discovered a way to organize magnetic-core memories into a grid, providing a more practical application than the previous serial connections. Computers became not only faster, but also more reliable and capable of containing larger memories.

In 1951, Mauchly and Eckert formed their own company to create a commercially usable general-purpose computer—UNIVAC I. When Mauchly and Eckert fell upon hard times, Remington Rand bought their company and completed it (Figure 9). UNIVAC I was designed specifically for business data-processing applications, and it was the first general-purpose computer used commercially. Previously, computers had been used solely for scientific or military applications. The U.S. Census Bureau immediately installed UNIVAC I and used it for more than twelve years. In Louisville, Kentucky in 1954, General Electric Company processed the first computerized payroll using a UNIVAC I.

It wasn't long before other companies including Burroughs (now called UNISYS), Honeywell, IBM, and others realized the commercial value of computers and began offering their own.

From 1950 to 1952, people in the U.S. Navy and at the Digital Computer Lab at MIT developed the Whirlwind, another vacuum tube, stored-program computer. The Whirlwind simulated high-performance trainer aircraft, contained self-diagnostics, and performed 50,000 operations per second; however, it was only about 85 percent accurate. During the early 1950s, the military used it for air surveillance.

Other innovators appeared on the scene in the late 1950s. Both Jack Kilby, at Texas Instruments, and Robert Noyce, at Fairchild Semiconductor, discovered that resistors, capacitors, and transistors could be made simultaneously from the same semiconductor material. Any number of transistors could be etched on silicon; the integrated circuit (Figure 10), christened the "chip," was developed and refined. These

FIGURE 9
The UNIVAC I correctly predicted that Dwight Eisenhower would defeat Adlai Stevenson in the 1952 Presidential Election. A young Walter Cronkite confers with J. Presper Eckert, Jr., and the computer operator. (Courtesy of UNISYS Corp.)

FIGURE 10
Comparison of size between vacuum tubes and integrated circuit (National Semiconductor Corp.)

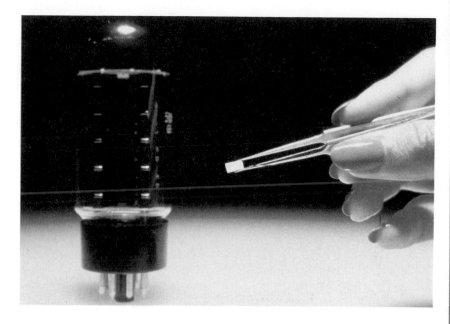

1959 discoveries were mass produced in 1962 and were included in 1964 computers.

The '60s also brought the arrival of Gene Amdahl's revolutionary IBM System/360 series of mainframe computers (Figure 11)—the first general-purpose, digital computers using integrated circuit technology. Because they were a "family" of computers and used compatible software, the series was a valuable addition to growing companies. Later, in his own company, Amdahl built a competitive computer that was faster, less expensive, and smaller in size.

The miniaturization of components developed through various technological innovations, coupled with the success of the commercial use of computers, led Ken Olsen and his Digital Equip-

FIGURE 11
IBM System/360 family of computers (Courtesy of International Business Machines Corp.)

ment Corporation (DEC) to the production of the first minicomputer, the PDP–1, in 1963. Less expensive than a mainframe, the minicomputer was for use by small companies.

At the other end of the spectrum, computers were becoming more powerful. In fact, the ILLIAC IV was a supercomputer, first used at the Ames Research Center in 1972 for solving aerodynamic problems that were too large and complicated for other systems.

Other supercomputers were being developed too. In 1976, Seymour Cray's Cray–1 super-computer was delivered to Los Alamos Scientific Laboratory in New Mexico, and a Control Data Corporation CYBER–205 was used by the Meteorological Service in the United Kingdom for weather predictions.

Meanwhile, advances were being made in the field of programming languages. High-level, English-like programming languages began to be developed in the mid-1950s. John Backus and a group of IBM engineers developed FORTRAN (FORmula TRANslator) as the first problem-oriented, algebraic programming language. Its orientation, therefore, was more toward mathematicians and scientists.

By 1959, Rear Admiral (ret.) Grace Murray Hopper was instrumental in developing COBOL (COmmon Business Oriented Language) as the first programming language designed for business data processing. Hopper also helped to invent the UNIVAC I's compiler, a program that could translate other programs into machine language—the 1s and 0s that the computer "understands."

Dr. John Kemeny, a mathematics professor at Dartmouth, and his colleague, Dr. Thomas Kurtz, developed the computer language BASIC (Beginner's All-purpose Symbolic Instruction Code) in 1965. They later presented a version called True BASIC, which uses structured programming techniques to make programs easier to read, debug, and update.

Today, numerous high-level languages are in use, including Pascal, C, and Logo.

By 1970, Intel had created a memory chip that could store a kilobit of information. A kilobit translates roughly into 25 five-letter words. Another innovation at Intel came from Ted Hoff,

who in 1970 further improved the integrated circuit by compressing twelve chips into four. The arithmetic and logic functions of several chips could be contained on one chip, called a microprocessor. Hoff's microprocessor, called the Intel 4004 ("forty-oh-four"), made the development of the small computer, or microcomputer, a reality.

The first hobbyist microcomputer became available in 1975. H. Edward Roberts, an electrical engineer who is now generally known as the "father of the microcomputer," designed the Altair 8800. It sold in kit form for approximately $395 and required some electronics knowledge to assemble. To the buyer, the novelty of owning a computer far outweighed the inconvenience of a memory that could hold only 256 bits.

Competition for the Altair 8800 appeared in 1977 from the TRS–80 Model 1 by Tandy Radio Shack and the Personal Electronic Transactor (PET) by Commodore Business Machines.

Many microcomputer companies have come and gone, but one of the great rags-to-riches stories is Apple Computer, Inc., founded by Steven Jobs and Stephen Wozniak. Apple Computer's first headquarters was a garage.

Wozniak, the technical expert, made a microcomputer that was affordable and small enough for both individuals and owners of small businesses. Because he knew very little about circuitry or coding, Jobs provided the marketing impetus for the small company. Since the first commercial Apple computers went on sale in 1977, their popularity has increased.

In 1981, Adam Osborne introduced a truly portable microcomputer, Osborne 1. It weighed only 24 pounds, had memory capacity of 64 kilobytes, and cost approximately $1,795. Osborne 1 could be manufactured in just over one hour, using only forty screws to put together the easy-to-assemble parts.

As microcomputers gained popularity, many companies introduced their own versions—not only for hobbyists and small-business users, but also for the entire business community.

Time magazine annually honors someone who during the year has made a difference in the world. In 1982, however, *Time* chose the computer as its "Man of the Year." Table 1 lists many of the major contributors to the development of computers.

TECHNOLOGICAL EVOLUTION OF COMPUTERS

Computers changed over time; they improved in speed, power, and efficiency. Those changes are recognized as a progression of generations of discoveries, each characterized by specific developments (Table 2).

First Generation (1951–1959)

The early **first-generation computers** were powered by thousands of **vacuum tubes.** UNIVAC I and other similar computers were large

TABLE 1
Major contributors to computer development

Date	Person	Contribution
1642	Pascal	First mechanical digital calculator, the Pascaline.
1804	Jacquard	Used punched-cards with weaving loom.
1822	Babbage	"Father of the computer." Invented difference engine with mechanical memory to store results.
1840s	Augusta Ada	"The first programmer." Suggested binary rather than decimal for data storage.
1850s	Boole	Developed Boolean logic, which later was used in design of computer circuitry.
1880s	Hollerith	Built first electromechanical, punched-card, data-processing machine, used to compile information for 1890 U.S. census.
1939	Atanasoff and Berry	Built the ABC, world's first general-purpose, electronic, digital computer to solve large equations.
1943	Turing	Used vacuum-tube technology to build British Colossus, used to counteract the German code scrambling device, Enigma.
1944	Aiken	Built the Mark I, the first automatic, sequence-controlled calculator; used by military to compute ballistics data.
1940s	von Neumann	Presented a paper outlining the stored-program concept.
1947	Mauchly and Eckert	Built ENIAC, second general-purpose electronic, digital computer; used to compute artillery firing tables.

TABLE 1
(continued)

Date	Person	Contribution
1949	Wilkes	Built EDSAC, first stored-program computer.
1949	Mauchly, Eckert, and von Neumann	Built EDVAC, second stored-program computer.
1949	Wang	Developed magnetic-core memory.
1949	Forrester	Organized magnetic-core memory to be more efficient.
1950	Turing	Built the ACE, which some consider to be the first programmable, digital computer.
1951	Mauchly and Eckert	Built UNIVAC I, first computer designed and sold commercially, specifically for business data-processing applications.
1950s	Hopper	Developed UNIVAC I compiler.
1957	Backus	One of a group of IBM engineers to develop FORTRAN.
1959	Kilby and Noyce	Developed and perfected the integrated circuit to be used in later computers.
1959	Hopper	Instrumental in developing the COBOL programming language.
1960s	Amdahl	Designed IBM System/360 series of mainframe computers, the first general-purpose, digital computers to use integrated circuits.
1963	Olsen	With DEC produced the PDP–1, the first minicomputer.
1965	Kemeny and Kurtz	Developed BASIC programming language. True BASIC followed later.
1970	Hoff	Developed the famous Intel 4004 microprocessor chip.
1975	Roberts	"Father of the microcomputer." Designed the first microcomputer, the Altair 8800 in kit form.
1976	Cray	Developed the Cray–1 supercomputer.
1977	Jobs and Wozniak	Designed and built the first Apple microcomputer.

TABLE 2
Generations of computers and
their characteristics

First Generation (1951–1959)
- ☐ Vacuum tubes
- ☐ Magnetic tape for external storage—some magnetic drum
- ☐ Punched cards for input
- ☐ Punched cards and paper for output
- ☐ Machine and assembly languages
- ☐ Human operators to set switches
- ☐ UNIVAC I typical example

Second Generation (1959–1965)
- ☐ Transistors
- ☐ Magnetic-core storage
- ☐ Magnetic tape most common external storage, but magnetic disk introduced
- ☐ Punched cards and magnetic tape for input
- ☐ Punched cards and paper for output
- ☐ High-level languages—FORTRAN, COBOL, BASIC, PL/I and others
- ☐ Human operator to handle punched cards
- ☐ Honeywell 200 typical example

Third Generation (1965–1971)
- ☐ Integrated circuits
- ☐ Improved disk storage
- ☐ Monitors and keyboards for input and output
- ☐ More high-level languages, including RPG and Pascal
- ☐ First complete operating systems meant less involvement for human operators
- ☐ Family of computers introduced allowing compatibility
- ☐ Minicomputers used commercially
- ☐ IBM System/360 typical example

Fourth Generation (1971–Present)
- ☐ LSI and VLSI
- ☐ Magnetic disk most common external storage
- ☐ Introduction of microcomputer
- ☐ Fourth-generation languages emerged and application software for microcomputers became popular
- ☐ Microcomputers used—Compaq Deskpro 386 typical example
- ☐ Burroughs B7700 and HP 3000 (minicomputer) typical examples

Fifth Generation (Future)
- ☐ Development of true artificial intelligence

because of the massive number of tubes required to operate the machines. The tubes themselves were large (the size of today's light bulbs); they required a lot of energy and generated a great deal of heat. The computer's memory was stored on magnetic storage devices primarily magnetic tapes and magnetic drums. Most of the data were entered into the computer on punched cards similar to Jacquard's loom process. Output consisted of punched cards or paper, and binary (machine) and assembly languages were used to program the computers. However, a human operator physically had to reset relay switches and wiring before a program could be run.

Second Generation (1959–1965)

The transistor characterized the **second-generation computers. A transistor** was made of a semiconducting material, and it controlled the flow of electricity through the circuits. A breakthrough in technology, the transistor made it possible to produce a computer that was faster, physically smaller, more powerful, and more reliable than before. William Shockley, J. Bardeen, and W. H. Brattain developed the transistor at Bell Labs in 1947 and displayed it to the public in 1948. They won a Nobel Prize in 1956, but their transistor was not used in conjunction with computers until 1959.

Transistors were smaller, less expensive, required less electricity, and emitted less heat than vacuum tubes; and fewer transistors than tubes were required to operate a computer. They were not as fragile as vacuum tubes, and they lasted longer. Because the components were substantially smaller, the size of the computer considerably decreased as well.

Although magnetic tape was still the most commonly used external storage medium, magnetic-disk storage was used so that data could be located more rapidly. MIT developed magnetic-core storage where each core stored one bit of information. Data stored this way were instantaneously available, contrasted with tape and drum storage where the data's place had to be found first.

Punched cards and magnetic tape were the primary means for input; punched cards and paper constituted the output.

Programming languages also became more sophisticated. High-level languages that resembled English, including FORTRAN, COBOL, BASIC, and PL/I, were being developed. Like the first-generation computers, second-generation computers were primarily under the control of human operators.

Third Generation (1965–1971)

The use of **integrated circuits** (ICs) signified the beginning of **third-generation computers.** Again, they were smaller, more efficient, and more reliable than their predecessors. Unlike transistors and circuit boards that were assembled manually, ICs could be manufactured. Ultimately, this method of production resulted in a lower cost.

Memory technology was improved, too. By 1969, as many as 1,000 transistors could be built on one chip of silicon. Magnetic disks had been improved and were being used more for storage. Monitors and keyboards were introduced for data input and output, while punched cards began losing their preeminence as the input or output device.

A new computer program, the operating system, effectively controlled the computer and its resources. Human operators were no longer required, and processing could be done at "computer speeds" rather than "human speeds." High-level programming languages continued to be developed, including RPG and Pascal.

Another phenomenon of this third generation involved the introduction of a concept of computer "families." Prior to this concept, businesses would buy computers and programs only to find that almost before the system was fully adapted, it was outdated, or unable to grow with the user's needs. IBM recognized this problem and created an entire product line, the IBM/360 series, that allowed for necessary upgrading or expansion. Programs written for one computer were compatible with any of the machines in the line. Businesses could upgrade or expand their data processing operations as necessary.

Digital Equipment Corporation introduced the first minicomputer in November 1963. Their PDP–1 was substantially cheaper than mainframes, thus making these smaller computers available to yet another business market.

Fourth Generation (1971–Present)

The significant distinction for the **fourth-generation computers** is the development of **large-scale integration (LSI).** LSI placed several thousand transistors onto a single chip. This advancement was followed in the mid-1970s by the development of **very large-scale integration (VLSI),** the incorporation of several hundred thousand transistors onto a single chip. VLSI made the development of the first microprocessor, and thus the microcomputer, possible. This development was followed by the creation of faster, more powerful microprocessors, such as the Intel 80386.

Magnetic disks became the primary means of external storage. The proliferation of application programs for microcomputers allowed home and business users to adapt their computers for word processing, spreadsheet manipulating, file handling, creating graphics, and much more.

Fifth Generation (Future)

Although many people disagree on the beginning date of **fifth-generation computer** technology, some say that the creation and use of a computer with **artificial intelligence** will represent the next step. The unofficial, original goal was a "thinking" machine by 1990. Although expert systems are already being used for spe-cialized applications, true artificial intelligence, or computers that can "think," are still concepts in the minds of tomorrow's Babbage, Lovelace, Turing, and von Neumann.

The future may hold the following possibilities: supercomputers capable of billions of calculations per second; advances in artificial intelligence; a computer that can "think" and "reason;" or further miniaturization of hardware.

Since you are part of the future, you may have some ideas or innovations of your own.

KEY TERMS

artificial intelligence (p. 41)

fifth-generation computers (p. 41)

first-generation computers (p. 37)

fourth-generation computers (p. 41)

integrated circuits (p. 40)

large-scale integration (LSI) (p. 41)

second-generation computers (p. 40)

third-generation computers (p. 40)

transistor (p. 40)

vacuum tubes (p. 37)

very large-scale integration (VLSI) (p. 41)

QUESTIONS

1. Describe the characteristics that delineate the first and second generations of computers.
2. Compare the distinctions between third- and fourth-generation computers.
3. What characteristics will appear in the fifth generation of computers?
4. Write a thumbnail sketch of someone you found interesting in this InfoModule.
5. What invention or innovation do you think is most responsible for making the computer a successful product? Defend your choice.

OBJECTIVES

 Describe the parts of the central processing unit

☐ Explain the function of the central processing unit

☐ Describe the types of primary storage and the roles they play

☐ Explain the differences between bits, bytes, and words

2
The Central Processing Unit

PROFILE: M. E. (Ted) Hoff

It's hard to imagine where we would be today if it weren't for people with vision like Ted Hoff. Even he probably didn't realize what would become of the work he started on that fateful day in 1969.

Ted Hoff joined Intel Corporation in 1969, after working at Stanford University as a research assistant. At Intel, Hoff led a team that helped a Japanese firm, Busicom, to design a custom circuit for its calculator.

The Busicom design called for twelve integrated circuit chips, each with 3,000–5,000 transistors. The chips that made up the processor were matched to the specific tasks of the calculator. After reviewing the design, however, Hoff decided it was too complex and would be too expensive to produce; consequently, he creatively solved these problems by using a totally different approach. He decided to design the calculator around a general-purpose processor, relying more on software than on a lot of electronics. Although more memory space was needed to store the software, this approach enabled Hoff to put the entire processor on a single integrated circuit chip, called a microprocessor.

And what a chip it was! The Intel 4004 could handle four bits of information at a time, and its computational powers came close to those of the ENIAC, one of the early electronic, digital computers which required an entire room to house. This single microprocessor performed as well as some of the early 1960s IBM machines that cost around $30,000 and had processing units the size of a large desk. Hoff's microprocessor was about one-sixth by one-eighth inch and cost about $200. The reductions in size and cost made it possible to design small, relatively inexpensive computers. This discovery heralded the beginning of the microcomputer revolution.

Thanks to Ted Hoff's creativeness, microprocessors are everywhere—in our computers, homes, cars, factories, and yes, still in our calculators.

The basic operations of the computer have not changed much over the years. What has changed, however, is the technology used to accomplish those operations. In the 1950s, it took a roomful of vacuum tubes and equipment to perform the tasks that are now completed by a single chip no bigger than a child's thumbnail. As technology advanced, the size of the chip became smaller; as the chip continues to be perfected, its size may be reduced even more. Couple this change with the increase in computing speed brought about, in part, by miniaturization and you have a computer that keeps getting smaller, but can do more in less time.

Its compactness and tremendous power have put the computer into almost every aspect of today's world, so the more familiar you become with the use of a computer, the more comfortable you will be when coming into contact with it. You do not need to be an expert in all phases of computer operation, however. A secretary may need to know all about word processors and spreadsheets, but have very little, if any, knowledge about how the computer functions internally.

This chapter provides an overview of the central processing unit. In addition, some basic concepts of data representation are presented. You won't be able to build a computer after you've read this chapter, but you will know how its basic components interact with one another.

CENTRAL PROCESSING UNIT

The **central processing unit (CPU)** is comprised of the arithmetic and logic unit (ALU), the control unit, and the primary storage unit. Some sources define the CPU as being only the ALU and the control unit. However, because the ALU, the control unit, and primary storage are closely related and function as a whole, the CPU is defined here as containing all three elements (Figure 2–1).

Advances in semiconductor technology have reduced the size of the CPU. Depending on conditions, a semiconductor can serve as a conductor (allowing the transmission of electricity) or as an insulator (inhibiting the transmission of electricity). This ability is ideal, because data are repre-

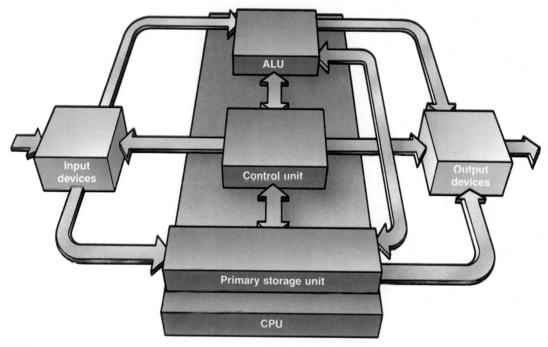

FIGURE 2–1

The relationship between a CPU and input and output devices is shown here. Arrows indicate the basic movement of data or instructions among these elements.

This technician is assembling a Motorola 32-bit chip at the company's Austin, Texas, facility. (Courtesy of Motorola, Inc.)

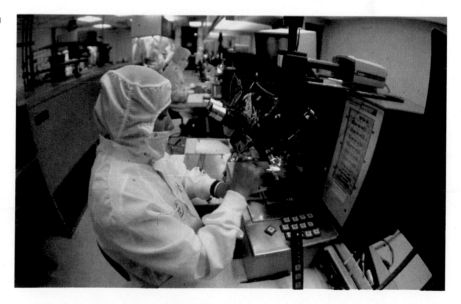

sented by combinations of high voltage states (conductor) or low voltage states (insulator).

One, complete, electronic semiconductor circuit contained on a small piece of silicon is called an **integrated circuit (IC). Large-scale inte-**

gration (LSI) and **very large-scale integration (VLSI)** technology have dramatically increased the number (from several thousand with LSI to over 100,000 with VLSI) of complete circuits residing on a small piece of silicon. An IC, also called a **microchip,** or just **chip,** is used for the design of both logic and memory circuitry. For example, an IC can be designed to function as part of the ALU or as part of primary storage.

Until the developmental work by Ted Hoff, all parts of the CPU were separate units; Hoff combined the ALU and the control unit on a single chip called a **microprocessor** (Figure 2–2). To be called a microprocessor, a chip must contain at least the ALU and control unit, but it may also contain primary storage.

In a microcomputer, the components of the CPU are mounted on the main circuit board, often called the "motherboard" (Figure 2–3).

Arithmetic and Logic Unit

The **arithmetic and logic unit (ALU)** is the part of the CPU where all mathematical and logical functions are performed. The basic mathematical functions include addition, subtraction, multiplication, and division. Software can be used to combine these four basic math functions to perform logarithmic, trigonometric, and other mathematical functions. A **logic function** is one where numbers or conditions are compared to each other. Examples of logic functions are greater than, less than, equal to, not equal to, greater than or equal to, and less than or equal to.

People make logic decisions every day. When you buy clothes for instance, you compare price, quality, and style from one garment to the next, and from one store to the next.

Often, comparisons are needed before calculations can be performed. For example, before overtime pay can be calculated, an employee's total number of work hours is compared to a base, such as 40 hours, to see if an overtime calculation is even necessary.

Main Components of a CPU

- Arithmetic and logic unit
- Control unit
- Primary storage unit

FIGURE 2–2
The Motorola MC68020 microprocessor in the protective ceramic package (Courtesy of Motorola, Inc.)

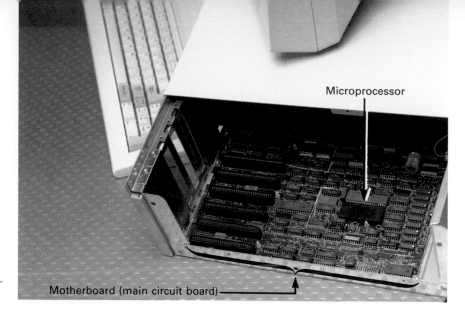

Microprocessor

Motherboard (main circuit board)

The Control Unit

The **control unit** interprets any instructions it receives from memory and directs the sequence of events necessary to execute the instruction. The control unit also establishes the timing of these events and is basically the "traffic cop" of the system.

To control all that is going on in the CPU, the control unit uses a **system clock,** which synchronizes all tasks by sending out electrical pulses. The number of pulses or cycles per second is a main element in determining the speed of the processor. The clock speed is measured in megahertz (MHz). Hertz is the unit of frequency that measures the number of cycles per second in a periodic signal; a megahertz is equal to one million hertz. All things being equal, an 8-MHz processor will do things twice as fast as a 4-MHz processor.

Circuit board designers use computers for the design, layout, simulation, and testing of circuits. (Reprinted with permission from Calma Co., a wholly-owned subsidiary of the General Electric Co., U.S.A.)

Other factors also affect processing speed; the instruction set is one. An **instruction set** consists of the group of commands available to the CPU which determines the basic computer operations (arithmetic, logic, and storage and retrieval functions) that can be performed. A CPU is designed with an instruction set that the control unit uses to direct and coordinate the computer's operations.

Each instruction takes a specific number of system clock cycles to complete. The same instruction may take ten clock cycles to complete on one processor but only five clock cycles on another. So even though both of these processors are running at 8 MHz, one takes twice as long to complete the same instruction.

Computer speed is also measured by the number of instructions completed per second, or **millions of instructions per second (MIPS).** This measurement is usually how large computer systems, such as minicomputers, mainframes, and supercomputers, are compared. Typical speeds for minicomputers are in the 5–10 MIPS range. Mainframe computers generally perform in the 20–50 MIPS range but the range can go to more than 100 MIPS. Supercomputers execute instructions from approximately 200 MIPS and up. Some microprocessors, such as the Intel 80386, can execute 3–4 MIPS. Most microprocessors, however, run at less than one MIPS and are usually classified only by their system clock speeds. A typical microcomputer can execute an instruction, such as adding two numbers, in a few milliseconds. Mainframes and supercomputers can execute in the microsecond and nanosecond ranges.

The difference between a millisecond and a microsecond may seem to be insignificant; however, it is roughly the same as the difference between one minute and one day, or one hour and one month. Just think of how much more you can accomplish in a month than you can in a hour. Table 2–1 shows how computer speeds compare to one second of time. These speed differences become important when running long programs that process volumes of data. On computers with varying processor speeds, a few millionths of a second can mean a big difference in the performance of a software package. For example, complicated accounting programs could take much longer to run on a computer with a slow rather than a fast processing speed.

TABLE 2–1
Computer speeds compared to one second of time

In:	There Are:
1 millisecond	.001 second
1 microsecond	.000001 second
1 nanosecond	.000000001 second
Put Another Way:	
1 second	1 thousand milliseconds
1 second	1 million microseconds
1 second	1 billion nanoseconds

Primary Storage Unit

The **primary storage unit** refers to the internal storage of the computer, where programs and their data are stored. Primary storage, or primary memory, provides temporary storage during program execution. Part of primary storage may also contain permanently stored instructions that tell the computer what to do when it is turned on. Because primary storage is located inside the computer and is linked directly to the other components of the CPU, access time to data is very fast.

The process of entering data into storage (primary storage or second ary storage) is called **writing.** When data are placed in, or written to, storage, they replace what was originally there; this procedure is equivalent to deleting a word with a pencil eraser and writing a new word in its

This scuba diver depends on the functions that the underwater decompression computer (the size of a wristwatch) can perform. The battery-operated computer keeps track of data such as dive depth and duration of dive. The appropriate rate of ascent is displayed numerically so that the diver avoids getting the ''bends'' when surfacing. (David Hiser/ Photographers Aspen. Inset: Merrill Publishing/Cobalt Productions)

HIGHLIGHT

THE EXPANDING TECHNOLOGY OF CHIP SHRINKING

To allow for faster computer processing, scientists are trying to reduce the distance the electrical signal must travel within the computer. The connections among microchips on today's integrated circuits are so bulky that they can be no closer than one-quarter inch or so. At the speed of light, however, that quarter inch multiplied by the number of connections becomes a vast distance.

The U.S. Navy is funding a research project to find a way to shorten this connecting span. One suggestion is to create a network of short, superfine metallic lines using a highly focused laser light to etch the lines. In early experiments using this technique, tungsten lines measuring only one micron—a thousandth of a millimeter—were used. To help you get a visual picture, a micron is $\frac{1}{100}$ the width of a human hair! Lines of this size allow the electrical components of a computer to be built closer together, shortening the distance the electrical signals must travel and, thus, increasing the processing speed.

place. The process of retrieving data from storage is called **reading.** The reading process does not change the data in any way.

Primary storage may take one of three forms: magnetic core memory; semiconductor memory; or bubble memory.

Magnetic Core Memory **Magnetic core memory** consists of small magnetic cores with wires running through them. Electric current flows through the wires; depending on the direction of current flow, electricity magnetizes the core in different directions (Figure 2–4). The direction of magnetization indicates certain data representation to the CPU. This form of memory has been in existence the longest, and because it is relatively bulky, magnetic core memory has given way to newer technologies such as semiconductor memories.

Semiconductor Memory Most primary storage today is comprised of semiconductor technology. **Semiconductor memory** is made by "etching" electronic circuits onto a silicon chip. The two most common forms of semiconductor memory are random-access memory and read-only memory.

Random-access memory (RAM) is that part of primary storage where data and program instructions are held temporarily while being manipulated or executed. This type of memory allows the user to enter data into memory (write) and then to retrieve it (read).

FIGURE 2–4
Magnetic core memory

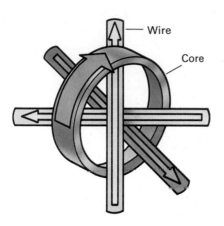

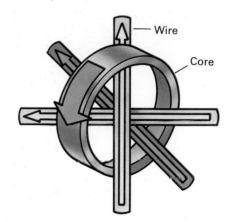

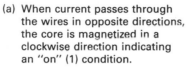

(a) When current passes through the wires in opposite directions, the core is magnetized in a clockwise direction indicating an "on" (1) condition.

(b) When current passes through the wires in the same direction, the core is magnetized in a counter-clockwise direction indicating an "off" (0) condition.

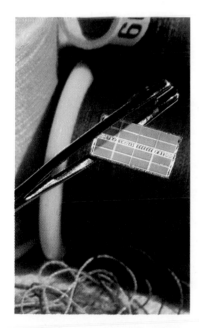

Chip sizes are shrinking. This IBM chip contains one megabit of memory, but it is so small it can fit through the eye of a needle. (Courtesy of International Business Machines Corp.)

RAM depends on a steady supply of electricity to maintain data storage. When the power to the computer is shut off, everything stored in RAM is lost. In other words, RAM is **volatile.**

As the name implies, the contents of **read-only memory (ROM)** can only be *read;* data cannot be *written* into it. ROM may contain information on how to start the computer and even instructions to the entire operating system. The actual contents of ROM are usually set by the computer manufacturer; they are unchangeable and permanent. Because the contents cannot be altered and they are not lost when the electric current is turned off, ROM is nonvolatile.

Several types of read-only memory can be programmed according to the user's specifications. **Programmable read-only memory (PROM)** allows a chip to be programmed by the user once; then it cannot be altered further. A type of ROM in which the contents *can* be changed is called **erasable programmable read-only memory (EPROM)** (Figure 2–5). An EPROM chip has the features of PROM, but it also has a transparent quartz window covering the internal circuitry. By removing the chip from the circuit and exposing the window to ultraviolet light, the contents are erased, and the chip can be reprogrammed for another application. Another type of ROM chip is the **electrically erasable programmable read-only memory (EEPROM).** This memory chip can be erased and reprogrammed electrically so there is no need to remove it from the circuit as with an EPROM.

To illustrate the use of RAM and ROM, let's look at how they might be used in a typical microcomputer. The primary storage unit is represented as the cube in Figure 2–6a. The cube is composed of two parts, RAM and ROM. ROM is shown as the thin portion along the top of the cube. When the computer is first turned on, ROM performs predetermined instructions, such as checking the system for errors. Notice that nothing is contained in RAM at this point.

Before a computer can be used, it must have operating instructions. The software that provides these instructions is called the **operating system (OS).** The typical microcomputer operating system resides on a disk and is referred to as a **disk operating system (DOS).** DOS must be transferred, or loaded, into RAM. Figure 2–6b shows the part of RAM that is occupied by DOS. (For more on operating systems, see Chapter 11.)

Now, let's say you want to write a letter. The computer needs programming instructions in the form of an application package that directs the computer to function as a word processor. This word-processing package also has to be loaded into RAM. Once it has been loaded, it is ready to use. These application programs usually take a lot of memory space (Figure 2–6c). Remember, though, that RAM is volatile. If you turn the computer off now, primary storage will contain only ROM and again look like Figure 2–6a.

FIGURE 2–5
By removing the chip and exposing the transparent quartz window to ultraviolet light, this EPROM chip can be erased and later reprogrammed.

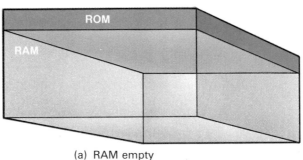

(a) RAM empty

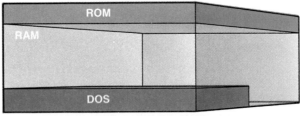

(b) DOS loaded into RAM

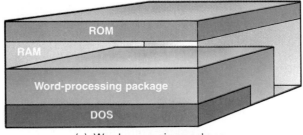

FIGURE 2–6
An example of RAM and ROM use in a microcomputer

(c) Word-processing package loaded into RAM

FIGURE 2–7
A RAM card for extending memory. Some RAM cards, such as this AST Six Pac Plus, offer additional functions, e.g., a parallel printer port and a battery-operated clock. Often, they are referred to as multifunction boards.

The amount of primary storage is very important in determining the capabilities of the computer. The more primary storage available means that more instructions and data can be loaded into the computer. Many applications require a specific amount of memory; if the computer doesn't have that amount, the application package cannot be used. Most computers have provisions for either adding individual RAM chips to the main circuit board or adding RAM cards (Figure 2–7). A RAM card is a group of integrated circuits already assembled on a printed circuit board. It can be plugged into the main circuit board of a computer to increase the amount of RAM.

Types of Primary Storage

- Magnetic core memory
- Semiconductor memory
  - ☐ RAM
  - ☐ ROM
- Bubble memory

Bubble Memory One attempt to overcome the volatility of RAM was the development of bubble memory. **Bubble memory** is built on a thin piece of the mineral garnet where certain sections are polarized (subjected to a magnetic field) to produce bubble-like areas. Data are represented by the presence or absence of these bubbles. Bubble memory is nonvolatile, but it is not used as widely as semiconductor memory because it is slower and more expensive.

Special-purpose Memories The two types of special-purpose memories in the computer are registers and buffers. These memories are vital to moving data in and out of primary storage and to processing the data. The CPU uses them to improve the computer's overall performance. Figure 2–8 shows the interconnections of the components of the CPU with these special memories.

A **register** holds an instruction or data that are to be worked on immediately. It is part of the CPU and can hold only one piece of data at a time. Because registers are part of the CPU, the transfer of data in and out

53

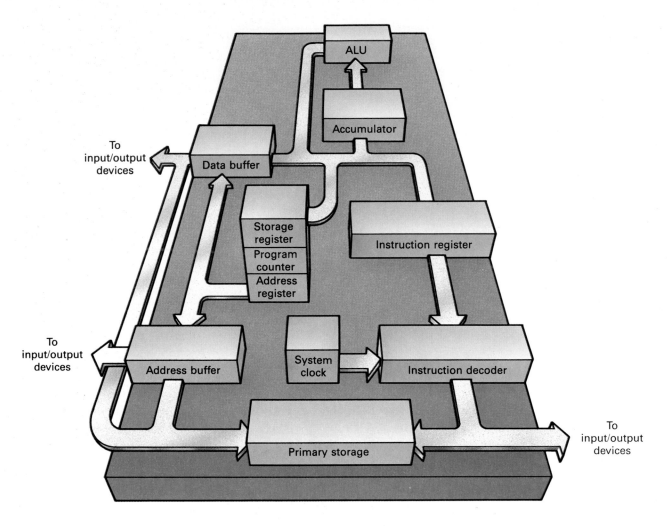

FIGURE 2–8
Arrows show the movement of data or instructions between registers and
buffers within the CPU.

of primary storage is a very high-speed operation. In fact, the size and
number of these registers help determine the overall speed of the computer. The names and functions of the registers used most often are

☐ Accumulator—Stores the result of the last processing step of the
ALU
☐ Instruction register—Holds an instruction in the control unit be-
fore it is decoded
☐ Address register—Holds the location of the next piece of data
☐ Storage register—Holds data on the way to or from primary stor-
age
☐ Program counter—Holds the location of the next instruction to
be executed

HIGHLIGHT

UNIVERSITIES: CASHING IN THEIR CHIPS

Although much of the research into microchip design and manufacture has been done by government and private industry, some of America's great universities are working on the front lines in these fields.

Stanford University and the University of California at Berkeley are pioneers in this research and development. More recently, the Massachusetts Institute of Technology (MIT) has joined in with its $22 million Microsystems Research Center. As with other university computer-centered programs, MIT's is heavily underwritten by government and industry. But industry will not be able to lay exclusive claims to MIT's developments and discoveries, all of which will be made public through the publishing of research documents.

Among the projects MIT faculty and students are working on are: (a) chip designs and integrated circuitry; (b) ways to speed up the conversion of data into digital form; (c) computer-assisted fabrication of chips; and (d) the continuing development of electronic sensors.

MIT's new facility is comprised of an Integrated Circuits Laboratory, a Sub-Micron Structures Laboratory, and a Technology Research Laboratory. A consortium of sixteen private companies paid for about half the cost of the facility. Most of the projected annual operating cost of $1.3 million also comes from industrial and government contracts.

Most of Stanford's new $26 million chip-making and design facility is also financed by computer and semiconductor firms.

The combination of outside money and inside brains is making the university a formidable testing ground for the computer-oriented society to come.

A **buffer,** another temporary holding space for data, may be part of the CPU, or it may be built into devices used to input or output data. Unlike a register, a buffer can hold more than one piece of data at a time. The buffer acts as an intermediary *between* the CPU and any input or output device. Input and output devices operate at much slower rates than the CPU, so it is necessary to have a temporary holding place for larger amounts of data. For example, a printer cannot print data as fast as the CPU can send them. Therefore, with no place to temporarily store the data, the CPU would be idly waiting for the printer to catch up. The CPU's operating speed would be reduced to the rate of the particular output device. Using a buffer allows the data to be stored temporarily, thereby freeing the CPU to do other tasks.

FIGURE 2-9
Communication pathways
within a computer

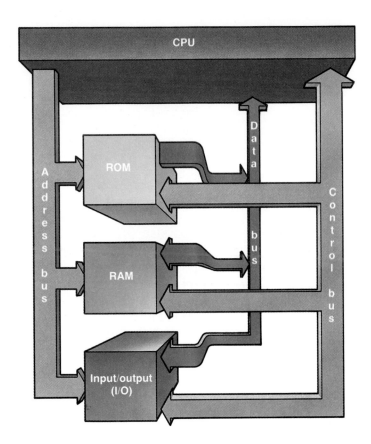

COMMUNICATION PATHWAYS

Communication Pathways

- Control bus
- Address bus
- Data bus

To function as a complete unit, the ALU, the control unit, and the primary storage unit must have a way to communicate. These links among and within the various units are called buses.

A **bus** is no more than an electrical path for data to flow from point to point in a circuit. A bus is classified by name according to its function. For example, the **control bus** is the pathway for all timing and controlling functions sent by the control unit to the other units of the system. The **address bus** is the pathway used to locate the storage position in memory where the next instruction to be executed or the next piece of data will be found. The **data bus** is the pathway where the actual data transfer takes place. The three bus paths are shown in Figure 2-9.

THE CPU AT WORK

Thanks in part to the control unit, the elements of the computer act with and react to one another with amazing precision. Depending on the instruction executed, certain computer components may or may not be used. In one instance, the instruction executed may involve computations within the ALU, while another simply looks into and displays the contents of some memory location.

Regardless of the actual instruction, the computer goes through two basic cycles to execute it: **instruction cycle** and **execution cycle.** The instruction cycle is made up of two distinct steps: **fetch** and **decode.**

Executing an Instruction

■ Instruction cycle
   □ Fetch
   □ Decode
■ Execution cycle

In general, during the instruction cycle, the fetch step locates an instruction in memory and sends it to the control unit. During the decode step, the instruction is decoded and sent to the ALU along with any necessary data. During the execution cycle, the instruction is executed by the ALU, and the result is stored in the accumulator until needed. The program counter is incremented to identify the location of the next instruction to be executed, and the instruction-execution sequence of operations is repeated for the next instruction and continues until the program ends. It may seem like a long process to fetch, decode, and execute a single instruction, but it is actually done in less than a blink of an eye—and it takes only about 200 milliseconds (.2 second) to blink an eye!

DATA REPRESENTATION

In Chapter 1, you learned that the computer only identifies signals in the form of digital pulses which represent either a high voltage state, "on," or a low voltage state, "off." The "on" and "off" conditions are commonly labeled with the numbers 1 and 0, respectively. The number system using only 1s and 0s is called the **binary system.**

The 1s and 0s can be arranged in various combinations to represent all the numbers, letters, and symbols that can be entered into the computer. While you see numbers and letters assembled to form English words and phrases, the computer sees things totally different. For example, the lowercase letter "d" appears as 01100100 to the computer.

Because the language of the computer, machine language, is based on the binary system, data entered into the computer must be interpreted into binary code before they can be used by the computer. There are programs to take care of this conversion (see Chapter 11).

Because the binary system is cumbersome for humans to work with, other number systems are used to represent data. These number systems are explained in more detail in this chapter's InfoModule.

Bits and Bytes

The smallest piece of data that can be recognized and used by the computer is the **bit,** a *bi*nary digi*t*. A bit is a single binary value, either a 1 or a 0. A grouping of eight bits is a **byte.** The term "nibble," which is one-half of a byte (four bits), is used occasionally. The byte is the basic unit for measuring the size of memory; although with today's memory sizes, it is more common to hear the term kilobyte (K or KB), or megabyte (MB). To give you an idea of how many English words are in a kilobyte, the text material in this chapter is approximately 60,000 bytes, or 60 kilobytes (60KB).

There is some confusion over the prefixes kilo- and mega-. In strict scientific notation, "kilo" means 1,000 and "mega" means 1,000,000. However, in the language of computers, kilo- actually means 1,024 and mega- is 1,048,576. The disparity occurs because the computer is a binary machine based on the powers of 2. If 2 is raised to the 10th power (2^{10}), the answer is 1,024. Since this is very near 1,000 (10^3), the prefix kilo- was adopted for computer use. The same reasoning is behind the prefixes mega- and giga- (1 billion). Before long, memory capacities in the

These Apple Macintosh micro-computers are being assembled at the factory. (Courtesy of Apple Computer, Inc.)

terabytes (1 trillion bytes) may be common in some of the largest computer systems.

Computer Words

A computer **word** is the number of adjacent bits that can be stored and manipulated as a unit. Just as English vocabulary words are of varying lengths, so are computer words. Some of the newer microcomputers have the ability to manipulate a 32-bit word, while older models have word lengths of 8 and 16 bits. Word lengths range up to 128 bits for super-computers.

The longer the length of the computer word that the registers can hold, the faster the computer can process the data. The word's length can be misleading, however. Even though a register may be able to handle 32 bits, the data bus may be able to handle only 16 bits at a time. A micropro-cessor such as the Motorola 68000, which has a 32-bit word size but only a 16-bit data bus, requires twice the time to load a 32-bit word as would a "true" 32-bit microprocessor. A "true" microprocessor is one in which the data bus can handle a number of bits equal to the number of bits in the register. The Motorola 68020 and the Intel 80386 are "true" 32-bit micro-processors. Both have a 32-bit word size and a 32-bit data bus. The micro-processor has come a long way from the 4-bit Intel 4004 that Hoff designed only a few short years ago.

Data Length
■ Bit
■ Byte
■ Word

SUMMARY

The central processing unit (CPU) is comprised of the arithmetic and logic unit (ALU), the control unit, and the primary storage unit. Modern tech-nology has put the ALU and the control unit (in some cases, all three units) onto one integrated circuit, or microchip (also known as chip), called a microprocessor. The ALU handles all the mathematical and comparison operations. The control unit regulates the timing and sequence of all pro-cessing within the computer. Primary storage is the internal storage unit of a computer where programs and data are stored.

There are three forms of primary storage, including magnetic core memory, semiconductor memory, and bubble memory. Semiconductor memory is the most common and is of two basic types: RAM and ROM. Program instructions or data can be stored internally in random-access memory (RAM) or read-only memory (ROM). RAM is used primarily for temporary storage and is volatile. ROM is used for permanent storage and is nonvolatile, i.e., it does not rely on a continuous source of power.

Two special-purpose memories are registers and buffers. A register is a temporary holding place for instructions or data to be worked on immediately. A buffer holds data on their way in and out of the CPU.

Data are transferred out of memory and into the ALU for processing through the control, address, and data buses. The process of executing an instruction involves the instruction cycle and the execution cycle.

Within the computer, data are represented as a binary system number. The smallest piece of data that the computer understands is a bit. The grouping of eight bits is a byte. A kilobyte is 1,024 bytes. The number of bits the registers can hold determines the length of the computer word. The size of the registers can vary from computer to computer and, therefore, so can the word length.

Key Terms

address bus (p. 56)

arithmetic and logic unit (ALU) (p. 46)

binary system (p. 57)

bit (p. 57)

bubble memory (p. 53)

buffer (p. 55)

bus (p. 56)

byte (p. 57)

central processing unit (CPU) (p. 44)

chip (p. 46)

control bus (p. 56)

control unit (p. 47)

data bus (p. 56)

decode (p. 56)

disk operating system (DOS) (p. 52)

electrically erasable programmable read-only memory (EEPROM) (p. 51)

erasable programmable read-only memory (EPROM) (p. 51)

execution cycle (p. 56)

fetch (p. 56)

instruction cycle (p. 56)

instruction set (p. 48)

integrated circuit (IC) (p. 45)

large-scale integration (LSI) (p. 45)

logic function (p. 46)

magnetic core memory (p. 50)

microchip (p. 46)

microprocessor (p. 46)

millions of instructions per second (MIPS) (p. 48)

operating system (OS) (p. 52)

primary storage unit (p. 49)

programmable read-only memory (PROM) (p. 51)

random-access memory (RAM) (p. 50)

reading (p. 50)

read-only memory (ROM) (p. 51)

register (p. 53)

semiconductor memory (p. 50)

system clock (p. 47)

very large-scale integration (VLSI) (p. 46)

volatile (p. 51)

word (p. 58)

writing (p. 49)

Review Questions

1. What three major units comprise the CPU?
2. The processing unit responsible for mathematical computations is the _____.
3. Describe an integrated circuit.
4. What is a microprocessor?
5. Give two examples of a logic function.
6. What is the function of the control unit?
7. Discuss the significance of using MIPS as a gauge of computer speeds.
8. What is the main purpose of primary storage?
9. What does the term "volatile" mean as it pertains to computer memory?
10. What type of memory is volatile?
11. The process of entering data into storage is called _____.
12. The process of retrieving data from storage is called _____.
13. Explain the differences among a ROM chip, a PROM chip, an EPROM chip, and an EEPROM chip.
14. Briefly describe the two cycles involved in the execution of an instruction.
15. What number system is used to represent the electrical conditions of "on" or "off" in computers?
16. The smallest unit of data that a computer recognizes is a(n) _____.
17. What is a byte?
18. A kilobyte is equal to _____ bytes.
19. Describe a computer word.
20. What is a "true" microprocessor?
21. Describe the purpose of the: (a) control bus; (b) data bus; and (c) address bus.
22. Name and briefly describe three forms of primary storage.
23. Discuss some of the factors involved in determining a computer's overall processing speed.
24. Describe the roles that RAM and ROM play within the computer, the main purpose of each, and what distinguishes the two types of memory.
25. What purposes do registers and buffers serve?

INFOMODULE
Number Systems

Most of you are comfortable counting and manipulating numbers with the decimal system and can picture in your minds the quantities that each number represents. But what if you were asked to picture the quantity 6A7C? At first you might say this doesn't represent a quantity because it contains letters. You might have this perception if you are not familiar with other number systems. The number 6A7C is an example of a number in the hexadecimal number system. If you were to use the various number systems presented here as often as you use the decimal system, they would become second nature to you, too.

DECIMAL SYSTEM

Because the decimal system is the number system most familiar to us, let's begin our discussion there. The **decimal system** is a base-10 system, which means there are ten distinct digits—0 through 9—to represent any quantity. Any number greater than 9 can be represented by a combination of these digits. The value that the digits represent depends on the "weight," or position, they hold. The weights are based on powers of 10 as shown in Figure 1.

Now look at how to determine the value of a group of digits in the base-10 system using the digits 1, 0, 2, and 4. Many combinations of these four digits can be made. The exact position in which they are placed will determine the final value. In Figure 2, 4 will be in the first position, 2 in the second position, 0 in the third position, and 1 in the fourth position. The final value can be figured by multiplying each digit by the weight and then adding all the intermediate

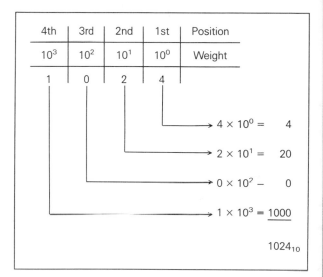

FIGURE 2
Representation of a decimal value

results to achieve the final value. This same technique can be applied to the other number systems.

To distinguish one number system from the next, a subscript is used to indicate the base. For example, 1024_{10} is a base-10 or decimal number, while 1001_2 is a base-2 number. In common use, however, the subscript is usually not shown.

BINARY SYSTEM

As you read earlier in this chapter, computer circuitry represents data as a pattern of "on" or "off" electrical states. Because there are only two states, they are represented by a 1 for

FIGURE 1
Position weights in base 10

4th	3rd	2nd	1st	Position
$10^3 = 1000$	$10^2 = 100$	$10^1 = 10$	$10^0 = 1$	Weight

"on" and a 0 for "off." This two-state digit representation is called the **binary system**.

The binary system is a base-2 system, meaning the position weights are based on the powers of 2 (Figure 3).

Again, let's evaluate a group of digits using the same procedure applied to the decimal system. Use the binary number 10000000000_2. Remember, you are in base 2, so this number is not 10 billion. Notice that commas are not used in base-2 numbers. The number 10000000000_2 is evaluated in Figure 4.

From our calculations, it can be determined that $1024_{10} = 10000000000_2$. Now, let's look at

FIGURE 3

Position weights in base 2

8th	7th	6th	5th	4th	3rd	2nd	1st	Position
$2^7 = 128$	$2^6 = 64$	$2^5 = 32$	$2^4 = 16$	$2^3 = 8$	$2^2 = 4$	$2^1 = 2$	$2^0 = 1$	Weight

FIGURE 4

Evaluation of a base-2 number

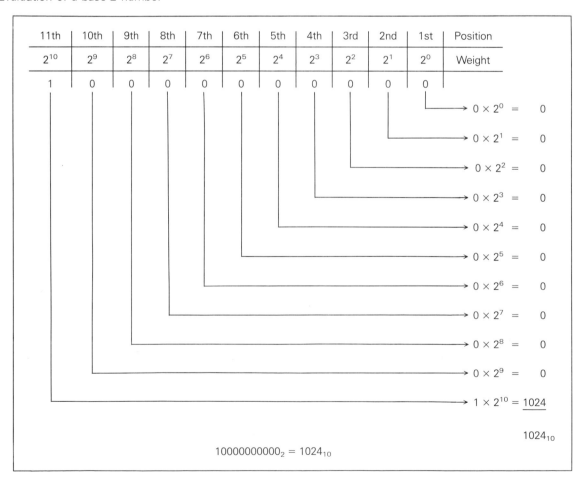

11th	10th	9th	8th	7th	6th	5th	4th	3rd	2nd	1st	Position
2^{10}	2^9	2^8	2^7	2^6	2^5	2^4	2^3	2^2	2^1	2^0	Weight
1	0	0	0	0	0	0	0	0	0	0	

$0 \times 2^0 = 0$

$0 \times 2^1 = 0$

$0 \times 2^2 = 0$

$0 \times 2^3 = 0$

$0 \times 2^4 = 0$

$0 \times 2^5 = 0$

$0 \times 2^6 = 0$

$0 \times 2^7 = 0$

$0 \times 2^8 = 0$

$0 \times 2^9 = 0$

$1 \times 2^{10} = \underline{1024}$

1024_{10}

$10000000000_2 = 1024_{10}$

FIGURE 5
Conversion of 1011011_2 to its decimal equivalent

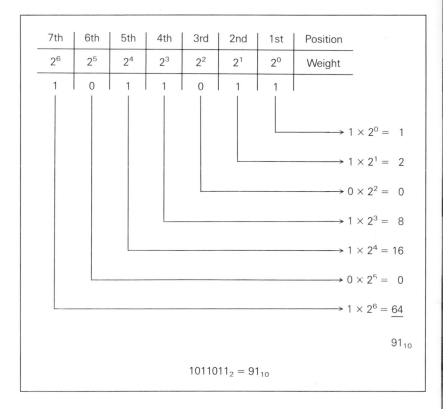

7th	6th	5th	4th	3rd	2nd	1st	Position
2^6	2^5	2^4	2^3	2^2	2^1	2^0	Weight
1	0	1	1	0	1	1	

$$1 \times 2^0 = 1$$
$$1 \times 2^1 = 2$$
$$0 \times 2^2 = 0$$
$$1 \times 2^3 = 8$$
$$1 \times 2^4 = 16$$
$$0 \times 2^5 = 0$$
$$1 \times 2^6 = \underline{64}$$

$$91_{10}$$

$$1011011_2 = 91_{10}$$

one more; the next example converts the binary number 1011011_2 to its decimal equivalent (Figure 5).

OCTAL SYSTEM

Octal and hexadecimal systems are used to provide a shorthand way to deal with the long strings of 1s and 0s created in binary.

As the name suggests, the **octal system** is a base-8 system using the digits 0 through 7. For evaluating purposes, you can again use a weighted system to convert from base 8 to decimal. Figure 6 shows the conversion of 3137_8 to its decimal equivalent.

Converting Octal Numbers to Binary Numbers

As shown in Figure 7, an octal number can easily be converted to a binary number by replacing each octal digit with the corresponding group of three binary digits. Groups of three are used because any octal number (0–7) can be represented by three binary digits. For example, 7_8 is 111_2 in binary.

HEXADECIMAL SYSTEM

The **hexadecimal system** is a base-16 system. It contains the digits 0 through 9 and the letters A through F. The letters A through F are used because sixteen placeholders are needed, and there are only ten distinct digits in the decimal system. The letters A through F represent the decimal numbers 10 through 15, respectively. This system is often used in programming as a shortcut to the binary number system. Figure 8 is an example of some position weights in the hexadecimal system and a conversion of $1D7F_{16}$ to its decimal equivalent.

FIGURE 6
Conversion of 3137_8 to its decimal equivalent

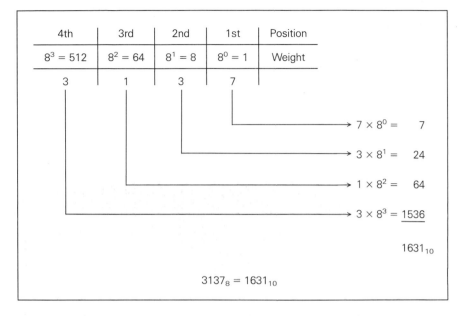

FIGURE 7
Conversion of an octal number to a binary number

$$
\begin{array}{ccc}
1 & 3 & 4 \\
\underbrace{001} & \underbrace{011} & \underbrace{100}
\end{array}
\qquad \text{therefore } 134_8 = 001011100_2
$$

$$
\begin{array}{cccc}
7 & 4 & 3 & 2 \\
\underbrace{111} & \underbrace{100} & \underbrace{011} & \underbrace{010}
\end{array}
\qquad \text{therefore } 7432_8 = 111100011010_2
$$

FIGURE 8
Conversion of hexadecimal number to a decimal number

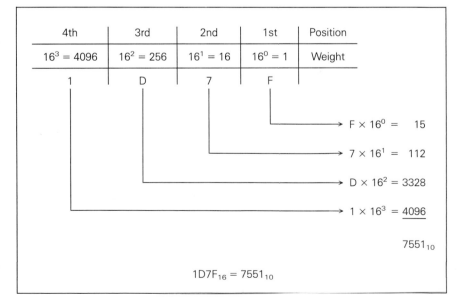

Number Systems

- Decimal—base 10
- Binary—base 2
- Octal—base 8
- Hexadecimal—base 16

Converting Hexadecimal Numbers to Binary Numbers

Hexadecimal numbers can be transposed to binary numbers in the same way as octal to binary conversions. This time, though, the binary digits are organized into groups of four because that many digits are needed to represent 15 (1111_2), the largest hexadecimal digit. Examples are shown in Figure 9.

Converting Binary Numbers to Hexadecimal Numbers

To reverse the operation, break the binary number into groups of four and replace them with the hexadecimal equivalent. Two examples are shown in Figure 10.

ENCODING SYSTEMS

Computers must be capable of interpreting more than just numbers. Letters of the alphabet as well as symbols, such as @, #, *, +, are used when programming. In fact, any character that can be entered from the keyboard must be converted into 1s and 0s before it can be used by the computer. The combination of letters, numbers, and symbols is collectively called alphanumeric characters.

To make this conversion, **encoding systems**, which permit alphanumeric characters to be coded in terms of bits using 1 and 0, were developed. The two most widely used encoding systems are EBCDIC (Extended Binary Coded Decimal Interchange Code) and ASCII (American Standard Code for Information Interchange). Table 1 provides a listing of the alphanumeric characters and their ASCII or EBCDIC codes. Table 2 provides a listing of the decimal, binary, octal, and hexadecimal codes.

FIGURE 9
Conversion of hexadecimal numbers to binary numbers

6   B   2
0110 1011 0010   therefore $6B2_{16} = 011010110010_2$

9   3   F   A
1001 0011 1111 1010   therefore $93FA_{16} = 1001001111111010_2$

FIGURE 10
Conversion of binary numbers to hexadecimal numbers

1101 1001 1111 1000
D   9   F   8   therefore $1101100111111000_2 = D9F8_{16}$

1010 0001 0111
A   1   7   therefore $101000010111_2 = A17_{16}$

TABLE 1
ASCII and EBCDIC
alphanumeric chart

Symbol	ASCII	EBCDIC	Symbol	ASCII	EBCDIC
(space)	0100000	01000000	N	1001110	11010101
!	0100001	01011010	O	1001111	11010110
''	0100010	01111111	P	1010000	11010111
#	0100011	01111011	Q	1010001	11011000
$	0100100	01011011	R	1010010	11011001
%	0100101	01101100	S	1010011	11100010
&	0100110	01010000	T	1010100	11100011
'	0100111	01111101	U	1010101	11100100
(	0101000	01001101	V	1010110	11100101
)	0101001	01011101	W	1010111	11100110
*	0101010	01011100	X	1011000	11100111
+	0101011	01001110	Y	1011001	11101000
,	0101100	01101011	Z	1011010	11101001
−	0101101	01100000	[	1011011	01001010
.	0101110	01001011	/	1011100	
/	0101111	01100001	]	1011101	01011010
0	0110000	11110000	^	1011110	
1	0110001	11110001	—	1011111	
2	0110010	11110010	a	1100001	10000001
3	0110011	11110011	b	1100010	10000010
4	0110100	11110100	c	1100011	10000011
5	0110101	11110101	d	1100100	10000100
6	0110110	11110110	e	1100101	10000101
7	0110111	11110111	f	1100110	10000110
8	0111000	11111000	g	1100111	10000111
9	0111001	11111001	h	1101000	10001000
:	0111010	01111010	i	1101001	10001001
;	0111011	01011110	j	1101010	10010001
<	0111100	01001100	k	1101011	10010010
=	0111101	01111110	l	1101100	10010011
>	0111110	01101110	m	1101101	10010100
?	0111111	01101111	n	1101110	10010101
@	1000000	01111100	o	1101111	10010110
A	1000001	11000001	p	1110000	10010111
B	1000010	11000010	q	1110001	10011000
C	1000011	11000011	r	1110010	10011001
D	1000100	11000100	s	1110011	10100010
E	1000101	11000101	t	1110100	10100011
F	1000110	11000110	u	1110101	10100100
G	1000111	11000111	v	1110110	10100101
H	1001000	11001000	w	1110111	10100110
I	1001001	11001001	x	1111000	10100111
J	1001010	11010001	y	1111001	10101000
K	1001011	11010010	z	1111010	10101001
L	1001100	11010011	{	1111011	
M	1001101	11010100	}	1111101	

Note: Blanks in EBCDIC column mean symbol is not represented in EBCDIC code.

TABLE 2

Decimal, binary, octal, and hexadecimal number chart

Decimal	Binary	Octal	Hexadecimal	Decimal	Binary	Octal	Hexadecimal
0	0	0	00	50	110010	62	32
1	1	1	01	51	110011	63	33
2	10	2	02	52	110100	64	34
3	11	3	03	53	110101	65	35
4	100	4	04	54	110110	66	36
5	101	5	05	55	110111	67	37
6	110	6	06	56	111000	70	38
7	111	7	07	57	111001	71	39
8	1000	10	08	58	111010	72	3A
9	1001	11	09	59	111011	73	3B
10	1010	12	0A	60	111100	74	3C
11	1011	13	0B	61	111101	75	3D
12	1100	14	0C	62	111110	76	3E
13	1101	15	0D	63	111111	77	3F
14	1110	16	0E	64	1000000	100	40
15	1111	17	0F	65	1000001	101	41
16	10000	20	10	66	1000010	102	42
17	10001	21	11	67	1000011	103	43
18	10010	22	12	68	1000100	104	44
19	10011	23	13	69	1000101	105	45
20	10100	24	14	70	1000110	106	46
21	10101	25	15	71	1000111	107	47
22	10110	26	16	72	1001000	110	48
23	10111	27	17	73	1001001	111	49
24	11000	30	18	74	1001010	112	4A
25	11001	31	19	75	1001011	113	4B
26	11010	32	1A	76	1001100	114	4C
27	11011	33	1B	77	1001101	115	4D
28	11100	34	1C	78	1001110	116	4E
29	11101	35	1D	79	1001111	117	4F
30	11110	36	1E	80	1010000	120	50
31	11111	37	1F	81	1010001	121	51
32	100000	40	20	82	1010010	122	52
33	100001	41	21	83	1010011	123	53
34	100010	42	22	84	1010100	124	54
35	100011	43	23	85	1010101	125	55
36	100100	44	24	86	1010110	126	56
37	100101	45	25	87	1010111	127	57
38	100110	46	26	88	1011000	130	58
39	100111	47	27	89	1011001	131	59
40	101000	50	28	90	1011010	132	5A
41	101001	51	29	91	1011011	133	5B
42	101010	52	2A	92	1011100	134	5C
43	101011	53	2B	93	1011101	135	5D
44	101100	54	2C	94	1011110	136	5E
45	101101	55	2D	95	1011111	137	5F
46	101110	56	2E	96	1100000	140	60
47	101111	57	2F	97	1100001	141	61
48	110000	60	30	98	1100010	142	62
49	110001	61	31	99	1100011	143	63

ASCII and EBCDIC codes allow the computer to distinguish between a number, letter, or symbol. When a computer sees the ASCII bit pattern 1001011, it interprets this pattern as a capital letter "K." A system using EBCDIC, however, sees the capital letter "K" as 11010010.

Encoding Systems

- EBCDIC
- ASCII

KEY TERMS

binary system (p. 62)

decimal system (p. 61)

encoding system (p. 65)

hexadecimal system (p. 63)

octal system (p. 63)

QUESTIONS

1. Why is the binary number system used for computers?
2. Convert the binary numbers 10101010_2 and 1111001_2 into their decimal equivalents.
3. What is the purpose of using the hexadecimal and the octal numbering systems?
4. Explain why it is necessary to have an encoding system.
5. Convert your age to a binary, octal, and hexadecimal number.

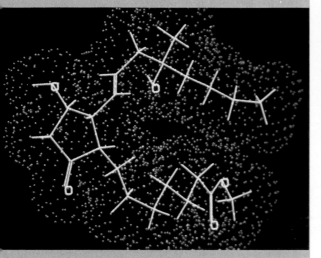

OBJECTIVES

- ☐ Define and distinguish between the following pairs of input concepts: batch and transaction processing; and transcriptive and source data entry
- ☐ List and briefly describe various input methods and devices
- ☐ List and briefly describe various output methods and devices
- ☐ Describe how data are transferred using serial and parallel interfaces

OUTLINE

3

Input and Output Devices

PROFILE: Douglas Engelbart

People who were there say it was more like a rock concert than a scientific demonstration. But what Douglas Engelbart was doing up there on the platform in 1968 was giving his audience a preview of their future as well as that of the computer. When computers were still in their infancy and viewed primarily as just machines to manipulate numbers rapidly, Engelbart had the notion that computers could also be used as extensions of the human mind. At this major computer conference in San Francisco, he was given the opportunity to demonstrate some of his ideas.

In 1968, Engelbart was working for the Stanford Research Institute (SRI) in Menlo Park, California. He had joined SRI in 1957, after having been a radar technician during World War II and subsequently a graduate student in electrical engineering at the University of California at Berkeley. After a few months at SRI, he convinced its administration that he should be allowed to set up a unit within the famed "think tank" which would be devoted to "human augmentation technology." This unit was the start of the Augmentation Research Center (ARC) at the institute

As the head of ARC, Engelbart began experiments to find a way to harness computers to a monitor instead of a teletype. At a time when some offices were still using only typewriters, he theorized about using computers as word processing units. He also experimented with computer-generated graphics.

Engelbart's use of a monitor screen presented the problem of how best to move a cursor around the screen to activate the various processes. He tried light pens and joysticks and even knee-activated controls to shift the cursor, but none of these proved satisfactory. So in 1964, Engelbart developed a handheld device that could roll across a flat surface on wheels and cause a corresponding movement on the screen. The device was hooked to the screen by an electric cord that looked something like a tail. He named this device a "mouse."

But it wasn't only the mouse that inventor Engelbart demonstrated in San Francisco in 1968. Using a giant screen that was connected by microwave transmission to his ARC computer forty miles away, Engelbart showed the audience how graphics could be generated and text manipulated, using the mouse as a right-hand control and a five-key "chord keyset" for inputting with the left hand. It was a stunning display of human and computer interaction, and it earned the scientist, who had so often worked in isolation, a standing ovation from an audience of his peers. From that day on, his peers would firmly believe in the computer potentials that Engelbart had so long visualized.

In Chapter 2, you learned that the CPU provides the means for the fast and efficient processing of data into usable information. But how are data entered into the computer for processing, and how are the results of processing communicated to the user?

Many traditional ways to input and output data were designed more with the machines in mind than the humans who used them. However, the trend in input and output (I/O) devices is to move toward a more natural means of communication. The most natural way for humans to communicate with a computer is to use the same techniques that people use to communicate with each other. For example, entering data into the computer might be accomplished by speaking, handwriting, or physically pointing at specific objects on the screen. Speech, written text, and visual images such as color graphs are forms of output that humans find easiest to interpret and use. Advances such as voice recognition and speech synthesis have only begun to reach their potential. This chapter will present some basic I/O concepts as well as look at the more common I/O devices.

INPUT CONCEPTS

Input is the process of entering and translating incoming data into machine-readable form so that they can be processed by a computer. The data to be entered are also often referred to as input. But before discussing concepts involving input, let's recall the meanings of some terms and introduce a new one so we can share a common language as concepts are discussed. **Hardware** is all the physical components of a computer system. Any hardware item that is attached to the main unit of a computer that houses the CPU is referred to as a **peripheral device.** An **input device** is a peripheral device through which data are entered and transformed into machine-readable form.

Three things to be concerned with during the input process are

1. The method of data preparation (transcriptive or source)
2. The type of processing to be used (batch or transaction)
3. The accuracy of the data being entered

Data Preparation Methods

Two concepts relating to data preparation methods are on-line and off-line. **On-line** refers to an operation or device in which data are transferred directly to or from a computer, e.g., when employees enter payroll data, such as hours worked, directly into the computer. **Off-line** refers to an operation or device in which data are *not* immediately transferred to or from a computer, e.g., when employees punch a time card or fill out a time sheet and these data are entered into the computer only once a week. The end product of an off-line input operation may be used as data for an on-line input operation. Traditionally, off-line input devices were most common; however, today the trend is toward on-line devices and operations.

Two basic ways in which data are prepared for input are transcriptive data entry and source data entry. In **transcriptive data entry,** the data are prepared on documents (e.g., hand-written or typed sales invoices) at the source, or place of origin, of the data. The data must then be transcribed to another medium that can be read and interpreted by a computer. In **source data entry,** the data are prepared at the source in a machine-readable form that can be used by a computer without a separate intermediate data transcription step.

One main advantage of the source data entry method is that it reduces the number of errors made during input by eliminating the transcription process. Various studies have shown that of all the errors detected in data approximately 85 percent are due to transcription errors and only 15 percent actually occur in the source data.

Batch and Transaction Processing

While many devices are used to enter data into a computer, the two main data processing methods are batch processing and transaction processing.

Batch processing is a method in which data are gathered and batched through either an on-line or off-line data-gathering process, and processed periodically without user intervention. A classic example of batch processing is payroll preparation in a business. The number of hours a person works is maintained throughout the pay period either on paper or punched cards through an off-line data-gathering process or in separate employee computer files through an on-line data-gathering process. At the end of the pay period, these data are input to the CPU and processed to determine the employee's paycheck amount.

Transaction processing is an on-line method in which data are processed immediately, and files are updated as a transaction takes place. On-line processing permits the use of **interactive programs,** which allow the user to communicate with the computer during processing. When an interactive program supplies the results of processing so they can be used when needed to control an operation, modify a process, or answer a customer's question, the procedure is referred to as **real-time processing.** Real-time processing transactions are found in the system used by an airline agent to book and prepare a ticket. The agent interacts with the computer asking the program to supply information about flights that fit the customer's schedule. When an available flight is found, the computer immediately records the sale of the seat desired and automatically reduces the number of seats available on that flight. Because more than one terminal is used to make reservations for a flight, the ability to record a transaction immediately prevents agents from duplicating a sale that already has been made.

No matter which data-entry or processing method is used, attention needs to be paid to the accuracy of the data being entered.

Data Accuracy

Given the vast amounts of data entered into computers, errors are bound to occur. Let's look at two of the various methods used to help eliminate errors: (a) verification, which is performed by an operator or user; and (b) validation, which is programmed into the computer.

Even if data are carefully entered by a user, mistakes can occur. One way to find mistakes is by **verification**—corroborating the data entered by checking them against a known source. For example, the user can match the computer input data against the original paper document that provided the data.

Error checking can also be accomplished by the computer. The computer can be programmed to accept only a certain range of data. Checking for data items that deviate from this range is called **validation.** For example, if the input calls for a number corresponding to a day of the year to be entered, the computer can be programmed to give an error message immediately if a negative number, number greater than 365, or an alphabetic character is entered instead. The computer does not proceed until data in the proper range are entered.

Input Concepts

- On-line and off-line
- Transcriptive and source data entry
- Batch and transaction processing
- Verification and validation

INPUT DEVICES

Recall that before data can be processed by the computer, they must be translated into a machine-readable form and entered into the computer by an input device. This section will introduce you to a variety of input devices, including card readers, keyboards, mouse, voice-recognition devices, and optical-character readers.

Punched Cards and Card Readers

A **punched card** is a rigid piece of paper containing rows and columns of numbers. These cards are put into a keypunch machine. As the operator keys in the data to be stored, the keypunch machine places holes in the card to represent the data. Figure 3–1 shows a standard 80-column punched card. The pattern of punched holes used to represent characters on the card is called the Hollerith code, named after its inventor, Herman Hollerith.

The holes punched in the cards are interpreted by a **card reader** that translates the punched information into a machine-readable code, then sends it to the CPU for processing.

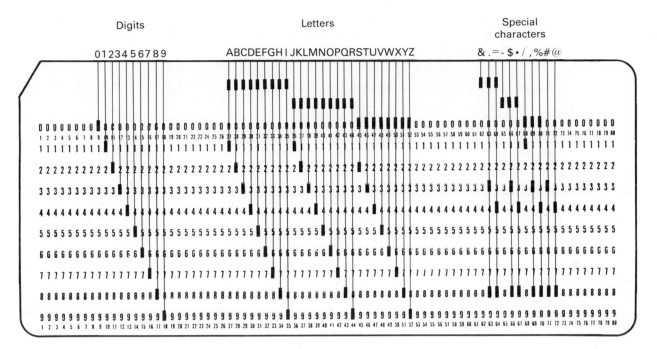

FIGURE 3–1

An 80-column punched card showing the Hollerith code (Courtesy of International Business Machines Corp.)

The punched-card system was one of the first methods used to input data. It has been almost totally replaced by newer, more efficient input devices.

Keyboards

One of today's most common and familiar input devices is the standard keyboard. The traditional QWERTY (so called because the first six letters on the top row are Q, W, E, R, T, and Y) typewriter keyboard comprises the basic portion of today's computer **keyboard** (Figure 3–2). A typical computer keyboard contains all the letters, numbers, and symbols of a regular typewriter, plus a variety of other keys. The other keys may include: (a) a numeric keypad that looks and functions much like a calculator; (b) function keys whose operation can be determined by the user or preprogrammed by the software being used; and (c) special keys such as those used to control the movement of the cursor on the computer screen.

A **cursor** is a special character or symbol that indicates the user's position on the screen or focuses attention to a specific area to allow communication and interaction between the user and the program. Cursor-movement keys typically include four directional arrow keys which move the cursor one space at a time in either an up, down, left, or right direction. Other keys, typically named Home, End, PgUp (page up), and PgDn (page down), move the cursor over longer distances quickly. The cursor move-

■ = QWERTY keyboard containing alphabetic, numeric, and special character keys

■ = Numeric keypad

■ = Function keys

□ = Other special keys

Note: Some keys have more than one function.

FIGURE 3–2
A typical computer keyboard

ment keys are often part of the numeric keypad. If this is the case, a key, such as the NumLck, acts as a toggle switching the function of these keys between cursor movement and numeric operations. Other special keys common to many keyboards are ESC (escape), CTRL (control), INS (insert), DEL (delete), and PRT SC (print screen). Many of these keys were added to increase efficiency in programming and in using applications such as word processing packages.

Joysticks and Trackballs

A **joystick** uses a lever to control the position of the cursor (Figure 3–3). It internally translates the lever position and speed with which the joystick is moved into digital signals that are sent to the computer to control the cursor movement. Most people are familiar with the joystick as a device used to play video games.

A **trackball** uses a hard sphere to control cursor movement (Figure 3–4). The ball can be rotated by hand in any direction. The trackball translates the sphere's direction and speed of rotation into a digital signal used to control the cursor.

Mouse

The mouse has been around for more than twenty years. Doug Engelbart developed the mouse as an alternative to the keyboard in the 1960s. The **mouse** usually contains one to three buttons; as the user rolls it on a flat surface, the mouse controls cursor movement on the screen. When the user presses one of the buttons, the mouse either marks a place on the screen or makes selections from data on the screen.

The mouse operates either electromechanically or optically. An electromechanical mouse uses the same principle as the trackball (Figure 3–5). The partially enclosed ball of the mouse, however, is on its underside; as the mouse is rolled along a flat surface, its movement is translated into a position on the screen.

An optical mouse travels over a special tablet of grid lines (Figure 3–6). The computer senses the location of the mouse on the grid and turns this data into a relative position on the screen.

A mouse can be used for many applications ranging from games to designing products with graphics. It provides an alternative for people who are uncomfortable with a keyboard, or it can be used in combination with a keyboard to enhance input operations.

Touch Screens

A **touch screen** registers input when a finger or other object comes in contact with the screen. Two touch-screen techniques involve infrared beams and ultrasonic acoustic waves. Infrared beams crisscross the surface of the screen, and when a light beam is broken, that location is recorded.

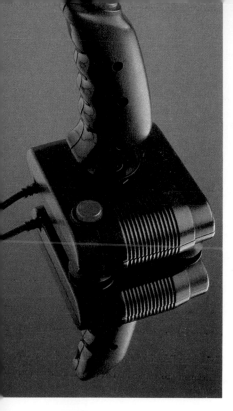

FIGURE 3–3
Joystick

FIGURE 3–4
Trackball

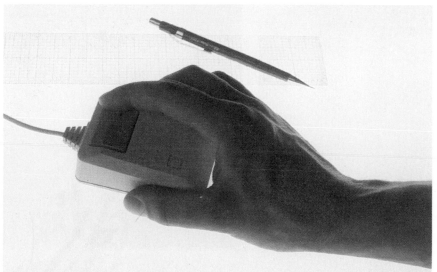

FIGURE 3–5
Electromechanical mouse

The other technique involves ultrasonic acoustic waves that pass over the surface of the screen. When the wave signals are interrupted by some contact with the screen, that location is recorded. Because the acoustic waves bend with the curved surface of the screen, they are closer to the screen, thus giving more precision when locating the point of contact.

Touch screens have long been used in military applications. Today, because they have become less expensive, touch screens are found in many other applications. Touch screens have provided information and directions to visitors at EPCOT Center at Walt Disney World since 1982. Visitors simply touch the items on the screen that they would like more information about, and the computer displays a screen that supplies them with the details. Automated lottery machines that use touch screens are becoming popular in supermarkets, carryouts, and retail stores. By touching the screen, selections, such as the type of game and the numbers to play are made. The computer registers the choice, then generates and prints the lottery ticket. Hewlett-Packard is one computer company that offers a series of microcomputers that have touch-screen capabilities. Figure 3–7 shows two examples of touch screens.

The touch pad is related to the touch screen, but activated by different means. The **touch pad** uses pressure-sensitive materials to record data at the point where the pad is touched. Many appliances around the home,

FIGURE 3–6
Optical mouse

(a)

(b)

FIGURE 3–7
(a) Hewlett-Packard touch screen. (b) Touch-screen lottery machine [(a) Photo courtesy of Hewlett-Packard Co. (b) Merrill Publishing/Cobalt Productions]

such as microwave ovens, use touch pads for programming time or temperature.

Light Pens and Digitizers

A **light pen** can make selections, place objects, or indicate dimensions by simply touching the screen (Figure 3–8). A light pen does not emit light; rather, it reacts to light through a photosensitive detector at its base. A **digitizer,** or graphics tablet, is similar to a light pen; however, instead of drawing on the screen, a separate tablet is used on which a special stylus is moved (Figure 3–9). By selecting commands on the digitizer, objects can be drawn or erased, and coordinates can be marked on the screen. Light pens and digitizers are often used in the mechanical and architectural fields for drawing.

Voice Recognition

Voice recognition is one of the newest, most complex input techniques used to interact with the computer. The user inputs data by speaking into a microphone (Figure 3–10). The simplest form of voice recognition is a one-word command spoken by one person. Each command is isolated with pauses between the words.

With a voice-recognition device, a doctor can ask the computer for information about a patient and not interrupt a surgical operation. Some quality-control inspections can be performed more productively if inspectors can verbally list possible defects into the microphone of the computer instead of stopping to write them down. Any procedure that requires using

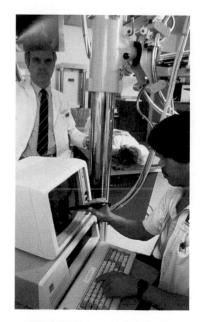

FIGURE 3–8
An X-ray technician uses a light pen to enter data into the computer. (Courtesy of Travenol Laboratories, Inc.)

FIGURE 3–9
A digitizer is used to transfer images to a computer screen. Here, the Harris Digital-Terrain Modeling System has digitized the rough terrain from a mechanical drawing and displayed it on a computer screen. (Courtesy of Harris Corp.)

FIGURE 3–10
With a voice-recognition, data-entry system, the operator's hands are free to write while commands are spoken to the computer. (Courtesy of Texas Instruments)

both hands and recording data simultaneously can benefit from voice input. Voice recognition also opens up the world of computers to people who are physically challenged and are unable to use traditional types of input devices.

Voice-recognition systems can recognize a few hundred words; however, regional accents and words that sound alike but have different meanings, such as ''hear'' and ''here,'' are difficult to decipher and, thus, cause the system problems. Although research continues in this area, computer voice recognition of continuous speech or normal conversation is not currently available for widespread use.

Source Data Input

Recall that data entered directly into a computer system without a transcription process is referred to as source data. Methods of source data input include magnetic-ink character recognition, magnetic strips, and optical recognition.

Magnetic-ink Character Recognition **Magnetic-ink character recognition (MICR)** is the interpretation by a computer of a line of characters written in a special magnetic ink. These characters can be read by humans as well. You may have noticed a line of numbers and some odd-shaped characters on the bottom of your personal checks. These magnetic-ink characters are bank processing symbols representing the check number, customer account number, and bank identification number (Figure 3–11). When the bank receives the check, the amount of the check is also printed in magnetic ink. The checks are sent through a MICR reader to interpret the information, update the appropriate accounts and, in some cases, sort the checks afterwards.

FIGURE 3–11
Banks use magnetic-ink characters on checks to ensure fast and efficient processing.

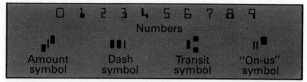

(a) Magnetic-ink character set

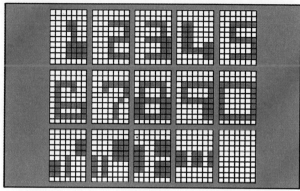

(b) Matrix patterns for magnetic-ink characters

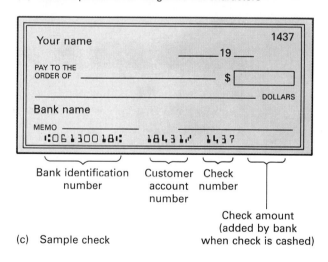

(c) Sample check

Magnetic ink is used on documents such as bank checks and credit card slips because a MICR device can easily distinguish the appropriate magnetic characters no matter how much a user might have written over them.

Magnetic Strips **Magnetic strips** are thin bands of magnetically encoded data that are found on the backs of many credit cards and automated teller cards (Figure 3–12). The data stored on the card vary from one application to another, but they include account numbers or special access codes. Magnetic strip cards can also be used to limit access to high security areas. To enter a security area, a person inserts the card into a computerized "read" device; if the card contains the right code, the door automatically opens. Because data cannot be seen or interpreted by simply looking at the card, the stored data can be highly sensitive or personal.

FIGURE 3–12
This Handi-Bank Plus automated teller card has a magnetic strip on which data, such as the card number and customer password, are recorded. (Courtesy of The Huntington National Bank)

Optical Recognition Optical recognition occurs when a device scans a printed surface and translates the image the scanner sees into a machine-readable format that is understandable by the computer. The three types of optical recognition described here are: optical-mark recognition; optical-bar recognition; and optical-character recognition.

FIGURE 3–13
Multiple-choice test form that uses optical-mark recognition to score test results (NCS General Purpose Answer Sheet reprinted courtesy of National Computer Systems, Inc. © 1977.)

SIDE 1

GENERAL PURPOSE - NCS - ANSWER SHEET
FOR USE WITH ALL NCS SENTRY OPTICAL MARK READING SYSTEMS
SEE IMPORTANT MARKING INSTRUCTIONS ON SIDE 2

	A B C D E		A B C D E		A B C D E		A B C D E		A B C D E
1	① ② ③ ④ ⑤	11	① ② ③ ④ ⑤	21	① ② ③ ④ ⑤	31	① ② ③ ④ ⑤	41	① ② ③ ④ ⑤
2	① ② ③ ④ ⑤	12	① ② ③ ④ ⑤	22	① ② ③ ④ ⑤	32	① ② ③ ④ ⑤	42	① ② ③ ④ ⑤
3	① ② ③ ④ ⑤	13	① ② ③ ④ ⑤	23	① ② ③ ④ ⑤	33	① ② ③ ④ ⑤	43	① ② ③ ④ ⑤
4	① ② ③ ④ ⑤	14	① ② ③ ④ ⑤	24	① ② ③ ④ ⑤	34	① ② ③ ④ ⑤	44	① ② ③ ④ ⑤
5	① ② ③ ④ ⑤	15	① ② ③ ④ ⑤	25	① ② ③ ④ ⑤	35	① ② ③ ④ ⑤	45	① ② ③ ④ ⑤
6	① ② ③ ④ ⑤	16	① ② ③ ④ ⑤	26	① ② ③ ④ ⑤	36	① ② ③ ④ ⑤	46	① ② ③ ④ ⑤
7	① ② ③ ④ ⑤	17	① ② ③ ④ ⑤	27	① ② ③ ④ ⑤	37	① ② ③ ④ ⑤	47	① ② ③ ④ ⑤
8	① ② ③ ④ ⑤	18	① ② ③ ④ ⑤	28	① ② ③ ④ ⑤	38	① ② ③ ④ ⑤	48	① ② ③ ④ ⑤
9	① ② ③ ④ ⑤	19	① ② ③ ④ ⑤	29	① ② ③ ④ ⑤	39	① ② ③ ④ ⑤	49	① ② ③ ④ ⑤
10	① ② ③ ④ ⑤	20	① ② ③ ④ ⑤	30	① ② ③ ④ ⑤	40	① ② ③ ④ ⑤	50	① ② ③ ④ ⑤

HIGHLIGHT

TALKWRITERS In spite of the roadblocks to voice-recognition technology, computer experts have been making some headway at creating machines that can "listen" to a person speak and then translate the speech into print. Although they carry different trade names, these machines are referred to generically as "talkwriters."

As commercially useful machines, talkwriters are still in the experimental stages, but they are getting better and more versatile. Eventually, they will speed up typesetting. When perfected, they will enable people who can't type to "type" messages just by speaking them—a godsend for those who have lost the use of their hands.

Talkwriters recognize speech patterns in various ways. Some store common patterns in their memories and match them to electrical signals (like spectographs) generated by words spoken into a microphone. Others rely on memory banks into which programmers have stored statistical analyses of the language. These analyses allow the computer to predict which word in its vocabulary will follow the one just uttered and to recognize a variety of voice intonations.

IBM's experimental model can "understand" 5,000 words, and the Kurzweil VoiceWriter can decipher twice that many. Both models require the user to read several minutes of text into the computer to acclimate it to that particular voice. Other companies in the U.S. and in Japan are also racing to perfect the talkwriter and to tap the business and educational markets such a device would create.

Because research is a time-consuming endeavor, however, industry observers say that stenographers and court reporters can feel safe in their jobs for years to come.

Optical-mark recognition (OMR) employs mark sensing, one of the simplest forms of optical recognition, to scan and translate, based on its location, a series of pen or pencil marks into computer-readable form. For example, answers to multiple-choice questions can be marked in pencil on a form such as the one in Figure 3–13. A computerized optical-mark reader scores the tests by identifying the position of the mark, not its shape.

A slightly more sophisticated type of optical recognition is **optical-bar recognition (OBR).** An optical-bar reader recognizes and interprets a pattern of lines that form a bar code. **Bar codes,** also called product codes, appear on products as a series of thick and thin black bars and spaces that are arranged to represent data, such as the name of the manufacturer and the type of product (Figure 3–14a). Interpretation of the code is based on the width of the lines rather than the location of the bar code. The bar code does not contain the price of the item. Prices are stored in the computer where the amount can be easily reprogrammed to reflect sales or special offers. The bar code is read by a scanner, and the price and product are then matched by the computer. The price may be displayed at a checkout counter by a point-of-sale terminal (Figure 3–14b). A **point-of-sale (POS) terminal** is a device that reads data at the source of a transaction and immediately turns them into usable information (Figure 3–15). These terminals record data found on bar codes or MICR price tags on each product, calculate cost, and provide the consumer with a detailed receipt of the transaction. Some also directly update inventory files.

There are various bar-coding schemes in use; however, the most common is the Universal Product Code (UPC). Department and grocery stores have long used OBR, but other types of stores, factories, and manufacturing operations are starting to use bar codes to provide more efficient, cost-effective control of inventory.

The most sophisticated type of optical-recognition is **optical-character recognition (OCR).** An optical-character reader works in much the same way as the human eye. It does not rely on the magnetic quality of the character such as MICR does; rather, it recognizes specially-shaped alphabetic and numeric characters. Capital and lowercase letters, as well as a variety of different optical-character typesets, can be read.

A set of optical characters may be used to print merchandise tags that can be read using an OCR wand (Figure 3–16). To process the sales trans-

---

Source Data Input

- Magnetic-ink character recognition (MICR)
- Magnetic strips
- Optical recognition
  - ☐ Optical-mark recognition (OMR)
  - ☐ Optical-bar recognition (OBR)
  - ☐ Optical-character recognition (OCR)

FIGURE 3–14

(a) The Universal Product Code (UPC) is typically found on consumer products. (b) This employee uses a bar-code scanner to enter inventory data into a computer. (Courtesy of Intermec Corp.)

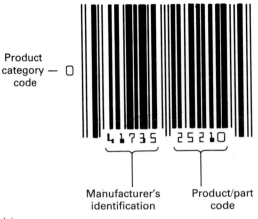

Product category code — 0

Manufacturer's identification

Product/part code

(a)

(b)

(a)

(b)

FIGURE 3–15
(a) This point-of-sale terminal enables the salesclerk to enter data about a product by simply passing the item's UPC bar code over a bar-code scanner connected to the POS terminal. (b) Laser beams from this scanner encircle an item and read its UPC bar code. [(a) Courtesy of Albertson's Inc. (b) National Semiconductor Co.]

FIGURE 3–16
Salesclerk using an OCR wand

action, the information on the tag, such as the item price and the inventory number, can be automatically entered at a point-of-sale terminal. Pertinent data can be saved and transferred to the company's main computer system to be used in activities such as managing inventories and analyzing sales. State-of-the-art scanners translate both graphics and text material. Technical drawings can be scanned and entered into a computer-aided design system for easy editing. Because of the variety of applications with which it can be used, optical-character recognition technology is steadily increasing its role as an input method.

OUTPUT CONCEPTS

Output is the process of translating data in machine-readable form into a form understandable to humans or readable by other machines. The information that is the result of processing is also often referred to as output. An **output device** is a peripheral device that allows a computer to communicate information to humans or another machine by accepting data from the computer and transforming them into a usable form.

Output is divided into two general categories: (a) output that can be readily understood and used by humans; and (b) output to secondary-storage devices that hold the data to be used as input for further processing by a computer or for use by another machine.

This chapter focuses on the devices that produce output that can be understood and used by humans. Chapter 4 focuses on output sent to secondary-storage devices.

In today's information society, people require clear, legible output—a major consideration when purchasing output devices. Output that can be understood by humans can be categorized as hard copy and soft copy. **Hard copy** is output, such as paper, that can be read immediately or stored and read later. It is a relatively stable and permanent form of output. **Soft copy** is usually a screen-displayed output. It is a transient form of output and is lost when the computer is turned off. But if the data needed to create the soft copy have been saved on disk or tapes, the soft copy can be reproduced on the screen anytime.

Output Concepts

- Human-readable output
  □ Hard copy
  □ Soft copy
- Secondary storage

HARD-COPY DEVICES

Graphics and text material can be produced with a wide selection of printers and plotters. A **printer** produces output, usually in the form of text, on paper; however, some printers produce graphics. A **plotter** produces graphic images on paper. Printers and plotters range in price from around one hundred dollars to tens of thousands of dollars. The speed of the devices and the quality of the hard copy are the main features that determine the various prices. A printer or plotter for home use might not have the same quality requirements as one for business.

There are enough different printers and plotters that descriptions could fill this chapter. In this section, however, we will look at only the major categories. First, let's consider print quality, an important feature of any hard-copy device.

Print Quality

The print quality available from hard-copy output can vary considerably. You may have heard the terms "near-typeset quality," "letter-quality," "near-letter quality," "standard-quality," and "draft-quality." But, just what do these terms mean?

At the top-of-the-line is **near-typeset quality print.** This print is similar in quality to what is produced by a typeset machine, such as the print found in a magazine or this text.

Letter-quality print is the equivalent of good typewriter print. This print is made using fully-formed (solid line) characters as opposed to characters made up of dots or lines (Figure 3–17). Letter-quality print is used traditionally in business letters and in formal correspondence.

Printers that don't produce the fully-formed characters can still print high-quality documents using a **near-letter quality print.** On some printers this is done when the print head makes multiple passes over the same letters, filling in the spaces between the dots or lines.

Standard-quality print is produced when characters composed of dots or lines are formed by a single pass of the print head. Generally, standard quality is suitable for most informal applications.

At the low end of the quality scale is **draft-quality print,** sometimes called compressed print. This print is sometimes used for rough drafts, informal correspondence, or computer program listings. The characters are formed with a minimum number of dots or lines and are smaller than the standard-quality characters. Figure 3–18 compares print qualities.

The quality of type that a printer produces is determined by its printing mechanism. Printers have two basic types of printing mechanisms: impact and nonimpact.

Impact Printers

An **impact printer** produces characters by using a hammer or pins to strike an ink ribbon, which in turn presses against a sheet of paper leaving

FIGURE 3–17

A comparison of fully-formed characters to characters composed of dots or lines

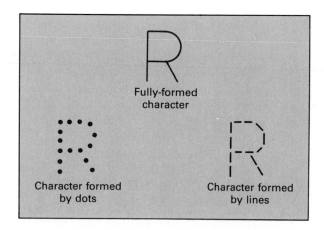

FIGURE 3–18
A comparison of the different qualities of print

```
        This is an example of near-typeset quality print.

     This is an example of letter-quality print.

       This is an example of near-letter quality print.

        This is an example of standard-quality print.

      This is an example of draft-quality (compressed) print.
```

an impression of the character on the paper. This is also how an ordinary typewriter works.

Two popular impact printers most often used with microcomputers are the dot-matrix printer and the daisy-wheel printer. They are both character-at-a-time printers, meaning they print one character at a time.

Dot-matrix Printers   The **dot-matrix printer** uses print heads containing from nine to twenty-four pins. These pins produce patterns of dots on the paper to form the individual characters. The 24-pin dot-matrix printer produces more dots than a 9-pin dot-matrix printer, which results in much crisper, clearer characters (Figure 3–19). Some dot-matrix printers can print better quality letters by using a near-letter quality mode. However, this mode drastically reduces printing speed because it makes multiple passes over the same line. The general rule is: the more pins, the crisper the letters. Dot-matrix printers are very popular with home computer users because they are relatively inexpensive (approximately $150 and up) and typically print at speeds of 100–600 characters per second.

Many printers have built-in buffers to store succeeding lines of text. Buffer storage allows bidirectional printing, i.e., printing in both directions as the print head moves back and forth across the paper. This capability significantly increases print speed.

Daisy-wheel Printers   In order to get the quality of type found on typewriters, a daisy-wheel impact printer can be used. The **daisy-wheel printer** is so called because the print mechanism looks like a daisy; at the end of each "petal" is a fully-formed character which produces solid-line

FIGURE 3–19
A comparison of print quality between 9-pin and 24-pin dot-matrix printers

```
      This is an example of 24-pin dot-matrix print.

      This is an example of 9-pin dot-matrix print.
```

FIGURE 3–20
Daisy-wheel element

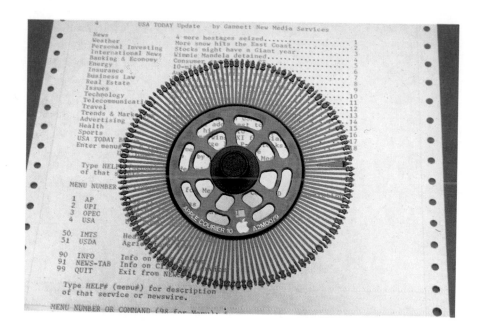

print (Figure 3–20). A hammer strikes a "petal" containing a character against the ribbon, and the character prints on the paper.

The daisy wheel can be replaced to change styles and sizes of typeface (fonts). For example, daisy wheels can be changed to go from pica to elite and from characters to symbols, or to print text in a foreign language.

When one feature of a printer, such as the print quality, is enhanced, it is usually at the expense of another. Letter-quality printers are much slower, typically 35–55 characters per second.

Line Printers In businesses where enormous amounts of material are printed, the character-at-a-time printers are just too slow; therefore, these users need line-at-a-time printers. **Line printers,** or line-at-a-time printers, use special mechanisms that can print a whole line at once; they can typically print in the range of 1,200–6,000 lines per minute. Drum, chain, and band printers are line-at-a-time printers.

A **drum printer** has complete character sets engraved around the circumference of each of the print positions of the drum (Figure 3–21). The number of print positions across the drum equals the number available on the page. This number typically ranges from 80–132 print positions. Individual print positions rotate until the desired letter is in the proper place, then a bank of hammers strikes the paper against the ribbon and drum, producing an entire line of print.

A **chain printer** uses a chain of print characters wrapped around two pulleys (Figure 3–22). Like the drum printer, there is one hammer for each print position. Circuitry inside the printer detects when the correct character appears at the desired print location on the page. The hammer then strikes the page, pressing the paper against a ribbon and the character located at the desired print position. An impression of the character is left

FIGURE 3–21
Print mechanism of a drum printer

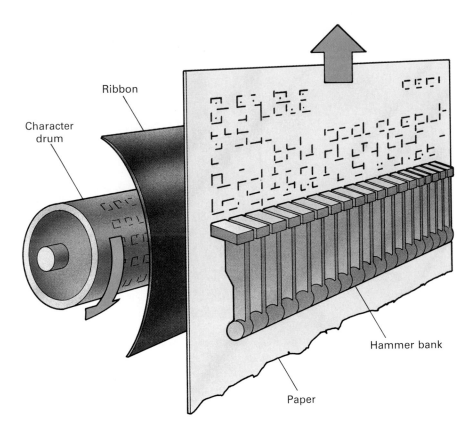

FIGURE 3–22
Print mechanism of a chain printer

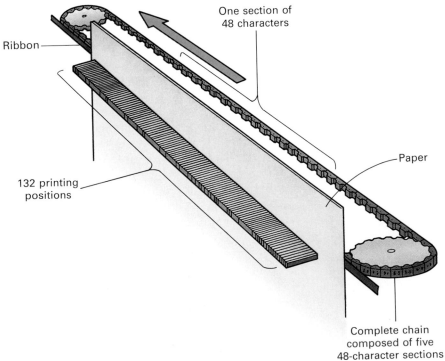

on the page. The chain keeps rotating until all the required print positions on the line have been filled. Then the page moves up to print the next line.

A **band printer** operates in a similar way except it uses a band instead of a chain and has fewer hammers (Figure 3–23). The hammers on a band printer are mounted on a carriage that moves across the paper to the appropriate print positions. Characters are rotated into place and struck by the hammers. Font styles can easily be changed by replacing a band or chain.

Nonimpact Printers

Nonimpact printers do not use a striking device to produce characters on paper; and because these printers do not hammer against the paper, they are much quieter. Major technologies in this area are the ink-jet, thermal-transfer, and laser printers.

Ink-jet Printers **Ink-jet printers** form characters on paper by spraying ink from tiny nozzles through an electrical field that arranges the charged ink particles into characters at the rate of approximately 250 characters per second. The ink is absorbed into the paper and dries instantly. Various colors of ink can also be used. Although this might sound like a messy way of printing, ink-jet printers are reliable, but expensive.

Thermal-transfer Printers An inexpensive alternative to the ink-jet printer is the **thermal-transfer printer** which uses heat to transfer ink to

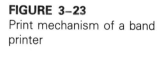

FIGURE 3–23

Print mechanism of a band printer

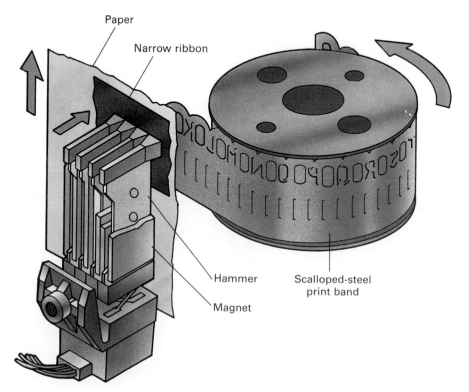

Paper

Narrow ribbon

Hammer

Magnet

Scalloped-steel print band

Hard-copy Devices

- Impact printers
  - Dot-matrix
  - Daisy-wheel
  - Line
- Nonimpact printers
  - Ink-jet
  - Thermal-transfer
  - Laser
- Plotters
- Computer output
  microform (COM)

paper. For about $150 to $300, a thermal-transfer printer produces near letter-quality characters. These printers bond the ink onto the paper by heating pins which press against a special ink ribbon. Thermal-transfer printers can produce color printouts by using a color ribbon.

Laser Printers When speed and quality comparable to typeset material are required and cost is no factor, a laser printer is the solution.

Laser printers (Figure 3–24) produce images on paper by directing a laser beam at a mirror which bounces the beam onto a drum. The laser leaves a negative charge on the drum to which positively charged black toner powder will stick. As the paper rolls by the drum, the toner is transferred to the paper. A hot roller bonds the toner to the paper.

Laser printers use buffers that store an entire page at a time. When a whole page is loaded, it will be printed. Many home-use laser printers can print eight pages per minute, but commercial printers are much faster and print approximately 21,000 lines per minute, or 437 pages per minute if each page contains 48 lines. Laser printer prices start at $2,000 but can go to the tens of thousands of dollars. Developments in the last few years have provided relatively low-cost laser printers for use in small businesses.

Plotters

The growth of computer-aided design and drafting has created a demand for devices that can produce high-quality graphics in multiple colors. A plotter reproduces drawings using pens that are attached to movable arms (Figure 3–25). The pens are directed across the surface of a stationary piece of paper. Many plotters, however, combine a movable pen arm with paper that can also roll back and forth to make the drawing. This two-way movement allows any configuration to be drawn.

FIGURE 3–24
Desktop laser printers have made near-typeset quality printing affordable for many small-business microcomputer users. (Courtesy of Okidata, an Oki America company)

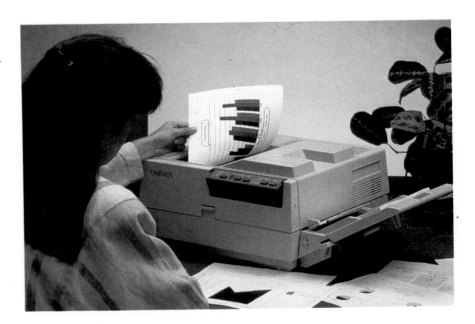

(a)

(b)

FIGURE 3–25
(a) Desktop plotters are used in offices to generate graphics that enhance business presentations. (b) Large plotters allow images such as this circuit diagram to be drawn to a size that enables users to view the image in detail. (Courtesy of Houston Instrument)

Plotter applications are not limited to computer-aided design. High-quality bar graphs and pie charts created with a plotter can also enhance business presentations.

Computer Output Microform

Computer output microform (COM) is hard copy in the form of photographic images recorded on a microform such as microfilm or microfiche cards. In some cases, the computer can output directly to a COM machine. In other cases, data are first recorded on magnetic tape, and the tape is used as input to a COM machine.

The advantage of COM is that it gives a low-cost storage option for large amounts of data requiring infrequent access. It is ideal for businesses such as hospitals that must keep old data for patients' medical, financial, and insurance claim records. Microfilm and microfiche readers are used to read the data.

SOFT-COPY DEVICES

Usually, a user prefers to see what the output looks like before making a permanent copy of it. Viewing the work allows corrections or rearrangement of material to suit specific needs. While most soft-copy output is seen on a display device, voice synthesis devices let us hear it as well.

HIGHLIGHT

THE LADY AND THE COMPUTER

In 1986, a massive celebration was held to honor the 100th anniversary of the Statue of Liberty. To get "The Lady" ready for this celebration, complete restoration of the statue was undertaken. Computers aided in the restoration process, as well as with other activities surrounding this event.

The event might never have taken place without the use of computers. Just the fund-raising required to finance this $265 million project was a major undertaking. To help raise money, computers with sophisticated data-base programs were used to compile the names and addresses of thousands of potential donors.

The organizers of the event used different kinds of software packages to assist them in their jobs. Spreadsheets were used to monitor contributions and distribution of monies. All activities, including work schedules, were monitored so adjustments could be made if required. Each phase of construction was updated on hard disk. At any time, the status of any part of the project could be checked from any work site via a modem.

Computers were also used in the actual design of the restoration. Sensors were attached to various parts of the statue to communicate to computers such details as wind velocity and structural stress.

Once the data were collected, detailed models of the statue were drawn using computer graphic systems. By using scanners, the engineers drew three-dimensional representations of the statue's torch and flame. These drawings helped the craftsmen restore its original design.

With the help of computers, "The Lady" was on time for her 100th birthday.

Monitors

The most popular and certainly the most viewed form of output is found on the monitor (Figure 3–26). A **monitor** is a television-like device used to display data or information. Just like other output devices, monitors come in many styles and price ranges. Monitors allow users to view the results of processing, but they can be combined with keyboards so that input data can be viewed and checked as they are entered. This combination of keyboard and monitor is often called a **terminal** or **workstation.**

Monitor quality is often judged in terms of **resolution,** a measure of the number of picture elements, or pixels, that a screen contains. A **pixel** is the smallest increment of a display screen that can be controlled individually—the more pixels, the clearer and sharper the image. A 640 × 460

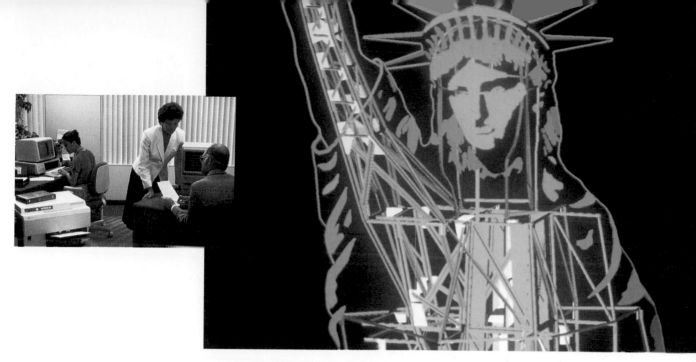

In 1986, the renovation of the Statue of Liberty was dependent on computer systems. Structural analyses and daily work schedules were monitored by larger systems; fund-raising donation letters and public relations advertising were prepared on smaller systems. (Courtesy of Intergraph Corp. Inset: Photo courtesy of Hewlett-Packard Co.)

pixel screen means 640 horizontal pixels and 460 vertical pixels. There are two kinds of viewing screens used for monitors: cathode-ray tube and flat-panel display.

Cathode-ray Tube To produce a data image on a **cathode-ray tube (CRT),** an electron beam moves across a phosphor-coated screen. By intensifying the strength of the beam, the phosphor coating glows in certain places, forming the characters. The most common type of CRT has a display screen of twenty-five lines of eighty characters each. Other sizes are available including those that can display a full $8\frac{1}{2}$-by-11 inch page.

The least expensive of the CRTs is the single color, or monochrome, monitor. Monochrome monitors are used where output is mainly text and numbers; although, with the appropriate circuitry, some monitors can display graphics. Monochrome monitors usually display either green, amber, or white characters on a black screen.

A color monitor is often preferable for output containing graphics. Three colors of phosphor dots form a pixel on color monitors (Figure 3–27). These colors are blended to make other colors by varying the intensity of the electron beam focused on the phosphor dots.

Two types of color monitors are commonly used: composite and red-green-blue. A composite color monitor uses only one electron gun to control the intensity of all three phosphor dots in each pixel. In a red-green-blue (RGB) monitor, three electron guns, one for each dot in a pixel, are used to control the intensity of the phosphor dots. A much sharper picture

FIGURE 3-26
Shown here are several monitors used to view output. Note the difference between the color display of the monitor on the left and the monochrome (single color) display of the monitor on the bottom right. (Courtesy of TRW, Inc.)

FIGURE 3-27
Each pixel contains three phosphor dots—one red (R), one green (G), and one blue (B).

Color monitors have one red, one green, and one blue phosphor dot in each pixel.

is produced with the RGB monitor because the three electron guns allow finer control over the intensities of the phosphor dots.

Artists may wonder why red, green, and blue are used as the primary colors instead of red, yellow, and blue. Simply stated, the difference between electronic waves and color pigments requires that green be used instead of yellow to get the appropriate color mixes.

Flat-panel Display Computers are becoming smaller and more powerful. A CRT is cumbersome for use with portable computers. However, a **flat-panel display** does not have a picture tube and can be manufactured small enough to fit on the small, battery-powered portables. Some desktop microcomputers also use flat-panel displays.

The most common type of flat-panel display is the liquid-crystal display (LCD), which produces images by aligning molecular crystals. When a voltage is applied, the crystals line up in a way that blocks light from passing through them; that absence of light is seen as characters on the screen.

Besides size, another advantage of LCDs over CRTs is that flat panels do not flicker. The flicker of a CRT is caused by the electron beam moving across the screen. It can cause eye strain and fatigue during prolonged sessions at the computer.

The flat-panel display is still in its infancy; better resolution and contrast, as well as other new features, are being developed. One advance is the gas-plasma screen. These displays offer flicker-free viewing and have a much higher contrast than LCDs. Gas-plasma displays contain an ionized gas (plasma) between two glass plates. One glass plate contains a set of horizontal wires; the other has a set of vertical wires. The intersection points of each horizontal and vertical wire identifies a pixel. A pixel is turned on when current is sent through the appropriate vertical and horizontal wires. The plasma at the pixel emits light as the current is applied. Characters are formed by lighting the appropriate pixels. Figure 3–28 shows a comparison between flat-panel display and gas-plasma display screens.

FIGURE 3–28

Comparison between (a) flat-panel display and (b) gas-plasma display screens

(a)

(b)

Voice Synthesis

Another emerging technology is voice synthesis and the computers that produce it. **Voice synthesis** is the process of electronically reproducing the human voice in recognizable patterns. Producing these patterns is not an easy task. The English language and its rules of syntax are enough to confuse many humans; imagine the difficulty in programming a computer to decipher how to say: "I can record a record."

Remember Hal, the computer, in the movie *2001: A Space Odyssey?* Hal talked to the astronauts just as we speak. While technology has yet to reach this point, it is slowly approaching this clarity of speech. There are still many obstacles to overcome.

Soft-copy Devices

- Monitors
  - ☐ Cathode-ray tube (CRT)
  - ☐ Flat-panel display
- Voice synthesis

MAKING THE CONNECTION

Computers require special hardware to connect the CPU and any peripheral device, such as a printer. The connection is called an **interface.** Data are transferred in one of two ways: serial or parallel.

When a **serial interface** is used, data are transferred either to or from the CPU and a peripheral device one *bit* at a time (Figure 3–29a). The most common serial interface found on microcomputers is called the RS–232C. It is usually available as a plug-in card, but is sometimes built into the circuitry of a computer by the manufacturer.

In a **parallel interface** data are transferred either to or from the CPU and a peripheral device one *byte* at a time, i.e., eight bits at a time (Figure 3–29b). Parallel interfaces are faster and more expensive than serial interfaces. The term "parallel" is used because data are sent over conductors running next to each other. The Centronics standard and the IEEE–488 standard are parallel interfaces used in many microcomputers. These are also either built in by the manufacturer or available as plug-in cards.

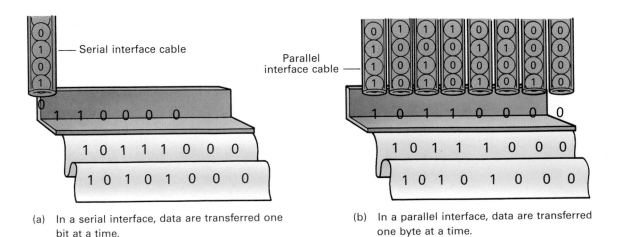

(a) In a serial interface, data are transferred one bit at a time.

(b) In a parallel interface, data are transferred one byte at a time.

FIGURE 3–29
Serial versus parallel data transfer

SUMMARY

Before the CPU processes data and makes the results available, there must be a way of communicating data to and from the computer. The process of entering and translating data into machine-readable form is called input. The data to be entered are also often referred to as input. Input devices are the hardware used to enter and translate data.

Data are prepared for input in two general ways. In transcriptive data entry, the data are first written on documents at the source, or place of origin, of the data. The data on these documents are transcribed to another medium that can be read and interpreted by a computer. In source data entry, the data are prepared at the source in a machine-readable form that can be used directly by a computer without the necessity of a data-transcription process.

Two basic data-processing methods are used to input data. Batch processing involves gathering data and then submitting it to the computer in a batch to be processed without user intervention. Transaction processing involves processing each data transaction as it occurs.

Any data being input should be checked for accuracy. Two methods of accuracy checking are verification and validation.

There are many kinds of input devices, including card reader, keyboard, mouse, light pen, voice recognition, optical-mark recognition, optical-bar recognition, and optical-character recognition.

The process of translating machine-readable data into a form that can be understood by humans or a form that can be read by other machines is called output. The information that is the result of processing is also often referred to as output. An output device is the hardware that performs the translation and produces a hard or soft copy of the processing results.

Output that humans can read can be separated into hard copy and soft copy. Hard-copy output devices include printers, plotters, and computer output microform devices. Printers are divided into impact and nonimpact categories based on how characters are printed. Soft-copy output devices include monitors and voice-synthesis systems. Two popular types of monitors are cathode-ray tube (CRT) and flat-panel display.

Peripheral devices are connected to the CPU through a connection called an interface. Two basic types of interfaces are used. A serial interface transfers data one *bit* at a time. A parallel interface transfers data one *byte,* or eight bits of data, at a time.

Key Terms

band printer (p. 91)

bar code (p. 83)

batch processing (p. 73)

card reader (p. 74)

cathode-ray tube (CRT) (p. 95)

chain printer (p. 89)

computer output microform (COM) (p. 93)

cursor (p. 75)

daisy-wheel printer (p. 88)

digitizer (p. 79)

dot-matrix printer (p. 88)

draft-quality print (p. 87)

drum printer (p. 89)

flat-panel display (p. 97)

hard copy (p. 86)

hardware (p. 72)

impact printer (p. 87)

ink-jet printer (p. 91)

input (p. 72)

input device (p. 72)

interactive program (p. 73)

interface (p. 98)

joystick (p. 76)

keyboard (p. 75)

laser printer (p. 92)

letter-quality print (p. 87)

light pen (p. 79)

line printer (p. 89)

magnetic-ink character recognition (MICR) (p. 80)

magnetic strips (p. 81)

monitor (p. 94)

mouse (p. 77)

near-letter quality print (p. 87)

near-typeset quality print (p. 87)

nonimpact printer (p. 91)

off-line (p. 73)

on-line (p. 73)

optical-bar recognition (OBR) (p. 83)

optical-character recognition (OCR) (p. 84)

optical-mark recognition (OMR) (p. 83)

output (p. 86)

output device (p. 86)

parallel interface (p. 98)

peripheral device (p. 72)

pixel (p. 94)

plotter (p. 86)

point-of-sale (POS) terminal (p. 84)

printer (p. 86)

punched card (p. 74)

real-time processing (p. 73)

resolution (p. 94)

serial interface (p. 98)

soft copy (p. 86)

source data entry (p. 73)

standard-quality print (p. 87)

terminal (p. 94)

thermal-transfer printer (p. 91)

touch pad (p. 78)

touch screen (p. 77)

trackball (p. 76)

transaction processing (p. 73)

transcriptive data entry (p. 73)

validation (p. 74)

verification (p. 74)

voice recognition (p. 79)

voice synthesis (p. 98)

workstation (p. 94)

Review Questions

1. What does it mean to input data into a computer?
2. What is the purpose of an input device?
3. Explain the differences between on-line and off-line.
4. Distinguish between batch and transaction processing.
5. What are the two basic ways in which data are prepared for entry? Describe them.
6. Describe two methods used to check data accuracy during the input process.
7. Name and describe at least five input devices.
8. Briefly describe how magnetic-ink character recognition (MICR) works.
9. List three types of optical recognition.
10. Define output.
11. What is the purpose of an output device?

12. Output can be divided into two categories. What are they?
13. Output that can be understood by humans can be divided into _____ and _____.
14. Name and describe the different degrees of print quality available.
15. How does an impact printer form characters?
16. Name and describe three types of impact printers.
17. How does a nonimpact printer form characters?
18. Name and describe three types of nonimpact printers.
19. What is a plotter?
20. Describe computer output microform (COM).
21. List two kinds of monitors and tell how they work.
22. How do resolution and pixels relate to monitors?
23. What are some of the problems of voice recognition and voice synthesis?
24. Describe the difference between serial and parallel interfaces.
25. If a computer system is available for your use, identify the input and output devices connected to that system. Alternatively, use a photo from a magazine or advertisement.

INFOMODULE

Computers in Design and Manufacturing

As you probably have suspected by now, there are very few areas for which a computer cannot be adapted. This is especially true in the areas of design and manufacturing.

As the computer has become more powerful over the years, it has become capable of handling more sophisticated tasks than simply processing numerical data. As modern manufacturing plants are built, or older ones are remodelled, they have incorporated an impressive array of computer-controlled machinery. This section will discuss how computers are used: (a) to design products and parts of products; (b) in computer numerical control; (c) with industrial robots; and (d) in programmable controllers that monitor assembly or manufacturing processes. Computers are used in these operations for very practical reasons: (a) to increase productivity; and (b) to reduce costs.

COMPUTER-AIDED DESIGN

Just a few years ago if you walked into a designing work area, you would have seen numerous drafting tables with designers or engineers hovering over them. Planning and drawing a proposed new product was a pencil and paper operation. Walk in that same room today and you will probably see a different scene. What was once a room full of drafting tables is now a room with design and drafting workstations, plotters, graphics tablets, and digitizers.

The computerized tools used to design and draw the various items might be either individual microcomputers or terminals connected to the company's large computer system.

Computer-aided design (CAD) is the integration of the computer and graphics to aid in the areas of design and drafting. Computer-aided design and drafting software was originally developed as a "tool" for mechanical designers and draftsmen. But professionals in other disciplines soon saw the advantage of using the computer as a design tool. Before

long, CAD packages were written for other areas. Electrical and electronic packages help design wiring layouts and printed circuit boards. For example, TRW, Inc., used CAD to design a new "superchip" circuitry containing 35 million transistors (Figure 1).

It is estimated that most architectural firms use some form of CAD. Architects are able to draw a floorplan and lay out all structural details, as well as plumbing and electrical fixtures, when designing a room or a whole building. Manufacturers of footware, such as Brooks Shoe, Inc., also use CAD systems to design their running shoes (Figure 2).

FIGURE 1
TRW employees use CAD systems to design chip circuitry. (Courtesy of TRW, Inc.)

(a)

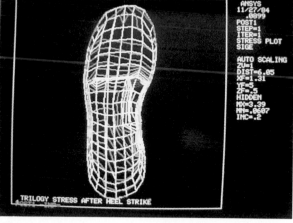
(b)

(c)

FIGURE 2

(a) A computer-generated model of the human foot is used to help design athletic shoes. (b) A computer generates a three-dimensional finite element model of an athletic shoe midsole that can be tested for stress points. (c) A two-dimensional cross-section of athletic shoe midsole. (All photos courtesy of Brooks Shoe, Inc., and Michigan State University)

The advantages of this new application of computers into product engineering are:

1. It makes the designing and drafting easier, more accurate, and better planned.
2. It increases productivity because design and drafting time are significantly shortened.

A CAD system has two parts: hardware and software. The CAD operator uses an input device, such as a mouse or light pen, along with computer commands of the CAD program to draw **entities,** or objects. These entities appear on a monitor, or display screen, so the operator can see them. The designer finds this drawing method much easier than the pencil and paper method because mistakes can be corrected eas-ily and the designs can be done and redone many times until they are just right.

The computer lets the designer draw the product or object to appear in three-dimensions (3-D). By drawing in 3-D, the designer can rotate the item on any axis on the display screen to view it from all angles (Figure 3). The designer can "zoom in" to see small details or can "pull back" to see the whole object, providing a clear view of any design flaws and showing how the item will look when it is finished.

Other features of CAD allow the designer to move, copy, mirror, and erase sections or entire images—all without eraser marks, of course. Drawings can also be scaled to any size and plotted on all sizes of paper.

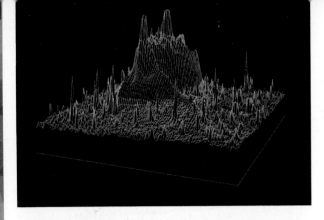

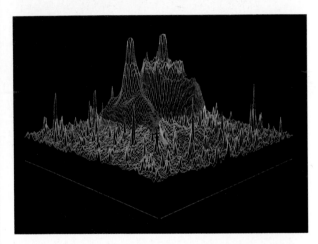

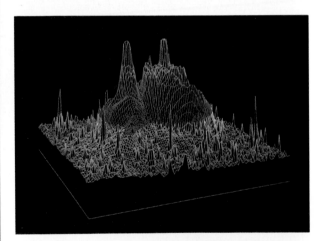

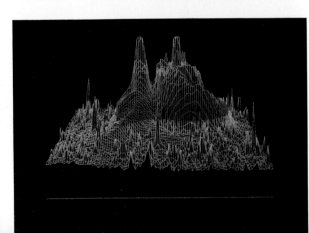

The use of a CAD system reduces production time from initial conception to finished product because: (a) the initial drawing can be done easier and faster; and (b) it avoids repetition. Each design can be filed and used later to create different products. Often-used items or images can be created and stored in libraries. Whenever these images are needed, the designer simply retrieves them from the library file and inserts them into the current drawing.

Individuals, too, can use CAD. An aeronautics student at Massachusetts Institute of Technology, used an IBM PC XT (a microcomputer) to design the wing ribs of a human-powered plane. The computer was programmed to determine the best shape of the wings for the 88-pound plane to get maximum lift with the least drag.

Automobile designers at large auto manufacturing plants, such as General Motors, use CAD to draw the many prototypes of a new car before creating solid models. Engineers at Ikeda Bussan Company, Ltd., in Tokyo, Japan, use a

FIGURE 3

Created at Los Alamos National Laboratory, a 3-D computer-generated image of the Whirlpool Nebula can be rotated to show the image from different angles. (Courtesy of Los Alamos National Laboratory)

Architects use a CAD system with an Apple Macintosh to plan a new structure. (Courtesy of Apple Computer, Inc.)

CAD system to design automotive seats, most of which are used in Nissan's passenger cars. One facet of their system allows them to design and perform tests that measure body pressure on the seats and analyze road-induced vibrations. CAD systems are even being used by clothing designers, such as Escada, to design the patterns and fabrics for their very expensive and unique sweaters.

COMPUTERS IN MANUFACTURING

Most companies have come to realize that they must either partially or fully computerize their factories to be competitive. The use of computers to control the factory machines in the manufacturing process is called **computer-aided manufacturing (CAM).** When the design process (CAD) and the manufacturing process (CAM) are combined, they are referred to as CAD/CAM.

To be truly automated and integrated, though, a company must link *all* the different parts of the manufacturing process with *all* other aspects of the company. This automation and integration of an entire manufacturing enterprise is called **computer-integrated manufacturing (CIM).**

With CIM, companies link not only product design to the manufacturing process, but they also link those processes to the company's computers that handle word processing, project management, general accounting, inventory control, order processing, factory-floor scheduling, and other operations within the factory itself.

Only a few companies have fully implemented CIM. Cone Drive Division of Ex-cell-o Corporation implemented CIM to automate its operation and to control products and processes so that its customers would receive their products in a timely fashion. At Cone, microcomputers, which are linked to their main computers, are placed not only in office areas, but also on the shop floor. An operator in the shop or a manager in the office can each view a drawing or request shipping. Volvo Car Corporation is designing its new plant in Uddevalla, Sweden, with the most advanced CIM technologies to keep Volvo competitive for many years to come.

The key to CIM is in the communication that must take place between all the different makes and types of computers and peripheral devices. All the computer systems in the company must be linked together by data communications. A problem can occur when a company uses one type of computer in one part of the company and another to control other aspects of operations.

Rockwell International's Graphic Systems Division in Reading, Pennsylvania, which manufactures newspaper printing presses, monitors factory time, attendance, and labor productivity with its computer system. Terminals on the factory floor and in managers' offices supply factory employees with timely information on job status, job cost, and payroll. (Courtesy of Honeywell, Inc.)

To integrate all computer-controlled operations and to make sure the equipment can communicate with each other, equipment manufacturers must agree upon communication links. One such communication link that is becoming the industry standard was developed by General Motors and is called **manufacturing automation protocol (MAP).** Although developed by an automaker, MAP standards can be implemented in other manufacturing environments.

Computer Numerical Control (CNC)

Manufacturing techniques have been through a tremendous transformation in recent years. A common task in the manufacturing process is the milling of parts. In the past, all operations of this sort were controlled by individual machine operators. The quality of the end product was often directly related to the skill of the operator. Today, many of these milling operations have been turned over to **computer numerical control (CNC),** a system in which an operator programs a computer that controls the milling process apparatus. The actual machine is not attended by a human.

Unlike a human, a computer-controlled drill bit, for example, can perform the same task

Information can flow from the factory floor to the boardroom with computer-integrated manufacturing (CIM) systems similar to the one used by this manufacturing company. (Courtesy of Honeywell, Inc.)

exactly, over and over again. This ability is particularly beneficial to repetitive part formation.

The use of CNC devices makes it possible to cut more difficult parts and with greater precision. The computer-controlled machines are even becoming easier to use. When programming is required by the operator, the commands usually appear as simple English words rather than complex computer codes.

The computer in the CNC machine can be programmed to change drill bits during a cutting operation. Operators no longer have to stop the manufacturing process to change drill bits and are free to perform other duties.

Often a CNC machine is connected to a CAD workstation. By watching the monitor, the CNC operator can view the part as it is being made by the machine.

Robotics

Many people perceive robots to be walking, talking androids or highly intelligent machines capable of carrying out all kinds of unusual deeds. These are the robots of science fiction and of modern-day movies rather than reality.

To clarify what is meant by a **robot,** since there is no uniformity by appearance, robot has been defined by the Robotics Institute of America as '' . . . a reprogrammable, multifunctional manipulator designed to move material, parts, tools, or specialized devices through variable programmed motions for the performance of a variety of tasks.'' More simply put, they are machines that can be programmed to do a variety of useful tasks.

While some experimental robots are made into human-like forms, most industrial robots resemble nothing of the sort, and it would be impractical to make them so. Far from being intelligent, robots are capable of completing only preprogrammed instructions. But they can be programmed to do some rather complicated tasks; and they can turn out products in a factory with unsurpassed precision.

They are used in manufacturing mainly to reduce costs and to increase productivity. Robots are also excellent at repetitive tasks that humans find boring; they never tire. Robots are ideal to replace humans on many jobs that are hazardous, providing welcome relief from the possibility of injury.

The first industrial robots were simply computer-controlled mechanical arms, performing a single, simple task. Today, industrial robots are still used for mainly assembly-line tasks, but some can do multiple tasks and move along on wheels or a track or belt system. Many robots have an elementary sense of touch and vision that gives them more precision.

Robots generally are delegated to three types of jobs: (a) operating tools; (b) lifting and handling materials or parts; and (c) assembling parts.

Operating Tools The operation of tools is the most common application of robots. Spot or arc

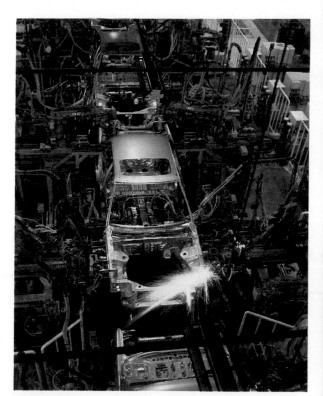

FIGURE 4
Robots are used for welding automobile parts at this Honda plant. (Courtesy of Honda America, Marysville, Ohio)

welding and spray painting automobile parts are typical tasks (Figure 4). The robots at Fey Manufacturing in California weld bumpers for small trucks. Drilling of the hundreds or thousands of rivet holes in aircraft components is a natural task to assign to robots. General Dynamics does just that.

Lifting and Handling Materials
Lifting and handling materials are also fairly uncomplicated tasks for robots. Most robots tend to be of the "pick and place" variety (Figure 5). These robots simply pick up an object and place it somewhere else, such as picking up a piece of metal and placing it in a stamping machine.

Another example is demonstrated by Metal Casings of Worcester, England, which makes aluminum cast parts for car and consumer-goods industries. Their robots are precisely

FIGURE 5
"Pick and place" robot (Courtesy of Martin Marietta)

timed to ladle a volume of molten aluminum into the machines and then remove the hardened component and place it in a cool water bath.

Flymo, an English lawnmower manufacturer, uses robots to box mowers that come off the production lines at its plant in Darlington. Flymo's robots lift very heavy objects; but some robots can handle very delicate objects. One chocolate manufacturer uses robots to carefully pick up pieces of candy and pack them into boxes.

Assembling
Assembly is still difficult for robots; however, inroads have been made in some areas. Some companies use robots to insert electrical components of standard shapes into printed circuit boards that eventually will be placed into many types of electrical equipment. IBM not only sells robots that can handle this type of assembly task, but also uses them to assemble products in their computer and terminal plants.

Robots are used in automobile factories to assemble steering gear tie rods or to insert valves into cylinders. One major U.S. auto plant uses 260 robots to weld, paint, and assemble their luxury model automobiles as they move down a twenty-one-mile production line.

> **Robot Tasks**
>
> - Operating tools
> - Lifting and handling materials
> - Assembling

As computer capabilities grow, so does the number of applications for robots. Robots can now be adapted with sensors that, together with the computer, help the robot "see" and "feel" its way around the workplace. An elementary sense of "sight" is accomplished with digital-imaging cameras or by bouncing infrared or microwave signals off the object. These signals are received by a robot's computer and matched with previously stored images for the purpose of identification and inspection.

Robots can be programmed to pick up heavy objects or objects as delicate and lightweight as an egg without damaging either. The sense of touch, **tactile sensing,** is in its elementary stages of development, but robots now can distinguish many different shapes, handle each appropriately, and perform various operations. These tasks are possible because the robot's "hands," called **end effectors,** are designed in many varieties and are often interchangeable (Figure 6).

Many robotic hands have been developed. Early robotic hands did not move independently of the arm. Recently, they have been modified

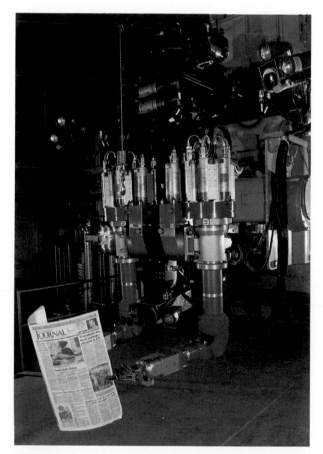

FIGURE 6
Robotic hand (end effector) (Courtesy of Martin Marietta)

to hold and manipulate fragile objects, turn doorknobs, and change ceiling light bulbs.

Researchers at Stanford University have designed a robotic hand that can move independently of the arm and even has fingers; one finger is similar to a thumb and greatly improves the dexterity of the device.

MIT designed a type of rubber "skin" for a robotic hand which contains a layer of fine wires that can sense the items being handled more precisely than earlier devices. The computer system connected to the hand constructs and displays the image of the object being touched.

Robots are emerging in nonindustrial areas of our lives, such as domestic use, medical applications, and earth, sea, and space exploration.

Japan is the world's leader in the manufacture and use of industrial robots. About 65 percent of the robots are in Japan; the United States is the next largest user. Statistics show that in 1986 there were over 100,000 industrial robots in the world. Projections indicate that at the current growth rate there will be over 200,000 robots in 1990. The cost of an industrial robot is anywhere from $25,000 to $125,000. Major suppliers of robots include: Hitachi, Kawasaki, and Mitsubishi in Japan; Cincinnati Milacron, GMF Robotics, and DeVilbiss in the U.S.; Volkswagen in West Germany; and Renault in France.

Programmable Controllers

Two important aspects of running an industrial plant are monitoring and controlling the activities of the machinery. These jobs are being taken over by the **programmable controller.** A programmable controller is a computer-regulated unit that consists of a microprocessor, an input and output module, and a power supply (Figure 7).

A programmable controller is used: (a) to control on/off functions of switches and relays; and (b) to control processes (process control).

The microprocessor of the programmable controller is programmed with a keyboard that can be attached to it when needed. The keyboard is not actually part of the controller; once

FIGURE 7
The Babcock & Wilcox Company's Loose Parts Monitoring System III, a programmable controller, uses sophisticated computer analysis techniques to evaluate metal-to-metal impacts of loose parts caught in the high velocity flows of nuclear steam systems. It provides real-time estimates of the location and damage potential of loose parts. (Courtesy of The Babcock & Wilcox Co.)

the programming is complete, the keyboard can be removed, and the programmable controller is still functional.

The advantage of the programmable controller is that its microprocessor can be programmed to reflect any desired cause and effect relationship, e.g., throwing Switch 1 starts Motor 2. The programmable controller can also be reprogrammed should any changes be necessary.

Here is a simple description of how the programmable controller is used to regulate on/off functions of two motors. Suppose two separate switches control two separate motors: S1 (Switch 1) controls M1 (Motor 1); and S2 (Switch 2) controls M2 (Motor 2). Rather than directly connecting S1 to M1, they are connected via the programmable controller; the same is true for S2 and M2. When the programmable controller receives the signal that S1 is switched on, it processes that signal and outputs it to start M1.

Why not directly connect the input to the output? What if you wanted Switch 1 to control Motor 2? It is much easier to reprogram the programmable controller than it is to rewire the circuit. Imagine if there were ten or twenty or even one hundred inputs and outputs. It is much easier to direct a programmable controller than to redesign the physical system.

Process control is the monitoring and controlling of various processes in a system's operation. For example, a programmable controller can play an important part in regulating furnace temperature for melting glass. Basically, a "set point" is programmed into the programmable controller, such as a specific temperature for the glass-melting furnace. The furnace continually sends temperature data signals back to the programmable controller. The programmable controller compares these signals to its preprogrammed set point. If the signals do not match—perhaps the temperature has risen—the programmable controller sends a signal to a control element that adjusts the furnace temperature accordingly. One programmable controller can control many process-control systems, a more complex task than controlling on/off operations.

Because of fierce worldwide competition, more factories are becoming automated with the latest computer technologies. Factories need to keep their costs down. With the aid of computers, the productivity of each person can be increased, and the precision of computer-controlled machinery reduces defects in the product, which also affects operating costs.

In manufacturing companies, process control can be integrated with plant data. The system used by this factory offers touch-screen access to thousands of terminals along the plant-wide reporting network. (Courtesy of Honeywell, Inc.)

KEY TERMS

computer-aided design (CAD) (p. 102)

computer-aided manufacturing (CAM) (p. 105)

computer-integrated manufacturing (CIM) (p. 105)

computer numerical control (CNC) (p. 106)

end effector (p. 109)

entities (p. 103)

manufacturing automation protocol (MAP) (p. 106)

process control (p. 110)

programmable controller (p. 109)

robot (p. 107)

tactile sensing (p. 109)

QUESTIONS

1. Explain how industry can benefit by automation.
2. What does the acronym CAD stand for? How is CAD used in industry?
3. Why must a common method of data communication, such as MAP, be implemented in a factory that uses CIM?
4. Describe a robot, and list the three jobs for which robots are generally used.
5. Explain a programmable controller's function.

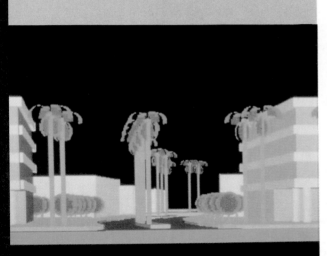

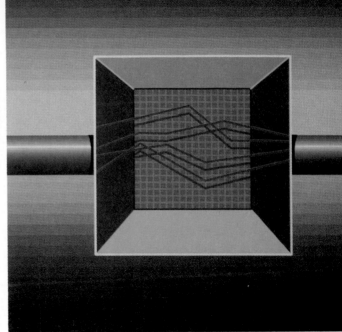

OBJECTIVES

☐ Define and identify the purpose of secondary storage

☐ Name and describe several different forms of secondary storage

☐ Describe the basic hierarchy of data organization

☐ Define three file-access methods

4

Storage Devices and File Organization

PROFILE: John von Neumann

"You know that he's a martian disguised as a human being." That's what the neighbors said.

Who was this alleged alien whose findings would have a resounding impact on the future of computers? Well, in a 1945 scientific draft paper that has served as the basis for the logic structure of subsequent computers, he explained how the computer processed information. This man among men was John von Neumann—one of the pioneers of the "stored-program concept." He based his theory on the idea that an internally stored program would save many hours of laborious, manual work needed to reset switches and wiring that were required to reprogram the early computers.

Von Neumann was born in Budapest, Hungary, in 1903, the oldest son of a well-to-do Jewish family. He studied in Germany at the Gottingen, a prestigious center of mathematical research, spoke German fluently, and even thought in German, translating those thoughts to English.

Friends and acquaintances were baffled by his ability to calculate complex mathematical problems in his head. He had the power of total recall and could recite entire books from memory many years after he had read them. Von Neumann employed this ability to accumulate a vast array of jokes, anecdotes, stories, and limericks to amuse his friends. On the other hand, the highways were unsafe with the reckless von Neumann behind the wheel because he was known to drive on either side of the road; once he even asserted that a tree jumped in front of his car causing an accident. Perhaps his combination of awe-inspiring recall and creative intellect is why neighbors gossiped!

In the 1930s, von Neumann moved to the United States to escape the Holocaust in Germany. He went to Princeton and soon immersed himself in studying hydrodynamics—the principles of fluid motion. His knowledge of hydrodynamics, a crucial aspect in designing atomic bombs, enabled von Neumann to produce a mathematical model that showed exactly how bombs would perform. This work apparently appealed to von Neumann as a "problem" to be solved, not a question of lives to be lost. Bombs and their power were a delight to von Neumann; he attended many nuclear tests.

Was it chance, in 1944, that brought Herbert Goldstine and von Neumann together at a train station? Regardless, it was there that the two mathematicians met and talked about a computing machine that Goldstine was working on—the ENIAC, one of the first operational electronic digital computers. The ENIAC fascinated von Neumann; he now devoted his energies to thinking about something more important than bombs—computers.

Von Neumann viewed the living brain as more than a highly complicated digital computer, and he doubted that a computer could duplicate its functions. But, he did not live to see the miniaturization of parts that may someday make artificial intelligence a reality.

While examining von Neumann's shoulder injury in 1955, doctors discovered he had bone cancer. His life prognosis was six months. Perhaps the radioactivity during the atomic bomb testing was responsible. At any rate, von Neumann's death at 54 was a tremendous loss.

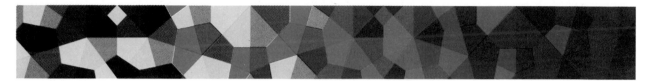

In some data processing, all of the instructions and data are entered in primary storage, the computer completes its processing, results are presented, and the application ends. The computer may have sufficient primary storage to hold all the instructions and data that are needed during processing. John von Neumann realized the importance of having instructions and data readily available in internally stored programs for the computer to process. However, in some applications, a computer's primary-storage capabilities are insufficient and unable to handle the instructions and data needed for processing. For example, consider the volume of data involved in processing the tax returns of all the taxpayers in the United States.

Another limitation of primary storage is its volatility. In many cases, a particular set of data is used more than once. When the power is turned off, the data in primary storage are lost and require reentry for each new use. This is a time-consuming and costly way to process data. As discussed in Chapter 3, often it is desirable to save the results of processing so that they can be used as input for further processing or printed as hard or soft copy later.

So, because primary storage may not be large enough to hold all the required instructions and data, and because RAM is volatile and doesn't provide long-term memory, supplemental storage is necessary. The solution to these limitations is found in the use of secondary storage. This chapter will discuss some devices and media used for secondary storage, as well as several methods of file organization.

SECONDARY STORAGE

Secondary storage is the nonvolatile memory that is stored externally to the computer. A secondary-storage medium is usually used for the storage of large amounts of data or for permanent or long-term storage of data or programs. Secondary storage is also used for storing backups, or copies, of data and programs so that they are not permanently lost if primary-storage power is interrupted.

Three secondary-storage media used with all sizes of computers are: magnetic tapes; magnetic disks; and optical technology. While these media can hold much more data than primary storage, access to the data is slower.

Magnetic Tape

Typically, **magnetic tape** is a one-half or one-fourth inch ribbon of mylar (a plastic-like material), coated with a thin layer of iron-oxide material. An I/O device, the **tape drive** reads and writes data to tape. The tape passes by a **read/write head** (Figure 4–1), the electromagnetic component in the drive. When the tiny, haphazardly arranged particles of iron oxide are aligned through magnetization, data are stored as magnetized spots. Magnetic tape is usually divided into nine separate strips, or tracks. Eight of these tracks are usually used for the codes that represent data characters. The ninth track is reserved for an error-checking bit. To store data, the write head aligns the iron-oxide particles. If they are aligned (polarized) in one direction, the particle represents a 1; in the opposite direction, the iron-oxide particle represents a 0. To read the tape, the drive passes the tape by the read head and the patterns of 1s and 0s are interpreted as pieces of data.

Magnetic tape stores records, or groups of related data, sequentially, i.e., one after another. To get to the data you're looking for, every record preceding them must be read. Not every inch of tape is used for data, however. Between each record is a space called an **interrecord gap (IRG)** (Figure 4–2). The IRGs are the spaces where the tape starts and stops. This space allows the tape to attain the proper speed before data are read from or written on it.

When an IRG is located between each record, the tape is referred to as unblocked, and much of the tape is unavailable for data storage because of the space needed for the IRGs. Data access is also slow because the tape drive has to start and stop between each record. In practice, more than one

FIGURE 4–1

The read/write head is the mechanism that can write or read bits of data from magnetic tape.

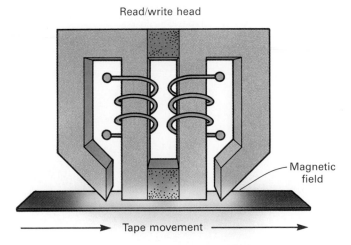

Read/write head

Magnetic field

Tape movement

FIGURE 4-2
An unblocked tape with inter-record gaps (IRG) between each record

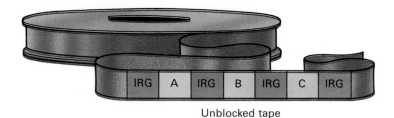

Unblocked tape

FIGURE 4-3
A blocked tape with a blocking factor of 5

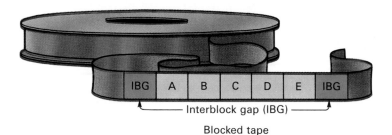

Interblock gap (IBG)

Blocked tape

record is usually stored between two IRGs. In this case, the tape is said to be **blocked tape** (Figure 4–3) and the space is referred to as an **interblock gap (IBG)**. The number of records stored between IBGs is referred to as the **blocking factor**. Blocking increases the storage capacity of a tape because it decreases the number of IRGs needed. Since an entire block of records is written on or read from tape all at once, blocking also increases the speed of writing data on or reading data from tape.

Tapes can store large quantities of data inexpensively and so are often used as backup storage media. Magnetic tapes are erasable, reusable, and durable. They can easily be cataloged and stored in a tape library (Figure 4–4). However, magnetic tape is not well-suited for data files that are revised or updated often. These files should be stored on a medium where

FIGURE 4-4
This magnetic tape library is located in the Santa Fe Railway Computer Center at Topeka, Kansas. (Courtesy of Santa Fe Southern Pacific Corp.)

access to data is faster and more direct. Some media that allow for this type of access will be discussed in this chapter.

Although mainly found with large computers, magnetic tapes can be used with all sizes of computers. They are made in reel-to-reel, cassette, and cartridge forms. Each form stores data magnetically, but each holds different amounts of data and accesses them at different rates.

The amount of data that can be held depends on the length of the tape, the number of interrecord gaps, and the density of the tape. **Density** refers to how tightly the data can be packed and stored on a storage media. Here it is a measure of the number of characters or bytes of data that can be recorded on one inch of tape. Data transfer rate—the number of characters or bytes per second that can be transferred from the tape drive to the media or vice versa—also varies.

Reel-to-reel Tape A **reel-to-reel tape** is magnetic tape placed on reels about $10\frac{1}{2}$ inches in diameter (Figure 4–5). A typical tape is about 2,400 feet long, $\frac{1}{2}$ inch wide, and holds about 40 megabytes of data. Data transfer rates vary from approximately 5,000 bytes per second to over one million bytes per second. The more common tape drives have rates of 60,000 bytes per second. These tapes usually store data at a density of 1,600 bytes per inch, but it can range from 800 to 6,250 bytes per inch. Reel-to-reel tapes are relatively inexpensive, durable, and can hold a large quantity of data. They are used mainly with large-computer systems.

Cassette Tape **Cassette tape** (Figure 4–6) resembles the cassette tape used for audio recording. The tape is about one-fourth inch wide, enclosed

(a)

FIGURE 4–5

(a) Magnetic reel-to-reel tape.
(b) Magnetic reel-to-reel tape mounted on tape drives [(a) BASF Corporation Information Systems. (b) Courtesy of Boise Cascade Corp.]

(b)

FIGURE 4–6
Cassette tapes for data storage are similar to cassette tapes used for audio recording.

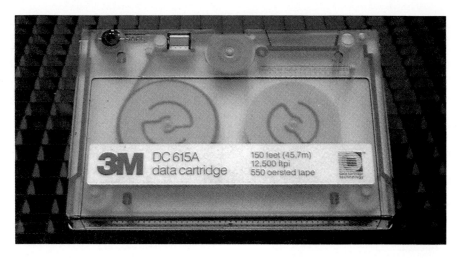

Forms of Magnetic Tape

■ Reel-to-reel
■ Cassette
■ Cartridge

FIGURE 4–7
This tape cartridge is approximately one-half the size of a videocassette and holds about 20,000 pages of information. (BASF Corporation Information Systems)

in a plastic case, and used mainly with small computers. They are inexpensive, but cannot hold much data, and access to the data stored on them is fairly slow. Cassette tape storage, once very popular with personal computer users, has been largely replaced by the more popular and versatile disk storage systems which will be discussed shortly.

Cartridge Tape **Cartridge tape** (Figure 4–7) is another form of magnetic tape. It is packaged similar to cassette tape but has a much greater data storage density (more storage in less area). Cartridge tapes and reel-to-reel systems are popular as the secondary-storage media for large computer systems.

Magnetic Disk

A **magnetic disk** is a mylar or metallic platter on which electronic data can be stored. Although disks resemble phonograph records, they do not have the characteristic spiraling groove; however, data are accessed in much the same way as an individual song is selected on a record.

Data files on the disk can be read sequentially or directly. A magnetic disk's main advantages over magnetic tape include

1. The ability to access the data stored on it directly
2. The ability to hold more data in a smaller space
3. The ability to attain faster data transfer speeds

Magnetic disks are manufactured in both floppy diskette and hard disk styles.

Floppy Diskette A **floppy diskette**, also called simply a diskette or disk, is a small flexible mylar disk coated with iron oxide (similar to magnetic tape) on which data are stored. It has been around since the early 1970s and was originally 8 inches in diameter. Today it is available in three sizes—the 3½-inch microfloppy, as well as the 5¼-inch size and 8-inch size (Figure 4–8).

FIGURE 4–8
Floppy diskettes are available in three different sizes: 8-, 5¼-, and 3½-inch.

The 8-inch and 5¼-inch diskettes are covered by a stiff, protective jacket with various holes and cutouts that serve special functions (Figure 4–9). The hub ring is where the disk drive (the I/O device) holds the disk to rotate it. The elongated read/write window allows the read/write head of the drive to write data on or read data from the floppy diskette. The small hole next to the hub ring is the index hole through which the computer determines the relative position of the disk for locating data. The cutout on the side of the floppy diskette is the write-protect notch. By covering this opening with a piece of tape, data on the diskette are protected from being erased or written over.

The 3½-inch diskettes have a hard plastic covering and a protective metal piece that covers the read/write window when the disk is not in use.

FIGURE 4–9
A floppy diskette jacket

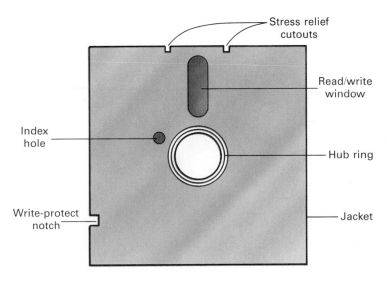

119

This additional protection makes the disk less prone to damage from handling, dust, or other contaminants. The 3½-inch disk is growing in popularity.

A diskette must be prepared for use before data or programs can be stored on it. Each diskette, regardless of size, is divided into concentric circles called **tracks** where data are stored. The diskette is also divided into pie-shaped wedges called **sectors** (Figure 4–10), which further specify data storage locations on the diskette. The number of tracks and sectors is usually determined by the computer's operating system during a formatting operation. The operating system labels each sector of each track with an address so that the computer can go directly to a specific area, rather than starting at the beginning, as with magnetic tape.

A diskette may be: (a) single-sided, in which case data are recorded on only one side of the diskette; or (b) double-sided, in which case data can be recorded on both sides of the diskette. All diskettes have two sides, but the difference depends on whether the diskette has been certified free of errors on one or both sides.

In addition to single- and double-sided, floppy diskettes are also available in several densities. The three most common densities for floppy diskettes are single, double, and quad densities. For example, a typical double-sided, single-density, 5¼-inch floppy diskette holds 180 kilobytes; a double-sided, double-density, 5¼-inch diskette holds 360 kilobytes; and a double-sided, quad-density, 5¼-inch diskette holds 1.2 megabytes. Advances in technology are steadily increasing the density of data storage on diskettes.

Diskettes must be used with the appropriate drive. If a double-sided diskette is used in a single-sided drive, the user is not taking advantage of the diskette's extra storage capacity. If a single-sided diskette is used in a double-sided drive, data can be stored as if the diskette were double-sided. However, this use is not recommended, because data may be lost on the second (uncertified) side of the single-sided diskette.

FIGURE 4–10
A diskette divided into tracks and sectors

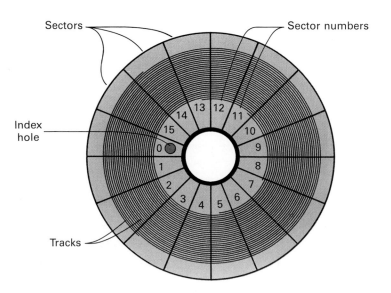

Data recorded on a double-sided diskette by a double-sided drive cannot be read on a single-sided drive because of the way data are stored. A double-sided drive has two read/write heads, one for each side; a single-sided drive has only one read/write head.

When a double-sided drive records data on a diskette, it does not fill up one side first and then the other. Instead, it will use the first available data track on side 0. When that track is filled, it will use the first available track on side 1, then the next available track on side 0, and so on. Note that the sides are usually labeled 0 and 1, rather than 1 and 2. Because of the above method of recording data, a single program or set of data will often reside on both sides of a diskette making it impossible for a single-sided drive to read all the necessary data.

Usually, a computer will have all single or all double-sided diskette drives. Double-sided is the most common, and nearly all new diskette drives are double-sided. Many computer models will use drives of equal density, however, some have a combination of two different densities. For example, the IBM PC AT is often configured with a double-sided, double-density drive and a double-sided, quad-density drive. A lower density disk can usually be read by a higher density drive. However, the reverse is not true.

Floppy diskettes are more convenient to use with a small computer than their cassette tape counterparts. They also cost less—$1 to $3 each for a $5\frac{1}{4}$-inch disk. Although the 1.2 megabytes of a quad-density disk may sound like a lot of memory, it represents only about 500 pages of text. This may be adequate for home computer or small business users, but for larger businesses a system using only floppy diskettes would be highly inefficient, inadequate, and expensive. To compensate for the limited space on the floppy diskette, another type of disk is used—the hard disk.

Hard Disk   A **hard disk** is just that—hard and inflexible. The hard disk is made from materials such as aluminum instead of mylar. The I/O device used to transfer data to and from a hard disk is called a **hard-disk drive**. The read/write head of a hard-disk drive floats above the surface of the disk at a height of about 50 millionths of an inch (0.00005 inches). In comparison, a human hair is a hundred times larger in diameter (Figure 4–11). Because of the high rotation speed of the hard disk [approximately 3,600 revolutions per minute (rpm)] if the read/write head runs into any particles of dirt, dust, or even smoke, a **head crash** results. When this occurs, a foreign particle is pushed into the disk, and the head actually bounces and comes into physical contact with the disk. Severe damage can result to the head or the disk, destroying the data stored there.

The hard disk has several advantages over a floppy disk. The rigid construction of a hard disk allows it to be rotated very fast (3,600 rpm) as compared to a floppy diskette (360 rpm). Thus, data can be transferred much faster to or from a hard disk because it takes less time to find the storage location. Also, because of its hard construction, this disk allows data to be stored more densely. More data can be placed in a smaller area giving the hard disk more storage capacity than a floppy diskette of the same size.

FIGURE 4–11
Notice the size of the disk contaminants compared to the distance between the read/write head and the hard disk.

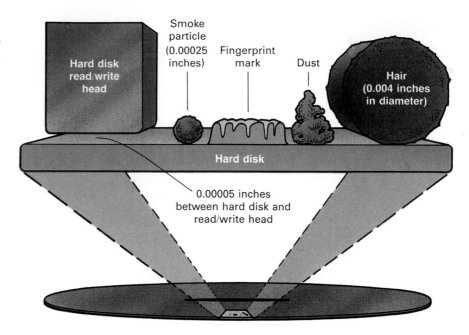

Hard-disk drives are available for all sizes of computers, from home-user microcomputers to business-oriented large system computers. Hard disks may be permanently installed in a drive or may be in the form of a removable cartridge or disk pack that can also be removed from the drive.

A **fixed disk** is enclosed permanently inside a sealed case for protection from the elements (Figure 4–12). Fixed-disk systems contain one or more hard disks and can be used in all types of computers. Home computer users may be familiar with the 5¼-inch fixed-disk systems used with microcomputers, having typical storage capacities of between 10 and 70 megabytes. In large computers, the fixed-disk system provides storage capacities in the gigabyte (billions of bytes) range.

A storage system using **removable cartridges** (Figure 4–13) has the same speed and capacity as a hard disk. These cartridges usually contain only one or two disks. Many hard-disk drives used with small com-

FIGURE 4–12
The case has been removed from this fixed disk to show the hard disk and a read/write head. (Photo courtesy of Seagate)

FIGURE 4–13
Removable-cartridge storage systems allow users more flexibility than fixed-disk systems. The cartridges can be removed and stored in a secure location.

Forms of Magnetic Disk

■ Floppy diskette
　□ 8-inch
　□ 5¼-inch
　□ 3½-inch
■ Hard disk
　□ Fixed disk
　□ Removable cartridge
　□ Disk pack

The Bernoulli Box is a removable-cartridge storage device.

puters are designed to use removable cartridges. The advantage of the removable cartridge is that it may be removed at any time and a new or different cartridge may be inserted. For example, a user can have a separate cartridge for each application.

A **disk pack** (Figure 4–14) is another removable device in which several hard disks (a common number is eleven) are packed into a single plastic case. The disk-pack drives are designed for large systems that require larger storage capacities. Because a disk pack is susceptible to damage by scratching, the top of the first disk and the bottom of the last disk are generally not used. This still leaves twenty sides for storage of hundreds of megabytes on a disk pack containing eleven disks. Disk packs can be interchanged, giving the computer a virtually unlimited amount of secondary storage.

FIGURE 4–14

An operator installs a disk pack for mainframe computer storage. (BASF Corporation Information Systems)

Optical Technology

Optical technology involves the use of laser beams—highly concentrated beams of light. This technology has created new types of secondary-storage media for the computer, including optical laser disks, optical cards, and optical tape.

Optical Laser Disk Sometimes technological developments created for one application will result in an improvement in other areas. **Optical laser disks** (Figure 4–15) are hard metal disks ranging in size from 4.72 inches to 14 inches; they were originally developed as compact disks for video and audio applications. The same method of using laser beams to encode binary data by burning microscopic "pits" on audio and video disks to represent 1s and 0s is used to encode the data stored on optical laser disks.

FIGURE 4–15

A CD–ROM optical laser disk

Most optical disks are read-only storage devices; however, some of the more expensive optical disks can be written on and erased. A common version of the optical disk is the CD-ROM (compact disk, read-only memory). While not suited to applications where data changes, they are very convenient for storing data that remains constant.

The laser technology used gives these devices tremendous storage capacities. For example, *American Academic Encyclopedia,* a nine-million-word (20-volume) encyclopedia, is stored on a compact disk less than five inches in diameter, with room to spare. Grolier Electronic Publishers sells it to consumers for about $200. A typical 14-inch disk can store as much as twenty reel-to-reel tapes. Libraries have started converting from traditional card catalogs and microfilm to CD-ROM systems. Los Angeles County has one of the largest library systems in the country; it was able to get its more than 5 million titles on a single disk. The search for references is faster than with either a card catalog or microfilm.

The increase in storage densities of hard disks and the availability of removable disk cartridges have made small systems suitable for very-high
resolution graphics applications that require large amounts of data to be
stored. Here, a high-resolution color graphics computer and display system
is used to create animation. Using cameras or recorders, individual images
are digitized and stored on disk. The images can then be retrieved from
disk and displayed by the user. (Visual provided courtesy of Chromatics,
Inc. Inset: Photo courtesy of Seagate)

Optical Storage Media

- Optical laser disk
- Optical cards
- Optical tape

Optical Card The **optical card**, or laser card, is the size of a credit card
and has an optical laser-encoded strip that can store approximately 2
megabytes of data. These cards have many potential uses, most notably for
storing credit records or medical histories. Some people predict that these
cards may one day lead to a cashless and checkless society. Optical cards
have the potential to store an individual's entire financial history, adding to
or subtracting from the appropriate accounts as a person makes, saves, or
spends money. These cards might also supply a hospital with the holder's
complete medical history. If emergency treatment is required, this information could expedite care.

HIGHLIGHT

WINNING CARDS

It has not happened as quickly as developers predicted, but before too long, the wallets of the world are almost certain to be bulging with two handy computer-age inventions: the smart card and the laser memory (optical) card.

A smart card is essentially a piece of plastic the size of a credit card with a built-in microprocessor and memory circuits which can interact with computer terminals installed at locations where the card-carrier does his or her business. The laser card, which is credit-card size, also can hold hundreds or even thousands of pages of information about the person to whom it belongs. Ideally, both cards can simplify a person's life. Promoters of smart-card technology say it has three main features that make it valuable to businesses: (a) it keeps a running account of how much a customer has left to spend because each transaction produces a new and current total; (b) it guards against theft because the user has to provide an individual code number at the time of transaction, just as is done with automated teller cards; and (c) since the totals are accurate and up-to-date, stores don't have the expense and time of authenticating the card and authorizing the transaction by long-distance telephone calls.

The spread of smart cards has been slow because of the enormous start-up costs involved. While the cards themselves are not excessively expensive, the computer systems needed to read them are; and one can't work without the other. Still, manufacturers in the U.S., Japan, and Europe are already turning out models on a limited basis.

Laser cards use the same technology that puts music onto a compact disk. The laser burns tiny holes through a layer of silver particles, and the holes form machine-readable messages. One such card, created by Drexel Technology, can hold 800 pages of single-spaced information on one wallet-size card. Others hold even more data.

This massive storage capability makes the cards ideal for holding a person's entire medical history. Various prototypes have been experimented with, but none have consistently been put to use. Proponents say these cards can eventually become minilibraries. One plan calls for the cards to be available for purchase for a fixed price at convenience stores. Each such card would have a certain amount of credit built in. Then the card would be used to purchase items from vending machines until all its credit was depleted.

Optical Tape   Continuing developments and refinements in optical technology include optical tape. **Optical tape** is similar in appearance to magnetic tape, but data are stored by optical-laser techniques. Optical tapes which are in cassette form can store over 8 gigabytes each, and the tape drives can hold 128 cassettes, providing a total data storage of about 1 terabyte (1,000 gigabytes). Like other optical methods of data storage, optical tape is read-only. As optical technology develops, higher densities and expanded uses will result.

FILE ORGANIZATION

So far in this chapter, various media and devices that store data outside of the computer were discussed. Some of the devices access data directly; others access data sequentially. In this section you'll explore some of the ways in which files are organized on and accessed from secondary storage.

Files, Records, and Fields

Organization of ideas or tangible objects is the key to productivity. Finding the right size wrench is a snap if they are laid out smallest to largest rather than scattered in a box. The same logic applies to data stored on tape or disk.

Imagine for a moment that you are the instructor of a class. Let's assume there are thirty students in your class and grades are assigned weekly for tests, homework, and computer lab reports. During each week of a sixteen-week semester, you collect and grade material from all three sources. When you are finished grading each piece of work, you mark the student's name and grade on a piece of paper and toss it on your desk. Each week you accumulate another ninety pieces of paper.

Now it's the end of the semester, and grades are due by noon today. You have to find over 1,400 pieces of paper, organize them, and calculate a grade for each student. Not a very productive method, is it?

The same haphazard data entry into a computer would render the data virtually useless. In order to be effective and achieve the most efficiency, data must be systematically organized.

In the example, by initially setting up a plan of organization, the instructor could have prevented many problems. The instructor could have kept a gradebook with rows for each student's name. The columns following the name could be broken down into areas where grades for each category of test, homework, and computer lab reports could be recorded. At the end of the semester, it would be much easier to locate and average grades.

Special names are given to data organized in this type of hierarchy. The basic hierarchy of data organization, going from the most general to the most specific, is data base, file, record, and field. A **data base** is a collection of related files stored together in a logical fashion. (The discussion of a data base is found in Chapter 9.) A **file** is a collection of similar groups of data that fit under one name or heading. The instructor's gradebook is an example of a file. All data in the gradebook deal with students and their grades.

Data Hierarchy

- Data base
- File
- Record
- Field

A file may be further separated into more descriptive subdivisions called records. The material in a **record** is specific to that record but falls under the general topic of the file name. Data about a particular student, such as name and test scores, are an individual record. All the information in the record pertains only to that student, but all those data are related to class grades.

In the record, space must be allocated for data. Each individual item of data stored in the record is called a **field**. Each record may contain one or more fields. Once again, in the instructor example, there are many fields: one for the student's name; one for each test; one for each homework paper; and one for each computer lab report grade (Figure 4–16).

Records may be of fixed or variable lengths. A **fixed-length record** is one where each record is set to a specific number of characters. If the record length is set at 20 characters and only 15 are used, 5 empty spaces are stored with the data.

A **variable-length record** is one in which places are allotted only to data. If only 15 characters are used, only 15 characters of data are stored. This method saves storage space. Fixed- and variable-length characteristics also apply to fields.

File-access Methods

Data items are organized into files; let's examine some methods in which these files are placed on the secondary-storage medium and accessed. Files are stored and accessed in many ways. Three common ways are: sequential access; direct access; and indexed-sequential access.

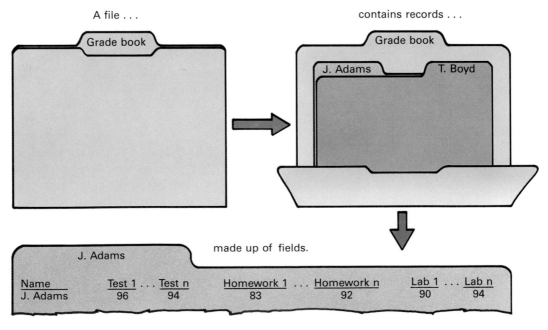

FIGURE 4–16
Organization of data by file, record, and field

The records in a **sequential access** file are stored and accessed in a row (sequentially), one after another (Figure 4–17a). Magnetic tape is a storage medium that is sequential in nature. To access a particular record, all preceding records must be read first. The sequential-access method could be used when recording the individual student grades each week because all students' records must be accessed and updated anyway.

A faster type of access that is used with disks is direct access. **Direct access** allows a record to be read directly from a disk without reading all preceding records (Figure 4–17b). It does not matter in what order the records were stored. Direct access is the fastest of the three access methods.

The third and final technique, **indexed-sequential access,** allows both sequential and direct access. An indexed-sequential file can be set up in many ways. A very elementary view of one type is shown in Figure 4–18.

Basically, the records are stored sequentially when the indexed-sequential file is initially created. But, when additional records are added to the file, they are stored in an overflow area on the disk. These additional records are stored out of sequence. In Figure 4–18 the "O" entries are stored out of sequence in the overflow area. Each record has a **key field** which contains data that uniquely identifies a record in a file. The key field in the example is indicated by a letter in parentheses. An index of the key fields from each record is kept. Each key field in the index is associated with an address that specifies where the record is stored on disk. The index is usually automatically kept sorted and updated to allow both sequential and direct access. The index then is searched by key field to access a record. When the key field is found, the record can then be accessed directly using

File-access Methods

- Sequential
- Direct
- Indexed-sequential

FIGURE 4–17
(a) With the sequential-access method, records are stored and accessed in a row (sequentially). When accessing a record, all preceding records in the file must be accessed first. Here, to access Record 4, Records 1, 2, and 3 must be accessed first. (b) With the direct access method, records can be accessed directly without having to access all preceding records. Here, Record 4 can be accessed directly without having to access any other records.

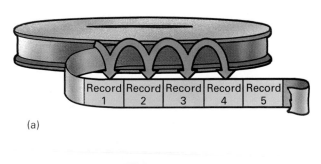

(a)

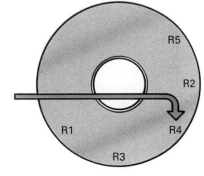

(b)

FIGURE 4–18
The indexed-sequential access method allows records to be accessed either sequentially or directly.

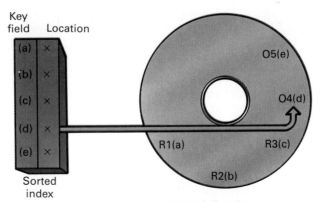

Record 4 may be accessed directly.

R = Record
O = Record stored
    in overflow area

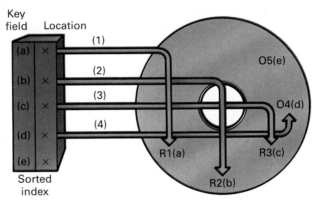

Record 4 may be accessed sequentially.

the address associated with the key field. To search sequentially, the record associated with the first key field in the sorted index is accessed followed by the rest of the index in sequential order. The sorted index allows records to be found in sequence no matter where they are physically located on the disk. In practice, there are usually multiple indexes that narrow the location of each record. This type of file access does not work with tape because tape is a sequential-access medium only.

SUMMARY

Primary storage is often not adequate for data storage needs because of its limited size and its volatility. To supplement primary storage, secondary storage—memory which is external to the computer and nonvolatile—is used.

Three types of secondary-storage media are: magnetic tape; magnetic disk; and optical technology. Magnetic tape is a ribbon of mylar, coated with a thin layer of iron-oxide material. It is available in three forms: reel-to-reel, cassette, and cartridge. Magnetic disks are mylar or metallic platters coated with iron oxide. Two types of magnetic disks are floppy

HIGHLIGHT

COMPACT DISKS

A new trend has emerged and it involves those little silver-colored disks called CD-ROMs (compact disk, read-only memory). You may know them as producing some of the best sounding music you've ever heard. The same laser technology that made the music so great made these disks available for many other applications.

The Rocky Mountain Poison Center maintains a CD-ROM list, called Poisindex, of 370,000 poisons and their antidotes that is distributed to hospitals. When the nurse or doctor types the name of the poison and the person's weight into the computer, the correct treatment and dosage are displayed on the screen. Because of the life-and-death nature of poisoning, immediate access to medical information is essential. This system of data retrieval is faster than the old one—microfilm.

How about finding your way around town with a CD-ROM mapping system? An onboard computer in your car contains a CD-ROM disk with a map of the entire city and surrounding area. Just tell the computer where you want to go, and it shows you the best route to take. These devices are available, but are expensive and, as yet, not available in all areas. Designers of these systems are hoping to tie into the navigational satellite system, NAVSTAR. Look for mapping systems to be added as options on new cars.

A new type of compact disk, the CD-I (compact disk, interactive), combines features such as audio and video. The drives used to read the CD-I have a microprocessor built in allowing animated video and speech-quality audio to be produced. Consulting the dictionary could be both a sight and sound experience.

A 4.72-inch CD can store as much data as 1,000 floppy diskettes; but compact disks cannot be conveniently or inexpensively written on more than once, so don't throw away the floppy diskettes yet.

diskettes and hard disks. Floppy diskettes are available in $3\frac{1}{2}$-, $5\frac{1}{4}$-, and 8-inch sizes. Hard disks are available as fixed disks, removable cartridges, and disk packs. Optical technology involves the use of a laser to store data on various media. Optical media include optical laser disks, optical cards, and optical tapes.

Data are organized in a hierarchy which includes data base, file, record, and field designators. A data base is a group of related files stored together in a logical fashion. A file is a collection of similar groups of data that fit under one category. A record contains data related to one particular item of that category, such as a person's name. A field is the name given to each piece of data in a record. Three common file-access methods are: sequential access; direct access; and indexed-sequential access.

Key Terms

blocked tape (p. 116)

blocking factor (p. 116)

cartridge tape (p. 118)

cassette tape (p. 117)

data base (p. 127)

density (p. 117)

direct access (p. 129)

disk pack (p. 123)

field (p. 128)

file (p. 127)

fixed disk (p. 122)

fixed-length record (p. 128)

floppy diskette (p. 118)

hard disk (p. 121)

hard-disk drive (p. 121)

head crash (p. 121)

indexed-sequential access (p. 129)

interblock gap (IBG) (p. 116)

interrecord gap (IRG) (p. 115)

key field (p. 129)

magnetic disk (p. 118)

magnetic tape (p. 115)

optical card (p. 125)

optical laser disk (p. 124)

optical tape (p. 127)

read/write head (p. 115)

record (p. 128)

reel-to-reel tape (p. 117)

removable cartridge (p. 122)

secondary storage (p. 114)

sectors (p. 120)

sequential access (p. 129)

tape drive (p. 115)

tracks (p. 120)

variable-length record (p. 128)

Review Questions

1. Describe secondary storage and explain why it is needed.
2. Describe magnetic tape and tell how data are stored on it.
3. Illustrate the differences between a blocked and an unblocked tape.
4. The number of records stored between IBGs is referred to as the _____.
5. List three forms of magnetic tape.
6. Describe a magnetic disk.
7. What are the advantages of magnetic tapes over magnetic disks?
8. What purposes are served by the cutout areas of a floppy diskette jacket?
9. Can a diskette recorded on a double-sided drive be read on a single-sided drive? Why or why not?
10. True or False: A hard disk can only store data sequentially.
11. What might cause a head crash?
12. A hard disk that contains one or more disks, permanently enclosed in a sealed case, is called a(n) _____.
13. Describe a removable-cartridge storage system. What advantage does it have over a fixed drive?
14. Describe a disk-pack storage system.
15. Describe an optical laser disk. How does its storage capacity compare to a magnetic hard disk?

16. Describe the hierarchy of data.

17. What is the relationship of a record to a file?

18. Each individual data item stored in a record is called a(n) _____.

19. Distinguish between a fixed-length record and a variable-length record.

20. How are records accessed using a sequential-access method?

21. How are records accessed using a direct-access method?

22. What is the method that allows both sequential and direct access?

23. Which secondary-storage medium would be appropriate for a file from which individual records are accessed often?

24. Which data-storage medium allows both sequential and direct access?

25. Which storage medium and which access method would be most appropriate to store data that are frequently accessed, but rarely updated or changed?

INFOMODULE

The Care and Handling of Microcomputers

The larger, more expensive computer systems are protected by special rooms where heat, dust, smoke, and static electricity are closely controlled or eliminated. Smaller systems can also be damaged by these elements. Although microcomputer systems don't have to be treated quite as gently as large systems, some precautions are necessary. (Specific precautions may be listed in the owner's manual.)

ENVIRONMENT

The area chosen for the system should be comfortable for the user and offer substantial support to accommodate the weight of the computer and its peripheral devices. The table or desktop should be sturdy and not subject to jostling or moving. Once the computer is set up, any other movement should be kept to a minimum; anytime the computer is to be moved a considerable distance, it should be repacked in its original box to afford maximum protection.

Temperature

Usually, an environment that is comfortable to the user will also be appropriate for the microcomputer. Since computers work most effectively if temperatures do not rise above 85 degrees Fahrenheit, the computer should be located away from a heat source. Placement in front of a sunny window, air conditioning unit, or radiator could mean exposure to extremes in temperatures, which are to be avoided. Heating adjustments in the winter and air conditioning for cooling in the summer months may be required to keep both the user and the system operating effectively.

Humidity

Humidity that ranges between 50 and 70 percent is best. Lower humidity levels allow a buildup of static electricity that can cause damage to chips inside the computer and destroy the data created. Higher humidity levels can ultimately lead to rusting of the metallic parts of the computer. Humidifiers can significantly reduce the effects of static electricity. If the computer system is placed in a basement office, a dehumidifier might be needed to remove the excess moisture in the air.

Magnetic Fields

The computer's data are encoded electromagnetically; therefore, they can be changed or destroyed when exposed to a magnetic field. Common sources that generate magnetic fields when they are turned on are electric motors, television sets, and computer monitors. Data on a magnetic disk stored nearby could be scrambled or destroyed. Particular care should be taken to store disks or tapes that contain data in areas away from any electrical appliances and magnetic fields.

Static Electricity

Static electricity can cause problems for data too. High-pile carpets can be a source of static electricity, but touching a static mat or another piece of furniture before touching the keyboard grounds that electricity. Antistatic sprays, rugs, and mats are available to eliminate the static charge. An antistatic spray also can be applied to a cloth to clean the area around the computer.

Static electricity can be generated by opening software packages that have been shrink-wrapped in plastic.

Environmental Considerations

- Temperature
- Humidity
- Magnetic fields
- Static electricity
- Dust, smoke, and other debris

Even if the area around your computer seems to get especially dirty, don't invest in an ionizer. Although the air-cleaning ionizers effectively remove dust from the air, they also increase the amount of static electricity. So, the area might be cleaner, but the data stored magnetically may be jeopardized.

Dust, Smoke, and Other Debris

The presence of dust and dirt are unavoidable, but the microcomputer system should not be situated near an open window where winds blowing cooling breezes contain particles of dust and debris. Even minute bits of dust can cause machines to fail and data to be misread.

Tobacco smoke contains particles of tar and nicotine that can build up on the computer equipment, too. But, the greatest damage that smoke causes occurs on disk drives and other storage media. (Figure 4–11 on p. 122 graphically illustrates the comparative size of these particles on a hard-disk drive.)

Animal hair and dander that gets into the equipment can also cause damage. In fact, even fumes from chemicals such as nail polish remover, glue, or cleaning agents such as ammonia may produce adverse reactions on the magnetic surfaces of disks or cassettes.

Food crumbs cause problems similar to dust and smoke particles, and drops of spilled beverages or other liquids can damage the delicate equipment or cause a short circuit. Additionally, food or beverage spills can damage working papers, final copy, or the storage media containing the final copy, creating yet another series of problems.

CLEANING AND OTHER TIPS

To avoid an electrical shock, before any cleaning or housekeeping chores are begun, unplug the computer system. The system packs up to 25,000 volts of electricity, but the primary danger comes if liquid cleaners get inside the monitor or computer. In general, sprays or liquid cleaners should not be used around the computer because spilling even a drop of liquid on the keyboard could cause problems, ranging from sticking keys to damaged circuit boards.

Unexplainable problems can occur if timely, preventive maintenance is not done, and the equipment becomes dirty. Erratic printing can be caused by dirty contacts or bits of paper or lint stuck inside the printer; if proper preventive maintenance is done, a service call can be avoided.

Since a typical microcomputer system is made up of hardware items and software, let's discuss care for each part separately.

Computer System Unit

Computer systems are powered by electricity; therefore, of course, the general guidelines concerning electrical appliances also apply. It is usually recommended that electrical appliances be unplugged from the source of electricity before any cleaning is done. Additionally, the computer should not be turned on before it is plugged in; this precaution avoids a surge of electricity that can damage the system. A surge protector is a device recommended to guard against power-line disturbances that can occur when lights flicker due to electrical use by other appliances or when electricity is actually cut off during a thunderstorm or other power outage. If the electricity should go off, unplug the system so that when electrical power is restored, the surge of electricity that is created will not place the sensitive circuits at risk. In some instances, a back-up generator system may be an appropriate, if expensive, addition to prevent the loss or destruction of valuable data.

If the computer system is connected to an electrical strip on the floor, the strip should be placed out-of-the-way so that it does not create a safety hazard or cause the system to be inadvertently turned off. Special precautions should be taken if a wall switch activates the electricity so that the computer system is not accidentally turned off at an inopportune time, i.e., before work is saved or backed up.

Computers that can be opened to allow access to the internal circuitry can be cleaned inside. Some computers do not open and cannot be cleaned inside. Cleaning inside the system should be done with extreme care, because circuit boards should not be bumped or damaged. However, if dust is not removed, the buildup over time can cause the retention of heat inside the machine and that can cause damage, too. Special compressed air canisters can be purchased to blow out dust particles without touching anything.

A household vacuum cleaner equipped with a crevice cleaning device can be used externally on air vents, disk drive openings, or any other cracks or openings where dust could accumulate. Special computer-cleaning kits, complete with miniature vacuum cleaners, brushes, and other cleaning apparatus, are also available.

Disk Drives

Expert advice on cleaning disk drives ranges from some people who suggest that drive heads should be cleaned twice a year to others who say once a week. One way disk drives are cleaned is with kits purchased from computer stores. A special cleanser is sprayed on a fiber disk and then inserted into the drive where it spins and removes dust, oxide, and grease on the read/write head. The safest way to have disk drives cleaned is by returning them to the computer store.

One special rule in caring for a hard disk drive is to keep it "parked" when not in use. When the drive is parked, it pulls the read/write head away from the disk and locks it into place, preventing the read/write head from bouncing into and damaging the disk if the computer is bumped or moved.

Monitors

A monitor screen, like a television screen, contains a certain amount of static electricity that causes dust to cling to it. To remove this built-up dirt, any commercial glass-cleaning product can be used. Care should be taken to avoid spraying or dripping any liquid onto other parts of the system, however. Spray the liquid cleaner on the cloth away from the system, and then rub the screen with the dampened cloth.

Keyboards

Probably the most exposed of all computer parts, keyboards are subjected to all manner of dirt and debris. Dead skin particles, eyelashes, dust, and dirt drop onto the keyboard and fall onto or become wedged under the keys. Even clean hands leave oily residue. Once again, a vacuum cleaner equipped with a crevice tool or a can of compressed air can be used to blow out bits of dust. When using compressed air canisters, be careful that you do not blow dust from one part of the computer system into another.

A moist, but not dripping, cotton swab or small brush can be used to remove soil from the tops and sides of the keys. Routine cleaning can avoid expensive repairs or replacement of the entire keyboard.

Connections

It is easy to overlook some obvious areas where dirt and grime collect. One of those areas is in the connectors linking computer to monitor, printer, modem, and other peripherals. Contact cleaner on cotton-tipped swabs can be applied to the edge and pin connectors, around plug screws, and on cable ends to ensure that proper electrical contact is being made.

Printers

Printers are subjected to room dust, as well as the fuzz, lint, and scraps that are generally associated with paper. Printer ribbons become frayed and leave debris too. Use the vacuum cleaner with crevice tool or a compressed air canister to blow the loose particles away.

Paper should always be advanced by using the line feed and page feed options. Manually moving the platen while the printer is on can damage the motor. If the print head is moved manually while the machine is on, the motor that controls the stepper could be damaged. A cloth sprayed with a Teflon-like spray can be used to lubricate the rod that the print head slides on.

To remove ink buildup, daisy-wheel print heads should be cleaned by using a typewriter cleaning solution or rubbing alcohol applied with a cotton swab.

Once all the equipment is cleaned, protect it with dust covers when not in use.

Diskettes

Diskettes are particularly delicate and should never be bent, folded, twisted, subjected to temperature extremes, or paper clipped. They should be handled only by touching the cardboard or plastic protective jacket. Even clean hands leave a fingerprint that can obstruct the drive head when it tries to read that part of the diskette. Unless the label has not yet been affixed to the diskette, use only felt-tip pens to write diskette labels.

Paper file jackets should be used to protect the exposed surfaces of the diskette, and diskettes should then be stored in cardboard or plastic boxes. To protect them from magnetic fields, diskettes containing data should not be stored on or near the computer, disk drive, or other electrical device or appliances.

Additional protection may be required in the form of safe-deposit boxes or specially-built diskette vaults. Some vaults are merely tamper proof, but others are designed and insulated to withstand the high temperatures generated by a fire. This type of storage should be considered for diskettes that contain valuable data.

Protecting Software and Data

External-storage media can be damaged; so, one of the best ways to protect important software and data is to make backup copies periodically and store at least one copy away from the computer. The safest practice is to make backup copies every fifteen minutes. Although they may take extra time and be a nuisance to make, backup copies of an afternoon's work may save you half the night trying to reconstruct lost data.

Equipment, Warranties, Service, and Insurance

Even with the best of care, a machine may require a service call. Most equipment is covered initially by limited warranty agreements for a specified period of time, usually ninety days. Some manufacturers offer extended warranties, on-site repair, and loaner machines.

A maintenance contract is a form of extended warranty where, for a set fee, authorized service on specified equipment will be performed for a period of time. These contracts are particularly useful for any equipment that contains moving parts, such as the printer and disk drives.

Remember that most warranties will be invalidated if you, or any other unauthorized person, try to make repairs.

Some people choose to take the risk of theft or loss of their computer equipment, and others decide to pay a premium and let an insurance company take that risk. Carrying insurance and paying for a service contract on a home computer are personal choices. Some homeowner's policies include coverage of computer equipment automatically, but an agent should be consulted to verify individual policies.

QUESTIONS

1. Describe an ideal environment for a microcomputer system.
2. Why are extremely high or low humidities dangerous to a computer?
3. Explain what happens to data if they are exposed to a magnetic field. How might that happen?
4. Why is smoke harmful to computer equipment?
5. Give examples of how people protect their computer from breakdowns, theft, loss of equipment, or loss of data.

Protection

- ■ Equipment
  - □ Warranty
  - □ Service agreement
  - □ Insurance
- ■ Data
  - □ Backup copies

PART TWO
Computer Systems

For the first time in history, we have a technology capable of adjusting to human needs, rather than the human being having to adjust to the machine.

John Diebold, author of Automation *and* Making the Future Work

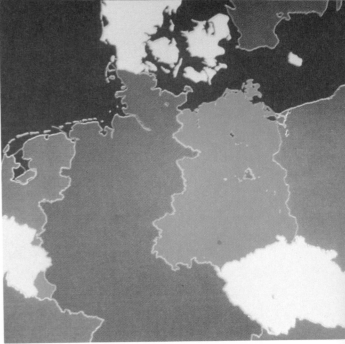

OBJECTIVES

☐ Recognize the differences between special-purpose and general-purpose computers and give examples of each

☐ List the categories of large systems

☐ Tell who uses the large system computers and how they are used

☐ Explain how uniprocessing and multiprocessing concepts differ

☐ Distinguish between time sharing and distributed data processing

OUTLINE

5

Large Computer Systems

PROFILE: Seymour Cray

In an age where particular emphasis has been placed on making small, personal computers, there is one man who continues to do quite the opposite. Seymour Cray marches to a different drummer; he works to create the fastest, most powerful computers in the world. Cray first worked at Control Data Corporation (CDC) where he helped invent computers that were called supercomputers. In 1972 he left CDC and, using half of a million dollars of his own plus over $2 million from venture capitalists, he formed his own company, Cray Research, in Minneapolis, Minnesota. Cray's primary objective was to build large computers.

By 1976, Cray Research delivered the first in a series of Cray supercomputers. The Cray–1 computed at the rate of roughly 160 million floating-point operations per second. The price tag of approximately $7 million made it affordable and useful primarily by government agencies and large corporations.

Cray resigned from his company in 1981 and now works as an independent contractor from his laboratory in Chippewa Falls, Wisconsin.

Cray's offices are designed for extreme quiet. "I just can't think when it's noisy," he once said. In fact, to be alone, he often works in the late afternoons and evenings. An interesting anomaly is that Cray usually prefers to work using paper, pencil, and occasionally a desktop sized computer, not his own high-tech products.

Cray designs and builds his own sailboats by hand. He may be seen as a bit of an eccentric, because after sailing the craft all summer, he burns it in the fall. Whether they're for a sailboat or a computer, his designs, he says, are for simplicity.

No one has designed more supercomputers than Cray, and without his contributions, the United States would not have technological supremacy in this area. Competitors in the field of supercomputers learned that Cray's products were the ones to beat.

Cray continues doing what he does best—thinking, and working on the next supercomputer, the Cray–3.

There are both large and small computer systems. This chapter is devoted to large systems. Even though the terminology "large computer system" would indicate that the physical size of the equipment may be large, you can see from Figure 5–1 that the most powerful computer today takes up much less space than the 1940s computer, ENIAC.

Those room-sized ancestors were larger, but not nearly as powerful as many of the small, personal computers being used today. The ENIAC computer was 80 feet long, 18 feet high, and contained over 17,000 vacuum tubes and 100,000 electronic components. The computing power of the ENIAC now fits on a chip measured in hundredths of an inch and is dwarfed by a postage stamp.

Large computer systems have been traditionally divided into three main categories: supercomputers; mainframe computers; and minicomputers. Many of the functional distinctions of large systems have overlapped over time because advances in technology allowed the smaller machines to take on the characteristics and capabilities of the larger machines. Some of the more sophisticated minicomputer characteristics are similar to the low-powered mainframes. Machine size, power, and capability overlap from one category to another. In the near future, the specific categories may be eliminated entirely; but for ease in identification now, let's use these three labels for discussion.

CLASSES OF COMPUTERS

The two classes of computers are: general-purpose and special-purpose machines. Let's see how they differ.

General-purpose Computers

Most computers in use today are **general-purpose computers**—those built for a great variety of processing jobs. Simply by using a general-purpose computer and different software, diverse tasks can be accom-

FIGURE 5–1
Although it is not very much larger than the microcomputer on the table in the background, the Cray–2 supercomputer can perform over one billion instructions per second. (Courtesy of Cray Research, Inc.)

plished, including writing and editing (word processing), manipulating facts in a data base, tracking manufacturing inventory, making scientific calculations, or even controlling an organization's security system, electricity consumption, and building temperature. Most of the large system, digital computers described in this chapter are general-purpose computers.

Special-purpose Computers

Special-purpose computers are built for specific processing jobs or applications. Special-purpose computers start out as general-purpose machines, but are adapted by using a specific configuration of peripheral equipment or by modifying the internal circuitry to achieve particular capabilities.

One example of a special-purpose computer configured to be used with a large computer system is a **front-end processor;** it controls the input and output functions of a main computer. Another example is the special-purpose computer called a **back-end processor** that retrieves data from storage and replaces them back into storage. These special-purpose computers free the main computer to complete its calculations without having to spend valuable time managing operations and data tracking. Figure 5–2 illustrates how a supercomputer can be set up with both front-end and back-end processors.

Dedicated processors are special-purpose computers whose internal circuitry has been modified to perform specific functions. They are designed to perform specific processing tasks, such as those found in:

FIGURE 5–2
A large computer system can be configured using a front-end processor to control input and output and a back-end processor to retrieve and store data.

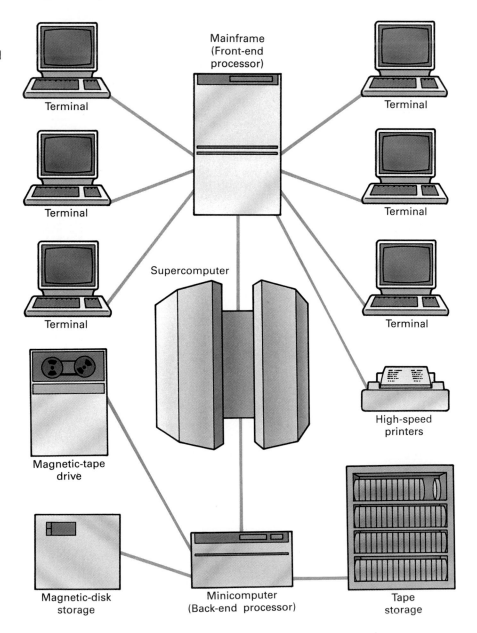

Classes of Computers

- General-purpose
- Special-purpose

☐ Robots used in manufacturing
☐ Hospital testing machinery such as CAT scanners
☐ Video games

Although all general-purpose computers can be programmed to perform the same basic functions, each size has its uses, special requirements, and limitations. A supercomputer would not be used to word process a term paper. A minicomputer would not be used to process all the statistical calculations needed for forecasting weather or testing aircraft. Computers have traditionally been divided into categories based on power, speed, and cost. Let's start with the top of the line.

SUPERCOMPUTERS

A **supercomputer** is generally characterized as being the fastest, most powerful, and most expensive computer.

One of the most powerful supercomputers today, the Cray–2, is set up in a C-shape, is not as tall as a person, and is small enough to fit in the space of a large business desk.

As many as sixty miles of wiring are closely-packed inside these supercomputers, and tremendous amounts of heat are generated. A supercomputer builds enough internal heat that it has special cooling requirements. Not only must the room that houses the supercomputer be air conditioned, but special plumbing is usually required to circulate fluid around the circuitry to protect it. The CPU of Seymour Cray's Cray–2, nicknamed "Bubbles," is immersed and cooled in an aquarium-like tank containing liquid fluorocarbon.

Some supercomputers require extra floor support to hold the extreme weight of the complete system which includes external storage units. Additionally, highly trained data-processing professionals are required to operate supercomputers.

The primary storage of the supercomputer contains many **gigabytes,** or billions of bytes of data. The secondary storage, however, can be expanded and is limited only by the number of additional storage devices that are part of the configuration.

Supercomputers recognize the largest word lengths of 64-bits or more. (See Chapter 2 for a review of the discussion on word sizes.) The supercomputer calculates at rates up to 1.2 billion instructions per second. These speeds are expected to keep increasing in the future.

The supercomputer can take input from over 10,000 individual workstations. To do this, however, a supercomputer needs a smaller computer to coordinate the input and output activities. The smaller computer, either a mainframe or a minicomputer, acts as a front-end processor and frees the supercomputer for the high-speed processing of large numbers which it does best.

Supercomputer prices start at about $4 million, with the Cray–2 going for approximately $17 million. Maintenance engineering service for the life of the computer is included by some manufacturers as part of the substantial price tag.

Because each supercomputer costs millions of dollars to manufacture and install, not many are made each year. In 1985, Cray, the largest manufacturer, contracted for thirty-nine new or used systems. In fact, of the more than 150 supercomputers in use today, more than half are Crays. The market for supercomputers is growing, in part, because of the need to produce prototype models or simulate conditions instead of conducting actual experimentation. Actual physical experimentation is considerably more expensive, and creating models or simulations and having them available via the terminal allows an experiment to be observed in more detail.

ETA Systems, Fujitsu, Hitachi, and Control Data Corporation also produce supercomputers (Figure 5–3), but Seymour Cray was the innovator and Cray Research still produces the most. Floating Point Systems, a company in Oregon that sells scientific computers, offers a supercomputer that performs many calculations simultaneously using several processors. This ability, the company claims, makes theirs the fastest supercomputer and allows the solution of problems that were previously considered unsolvable.

The federal government uses most of the existing supercomputers for a variety of tasks. They control the nation's defense system, break cryptographic codes, keep track of the huge volumes of data generated by both the Internal Revenue Service and Social Security offices, and make space exploration possible. Because of the supercomputer's sophistication and its adaptability and importance for use in weapons design, the United States government forbids their sale to Communist countries.

Supercomputers are widely used in scientific applications, such as aerodynamics design and simulation, processing of geological data and data regarding genetic coding, and collecting and processing weather data.

In aerospace, aerodynamics and structural design are traditionally studied. Three aerospace programs that will benefit from the super-

FIGURE 5–3
A Control Data ETA 02P supercomputer (Courtesy of Control Data Corp.)

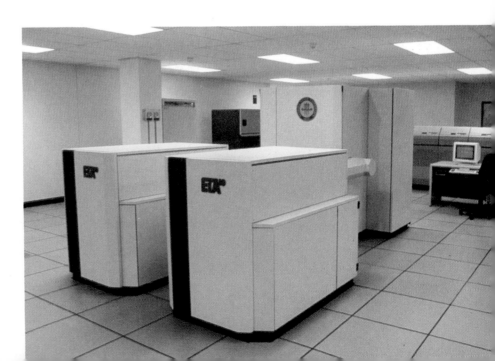

A programmer analyst uses the Chevron Exploration Viewing and Interpreting System to explain three-dimensional seismic exploration data that will help determine the location for offshore oil derricks. (Courtesy of Chevron Corp.)

computer's capabilities are the Strategic Defense Initiative (SDI), a proposed space station, and a space plane (transatmospheric vehicle).

These three projects require extensive experiments, some of which are physically impossible. For example, the proposed space station would collapse under its own weight if built in Earth's gravity. The space plane, the X–30, must be able to take off from a runway on Earth and accelerate directly into orbit at speeds over 8,800 mph. Many of these conditions cannot even be duplicated in a wind tunnel. Testing in space could be accomplished, but the expense would be prohibitive.

The simulations and modeling for these designs and tests include processing billions of pieces of data and solving numerous, complex math-

HIGHLIGHT

ONE OF THE WORLD'S FASTEST COMPUTERS

In March 1987, a new, National Aeronautics and Space Administration (NASA), $120-million supercomputer complex was completed. At the heart of the system is the Cray–2, a 240,000-chip machine with a 256 million-word memory; it immediately began making 250 million computations per second. The NASA network expects to reach one billion computations per second by 1989. These incredible speeds make this supercomputer thousands of times faster than the early 1940s machines such as the ENIAC.

NASA's Ames Research Center at Moffett Field, California, proposes to use the Cray–2 to design an aerospace plane that will fly from Washington, D.C., to Tokyo, Japan, in two hours. The computer simulates wind-tunnel tests to calculate stress areas that may be created by the high speeds the aircraft will encounter. The computer simulation allows potential design changes to be introduced and their effects examined before incurring the expense of actually building prototypes.

At NASA, the supercomputer also investigates galaxies, models weather phenomena prior to prediction, simulates chemical reactions, and studies artificial intelligence.

Although the Cray–2 appears to be the world's fastest computer, work began on its successor almost before it was completed. The Cray–3, with a proposed memory of a billion words and a promise of several billion calculations per second, will soon be available.

ematical calculations in a timely fashion—the perfect application for supercomputers (Figure 5–4).

Oil companies process millions of pieces of geological data to determine which exploration sites have the best chance of yielding productive oil reserves (Figure 5–5). Scientists use the supercomputer to sort through the maze of biological data involved in genetic coding. Meteorologists digest volumes of atmospheric phenomena, including worldwide data from satellite communications, in order to make weather forecasts.

In Los Angeles, Digital Productions generated commercials for the Mattel Company. Turner Broadcasting created rock videos, and Lorimar used Digital's special effects in the movie *The Last Starfighter*. All of these various feats were accomplished with the help of supercomputers.

Processing speeds for large computers are generally measured in millions of instructions per second (MIPS). These speeds make it appear that operations are occurring simultaneously; but even the central processing unit in a supercomputer can operate on only one instruction, or unit of work, at a time. **Uniprocessing,** using only one CPU in a computer system, limits a computer's processing speed. Early computers and many of

FIGURE 5–4
To train personnel, the United States Armed Forces use supercomputers to create simulations of actual battle situations. (Courtesy of Department of the Army)

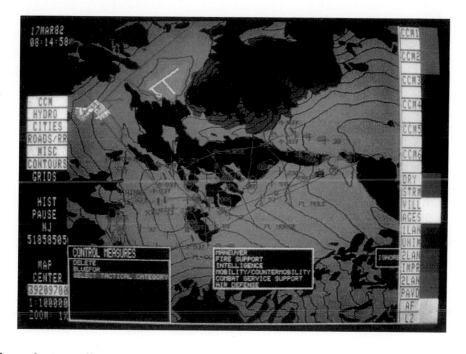

Supercomputer Users

- United States government
- Oil companies
- Science
- Weather service
- Film companies

today's smaller systems still use the uniprocessing approach. To get around its limitations, multiprocessing computer systems were developed. They enable supercomputers to reach their millions of instructions per second speed.

Multiprocessing involves using two or more CPUs, and because each CPU executes its own instructions, several sets of instructions can be executed simultaneously. The concept of multiprocessing is used not only in supercomputers, but also in other large computer systems.

Seymour Cray's work was specifically directed toward the development of supercomputers. However, many supercomputer design ideas have found their way down to other sizes of computers, creating greater capabilities for them also. Now, Cray and other manufacturers build

FIGURE 5–5
Chevron links supercomputers and sophisticated recording equipment to accumulate seismic data for oil exploration crews that are based on remote barges. (Courtesy of Chevron Corp.)

minisupercomputers—smaller scale, cheaper supercomputers. Cray's minisupercomputer entry, the X-MP/14se sells for approximately $2.5 million and can run simulations in areas such as aerodynamics and mechanical design and analysis. These minisupercomputers will handle similar word sizes and run many other supercomputer applications, but not with as much speed. The ETA Systems' ETA[10] is another entry in the minisupercomputer category. The emergence of these computers further blurs the line between supercomputers and the next large system, known as a mainframe.

MAINFRAME COMPUTERS

A **mainframe computer** is usually slower, less powerful, and less expensive than a supercomputer. It was so named because it was first built by incorporating modules on a chassis, or "main frame." IBM introduced the concept of building entire families of compatible mainframe computers—small, medium, and large—all with interchangeable software and computing abilities suggested by their sizes. Organizations could start with a small, relatively inexpensive system and add to it, building a larger computer system as computing needs grew. Some mainframe configurations rival the supercomputer's speed, power, and even expense.

A mainframe computer (Figure 5–6) is generally found in a special computer room where environmental factors such as temperature, humidity, and dust are closely monitored. Because of the computer's cost and the value of the information stored there, these rooms usually have a security system allowing only authorized personnel to enter.

The mainframe's primary storage is measured in megabytes, and it can grow substantially depending on the configuration. External memory (secondary storage) depends on the number and types of storage devices chosen. Smaller mainframes generally recognize 32-bit words, but some of the more powerful machines manipulate words up to 64 bits. Mainframes

FIGURE 5–6
An Amdahl mainframe (Courtesy of Amdahl Corp.)

This CRT is on-line to an IBM 3081 mainframe computer and runs profit and loss models for evaluating new Albertson's supermarket locations. (Courtesy of Albertson's, Inc.)

process data at several million instructions per second. More than 1,000 remote workstations can be accommodated by a typical mainframe computer.

Mainframe systems can be rented from the manufacturer, leased through leasing companies, or purchased for amounts ranging from several hundred thousand dollars to several million dollars.

Control Data Corporation builds mainframe computers. Other manufacturers include National Cash Register Company, Digital Equipment Corporation, UNISYS (formerly Burroughs and Sperry), and Amdahl. But the largest supplier, IBM, has produced mainframes for over twenty-five years and still accounts for 60 percent of mainframes sold in North America. One of their products, the powerful IBM 3090 mainframe, contains a tiny computer chip that retrieves information faster than any previous IBM chip. The chip stores one million bits of information and takes only 80 billionths of a second to retrieve data.

Federal and local government agencies, large banks and hospitals, and commercial and industrial users need a mainframe's capabilities. Mainframes typically coordinate and manage an organization's vast amounts of data in giant data banks.

A technique that allows many people at terminals to access the same computer at one time is called **time sharing.** In a time-sharing environment, the CPU gives its attention to only one user at a time, for a short period of time, and then switches to the next user. But it switches so quickly between users that it gives the appearance that the CPU is devoted to only one user's task. Some companies offer to sell time-sharing services to others outside their organizations.

During the 1950s, American Airlines and IBM joined forces to develop the SABRE system, a time-sharing plan that allowed airline reservations to be made from hundreds of widely distributed terminals. Airline companies and travel agents access the same computer system to confirm

A mainframe at Santa Fe Southern Pacific's operating center in Clovis, New Mexico, monitors the movement of trains. (Courtesy of Santa Fe Southern Pacific Corp.)

reserved seats, write tickets, and track baggage. Although the SABRE system had one particular purpose, time sharing now occurs in many different applications.

Using a mainframe system, the Metro Toronto (Canada) Police store hundreds of thousands of fingerprints. They also monitor and service the emergency 911 telephone number for police, fire, and ambulance calls. A time-sharing system allows arresting officers, managing officers, and dispatchers to access the computer data bank at the "same" time.

Banks depend on mainframes and time-sharing systems for managing checking and savings accounts, generating amortization schedules, and preparing monthly statements. Because a mainframe can be accessed by many people at different locations, it is especially valuable to banks where tellers from several different branch offices make debits and credits to accounts, loan officers verify account balances, and data processing personnel handle other transactions all, seemingly, at one time. Figure 5–7 shows a mainframe computer layout that could be implemented for a banking application.

Mainframes are used by many businesses to update inventory, schedule production, prepare bills, and generate sales and management reports.

Mainframes at Johnson Spaceflight Center manage operations, assist engineers, and provide support for missions from the planning stage through flight and post-flight evaluation. The United States Air Force Military Airlift Command (MAC) uses mainframes for situation modeling. MAC is responsible for airlifting personnel and equipment in emergencies,

Mainframe Computer Users

- Federal and local government
- Banks
- Industry/manufacturing
- Hospitals

FIGURE 5–7
A mainframe can be set up with multiple workstations for use by several branches of a bank.

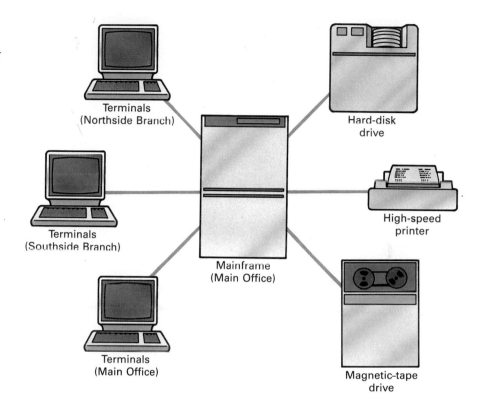

Terminals
(Northside Branch)

Hard-disk
drive

Terminals
(Southside Branch)

High-speed
printer

Mainframe
(Main Office)

Terminals
(Main Office)

Magnetic-tape
drive

handling Presidential transportation, and coordinating aerial search and rescue operations. Modeling emergency situations where their special services could be called into use provides valuable training before a real emergency arises. Contingency plans can be suggested, tested, and modified, as necessary, without risking lives.

Beech Aircraft Corporation coordinates and processes the design and production of its nine-passenger executive aircraft, Starship, with a mainframe to handle the mathematical operations for aerodynamic and structural analysis efficiently.

MINICOMPUTERS

Minicomputers are smaller-than-mainframe, general-purpose computers, that give computing power without adding the prohibitive expenses associated with larger systems. In the mid-1960s, Digital Equipment Company (DEC) introduced the first commercially successful minicomputer, the 12-bit PDP–8. It was a small-scale mainframe computer; it did not have as much power or speed, but it did have a lower price—approximately $20,000—and it created a fast-growing market.

The minicomputer's size prevents it from being portable, but it can be moved more easily than a mainframe. Although some are still kept in special computer rooms with dust and humidity controls, most minicomputers are free of the elaborate environmental constraints of the larger

HIGHLIGHT

WHAT A COLLECTION!

In Houston, Texas, a 30-year-old company is thriving despite slumps in other industries. The Gulf Coast Collection Agency started out collecting past-due accounts. The first account was for $57; but to date, overall collections total $2 billion.

Who owes all this money? To whom is it owed? Well, it's no surprise that quite a bit is payable to Uncle Sam. Yes, the Internal Revenue Service (IRS) has teamed up with Gulf Coast and, with the help of several mainframe computer systems, they are collecting past-due taxes. An estimated $47.3 billion is due; they are billing approximately 13.2 million taxpayers.

Through a computerized automated collection system, when a delinquent taxpayer refuses to acknowledge late notices, an IRS agent is put on the case. The collection program is devised so that the IRS employee instantaneously views a taxpayer's records on the monitor, and the computer automatically dials the appropriate person's telephone number. Information in the records includes what real estate you own, if and where your spouse is employed, how much you both earn, the balances of your mortgage and bank accounts and, of course, the complete record of previous tax filings.

The computer is tireless; if no one answers its telephone calls, it automatically tries again at designated times. The computer can even try to reach you at a business phone during the hours of 9 AM to 5 PM.

If you are lucky enough to avoid the phone contact, the computer can then be programmed to generate letters to past employers, neighbors, or others who might know and share the details of your whereabouts.

Even though the collection of back taxes by this computerized system is so far marginal, the IRS has saved $32 million by using it and, thus, has improved its efficiency.

systems (Figure 5–8). Minicomputer operators do not require as much training as those of larger systems.

Primary storage can consist of several million bytes of data and can expand memory capabilities by using external storage media such as tape, floppy diskettes, or removable disk packs. Minicomputers generally recognize 16- and 32-bit words and hundreds of terminals can access some minicomputers.

Although minicomputers have limited power and capabilities and accommodate fewer peripherals, they are generally less expensive than larger systems. Pricing begins at several thousand dollars and can range into the hundreds of thousands of dollars.

Large computer systems are usually found in special computer rooms similar to this one. The operators at these workstations are among the hundreds that can use the same system.

FIGURE 5–8
The Hewlett-Packard and other minicomputers with lower price tags offer computing capabilities for smaller offices and businesses. This operator makes a back-up copy of the day's transactions on a cartridge tape. (Photo courtesy of Hewlett-Packard Co.)

Minicomputers are manufactured by many companies, including Hewlett-Packard, Data General, Texas Instruments, Honeywell, Burroughs, Wang, IBM, and Prime; however, DEC, the minicomputer's innovator, continues to be the leader.

Some people are concerned that the minicomputer will become obsolete because mainframe capabilities are encroaching on the minicomputer market from the top, and high-power microcomputers are threatening the lower end. This development may not happen soon because:

1. The minicomputer integrates commercial and technical operations better than the more powerful computers.
2. The minicomputer is still generally easier to use.
3. The microcomputer is not yet powerful enough to handle the processing demands of larger multiuser systems.

The minicomputer's reasonable price makes it available to smaller organizations such as the American Association of University Women. A minicomputer in their Washington, D.C., headquarters keeps 175,000 members in 2,000 communities in touch with issues important to them, their communities, and the nation.

Scientific laboratories, research groups, some colleges, engineering firms, and even industrial and manufacturing plants also use minicomputers. At the University of Miami's Rosenstiel School of Marine and Atmospheric Science, minicomputers condense more than 2 billion bytes of information daily. Research there includes image processing. Complex images are compiled from satellite observations of the Earth's oceans to create color photographs that indicate the oceans' surface temperatures, winds, and even chlorophyll content.

Minicomputers are well-adapted for functions such as accounting, word processing, data-base management, and specific industry applica-

Prime Computer, Inc., sells and supports an advanced computer-aided design system for minicomputers. It is used primarily for CAD/CAM design, drafting, and three-dimensional solids modeling. (Courtesy of Prime Computer, Inc.)

tions. These varied uses brought computers out of the realm of scientific and engineering applications and into the corporate world.

Employees at Wright Schuchart Harbor Company work in the oil fields at Prudhoe Bay, Alaska. Oil companies have strict government reporting requirements, and labor costs are extremely high in Alaska. Wright Schuchart had always physically delivered the payroll figures that were to be processed by a mainframe at corporate headquarters in Seattle, Washington. Getting the checks returned in time for payday and not having ready access to the data in the reports proved to be problematic, however.

With an on-site Texas Instruments minicomputer programmed with construction management software, they now process the payroll and print the checks on time. More importantly, they also generate the job-cost reports, equipment-cost reports, accounts payable information, and purchase orders on the spot.

A separate mainframe for the Alaskan operation would have been extremely expensive. Additionally, a mainframe would have had problems operating in a construction trailer where outside temperatures dropped to as much as −75 degrees Fahrenheit.

The minicomputer's capabilities and lower price made the idea of **distributed processing,** a method where two or more computers are used to process data at different geographic locations, feasible. Distributed computers are tied together through a telecommunications link and function as one system. (See Chapter 7 and its associated InfoModule for more information about telecommunications and distributed processing.)

DEC introduced a VAX system minicomputer in 1977. The VAX expanded into a line of minicomputers that had compatible hardware and software.

VAX systems are now found being grouped into units called VAXclusters, so that as a user's business grows, data processing activities can expand. A single software system works on all the VAX systems. By

Minicomputer Users

- Smaller businesses
- Colleges and universities
- Scientists

FIGURE 5–9
Because computer capabilities are increasing and prices for those systems are decreasing, the categorical distinctions are not easily defined.

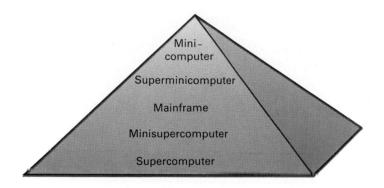

Large Computer Categories

- Supercomputer
- Mainframe computer
- Minicomputer

linking systems that share a common data base, the VAXcluster arrangement delivers more power and performance than some of the largest mainframes.

VAXclusters in the Volvo Car Corporation's manufacturing plant in Uddevalla, Sweden, are used throughout the entire company—from designing and testing right through the manufacturing process.

The DEC VAX 8800 and Data General's Eclipse MV/20000 Models 1 and 2 are superminicomputers—faster, more powerful, high-end minicomputers. These superminicomputers recognize 32-bit words and have a primary storage capacity approaching that of the mainframe. Other superminicomputer manufacturers include Honeywell Information Systems, Prime Computer, UNISYS, and Wang Laboratories. The superminicomputers range from several thousand dollars to several hundreds of thousands of dollars.

Characteristics of superminicomputers overlap those of mainframes and minicomputers. Figure 5–9 graphically shows the obscuring and overlapping among all the large computer systems.

SUMMARY

Large computer systems are divided into three categories: supercomputers; mainframe computers; and minicomputers. The distinctions between these systems are primarily the speed, power, and price.

Computers that are built for specific applications processing are called special-purpose computers. Examples of special-purpose computers configured to perform a specific task are: a front-end processor that controls the input and output functions; and a back-end processor that retrieves and replaces information in storage. These processors allow the main computer CPU to operate more productively. Some special-purpose computers are dedicated processors that perform specific tasks, such as robots used in manufacturing, hospital testing machinery, video games, or other single applications. Most computers, however, are general-purpose computers and can be programmed to perform many functions.

Supercomputers are the fastest, most powerful, and most expensive computer. Some can perform over one billion instructions per second. The

HIGHLIGHT

LEO OF THE LIONS   Leo works for the Detroit Lions football team and has the primary job responsibility for compiling over 15,000 reports on the 7,500 players eligible for the annual pro football draft, tracking players' health and injuries, and analyzing their game plans. On Monday afternoons, all the play-by-play information from the weekend games must be organized for detailed analysis. The Lions have many application programs for Leo, some of which may be used as teaching tools to instruct players on the more than 5,000 formations used by and against the Lions.

When conducting physical examinations, the team physician uses information collected about team members' injuries. If a player is injured, special notes are recorded on over 100 variables, such as the player's position, specific injury, playing surface, what equipment was in use, and even what the weather was at the time.

Sifting through all this data could be a time-consuming task; but, luckily, Leo is a Prime minicomputer with plenty of memory capability for maintaining all these statistics.

Leo even won a game ball after the Lions led the National Football League in rushing defense in 1981.

great speed and the volume of circuitry needed in the supercomputer also demand environmental controls in the form of air conditioning and special internal cooling. Supercomputers are operated by trained professionals.

Supercomputers recognize the largest word sizes and have the largest primary storage capacity which is measured in gigabytes, or billions of bytes.

A supercomputer can be linked to over 10,000 workstations. Primary users are: the federal government for manipulating large volumes of data in scientific and defense projects; and large corporations where the great number of computations required justifies the price tags which range in the millions of dollars.

Uniprocessing is when one processor makes calculations. Multiprocessing involves several processors linked through electrical connections to share input, processing, output, and storage devices and allows execution of several instructions at one time.

A mainframe computer is usually less powerful, slower in speed, and not as expensive as a supercomputer. It calculates at several millions of instructions per second (MIPS). Mainframes are usually placed in special environmentally-controlled computer rooms where they are operated by trained personnel.

Mainframes contain many megabytes (millions of bytes) of memory and recognize 32-bit size words. Some larger, more powerful mainframes manipulate 64-bit word sizes. They can organize all the required information in large data banks. A mainframe computer can control the operations of more than 1,000 workstations linked in a time-sharing format.

With prices ranging from several hundred thousand dollars to several million dollars, businesses and industries can afford mainframe systems.

Time sharing occurs when many terminals are attached to the same computer and all users have what appears to be uninterrupted use. Actually, the computer handles only one instruction at a time and switches among users, although it appears that the computer is devoted to only one user.

Minicomputers are the smallest of the large computers. They operate on fewer instructions per second. Since the circuitry is not as tightly packed, they usually do not require extensive environmental controls.

Minicomputers contain several million bytes of primary storage and generally recognize 16-bit word sizes. Some minicomputers and super-minicomputers read 32-bit words.

Several hundred workstations can access some minicomputers; therefore, the minicomputer is ideal for use by smaller businesses and industries and is widely used in applications such as time sharing and distributed processing networks. Distributed processing is a method of processing where two or more computers are used at different geographic locations.

The future of large systems appears to be that supercomputers will become more powerful, and the other categories of large computers will continue merging, becoming less and less distinct.

Key Terms

back-end processor (p. 144)

dedicated processor (p. 144)

distributed processing (p. 156)

front-end processor (p. 143)

general-purpose computer (p. 142)

gigabyte (p. 145)

mainframe computer (p. 150)

minicomputer (p. 153)

multiprocessing (p. 149)

special-purpose computer (p. 143)

supercomputer (p. 145)

time sharing (p. 151)

uniprocessing (p. 148)

Review Questions

1. Describe a general-purpose computer and explain what it does.
2. Describe a special-purpose computer and tell what it does. Give examples of special-purpose computers.
3. Describe a dedicated processor.
4. List the characteristics of a supercomputer.
5. Why are the supercomputer's capabilities often used for modeling and simulations?
6. Who are the primary users of supercomputers?

7. Large-system computer calculations are measured in _____.

8. Describe uniprocessing.

9. Describe multiprocessing.

10. A mainframe computer is usually _____, _____, and _____ than a supercomputer.

11. Give examples of users and uses of mainframe computers.

12. How did the mainframe get its name?

13. What is the word that means one billion bytes?

14. How many instructions can the CPU of a supercomputer execute at one time?

15. What is time sharing? Explain how it works.

16. What is the PDP–8?

17. Give examples of users and uses of minicomputers.

18. Explain distributed processing. Why would a company use it?

19. A small business or organization would probably choose what kind of system? Explain why.

20. List the categories of computers starting with the most powerful.

21. Compare the three categories of large computer systems.

22. Describe what causes the blurring of the categorical distinctions between the computer systems.

23. List three reasons why mainframes and high-powered smaller systems have not made minicomputers obsolete.

24. For what tasks are supercomputers best suited?

25. Describe the environmental constraints of the large computers, and tell why they are necessary.

INFOMODULE
The Value of Information and Computer Technology

The power structure during the latter part of the 20th century has moved forward dramatically from a muscle orientation toward a knowledge orientation. Today, people need to work smarter, not harder, and they can do this using information and information technologies.

Education for jobs in today's information society is geared more toward preparing people for providing services and information rather than teaching physical or industrial skills. Some experts think that those people who are not part of the revolution to learn about computers—those people who remain computer illiterates—will find few opportunities in the job market.

Various studies indicate that those organizations or businesses that take advantage of computer technology and that manage their information efficiently and creatively will have a competitive edge in today's marketplace. Those who do not, won't be able to keep pace, whether it's in the world market or locally.

COMPETITION

It is not necessarily the first idea—or the first user of a new idea—that becomes a winner. In retail banking for instance, the Chemical Bank of New York was the first to automate the teller's job using automated teller machines (ATM). Unfortunately, their machine didn't seem to work properly or live up to their expectations, so they shied away from making the most of the idea. Citibank of New York, though, thought there was a definite market for the ATM. Extensive research proved that by making the equipment easier to use, the customers themselves were able to take advantage of the services offered. Having the right information helped successfully match an idea with the consumer's needs. The modified ATM idea obviously works; ATMs can be found at most banks, in shopping malls, on campus, and even at walk-up banking sites designed especially for them.

Well-established businesses also benefit from the right information. Rivalry among businesses is intense. Because the supply of customers is limited, and those customers tend to be fickle, businesses must sell either new products or find new uses for their old standbys. The competitor who makes use of any tool to increase production or profit will benefit. It will be that way for the competitor who uses the new tools—computers and information technology.

INFORMATION'S VALUE

Society seems to hunger for and thrive on information. But decisions concerning the value placed on particular information must be made individually, because what may be valuable information to one person or business may have little or no value or interest to others. That same information may not have the same value at another time; therefore, true value must always be decided on a case-by-case basis. For example, miscellaneous data such as 40–33–11–7–28–24 may seem worthless to you; however, the owner of a winning lottery ticket with those numbers will realize increased worth and will probably remember that particular number combination forever. By the same token, the owner of a lottery ticket for the next drawing will not have any use for that combination of numbers.

Some recorded information has more value to a greater number of people. Road maps are used by millions of travellers, telephone directories of large cities are used by millions of people daily, and dictionaries have proved valuable to all of us at one time or other. However, none of us will need *all* of the miscellany encompassed by any of the above sources. It would be senseless to memorize all the data in a dictionary when you need only reference specific words or meanings as needed. Each of us must be selective in the information we collect, update, and remember.

Here are some guidelines to help determine the value of information. Valuable information is on time, relevant, accurate, and communicated to the appropriate person(s).

These principles apply to setting value on computerized business information. A business manager should not have to wade through the reams of paperwork explaining the factory production schedule or an inventory of office furniture if the only information needed at the time is a total of how many hours of overtime are expended for a particular week.

Computers can provide managers with very specialized summaries of only the information they need to help them make better decisions. However, what has been noticed is that many managers request more information than they need, just because they know it is readily available. Many systems are designed to store and summarize more data than are ever used. This processing not only ties up valuable computer time, but it is very expensive to maintain and store in the system. There is very little value to the information contained in any reports that pile up unread and unused by anyone.

MAKING THE MOST OF INFORMATION TECHNOLOGY

Access to the right information and the latest computer technology no doubt gives a company a competitive weapon and a potential for growth. But too much information or unnecessary information can become overwhelming and counterproductive. So, it appears that there is a fine balance in reaching the bottom line, i.e., getting the right information to the right person at the right time. How can this be done?

Unfortunately, some large organizations still have data-processing managers who do not have good business acumen and business managers and other managers who do not have the necessary background in computer technology or information systems. It's a classic example of the right hand not knowing what the left hand is doing.

Some companies recognize this deficiency and include all managers in the planning and use of their information systems. Large

amounts of money are spent on data processing; therefore, a system must be designed that will provide the information that each manager needs for decision making that can make a difference in the company's profits.

Information technology brings with it changes, both in the way business is done and how decisions are made. Some of the areas in which organizations use computers to make the most of the new information technology and improve their competitive standing include

- [ ] Management
- [ ] Sales
- [ ] Telecommunication and telemarketing
- [ ] Expansion
- [ ] Production
- [ ] Customer service

Management

Data-processing managers should improve their technological skills and learn more about business strategies. Managers in other areas cannot ignore the importance of honing their hard-won skills to include learning how to use information technology to formulate their decisions. With quality information available for management decision making, sales could increase, production improve, and profits increase.

Sales

The cost of supporting computer and information technology has declined enough to make its use a viable tool for sales managers and sales representatives.

One way some companies try to stay on top in sales is by providing their salespeople who work in the field with portable computers. A portable computer can be used on the spot for keeping an updated, easily-referenced catalog of the items in stock, lists of items on sale, and items on back order. The salesperson can place orders, add new customers, and even change incorrect information in a customer's file that is maintained by a larger computer back at the home office.

When the salesperson directly enters information about a sale, shipments can be scheduled quickly, and inventory can be appropriately reduced. With less paperwork to be shuffled back at the office, there is also less chance for error. Even an independent salesperson should explore the advantages of using a computer for on-site ordering.

Communication and Telemarketing

The vast expanse of the globe seems to have shrunk, not only because of advances in air travel, but also because of the new communication technologies. An organization can easily send and receive information to its branch offices anywhere using satellite dishes and data communication hookups. With the world at its fingertips, a company's goods and services can potentially find a market anywhere.

Telemarketing, a relatively new idea in marketing that has proved to be very successful, is a way of reaching previously untapped markets. Instead of sending a sales representative to the customer, the business uses the telephone, a computer system, and lists of leads for prospective customers to make the contact and record the sale. Addresses and phone numbers of these leads are usually furnished (for a price) by many different organizations who have also used computers to compile, organize, and maintain those lists.

For example, when someone buys an item from a sporting goods catalog, that name usually gets added to the company's computerized address list of sports enthusiasts. The list could eventually be sold to a sports magazine as a lead list. Other sporting goods manufacturers could then buy that list of names assuming that many of the people who had purchased from other sporting goods companies could possibly have an interest in their products. When someone makes a contribution to a particular charity, that name may get added to a computerized address list of other foundations seeking donations. If someone orders information from a computer trade magazine, that name undoubtedly gets added to address lists available to other computer magazine promotionals, com-

puter-catalog suppliers, and possibly even unrelated categories of mailing lists. You can see that a consumer's name and address could very quickly be added to more than one list for future sales.

Expansion

For many years, transportation and financial service industries were regulated. Deregulation offered opportunities for these and other businesses to explore new options, change product lines, and expand markets for exploration into other services and products.

The advent of the computer and information systems also makes exploration and expansion of new areas possible.

A computer with the appropriate software can survey new markets for a particular business or industry and can forecast trends and competitor's plans. It is used to collect and categorize the historical facts, taking into account economical or social factors that could adversely or positively affect the market. Most programs analyze the total financial situation and weigh the information before making predictions; however, the manager must still also use personal information, experience, judgment, and knowledge of current conditions before finalizing business decisions.

One way the J. C. Penney Company developed a new market was by selling a new service—its computing power. A chain of retail stores, Penney's uses computers for operations that are similar to other normal retail store applications—ordering, billing, inventory, accounting, and personnel functions. They also process several gasoline companies' credit-card transactions. This service helps them recover some of the initial equipment expense.

Production

Computers and the information they provide can increase efficiency and productivity in any industry—from selling and manufacturing through packaging and shipping. The computer that takes a customer's order not only records the order, but at the same time creates a packing list, shipping label, and the billing papers required to complete each transaction.

Computers help engineers build the most effective equipment, while in manufacturing plants, the computer's skills augment or replace machines for the most efficient production. Computer-generated production control statistics provide valuable information from which management can make decisions, e.g., which products should be removed from inventory and which product lines might be added or increased.

Customer Service

For a long time, many businesses have offered customers toll-free phone numbers to open the lines of communication. A customer can provide valuable information and feedback about products, offer suggestions for improvement, and even spark the idea for a new product.

Some organizations have allowed customers to use their own compatible computers to gain direct access to information in the corporate computer to check on their own orders and shipments. Still other companies furnish their customers with terminals to place their orders. The customer can place orders directly, easily, and efficiently, and at the same time, the vendor has made it easy for that customer to place all, or many, of its orders with them.

THE COST

Currently, banks and other financial institutions use about one dollar of computer hardware for every $30 to $40 of value they gain. This return usually comes after many years of computer use by those institutions; however, if computers had never been purchased, the additional services and profits from those services could not have been generated. Being daring enough to venture into the realm of computers and information technology certainly proved worth the risk.

An investment in an information system can be incredibly expensive for a business, and the initial financial outlay cannot be estimated easily. Prudent business strategists would insist the cost effectiveness of any new equipment be proved based on a dollar-for-dollar return against the cost of the equipment. However, some of today's computer applications were barely dreamed of five years ago, and their uses today could not have been foreseen. So, trying to justify the computer's expense and predict the value of its information in future situations is nearly impossible.

THE INDIVIDUAL

Computer technology adds value to a person's life in many ways. Innovations in computer technology have been incorporated into products that make day-to-day living a little nicer through such things as faster check-out service at the supermarket, microwave ovens for meals prepared in a short time, and high-tech watches to keep you on time for scheduled appointments. On a larger scale, however, computers and information technology have freed us from many mundane, dull, boring, dangerous jobs and, at the same time, allowed us the opportunity to maintain control over those jobs.

Information technology will bring changes. But, there will undoubtedly be those who resist any changes. They'll use the least favorite sentence of computer pioneer, retired Rear Admiral Grace Hopper: ''But we've always done it that way.'' Those individuals or organizations will miss the opportunity to move forward.

We now live in a time when a nation's, or even a single corporation's, economic health can have worldwide implications. The potential for computer technology is astounding. The owner and user of the latest in this technology, and the information that can be delivered as a result, will undoubtedly be in possession of a powerful, strategic, and competitive weapon.

QUESTIONS

1. Explain why the value of information must be decided on a case-by-case basis.

2. Why is it important for data-processing managers to work closely with other managers?
3. Is it true that the more information you have available, the more valuable that information is? Explain.

4. List several areas where organizations can use information technology.
5. What valuable information might a salesperson get from a computer?

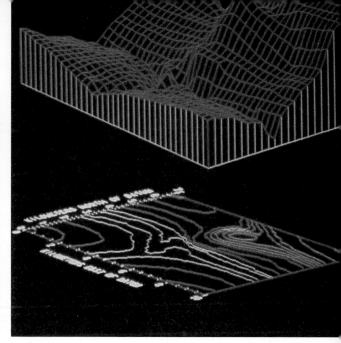

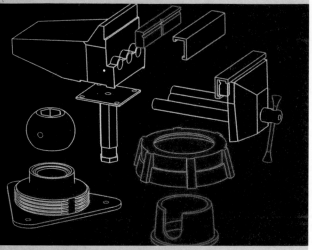

OBJECTIVES

OUTLINE

6

Microcomputers

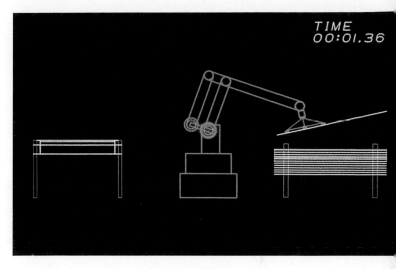

PROFILE:
Stephen Wozniak and Steven P. Jobs

When Stephen Wozniak and Steven P. Jobs joined forces in the mid-1970s to form Apple Computer, Inc., it was an ideal partnership of science and salesmanship. While both men were well-versed in the computer technology of the time, Wozniak was the scientific whiz kid. Jobs had a vision of creating a computer so small, powerful, and easy to use that it would have the sales appeal of a handy home appliance.

That his vision was more fact than fantasy was demonstrated within a remarkably short time. The first Apple computer went on sale in 1977; by 1980, when Apple stock became available to the public, the company registered sales of $139 million—not a bad record for an enterprise that was founded on just $1,300.

Neither Wozniak nor Jobs was a college graduate when their company was established. Wozniak had attended the University of California at Berkeley before dropping out in 1972, and Jobs had spent one semester at Reed College in Oregon.

In 1974, Jobs went to work briefly for Nolan Bushnell's video game company, Atari. There he witnessed the intellectually demanding but socially loose workstyle that would become a trademark at Apple.

A year after joining the Atari staff, Jobs began dropping in on meetings of the Home Brew Computer Club, a group of computer and software en-

thusiasts that included Wozniak. At the time, Wozniak was on the payroll of the Hewlett-Packard computer company, but Jobs (already with visions of microcomputers dancing in his head) persuaded "Woz" to leave his job and go in business with him.

The result was Apple Computer, Inc., a firm devoted from the start to changing the computer from an exotic and scary piece of mysterious hardware into a small, attractive, "user-friendly" workhorse for the office and home.

Success eventually drove the pair of pioneers from the top of the Apple barrel. As early as 1982, Wozniak was experimenting with rock concert promotion—an interest that cost him $30 million in two years. He returned to college at Berkeley and graduated in 1986 with a bachelor's degree in computer science.

Wozniak left Apple in 1985 and has since joined forces with fellow computer wizard Nolan Bushnell to produce and market a line of toy robots that are directed by audio signals encoded on the soundtracks of television programs or videocassettes.

Jobs also left Apple in 1985 and has since formed Next, Inc., a company that builds powerful personal computers for university scholars and educators.

Entry into a new generation of computer technology occurred with the introduction of the microprocessor. Changes have occurred so fast in the last few years that some people describe the time since 1975 as a "Microcomputer Revolution," a smaller revolution within the larger Information Revolution.

By varying size, capacity, and speed, microcomputers with microprocessor technology are being designed and made to meet many users' needs. Hundreds of different models and configurations are being promoted to accommodate anyone's budget.

When microcomputers were first brought into homes, people used them mainly as game machines and for entertainment. Today, the possible applications for microcomputers have increased, and the excitement has spread. Microcomputers are used not only for entertainment, but also for education and productivity. They are used by hobbyists and game players, as well as by people conducting their personal business and finances, students, educators and other professionals, small and large businesses, and even corporate executives (Figure 6–1). This chapter describes some of the sizes and types of microcomputers that people use.

THE MICROCOMPUTER— A PERSONAL COMPUTER

A **microcomputer** is the smallest, least expensive of all the computers. But don't let the prefix "micro" or the word "small" fool you. "Micro" refers mainly to the physical size of the computer and its circuitry rather than its capabilities. It *is* a small computer, and originally, it had rather limited capabilities compared to the large mainframe computers. Now microcomputers are more powerful than the early mainframes.

All computers, whether microcomputers or large computers, have the same basic elements—input devices, CPU (ALU, control unit, and primary storage unit), output devices, software, and usually, secondary storage. The essential differences today between microcomputers and mainframes or minicomputers are that microcomputers do have smaller memory and less power, are physically smaller, and permit fewer peripher-

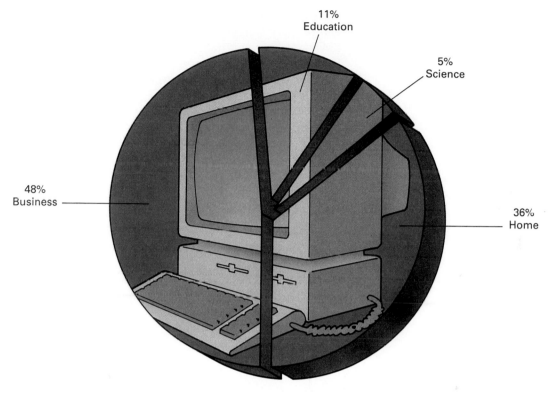

FIGURE 6–1
Approximate distribution of personal computer use [Source: *USA Today*
(12 August 1986): 6B]

als to be attached. Even these differences are diminishing as the distinctions of size, power, and capability gradually blur between all computers.

Microcomputers range in price from a few hundred dollars for the simplest ones to several thousand dollars for more powerful systems with all the peripheral equipment and software.

Microcomputers have also been called **personal computers**—a personal workstation where one person decides how one computer will be used. That's what Jobs and Wozniak had in mind when they were designing their first Apple—a computer to put on your desk, ready for you to use. Today, however, some microcomputers can be used by several users, each with a terminal connected to a central microcomputer.

A MICROCOMPUTER SYSTEM

A microcomputer and its peripheral devices and software are called a **microcomputer system.**

Depending on its purpose, a microcomputer system can be configured using a variety of different input and output devices. Figure 6–2 shows a plan for a typical microcomputer system. The major components are

☐ System unit (the basic computer, containing the microprocessor and primary storage)
☐ Keyboard for input
☐ Disk drive(s) for secondary storage of data and programs
☐ Monitor (display screen) for soft-copy output
☐ Printer for hard-copy output
☐ Serial or parallel interface card to permit printer and other peripheral device connections
☐ Connecting cables to connect all hardware components
☐ Software (including the operating system and application software)

Other components usually needed to complete a system include

☐ Modem connected to telephone line for telecommunication
☐ Serial interface card to permit modem connection

Most of these components have been described in more detail in earlier chapters. Modems are described in Chapter 7.

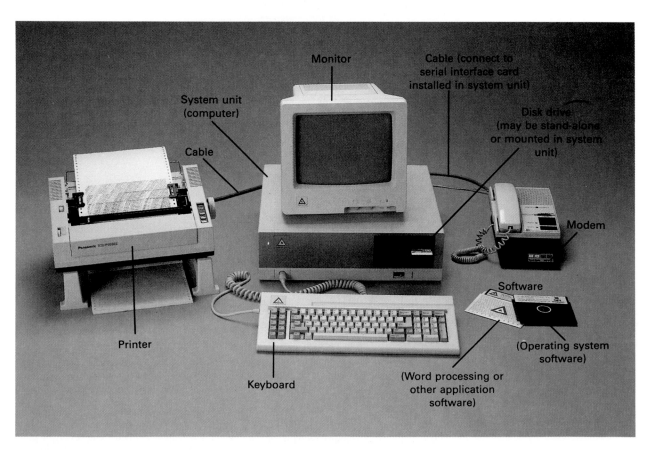

FIGURE 6–2
A typical microcomputer system

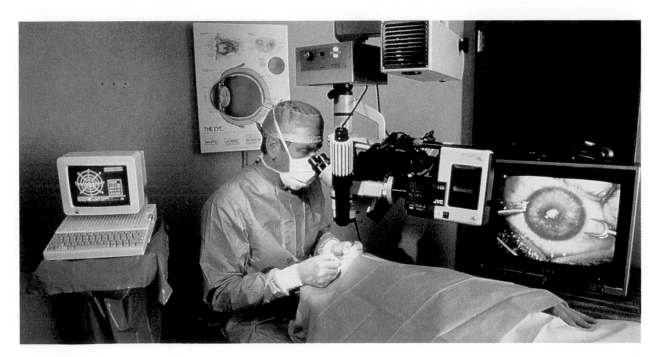

FIGURE 6–3
Physicians can access lab reports and other vital patient information during surgery with a microcomputer placed in the operating room. (Courtesy of Apple Computer, Inc.)

Some organizations and businesses use **multiuser microcomputer systems.** In this type of system, a number of terminals (workstations), typically eight to thirty, are attached to one powerful microcomputer, hard-disk drive, and printer. These workstations, usually in the same office or building, can also have individual disk drives. A microcomputer used in this way needs to have a lot of primary storage in order to handle input from each station.

The advantage of a multiuser system is that several people can use the same computer and peripheral equipment and share the data; this configuration is similar to a minicomputer or mainframe system with multiple terminals.

WHY MICROCOMPUTERS ARE POPULAR

Since Jobs and Wozniak put the first Apple II personal computer on the market in 1977, people have been excited about the possible uses of microcomputers. Why the excitement? Why do people want computing capability? Why have microcomputers gained such acceptance?

One reason is that they are useful tools. They help solve problems, accomplish specific tasks, and increase productivity. After a network of microcomputers was installed, Gulfstream Aerospace Corporation of Savannah, Georgia, found that productivity increased 25 percent in its Vehicle Design and Flight Sciences departments. Engineers used microcomputers to test aircraft design, thereby reducing time-consuming and expensive wind tunnel tests. Overall, Gulfstream was able to speed up its production schedule.

Computing power is no longer just a corporate tool in the hands of professionals. By using microcomputers, individuals and small businesses can increase productivity or accomplish tasks that would ordinarily take too much time or too much effort to even attempt manually.

Second, computers can be useful to a variety of people for a variety of tasks. They can be used to play games, teach children math, create new musical sounds, predict stock market trends, or serve as a handy reference resource (Figure 6–3). In fact, if you are interested, *you* can even program the computer to perform other tasks.

A third reason is that they are inexpensive. Young students can save allowances to buy a simple computer for under $300. Families or home businesses can afford to buy a small system to use at home (Figure 6–4).

Because of low prices and the abundance of ready-to-use software, the capabilities of computers are available to almost anyone who wants to use them. People can own a microcomputer or have access to one in schools, the public library, or even the neighborhood photocopy shop.

Fourth, microcomputers are relatively easy to use. Typically, people don't need to know how a computer actually operates internally to use one (Figure 6–5). Some computers are easy to use because many of the ready-to-use software packages have instructions that appear on the computer screen to guide you through the task at hand.

The operation of input and output devices has also been simplified. Some computers accept commands when you touch the screen. Others, with the appropriate hardware and software, respond to voice commands.

In the same way that most people drive an automobile without having to give much thought to its complex machinery or the way it works

FIGURE 6–4
Computers are used in homes for entertainment, education, and home business tasks. These young people are learning to use a microcomputer to type reports for class.

FIGURE 6–5
This photographer uses a microcomputer to keep track of all his photographs
as well as files of client data for billing purposes.

internally, people can use a computer without giving much thought to the
fact that it is a complex, high-tech machine.

BENCHMARKS IN THE MICROCOMPUTER INDUSTRY

The microcomputer industry became feasible after Ted Hoff, an engineer at
Intel, developed the Intel 4004 microprocessor, which was introduced in
1971. This chip could handle only four bits of data at a time. Eventually,
eight-bit microprocessor chips were developed, and those were used in the
early microcomputers.

The earliest microcomputer was developed in 1975 by Ed Roberts,
founder of a company called Micro Instrumentation Telemetry Systems
(MITS) and called by many the "father of the microcomputer." He developed the Altair 8800, a computer that the buyer had to assemble from a kit,
and sold it to consumers (mainly hobbyists) for $395. This computer used
an early Intel microprocessor and had less than 1K of memory.

The Apple II followed right behind the Altair 8800, and since then,
the microcomputer industry has grown rapidly, sending millions of microcomputers into our homes, schools, and businesses. Commodore Business
Machines also entered the market in 1977 with the Commodore PET. Atari
followed and so did the Tandy Corporation. Tandy marketed their first
microcomputer, the TRS-80 Model I, through their Radio Shack stores in
1977; this was the first time that consumers could walk into a retail store
and buy a computer.

Even though business was booming, until IBM came along, the total
sales of microcomputers was still fewer than one million units. IBM had
been in the business of manufacturing and marketing office equipment and
larger computer systems for years. In 1981, they introduced their IBM
Personal Computer (IBM PC); it used a 16-bit microprocessor. That year
other computer giants, Xerox and Digital Equipment Corporation (DEC)

173

also entered their versions of microcomputers. Sony, Hewlett-Packard, NEC, North Star, Zenith, and others now have microcomputers on the market.

By 1984, the IBM PC had become the industry standard; hundreds of companies designed software for it. IBM did not stay at the top for long, however. Because it was the most popular, almost every microcomputer manufacturer presented its version of the IBM PC design.

These other versions are called **IBM PC compatibles,** or "clones"—machines that run the IBM PC software and work with other IBM PC equipment. Because of the number of PC compatibles introduced into the marketplace, IBM sales dropped drastically in 1986. Some IBM PC compatibles are made by Leading Edge, Tandy, Epson, Kaypro, and Compaq.

Another benchmark in the microcomputer revolution is the introduction in 1984 of the Apple Macintosh. The Macintosh was visually-oriented and its mouse made it remarkably easy to use. It was praised for its ability to produce graphics and print text of near-typeset quality using Apple's LaserWriter. In 1986, the Compaq Deskpro 386 computer, the first to use the powerful, 32-bit Intel 80386 microprocessor, was introduced.

About 300 American computer makers are competing for the microcomputer market. Because of the heavy competition and partly because the costs of manufacturing computers has decreased, IBM and other companies have lowered the prices for their machines—good news for consumers. Approximately 30 million personal computers are in use in the U.S. today. In 1986 alone, almost 4 million personal computers (each costing $2,000 or less) were sold, and 65 million software packages were sold to go along with them. Those numbers are still growing (Figures 6–6, 6–7, and Table 6–1).

FIGURE 6–6

Approximate number of microcomputer manufacturers in the U.S. [Source: *USA Today* (12 August 1986): 6B].

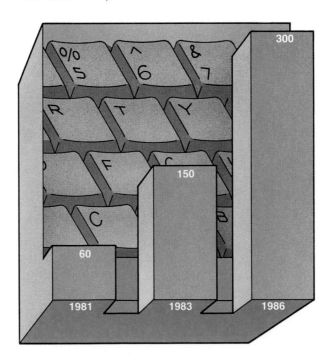

HIGHLIGHT

**MICRO MAVERICKS
GET TOGETHER**

It was the computer world's equivalent of America's first Continental Congress. The meeting was part strategy and part philosophy—an attempt to make the unknown world that lay ahead a better place for everyone. The first Hackers Conference took place in Marin County, California, on a winter weekend in 1984.

Some movies and newspaper stories have given hackers a bad name, reducing them to the status of criminals or precocious kids whose aim is to create chaos with someone else's computer system. However, the traditional definition of computer hacker is "skilled hobbyist." The computer hackers of this early generation were, in fact, the pioneers in microcomputer development and application. They designed the early video games, created the understandable and useful software for everyday uses, and dreamed of a society in which computers are as vital and commonplace as running water.

Unlike the Continental Congress of 1774, though, the Hackers Conference of 1984 did not lay out political plans for its representatives or issue manifestoes about the computer's rightful place in the world. But it did bring together some of the best and brightest minds in the country: Steve Wozniak, Apple computer designer and cofounder; Bob Frankston, VisiCalc developer; and Lee Felsenstein, leader of the Home Brew Computer Club, a pioneering, computer brainstorming organization.

Except for being unanimous in their beliefs in the benefits and usefulness of computers, the 150 hackers agreed on virtually nothing else. Some thought that all software should be free and available to everyone; others argued that the software their brains had created was as much their own property as their souls.

But the important part of this historic meeting was not on what the representatives agreed or disagreed. Rather, for the first time, the leading minds of the computer revolution met to talk, plan, inspire, and challenge each other. They were finally able to see themselves as members of a community—not as isolated thinkers.

Just as the second Continental Congress was destined to lay out the blueprints for a free America, so subsequent meetings of these creative minds (and those who follow their lead) are destined to liberate the potential that computers hold for us all.

MICROPROCESSORS

A microcomputer runs under the control of a **microprocessor.** Sometimes referred to as "a computer on a chip," the microprocessor is the significant feature of a microcomputer. As a result of miniaturization of electronic circuitry, a microprocessor is a logic chip on which parts of a

FIGURE 6–7

Approximate number of microcomputers in the U.S. [Sources:
Electronics Industries Association, *Consumer Electronics:
U.S. Sales* (June 1987):14 and
USA Today (12 August 1986):
6B]

CPU (the ALU and the control unit) are placed. This small chip, along with the RAM and ROM chips (primary storage), comprise the central processor of a microcomputer. Some advanced microprocessor designs include the ALU, control unit, and primary storage all on a single chip.

Often, a microcomputer is identified by the microprocessor that controls it. Four series of microprocessors dominate the microcomputer industry: (a) Zilog Z–80; (b) MOS Technology 6502; (c) Motorola 68000; and (d) Intel. These companies introduce new microprocessors in their lines as technology advances (Table 6–2).

Zilog's Z–80 microprocessor popularity has dwindled, but the MOS Technology 6502 series has remained popular because a lot of software for the Apple II series of computers has been written for it. Intel's advanced

TABLE 6–1

Number of personal computers and software sold

	Year					
	1982	1983	1984	1985	1986	1987*
Computers sold	2,000,000	4,800,000	5,100,000	4,100,000	3,800,000	4,100,000
Software packages	—	35,000,000	40,000,000	50,000,000	65,000,000	80,000,000

Source: Electronics Industries Association, *Consumer Electronics: U.S. Sales* (June 1987): 14.
*Estimated

TABLE 6–2
Microcomputers and their microprocessors

Microcomputer	Microprocessor
Apple Macintosh	Motorola 68000
Apple Macintosh II	Motorola 68020
Apple II	MOS Technology 6502
Apple IIc	MOS Technology 65C02
Atari 520ST	Motorola 68000
AT&T UNIX PC	Motorola 68010
AT&T 6300	Intel 8086
Commodore Amiga	Motorola 68000
Compaq Deskpro 286	Intel 80286
Compaq Deskpro 386	Intel 80386
Compaq Portable Computer	Intel 8088
IBM PC AT	Intel 80286
IBM PC XT	Intel 8088
IBM PS/2 Model 80	Intel 80386
Kaypro II	Zilog Z–80A
Leading Edge Model D	Intel 8088
Tandy 1000	Intel 8088
Tandy 3000	Intel 80286
TRS–80 Model 4	Zilog Z–80A
TRS–80 Model 16	Intel 8086
Zenith Z–150	Intel 8088

FIGURE 6–8
A microprocessor embedded in the circuit board controls this microwave's functions.

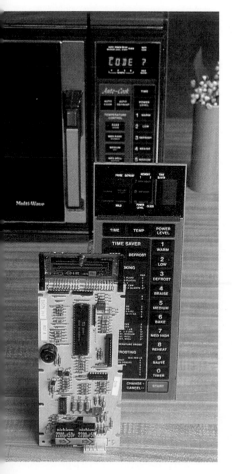

32-bit chip, Intel 80386, and other 32-bit chips such as Motorola's 68000 have brought large computer power to microcomputers.

The first microprocessor was not intended for use in a computer at all, but for use in a line of Japanese calculators. The same type of microprocessor is also found in a large array of modern automatic devices and appliances. These **embedded microprocessors** control certain functions of the devices, making them "smart." The chips are preprogrammed by the manufacturer so that the user usually does no more than turn on the device or press a button to choose a feature or function.

In microwave ovens, the embedded microprocessor controls both cooking time and temperature. All you do is set the amount of time you want the food to cook and select the temperature. The microprocessor does the rest (Figure 6–8).

In some automatic cameras, a microprocessor senses the light level at several points on the viewing screen, averages the light, and computes and sets the correct lens opening and shutter speed.

Some automobile engines use one or more microprocessor chips to monitor and control certain engine functions. The microprocessor receives information from strategically located sensors about functions such as speed, temperature, or pressure. It also controls the air and fuel mixture, injection, spark timing, and emission control to get the best engine economy and efficiency.

In offices, most modern typewriters and photocopiers contain microprocessors. The control panel on a modern copier reflects its many microprocessor-controlled functions, such as the size of reductions or enlargements, the paper feed, automatic exposure that controls the degree of contrast on the copy, and the copy counters. Most copiers even have self-diagnostics to explain problems when they are encountered (Figure 6–9).

In gasoline pumps, microprocessors measure the amount of gasoline pumped and calculate the price. Some pumps are programmed to stop when a certain dollar amount or number of gallons is reached.

Many modern toys use microprocessors. Toy robots, for example, can walk, pick up and carry items, and respond to the user's commands.

DESKTOP MICROCOMPUTERS

The typical microcomputer fits nicely on the top of a desk at home or in an office. These **desktop microcomputers** are the most common microcomputers used. They average about thirty to fifty pounds, a little too heavy and cumbersome to carry around easily, but certainly more portable than a mainframe.

At the core of a desktop computer is the main circuit board known as the **motherboard.** Mounted on this circuit board are the microprocessor, memory chips, and the chips that handle input, output, and storage. This circuit board is placed inside the system unit at the factory.

There are usually slots for adding other circuit boards or cards, e.g., a card that adds graphics capabilities, or a card that expands memory capacity.

In contrast to the Altair 8800's small memory, today's microcomputers contain memory ranging from 64K bytes to several megabytes. For example, Apple's Macintosh II has 4 megabytes of primary storage; the IBM Personal System/2 Model 40 has 1 megabyte.

FIGURE 6–9
This photocopier's functions are controlled by a microprocessor.

Musician and entertainer Steve Loren of Columbus, Ohio, uses eight pieces of computerized equipment, a microcomputer, a keyboard, and a MIDI, such as "The Box," to make his synthesized music. With this equipment, he records demonstration tapes and gives live performances as well. Loren records all the instrumental music tracks himself, stores the sounds on disk, and plays them back, as needed, during his performances. As he sings, the system provides all the background music he needs (sometimes replicating the sounds of an entire orchestra), eliminating the need for other musicians to travel with him. (Merrill Publishing/Cobalt Productions. Inset: Courtesy of Decillionix Co.)

Some companies incorporate a 32-bit microprocessor. The 32-bit Intel 80386 chip, a high-speed microprocessor, is used in the most powerful desktop computers. Introduced in late 1986 in the Compaq Deskpro 386 computer, the Intel 80386 chip created a lot of excitement. This chip provides multiprocessing capabilities, gives more speed, and accommodates more powerful programs than the 8- or 16-bit chips. Completing complex tasks, such as speech recognition and human-like decision-making functions, will become possible with microcomputers as software becomes available for them to take advantage of the 32-bit chip's power.

On the outside of a desktop computer and most all microcomputers, openings, or **ports,** allow peripheral devices such as printers or modems to be attached.

Popular desktop computers whose names you might recognize are the IBM PS/2, IBM PC XT, AT&T 6300, Kaypro II, Leading Edge Model D, Tandy 1000, Zenith Z–150, Macintosh II, Commodore Amiga, Atari 1040ST and 520ST, Epson Equity, and Apple IIc. These name brands are just a few among many desktop computers available to consumers for home use and for businesses.

SUPERMICROCOMPUTERS

Some desktop-sized, high-performance computers are called **supermicrocomputers.** They are used mainly by businesses to support a multiuser system, where a number of workstations (typically eight to thirty) are connected to the same microcomputer.

Supermicrocomputers usually contain 32-bit, high-speed microprocessors and include extensive memory. Because microprocessors are rela-

IBM introduced its PS/2 (Personal System/2) family of personal computers in 1987. (Courtesy of International Business Machines Corp.)

tively inexpensive, manufacturers build supermicrocomputers with several microprocessors, each dedicated to a specific task, such as one microprocessor per workstation to handle input and output, and one to handle all processing. Here, too, primary storage can be expanded by adding memory cards.

These fast and powerful microcomputers come close to matching the speed and power of minicomputers. In fact, the two are competing in the marketplace because of their comparatively low price and their ability to handle multiple users. To compete with a minicomputer, a supermicrocomputer must also store large amounts of data. Because large-capacity, hard-disk drives are available for microcomputers, they are the usual storage device used with supermicrocomputers.

Examples of systems that are considered to be supermicrocomputers are the IBM Personal System/2 Model 80, AT&T UNIX PC, Hewlett-Packard Vectra, and DEC's Microvax I and II.

PORTABLE MICROCOMPUTERS

For some people, such as a writer on assignment, a salesperson who types orders and sends them in by telephone communication, or a student who uses a computer on campus, the need arises for a small computer, lightweight enough to carry easily—a **portable computer.** In fact, a Hewlett-Packard portable computer supplied data to the hundreds of journalists covering the 1986 Wimbledon tennis tournament.

"Transportable" computers are microcomputers that are lightweight enough to move, but still need an external power supply. The truly portables, those small enough to be carried around easily, use either replaceable or rechargeable batteries. Some have the option, though, of using either electrical current or batteries.

Most portables use microprocessors as powerful as those found in a full-sized (desktop) microcomputer.

(a) The Compaq Deskpro 386 was the first of a new generation of personal computers in 1986 to use the powerful (b) Intel 80386 microprocessor. [(a) Courtesy of Compaq Computer Corp. (b) Courtesy of Intel Corp.]

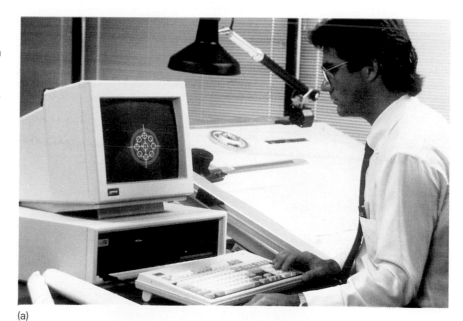

(a)

(b)

The Macintosh II GS computer appeared in 1987 with dazzling color graphics and the computational power of machines three times the price.

FIGURE 6–10
Laptop computers are convenient for salespeople who have to make client contacts either in person or by telephone. This salesman is able to give his client current prices which are stored in the computer and to key in the client's order as it is placed.

Although features and costs vary from computer to computer, some portables have the same full range of features as a desktop computer. The display screens are generally smaller to save space, but most can display twenty-five lines of text. One disk drive is usually standard, but sometimes even hard-disk drives and expansion slots are available where other peripheral devices can be added.

Prices range from approximately $1,000 to $5,000, and they weigh from ten to thirty pounds. Many portables are about the size of a suitcase, but they are becoming even smaller and can be further categorized as laptop computers, handheld computers, and sizes in between.

Laptop Computers

Laptop computers, sometimes called briefcase computers, can be used on your lap and are very portable (Figure 6–10). Some models, such as the Radio Shack Model 100 and the NEC 8201, cost under $500 and weigh about four pounds. Others weigh more: the IBM PC Convertible weighs thirteen pounds; and Toshiba's T3100 weighs fifteen pounds. Like desktop microcomputers, laptop computers have a full typewriter keyboard. Even these laptops come close to or equal the primary storage of some desktop models. Primary storage ranges from 64K bytes to several megabytes, and most are IBM PC compatible. The display screen typically has several lines of display on a flat, liquid crystal display (LCD) screen. Some laptops, such as the Toshiba T3100, now have the advanced gas plasma display screens, which provide greater contrast and clearer images than LCD screens.

Most laptop computers have a built-in modem or serial interface so the user can send data to or receive data from a larger computer. Some have built-in software packages (such as word processors) and built-in tape or disk drives. Back at the office, laptops can be connected to larger peripherals—a regular size printer or a larger monitor, for example.

The manageable size enables business people to work while traveling on a commuter train or journalists to file stories from the field. IRS auditors using Zenith–171 laptops perform audits at the taxpayer's location. Today, a business traveler sitting in an airport working with a laptop computer while waiting for a flight is a common sight. When the flight is announced, the person slips the computer into the case with a few disks and papers, and later places the case under the seat in the airplane. Some airlines permit passengers to use laptops during flights.

Handheld Computers

Although rather small and usually with only one line of LCD display, **handheld computers** have a full keyboard and sometimes include a built-in printer. The cost ranges from $200 to $1,000 (Figure 6–11).

Handheld computers have been around since 1981 when Radio Shack introduced one about the size of a small book; it weighed only seven ounces.

The handheld size is particularly appropriate for people such as engineers or repair and maintenance personnel, who work on location. Marquette Electronics, Inc., a manufacturer of high-tech computerized electrocardiogram equipment, supplies its service technicians with handheld computers to compile and transmit service call reports. Instead of handwriting and mailing work orders to headquarters each day, the technicians file the reports by computer. Each technician includes data such as his or

FIGURE 6–11
Here, a pocket computer is being used to design new pricing strategies for service station dealers. (Courtesy of Chevron Corp.)

This student takes a portable computer to the library to make research notes. Back at her room, she will organize the notes, prepare a rough draft, revise the text, and then print a final copy for her class assignment.

her identification number, expenses incurred, customer's account number, part numbers, and quantities used on the service call.

Table 6–3 compares several sizes of microcomputers.

THE PROBLEM OF COMPATIBILITY

One major problem that affects the microcomputer industry, and users too, is the lack of compatibility of equipment and software among manufacturers. **Compatibility** is the capability of hardware and software from one computer to work with another computer.

The disk size varies from computer to computer. For example, the Apple Macintosh uses a $3\frac{1}{2}$-inch disk enclosed in hard plastic, but other Apple microcomputers use a standard $5\frac{1}{4}$-inch floppy disk. Using the same size floppy disk does not guarantee compatibility. A program designed to work with a particular microprocessor and with a particular operating system will run *only* under those conditions.

Even disk drives, printers, and software applications are designed to operate with specific computers.

TABLE 6–3
Comparison of microcomputers

	Supermicrocomputer	Desktop	Typical Portable	Laptop	Handheld
Price range	$7,000–$10,000	$300–$6,000	$1,000–$5,000	$500–$3,000	$200–$1,000
Size	Desktop	Desktop	Suitcase	Briefcase	Book or pocket
Weight	30–70 lbs.	30–50 lbs.	10–30 lbs.	4–15 lbs.	Several ounces
Display screen	25 lines	25 lines	25 lines	8–25 lines	One line
Processor	16-, 32-bit	8-, 16-, 32-bit	8-, 16-, 32-bit	8-, 16-bit	8-, 16-bit
Power source	External	External	Battery/external	Battery/external	Battery/external

THE SOURCE OF HANDS

When more than 5 million people lined up May 25, 1986, to hold hands for the record-breaking Hands Across America fund-raising event, it seemed to be a very basic and technically simple effort. But it wasn't. To get that many people together in the right place at the right time and to collect the $10 minimum fee each of them pledged to pay were challenges that required the technical assistance of a lot of computers.

To help the organizers succeed, The Source information service set up and donated a private communication network. Messages were sent between the regional offices that organized each link of the 4,152-mile human chain between New York and Los Angeles. The system also enabled the national planners to place group messages to regional planners on an electronic bulletin board.

Computer owners who subscribed to The Source were allowed to sign up for Hands Across America by typing "HAA" on their personal computers. Then The Source would take the subscribers' pledges and make a note of where in line they preferred to stand. This information was then sent to national headquarters to keep an ongoing estimate of donation totals and to see in advance where the line would have too few or too many people.

While the line was not an unbroken one, millions of dollars were raised to fight hunger—thanks, in large part, to the unseen computers behind the hands.

For a consumer, this means that links from one computer to another to exchange data, or to share equipment or data in a network, can occur only when the hardware and software of the two computers are compatible. A lot of planning needs to go into the purchase of a system, its peripheral equipment, and software.

Because the IBM PC was, for a time, the most popular desktop microcomputer, many other microcomputer makers introduced versions of an IBM PC compatible. These machines are compatible in varying degrees; they run IBM PC software and work with other IBM PC peripherals. Manufacturers also make portables compatible with the IBM PC. Compatibles generally use the same microprocessors as the IBM PC/XT/AT series (Intel 8088/80286) and the same operating system (Microsoft Corporation's MS DOS or PC DOS).

IBM PC software and hardware are not, however, always compatible with the clone and vice versa. Some software can be used on the IBM PC and its clone because that software is designed to run on the same operating system. Other IBM-designed software is not interchangeable because of differences in portions of the operating system that reside in ROM [the

ROM-Basic Input Output System (ROM-BIOS)]. This portion of the operating system is built into the computer. It is protected by copyright laws, and IBM has chosen not to make it available to other manufacturers. However, software developers such as Phoenix Software Associates, Limited, have designed a ROM-BIOS that is nearly 100 percent compatible and have made this available to the IBM PC-compatible manufacturers.

Some peripherals or other hardware that claim that they are compatible actually need modification before they will work.

One way the computer industry is helping consumers handle the compatibility problem is with the insertion of a second microprocessor on a plug-in board. This board lets the system switch between the two microprocessors, permitting software designed for both as well as their respective operating systems to be run.

Another way compatibility problems are being addressed is with the creation of industry standards. Various organizations are making recommendations for standardization of hardware and software. Standard interfaces and data formats for input and output devices, as well as standards for programming languages, would go a long way toward alleviating some of these problems.

With the advent of the first microprocessor and the first microcomputer, technological changes have occurred very rapidly. The development of the powerful 32-bit processor, which allows microcomputers to be compared to minicomputers with regard to their capabilities, may herald the dawning of a "second generation" of microcomputers.

SUMMARY

The development of the microprocessor ushered in a new generation of computer technology, making the invention of the microcomputer possible.

A microcomputer, sometimes called a personal computer, is the smallest, least expensive computer. Its capabilities are nearing the proportions of large computers.

Several items comprise a basic microcomputer system: system unit, keyboard, disk drive(s), monitor, connecting cables, and software. Other items that are often needed include modem, printer, and serial and parallel interfaces. A multiuser microcomputer system is one in which several terminals are connected to a single powerful microcomputer.

Microcomputers have become popular because they are useful, inexpensive, easy to use, and offer something for almost everyone.

The introduction of the Apple II spurred the microcomputer industry on and moved microcomputers into our homes, schools, and businesses. The industry received an even greater boost when IBM presented its version of the microcomputer.

Today, there are many imitations (clones) of the IBM PC. An owner of one of the IBM PC compatible machines can use equipment and software originally intended for the IBM PC.

A microprocessor, sometimes called a "computer on a chip," is a logic chip on which parts of a CPU are placed. Microprocessors are used not only in computers, but also in electronic devices and appliances that are not computers themselves. You can find these embedded microprocessors in automobile engines, photocopiers, electronic typewriters, and many appliances.

Desktop computers are the most common type of microcomputer; they weigh about thirty to fifty pounds and are small enough to fit on a desk. Some businesses use very powerful desktop-sized supermicrocomputers, which have almost as many capabilities as minicomputers.

There are various sizes of portable computers, the small microcomputers that are lightweight enough to be carried from place to place. Some portables weigh as much as thirty pounds, but some laptop computers weigh as little as ten pounds; handheld computers weigh only several ounces.

Portable computers have similar, but sometimes smaller, components as desktop computers. However, many portables are as powerful as desktops and can be connected to large peripheral devices, such as a standard monitor or printer.

Compatibility of equipment and software from one computer to another has always been a problem for users. New hardware developments and the creation of hardware and software standards are helping to relieve the problem.

Key Terms

compatibility (p. 184)

desktop computer (p. 178)

embedded microprocessor (p. 177)

handheld computer (p. 183)

IBM PC compatible (p. 174)

laptop computer (p. 182)

microcomputer (p. 168)

microcomputer system (p. 169)

microprocessor (p. 175)

motherboard (p. 178)

multiuser microcomputer system (p. 171)

personal computer (p. 169)

portable computer (p. 180)

ports (p. 179)

supermicrocomputer (p. 179)

Review Questions

1. So many technological changes occurred after 1975 that the period is sometimes called the _____.

2. The first typical use of microcomputers in homes was _____.

3. Why are microcomputers sometimes called personal computers?

4. List the basic components of a typical microcomputer system.

5. True or False: Microcomputer systems cannot be used in situations where more than one user is connected and has access.

6. Microcomputers are easy to use because of the availability of pre-packaged ＿＿＿＿＿＿＿.

7. Which two men introduced the Apple II and are attributed with making computers user-friendly?

8. Microprocessors were originally developed to be used in a line of ＿＿＿＿＿＿＿.

9. Describe the features of a microprocessor.

10. What are some devices or appliances with embedded microprocessors? Give examples of their functions.

11. True or False: Microprocessors in appliances are preprogrammed at the factory before installation.

12. With regard to size and cost, how does a microcomputer compare to other computers?

13. True or False: The typical desktop microcomputer is very portable.

14. What is a motherboard and where is it found?

15. A(n) ＿＿＿＿＿＿＿ is a very powerful desktop microcomputer.

16. A(n) ＿＿＿＿＿＿＿ -bit chip is used in the most powerful desktop computers.

17. Any computer that is small and lightweight enough to be easily carried or moved around is a(n) ＿＿＿＿＿＿＿ computer.

18. Describe a laptop computer. What are some typical uses?

19. The ＿＿＿＿＿＿＿ is even smaller than a laptop computer.

20. Describe the first microcomputer available to consumers.

21. Explain why microcomputers have become so popular in the U.S.

22. How are supermicrocomputers and minicomputers used similarly?

23. Describe the problem of compatibility as it relates to microcomputers. How is this problem being addressed?

24. Relate some of the key events in the development of the microcomputer industry beginning with the invention of the microprocessor.

25. What is the main difference between a typical microcomputer system and a multiuser microcomputer system?

INFOMODULE
A Buyer's Guide

Buying a microcomputer system can be a fun and exciting experience for some people. For others, it can be a difficult and unpleasant chore. There are hundreds of computers and thousands of ready-to-use programs from which to choose. Where do you begin? Without prior experience, you might feel lost amid that huge array of products.

Regardless of where you will use the system, some preparation and homework on hardware and software will ensure that you get what you need. It will also ensure that after the purchase, your computer doesn't sit idle because it doesn't do what was expected after all.

PREPARATION

Become computer literate. By the time you've finished this course, you will know many of the computer's capabilities and have ideas of what it might do for you. You'll know the names of the components that comprise a typical system, major applications, and how to run some software. You may even learn how to do some programming in the BASIC or Pascal languages.

Determine what you want a computer to do for you. This decision is the first and probably most important one to make before shopping. You cannot evaluate the various computers or the software if your goals aren't clear.

Perhaps you want a computer to do two or more different tasks. Which one is the most important? For example, if word processing business letters will be the computer's primary function, then a quality printer is an important consideration. If large spreadsheet calculations are its main task, then large primary storage is important.

Because hardware and software work together and because all software won't run on all computers, coordinate the software purchase with the computer purchase. Investigate and select the software first, then choose the hardware. If you are planning to program in a specific computer language, make sure that language is available on the computer you choose.

SELECTING AND EVALUATING SOFTWARE

There is an astounding array of **application packages** (programs designed for a specific task) from which to choose. For example, for the IBM PC, its clones, and the Apple IIe and IIc, over 100,000 commercial programs are available. Here are some guidelines to help you make informed choices.

Make sure the software is available for the tasks you have decided upon (and for your computer if you already own one). The software that perfectly fits your task may not be available for a computer you have in mind. Read software reviews in trade magazines, home-computing magazines, and software directories. Visit computer stores, contact people who are using the software, and ask friends who have computers to see if they recommend certain packages for your job. Other users can often tell you about helpful features and limitations of packages with which they've had experience.

Know what operating system controls your computer. The software you buy must be able to run on that operating system.

Decide how much money you want to spend. At this point, the cost of the package sometimes becomes a determining factor for

---

Preparation

- Become computer literate
- Decide on tasks
- Select software first
- Coordinate hardware and software

many consumers. Determine if the package requires the purchase of additional hardware or software to use it.

Examine the specific features of the package.
Make sure they are the ones you need. If possible, ask to see the package demonstrated with your data to make sure that it can do all you need it to. Keep in mind that the most expensive and feature-loaded package may not be the best for you. Most users need only a portion of the features offered. You may pay for more than you need.

Determine if the package will be easy to learn and use.
Are the commands, especially the ones you'll use most often, simple to use and remember? Is the display screen clear and easy to read? Does the program have a menu orientation, a command orientation, or a combination of both?

Most novices prefer a program with a **menu orientation,** which is easier to learn because it displays the choices and options in lists (menu form) on the screen. A **command orientation** requires that you either refer to a manual or memorize the choices and their corresponding keystrokes. This process may be more difficult for some people to learn. A more experienced user may prefer it, however, because it can be faster and less cumbersome once the commands have been memorized. These shorter, cryptic commands without menus also allow for a smaller program that executes faster and takes up less RAM.

Examine the written and graphic descriptions for the software, known as **documentation.**
Make sure that they are clear, accurate, and complete. This can be difficult to determine at first, especially if you have never used computers and application software. Notice if the package has appropriate ''help'' manuals or hints and instructions that appear on the computer screen when requested. These aids are valuable tools that assist you in learning and using the package.

Determine the amount of support or assistance you will receive from the vendor or developer in troubleshooting or solving problems you might have.
Who will supply the support—the dealer or the manufacturer? Many vendors charge fees for support because of the high cost of maintaining the personnel and facilities to answer questions. User groups in your area are also a good source of information if you have questions.

Compare cost to value received.
In the past, a higher price usually meant one or more of the following: greater capability; better documentation and support; and greater flexibility. Today, it's not so clear. A number of programs with lower price tags are every bit as good as some higher-priced programs.

Program flexibility.
Can the package be adapted to a wide variety of situations and hardware configurations? If you already have a system, will the package run on it?

Many programs require large amounts of RAM to operate. Generally, to operate a program most efficiently, you'll want to have more than the minimum required RAM. Some programs only work with certain printers or plotters; make sure that the package you choose is compatible with equipment you already have.

Ability to upgrade the package.
Does the manufacturer revise and upgrade the program to incorporate the latest technology and advances in programming techniques? If so, will the manufacturer provide the new program to you? Are old files then compatible with new versions of the program? What are the pricing policies of new versions for owners of previous versions? If it is a new program in its first version, check the credibility of the company on its other products (if there are any).

Careful evaluation and selection of the application packages ensure enjoyable and productive operation of your computer and effective use of the money spent. Table 1 is a checklist of criteria to be considered when selecting new software.

TABLE 1
Software buyer's checklist

Tasks planned:
1. _____
2. _____
3. _____
4. _____

Name of supplier:
Retail _____
Mail-order house _____
Public domain/shareware _____

Name of package _____

Operating system required _____

RAM required _____

User orientation:
Menu _____
Command _____
Combination _____

Additional hardware or software needed _____

Features available _____

Quality of documentation _____

Vendor support _____

Return policy _____

Warranty _____

Flexibility _____

Ability to upgrade the package _____

Price:
Package _____
Shipping, tax, etc. _____

Comparison of cost to value received _____

SELECTING A MICROCOMPUTER

You have decided what you want the computer to do, and you may have made a final selection on the programs you need for your applications. Now look at some computers.

Decide how much money you want to spend. Computer prices vary greatly. If you cannot afford an elaborate system now, perhaps some of the components could be added later. Be sure to ask which components are included in the price quoted. Sometimes the price tag includes only the basic computer; at other times the monitor, printer, and other peripherals are included in the price.

Look at the equipment that is available. Table 2 lists some manufacturers that make microcomputers. Talk to friends or associates who already use or own computers for their recommendations. Often, they'll be able to tell you about the limitations of a particular computer as well as the good features. Read reviews of computers and other hardware in computer magazines or newspapers.

TABLE 2
Popular microcomputer manufacturers

Apple	Epson	Sony
AT&T	Hewlett-Packard	Tandy (Radio Shack)
Atari	IBM	Wang
Commodore	Leading Edge	Xerox
Compaq	NEC	Zenith
DEC	North Star	

Check the primary storage (RAM) capacity of the system. Does the system have enough storage to run the software you have selected? The software package usually indicates the minimum amount of memory needed to use it. You'll probably want more than the minimum memory because larger memory capacity lets more or all of the program and your data reside in primary storage, thereby allowing the program to work faster.

Make sure the system can be expanded later. As you use your computer, you will probably find other applications for it and want to add that capability. You might want to run larger programs later—programs that demand more RAM. Can primary storage of the system you've selected be expanded? How many ports and expansion slots are there to accommodate more memory and peripherals? Can more disk drives be added? Can a hard-disk drive be added? Can you add graphics capabilities? If you can't anticipate future needs, at least know just how much the system can be expanded so that you won't be disappointed later.

Look at the documentation provided with the system. Read some or all of it. Reference manuals and user's manuals should be clearly written, illustrated, and easy to understand. Some vendors offer classes in the use of the hardware and software packages they sell.

Decide specifically which hardware features you'll need. Will you need a color monitor to run color graphics? Or, will monochrome do? Do you prefer the amber screen characters or green? The type of printer selected depends on the printed matter. If you are printing business letters, for example, letter-quality (typewriter

quality) print may be needed. If you create rough drafts or print very little, a cheaper, dot-matrix printer will suffice. You will need a fast printer if you have many pages or letters to print.

Test the equipment or ask for a demonstration. Once you sit at the computer, you might find that you prefer one computer over another. Try out the keyboards. Perhaps one keyboard is more comfortable for you than another. You may even find that one type of monitor is preferable over another.

Determine the level of service and maintenance the vendor provides. It might be important to know that someone at the store is willing to answer questions if you get home and something does not work.

Learn about the company's service contract. Some companies offer service agreements that cover repairs after the warranty period has ended. These agreements cover a specified time period—usually one year—and include repairs on certain parts and equipment. Investigate the prices for this service. It may seem expensive to pay the lump sum cost, but that choice may cover all repairs. Or, you can choose to pay for any repairs yourself and hope that the total amount required ends up being less than you would have paid for the service agreement. Table 3 is a checklist of criteria to be considered when shopping for a microcomputer system.

WARRANTIES

Become familiar with the warranty. Before you buy anything or sign any documents, read the sales order, and anything else you are asked to sign, front and back.

TABLE 3
Microcomputer buyer's checklist

Tasks planned:

  1. _____

  2. _____

  3. _____

  4. _____

Select the software _____

Microprocessor:

  8 bit _____

  16 bit _____

  32 bit _____

Amount of RAM _____

Hard-disk capacity _____

Disk drives included _____

Monitor:

  40 or 80 columns _____

  Color: Composite _____

       RBG _____

  Monochrome: White _____

          Amber _____

          Green _____

Printer:

  Tractor/single sheet feed _____

  Daisy-wheel/dot-matrix/laser _____

  Carriage _____

    Width: 80 columns, 132 columns _____

    Bidirectional printing _____

Quality of documentation _____

Name of vendor:

  Mail-order house _____

  General discount/department store _____

  Retail computer store _____

Vendor support _____

Maintenance _____

Service contract _____

Warranty _____

Price:

  System (includes which components) _____

  Other charges (shipping, tax, etc.) _____

A computer warranty states what rights you have and the degree to which the company is liable for repairs. It covers repairs during a set period of time (the warranty period) unless the damage results from improper handling, abuse, or accident. Some warranties are automatically voided if anyone other than an authorized technician repairs the equipment. Most companies guarantee hardware for ninety days. Check carefully, however; you may have as much as eighteen months of protection. Software and disks are usually not covered in that agreement.

Legal experts have established a set of guidelines, the Uniform Commercial Code, relating to commercial transactions that provide some protection to the consumer. Article II of this code has been accepted and adopted as law in all states in the U.S. except Louisiana. Article II basically grants certain **implied warranties** on goods (not services) sold (not leased). These laws imply that the computer (goods sold) is merchantable, i.e., reasonably fit and of average quality. However, some companies' printed sales agreements try to disclaim merchantability.

If you have already signed an agreement, you may have forfeited or waived some rights; however, all is not lost. **Express warranties** may have been created during the sale's negotiations. An express warranty can be based on a salesperson's claims for the product. Document these claims by taking notes—sales personnel names, dates, and specific promises or claims. Also, check any advertisements or brochures where promises or guarantees of performance may have been made.

If problems arise in getting repairs made, negotiate with the company to the best of your ability. If that discussion brings no equitable settlement, you should contact an attorney to find out about other alternatives available to you.

Software warranties rarely make promises that the software will work as described or do all that the advertising claims; usually you buy software "as is." However, there are guarantees against physical defects of the tape or disk itself. Although many programs have been on the market long enough to have a good track record of reliability and workability, sometimes software is rushed into the marketplace before it is fully tested. At other times, software is released, and the users find the problems and report them to the company. Eventually, the company comes out with a new, corrected version. These facts are all the more reason to read those reviews and get recommendations from reliable sources.

USER GROUPS

After you've become a microcomputer owner, you might want to contact a **user group,** an informal organization of owners of microcomputers like yours.

People in these organizations exchange information about hardware and software and help each other find solutions to problems they encounter. Often, members share programs they have written.

A user group is a valuable resource when you are planning to buy another piece of equipment or a new software package. More than likely, someone in the group will have used that item and can give you inside information about it.

Ask your computer dealer for the name of the contact person for a local user group. Sometimes, the name and address of a national user group is included in the package with your new computer.

COMPUTER MAGAZINES

Dozens of magazines at the local newsstand are written for microcomputer users. They contain reviews of software packages, descriptions of the latest technological advances, critiques of the latest hardware, and many ideas for new ways to use your computer (Figure 1).

Some magazines include prewritten programs that are printed and free for anyone to use. Columns and special features of interest appear in each issue. Many magazines present ideas and information from other readers on how they use their computers.

There are even magazines for specific computers and for specific concerns. Some publica-

FIGURE 1
This display shows the variety
of computer-related publications
available to consumers.

tions are more technical than others. Here is a
list of the more popular magazines:

- ☐ *Family Computing*—monthly ⎫
- ☐ *Personal Computing*—monthly ⎬ General
- ☐ *Byte*—monthly ⎫
- ☐ *PC World*—monthly ⎪ More
- ☐ *PC Magazine*—biweekly ⎬ technical
- ☐ *Macworld*—monthly ⎭
- ☐ *Computerworld*—weekly ⎫ Industry
- ☐ *InfoWorld*—weekly ⎬ news

WHERE TO SHOP

Buyers can make their software purchases at
different locations—retail computer stores,
mail-order houses, general discount and department stores, or special discount software
stores. Users can also acquire public domain
software and shareware programs. Hardware
buyers can shop at retail computer stores, mail-
order houses, and general discount and department stores.

Retail Stores

Microcomputers and software can be purchased
at local, general discount stores such as K-Mart
and at most large department stores. Radio

Shack sells its own line of computers; computer
retail chains such as Entré and ComputerLand
specialize in computers. ComputerLand, which
has over 800 stores, sells many name brands
and models, peripheral devices, software, computer supplies, and even books and periodicals
relating to computers (Figure 2).

Here are some advantages to buying your
computer at a computer store:

1. Computer stores usually provide the most
   service and support. They are usually willing
   and able to answer questions or help solve
   any problems you encounter in using your
   new equipment.
2. Some have repair centers right in the store.
   If not, they will send the computer to service
   centers if a repair is needed.
3. You can examine what you are buying, get a
   demonstration, and even try the computer
   out.

A major disadvantage is that you will probably
pay more.

Software can be purchased at computer
stores, also. Advantages include

1. Computer stores often provide the name of a
   contact person to answer questions and help
   troubleshoot.
2. You can get a demonstration in the store.

FIGURE 2
Micro Center is one of many retail computer stores across the nation.

Disadvantages include

1. A software selection that is not extremely large (they usually stock only the best-selling programs)
2. Fewer discounts, unless you are also buying equipment

For software purchases, a good alternative to the computer store is a specialized software discount store. For example, Egghead Discount Software has forty stores in the Pacific Northwest, California, and Chicago. These stores stock almost every kind of software imaginable and sell at discount prices.

Mail-order Houses

Another option when purchasing hardware or software is to order by mail. There are plenty of advertisements in magazines offering lower-priced computers and software. Some of the products are brand-name computers; you may not recognize the names of others. Ordering computers and software by mail is part of a major trend in this country of buying consumer products by mail.

The advantage to buying by mail is the lower price—sometimes 15–50 percent below store prices. Some disadvantages are

1. You don't get the customer service and support that you would in a computer store.
2. You can't see what you are getting or get a demonstration. (If you don't know exactly what you want or understand the description of the equipment or software, you may be surprised when the package arrives.)

It is usually less risky to buy software, computer accessories, and supplies by mail order than it is to buy a computer. Here are a few tips when ordering hardware or software by mail:

☐ Check the reputation of the company selling the computer or the software. Consult a reputable computer magazine for articles and suggestions. Most magazines will not run an ad from a company with a bad reputation. Contact your local Better Business Bureau; they have records on mail-order companies that have given consumers problems. Call the company if you need to find the answers to questions the advertisement doesn't answer. Often, the cooperation you receive from people over the phone is an indication of what to expect if problems develop. If they respond with "we just take orders," and cannot direct you to anyone who can answer your questions, beware. Reliable companies often offer a free trial period, a money-back guarantee, and provide you with a toll-free telephone number to call in the event a problem arises.

☐ If it's your first time ordering from a particular mail-order house, place a small order to see if service is good.

☐ Ask the company how long it will take for the order to be shipped. Usually the wait is

---

Acquiring Hardware

■ Computer stores
■ General discount and department stores
■ Mail-order houses

a week or more. If orders are backlogged (for example, during certain seasons), it might take four to six weeks.

☐ Ask what the price of a computer system includes. Sometimes the price listed does not include the disk drive, printer, or other peripherals.

☐ Ask about their policy and procedures if something does not work properly. What kind of warranty is provided? Is it a manufacturer's warranty or does the mail-order house offer its own warranty?

☐ Consider the delay in repair time and the time involved in shipping the equipment back and forth. You will be without your computer for that period. Usually, you will have to pay the shipping cost if an item is returned for repairs. You might want to take the machine to a local repair center.

Other Low-cost Sources of Software

Literally thousands of public domain software and shareware programs are available to users free or for prices up to $100.

Public domain programs, or freeware, are those that are not copy-protected or copyrighted and are made available by their authors for anyone to use. The Boston Computer Society, among other user groups, is a good source of free programs, programs that cost a few dollars, or programs for which you are charged just for the cost of the disk and mailing. Some information services such as CompuServe offer their subscribers public domain programs in just about any category.

Shareware programs are available for anyone to use free, but authors request that you send a donation if you have found their particular program useful. Quicksoft in Seattle, Washington, and Buttonware in Bellevue, Washington, are two shareware companies.

The advantages of acquiring software this way are

1. Its low cost
2. The possibility of experimenting with different types of programs

> **Acquiring Software**
>
> - Computer stores
> - General discount and department stores
> - Special discount software stores
> - Mail-order houses
> - Public domain programs and shareware

The disadvantages are

1. The programs are not name-brand software and thus may not be widely used, thereby limiting the number of other users who can exchange information and ideas about using the product.
2. If you have problems with the software, you may not have access to the authors to answer your questions or help you troubleshoot.

KEY TERMS

application package (p. 189)

command orientation (p. 190)

documentation (p. 190)

express warranty (p. 194)

implied warranty (p. 194)

menu orientation (p. 190)

public domain programs (p. 197)

shareware (p. 197)

user group (p. 194)

QUESTIONS

1. How can a consumer prepare to make an informed decision before shopping for and evaluating software or hardware?
2. What is the purpose of user groups?
3. List several popular computer magazines.
4. What are the advantages of buying a computer at a computer store?
5. Compare public domain software, shareware, and the software found in a retail store.

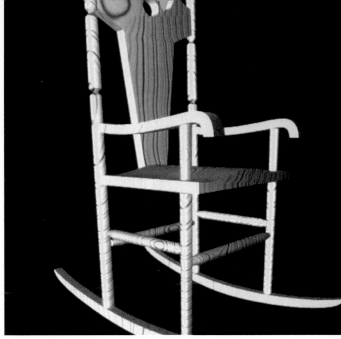

OBJECTIVES

☐ Define data communication and describe several applications

☐ Explain the differences between analog and digital data transmissions and describe the process of converting one to the other

☐ Describe a communication channel and discuss the three basic types

☐ Describe two ways in which communication channels are configured

☐ Identify factors that determine the speed at which data are transmitted through a communication channel

☐ Name and describe the three modes of data transfer

OUTLINE

DATA COMMUNICATION
    Analog and Digital Data Transmissions
    Modulation, Demodulation, and Modems

COMMUNICATION CHANNELS
    Channel Configurations
    Channel Sharing
    Front-end Processors
    Common Carriers

RATE OF DATA TRANSMISSION
    Communication Channel Bandwidths
    Asynchronous and Synchronous Transmissions

MODES OF TRANSMISSION

MICRO-TO-MICRO LINK

MICRO-TO-MAINFRAME LINK

COMMUNICATION CHALLENGES

DATA COMMUNICATION AT WORK

INFOMODULE: Networks and Distributed Data Processing

LOCAL-AREA NETWORKS

WIDE-AREA NETWORKS

NETWORK TOPOLOGY
    Star Network
    Ring Network
    Tree Network
    Bus Network

DISTRIBUTED DATA PROCESSING

7

Communication and the Computer

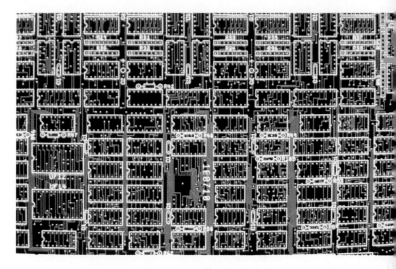

PROFILE: Andrew Fluegelman

A lawyer by training, an editor by profession, and a professional baseball fan by day and night, Andrew Fluegelman left several bright marks on the computer world before his death at age forty-one.

Fluegelman made his first major contribution in the field of data communication when he wrote his own computer program to transfer files between his IBM PC and an acquaintance's North Star computer. The program worked so well that friends and colleagues suggested he publish it.

Because he was familiar with the software publishing process, Fluegelman had some reservations about putting his own program through it. Instead of following this traditional route, which he had little patience for, he wanted to try a new way of getting the program out to users—a way that would retain the excitement then being felt about the many promises of computers. The standard way of publishing a program involved the insertion of an element that prevented the software from being copied. However, all the elements being used at that time for copy protection were easily broken, and he did not have the technical skill to create a better form of protection.

After watching a local public television station carry on its fundraising drive, Fluegelman decided that he would develop the concept of "user-supported software," similar to the TV station's viewer-supported programming. Thus, he began encouraging people to copy the PC Talk program and to send him a voluntary contribution of $35 for each copy. He referred to this software as "freeware."

A graduate of Yale Law School, Fluegelman practiced law for five years before turning to book publishing. His new profession made it necessary for him to learn such skills as publishing, distribution, and advertising—all of which he was able to use when he developed and marketed his own software.

Fluegelman also became a gifted writer and editor near the end of his life. He coauthored the book *Writing in the Computer Age* and served as editor-in-chief of *PC World* and *Macworld*.

Throughout his life, Fluegelman took great delight in baseball, particularly in the fortunes of the San Francisco Giants. He once told a friend that if he ever became disabled, wheeling him out to the ballpark would restore his happiness.

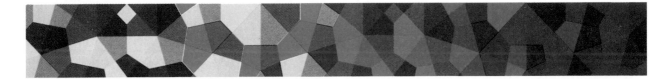

I n the previous two chapters you were introduced to the different classes of computers—supercomputers, mainframes, minicomputers, and microcomputers. These computers offer a wide range of computing power. If more computing power is needed, however, one way to get it is to buy a larger system. That's fine if you have the money and necessary facilities, but many individuals and businesses simply can't afford to purchase a larger system.

Another problem arises for corporations and others who are geographically dispersed. They may need to send data to, or use the same data at, many different locations. One answer to this problem is to keep separate files of the data at each location, but this method can be a costly and potentially dangerous solution. It is expensive to maintain these redundant data files and difficult to ensure the continuing accuracy of data at any one location.

What then are the answers to these problems? The solutions to both the need for more power and the ability to exchange and share data are found in data communication technology.

DATA COMMUNICATION

Data communication is the process of electronically sending data from one point to another. Linking one computer to another permits the power and resources of that computer to be tapped. It also makes possible the sharing and updating of data at different locations.

Computers that are physically located close to each other, either in the same room or building, can communicate data through a direct-cable link. Computers located far apart use a special form of data communication—telecommunication. The process of using communication facilities such as the telephone system and microwave relays to send data between computers is a form of data communication sometimes referred to as **telecommunication**, or teleprocessing.

**Forms of Data
Transmission**

- Analog
- Digital

Analog and Digital Data Transmissions

The two forms of data transmission are analog and digital. **Analog data transmission** is the transmission of data in a continuous waveform (Figure 7–1a). The telephone system is an example of a system designed for analog data transmission.

Digital data transmission is the transmission of data using distinct on and off electrical states (Figure 7–1b). Recall from Chapter 2 that data in digital form are represented as either on (1) or off (0). Because the computer "understands" and works in digital form, and because digital data communication is faster and more efficient than analog, it would seem that all data communication between computers would be in digital form; however, that is not the case. Totally digital is possible; however, the telephone system, an analog system, is used for a great percentage of data communication because it is the largest and most widely used communication system in place. Because of the expense involved in converting to a digital system or running a duplicate digital system, a method was devised allowing the digital data to be transmitted over telephone lines. The process is called modulation-demodulation.

Modulation, Demodulation, and Modems

Data in a computer are formatted as digital signals. However, because telephone lines were designed to transmit the human voice, they format data as analog signals. For communication between computers to take place over a telephone line, the digital signal must be converted to an analog signal before it is transmitted. After its journey over the telephone lines, the analog signal must then be reconverted back to a digital signal so that it can be used by the receiving computer. The process of converting a digital signal to an analog signal is called **modulation** (Figure 7–2a). **Demodulation** is the process of reconverting the analog signal back to a digital signal (Figure 7–2b). The device that accomplishes both of these processes is a **modem**, short for *mo*dulator-*dem*odulator.

FIGURE 7–1
Analog and digital data transmissions

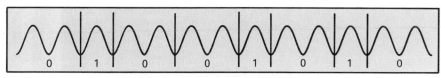

(a) Analog data transmission

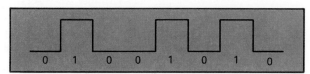

(b) Digital data transmission

FIGURE 7–2
Modulation is the conversion of a digital signal to an analog signal. Demodulation is the conversion of an analog signal to a digital signal.

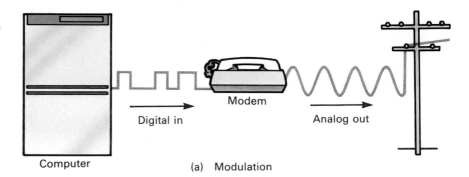

(a) Modulation

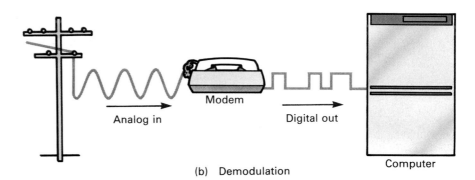

(b) Demodulation

The three basic types of modems used in microcomputers are: acoustic; external direct-connect; and internal direct-connect. The **acoustic modem**, or acoustic coupler as it is sometimes called, has two cups into which the handset of your telephone is placed (Figure 7–3). The acoustic modem sends data through the mouthpiece and receives data through the earpiece of the handset. This type of modem is not used very often today because: (a) the signal is much more susceptible to distortion than with other types of modems; and (b) the carbon microphones used in a telephone handset limit the rate of data transmission.

An **external direct-connect modem** is external to the computer and connects directly to the telephone line with a modular phone jack (Figure 7–4). The direct connection greatly reduces the signal's distortion and permits faster data transfer rates. A popular external direct-connect modem is the Hayes Smartmodem. Most external direct-connect modems have a variety of features not found on acoustic modems, including the ability to:

- ☐ Check the operating status using status lights and speakers
- ☐ Change the speed at which data are transmitted
- ☐ Dial and answer the phone automatically
- ☐ Respond to commands from a communication program
- ☐ Self-test to verify the modem's ability to correctly transmit data

Because the specialized circuitry in these modems allows them (rather than the computer) to perform these and other functions, they are often called "smart" or "intelligent" devices.

FIGURE 7–3

An operator uses an acoustic modem to send data over telephone lines to another computer. (Photo courtesy of Hewlett-Packard Co.)

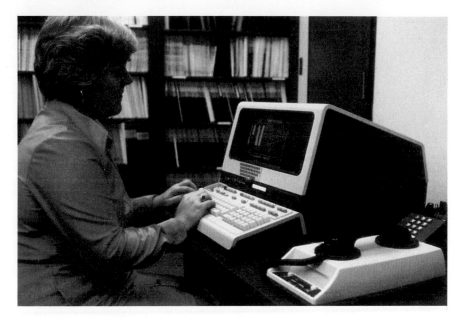

FIGURE 7–4

External direct-connect modems connect to the computer via a serial interface cable and to the telephone line via a modular phone jack.

Both the acoustic modem and the external direct-connect modem require that a computer be equipped with a communication adapter or other serial port with a connector used as a serial interface. This interface provides a standard method for serial transmission of data. A modem cable to connect the modem to the serial port is also needed. For example, the RS–232 interface is used on an IBM PC XT and most compatibles. It has twenty-five pins, called a male connector, and the modem's communication port has twenty-five receptacles, called a female connector. These pins carry specific electronic signals, although all twenty-five are not used in communications.

An **internal direct-connect modem** has all the needed communication circuitry on a plug-in board that fits into one of the expansion slots inside the computer (Figure 7–5). A separate communication board or serial port with an RS–232 interface is not needed. Internal direct-connect modems also link directly to the telephone line with a modular phone jack. These modems have many of the same special features as the external direct-connect modems. In addition, they take up no desk space and are ideal for use in portable computers.

COMMUNICATION CHANNELS

A **communication channel** is the medium, or pathway, through which data are transmitted between devices. Communication channels fall into three basic types: wire cable; microwave; and fiber optics.

Wire cable includes telegraph lines, telephone lines, and coaxial cables; it is the most common type of data communication channel in use. Because it is easier and cheaper to use the extensive wire-cable networks that already exist, wire cable channels are the most popular. Another reason for their popularity is that the technology used to transmit data over wire cables is standardized, thus reducing compatibility problems.

FIGURE 7–5
Internal direct-connect modems contain the necessary serial interface circuitry
and plug directly into the computer's main circuit board.

A disadvantage of wire cable is that data must be transmitted in analog form. Therefore, digital data must be converted to an analog signal before they reach the wire cable. This conversion not only requires special hardware but also slows down the transmission of digital data. Another disadvantage is that wire cable is subject to electrical interference making it less reliable than other types of communication channels. Finally, it is difficult to create the physical links needed where users are separated by large distances or natural barriers such as mountains or large bodies of water.

Another type of analog communication channel is **microwave**. Microwave signals are transmitted through the atmosphere rather than through wire cables, similar to the way radio and television signals are transmitted. Microwave signals must be transmitted in a straight line; they do not bend around corners or around the curve of the earth. Transmitter stations redirect and boost the signals. Satellites are also used to direct microwaves over large, geographically dispersed areas.

Compared to wire cable, microwave has a much lower error rate, making it more reliable. Also, because there are no physical links between the sending and receiving systems, communication links can be made over large distances and rough terrains. A disadvantage, however, is the high cost of ground stations and satellites to support a microwave network.

The third type of communication channel is **fiber optics**. Unlike wire cable and microwave, a fiber-optic channel transmits data in digital form. It uses light impulses that travel through clear flexible tubing. The tubing is thinner than a human hair and hundreds of them can fit in the same amount of space required for one wire cable.

HIGHLIGHT

TELECOMMUNICATION FOR MUSICIANS

Musicians and other people in the music industry are finding the combination of music, computers, and the telephone to be a valuable tool.

Musicians who are frequently "on the road" find it difficult to keep in touch with their management services, studios, other musicians, or friends. Often, they need to communicate immediately or lose a career opportunity. Some entertainers are finding that telecommunication services can help them stay in touch easily and on a timely basis.

A number of telecommunication services geared toward the music and entertainment industry have opened. These include Entertainment Systems International (Esi Street), MusicNet, and Performing Arts Network (PAN). These services, as well as many others, offer electronic mail services that enable messages to be sent and received at the convenience of the users. For the musician who travels worldwide, electronic mail eliminates the problems of time differences. An electronic-mail message can be sent from a hotel one night and an answer can be returned by electronic mail as soon as it is received. This service eliminates the hassle of continually trying to return a call, or long mail delays.

Some musicians, such as Graham Nash of Crosby, Stills, and Nash fame, use electronic mail systems to send ideas to friends for comments and suggestions. While on tour, Tony Levin, a bass and stick player who has played or recorded with Peter Gabriel, John Lennon, James Taylor, and Dire Straits, uses electronic mail to stay in touch with his England-based management firm and other musicians.

Fiber optics are very reliable communication channels; data can be transmitted at very high speeds with few or no errors. Unlike wire cables, fiber-optic cables are not subject to electrical interference. They do, however, require repeaters to read and boost the signal strength because light pulses will lose signal strength over long distances. Technical developments continue to drive down the costs of installing, using, and manufacturing fiber optics so that they are becoming competitive with traditional cabling. Some long-distance telephone companies such as Sprint have already converted to a fiber-optic system, and others are in the process of converting.

Channel Configurations

The two principal communication channel configurations are point-to-point and multipoint (Figure 7–6). In a **point-to-point channel config-**

Types of Communication Channels

- Wire cable
- Microwave
- Fiber optics

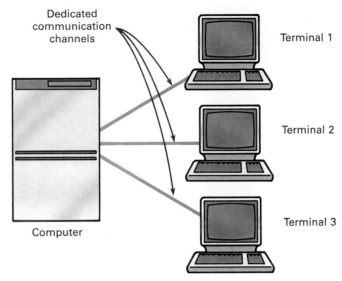

(a) Point-to-point channel configuration

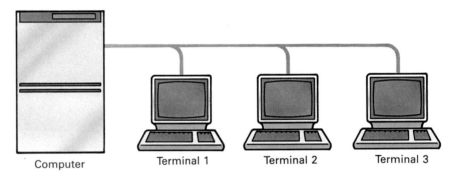

(b) Multipoint channel configuration

uration, a device (e.g., a terminal or computer) is connected directly to another device by a dedicated communication channel, giving those devices sole use of that channel. Point-to-point can be an inefficient and costly configuration if a terminal is not active enough to keep the line busy.

An alternative is the **multipoint channel configuration** in which three or more devices are connected to the same line. The multipoint configuration uses the communication channel more efficiently and reduces the amount of intercabling needed, thus lowering costs.

What keeps more than one device from sending messages over the communication channel at a time? Two methods are used to determine which device gets access to a channel: polling and contention. In **polling**, the computer checks with each device, one at a time, to see if the device has a message to send. If the device has a message ready, transmission begins; if not, the computer moves on to the next device to poll it. After all devices have been individually polled, the process begins again. A disadvantage to polling is that if there are no messages to be sent by the device

Communication Channel Configurations

- Point-to-point
- Multipoint

being polled, the computer's processor will be idle, wasting expensive processor time.

A second method, **contention**, puts the devices in control, i.e., each device monitors the communication channel to see if the channel is free. If the channel is free, the device will send its message. If the communication channel is being used, the device will wait a predetermined amount of time and try again. This process is repeated until the channel is free. A problem with this approach is that although the processor is not idle, one device can tie up the communication channel for long periods of time.

Channel Sharing

Two methods are used to regulate the flow of data from communication channels into a computer: multiplexing and concentration. Their purpose is to increase the efficiency of use of a communication channel.

Multiplexing   **Multiplexing** is the process of combining the transmission, character by character, from several devices into a single data stream that can be sent over a single communication channel. A **multiplexer** is hardware that produces multiplexing. It is also used at the receiving end to separate the transmissions back to their original order for processing (Figure 7–7). The rationale for this process is that most communication channels can transmit much more data at any one time than a single device can send. A multiplexer allows the communication channels to be used more efficiently and thus reduces the cost of using the channel.

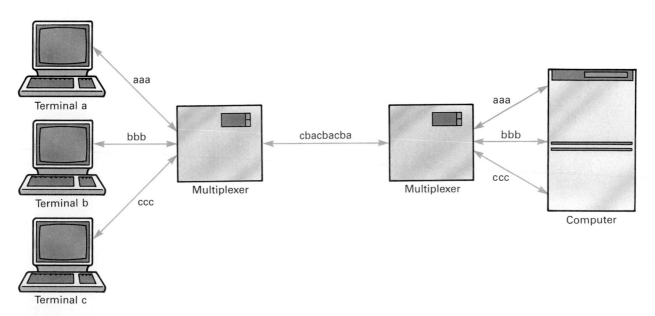

FIGURE 7–7
A multiplexer allows several terminals to share a communication channel.

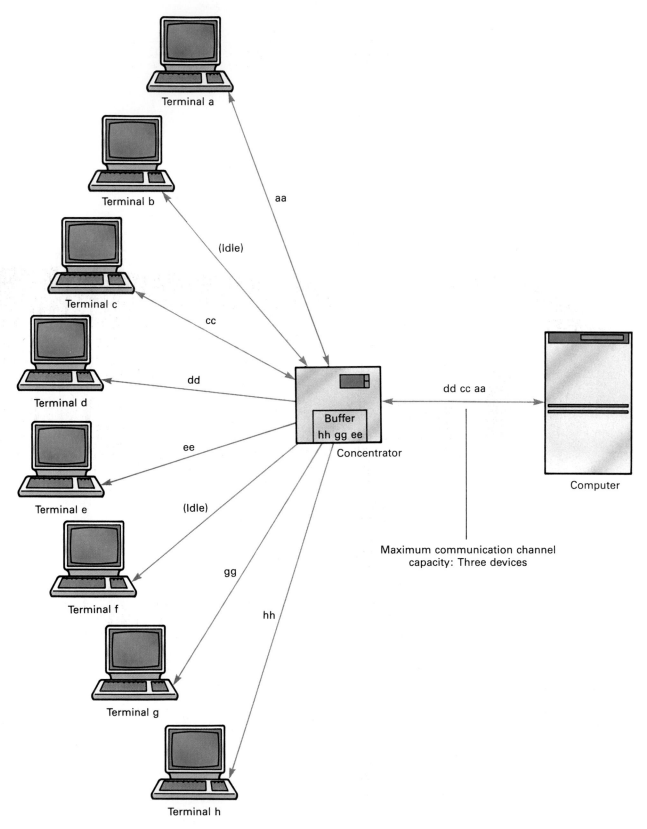

Terminal a

Terminal b

(Idle)

Terminal c

cc

Terminal d

dd

Terminal e

ee

(Idle)

Terminal f

gg

Terminal g

hh

Terminal h

aa

Buffer
hh gg ee

Concentrator

dd cc aa

Computer

Maximum communication channel
capacity: Three devices

Concentration Frequently, it is necessary to connect more devices to a computer than the communication channel can handle at once. **Concentration** is the process of connecting and serving these devices. A **concentrator**, often a minicomputer, is the hardware that provides concentration (Figure 7–8). When the number of devices transmitting exceeds the capacity of the communication channel, the data are stored in a buffer for later transmission. Many multiplexers also provide concentration.

Front-end Processors

A **front-end processor** is a computer that handles all the data-communication control functions (Figure 7–9). While the CPU in the front-end processor handles all the communication tasks, the CPU of the main computer is free to work on other tasks. The two processors interact only when data need to be passed between them. A typical front-end processor might control scores of communication channels of varying types and speeds coming from a number of diverse remote terminals.

The front-end processor can be programmed to perform a variety of functions such as concentration, error control, code conversion, buffering, and other functions related to data and message control.

Common Carriers

A **common carrier** is a company that is licensed and regulated by federal or state government to transmit the data-communication property of others at regulated rates. There are thousands of licensed common carriers of data communication. Three of the largest are American Telephone and Telegraph (AT&T), Western Union, and General Telephone & Electronics (GTE). All common carriers dealing with communication are regulated by the Federal Communications Commission (FCC) and by various state agencies.

Two alternatives to the major common carriers are specialized common carriers and value-added carriers. **Specialized common carriers** are companies that supply only a limited number of data-communication services. They are usually limited to communication in and between selected areas. MCI Communications, for example, is a specialized common carrier. A **value-added carrier** is a company that leases communication channels from the common carriers and adds extra services over and above what the common carriers provide. Tymnet and Telenet are both value-added carriers.

FIGURE 7–8
A concentrator allows connection and service to a greater number of devices than the communication channel is capable of transmitting to at one time.

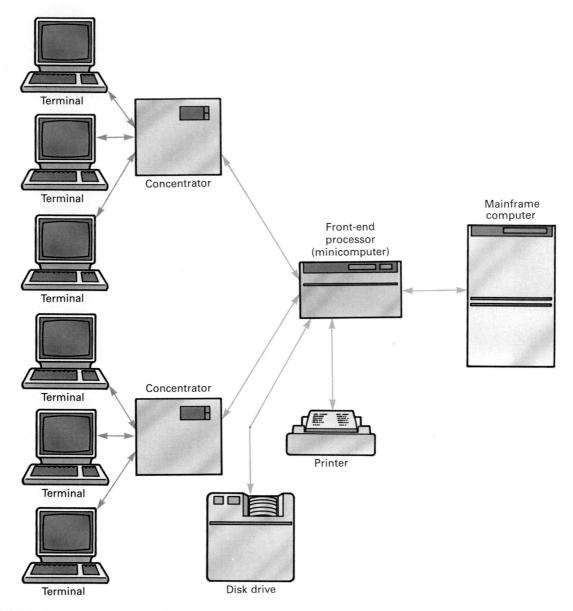

FIGURE 7–9
A front-end processor processes and routes all input and output operations.

RATE OF DATA TRANSMISSION

As people become accustomed to the speeds at which computers can trans-fer data, they seem to want to be able to make that transfer even faster. Information that once took days to receive now seems slow in coming even though it has only taken a couple of minutes by computer. The rate that data are transferred is the baud rate. **Baud rate** is the number of times per second that the signal being transmitted changes (modulates or demodu-lates). Baud is often equated with bits per second (bps); however, this comparison is not entirely accurate because a signal does not always carry one bit.

Although higher speeds are possible, typical data transmission speeds are 300, 1200, 2400, 4800, and 9600 bps. Modems used with microcomputers typically use 300, 1200, or 2400 bps. Larger computer systems used for communications in business typically transmit data at speeds of 4800 bps or higher using high-speed modems. Two factors that determine the rate at which data can be transmitted over communication channels are: (a) the bandwidth of the channel; and (b) the method of data transmission—asynchronous or synchronous.

Communication Channel Bandwidths

The **bandwidth**, or grade, of a communication channel determines the rate, or speed, that data can be transmitted over a channel. The term

Data communication between a space shuttle and Earth stations is accomplished with the help of computers, satellites, and satellite dishes. (Courtesy of Chromatics, Inc. Inset: Photo courtesy of American Satellite Co., part of Contel's Information Systems sector)

"bandwidth" is often shortened to "band." There are three bands for communication channels: narrow-band; voice-band (also called voice-grade); and broad-band.

The slowest of these is the **narrow-band channel**, which transmits data at rates between 40 and 100 bits per second. A telegraph line is a narrow-band channel.

Voice-band channels can transmit data at rates between 110 and 9,600 bits per second. Telephone lines are voice-band channels.

The fastest of these channels is the **broad-band channel**, which can transmit data at rates up to several megabits per second. Advances in technology will soon allow data to be transmitted on some types of broad-band channels in the billions-of-bits-per-second range. Microwaves, coaxial cables, and fiber optics are broad-band channels.

Asynchronous and Synchronous Transmissions

Asynchronous transmission of data is a method in which one character is sent at a time. The transfer of data is controlled by start bits and stop bits. Each character is surrounded by bits that signal the beginning and end of the character. These characters allow the receiving terminal to synchronize itself with the receipt of data on a character-by-character basis. Asynchronous transmission is the least expensive of the two methods. It is often used in low-speed transmission of data in conjunction with narrow-band and some slower speed (less than 1200 bps) voice-band channels where the transmitting device operates manually or intermittently.

In **synchronous transmission**, blocks of characters are transmitted in timed sequences. Rather than using start and stop bits around each character, each block of characters is marked with synchronization characters. The receiving device accepts data until it detects a special ending character or a predetermined number of characters at which time the device knows the message has come to an end.

Synchronous transmission is much faster than asynchronous transmission. It commonly uses the faster (greater than 1200 bps) voice-band and broad-band channels and is usually used when data-transfer requirements exceed several thousand bits per second. Synchronous transmission is used in direct computer-to-computer communication for large computer systems because of the high data-transfer speeds required.

The equipment required for synchronous transmission of data is more sophisticated than that needed for asynchronous devices. The special characters used by asynchronous (start/stop bits) and synchronous (synchronization characters) transmissions to alert the modem when data are being sent and when the transmissions are finished are called **message characters**.

Before data are transmitted, however, a set of traffic rules and procedures, called **protocol**, must be established. The same protocol must be followed by all devices participating in the communication session. These rules may vary depending on the devices being used. Prearranged signals defining the protocol to be followed when transmitting and receiving data are sent between computers in an exchange called **handshaking**.

MODES OF TRANSMISSION

The three modes in which the transfer of data over communication channels occurs are: simplex; half-duplex; and full-duplex. In the **simplex mode**, data can be transmitted in only one direction (Figure 7–10a). A device using the simplex mode of transmission can either send or receive data, but it cannot do both. This mode might be used in a burglar alarm system whose source is located in a building and whose destination is at the local police station. The simplex mode allows no means of feedback to ensure the correct interpretation of the received signal. For example, police officers would have no way of knowing if the alarm was set off by a test, a malfunction, or by a burglar.

The **half-duplex mode** allows a device to send and receive data, but not at the same time. In other words, the transmission of data can occur in only one direction at a time (Figure 7–10b). An example is a citizens band (CB) radio where the user must either talk or listen, but cannot do both at the same time.

Modes of Data Transfer

■ Simplex
■ Half-duplex
■ Full-duplex

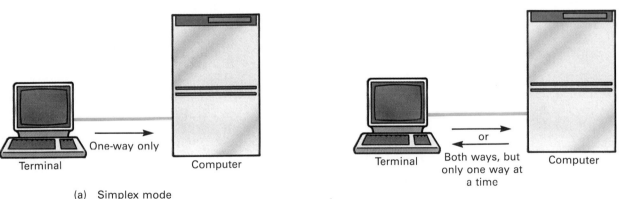

(a) Simplex mode

(b) Half-duplex mode

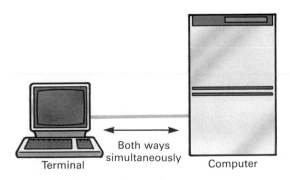

(c) Full-duplex mode

FIGURE 7–10
The transfer of data over a communication line can take place in one of three modes: simplex; half-duplex; or full-duplex.

The most sophisticated of these transmission modes is the **full-duplex mode**, which allows a device to receive and send data simultaneously (Figure 7–10c). For example, a telephone system using full-duplex mode allows the user to talk and listen at the same time. Telephone systems use either the half-duplex or full-duplex mode.

MICRO-TO-MICRO LINK

Microcomputers are often connected for data communication in a **micro-to-micro link** so microcomputer users with incompatible data formats can share data. For example, data on an Apple IIc disk can't be used by an IBM PC XT drive because the data are not saved on the disk in a format that the IBM can read. However, that data, provided they are in a standard format such as ASCII, can be sent via modem and telephone line to the IBM, saved on disk by the IBM, and used in that format. The reverse, sending data from the IBM to the Apple computer, is also possible. If the two computers are located near each other, another option is to directly connect, or hard wire, them using a **null modem** cable. The null modem cable uses a different pin configuration from a modem cable and eliminates the need for a modem by directly matching the data transmit pin from one computer to the data receive pin on the other computer. The advantages of hard wiring are that: (a) it allows incompatible computers to transfer data; (b) it eliminates the need for modems at each computer; and (c) it allows data transfer to take place at speeds up to 9,600 bps. However, there are no error detection capabilities with hard wiring.

MICRO-TO-MAINFRAME LINK

To share data and computing power, microcomputers can also be connected to large systems in a **micro-to-mainframe link**. As the number of microcomputers used in business increases, this connection is being seen more and more. As with micro-to-micro communication, micro-to-mainframe communication can be accomplished via modem and telephone lines or by hard wiring.

However, the connection is not as simple because large systems use different formats for communication, and they handle data differently internally. To complicate the problem, the communication and data formats used among the various large systems also differ. Specialized hardware designed for the particular type of computer being used is usually needed to make the data compatible. For a microcomputer to communicate with a large system, three facts must be known: (a) the type of mainframe to be communicated with; (b) the mainframe's specific data format: and (c) the mainframe's specific communication protocols.

COMMUNICATION CHALLENGES

The use of data communication is not without its challenges. Data sent over communication channels are subject to various kinds of interference which may alter or destroy some of that data. In addition to ensuring the security of the data, privacy of the data must often be protected. However, unauthorized access to data files can be limited by the use of passwords

HIGHLIGHT

THE NYSE AND TELECOMMUNICATION

Most brokers and specialists use preprinted slips and pencils to note the deals they make on the floor of the New York Stock Exchange (NYSE). They keep track of details such as how much stock is involved, who the parties in the deal are, and what the price per share is.

However, the paper method doesn't allow the trader the opportunity to review the details of the deal to make sure the broker wrote down and used the correct information. This paper method results in about 15 percent of the trades being questionable.

Now, there is a push for computerized trading. The person who acts as the auctioneer uses an electronic workstation while the brokers use hand-held terminals (a combination of laptop computer and telephone). The brokers enter the details of each deal on their terminals; the traders immediately see the transactions on the LCD and lock them in or fix any mistakes. Besides eliminating the paper mess at the end of a day of trading, stockbrokers would like to see the percentage of questionable trades drop to near zero.

and access codes. To prevent highly sensitive data from being accessed and used from the communication channels, the data are often encrypted, or scrambled, based on some code before they are sent. Then they are unscrambled using that same code after they are received.

DATA COMMUNICATION AT WORK

Most of us deal with a business that uses some form of data communication every day. For example, many of the stories in the newspaper and magazines that you read are filed by journalists from remote locations using portable computers and data-communication channels. Airlines and travel agencies receive and send information on flight schedules and reservations through data-communication channels. The supermarket may have its cash registers linked to the store's large computer at a remote location to keep track of inventories.

Electronic funds transfer (EFT), the electronic movement of money among accounts, is a widely used data-communication application. A large portion of money in the business and financial communities changes hands through EFT. A popular application of EFT is the automated teller machine.

In fact, Society for Worldwide Interbank Financial Telecommunications (SWIFT), the most sophisticated private interbank system in the world, averages 750,000 transactions daily for 1,300 member banks in 46 countries. After being upgraded, their mainframe and communication network will process one million messages daily.

Some companies have adopted a method of employment, called **telecommuting**, where some personnel work at home and use their computers to communicate with the office computer.

Electronic mail is a system used by computers and communication channels to store and send messages. Many businesses use electronic-mail systems to reduce paperwork and to save the time it takes for a message to reach its destination. At home, Bill Machrone, editor at *PC Magazine*, uses his Compaq Portable Plus microcomputer to write his "Editor's Notes" column, edit stories, and communicate with contributors through the MCI electronic-mail service.

Information services and **data-base services**, such as The Source, CompuServe, Dow Jones News Retrieval, and Dialog use data communication so their subscribers can access one or several large computers containing data banks on various topics. The services can be accessed easily from microcomputers equipped with the proper communication hardware and software. (Chapter 16 gives more information on communication software for microcomputers, and the InfoModule in Chapter 16 discusses electronic networks.)

Data communication has made the computer one of the most vital tools in our information-seeking society. It links two or more computers via telephone lines or direct cabling and enables users to send and receive electronic data without regard to the boundaries of time or distance.

SUMMARY

Data communication is the process of electronically sending data from one point to another. Using communication facilities such as the telephone system and microwave relays to send data between computers is a type of data communication often referred to as telecommunication.

The transmission of data takes one of two forms: analog or digital. Analog data transmission is the passage of data in a continuous waveform. Digital data transmission is the passage of data in distinct on and off pulses.

Modulation is the process of converting a digital signal into an analog signal. Demodulation is the process of converting the analog signal into a digital signal. A modem (*mo*dulator-*dem*odulator) is the device that converts the signals.

A communication channel is the pathway through which data are transmitted between devices. There are three basic types of communication channels: wire cable; microwave; and fiber optics. Communication channels are found in two principal configurations: point-to-point and multipoint. Two methods, polling and contention, are used to determine which terminal gets access to the communication channel. Polling is the process whereby the computer checks each terminal to see if it is ready to send data. In contention, when the terminal is ready to send a message, it monitors the communication channel to see if the channel is free. The terminal keeps monitoring until the channel is free, and then it can send its message.

Multiplexing is the process of combining the transmissions from several computers or other devices so the transmissions can share the same communication channel. A multiplexer is the hardware that accomplishes multiplexing. Concentration is a process that allows a communication channel to be connected to and serve more devices than the capacity of the channel normally allows. A concentrator is one type of device that accomplishes concentration. A front-end processor is a computer that handles all the data-communication control functions, freeing the CPU of the main computer to work on other tasks.

Common carriers are companies that are licensed and regulated to transmit the data-communication property of others. Specialized common carriers and value added carriers are two alternatives to using the major common carriers for data communication.

The baud rate of a communication channel is the number of times per second that the signal being transmitted changes (modulates or demodulates). Typical bps rates are 300, 1200, 2400, 4800, and 9600. The bandwidth, or band, of a communication channel determines the speed at which that channel can transmit data. There are three different bandwidths: narrow-band; voice-band; and broad-band.

Asynchronous transmission transmits data one character at a time. Synchronous transmission transmits data as a block of characters in timed sequences. Message characters alert the modem when data are being sent and when they are finished. The exchange of prearranged signals defining the rules to be followed when transmitting and receiving data is known as handshaking. Protocol is the set of rules and procedures defining the technical details for data transfer between two devices.

Data transfer can occur in three modes: simplex; half-duplex; and full-duplex.

Data communication has allowed the linking of microcomputer-to-microcomputer and microcomputer-to-mainframe so data and capabilities can be shared.

Ensuring the security and privacy of data are two important challenges facing users of data communication.

Data communication has allowed computers to share data in spite of the boundaries of time or distance and has found many applications in our society, including information services, data-base services, electronic funds transfer, electronic mail, telecommuting, reservation systems, and other business systems.

Key Terms

acoustic modem (p. 202)

analog data transmission (p. 201)

asynchronous transmission (p. 212)

bandwidth (p. 211)

baud rate (p. 210)

broad-band channel (p. 212)

common carrier (p. 209)

communication channel (p. 203)

concentration (p. 209)

concentrator (p. 209)

contention (p. 207)

data-base service (p. 216)

data communication (p. 200)

demodulation (p. 201)

digital data transmission (p. 201)

electronic funds transfer (EFT) (p. 215)

electronic mail (p. 216)

external direct-connect modem (p. 202)

fiber optics (p. 204)

front-end processor (p. 209)

full-duplex mode (p. 214)

half-duplex mode (p. 213)

handshaking (p. 212)

information service (p. 216)

internal direct-connect modem (p. 203)

message characters (p. 212)

micro-to-mainframe link (p. 214)

micro-to-micro link (p. 214)

microwave (p. 204)

modem (p. 201)

modulation (p. 201)

multiplexer (p. 207)

multiplexing (p. 207)

multipoint channel configuration (p. 206)

narrow-band channel (p. 212)

null modem (p. 214)

point-to-point channel configuration (p. 205)

polling (p. 206)

protocol (p. 212)

simplex mode (p. 213)

specialized common carrier (p. 209)

synchronous transmission (p. 212)

telecommunication (p. 200)

telecommuting (p. 216)

value-added carrier (p. 209)

voice-band channel (p. 212)

wire cable (p. 203)

Review Questions

1. What is data communication?

2. The process of using communication facilities such as the telephone system to transmit data is called _____.

3. Describe the difference between analog and digital data transmission.

4. The conversion of an analog signal to a digital signal is called _____.

5. What is a modem's function?

6. Describe the purpose of a communication channel.

7. _____, _____, and _____ are the three basic types of communication channels.

8. Which type of communication channel can transmit data in digital form?

9. Describe and sketch how a point-to-point configuration works.

10. A(n) _____ configuration has a number of terminals connected to the same communication channel.

11. _____ is the process whereby the computer checks each terminal, one at a time, to see if it is ready to transmit data.

12. The process whereby each terminal monitors the communication channel to see if it is free is known as _____.

13. Describe the function of a multiplexer.

14. Describe the process of concentration.

15. What is the function of a front-end processor?

16. The number of times a signal being transmitted changes (modulates or demodulates) is known as its _____.

17. What is a common carrier?

18. The transmission of blocks of characters in timed sequences is known as _____ transmission.

19. Describe protocol.

20. The three modes in which the transfer of data can occur are _____, _____, and _____.

21. List and describe three types of modems.

22. Describe the three types of communication channels.

23. What are the three bandwidths for communication channels? Discuss their differences.

24. Describe the three modes in which the transfer of data can occur.

25. List three facts that must be known in order to communicate with a large system computer.

INFOMODULE

Networks and Distributed Data Processing

One application of the data communication technology discussed in Chapter 7 is the development of computer networks. A **computer network** is created when several computers are linked by data communication channels. Each computer in a network can have its own processing capabilities and can also share hardware, data files, and programs. The two basic types of networks are local-area and wide-area.

LOCAL-AREA NETWORKS

A **local-area network (LAN)** is two or more computers directly linked within a small well-defined area such as a room, building, or group of closely placed buildings. A LAN may be made up of only microcomputers or any combination of microcomputers and large systems.

In Chapter 6 you were introduced to multiuser systems. The difference between a LAN and a multiuser system is that a LAN is made up of stand-alone computers whereas a multiuser system typically has one computer that is shared among two or more terminals.

A LAN usually consists of the following:

- Two or more computers
- Peripheral devices such as printers and hard-disk drives
- Software to control the operation of the computers or other devices connected to the LAN
- Special cables, usually coaxial or fiber optic, to connect the computers and other devices
- A plug-in board to handle the data transmissions (usually when a microcomputer is part of a LAN)

A benefit of a LAN is the reduction of hardware costs because several computers and users can share peripheral devices such as laser printers, hard-disk drives, color plotters, and modems. Another advantage is that the users can share data.

Ensuring the security and privacy of data are two concerns of LAN users. The LAN must get the data to its destination, transmit the data correctly, and prevent unauthorized users from gaining access to that data. These tasks are accomplished through both the hardware and LAN software.

Popular LANs available for microcomputer users include Novell, Ethernet, Corvus, ARCnet, PC Network, and Omninet. They vary in the type and number of computers that can be connected, the speed at which data can be transferred, and the type of software used to control the network. Some LANs require that all the computers be of a certain brand, while others allow a variety of brands to be connected. The number of computers in a LAN varies widely from smaller LANs that typically connect two to twenty-five computers, to larger LANs that can connect as many as 10,000 computers.

The length of the cable connecting a computer to a LAN also varies depending on the LAN. Most LANs allow cables of about one thousand feet, but some allow cables of several miles to be used. The data transfer speeds range from several thousand bits per second to around 10 million bits per second. The programs that control the LANs also vary in the features they offer. Some programs allow the use of more than one operating system; others allow only one. On some LANs, file access is limited to one user at a time; on others, more than one user can access a file simultaneously.

WIDE-AREA NETWORKS

A **wide-area network** is two or more computers that are geographically dispersed, linked by communication facilities such as the telephone system or microwave relays. This type of network is usually limited to use by large corporations and government agencies because of the high costs involved in building and maintaining them.

Network Topologies

- Star network
- Ring network
- Tree network
- Bus network

NETWORK TOPOLOGY

Each computer or device in a network is called a **node**. How these nodes are connected is the network's **topology**. A network can be arranged in one of four different topologies: star network; ring network; tree network; and bus network.

Star Network

A **star network** consists of several devices connected to one centralized computer (Figure 1). All communication first goes through the centralized computer allowing it to control the operation, workload, and resource allocation of the other computers in the network. For example, a bank with several branch offices would typically use a star network to control and coordinate those branches. The advantage is relative simplicity, but a problem exists with the single-point

FIGURE 1
Star network

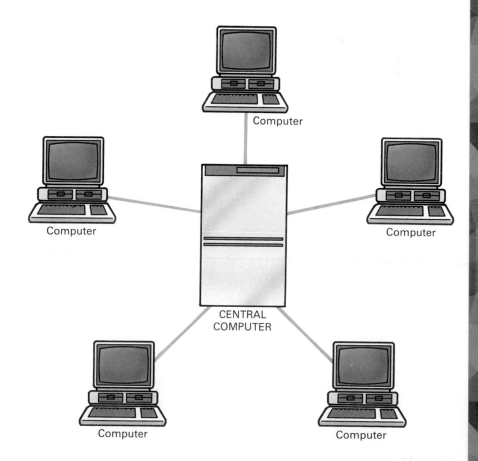

Computer

Computer

Computer

CENTRAL
COMPUTER

Computer

Computer

vulnerability of the network. If the central computer breaks down, none of the other computers can communicate with each other.

Ring Network

A **ring network** consists of several devices connected to each other in a closed loop by a single communication channel (Figure 2). There is no central, or predominant, computer in this network. The data must travel around the ring to each station in turn until they arrive at the desired station. A ring may be unidirectional or bidirectional. A unidirectional ring moves data in one direction only; a bidirectional ring moves data in both directions, but only one direction at a time. In a unidirectional ring, if one computer should break down, special software is required to keep the network functional. When one node malfunctions in a bidirectional ring, a message

can usually be sent in the opposite direction, still allowing the node to communicate with all the other active nodes in the network.

Tree Network

A **tree network** links computers in a hierarchical fashion and requires information to flow through the branches (Figure 3). To move from the computer at Node 1 in Figure 3 to Node 7, data would have to go through Nodes 3, 5, and 6 before arriving at 7.

An advantage of a tree structure is that functional groupings can be created. For example, one branch could contain all the general ledger terminals, another branch all the accounts receivable terminals, and so on. If one branch stops functioning, the other branches in a tree network are not affected. However, data movement through this network can be slow.

FIGURE 2
Ring network

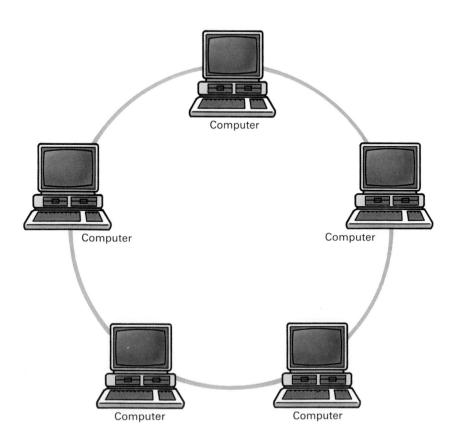

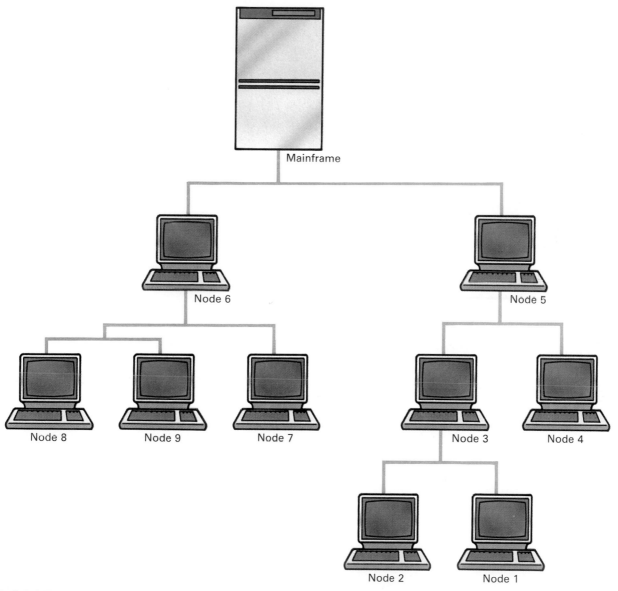

FIGURE 3
Tree network

Bus Network

In a **bus network**, each computer is connected to a single communication cable via an interface; every computer can communicate directly with every other computer or device in the network (Figure 4). Each node is given an address. To access a particular node, a user just needs to know its address. This topology is frequently used with local-area networks. Going through a hierarchy of nodes is not necessary.

DISTRIBUTED DATA PROCESSING

Distributed data processing (DDP) is the concept of dispersing computers, devices, software, and data connected through communication channels into areas where they are used. The

FIGURE 4
Bus network

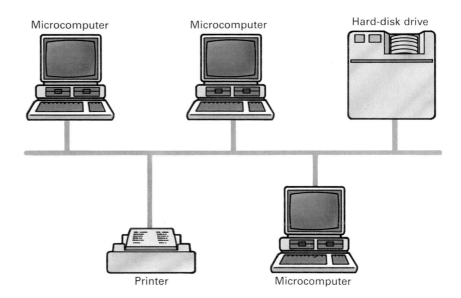

Microcomputer   Microcomputer   Hard-disk drive

Printer   Microcomputer

DDP Advantages

- Cost efficiency
- User-control of computer facilities
- Shared resources

---

computers are organized on functional and geographical bases and work together as a cohesive system to support user requirements.

This approach is in contrast to a centralized system where all the data-processing resources are in one location. Typically, a centralized system has one large general-purpose computer with many terminals attached to it. While the centralized computer can do many tasks, it may not be the most efficient or cost-effective way to do many of them. A DDP system allows the use of many smaller, more specialized computers that can be tailored to complete a particular task or tasks efficiently and cost-effectively.

Three advantages of using a DDP are: (a) cost efficiency; (b) user-controlled computing facilities, resulting in shorter response times; and (c) shared resources.

In the past, the cost of computing was a major argument for not using DDP. Most components in a computer system have decreased in cost and improved in performance; however, the cost of using communication channels has not decreased as much as computing costs. Because computers and data-storage device costs have decreased, many organizations have discovered that distributing computers and data storage to local areas can actually save them money by decreasing their use of expensive communication channels. In addition, because a DDP network allows remote sites to share equipment and data, proper management and control of the DDP system can reduce redundancy of both of these.

DDP has also become popular because the users have more control over individual data-processing needs. They no longer have to count on a centralized computer staff that fulfills all the organization's needs. A DDP system typically uses many minicomputers and microcomputers; it is not as complicated and does not require as much maintenance as a centralized computing system. The users of the smaller systems access them directly and take advantage of their full power. For tasks such as managing extremely large and complicated data bases, however, mainframes still play a vital role in many DDP systems.

Response times for many applications are shorter in a DDP. While distribution of the equipment and data are referred to as DDP, the concept of distributing management is referred to as decentralized management. When a DDP system has its management decentralized, it is often referred to as a fully distributed system. Of course, there are varying degrees of both DDP and decentralized management. As with many things, it is not a simple case of one or the other.

Finally, to meet their total information needs, users share equipment, software, and data with other computers in the DDP system.

There are five disadvantages of using a DDP They include: (a) a loss of organizational control; (b) redundancies of resources and data; (c) compatibility problems; (d) unskilled users; and (e) support difficulties.

First, problems can occur with a DDP system if it is not managed properly. If organizational control over the data-processing resources is lost, management has difficulty controlling costs and maintaining standards throughout the distributed areas of an organization.

A second problem that can arise is a redundancy of resources and data. Without proper management and control, each distributed site may try to develop separate data-processing facilities to meet all their needs. Several systems that are the same, or nearly the same, may result. This duplicity can lead to higher hardware and software costs than if the distributed sites shared these resources. Uncontrolled data redundancy can lead to differences in data at the distributed sites, causing discrepancies in reports. This problem can be difficult and expensive to resolve.

Third, if the distributed sites do not coordinate their selection of hardware and software, compatibility problems can arise. Different protocols at certain distributed sites may result in the inability of some hardware to communicate with hardware at other distributed sites. Designing

software to solve compatibility problems can be time-consuming and costly.

A fourth problem can occur when data processing is distributed. A site could fall under the control of untrained and inexperienced users, resulting in poor selection of hardware and software, inferior programming techniques, and little, if any, documentation. This circumstance could lead to a costly and overly complex system or, in some cases, to a system that is inappropriate for the job.

Finally, obtaining timely support at some distributed sites can be difficult because they are too far from the vendor's or the organization's support staff. Maintaining a separate support staff at each location can be too expensive for some organizations.

DDP is not appropriate for all applications. Large, centralized computing systems are still essential in some cases. However, many applications could be completed more efficiently and cost-effectively with distributed systems.

To ensure that it meets their needs, users should be integrally involved in the design of the DDP system. The success or failure of a DDP system ultimately depends on planning, commitment to, and control of the system by management, as well as user acceptance.

KEY TERMS

bus network (p. 223)

computer network (p. 220)

distributed data processing (DDP) (p. 223)

local-area network (LAN) (p. 220)

node (p. 221)

ring network (p. 222)

star network (p. 221)

topology (p. 221)

tree network (p. 222)

wide-area network (p. 220)

QUESTIONS

1. What is a computer network?
2. Describe a local-area network.
3. How does a wide-area network differ from a local-area network.
4. Name and describe the four different network topologies.
5. Explain distributed data processing and discuss some possible advantages and disadvantages.

DDP Disadvantages

- Loss of organizational control
- Redundancies of resources and data
- Compatibility problems
- Unskilled users
- Support difficulties

PART THREE
Information Systems and Programming Concepts

What the world *really* needs is a better way of handling information, because information is all-powerful . . . . Without information, nothing can happen. But *with* the right information, virtually anything is possible. And by coming up with the proper information, one can turn want and war into peace and plenty.

David Ritchie, author of The Binary Brain: Artificial Intelligence in the Age of Electronics

OBJECTIVES

- ☐ Explain why a system life cycle is initiated
- ☐ List and discuss the five stages in the system life cycle
- ☐ Know the kinds of documentation kept during the life cycle of an information system
- ☐ Describe some of the tools system analysts use in the analysis phase of the system life cycle
- ☐ Distinguish between the different methods of system conversion

OUTLINE

8

Information System Life Cycle

PROFILE: Kenneth Olsen

Though Kenneth Olsen has helped launch and has provided the Boston Computer Museum with several "gems," such as the Whirlwind computer, the man is a gem himself.

Olsen is also an innovator, which may have grown out of his boyhood hobby of tinkering in the basement with his dad's tools. Or, maybe it was in the U.S. Navy where he learned about electronics.

From his hometown of Stratford, Connecticut, he went to the Massachusetts Institute of Technology where he received his bachelor's and master's degrees in engineering. As a student at MIT in 1950, he helped build the Whirlwind Computer to coordinate New England military radar units that scanned the skies for Soviet planes.

In 1957, Olsen started American Research and Development (later changed to Digital Equipment Corporation [DEC], a leader in the minicomputer industry) with his brother, Stan, in an old textile mill in Maynard, Massachusetts. Here, they de-

signed circuit modules that were later used in the early 1960s in their first computer, the Program Data Processor (PDP–1). PDP–1 was the first in a long line of minicomputer systems. By 1965, Olsen introduced the $10,000 PDP–8, generally considered to be the first inexpensive minicomputer.

Olsen is still at DEC—over thirty years now—and still a top engineer. Throughout the company, he's known as Ken; his staff appreciates his leadership and good nature. At DEC, he does not permit reserved parking places and allows any employee to use the company helicopters for business.

Although his employees consider him a tough leader, they also like his "common-man" way of life. He drives a van (not a limousine) and owns no lavish possessions.

The motivating forces behind this leader and engineer are not glory and money, but competition and the sheer challenge of making things work.

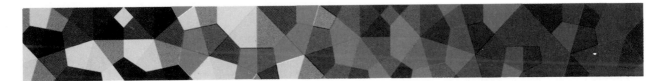

Every day people buy goods and services from businesses. Who buys what, why they buy it, how much it costs to make, what it is selling for, and how much inventory is left are all questions that, when answered, produce large amounts of data for businesses.

Because of computers, businesses now have the capabilities to collect and store vast amounts of data for use in conducting their business. These businesses require a method of turning data into useful information and a way to manage all that information. Successful businesses accomplish this task efficiently to achieve the maximum benefit from the processed data.

All businesses need an information system to operate, but all do not include a computer. For most modern businesses, however, the computer plays an integral part in this process. Simply buying a computer, however, does not automatically solve the data-to-information problem. A system that converts data to information must be carefully developed through the establishment of a systematic development process. This chapter overviews the system life cycle of an information system from inception to completion. The information presented is general in nature and is designed to give a basic understanding of the types of concerns that must be addressed when developing an information system.

THE SYSTEM LIFE CYCLE

For our purposes, a **system** is the combination of people, devices, and methods interrelated in working toward a common goal. The focus here is on business systems that include computers to reach the common goal. Because data are being converted into information, these systems are called **information systems.**

An information system is a computer-based business system that provides the data-processing capabilities and information that an organization needs to be informed about various aspects of its operations. Because information is a valuable asset to any business or organization, it must be carefully acquired and organized into a system that is useful. For a system to be useful and to have value, it must: (a) provide accurate information; (b)

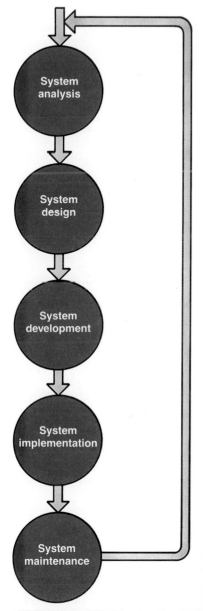

FIGURE 8–1
The system life cycle

provide timely information; and (c) be capable of communicating that information to the people in the company who need it.

An organization can have one or more information systems in operation. Among other tasks, businesses use information systems for sales and order processing, administrative record keeping, and accounting and payroll applications. An insurance company, for example, might use an information system to manage all the data it needs to issue policies and process claims. An oil company might use one information system to process and manage data about oil exploration, another system for refinery management, and yet another for customer accounts.

The **system life cycle** is the life span of an information system from its inception until it is removed or redesigned. It consists of five major stages (Figure 8–1) which are discussed in more detail throughout the chapter:

1. System analysis—an evaluation of the current system in response to a problem or new opportunity to determine if the current system should be modified or a new system developed
2. System design—a physical design of a proposed system is developed
3. System development—creating the new information system from the physical design; the programs of the new or modified system are written
4. System implementation—the organization installs and begins to use a new system
5. System maintenance—the system is continually monitored and adjusted as needed until it is time for a total reevaluation

Developing an information system throughout the system life cycle involves continual and clear communication among users and system personnel—the people responsible for designing and implementing the information system.

The **user** is the person or persons who will use the information system once it's been installed. For example, users include the operators who run the computers and managers who require information from the system. System personnel include system analysts, system designers, and programmers. A **system analyst** is the person who works with users to determine their information needs. A **system designer** is the specialist who designs a system to fulfill the users' information needs. A **programmer** is the person who codes the instructions that solve a problem in a programming language so that they can be used by the computer. In large organizations, these positions are usually separate and distinct jobs; however, in some companies, particularly the small ones, one person may do all or several parts of these tasks.

To help make the communication process easier and more efficient, a **project management team** is often established. The project management team usually consists of a project manager and, depending upon the size of the project, various numbers of users, system personnel, programmers, and other specialists (Figure 8–2).

FIGURE 8–2

A project management team composed of system personnel and users must first come to an agreement on the nature and scope of a problem. (Courtesy of Honeywell, Inc.)

Information Systems Involve
■ People
■ Devices
■ Methods
■ Conversion of data to information

The role of user involvement cannot be overemphasized. Users are the ultimate consumers of the information system and must accept and use it if it is to be successful. The best way to ensure this acceptance is through close communication between the team and the user throughout the development process.

The project manager is responsible for planning and coordinating the tasks to be accomplished by the team. The project manager breaks down a project into smaller tasks that have specific end points. These tasks can then be assigned a time frame in which to be completed by specific team members; then, tasks can be easily monitored to see if they are on schedule.

Two tools used by a project manager to help monitor schedules are Gantt charts and Program Evaluation Review Technique (PERT) diagrams. A **Gantt chart** (Figure 8–3) is a bar chart that depicts the timing of com-

FIGURE 8–3

A Gantt chart showing the planned timing of the stages for a system analysis

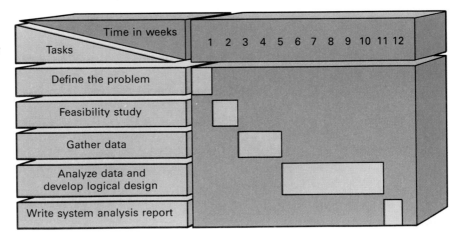

pletion of a series of tasks. A quick glance at the chart shows the project manager if the designated tasks are being completed on schedule. A **Program Evaluation Review Technique (PERT)** diagram shows both the timing and the relationships among a project's tasks (Figure 8–4).

Another important means of communication throughout the entire cycle is to keep accurate and complete documentation. **Documentation** is the written or graphic record of the steps carried out during the development of an information system. System personnel are responsible for accurately documenting each task they perform. The documentation is then compiled, maintained, and made available to other personnel by a **system librarian.** Keeping accurate and complete documentation is important for several reasons. First, many people are often involved in the development of an information system, and many tasks rely directly on work already completed by other members of the development team. Documentation allows system personnel and management to review what was previously done and why. A second reason is that many system development projects extend over a long period of time. During that time, there are personnel changes or additions to the team. New personnel can review documentation to understand what is going on and thus to be able to contribute right away, even in the middle of a project.

Several types of documentation that are typically kept during the project are: a project manual; a system manual; a programmer's manual; an operator's manual; and a user's manual. A project manual contains detailed descriptions of the steps taken to develop the information system, and a complete technical explanation of the information system is found in a system manual. A programmer's manual contains step-by-step descriptions of the programmer's work. An operator's manual contains amplified descriptions of the procedures required to operate the information system. This manual is designed to be used by personnel who actually operate and maintain the computer system itself. Finally, a user's manual contains a

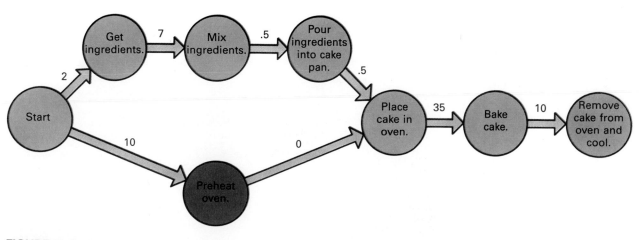

FIGURE 8–4

A PERT diagram showing the planned timing in minutes and relationships of events in preparing a cake

simplified, less technical description of the information system and details of how to use the information system. This manual is designed to be used by personnel who may or may not access the computer directly, but require information from the system.

The following sections explain each stage of the system life cycle and describe how system personnel go about the task of analyzing and solving a problem.

SYSTEM ANALYSIS

System analysis is the process of analyzing a system and trying to find a way to modify it or create a new system to meet the user's needs. The process is initiated by the recognition of a problem or new opportunity that the current system cannot handle. As used here, the term "problem" indicates that the current system is not functioning properly for tasks it was designed to handle. The phrase "new opportunity" indicates that circumstances have arisen, such as a new product line, that the current system was not originally designed to handle. A distinction is made to show that a system analysis is not always initiated in response to negative situations.

The need for a system analysis may be brought about by the routine business of doing business, such as adding or deleting a new product line. It can also occur because of the particular way a company runs its business. For example, for many years manufacturers would build huge inventories of stock so they would never run out of the product; however, this strategy proved to be costly. The trend is to the just-in-time (JIT) method of inventory control where just enough inventory is stocked to meet demands. As a business adopts JIT, its old inventory system would need to be analyzed and changed to fit the new method.

Changes in state laws or federal regulations also trigger a need for system analysis. Restructuring of tax laws has caused accounting and tax software packages to become outdated. Changes in environmental laws

The project manager and chief programmer review project documentation.

may cause a manufacturer to revise some operational aspects which may require changes to its information system.

A business' customers may also identify a problem area that needs attention. For example, customers constantly complaining about billing errors should alert a business that its billing system needs to be reevaluated and possibly redesigned.

Technology-related changes, such as redesigning an information system to include newer, more advanced computer systems, are often suggested by the system analyst.

A problem or new opportunity, however, does not always mean the present system must be scrapped. It may mean simply that new features are needed or no system currently exists to perform the functions needed by the business.

At this point, the system analyst is not looking for a solution so much as a clear understanding of the problem or new opportunity. After the area of concern has been recognized, the scope and purpose of the problem or new opportunity should be made clear to all involved parties, including management, system personnel, and the users (Figure 8–5). Once these parties have agreed on the scope and purpose, management must make the decision of whether or not to proceed with a feasibility study. If it is decided to go ahead with the feasibility study, a system analyst is called upon to conduct it.

Feasibility Study

A **feasibility study** is a preliminary study to determine if the information system should be developed. Three questions need to be asked:

1. Is the technology available to solve the problem or accommodate the new opportunity?
2. Would the system as proposed be accepted and used by the intended users?
3. Are the benefits of developing the appropriate information system greater than the costs?

Available Technology   The system analyst must determine if the technical capability exists to create the desired system. To do this, the analyst must keep abreast of current technology. The system analyst doesn't need to be a technical expert, but does need to have a good general background and knowledge of sources where the needed technological information can be obtained.

User Acceptance   It is important for the system analyst to design a system that fits the users' capabilities. A very technical and complex system may seem like the best solution to a problem, but it is worthless if the users cannot operate it, are intimidated by it, or are reluctant to use it.

Cost-to-benefit Relationship   A cost-to-benefit study is conducted by the system analyst to identify the anticipated benefits, as well as any anticipated costs to the company. The study determines how the system will benefit the company in terms of decreased costs or increased profits. Some benefits are easy to identify and measure. Those that reduce costs or increase profits can be easily quantified. Other benefits, such as improved customer service and employee morale, and better dissemination of information to managers, are more difficult to measure.

Some of the typical costs that concern companies include: (a) hardware; (b) software; (c) personnel (including the cost of training and lost production time while learning the system); and (d) operation (including the cost of storing data, CPU time, and supplies, such as paper). No organization wants to take on a project that loses money. If the benefits are found to outweigh the costs of developing a system, then approval is given by management to start the data-gathering phase of system analysis.

Data Gathering

If the project survives the feasibility study, the system analyst begins to gather data about the current system and the users' needs. Data are gathered from both internal and external sources. Internal data sources include employees, management, and any internally-generated business documents such as operator's manuals, financial statements, and job descriptions. Employees and management may be personally interviewed, observed, asked to keep a diary, or requested to fill out a questionnaire.

While these can all be effective data-gathering tools, there are dangers if used improperly. Observations can be incomplete or interpreted incorrectly. Diaries take a lot of time, and managers may refuse to keep them or keep inadequate records that are of little use to the system analyst.

Interviews require the analyst to have a high level of people-oriented skills, and questionnaires must be structured properly so they will be answered and so everyone interprets the questions the same way. External data sources include suppliers, trade journals, and competing organizations.

Data Analysis and Logical Design Development

After all pertinent data have been gathered by the system analyst, they are analyzed and the logical design of the system is developed. A logical design shows the flow of data through a system. There are two general steps in developing the logical design: (a) determining the purpose and objectives of an information system; and (b) determining the outputs, inputs, and processing requirements of the information system from the users' points of view without concern for how the requirements will be physically accomplished. Any anticipated conditions that may cause these to change are also outlined at this time.

The users and the system analyst work together to determine the logical design of the new system. Because the users are involved, each requirement can be checked immediately to ensure that their needs are being met.

The system analyst uses many tools in the analysis phase. Decision tables and data-flow diagrams help analyze data. Data-flow diagrams can also be used to communicate the logic design to users. Other tools that communicate the logical design include layout forms and system flowcharts.

A **decision table** lays out alternatives for different circumstances (Figure 8–6). A set of conditions and rules is described to determine an appropriate course of action. For each condition, there are rules that determine the action to take. By detailing decisions on paper, the system analyst can get a better understanding of the factors that lead to specific actions in the current system.

The symbols in Figure 8–7 are used to construct a data-flow diagram. A **data-flow diagram** shows the logical flow of data through the system (Figure 8–8). The data-flow diagram makes no reference to the data media

FIGURE 8–6

The decision table outlines the actions to be taken given the stated conditions and rules. For example, if the stock price is low and it is likely to go up, then buy the stock; however, if the stock price is low and it is not likely to go up, then don't buy the stock, and so on.

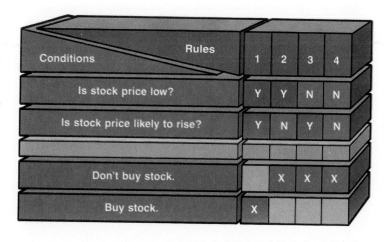

Conditions	Rules			
	1	2	3	4
Is stock price low?	Y	Y	N	N
Is stock price likely to rise?	Y	N	Y	N
Don't buy stock.		X	X	X
Buy stock.	X			

FIGURE 8–7
Data-flow diagram symbols

A box indicates input to
or output from a system.

A circle indicates a
processing function in
which data flowing in
are changed in form,
value, or location
before exiting.

An arrow indicates data
flowing through the system.

An open-ended rectangle
indicates a data store such as
a data-base file.

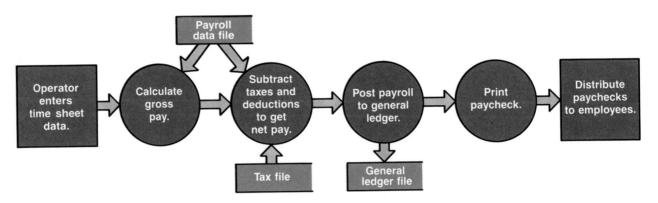

FIGURE 8–8
This data-flow diagram shows the general data flow through a payroll process.
First, data from time sheets are keyed into the payroll system by an operator.
Next, gross pay is calculated using the hourly rate or salary amount retrieved
from the payroll data file. Net pay is then calculated subtracting both the appropriate taxes as determined from the data in the tax file and any deductions
contained in the payroll data file. The payroll data are posted to the general
ledger file, the paychecks are printed, and finally distributed to the employees.

used, only to where in the system the data are entered, processed, or
stored.

A **layout form** is used to detail, on paper, the setup of the input and
output CRT screens and hard-copy reports (Figure 8–9). This form enables
system analysts and users to agree upon the design for the screens and
reports before they are actually implemented.

A **system flowchart** graphically illustrates the types of hardware
devices and storage media that are required to physically implement a

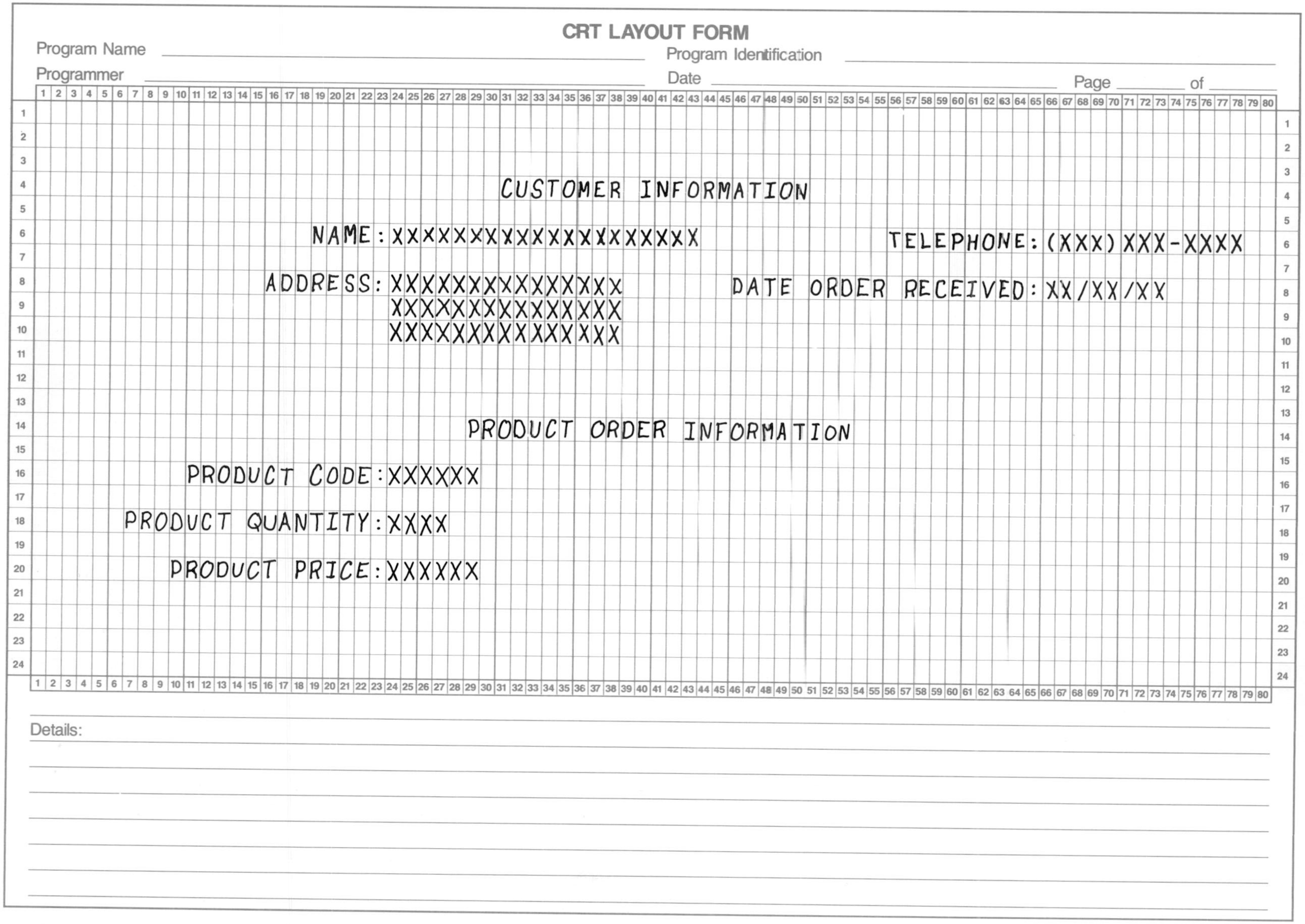

CRT LAYOUT FORM

Program Name
Programmer
Program Identification
Date
Page ___ of ___

```
CUSTOMER INFORMATION                           TELEPHONE:(XXX)XXX-XXXX

NAME:XXXXXXXXXXXXXXXXXXX
                                       DATE ORDER RECEIVED:XX/XX/XX
ADDRESS:XXXXXXXXXXXXXXX
        XXXXXXXXXXXX
        XXXXXXXXXXXX

                              PRODUCT ORDER INFORMATION

PRODUCT CODE:XXXXXX

PRODUCT QUANTITY:XXXX

PRODUCT PRICE:XXXXXX
```

Details:

239

FIGURE 8–9

A layout form showing a design for a CRT screen

logical information-system design. System flowcharts use a set of standardized symbols (Figure 8–10). Figure 8–11 is an example of a system flowchart.

When constructing a logical design, it is usually more productive to first determine what output is needed and *then* determine the input required to produce that output. By working with the users, the system analyst determines what output is needed and its format—hard copy or soft

FIGURE 8–10
Some commonly used system flowchart symbols

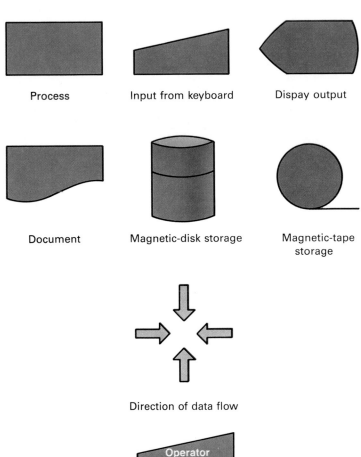

FIGURE 8–11
A system flowchart for a payroll-processing system

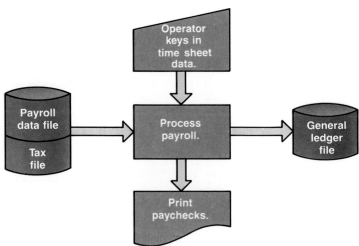

HIGHLIGHT

BOSTON'S COMPUTER MUSEUM

Over by the entrance squats the huge Whirlwind computer that coordinated the sky-scanning radar units that swept the New England skies in search of Soviet aircraft during the 1950s. There's a brontosaurus-class relic, the 175-ton SAGE (IBM Q–7) computer. Here's a UNIVAC I. What is this place? It's a retirement center for over-the-hill computer hardware—Boston's Computer Museum. Along with the Smithsonian Institution in Washington, D.C., this facility aims for nothing less than a complete display of history of computer development and use in the United States.

Established in 1982, the museum was funded initially by Digital Equipment Corporation. Since then, other companies and individuals have provided further support.

Digital's Ken Olsen had been a part of the 1950s Whirlwind project team and upon learning that MIT was getting rid of the Whirlwind, he came to its rescue by offering warehouse space. Before long the warehouse was overflowing with other finds—artifacts too valuable to be destroyed. The museum's collections staff knows that the crucial time for gathering the historically vital hardware is now, before the machines that led to today's tiny and more powerful models are lost or tossed onto a scrap heap.

Spurred on by its informal competition with the Smithsonian, the Computer Museum has found such cybernetic treasures as: the 1947 ENIAC, built at the University of Pennsylvania; Wang's first calculators and the laboratory notes he made at Harvard while developing the first magnetic-core memories; and the earliest Apples, donated by the firm's co-founder, Steve Wozniak.

Tools to Aid System Analyst

- Decision table
- Data-flow diagram
- Layout form
- System flowchart

copy. The users may require output to appear on the display screen or on preprinted forms, such as checks, inventory lists, invoices, or sales receipts.

After determining the required output, the system analyst determines what input is required to produce it and the source of that data.

Once the output and input requirements are known, the general processing requirements, including identifying what processing needs to be done and where, how much data will be handled, and how fast the data need to be processed, can be formulated. The specific formulas and procedures to convert input to output are not formulated at this point in the system life cycle.

Once the logical design is complete, a formal report with the system analyst's recommendations is presented to management. This report is often accompanied by an oral presentation to all involved parties. The report is reviewed by management in light of the feasibility study. Management then decides whether to: (a) continue to the system design step; (b) repeat the system analysis step; or (c) terminate the project. If management decides to continue to the next step, the system analyst or system designer now proceeds with the system design.

SYSTEM DESIGN

System design involves detailing the physical design of the system; it is the *how* of the process. Once the logical design is outlined during system analysis, the system analyst or a system designer determines the physical design, which describes the hardware, the software, and the operating procedures required to make the system operational.

The analyst may develop a prototype during the system-design phase. A **prototype** is a stripped-down model of the final system. It does not contain the frills of the final version, but it allows the analyst or the users to evaluate the basic operation or suitability of the system.

During the system design step, the logical design of the system is further refined and the physical design is developed.

The outputs that were developed during the system analysis are evaluated by the system designer and users, and any corrections or changes are made. The types of hardware and software needed to produce the outputs are identified and their costs are determined. For example, the analyst may have decided that minicomputers rather than mainframes are appropriate. Specific brands or models are not identified until system development.

Next, the inputs that were described in the system analysis are evaluated and appropriate corrections or changes are made. Once the input data have been verified, the system designer works with the user to design the input screens, determine whether data will be entered in a batch mode or as source data, and design any paper forms which will be used to write on or code input data.

The system designer then plans the required processing steps. These steps involve two basic tasks: file design and software design.

File design involves planning the way data used in the logical design are organized, stored, and controlled. The analyst consults with the users to determine how data will be organized into records and files.

All data items used in the files are defined using a data dictionary. A **data dictionary** describes the types of data, their structure, and how they are to be used in the system. The use of a data dictionary prevents confusion between departments or personnel as to the meaning of datum or its intended use (Figure 8–12).

Each user has specific system requirements and requires file storage and file access methods that reflect these needs. So the system designer now determines whether data should be stored in a file using batch or transaction methods and the type of file-access method to be used— sequential, direct, or indexed-sequential.

The system designer also plans control procedures to protect against errors that may occur in the information system. Control can be built into the system to monitor and check for errors caused by hardware, software, or the people that operate the system. For example, input controls, validation, and accuracy checking are necessary to ensure that data are entered

FIGURE 8–12

Partial data dictionary containing description of fields for employee records

Field	Field Description	Field Type	Field Width
EMPNUM	Employee number	Numeric	4
EMPNAM	Employee name	Character	25
EMPDAT	Date employee hired	Character	8
LSTR	Date of last raise	Character	8
DEPTNUM	Department number employee works in	Numeric	4
DEPTNAM	Department name employee works in	Character	20

correctly. Controls must also be designed to assure the security of the data used in the information system.

After the file design has been completed, the software design is developed. Software design involves devising programs to ensure that the available inputs will produce the desired output. The design should be easy to understand and maintainable by others. (Software development is discussed in more detail in Chapter 10.)

During this stage, work is also begun to design the procedures to be used to test the information system during the development and implementation steps. These procedures are established at this point because, in the development and implementation steps, there is often a great deal of pressure to get a system installed and running as soon as possible. If testing procedures have not already been designed, they are often done haphazardly or not at all.

After the physical design of the system has been determined, a report outlining all the system analysis and design work is submitted to management. This report is again reviewed in light of the original feasibility study. Management may choose to: (a) proceed to the system development phase; (b) redo the system analysis and/or system design; or (c) terminate the project.

SYSTEM DEVELOPMENT

By now the users and the system-design personnel should have a clear idea of how the information system will work. If the system personnel have been working closely with the users, the system should meet all their requirements. When everyone is satisfied with the system design, the actual system development can take place.

System development refers to creating the new information system from the physical designs established in the preceding phase.

The system analyst first determines if a suitable prewritten software package exists that can be purchased to implement the physical design or if new programs must be developed.

Depending on the system design and the users' needs, prepackaged software may be available. Prepackaged software is general in nature because it is intended for a wide range of users. If this type of package is chosen, the analyst must make sure it completely fulfills the requirements of the users. Development time is greatly reduced if prewritten software is available.

If a new set of programs is to be written to implement the system, the system designer calls on a computer programmer to write the code. Documentation from the analysis and design processes gives the programmer all the information needed to code the programs. When writing and coding a program, the programmer uses a structured approach to ensure the program can be easily understood and maintained. (Structured-programming concepts and the program development process are covered in Chapter 10.)

When the programs are completed, they are tested using actual data from the users and test data designed by system personnel to test the extremes of the system. To be sure mistakes can be detected by the system, the tests are performed not only with accurate data, but also with data that contain errors. During these tests and, in fact, anywhere in the system life cycle, modifications can be made to the design. However, the later in the cycle that the modification occurs, the more expensive and time-consuming it's likely to be.

The actual specifications of the hardware are also developed during this phase. For example, if minicomputers were to be used for the system, specific types of minicomputers are selected now. Printers or plotters are chosen, and all the cable needs are finalized. Costs of the equipment are investigated and purchase orders are approved.

Personnel needs, including the users and all support staff to operate the information system, are also determined at this time.

Again, a report of recommendations is compiled and presented to management and users. After all the involved participants agree, the next stage—system implementation—can begin.

SYSTEM IMPLEMENTATION

Everything in the design at this point may have passed all the preliminary tests, but the big one is yet to come—making the system work as a whole in the users' own environment.

System implementation involves testing the installed system, converting from the old system to the new one, and training the users.

Testing

Testing actually should take place during each stage of the system development. During system implementation, however, the system is tested as a whole rather than in parts. The hardware, software, and all other elements in the system must perform as well during normal everyday processing as they did in the controlled tests.

The users evaluate the new system, comparing it to the old one. At this point, any minor flaws can still be detected and corrected. If the new system performs well and is accepted, the process of replacing the old system begins.

The New York City Department of Transportation (DOT) designed and implemented a computerized system to prevent gridlock traffic jams such as the one shown. DOT employees monitor traffic from control centers. (Photos courtesy of New York City Department of Transportation)

Conversion

Conversion is the process of changing over from the old system to the new system. It can take one of four basic forms: direct; pilot; phased; and parallel.

Direct Conversion   The quickest way to replace an old system is with direct conversion. **Direct conversion** is the immediate changeover that results by dismantling the old system as soon as the new one starts operating. The danger in this method is that there is no temporary backup in the event that all the problems weren't worked out of the new system.

Pilot Conversion   With **pilot conversion,** the entire new system is installed, but it is used in only part of the organization's operation. For example, a supermarket changing from manual cash registers to on-line processing may commit only one or two of its checkouts to the new system. This conversion allows the users to fully evaluate the system and train employees while still operating the rest of the business on the old system.

245

System Conversion Methods

- Direct
- Pilot
- Phased
- Parallel

Phased Conversion   **Phased conversion** is the implementation of only part of the new system at one time. During phased conversion, the entire system is slowly introduced, piece by piece, over a period of time. This process of conversion takes longer but minimizes the risks of fully committing to a new system.

Parallel Conversion   **Parallel conversion** is the operation of the old system and the new system alongside each other. The cost of running two systems simultaneously may be high, but this type of conversion allows for direct comparison, and the users do not have to worry about shutdowns if the new system fails to perform.

Training

Even the most highly developed system will not benefit the users if no one can operate it. Training is very important if the users are to operate the new system successfully. Training programs and manuals should address all levels of personnel involved with the new system. Managers should learn what the system can do for them and their business (Figure 8–13). Operators need training in data entry, how to retrieve data stored in files, and even how to fix a paper jam in a printer.

Training can occur in several ways. A one-on-one training approach can be used where one trainer instructs a single individual in the use of a system. This method is expensive, but it may be necessary for complex systems. Group workshops, where one trainer instructs many individuals, is another method. Here, training costs are minimized, and numerous individuals can be trained simultaneously. A third technique, computer-aided instruction (CAI), uses specific software to instruct users through an interactive dialog in the operation of an information system. The advantage of

FIGURE 8–13
Middle-level managers attend a training class outlining a new management information system. (Courtesy of Electrohome Limited)

CAI is that users can learn at their own pace and can review the program whenever necessary.

Once the system is installed and operating in an organization, it enters the system maintenance stage of the system life cycle.

SYSTEM MAINTENANCE

System maintenance is the ongoing process of monitoring and evaluating the new system. Business needs and computer technology are constantly changing; therefore, an information system may need to be updated periodically to keep it current and ensure that it continues to meet the information needs of the business.

System maintenance involves identifying the need for change in the current system and making the appropriate changes. Even the best-designed system may some day need to be replaced. When a problem or new opportunity is discovered, the system analysis phase of the system life cycle begins again.

SUMMARY

Computers form part of a system along with other devices, people, and methods that are interrelated in working toward a common goal. A system established to convert data to information is called an information system.

The system life cycle is the life span of an information system consisting of five steps: system analysis; system design; system development; system implementation; and system maintenance.

The steps in the system life cycle involve not only computers, but also people including users, system analysts, system designers, and programmers.

A project management team is often established to coordinate system projects and facilitate communication between all involved parties. A project manager is the person responsible for planning and coordinating the tasks to be accomplished by the project management team. To plan and monitor work schedules, the project manager can use Gantt charts and Program Evaluation Review Technique (PERT) diagrams.

Documentation is another important means of communication throughout the cycle. Documentation is the written or graphic record of the steps carried out during the development of an information system.

System analysis is the process of analyzing a system to discover a way to modify it or create a new system to meet the users' needs. It involves identifying the problem or new opportunity, conducting a feasibility study, gathering data, analyzing data, and developing a logical design.

System analysts have many tools at their disposal to help them design a system. Among these are decision tables, data-flow diagrams, layout forms, and system flowcharts.

The system design step further refines the logical design and details the physical design required to implement it. Often, a prototype, or stripped-down version, of the final system is developed to allow the analyst and users to evaluate the basic operation or suitability of the system. The

System Life Cycle

- System analysis
- System design
- System development
- System implementation
- System maintenance

HIGHLIGHT

CAPTAIN COMPUTER

I must go down to the sea again,
To the lonely sea and the sky.
And all I ask is a tall ship
And software to steer her by.

Actually, poet John Masefield specified "a star" to steer his ship by, but progress rides on the deep as well as on the land. Today, sailing ships—those graceful vehicles that bring humanity and nature together in their most elemental forms—are being designed, outfitted, and guided by computer technology.

These applications were evident everywhere in the 1987 America's Cup Race in Australia. Several countries competing in the race began their work by using computers to simulate hull designs and predict how the ships might perform in the water. Designs that showed promise were made into scale models which were, in turn, tested in wind tunnels to find and trim their resistance. A team of people using a Cray supercomputer designed the winning yacht, U.S. entry *Stars and Stripes,* and a French group used a computer-driven laser to cut its specially-designed sails.

On board the yachts, computers extracted data from sensors placed on the masts and hulls and used the information to plot and replot the best course for the ships to follow.

It was enough to send the old sea-dogs Masefield praised grumbling back up the beach.

two major tasks to be accomplished during the system design step are file design and software design.

In the system development step, the system personnel select prewritten software packages, or they write new programs. If they fit the users' need, prewritten application packages can greatly shorten the development time. If a suitable package is not available, a programmer codes the specific software necessary to make the system operational.

System implementation is the next step of the system life cycle. In this phase, the system is further tested, personnel are trained, and the process of conversion from the old system begins. The process of conversion can be done by the direct, pilot, phased, or parallel method.

System maintenance, the final step of the system life cycle, is an ongoing process of monitoring and evaluating the new system. It involves identifying the need for change in a system and then making the appropriate changes. Eventually, a problem or new opportunity will require that a full-scale system life cycle begin again.

Key Terms

data dictionary (p. 242)

data-flow diagram (p. 237)

decision table (p. 237)

direct conversion (p. 245)

documentation (p. 233)

feasibility study (p. 235)

Gantt chart (p. 232)

information system (p. 230)

layout form (p. 238)

parallel conversion (p. 246)

phased conversion (p. 246)

pilot conversion (p. 245)

Program Evaluation Review Technique (PERT) diagram (p. 233)

programmer (p. 231)

project management team (p. 231)

prototype (p. 242)

system (p. 230)

system analysis (p. 234)

system analyst (p. 231)

system design (p. 242)

system designer (p. 231)

system development (p. 243)

system flowchart (p. 238)

system implementation (p. 244)

system librarian (p. 233)

system life cycle (p. 231)

system maintenance (p. 247)

user (p. 231)

Review Questions

1. What is a system?

2. What is the purpose of an information system?

3. Describe the role of the following people in the system life cycle: user; system analyst; system designer; and programmer.

4. What is the function of a project management team? Which personnel make up the team?

5. Describe two tools a project manager can use to monitor schedules.

6. What is documentation? Describe its function in the system life cycle.

7. What are the stages of the system life cycle?

8. What is the purpose of a system analysis?

9. Discuss the three concerns that are addressed during a feasibility study.

10. What sources are available to the system analyst for gathering data?

11. Describe the two general steps in developing a logical design of an information system.

12. Describe two tools that a system analyst can use to help analyze data.

13. In addition to a data-flow diagram, describe two other tools the system analyst can use to communicate the logic design to the users and other system personnel.

14. What is the purpose of the system design step?

15. What is a prototype and why is one developed?

16. Describe a file design.

17. Describe the purpose of a data dictionary.

18. What is the purpose of the system development step?

19. List the three processes involved in the system implementation step.

20. List and discuss the four basic types of conversion.

21. Describe three approaches to training personnel in a new information system.

22. What is the purpose of the system maintenance step?

23. Why is it important that the users be involved in the system life cycle?

24. Why should testing procedures to be used later in the development and implementation phases be designed earlier during the system design step?

25. Describe some possible situations in a business that might call for a system analysis.

INFOMODULE

Case Study: The System Life Cycle in a Small Business

In this case study, you will see how a small, upstart architectural firm develops an information system. This study simplifies many of the processes, but nevertheless you will see how the system life cycle might evolve in a small business environment.

Sprungl Designs was incorporated a little over a year ago. Laura Sprungl started the business and originally employed two full-time architects. The architects were paid a salary; Sprungl figured the payroll, wrote checks, and posted general-ledger entries by hand. At first, this system was manageable. But soon, the company's reputation grew and so did the number of clients and staff. Sprungl Designs now employs five full-time architects and fifteen part-time personnel, mostly architecture students from the local college.

In the early stages of the business, preparing the payroll and handling general-ledger entries had not significantly limited the amount of time Sprungl could spend on the company's architectural projects. However, as the company grew, more and more of her time was taken away from architectural clients and projects that demanded her attention. Deadlines were missed, delays were frequent, and some bids were not even submitted. These problems had a significant negative impact on the company's reputation. In addition, Sprungl felt she was losing control of how much time and money was being spent on each project.

SYSTEM ANALYSIS

At a meeting with the senior architects, everyone agreed that a computerized system was probably needed to manage all these tasks. They further decided to hire an outside consultant, a system analyst, to determine the best way to solve their problems.

The following week, the system analyst, Bob Alan, arrived. After preliminary talks with Sprungl, Alan called a meeting with Sprungl and the senior architects to determine the nature and scope of the problem. Alan discovered several important facts:

1. Payroll was calculated manually by Sprungl and checks were hand typed. This system was time-consuming for the owner; her efforts would be more productively spent overseeing the company's projects. In addition, Alan learned that due to miscalculations or typing errors the paychecks were often incorrect. As a result, employees were becoming disgruntled and losing confidence in the organization.
2. Part-time employees currently were not using time sheets. Hours were kept haphazardly and were not attributed to a project; they were submitted on improvised slips of paper. Sometimes, these scraps of paper were illegible and often misplaced.
3. Sprungl was also making entries in the general ledger and paying bills. She was spending fewer hours at the drawing board and was unhappy working on tasks that were not related to her field of interest.
4. Sprungl needed a way to track the employees' time and wages according to the particular project they were working on to make sure her bidding process was accurate. All employees, hourly as well as salaried, should submit time sheets that would reflect their hours by projects.

Alan and the company management agreed that purchasing a computerized information system and hiring an operator for the system would relieve Sprungl of the burden of working on the payroll and accounting; that, in turn, would allow her to monitor and control the amount of time and money being spent on each project. At the end of the meeting, Sprungl asked Alan to proceed with a feasibility study.

The first question that Alan needed to answer was: Could the system be physically and technically configured? From his previous experience and knowledge of the equipment and software available, Alan was sure it could be.

Next, he addressed the question: If developed, would a computerized system be used? From the meeting, Alan learned that Sprungl, although not proficient with computers, was eager to adopt a system and reap the benefits that a computerized system could bring.

Finally, Alan began the task of preparing a cost-to-benefit study. The results of this study follow.

Benefits

A computerized information system would:

☐ Free Sprungl's time for company projects where her expertise was needed (As a result, projects requiring her time and effort would not be delayed, and the company's credibility of delivering on time would be restored. The improved reputation and the fact that Sprungl could bid on and accept more jobs would enable the company to earn more revenues.)

☐ Increase accuracy and reduce the time spent on payroll and other accounting functions

☐ Increase employee morale and confidence due to prompt and accurate preparation of paychecks

☐ Provide management reports to help monitor and control time and expenses on projects that would increase their profitability

☐ Provide automatic production of monthly, quarterly, and year-end tax reports to assure the company's compliance with tax requirements, thus preventing the assessment of penalties for late or incorrect filings

☐ Allow the company to pay bills to creditors on time, thereby increasing their credibility and credit standing, and saving interest and service charges

Costs

☐ Software (prewritten or developed)
☐ Hardware (computer system, printer, cables, interface, etc.)
☐ Supplies (disks, paper, printer, ribbons, multiple-copy checks, etc.)
☐ Training new operator and current staff
☐ Wages for a new operator for the system

Alan compared the costs to the benefits. He found that the long-term increase in revenues gained by freeing Sprungl's time and providing her with increased control of time and money spent on the projects, combined with the improved attitude of the employees, considerably outweighed the costs, which were primarily one-time cost outlays. The costs were within the company's budget. The hourly wage paid to the new operator was negligible compared to the increased revenues that Sprungl anticipated.

Alan presented the results of the feasibility study to Sprungl who gave approval for the next step.

Alan then gathered facts about the current system—how it operates and what data the company needs to operate.

Alan used both internal and external sources to gather this information. From the internal sources, he gathered information by interviewing Sprungl, the full-time staff, and the part-time staff. He also gathered data from internally generated business documents such as the company's general ledger and payroll and employee records.

Alan used external sources too; he compared Sprungl Designs to other small companies and read computer and information systems journals to update his knowledge of the latest equipment and software available.

After gathering all this information, Alan began to analyze the data and to construct a logical design for the system. From the data, Alan determined the following outputs would be needed from a new system:

☐ Printed paychecks (hard copy)
☐ Printed general ledger (hard copy)
☐ Job-cost reports (hard copy and soft copy)
☐ Weekly payroll report (hard copy)
☐ Quarterly tax reports (hard copy)
☐ Year-end closing reports (hard copy)

The following inputs would be needed to produce these outputs:

☐ Employees' hours broken down by project numbers

☐ Employee data (name, pay rate, exemptions, deductions, etc.)

☐ Tax data (city, state, and federal tax rates)

☐ Quarterly and year-end tax information

Alan decided to use several tools to construct the logical design. First, he created a data-flow diagram to show the logical flow of data through the system. He outlined that as follows:

1. Employee writes hours and job numbers on time sheet daily and submits it to manager weekly.
2. Manager validates hours.
3. Manager submits time sheet to computer system operator.
4. Operator enters data into payroll program.
5. Operator runs payroll program to calculate paychecks and job-cost data and update general ledger.
6. Operator verifies that calculations are reasonable. (No zero or million dollar checks have been calculated.)
7. Operator loads paychecks into printer, prints checks and verifies amounts, and generates other reports as needed.
8. Operator delivers checks to owner for signature.
9. Owner signs checks and returns them to operator.
10. Operator distributes checks to employees.

Figure 1 shows the data-flow diagram.

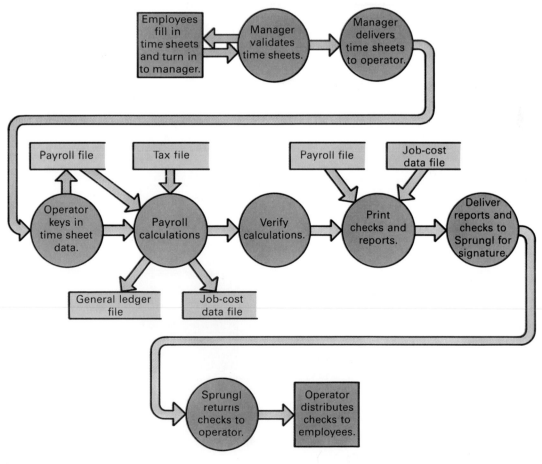

FIGURE 1
Data-flow diagram for Sprungl Designs

FIGURE 2
System flowchart for Sprungl
Designs

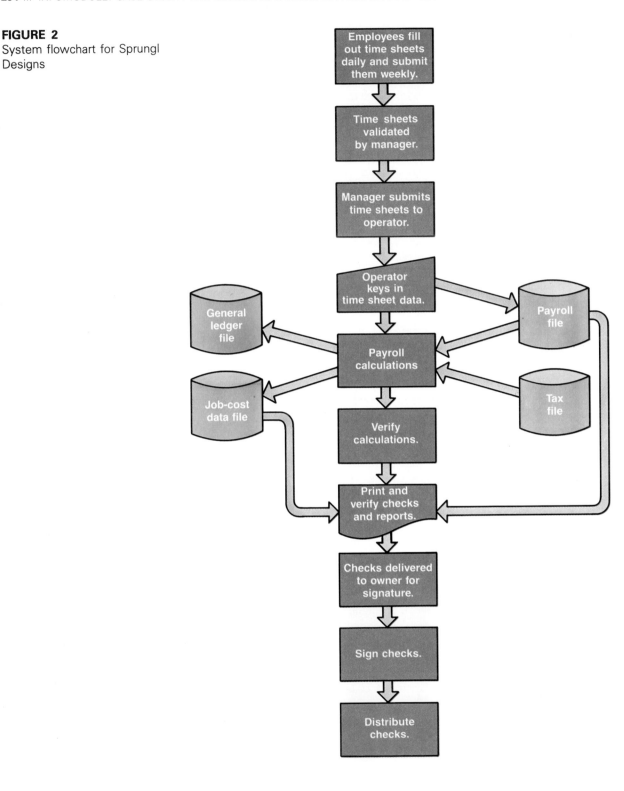

FIGURE 3
Data-flow diagram for payroll
calculation

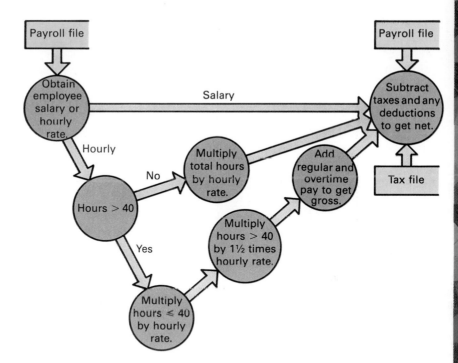

Alan also used a system flowchart to graphically illustrate the type of hardware devices and storage media that will be required to implement the logical design. Figure 2 shows the system flowchart he created.

Next, Alan detailed the processing steps. The processing steps shown in the data-flow diagram are very general in nature and can be broken down into separate and distinct tasks. Figure 3 is a data-flow diagram showing an expanded version of what happens during payroll calculation. Note that gross pay is calculated for salaried employees by simply using their existing salary amount. Gross pay for hourly employees involves determining if they have worked more than forty hours. All hours up to forty are multiplied by the employee's normal rate and added to overtime hours that are multiplied by one and one-half times their normal hourly rate. Figure 4 shows a decision table that outlines the conditions, rules, and actions to be taken when determining if an employee receives overtime pay.

After gross pay is calculated, taxes are subtracted to give the employee's net pay. Currently no other deductions are taken by employees of Sprungl Designs.

After completing the logical design, Alan writes a report outlining his findings and recommendations and presents it to Sprungl who reviews and approves the project for continuation to the system design step.

SYSTEM DESIGN
During the system design, Alan develops a physical design for the system. The outputs de-

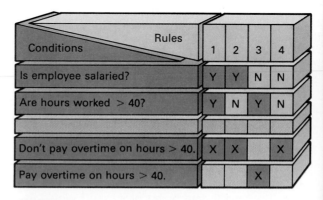

FIGURE 4
A decision table showing the rules, conditions, and actions to be taken when determining if an employee is to receive overtime pay

termined in the system-analysis phase are evaluated, and Alan decides that a microcomputer and a letter-quality printer are needed. The printer must print on multipage forms so that copies of checks, tax reports, and monthly reports can be printed simultaneously with the use of carbons. In addition, an accounting software package that includes general ledger, payroll, and job-cost modules is needed.

Next, Alan evaluates the inputs determined during the system-analysis step. He determines that payroll data should be entered in a batch mode and that an input form for hourly time sheets needs to be designed.

The next task is to create the file design. Alan first determines how data should be organized into records and files. Here is a list of the files and records that the company needs:

- ☐ Employee data file
- ☐ Records to contain employee information
- ☐ General ledger file
- ☐ Records to contain a list of categories to which expenses or revenues are debited or credited
- ☐ Tax files
- ☐ Records to contain tax rates for city, state, and federal
- ☐ Job-cost file
- ☐ Records to contain cost and time information related to a particular project
- ☐ Quarterly and year-end tax file
- ☐ Records to contain information for preparing quarterly and year-end city, state, and federal tax reports
- ☐ W-2s
- ☐ 940s
- ☐ 941s

To avoid any confusion in the meaning of datum or how it was to be used, Alan created a data dictionary. Alan confirmed that the data would be entered into the system in a batch mode. He also needed to determine which file-access method would be the best choice. Usually, the payroll data being processed would involve weekly entries for all employees; therefore, sequential access would be appropriate. However, occasionally personnel files are re-

viewed or bonus checks are prepared on an individual basis, so a direct-access method would be appropriate here. Alan decided that the best choice is an indexed-sequential method that allows both sequential and direct access to files.

Job codes for each project also needed to be designed. Each project was assigned a primary code, and each task in the project was assigned a secondary code. Alan kept these code numbers short, easy to write, and easy to remember. The list of code numbers would be typed and distributed to each employee.

The next task was to create the software design. Since Alan's experience told him that prewritten software was available, he did not work up detailed software specifications of how the software would process data. Instead, he made a list of the goals the software would be required to meet. This list included

- ☐ Calculate payroll accurately and print checks
- ☐ Calculate job-cost information
- ☐ Post payroll data automatically to general ledger
- ☐ Print payroll reports
- ☐ Print quarterly tax forms
- ☐ Print year-end tax forms and reports
- ☐ Be flexible (If mistakes are made, the software should allow the user to back out of them and reenter data. All appropriate modules should reflect the corrections automatically. These requirements would be used when evaluating software for the system.)

The final step was for Alan to design test procedures for the development and implementation steps. He decided that the hardware could be tested using the diagnostic software that the manufacturer includes with the hardware. For the software test, he decided to set up a miniversion of the general ledger and use data for one employee to cut a single check, thus verifying that the software was functional.

For the implementation step, he decided to use the past three months' data as test data to match the results against known, previously prepared data. Data for each month would be entered, payroll calculated, and then verified. Then, all three months would be totaled, and quarterly tax and management reports would be printed. Alan would also use some extremes such as negative numbers and outrageously high numbers to see if the program would bring these errors to the operator's attention.

After completing the system design, Alan wrote his report and presented it to the owner. Everything looked fine, and Sprungl gave her approval to start the system development step.

SYSTEM DEVELOPMENT

Normally, Alan's first decision would be to choose between using prewritten software and creating new software. Because prewritten software would be cheaper, available now, and presumably would have no errors, Alan determined that it was his choice. From his experience, he knew that prewritten software was available, and a search of the local computer stores confirmed this. Alan found several packages that met the software requirements. He examined a number of factors, including cost, vendor support, features, and ease of use for each package. He created a grid chart (Figure 5) to help make the decision. From the grid chart, it was clear that the choice should be the *Easy Works* accounting package. A purchase order was issued and presented to the owner for her approval.

Alan's next task was to choose the specific microcomputer and printer for the system. When shopping for the computer, Alan considered the speed and power of the computer, cost, available service, vendor's reputation, computer manufacturer's reputation, and location of the vendor (for fast service). Knowing the current requirements of Sprungl Designs and planning for future expansion, Alan determined that the IBM Personal System/2 Model 60 which uses the Intel 80286 processor would give the necessary processing speed and power needed now, yet allow expansion of the system without exceeding the computer's capabilities. He also decided to recommend the installation of a 70 megabyte hard-disk drive to allow adequate disk storage space. The hard-disk drive would also allow fast data-access speeds. A letter-quality printer was chosen because it could print multiple-form checks and reports. All other hardware, including interface cards and cables, was also chosen.

A high-resolution monitor was selected for its clarity in displaying text and numbers. The costs were comparable at all the vendors, but Alan found a respected, local dealer two blocks from the company that had a service department on site. He decided to recommend that the equipment be purchased there. The access of quick service which Sprungl Designs desired eliminated the cheaper mail-order houses from competition. A purchase order was issued and given to Sprungl for approval.

Both the software and the hardware purchase orders were approved. Alan made the purchases and then began testing each component. After it was clear that each component functioned properly, he prepared his system development report and submitted it for approval. Sprungl was satisfied with the results of the system development and gave her approval to begin implementing the new system.

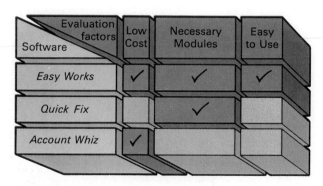

FIGURE 5
Grid chart for Sprungl Designs

SYSTEM IMPLEMENTATION

The first step in the system implementation was to set up the entire system and test it using the test data designed in the system design phase. The tests verified that the system was working properly.

The next step was to train the employees. The operator was hired and taught in a one-on-one training session. Alan, who was familiar with the accounting package, trained the new operator. The new operator took over the accounting functions, enabling Sprungl to concentrate on the company's projects. All employees met in a group workshop where the new system was explained to them. Here they were shown how to fill out their new time sheets properly.

After training was complete, the conversion from the old system began. Even though Sprungl was receptive to the new computer system, Alan sensed that she was uneasy about trusting it. Alan suggested that the new computer system be run parallel to the old paper system for the first three months to insure that the new system was working properly and that everyone was comfortable with it. At the end of this period, if everything was running smoothly, the old system would be completely dropped.

SYSTEM MAINTENANCE

Once the new system was running, the system maintenance step began, and Alan's job as a consultant was finished. During this step, the operator monitors the system to see if any changes are needed. Eventually new requirements may result in Alan being called back to initiate another system life cycle. That might occur when the company business grows so much that the current system can no longer support it or when new technological developments occur that improve business at Sprungl Designs.

In fact, maybe they're almost ready to discuss the possibility of buying computers for each architect to use in computer-aided designing!

QUESTIONS

1. In the case study of Sprungl Designs, what problem triggered the idea to hire a consultant?
2. What was the consultant's title and role in the project?
3. What did the cost-to-benefit study indicate in the feasibility study?
4. What tools did the system analyst use to detail the processing steps for the new system?
5. What advantages do you think there are to selecting prepackaged software as compared to developing your own?

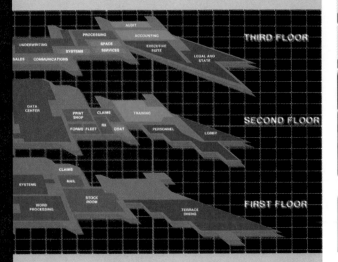

OBJECTIVES

- ☐ Describe a management information system and explain why it is used
- ☐ Describe a data base and discuss data-base design concepts
- ☐ List the levels of management and the types of decisions made by each
- ☐ List and describe the four general types of reports generated by a management information system
- ☐ Explain the difference between a decision support system and a management information system

OUTLINE

MANAGEMENT INFORMATION SYSTEMS

DATA-BASE DESIGN CONCEPTS
    Designing a Data Base
    Data-base Structures
    Data-base Query Language

MANAGERS AND INFORMATION NEEDS
    Role of a Manager
    Management Levels and Information Needs
    Information Provided by an MIS
    Information Quality, Value, and Cost

DECISION SUPPORT SYSTEMS

MICROCOMPUTER USE IN DECISION MAKING

INFOMODULE: Case Study: Overview of a Manufacturing MIS System

ORDER-ENTRY SYSTEM

INVENTORY-CONTROL SYSTEM

MATERIALS REQUIREMENTS PLANNING (MRP) SYSTEM

ACCOUNTS-RECEIVABLE SYSTEM

PAYROLL SYSTEM

GENERAL-LEDGER SYSTEM

9

Management Information Systems and Data-base Design Concepts

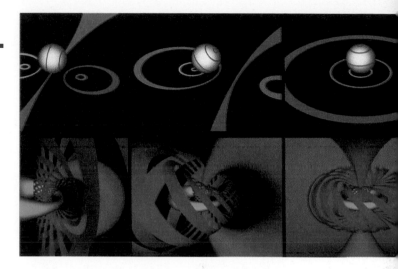

PROFILE: Grace Murray Hopper

Not many soon-to-be octogenarians make major career moves like this one, but in 1986, Grace Murray Hopper, at age 79, retired as a rear admiral in Naval Data Automation Command in the U.S. Navy, and serves as senior consultant at Digital Equipment Corporation.

Admiral Hopper is widely known in the computer field for helping to develop early computers, and she is well-known among students and members of the computer industry as a lecturer and spokesperson for innovation. During her presentations, she discusses data processing and the nature and importance of information.

Hopper, a native of New York City, attended Vassar College and went on to receive her master's degree and doctorate from Yale University. Her work in computer technology has been conducted in a mixed environment that includes the academic scene, the business world, and the military.

After joining the U.S. Naval Reserve in 1944, she worked with Howard Aiken to program the Mark I, the first sequence-controlled digital calculator. Besides teaching in colleges and universities, she was senior mathematician for Eckert-Mauchley Computer Corporation and worked for Sperry Corporation as a system engineer and later as a staff scientist in system programming. Part of this time Hopper was on military leave. She helped develop

UNIVAC I, the first large commercial computer, and she was instrumental in creating the COBOL programming language.

In 1966, she was retired at the age of 60 (the Navy thought she was too old) with the rank of commander in the U.S. Naval Reserve. Within seven months, however, Hopper was recalled to active duty. Much of her military service has been dedicated to helping run all the Navy's nonweapons computers and keeping the Navy at the leading edge of computer technology. Now, she has retired from the Naval Reserve a second time, once again moving into private industry.

Hopper has received world recognition and many honors as one of the outstanding contributors to the computer revolution. One unique honor was presented in 1969, when the Data Processing Management Association selected her as their first Computer Sciences "Man of the Year." There has been no higher award, she says, than that of the privilege and responsibility of service in the U.S. Navy.

When *Computerworld*'s senior editor Janet Fiderio asked her if society has become too dependent on computers, she replied, "Well, we used to be dependent on paper. What difference does it make that our information is on computer or paper?" Fiderio answered, "Computers can fail." Hopper responded, "And paper can burn."

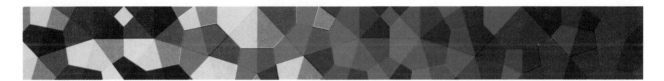

In the last chapter, you learned what an information system is and how one is developed. Information systems can provide a user with just about any kind of information needed.

To run a successful business, the people in charge must continually make decisions based on not only current information about their business but also information about the rest of the world. Managers often use an information system to help them plan, organize, and direct their organization. If this information is wrong, late, lengthy, or confusing, their decisions might be in error or not made at all. These types of blunders can cause a business to lose profits or fail altogether.

Since computers have entered the business scene, information can be produced and disseminated faster than ever before. However, managers don't have the time to sort through every piece of paper that comes into the office; besides, different levels of managers need different kinds of information. Computers and their associated programs must be properly organized and managed so managers will not drown in a sea of information.

This chapter examines a management information system, a type of information system that supplies managers with the information they need. Data bases, the heart of a management information system, are also described. In addition, an extension of a management information system, the decision support system, is discussed.

MANAGEMENT INFORMATION SYSTEMS

An information system that supplies information specifically to aid managers with decision-making responsibilities is called a **management information system (MIS).** In earlier times, an MIS simply was a system in which managers talked, discussed, and shared information about their departments to help in decision making. A modern MIS uses computers to generate reports from data stored about the company's daily activities and provides this information to managers in a timely fashion to assist in decision making (Figure 9–1).

FIGURE 9–1
This operator works at the division operating center, which is part of Santa Fe
Southern Pacific's MIS. (Courtesy of Santa Fe Southern Pacific Corp.)

Elements of an MIS

- Data
- Software
- Hardware
- Information
- People

The computer itself does not make the decisions, but with the application of an MIS, a manager is supported in the process of making informed decisions. Because more information is more readily accessed, better-informed decisions can be made much faster.

A management information system is composed of data, software, hardware, information, and people. Each is part of a total concept of integrated resources that can be used by an organization to reach its goals and objectives.

The data used in an MIS must be stored in an organized way. If data are unorganized, it becomes impossible to retrieve and use them in an efficient and timely fashion, rendering the MIS virtually useless. To ensure that data retrieval is uncomplicated and timely, a data base is used. The data base is the foundation upon which an MIS is built. The following section discusses some data-base design concepts.

DATA-BASE DESIGN CONCEPTS

A **data base** is a concept of file organization; it consists of related files stored together so that groups of data items can be easily accessed or retrieved by those who need them. The data are integrated so that individual datum can be accessed in a variety of ways. A **data-base management system (DBMS)** is the software that functions as the interface between users, other programs, and the data base itself. It allows the data to be stored, maintained, manipulated, and retrieved.

Prepackaged DBMSs are available from vendors for both large systems and microcomputers. However, some organizations using extremely

263

HIGHLIGHT

HIGH-TECH HAVENS   Silicon Valley near Palo Alto in the Santa Clara Valley of Southern California is known as a high-tech mecca, the place where many computer and computer-related industries first started. Now it's clear that there are other high technology pockets from coast to coast in the U.S. Some other areas where silicon, computers, and chips are found include

- ☐ Silicon Forest, the area southwest of Portland, Oregon, that has become a haven for large Japanese companies such as NEC, Epson, and Fujitsu
- ☐ Silicon Mountain, or Colorado Springs, Colorado, where chip production and technology reaches a "higher elevation"
- ☐ Silicon Prairie, the flatlands north of Dallas, Texas, that have been developed by entrepreneurs who started such companies as Electronic Data Systems and Texas Instruments
- ☐ Automation Alley, in Ann Arbor, Michigan, where more than 200 companies offer computer-aided design and advanced robotics for automakers
- ☐ Research Triangle, located southeast of Durham, North Carolina, on 6,500 acres of a high-tech, campus-like development
- ☐ Naperville, a Chicago suburb, that offers over 10,000 computer-oriented job opportunities and a place where sunbathing and roller skating along the River Walk are commonplace—a California-style culture with a mid-western-style forecast

Austin, Texas, has its High-Tech Hills, and over 600 research firms have made their homes in Fairfax County, Virginia.

Another area that is not quite as aptly named is Route 128, the highway around Boston where Massachusetts Institute of Technology and Harvard engineers and scientists have long been establishing companies, such as Wang Laboratories.

Many areas of the country are capitalizing on the computer boom. Maybe the next high-tech industry will be in your hometown.

large amounts of data and those with special data-handling requirements often must create their own DBMS in-house or hire outside consultants.

Designing a Data Base

Designing a data base in a business environment can be a complex project involving many people. In some companies, the **data-base administrator** is in charge of designing, implementing, and maintaining the data base and all related activities. The data-base administrator, along with the users and other specialists, analyze the requirements of the proposed data base. Of course, the main factor to be considered is the user's needs.

After determining the data base requirements, a schema and subschemas are developed. The **schema** is the conceptual, or logical, design showing the relationships among data elements in a data base. The schema and subschemas comprise the data base's logical design, which is the user's view of how the data appear to be arranged on the secondary storage media.

To help maintain data-base security, many users will be denied access to some of the information stored in a data base; therefore, the logical design must take this into consideration. With the overall schema developed, various subsets of the schema, or **subschemas,** can be designed to limit access of individual users. Users are then limited to accessing only the data in the subschemas that they are authorized to use (Figure 9–2).

To complete the design of the data base, the physical design—how the data are actually stored on a secondary storage media and how data are

FIGURE 9–2

A logical design of a data base showing subschemas, or the individual user's view of what the data base contains

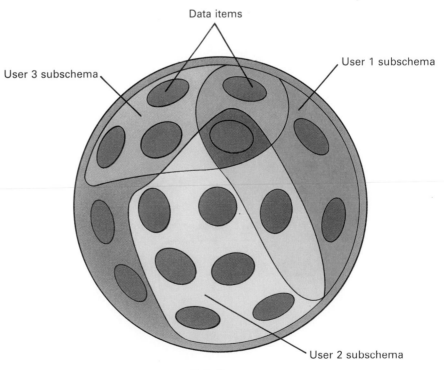

Data items

User 1 subschema

User 3 subschema

User 2 subschema

Data Base

accessed—has to be determined. Users of prepackaged DBMSs are not concerned with these issues because the physical design is already determined and implemented by the program. With prepackaged DBMSs, the user needs only to make sure that the software's physical design fits that company's needs.

Data-base Structures

The relationships outlined in a schema are often complex. Three basic structures are used to organize the data elements: hierarchical; network; and relational. In practice, the actual structure used is determined by the application and is sometimes a combination of points from all three basic data-base structures.

Hierarchical The **hierarchical data-base structure** resembles an organizational chart of a corporation. The president has many vice-presidents who, in turn, have many subordinates. Data can be structured in the same hierarchical way. One might view the structure as an upside-down family tree. At the top, or main, level of data is the **parent,** or root, level. Data found under the root level are at the **child,** or subordinate, level. Each parent can have numerous children, but each child can have only one

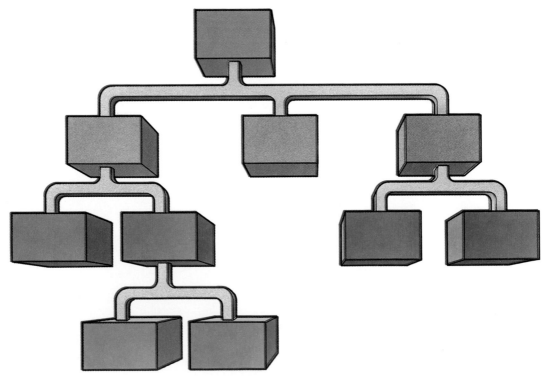

FIGURE 9–3
Hierarchical data-base structure

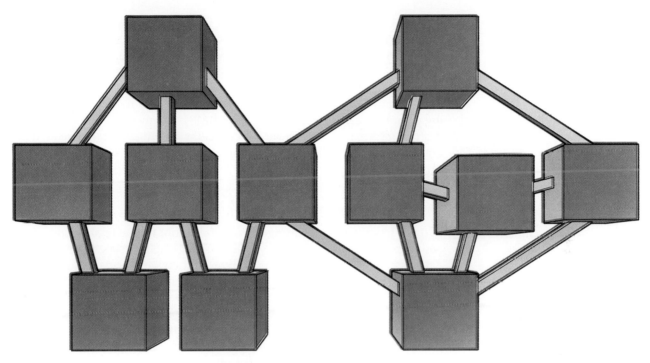

FIGURE 9–4
Network data-base structure

parent. Each child level may also be broken down into further levels with the child becoming the parent for the next level (Figure 9–3).

Because relationships between data items follow defined paths, access to the data is very fast. However, any relationships between data items must be defined when the data base is being created. If a manager wants to retrieve or manipulate data in a manner not defined when the data base was originally created, the costly, time-consuming step of redesigning the data-base structure is required.

Network The **network data-base structure** is similar to the hierarchical structure; it is more complex in nature, but also more flexible in accessing data items. Similar to a hierarchical structure, each parent can have more than one child, but in a network structure each child can have more than one parent (Figure 9–4). Therefore, more than one path can lead to the desired data level. The network data-base structure is a more versatile and flexible data-access structure than the hierarchical type because the route to data is not necessarily downward; it can be from any direction.

In the network structure, again similar to the hierarchical structure, data access is fast because relationships follow predefined paths, and any data relationships must be defined during the data-base design.

Relational The **relational data-base structure** does not rely on a parent-child relationship. Instead, the relational structure groups all the

---

Data-base Structures

- Hierarchical
- Network
- Relational

data into tables from which the actual data relationships can be built. A table consists of rows and columns. Each row specifies a record, each column represents individual data items, and the entire table represents a file (Figure 9–5). Tables can be linked to pull various data elements together.

The relationships between data items do not have to be defined during the data-base development. As managers require new ways of analyzing data, they can simply instruct the DBMS to extract and manipulate the desired information. However, because the relationships between data items are not predefined, access time can be relatively slow compared to the other two structures.

Data-base Query Language

A **data-base query language** is a helpful tool that acts as an interface between a user and the DBMS. The language helps users of a relational data base to easily manipulate, analyze, and create reports from the data contained in a data base. It is composed of simple, easy-to-use statements that allow people other than programmers to use the data base.

There are two basic query styles used: (a) query-by-example; and (b) structured query language. In **query-by-example,** a DBMS displays field information, and the user enters inquiry conditions in the desired fields. For example, if a user wants to list all the employees whose salaries are greater than $25,000 and sort the items in ascending order by department number, the screen might appear as in Figure 9–6.

Structured query language involves using commands in a structured format. For example, the inquiry in Figure 9–6 would appear as it does in Figure 9–7 using structured query language. This tells the DBMS to use the fields EMPNAM, EMPNUM, DEPTNUM, and SAL from each record in the employee file (EMPF) if the employee's salary is greater than $25,000 and to sort that list by department number.

MANAGERS AND INFORMATION NEEDS

In a business, decisions are made at all levels of management, each level having its own needs for specific types of information to handle its own

FIGURE 9–5
Relational data-base structure

EMPNAM	EMPNUM	EMPDEPT	EMPSAL
P. Bower	09135	07	22000
T. Mann	04216	11	17500
A. Sanchez	08961	04	28000
R. Bates	03032	06	25000
B. Wong	01196	07	22000

FIGURE 9–6
An example of a data-base query language that uses the query-by-example approach

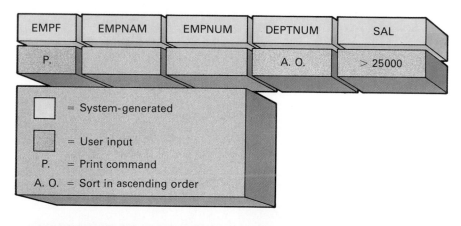

EMPF	EMPNAM	EMPNUM	DEPTNUM	SAL
P.			A. O.	> 25000

▢ = System-generated

▢ = User input

P. = Print command

A. O. = Sort in ascending order

FIGURE 9–7
An example of a data-base query language that uses the structured query language approach

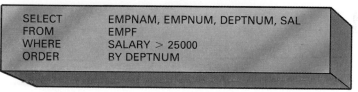

```
SELECT     EMPNAM, EMPNUM, DEPTNUM, SAL
FROM       EMPF
WHERE      SALARY > 25000
ORDER      BY DEPTNUM
```

Role of a Manager

- Plan
- Organize
- Direct
- Control

---

unique problems. Before defining the different levels of management, let's describe what a manager is and does.

Role of a Manager

A **manager** is a person responsible for using available resources to achieve an organizational goal. Resources include people, materials, and money. The overall organizational goal is usually to increase profits or reduce expenses. A manager works toward this goal through the four major functions of planning, organizing, directing, and controlling these resources.

Planning is the process of developing courses of action to meet short- and long-term goals of the organization. Organizing involves assembling people, materials, and money, and providing a structure in which personnel are responsible and accountable in working toward the organizational goal. Directing involves supplying leadership in supervising personnel through communication and motivation. Controlling involves making sure the organization is moving toward its goal. Evaluations are made of the organization's performance, and if needed, plans are provided for modifications.

Management Levels and Information Needs

Management is divided into three basic levels: top-level managers; middle-level managers; and low-level managers (Figure 9–8). Each level is involved to varying degrees in each of the four management functions and require different types of information to reach their goals. Let's look at the types of decisions made and at some of the informational needs of each level of management. Note that the amount of detail required by a man-

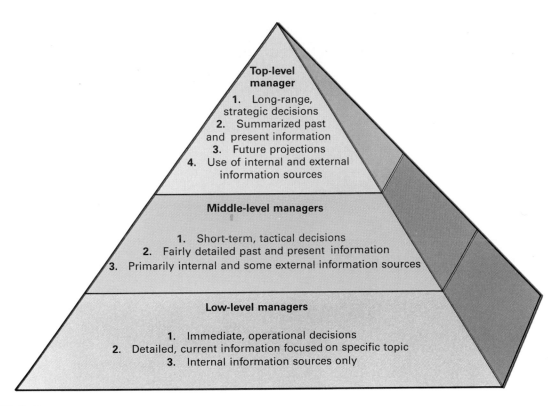

FIGURE 9–8
Levels of management, types of decision making, and information needs

ager increases from the top level downward. The higher the level of manager, the broader and less detailed the information needs to be.

Top-level Managers **Top-level managers** make decisions involving the long-range, or strategic, goals of the organization. Of the four major functions of a manager, top-level managers spend most of their time planning and organizing. A manager like Ken Olsen at DEC (see profile on p. 229) needs summarized information covering past and present operations and information projecting the future. This information is drawn from internal sources to give him a broad view of the company's internal situation. He also needs information drawn from external sources so that he can evaluate industry trends, world economic trends, government regulations, and other outside activities that influence the business health of a corporation.

Middle-level Managers **Middle-level managers** divide their time among all four general duties of management and are concerned with short-term, tactical decisions. Their decisions are directed toward accomplishing the overall organizational goals established by top-level managers. They work on such tasks as budgets, schedules, and performance evaluations and need information that is fairly detailed to compare present results

HIGHLIGHT

TOTALING THE TAXES

Some might call it the Computer Center for Bad Dreams. A few miles northwest of Washington, D.C., is the Internal Revenue Service's National Computer Center. It is located just outside the town of Martinsburg, West Virginia, and is the most essential link in the chain that takes in the nation's taxes and returns the overpayments.

Inside the rambling brick building, which is surrounded by a ten-foot-high barbed wire fence, are 263,000 reels of computer tapes. These reels are the master files of taxpayers.

The massive computers in the 35,000-square-foot building perform 1.5 billion transactions a year. Through the computers, a taxpayer's return is compared to financial data from that individual's employer, bank, and related sources. Consequently, here is where all the audits of accounts begin, all the penalties are calculated, and all the returns are assessed.

Relying on the Martinsburg operation are ten regional centers that process more than 100 million returns. In 1985, 81 million refund checks were generated, worth a total of $74 billion.

More than 500 people work at the center, but only 20 know the combination to the vault where the master files are kept.

with past results and make adjustments where necessary. They mainly require internally-generated information, but also use some external information.

Low-level Managers **Low-level managers,** or operational managers, are involved directly with the day-to-day operations of the business. They are responsible for seeing that the tactical decisions of the middle-level managers are implemented by directing personnel at the operations level. Their information must be detailed, current, and focused on a specific topic. It comes from sources such as inventory lists, historical records, and procedures manuals.

Information Provided by an MIS

Although all three levels of management work toward the organizational goals of the business, each requires different types of information to achieve the goals. That information is usually presented to managers in the form of reports. An MIS supplies information in four basic kinds of reports that aid managers in their decision making: predictive; demand; exception; and scheduled.

Predictive Reports   **Predictive reports** help top-level managers spot future trends. These reports generally contain an in-depth analysis of the data rather than just data. From the information in those reports, managers can answer "what if" questions, such as: "What if the present market trend continues; should we look to diversification?"

Demand Reports   **Demand reports** are issued only when a manager requests one, i.e., on demand. They are usually limited to one specific topic and may contain both data and analysis. For instance, if a business were in a budget crunch, the manager might request a report analyzing overhead expenses. Demand reports are generally requested by middle-level and top-level managers.

Exception Reports   **Exception reports** are usually oriented toward middle management and are issued only when an event occurs that deviates from its normal limits. This report might show that an inventory item is running dangerously low.

Scheduled Reports   The most often issued report is the **scheduled report** issued at regularly specified intervals (Figure 9–9). For example, the scheduled report gives details on weekly inventory lists, monthly financial

FIGURE 9–9
Managers discuss the results of a scheduled report produced by their company's MIS. (Photo courtesy of Hewlett-Packard Co.)

The United States Coast Guard Ice Patrol maintains records of potentially dangerous icebergs adrift in the North Atlantic by obtaining information using computerized side-looking airborne radar. Here, a technician monitors a computer display watching for and tracking the coordinates of icebergs such as the one pictured. (Wolfgang Kaehler. Inset: Courtesy of International Ice Patrol, United States Coast Guard)

MIS Reports

- Predictive
- Demand
- Exception
- Scheduled

reports, and weekly sales records. A scheduled report of sales might show a detailed outline of every item sold. Contrast this with a predictive report on sales that would show a top-level manager the sales trends rather than item sales. Scheduled reports are used by low- and middle-level managers.

Information Quality, Value, and Cost

Even when an MIS can supply a report, there is no guarantee it will be useful. For the document to have value for the manager in the decision-making process, the information must be timely, complete, free from inaccuracies, and communicated to the person who needs it. All the current information delivered today is useless if the decision was made yesterday. Reports must be delivered when they are needed.

A manager's time cannot be wasted sorting through lengthy reports. The reports from an information system should be concise and provide *only* the information that a manager needs to make the decision. Too often managers are flooded with reams of paper that only confuse the issue at hand.

As Grace Hopper points out in her lectures, in addition to the quality of information provided, the value and cost of keeping the information should also be carefully evaluated. Hopper states that emphasis should be placed on examining the total information flow through an organization, activity, or company, and decisions should be made about which information is the most valuable. Then, the best equipment should be used with the most valuable information.

Hopper also points out that information tends to lose its value, but the cost of storing and maintaining that information increases the further in time you get away from the event that generated it. She suggests that users look more closely at information to see if it really needs to be stored; if not, get rid of it to reduce costs.

DECISION SUPPORT SYSTEMS

An MIS provides managers with primarily historical information—what has already happened—in formats that were predefined at the time the system was originally created. A **decision support system (DSS)** is an extension of an MIS. It complements an MIS by allowing managers themselves to describe the information that they need, the processing to be done, and the format of the output. The emphasis is shifted from only supplying information about what has happened to allowing the manager to ask "what if" questions in order to predict what might happen in the future given certain circumstances. In other words, it provides an information and planning model for managers.

An MIS is an excellent source for information, but it is better at helping managers with routine or structured decisions at the low- and middle-management level. With an MIS, a manager simply receives printed reports and has no direct contact with the computer. A DSS, however, is an interactive system and requires that a manager directly interact with the computer when using it.

A decision support system can help middle- and top-level managers make decisions about nonroutine and unstructured problems and is one reason computers are found on the desks of more and more executives. A DSS uses sophisticated software that simulates potential outcomes using analysis and modeling. Data can be drawn from the computer data base, external sources, or both. The DSS does not actually make the decision, but can help predict outcomes for given situations. To be efficient, a DSS must have two key features. First, because of the higher degree of unstructured problems that the DSS is required to handle, a DSS must possess stronger analytical capabilities than an MIS. Second, the DSS must be user-friendly because it works by manager and computer interaction. Many managers have been in their jobs prior to computers being used in business, and some of these managers are still reluctant to sit and interact with the computer. Even managers who are comfortable with computers are usually not

HIGHLIGHT

COLORIZATION—NOT A BLACK AND WHITE ISSUE

With the growth of cablevision and the home-video industry, it eventually became obvious to program suppliers that they were running short of product. New programs were expensive and time-consuming to produce, and many of the recent television series and movies had been shown many times.

One answer to this shortage was to market the early black-and-white film classics. There was a fear, though, that an audience raised on color television and movies would be unwilling to buy, rent, or subscribe to a steady diet of black-and-white programs, no matter how well they might have been filmed and acted.

Enter colorization.

Enter controversy.

The colorization process first involves transferring the black-and-white film to videotape. The tape is categorized into its separate sequences, and then colors are assigned (under the guidance of an art director) to each shade of grey in the key frames. The data are then stored as electronic digital signals in a computer. Using the reference frames as a guide, the computer then assigns the colors electronically to subsequent frames. Once this laborious process is completed, the entire videotape may be color-balanced.

The cost of this process can range from $1,800 to $3,500 per minute of completed programming. Cable TV operators say it pays off in increased viewer interest; and video retailers maintain it accelerates sales and rentals. However, movie producers and critics insist that the colorization process ruins or diminishes the artistic impact of the film that was originally created. They argue that transmuting such black-and-white classics as *The Maltese Falcon* or *Citizen Kane* into color is artistic slaughter.

Naturally, such strong and contradictory opinions found their way into court. The movie companies and producers allege that the colorization process is a copyright infringement; the colorizing companies maintain that their work is legitimate *and* copyrightable in its own right.

system analysts or programmers. Therefore, the easier the DSS is to use, the more receptive managers will be and the more they will take advantage of what DSS offers.

United Telephone of Florida, operating in one of the fastest-growing regions of the country, requires a flexible data network that can provide important corporate information to the managers who need it at their fingertips. To provide this instant information, they use a decision support system based on Digital Equipment Corporation's All-In-One Office and

Information Systems software and DEC minicomputers. The DSS provides information such as status reports on the telecommunication network, number of calls routed through the long-distance switching centers, and quality control for service and repair requests.

MICROCOMPUTER USE IN DECISION MAKING

Microcomputers have made great inroads into traditionally large system MISs and DSSs. They have taken the control of computing power from a few individuals in a data-processing department and made it available to managers at all levels. Managers can have microcomputers in their offices for their own personal use, thereby having more control over the information they receive and how it is analyzed (Figure 9–10). Being comfortable using computers increases their confidence in and use of the MIS or DSS.

Microcomputers are used in two general ways in connection with MISs and DSSs. Many organizations use stand-alone microcomputers linked by a local-area network as part of their MIS or DSS. These microcomputer networks are popular among smaller organizations that cannot afford larger computer systems, but they are also used by larger organizations where the information stored is needed and controlled by only a few users.

The second way microcomputers are used with regard to MISs and DSSs is that microcomputers are also being linked to larger computer systems. This configuration gives managers the ability to transfer data to and from a larger computer system and then manipulate that data on the microcomputer in their offices.

Making decisions is the main task of modern-day managers. Even with microcomputers, MISs, and DSSs at their fingertips, managers still make the final decision.

SUMMARY

Managers are required to make many decisions in business. Systems have been designed to aid them in their task. One such system is the management information system (MIS).

At the heart of an MIS is a data base, which contains the data that the MIS uses. A data-base management system (DBMS) is the software that provides an interface between users and other programs to create, maintain, manipulate, and retrieve data from a data base. In a large organization, data-base activities are usually controlled by a data-base administrator.

To design a data base, the administrator develops a schema showing the relationships among data items. A schema can be divided into subschemas defining individual user's views of the data base. Three basic data-base structures are used for data-base design: hierarchical data-base structure; network data-base structure; and relational data-base structure. A data-base query language is an interface between the user and the DBMS of a relational data base which makes it easier for managers to use the DBMS to control the creation, manipulation, and retrieval of data.

A manager is responsible for achieving the goals of the organization through planning, organizing, directing, and controlling the available re-

FIGURE 9–10
Microcomputers have brought computing power directly to managers. (Courtesy of Dataproducts Corp.)

sources. There are three basic levels of management: top-level managers; middle-level managers; and low-level managers. One function of an MIS is to provide the needed information to the appropriate manager. An MIS provides information to managers in the form of reports. A predictive report helps top-level managers predict future trends. A demand report is issued when demanded by a manager for a specific purpose. When a condition occurs that greatly deviates from the norm, middle-level managers rely on exception reports. A scheduled report, such as an inventory or sales report, is routinely issued to keep low-level managers informed on day-to-day business.

An information system that is used by top-level managers to make decisions about nonroutine and unstructured problems is the decision support system (DSS). With a DSS, the manager interacts with a computer system that can simulate outcomes based on different criteria.

Key Terms

child (p. 266)

data base (p. 263)

data-base administrator (p. 265)

data-base management system (DBMS) (p. 263)

data-base query language (p. 268)

decision support system (DSS) (p. 274)

demand report (p. 272)

exception report (p. 272)

hierarchical data-base structure (p. 266)

low-level manager (p. 271)

management information system (MIS) (p. 262)

manager (p. 269)

middle-level manager (p. 270)

network data-base structure (p. 267)

parent (p. 266)

predictive report (p. 272)

query-by-example (p. 268)

relational data-base structure (p. 267)

scheduled report (p. 272)

schema (p. 265)

structured query language (p. 268)

subschema (p. 265)

top-level manager (p. 270)

Review Questions

1. Describe a management information system.

2. How is a data base related to an MIS?

3. Describe the function of a data-base management system.

4. Describe the role of a data-base administrator.

5. What is a schema?

6. Describe the purpose of developing subschemas.

7. Distinguish between the logical and physical designs of a data base.

8. How does the network data-base structure differ from the hierarchical data-base structure?

9. Describe the relational data-base structure.

10. What is a data-base query language?

11. Discuss the two basic query styles used by data-base query languages.

12. Describe the role of a manager.

13. List the three levels of management and discuss the types of decisions they make.

14. A(n) _____ report is issued only when a manager requests it.

15. A(n) _____ report is issued only when an event occurs that deviates from its normal limits.

16. Discuss some of the factors that determine the quality of information and make it useful to management.

17. Describe a decision support system.

18. What level of manager would you expect to use a DSS and why?

19. Name two ways in which microcomputers are being incorporated as part of an MIS or a DSS.

20. Discuss the role of the computer in a manager's decision-making process.

21. What type of data-base structure would you recommend when designing a data base for a DSS? Why?

22. Explain why it is important to examine the quality and value of information generated by an MIS.

23. Which is more appropriate for a manager who needs to make decisions that affect the future—an MIS or a DSS? Why?

24. If a manager needs information about the future, what type of report would he request from an MIS?

25. Why is data access generally faster with a hierarchical or network data-base structure than with a relational data-base structure?

INFOMODULE

Case Study: Overview of a Manufacturing MIS System

In this InfoModule, you'll look at a simplified model of a management information system (MIS) for Farrell Manufacturing, a typical manufacturing business. The MIS at Farrell is composed of a number of individual subsystems; each subsystem is composed of people, computers and other devices, and software. The subsystems in Farrell's MIS include

- ☐ Order-entry system
- ☐ Billing system
- ☐ Accounts-receivable system
- ☐ Inventory-control system
- ☐ Materials requirements planning (MRP) system
- ☐ Purchasing system
- ☐ Sales-analysis system
- ☐ Payroll system
- ☐ Accounts-payable system
- ☐ General-ledger system

Figure 1 shows how Farrell's subsystems are related. Each subsystem provides its managers with one or more types of management information on some portion of the company's operation. For example, the order-entry system provides information which is used by Farrell's low-level managers to fill an order, and provides information used by middle-level managers in designing, marketing, and advertising campaigns. Let's take a closer look at each subsystem to see examples of the types of information generated and how it is disseminated throughout Farrell.

Remember, a reference to any system throughout the case study refers to the data, software, hardware, information, and people that make up the system.

ORDER-ENTRY SYSTEM

The purpose of Farrell's order-entry system is to accept the customer's order and then begin the process of filling that order. The first step in the flow of information begins when the order is phoned in and the order-entry operator enters it at a computer terminal into the order-entry system. Personnel in the order-entry system then request information from the inventory-control system to verify that the items ordered are in stock. If the items are not, the materials requirements planning (MRP) system is consulted to see if the product can be ready by the time the customer needs it.

The order-entry system then requests information from the billing system to check the customer's credit standing. Credit information is formulated from in-house sources as well as outside credit bureaus. If the credit rating is poor, the order can be canceled, and the customer will be notified as to why the order was rejected. If credit is approved, the order information, including where and how to ship the product, is sent to the warehouse, and the product ordered is packaged and shipped to the customer.

The order information is then passed to the billing system. Here, the information is used to print an invoice that includes product information, quantity ordered, item prices, and a total price. One copy of the invoice is mailed to the customer as a bill and another copy is sent to the accounts-receivable system.

Notice that the outputs generated by one system at Farrell are often used as the inputs to another system. The order-entry system also sends the order information to the sales department where it is entered into the sales-analysis system. The sales-analysis system produces a number of management reports, such as salesperson performance and sales statistics. The salesperson performance reports are used by Farrell's middle management to evaluate performance and make decisions on staffing and bonuses. Reports that outline the sales for each particular product might be studied by top management to help determine future strategy at Farrell, such as dropping low sales items from the product line.

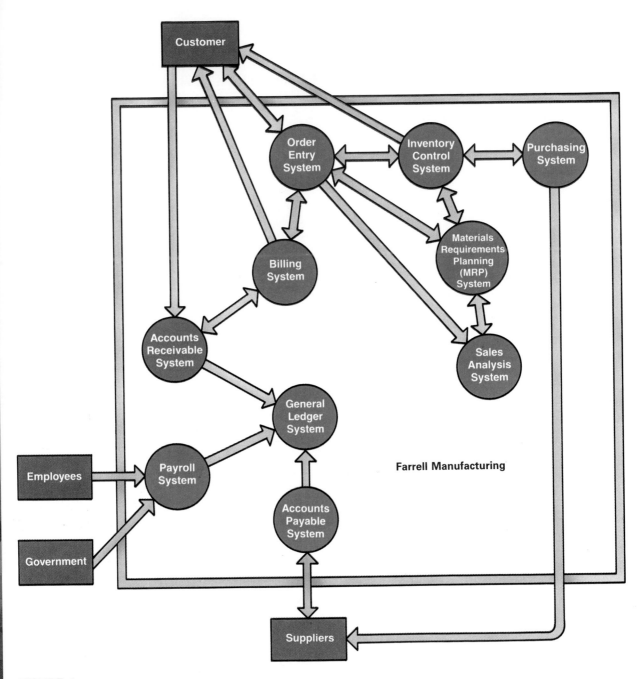

FIGURE 1
A simplified MIS model for Farrell Manufacturing

The order-entry system also provides feedback to customers when they inquire about an order. It can also be valuable for collecting data from customers, such as asking where they heard about a product (to determine the effectiveness of an advertising campaign), or to gather information for a profile of the type of customer buying specific products so advertising can be targeted to these segments.

In the discussion of the order-entry system, the inventory-control system and the MRP system were mentioned. Let's take a closer look at each one of these to see what kind of information it supplies.

INVENTORY-CONTROL SYSTEM

An inventory-control system manages inventory. Inventory is the amount of product that is kept on hand to fill manufacturing (parts to make a product) and customer (the final saleable product) needs. An inventory-control system monitors inventory so that costs are kept at a minimum by keeping only what is needed on hand while avoiding out-of-stock situations which can result in lost sales. One way to set up this system is to enter each product in a data base as a separate record containing fields, such as the product code, product description, quantity on hand, reorder point, reorder quantity, and supplier information. The system keeps track of each product, and when the quantity on hand reaches the reorder point, either a purchase order is automatically issued, or management is informed that one should be generated. Whether or not it is automatically issued, the purchase order is approved by management, typically a low-level manager. Middle-managers study reports of inventory movement to determine fast- and slow-moving inventory items and to spot problems and trends such as when sales for a previously fast-moving product have slowed down. They then use this information to help make decisions, such as informing manufacturing to slow production down so the costs of carrying all the extra inventory don't increase.

MATERIALS REQUIREMENTS PLANNING (MRP) SYSTEM

The order-entry system and the inventory system also interface with the MRP system. This system provides low- and middle-level management with information about orders and available resources to help plan and monitor the progress of the manufacturing process. Information passed from the order-entry system tells the MRP system what products need to be manufactured and the date by which they are needed. The MRP system interfaces with the inventory system to see which products are available. If a part or product is needed from a supplier, the MRP system sends this information to the purchasing system, and a purchase order is generated and mailed to the supplier.

The MRP system also interfaces with the sales-analysis system. The sales-analysis system provides forecasts of needs that the MRP system uses to help schedule manufacturing.

The MRP system produces a number of reports used by low- and middle-management, including a bill of materials report which contains a listing of all the components that are required to manufacture a product. This information is used to help determine upcoming demands on the manufacturing facilities and what parts will be required and when. All this information is used by low- and middle-level management to ensure the products are available when needed.

ACCOUNTS-RECEIVABLE SYSTEM

The accounts-receivable system handles collection of bills and generates reports related to the collections. It supplies the billing system with information relating to the credit standing of a customer. For example, if a customer is repeatedly delinquent in paying bills, a bad credit rating is reported to billing.

Accounts receivable provides information needed to compile monthly customer statements and past-due notices. Accounts-receivable systems also provide management with a report that forecasts when a customer is likely to pay. This type of information helps Farrell's middle management determine the company's available cash at any time. The aged-trial balance is another report that helps managers identify available cash and cash needs. This report lists outstanding balances, how many days a bill is overdue, current payments, and new purchases by each customer.

The accounts-receivable system also provides summary reports of sales, discounts, and finance charges. These summaries are reviewed by middle- and top-level management to see if changes need to be made in product strategy or company policies, such as discounts or finance rates. All payments and charges are passed by the accounts-receivable system to the general-ledger system.

The purpose of the accounts-payable system is to pay Farrell's suppliers in the most efficient way by taking advantage of discounts and conserving cash. The accounts-payable system provides management with reports to help monitor and control payments. One is a cash-requirements report, which informs management how much cash will be needed to meet the current period's payment requirements. A check-register report is also generated to allow management to review a list of all the checks that were issued for a particular period. The accounts-payable system also maintains a complete list of supplier information which can be printed on demand to help a manager decide which supplier to choose.

PAYROLL SYSTEM

To the average employee, payroll is probably the most important system. This system prepares and delivers paychecks. It maintains information on all checks issued enabling management to see which checks have been cashed, which are still outstanding, and which have been voided or canceled. The payroll system also generates the information, or in many cases the actual reports, required by federal, state, and local agencies. Payroll transactions are sent from the payroll system to the general-ledger system.

GENERAL-LEDGER SYSTEM

The final system in this model is the general-ledger system. This system is responsible for maintaining the financial records of the company and generating management reports summarizing the financial well-being of the company. The two primary reports produced by the general-ledger system are the balance sheet and the income statement, also called the profit and loss statement.

The balance sheet lists the company's assets and liabilities. Assets are anything the company owns, and liabilities are anything the company owes. The difference between the two is the company's net worth.

The income statement lists all the income and all the expenses incurred over a specified period. The difference between these two is the company's profit or loss for the period. Both of these reports are used by top-level management when making policy and strategic decisions about the company's future.

The general-ledger system also produces reports used by Farrell's middle management, such as sales journals and cash-receipts journals that list and summarize all financial transactions for a period.

Each of the subsystems described in this review of Farrell's MIS system is also made up of numerous other subsystems. Even though this case study only scratched the surface of Farrell's MIS, you can get the feel for the amount of information that is generated for just a single order. Without an MIS, it would be difficult to collect, analyze, and disperse the information so that managers can have it to make timely decisions. The MIS at Farrell also appropriately limits the amount of information flowing to any one manager so that each manager receives only that which is pertinent to his or her needs.

QUESTIONS

1. What are the advantages of using a computerized management information system at Farrell Manufacturing?
2. What are the essential elements of each subsystem of Farrell's MIS?
3. What type of information might top-level management request from their MIS at Farrell?
4. How do you think a DSS might help Farrell?
5. In your opinion, why must Farrell be concerned with the quality and amount of information reaching each manager?

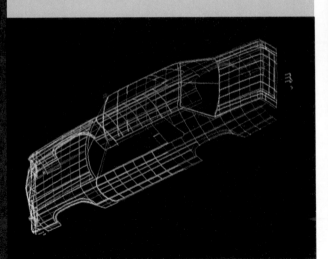

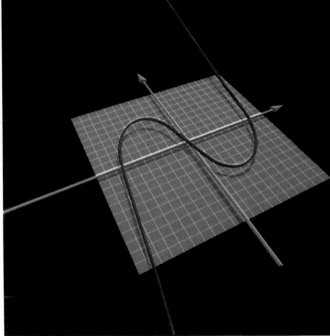

OBJECTIVES

☐ Explain how knowledge of the program development process can be helpful even to nonprogrammers

☐ Define and discuss structured programming concepts

☐ Explain the importance of documentation in the program development process

☐ List and describe the purpose of each of the six steps in the program development process

10

Structured Programming and the Program Development Process

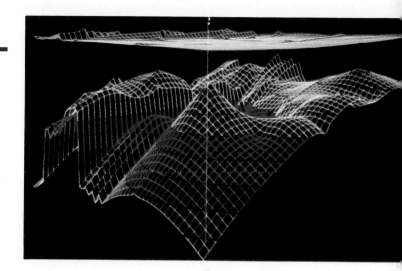

PROFILE: Edsger Dijkstra

Since the days of the earliest programming ef-forts, programmers assumed that errors were something that they always had to contend with—mistakes that couldn't be discovered until the program was tested or put into actual use. Edsger Dijkstra (pronounced Dike-stra) never had much sympathy for this viewpoint.

The Dutch scientist believes that programs should be written on a firm mathematical basis that increases the precision and reduces the randomness of results. His approach to the problem is called "structured programming."

Born in 1930 in Rotterdam, Dijkstra is the son of a father who was a chemist and a mother who was a mathematician. After completing studies at the University of Leiden in 1948, he planned to become a theoretical physicist. Fate intervened, however, when his father happened to see an advertisement in a science journal, *Nature*, for a summer school course on computing in Cambridge, England.

The computer used for the class was the EDSAC, the first automatic electronic computer in Europe. At the time, neither Dijkstra nor his father knew what an automatic electronic computer was. His curiosity and the thought that this invention might be something of interest to him as a theoretical physicist sent him to England. Although he eventually received his master's degree in physics,

Dijkstra decided to pursue programming and became the Netherlands' first professional programmer.

During the late 1960s, when Dijkstra came under fire from his colleagues for his unconventional notions about programming, he started writing his "Notes on Structured Programming." In this article, he showed how programs can be structured to lessen their complexity. He advocated the creation of programs that did not rely on the use of unconditional branch instruction (the GOTO statement), and he argued that by using three programming structures—sequence, selection, and repetition—any program could be written without GOTO statements.

To disseminate his ideas, Dijkstra began writing and distributing a series of newsletters on his theories and observations to prominent members of the computing community throughout the world. Ultimately, the programming community at large began to discover the advantages of structured programming. Dijkstra had laid the foundation for turning programming into a science.

Dijkstra has since returned to the question that had originally prompted his programming research: Why not prove programs correct? He believes it is possible and continues to work on a method that would allow even a large, complex program to be proven error-free mathematically.

B y themselves, computer hardware—the physical components of the computer—are of little use. In order to accomplish any task, the computer must be supplied with a series of instructions telling it what to do.

This chapter discusses how those instructions are developed using the concepts of structured programming.

SYSTEM AND APPLICATION SOFTWARE

The series of instructions telling the hardware what to do is called a **program**, or **software**. The two general types of software are system and application.

Programs that control and direct the operation of the computer hardware are **system software**. For example, system software controls the saving of data and its retrieval from secondary storage devices. (Chapter 11 looks at one of the most important examples of system software—the operating system.)

Programs that help the user and the system software work together are **application software**. For example, application software enables a user to perform such tasks as writing a letter or creating a graph. Application packages create a communication bridge whereby the user can tell the system software how to direct the hardware to perform the desired functions. Figure 10–1 shows the relationships among system software, application software, hardware, and the user. (Specific application packages for microcomputers will be examined in Chapters 12 through 16.) Let's begin our look at the program development process by examining how programming is relevant to you.

WHY YOU NEED TO KNOW ABOUT PROGRAMMING

Many of you have no intention of becoming a programmer or of programming your own software. You may be interested only in knowing how to use commercially available application programs, such as word processing,

FIGURE 10–1

Relationships among system software, application software, hardware, and the user

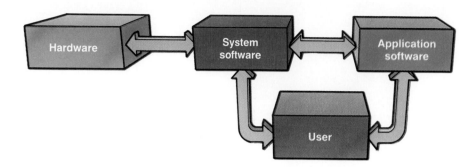

Types of Software

■ System software
■ Application software

data base, or spreadsheet packages. Why should you take the time to learn about programming concepts?

First, your basic knowledge of how a computer works and what it can do will increase. As your understanding increases, computers become less threatening and more useful.

Second, the chances that you will have to communicate with a programmer, directly or indirectly, are increasing because computers are becoming more prevalent. An understanding of the programmer's work and the information he or she needs will help the two of you work more effectively.

Third, many application programs, particularly data bases, incorporate fourth-generation languages (4GL) that can be easily used by nonprogrammers to help take full advantage of the program's power. (The 4GLs will be discussed further in Chapter 11.) Therefore, knowledge of the basic concepts of good program design and development can be beneficial even if you don't intend to program in a traditional programming language. With these points in mind, let's examine some structured programming concepts.

STRUCTURED PROGRAMMING CONCEPTS

As uses for computers become more sophisticated, the software required to accomplish these tasks becomes more complicated. Because of this complexity, a method to control the development of a program and assure its quality is needed.

Edsger Dijkstra is one of the major proponents of structured programming. He thinks that, ultimately, programming will be tested mathematically rather than by trial and error. According to Dijkstra, while the presence of "bugs," or errors, in many programming situations, such as fouled-up airline reservations, are merely annoying, their presence in others, such as the launching and guidance of space flights, are life-and-death matters. An example of this type of situation occurred in 1981 when the first launching of the U.S. space shuttle was halted because errors in the software caused the shuttle's computers to fall out of synchronization.

Dijkstra and others think that traditional programming is sloppy in design. Commonly, such programming relies on specific "GOTO" instructions. These commands tell the computer to go to another, sometimes distant, point in the program. The use of this command in extended program-

Structured programming techniques are used by programmers to design the complicated software required for the operation of space programs. (Photo courtesy of American Satellite Co., part of Contel's Information Systems sector. Inset: Official U.S. Navy photograph)

ming results in enormous structural complexity and creates innumerable opportunities for errors.

Structured programming is a methodology that takes a step in the direction of improving both the designing and testing processes to ensure that a program is error-free.

Qualities of a Good Program

A good program meets the following criteria; it is

- ☐ Correct
- ☐ Easy to understand
- ☐ Easy to maintain and update
- ☐ Efficient
- ☐ Reliable
- ☐ Flexible

A *correct* program is one that will do what it was designed to do in accordance with the specifications laid out during the design of the program. The program should be designed so that anyone who works with it

Qualities of a Good Program

- Correct
- Easy to understand
- Easy to maintain and update
- Efficient
- Reliable
- Flexible

finds its logic *easy to understand*. It should also be designed in such a way that program *maintenance and updating* can be made with relative ease. The program should run *efficiently* by executing quickly and using computer resources such as primary storage conservatively. The *reliability* of the program is its ability to operate under unforeseen circumstances, such as recovering from invalid data entries. For example, if the program expects a "yes" or "no" response, but the user types in a number, the program should recognize the error, inform the user that an invalid entry has been made, and indicate what is expected; then the user can reenter the data. Finally, a *flexible* program is one that can operate with a wide range of legitimate input. For example, if a program requests a "yes" or "no" answer, it should be able to accept as valid entries any combination of capital and lowercase letters for the words "yes" and "no" in addition to the single letters Y, y, N, or n.

Using structured programming concepts can help a programmer achieve these qualities in a program.

Need for Structured Programming

In the early days of computers, programming was more an art than a science. Developing a quality program was more of a hit-or-miss proposition than a planned goal. Programmers were given a task to program and were left on their own to come up with a solution any way they could. Often, this practice led to problems.

Three major problems which arose from this free-form method of programming were: (a) long development time; (b) high maintenance costs; and (c) low quality of the software.

Managers were finding that many software projects were taking too long to complete. They wanted to increase the productivity of the programmer.

Software development costs were also getting out of hand. As the computer age moved forward, hardware costs began to decrease, but software development costs, especially personnel costs, rose sharply. Most of the money invested in purchasing and operating a computer system was spent on software-related costs and, in particular, on maintaining software. Many organizations were spending more than 60 percent of their time repairing and enhancing systems that were already installed. In general, the cost of developing, testing, and maintaining programs was not only too high, it was continuing to increase. Management needed a way to control and reduce these costs. To avoid the high costs of program maintenance, program designs had to be right the first time.

Many of the programs were also of low quality; they were too complex and had poor documentation. As a result, they were difficult to test and maintain. Numerous errors went undetected in the testing process. In many cases, programmers also lost sight of the user's requirements; consequently, the programs did not meet the user's needs.

These problems forced people to search for ways to resolve them. Edsger Dijkstra's work and that of others led to the development of the structured programming concept.

Structured programming is a methodology that stresses the systematic design, development, and management of the program development process. Therefore, the purpose and overall goals of structured programming are to:

☐ Decrease development time by increasing programmer productivity and reducing the time to test and debug a program
☐ Decrease maintenance costs by reducing errors and making programs easier to understand by reducing their complexity
☐ Improve the quality of software by providing programs with fewer errors

Structured programming attempts to accomplish these goals by incorporating the following concepts:

☐ Use of only the sequence, selection, and repetition control structures
☐ Top-down design and use of modules
☐ Management control

> **Goals of Structured Programming**
>
> - Decrease program development time
> - Decrease program maintenance costs
> - Improve the quality of software

Control Structures

In the late '60s, two mathematicians, Corrado Bohm and Guiseppe Jacopini, proved that even the most complex program logic could be expressed by the use of three control structures: sequence; selection; and repetition (looping). Edsger Dijkstra also put forth this same theory in his article "Notes on Structured Programming." A control structure is a device in a programming language that determines the order of execution of statements in a program.

A **sequence control structure** executes statements one after another in a linear fashion as illustrated in Figure 10–2.

The **selection control structure** presents a number of processing options. The option chosen depends on the result of the decision criterion. Figure 10–3 depicts some variations of the selection control structure.

The **repetition control structure** (also called looping) is used to execute an instruction or group of instructions more than once without having to recode them. The two basic variations of this type of structure are DO WHILE and DO UNTIL. If the decision criterion is placed before the statements to be repeated, then it is a DO WHILE loop as illustrated in Figure 10–4. A DO UNTIL loop places the decision criterion at the end of the statements to be repeated as shown in Figure 10–5. In this structure the statements are always executed at least once.

A fourth type of control structure commonly being used in early programs was the unconditional branch. In many programming languages, this structure took the form of a GOTO statement. This statement allowed the execution of a program to indiscriminately jump to other points in the program. Programs designed with several of these unconditional branches were very confusing and difficult to follow, thereby earning them the name "spaghetti code."

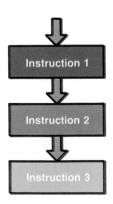

FIGURE 10–2
Sequence control structure

FIGURE 10–3
Selection control structures

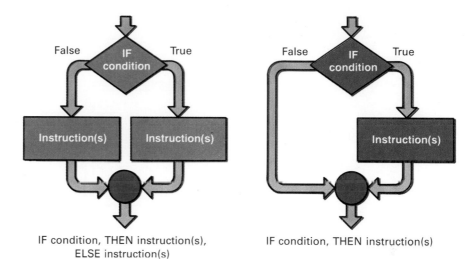

IF condition, THEN instruction(s),
ELSE instruction(s)

IF condition, THEN instruction(s)

CASE condition: CASE 1, CASE 2, CASE 3, CASE 4

The use of only the sequence, selection, and repetition structures and avoidance of unconditional branching are parts of the first step toward a structured programming methodology.

Top-down Design and Use of Modules

Structured programming advocates the top-down approach to solving a problem. **Top-down design** is the process of starting with the major functions involved in a problem and dividing them into subfunctions until the

---

Control Structures for Structured Programming

- Sequence
- Selection
- Repetition (looping)

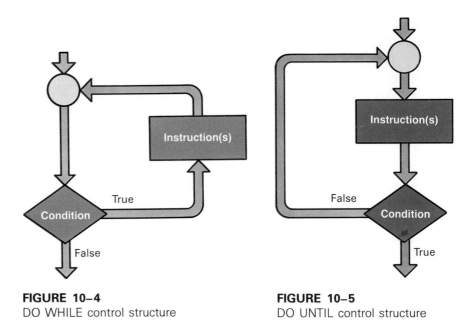

FIGURE 10–4
DO WHILE control structure

FIGURE 10–5
DO UNTIL control structure

problem has been divided as much as possible. Top-down design involves three major steps:

1. Defining the output, input, and major processing steps required
2. Step-by-step refinement of the major processing steps
3. Designing the algorithms

The first step involves three separate processes. First, the desired outputs are defined. Second, the required inputs are determined; and finally, the major processing tasks are determined.

In the second step, each major processing task is broken down into smaller and smaller tasks until it cannot be broken down any further. This method forces an examination of all aspects of a problem at one level before starting on the next level. The programmer is left with groups, or **modules**, of processing instructions that are easy to understand and code. Working from the top down (the general to the specific) rather than the bottom up (the specific to the general) avoids designing partial solutions that deal with only part of the problem.

A program broken into smaller modules is easier to read, test, and maintain. In the structured programming method, modules have the following features to ensure these qualities:

☐ Only one entrance and one exit
☐ After exiting a module, control returns to the module that called (passed control to) it. (For example, if module D called module G, then when module G is finished executing, control returns to module D.)
☐ Performs only one program function

The third step involves designing the algorithm for each module. An **algorithm** is the finite set of step-by-step instructions that solve a problem. The main module is first; development then moves down in one of two ways: (a) by level; or (b) by path. In programming by level, each level of modules is coded before the next level. In Figure 10–6, coding by level would follow the order of the numbered sequence. In programming by path, all modules along a path are coded in sequence. In Figure 10–6, coding by path would follow the order of the alphabetic sequence.

In many cases, top-down design has resulted in a lower error rate and shorter program development time.

Management Control

Management control is an essential part of the structured programming concept. It prevents the project from being sidetracked, keeps it on schedule, and assures that the user's needs are being met.

When many people are involved with the design and development of a large program, different ideas and ways of doing things surface. To provide consistency and coordinate all work, a **chief programmer team** is established. The team consists of a number of specialized personnel to design and develop a program. The type of specialists may vary depending on the project. A typical team might consist of the following:

- ☐ Chief programmer
- ☐ Assistant programmer
- ☐ Librarian
- ☐ Other specialists as needed

The chief programmer defines and assigns portions of the program development to various team members and takes responsibility for the

FIGURE 10–6
Coding by level and by path

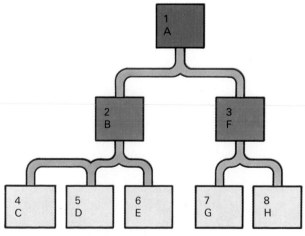

Coding by level: 1 2 3 4 5 6 7 8

Coding by path: A B C D E F G H

HIGHLIGHT

COMPUTERS AS COUNSELORS

Telling your troubles to a computer may seem the ultimate act of desperation, but psychologists have found that it works with a whole range of personal problems. Programs which enable people to relieve stress, recognize and handle marital difficulties, and treat alcoholism and other addictions are available everywhere.

Essentially, what the programs do is engage the patient in a "dialogue" with the computer to discover what the specific problems are and to suggest solutions. In some cases, the programs merely help diagnose the problems so that they can then be treated by a psychologist or psychiatrist. In other situations, however, the program provides direct counseling. Professionals who use these programs say they work best with adolescents and younger people who are already attuned to having computers in their lives.

However, people of all ages who have difficulty in discussing their fears and perceived weaknesses with other human beings will often relax more when they are "talking" to a computer.

When the elements of fear and intimidation are removed from the counseling scenario, diagnosis can proceed quickly. A counselor in New Jersey said he could get as much information in three hours of computer testing as he could in two months of direct interviewing.

There are at least two wholesome side effects of introducing computers into counseling: (a) they enable patients to be treated more quickly because they do not demand the usual one-on-one counseling; and (b) the cost of counseling comes down accordingly.

project (Figure 10–7). He or she reviews each member's work, coordinates the integration of the work, and is the liaison between management and the project. It is the chief programmer's responsibility to make sure the appropriate personnel are on the team and to make changes or additions to the team as needed.

The assistant programmer works directly with the chief programmer. Depending on the size of the project, there may be more than one assistant programmer. For very large projects, separate teams of programmers are sometimes established. Each team might have a group leader who reports to an assistant programmer or directly to the chief programmer.

The librarian's responsibility is to maintain and make available the records of the project, such as program listings and results of testing.

Other specialists, such as system analysts or financial analysts, may also be a part of the chief programmer team. The nature of each project determines their use.

The makeup of a chief programmer team does not have one set formula. Its composition depends on the nature of the problem, management philosophy, and cost factors.

FIGURE 10–7
An assistant programmer discusses a problem with the chief programmer.

One technique the chief programmer team may use before beginning to code a program is a **structured walk-through**—a meeting that consists of a system analyst, user(s), and possibly other system personnel. The system analyst discusses or "walks through" the program design with the team members present at the meeting. The rationale behind this presentation is to force the analyst to explain the design to others with the expectation that errors will be caught and corrected before programming begins.

The structured programming concepts presented in this section are used in the following discussion of the program development process to help create a program that adheres to the qualities of a good program.

PROGRAM DEVELOPMENT PROCESS

There are numerous ways to complete the tasks in any process. Some methods are more efficient and effective than others. For example, if you want to dig a swimming pool in your backyard, you could get out your spade and start digging, or you could use heavy, mechanical equipment designed for the task. Both methods would get the job done, but the second method is more efficient and effective. The same principle applies to programming.

The **program development process** is a recommended series of steps to follow when developing a program. It consists of the following six steps:

- ☐ Define the problem
- ☐ Design the algorithm
- ☐ Code the program
- ☐ Test and debug the program
- ☐ Implement the program and train users
- ☐ Maintain and upgrade the program

Program Development Process

- Define the problem
- Design the algorithm
- Code the program
- Test and debug the program
- Implement the program and train users
- Maintain and upgrade the program

This list does not include documentation as a separate step; however, documentation is an important requirement throughout *all* the steps, each of which will be examined below. Although each step is presented as a separate and distinct process, they are all related; in actual practice, there may not be a clear separation between the steps. Let's address the topic common to all the steps of the program development process—documentation.

The Importance of Documentation

Documentation is the text or graphics that provides specific instructions about, or records the purpose or function of, a particular step or instruction in a program. Each step throughout the programming process should be documented. Documentation is sometimes done as an afterthought rather than as an ongoing integral part of the project. Approached in this manner, it can become an overwhelming burden of paperwork. If documentation guidelines are established and followed from the beginning of a project, the process will take less time and effort in the long run.

There are two good reasons to document the program development process. First, documentation leaves a clear record for someone else to understand what was done. This record is extremely important in a business environment because it is likely that the person who later corrects an error or modifies the program will not be the same person who originally designed or coded it.

Second, documenting the steps as they are developed forces a reexamination of the actions taken. Problems might be discovered early enough to avoid costly alterations later. Documentation is important even if you are programming just for your own use.

For documentation to be of value, it must be clear and concise, and it must be available to those who need it. Many organizations maintain a library where copies of all documentation are accessible to authorized personnel.

Several types of documentation are kept during the course of the program development process. Here are a few:

- ☐ Program specifications
- ☐ Program description
- ☐ Program design charts (flowcharts, pseudocode, etc.)
- ☐ Description of testing done and errors found
- ☐ An operator's manual (user's guide)
- ☐ Maintenance documentation

Program specifications describe what the program is intended to accomplish; they help the programmer design the program. The program description details what the completed program actually does. Program design charts outline the specific steps used in the program to produce the desired results. The types of testing done, the data used, as well as the errors found are typically recorded in separate documentation. Details on how to operate a program are presented in an operator's manual. Maintenance documentation is a record of the changes made to the program and a detailed explanation of those changes.

The type of documentation kept depends on each programming department's various requirements.

Keeping in mind that each step of the program development process should be properly documented, let's take a look at each of the six steps.

Define the Problem

The first step in the program development process is to recognize that there is a problem, identify exactly what the problem is, determine the desired output and available inputs, and determine if the problem can be solved by a computer.

It is important to define the problem thoroughly so that the proposed solution will solve the problem and not just address itself to a particular symptom. For example, if you had an illness and were experiencing severe pain, you might take a pain killer. However, that would only alleviate a symptom (pain), not the real problem (the illness). Eventually, the real problem will surface, but it may be more difficult and costly to correct at this stage than it would have been to address earlier. The same principle applies to programming.

Communication with those involved in dealing with the problem and examining current practices and procedures could help shed light on what the true problem is.

Defining the problem involves determining the output's format and what information it should contain. Programmers must communicate with the intended users to ensure that the program will meet their needs. The inputs required to yield the desired output and how to obtain them also need to be determined. Some inputs may have to be gathered; others may be available in current files.

Once the programmers know the desired output and the available inputs, they can determine if a computer is needed to solve the problem. If it is, the next step is to design the steps that will convert the available inputs into the desired output.

Design the Algorithm

After the problem has been defined, an algorithm can be designed. Recall that an algorithm is the finite set of step-by-step instructions that solve a problem. There are many design aids to assist programmers when designing and documenting an algorithm. Several common ones are

☐ Structure charts
☐ HIPO charts
☐ Flowcharts
☐ Pseudocode

Design Aids

- Structure charts
- HIPO charts
- Flowcharts
- Pseudocode

Structure Charts **Structure charts** provide a visual means to show: (a) the purpose of each module in a structured program; (b) the relationships

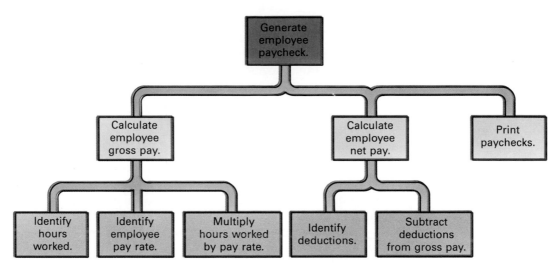

FIGURE 10–8
Structure chart

among the modules; and (c) the overall program logic flow. Each module (a small segment of a program) is represented by a box; the boxes are arranged in a hierarchy and are connected by lines to indicate the logic flow. Figure 10–8 is an example of a structure chart.

The **visual table of contents** is related to the structure chart. It is arranged exactly like the structure chart except each module is numbered for easy reference. Figure 10–9 is an example of a visual table of contents.

HIPO Charts A **Hierarchy plus input, processing, output (HIPO) chart** can enhance a structure chart by outlining the input, processing, and

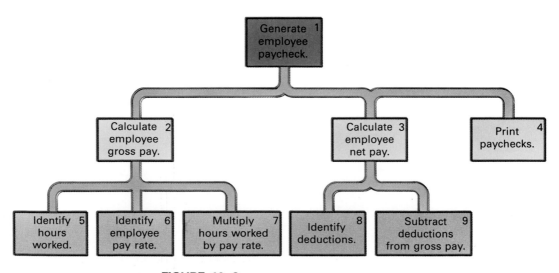

FIGURE 10–9
Visual table of contents

output needed by each module. An overview HIPO chart shows the types of input, processing, and output required and is usually completed for the main (most generalized) program module first. Detailed HIPO charts are then constructed for the rest of the modules to determine their specific input, processing, and output requirements. Figure 10–10 is an example of an overview HIPO chart that might accompany the structure chart in Figure 10–8.

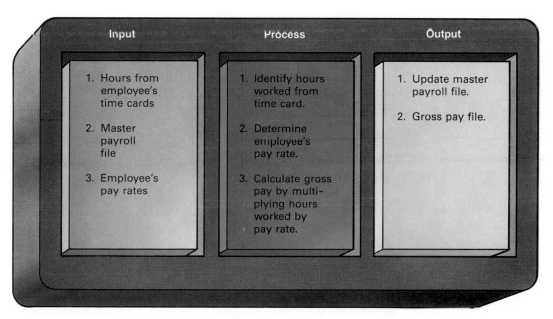

FIGURE 10–10
An overview HIPO chart

FIGURE 10–11
Programming flowchart symbols

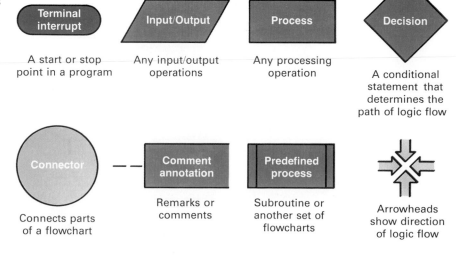

Flowcharts   Probably the most familiar program design tool is the flow-chart. A **flowchart** uses standardized symbols to show the components of a system or the steps in solving a problem, such as in a program. System flowcharts and program flowcharts are the two basic types of flowcharts. (System flowcharts were presented in Chapter 8.)

A **program flowchart** graphically details the processing steps of a particular program. Figure 10–11 (p. 299) shows some standard program flowcharting symbols. A flowchart is used to:

☐   Clarify the program logic
☐   Identify alternate processing methods available

FIGURE 10–12

A program flowchart

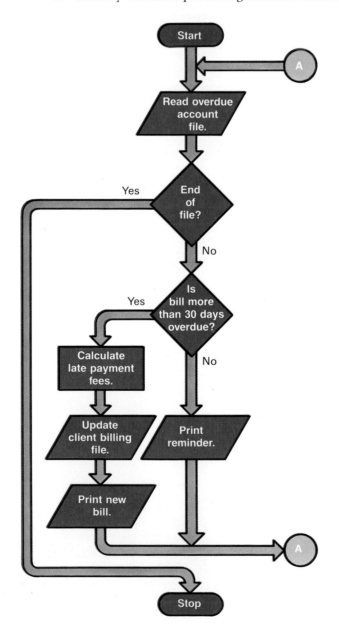

☐ Serve as a guide for program coding
☐ Serve as documentation

Figure 10–12 is an example of a program flowchart constructed for a program that checks a client's payment record.

A variation of the standard flowchart is the structured flowchart, also called a **Nassi-Shneiderman chart**, developed by Isaac Nassi and Ben Shneiderman.

A Nassi-Shneiderman chart uses the three basic program control structures (sequence, selection, and repetition) to illustrate the processing steps of a program. Various shaped boxes represent each control structure in a "box-within-a-box" format. Figure 10–13 illustrates the logic patterns of a Nassi-Shneiderman chart. Figure 10–14 shows how the flowchart in Figure 10–12 could be represented using a Nassi-Shneiderman chart.

Pseudocode   Another tool used to formulate the processing steps of a program is pseudocode. **Pseudocode** uses English phrases to describe the processing steps of a program or module. Pseudocode was designed as an alternative to flowcharts. Often, the phrases resemble the programming language code, hence the name pseudocode.

Processing steps are expressed in a simple straightforward manner so that the pseudocode can be easily converted to program code. Most programming departments establish rules and conventions to be followed when using pseudocode so that others will be able to read and interpret its meaning. Figure 10–15 is an example of pseudocode as it might be written for the problem in Figure 10–12.

After the solution has been clearly formulated, it is time to code (write) the program.

FIGURE 10–13
Nassi-Shneiderman chart logic patterns

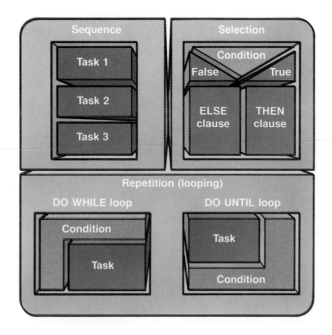

FIGURE 10–14

A Nassi-Shneiderman chart for problem in Figure 10–12

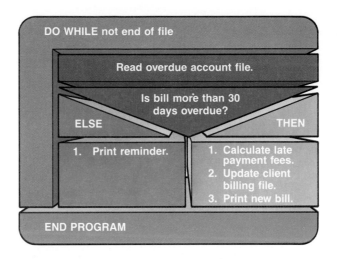

DO WHILE not end of file

Read overdue account file.

Is bill more than 30 days overdue?

ELSE   THEN

1. Print reminder.

1. Calculate late payment fees.
2. Update client billing file.
3. Print new bill.

END PROGRAM

FIGURE 10–15

Pseudocode for problem in Figure 10–12

```
Begin
   Read overdue billing file.
   DO WHILE not end of file
     IF bill more than 30 days overdue
       THEN
          Calculate late payment fees.
          Update billing file.
          Print new bill.
       ELSE
          Print payment reminder.
     End-if
     Read overdue billing file.
   End
```

Code the Program

Coding a program involves actually writing the instructions in a particular programming language that will tell the computer how to operate. The first question that arises is in what language should the program be coded. In many business situations, the choice will be made by the data processing department. The type of problem might also dictate the language choice. For example, certain languages are more suited to manipulating large data files, and others are more suited to numerical calculations. (Chapter 11 looks at some popular programming languages.)

Coding a program typically takes less time than any of the other steps in the development process. In a medium to large corporate environment, coding is performed by programmers, but the definition of the problem and the design of the solution are usually done by system analysts and system designers. In smaller companies, it's not uncommon for the analyst, designer, and programmer to be the same person. After the program is coded, it is entered into the computer for testing and debugging (Figure 10–16).

FIGURE 10–16
A computer programmer sits among a variety of microcomputers on which he codes, tests, and debugs software. (Photo courtesy of Hewlett-Packard Co.)

Test and Debug the Program

Now the program needs to be tested to ensure that it is correct and contains no errors. It is difficult, if not presently impossible, to test a complex program for every condition that may cause an error; however, sufficient tests can be made to be reasonably sure the program is correct and error-free.

Three types of program errors that may be encountered during the testing phase are

☐ Syntax
☐ Run-time
☐ Logic

The **syntax** of a programming language is the set of rules and conventions to be followed when writing a program; these rules are similar to the grammatical rules of the English language. When these rules are violated, a **syntax error** occurs. All syntax errors must be found and corrected before a program will execute.

A second type of error that may occur during testing is a **run-time error**. This error stops the execution of the program. It may be that invalid data were entered. For example, if the program was set up to expect numerical data, and alphabetical data were entered instead, a poorly designed program would "crash," i.e., stop executing. A properly written program would identify the problem and prompt the user with an error message and permit the data to be reentered.

The third type of error, and the most difficult to find, is the logic error. A **logic error** will not stop the execution of the program; however, the results will not be accurate. With luck, the error will be obvious. Often, it is not. Here's a simple example: The problem is to add 2 apples to 4 apples and determine the total number of apples. The formula should be $2 + 4 = 6$. But, what if the wrong symbol, such as a multiplication sign, is typed while entering the program into the computer? Actually, $2 \times 4 = 8$. The

Types of Program Errors

■ Syntax
■ Run-time
■ Logic

answer of 8 is correct for the formula as entered, but not for the problem intended to be solved—*adding* 2 apples to 4 apples. Finding the logic error in the above example is easy; however, finding a logic error in a complicated program can be like trying to find the proverbial needle in a haystack.

The process of finding any type of error and correcting it is called **debugging** (Figure 10–17). After a program is debugged, it can be installed and used.

Implement the Program and Train Users

After a program has been debugged, it is time to install the program in the users' computer(s) and train the users how to operate it. Without proper

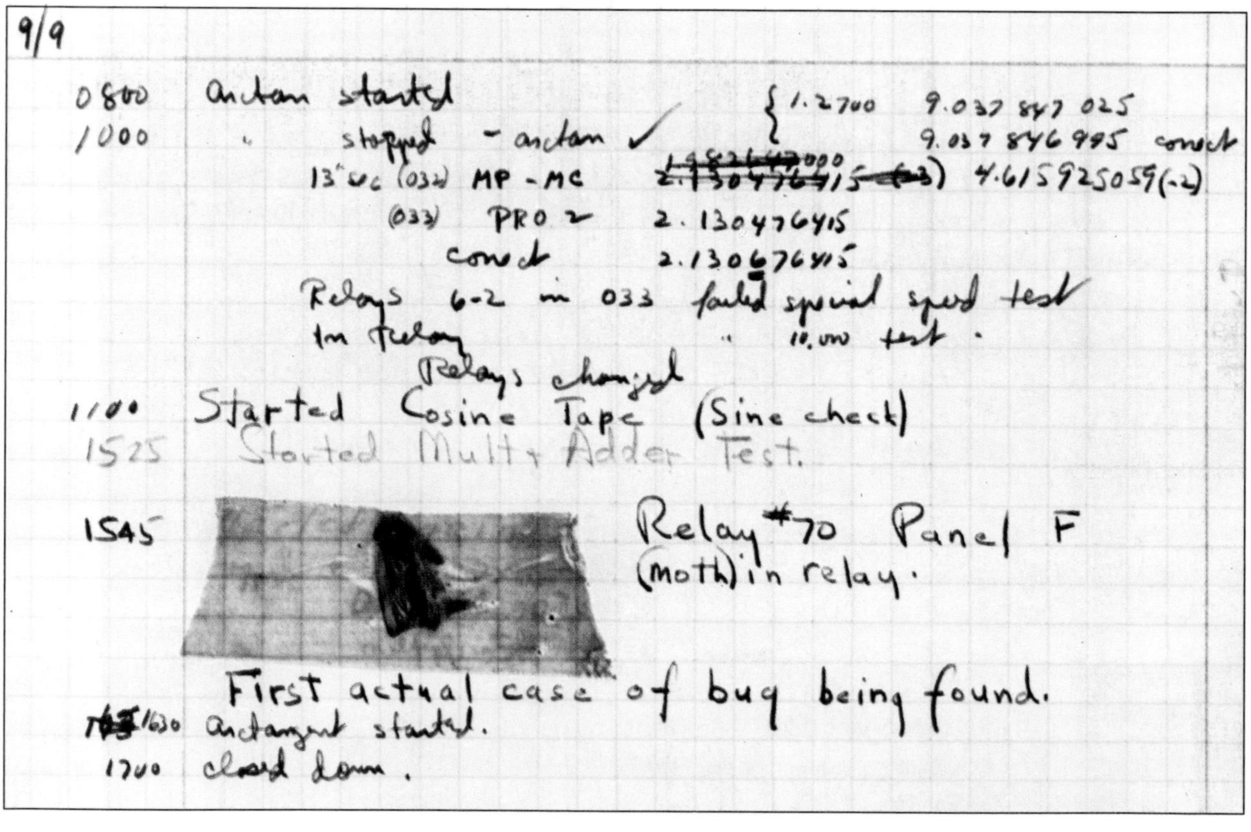

FIGURE 10–17

Grace Hopper relates the story that she and a team of programmers were working on the Mark II back in 1945 when the computer simply quit. They couldn't determine what was wrong; finally, they looked inside the computer and saw a large, dead moth in one of the signal relays. The moth, the first computer ''bug,'' was removed and saved for posterity in a log book now located at the U.S. Naval Museum in Dahlgren, Virginia. After that incident, when naval officers came in to check on progress when a computer was not operating, the personnel advised that they were ''debugging the program.'' (U.S. Navy photo)

HIGHLIGHT

WHERE THE BUGS ARE

Believe us—it's getting better. But there are a lot of bugs still out there in computerland. Bugs are the flaws that find their way into a computer or its software and lie in wait, so to speak, to cause trouble. In some cases, bugs are merely bothersome; but they can also be enormously expensive to businesses and catastrophic when they show up in military systems.

On the one hand, our increasing knowledge about computer construction and programming makes it easier to spot bugs; on the other hand, the spread of computers into all facets of society gives them more places to "hide."

According to one poll, computer glitches have complicated the lives of at least 91 percent of us whether it's at work, at the bank, with credit card companies or airlines, or in computerized appliances at home.

Bugs have delayed federal tax returns, wiped out financial records for an entire town, delayed space launches, caused gigantic overdrafts that have sent banks reeling, and raised the question of whether such a life-or-death military system as the Strategic Defense Initiative can ever be considered fool-proof in its operations.

To reduce the likelihood of bugs, designers, instead of leaving the building of computers and software in the hands of more fallible human beings, are turning to computers to perform these tasks. Large computer programs may use as many as 100,000 lines of code, and the space and defense programs use millions of lines. Without computer aid, even a seasoned programmer may be able to write only twenty lines of code a day.

In 1979, the General Accounting Office looked at computer use and reliability in government and learned that less than two percent of the $6.89 million spent for software programs could actually be used as bought. To address problems like this, there are now companies that will test programs for buyers before they are put into use.

Another defense against bugs—and probably the most realistic one—is to conclude that they are likely to be found, so safeguards have to be put in place to catch them. For example, the nearly 100 computers needed to fly the Boeing 767 duplicate essential operations so if a bug ruins a function, another computer can compensate for the error.

training, people tend to avoid using even a good program. A user's manual makes training easier, and it allows the users to study and review all they have learned during the training session.

Maintain and Upgrade the Program

It is difficult to catch all the errors in a complex program. Some errors appear only under very specific conditions. Sometimes, these conditions are not foreseen in the testing phase. **Program maintenance** is the process of correcting errors that are discovered in the program after it has been installed. However, the structured programming concepts introduced in this chapter are designed to reduce the number of errors that occur past the testing phase.

Most businesses operate in a dynamic and constantly changing environment. It is inevitable that most programs will require not only maintenance, but also upgrading to accommodate new user needs or new hardware designs.

SUMMARY

A program, or software, is the series of instructions that directs the hardware to perform various tasks. The two types of software are system software and application software.

A good program is one that is correct, easy to understand, easy to maintain and update, efficient, reliable, and flexible. Using a free-form approach to programming has resulted in lengthy development time, high costs, and low quality. In answer to these problems, structured programming was developed.

Structured programming is a programming methodology that involves systematic design, development, and management of the program development process. Structured programming concepts include the use of three control structures (sequence, selection, and repetition), top-down design, modules, and management control.

Top-down design identifies the major functions involved in a problem and then divides them into subfunctions until the problem has been divided as much as possible. A module is a group of processing instructions that performs a specific function. Structured programming also requires tight management control over the program development process. This control often takes the form of a chief programmer team—specialized personnel to design and develop a program. A structured walk-through is a technique that can be used to check the appropriateness of the system analyst's program design.

The program development process is the series of steps to be followed during the development of a program. The steps are: (a) define the problem; (b) design the algorithm; (c) code the program; (d) test and debug the program; (e) implement the program and train users; and (f) maintain and upgrade the program. Each step of the program development process needs to be documented.

Documentation is the text or graphics that provides specific instructions about, or records the purpose or function of, a particular step or instruction.

An algorithm is a set of step-by-step instructions that solve a problem. Structure charts, HIPO charts, flowcharts, and pseudocode are used to help design the algorithm.

Structure charts depict the relationships between modules in a hierarchical structure. A visual table of contents is structured similarly, the difference being that each module is numbered so that it can be easily referenced. A HIPO (hierarchy plus input, processing, output) chart outlines the input, processing steps, and output required. A program flowchart is a graphic representation of the steps of a program using standardized symbols. A variation of the flowchart is the structured flowchart or Nassi-Shneiderman chart. It uses various shaped boxes to represent control structures in a "box-within-a-box" format. Pseudocode is the use of English phrases to describe the processing steps in a program.

Coding is the process of writing the algorithm in a specific programming language so it can be entered into the computer and executed. Once the algorithm is coded and entered, testing and debugging the program begins. Testing is the process of checking the correctness and identifying the errors in a program. Three types of errors or "bugs" may be encountered when testing: syntax; run-time; and logic. The rules and conventions that must be followed when writing in a particular programming language are called syntax. Debugging is the process of finding and correcting any type of error in a program.

After a program has been tested and debugged, it is installed; then user training begins. The final step is ongoing and involves program maintenance and upgrading, as needed.

Key Terms

algorithm (p. 293)

application software (p. 286)

chief programmer team (p. 293)

coding (p. 302)

debugging (p. 304)

documentation (p. 296)

flowchart (p. 300)

HIPO (hierarchy plus input, processing, output) chart (p. 298)

logic error (p. 303)

module (p. 292)

Nassi-Shneiderman chart (p. 301)

program (p. 286)

program development process (p. 295)

program flowchart (p. 300)

program maintenance (p. 306)

pseudocode (p. 301)

repetition control structure (p. 290)

run-time error (p. 303)

selection control structure (p. 290)

sequence control structure (p. 290)

software (p. 286)

structure chart (p. 297)

structured programming (p. 290)

structured walk-through (p. 295)

syntax (p. 303)

syntax error (p. 303)

system software (p. 286)

top-down design (p. 291)

visual table of contents (p. 298)

Review Questions

1. A(n) _____ is a series of instructions telling the computer what to do.

2. Describe the difference between system software and application software.

3. List the six qualities of a good program and describe each.

4. The programming methodology that stresses the systematic design development and management of the program development process is called _____.

5. How does the selection control structure differ from the sequence control structure?

6. Name and describe the two basic variations of the repetition control structure.

7. Describe how the top-down approach to solving a problem works.

8. What is a module and how does the use of modules affect the development of a program?

9. The finite set of step-by-step instructions used to solve a problem is called a(n) _____.

10. What is the function of a chief programmer team?

11. What happens in a structured walk-through?

12. Describe the six steps in the program development process.

13. What is documentation and why is it important to the program development process?

14. Describe and draw an example of a structure chart. How does it differ from a visual table of contents?

15. For what is a hierarchy plus input, processing, output (HIPO) chart used?

16. What is the function of a program flowchart?

17. Name the three basic program control structures used in a Nassi-Shneiderman chart and draw the shapes used to represent them.

18. Why do most programming departments set standards to be followed when using pseudocode?

19. What is involved in coding a program?

20. The set of rules and conventions to be followed when using a programming language is called its _____.

21. List and discuss three types of program errors that may occur.

22. The process of finding and correcting errors in a program is called _____.

23. Why is a good training program important to the successful use of a computer program?

24. Explain why learning about programming can be beneficial even if you don't choose a programming career.

25. Discuss the three major problems associated with free-form programming that structured programming attempts to solve.

INFOMODULE
Expert Systems

Expert systems are one of the first and, so far, the most practical applications derived from the research on artificial intelligence. **Artificial intelligence (AI)** is that area of computer science in which scientists are striving to build machines to "think" and "reason" in a fashion similar to humans. An **expert system** is software, based on certain concepts of AI, that acts as a consultant, or an expert, in a specific field or discipline to help solve a problem or help make a decision. Expert systems are also referred to as knowledge-based systems.

Expert systems attempt to supply both the knowledge and reasoning of human beings. They are "expert" in only one field, topic, or discipline; they can help solve only a narrowly defined problem. The user provides data about a problem through a keyboard and the computer responds with an answer and explanation based on facts and rules that have earlier been extracted from human experts and stored in the computer.

An expert system cannot entirely duplicate a human expert's judgment or make the final decision; but it can offer opinions, suggest possible diagnoses, and suggest various solutions to a problem. These programs are usually used as a supplemental source of advice.

Because of their usefulness, expert systems are one of the first results of AI research to become a viable commercial product. Oil companies use expert systems to analyze geological data, while physicians use them to help diagnose and treat illnesses. People in other types of diagnostic fields, professional assistance, and emergency management also take advantage of expert systems.

Until recently, most expert systems were designed for use only on large computers because the programming demanded so much power and memory. Now, many expert systems can be used with microcomputers; however, these programs are still very expensive. Early work was done using PROLOG (*Pro*gramming in *Logic*), LISP (*Lis*t *P*rocessing), and other special-ized programming languages. Now the trend is toward designing these systems for microcomputers and with popular programming languages such as FORTRAN and C.

CONVENTIONAL PROGRAMS VERSUS EXPERT SYSTEMS

An expert system differs from a traditional program that is used to solve a problem (application software). In traditional software, there is the program, and there are the data that the program is given to work on. In expert systems, however, the program is called the inference engine and the data base has been replaced with a knowledge base. (The inference engine and knowledge base will be described in more detail later.)

Traditional computer programs are composed of a detailed set of sequentially organized instructions to be followed that comprise an algorithm for the processing steps. The computer can do nothing else but strictly follow the sequence of the instructions. Using heuristic programming, an expert system can group instructions in any order and allows different reactions to each situation it encounters. The exact processing activities are determined by the data that are entered during a "consultation" (a series of questions the expert system generates that the user answers), not by the sequence of processing statements (Figure 1).

Heuristic programming is a key feature of expert systems. The main difference between expert systems and traditional programs is the inclusion of heuristics, the rules of thumb about the problem. Heuristic programming is an attempt to emulate human intuition, judgment, and common sense. This type of program allows the computer to recall earlier results and include them in its programming. That newly gained knowledge is then added to its knowledge base and becomes a basis for the next problem and its solution. Here, the computer has learned from its own experience and mis-

FIGURE 1

Comparison of traditional application software to expert system software

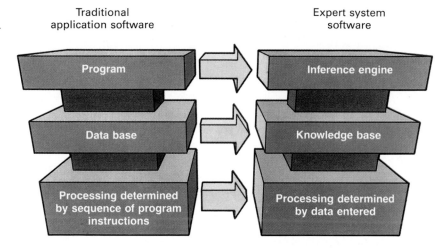

takes, so when it encounters a new problem, it will recall earlier results and consider them.

ORIGINS AND EARLY SYSTEMS

Human experts are expensive to hire and are sometimes hard to find; indeed, some are rare. In addition, they eventually die, taking with them worlds of experience and knowledge, much of which new generations will have to reassemble or learn for themselves. Early AI researchers began to wonder: What if all the experts' years of knowledge and expertise could be captured and preserved? Future generations could have access to that knowledge and expertise and build on that foundation.

For those who first started toying with the idea of electronically preserving wisdom, the

Differences Between Expert System and Conventional Programming

- Use of inference engine rather than program
- Use of knowledge base rather than data base
- Processing determined by data entered rather than by the sequence of program instructions

underlying premise was that the reasoning process that enables a human expert to think and make decisions about a problem could also enable a programmed computer to do the same. In addition to the programming, the computer needed the same pools of knowledge stored by the human authority on that particular subject.

Nearly fifteen years ago, during the early stages of expert systems development, researchers began to explore how the minds of human experts worked—how they used what they knew to solve a problem. These researchers soon realized that people attained expertise by acquiring knowledge and gaining experience. They also recognized that there was more to being an expert than just knowledge and practice; intuition and common sense are required, and these qualities are difficult to describe. Even experts have trouble explaining them. Therefore, because computers can operate only on explicit instructions, programming expert systems with human reasoning is complicated.

To make the process even more difficult, experts differ in the way they approach problems and reach decisions. An expert in one field, medicine for example, may not use the same methodology in problem solving as a geologist. Eventually, however, scientists found enough common aspects on which to base the design of expert systems.

Practically speaking, it would be quite a benefit to business and society in general to be able to preserve the unique individual experience and knowledge that cannot be easily passed on in books, classrooms, or training sessions. When the Campbell Soup Company learned that its expert in maintaining the complex sterilizers used to kill bacteria in Campbell's canned soup products was retiring, management decided to capture his many years of knowledge in an expert system program. Company officials wanted his expertise to be passed on to other workers, so developers of the program worked about seven months in an attempt to glean all his experience and knowledge. Campbell says the system can deal with about 95 percent of the problems that might arise, but it will be baffled when problems that are not covered in its knowledge base are presented.

The first applied use of an expert system was DENDRAL, software that interprets data produced by mass spectrometers to determine molecular structures of unknown compounds. In the early '60s, Edward Feigenbaum, a professor at Stanford University and expert system theorist, and Joshua Lederberg, a Stanford colleague and subsequently a Nobel Prize-winning geneticist, decided to try to apply expert system principles to finding how scientists analyze organic compounds. The result was DENDRAL. The system represented all the knowledge needed by

the program (inference engine) as "if-then," or situation/action, rules.

Since then, the system has been used and refined to such an extent that it has been declared almost as proficient as a human chemist in analyzing chemical structures. In fact, DENDRAL is so well-established as an "expert" that researchers even cite it as a contributor to some of their technical articles on chemistry.

Because of its diagnostic-type problems, medicine was also a promising area in which to apply expert systems. Feigenbaum, Bruce Buchanan, another Stanford colleague, and Edward Shortliffe, a computer enthusiast at Stanford Medical School, started working on an expert system called MYCIN that would help diagnose meningitis and blood infections and recommend antibiotics and proper treatment.

They discovered that the data (knowledge base) could be changed or even replaced without affecting the program as a whole, and the program section (inference engine) containing the logic could remain intact. They called the "empty" program EMYCIN (empty MYCIN, or essential MYCIN, as it was later called). The team then created a knowledge base to go with EMYCIN—one to deal just with lung diseases. Other researchers adapted this empty program to geological exploration and diagnosis of oil

Service people who maintain industrial and computer equipment use expert systems for assistance. This Honeywell service technician uses Mentor, an expert system that helps him repair installed control systems. (Courtesy of Honeywell Inc.)

drilling problems. This separation of the knowledge base from the inference engine led to the concept of just a **shell**, a general-purpose inference engine and a skeleton of the knowledge base into which users could add their own special data and if-then rules.

Medical applications of expert systems have allowed the knowledge of the world's foremost medical talent to become available to small hospitals and to paramedics. An even more ambitious medical project, CADUCEUS, was developed in the early '70s at the University of Pittsburgh by Harry Pople, a computer scientist, and Jack Meyers, a professor of internal medicine. It included diagnostic knowledge of more than 700 diseases. The size of its knowledge base limited its use, however, because it required a large, expensive computer system.

Researchers have been working hard creating expert systems in various fields. Business and industry, aware of the system's economic advantages, are also spending money in its development.

COMPONENTS OF AN EXPERT SYSTEM

An expert system consists of: (a) a knowledge base on a specific topic; and (b) an inference engine, the program that can probe that base to suggest solutions to a problem.

Knowledge Base

The **knowledge base** is the stored collection of facts on a particular subject and the hundreds or thousands of if-then (situation/action) rules by which the facts relate. The base includes maxims provided by a group of experts in that field and thousands of facts and rules of thumb (heuristics), as well as judgments, intuitions, and experiences.

The knowledge base differs from a traditional data base. A data base is a collection of related or unrelated facts. A knowledge base, on the other hand, includes not only facts about a particular subject, but also instructions on how to use the facts and on how they relate, i.e., the if-then rules that connect the pieces of data and draw conclusions.

For example, an extremely simplified if-then rule for a family physician might be: *If* patient complains of general aches and pains and if patient's age is greater than eighteen, *then* prescribe aspirin. Usually, if the knowledge can be expressed clearly in words, it can be presented in an if-then rule.

To create a knowledge base, special designers called **knowledge engineers** spend months working with the human experts to extract and structure the facts, rules, and knowledge. After the knowledge base is developed, then the program (inference engine) will be able to probe that base.

Inference Engine

The human expert has to be able to make inferences from pieces of evidence. The expert system also has to have a way to make inferences. An **inference engine** is the reusable program that allows the computer to intelligently apply the facts and information to a particular problem. It retrieves and manipulates the facts and rules, deciding in which order to make connections, associations, and inferences. An inference engine decides how to link the mental associations that a human expert makes instinctively when confronted with a problem and the order in which these decisions are made. It also has the capability of explaining its reasonings and conclusions to the user.

SHELLS

Sometimes an expert system takes the form of an empty shell in which the user company supplies additional facts. Remember EMYCIN, the shell from MYCIN? It is the expert system with

---

Components of an Expert System

- Inference engine
- Knowledge base

a structure for its knowledge base but it does not contain the knowledge base itself. It includes an inference engine that works well with a variety of different fields, and it prompts the user with questions until enough information is accumulated to fill the knowledge base.

With a shell, knowledge engineers, or sometimes the intended users themselves, can build a knowledge base and create an expert system for specific applications. Shell packages are becoming a popular way for developing expert systems for microcomputers.

HOW AN EXPERT SYSTEM WORKS

Several methods are used to structure knowledge in an expert system so that the inference engine can make its conclusions, but the most common one is with the set of if-then rules. Systems developed with this approach are called rule-based systems.

In a rule-based system, the computer moves through the symbols that describe the current situation, looking for patterns that correspond to the "if" sides of its stored rules. When the program finds such a pattern, the relevant rule is triggered. The program then takes an action, such as presenting the user with a conclusion or applying a succeeding chain of rules.

Generally, here is how it works when a user consults an expert system. The system interviews (asks questions of) the user and gets the facts about the problem at hand. During the interview, questions appear on the computer display screen, and the user responds by keying in answers or important data. Some systems, in order to simplify the user/program interaction, use a natural language; then the computer and the user communicate in a human language (e.g., English) rather than cryptic programming commands. The system keeps the user posted on its "analysis." The user guides the program to choose among sets of options, with each decision opening the gate to another group of choices.

Then, utilizing the user's responses, the system searches its knowledge base. The organized information in the knowledge base is probed and interpreted by the inference engine, which performs deductive reasoning, making inferences on the knowledge. It systematically searches through the various paths for a solution without becoming lost in the vast number of possibilities. Eventually, the program comes up with the advice and communicates it to the user. Sometimes, it will need to ask the user more questions to get additional information on which to base its advice. The system also explains its reasoning process and its conclusions.

Now, let's briefly go through the process using MYCIN, which analyzes bacterial blood infections and recommends proper treatment.

On the basis of symptoms presented to it by the user physician, the program first makes a reasonable guess regarding the patient's condition. That input includes data about the patient's history—lab test results, symptoms, and other observations. The physician also answers any questions the program asks.

The program then determines how well its "first reasonable guess" diagnosis fits the known facts about the behavior of the microorganism suspected to be involved. Once the system has identified the cause of the infection, it reviews all the antibiotics in its knowledge base and makes a recommendation as to which one should be administered to the patient.

EXPERT SYSTEMS IN USE

After DENDRAL, MYCIN, and CADUCEUS proved their usefulness, other expert systems started to appear in a variety of fields. Today, expert systems are used by fighter pilots to make tactical decisions, by mechanics to diagnose mechanical problems, by oil companies to analyze geological data, by computer companies to design new products, and even by credit card companies to assess credit risks.

Expert systems such as Authorizer's Assistant, a system that assesses credit ratings, could affect many of us. Faced with financial losses from unwise extension of credit and from the fraudulent use of its cards, American Express has resorted to Authorizer's Assistant to make precise credit authorizations for applicants. Under the old system, American Express authorizers had to rely on facts that were supplied by as many as twelve different data bases. The process was not only slow, it was also unreliable, as the mounting losses proved.

While the new system still goes back to data held in the original bases, it does so through a complex network of 800 different rules that result in: (a) accurate assessments of the size and nature of each credit risk; (b) a judgment on whether or not the credit should be given as it asks questions to resolve the matter; and (c) revisions of the recommendations when the questions are answered, while providing explanations for all its recommendations. Human authorizers can still overrule the credit decisions made by the expert system, but since these authorizers were the ones who provided the data from which the system was constructed, it is relatively rare for such an override to occur.

Here are some proven expert systems and the kind of assistance they provide:

- [ ] PROSPECTOR interprets geological data for use in mineral exploration. It predicts the potential for locating mineral deposits in the earth. This system is reported to have helped discover a vast, previously unknown, molybdenum (a metallic element used in strengthening steel) deposit in the state of Washington.
- [ ] CATS (Computer-Aided Troubleshooting System) is used by General Electric mechanics to help identify and repair problems with diesel locomotives. The mechanic keys in responses to questions from the program about the problem or malfunction. With this interactive questioning, the expert system identifies the cause of the problem and suggests and demonstrates repair procedures on the computer display screen.
- [ ] XCON contains about 500 facts and over 5,000 rules to assist sales personnel at Dig-

By analyzing masses of collected data, expert systems help petroleum companies determine the best way to extract and move oil from the geological formation where it is found. (Courtesy of Marathon Petroleum Co.)

ital Equipment Corporation when ordering computer systems for customers.

☐ Management Adviser is an expert system that helps managers evaluate the financial impact of decisions such as new investments, cost reduction programs, and changes in prices.

☐ PROTEAN, developed at Stanford University, figures out the structures of molecules.

Many other expert systems are also appearing. One system used by oil companies evaluates 500 variables to diagnose problems at drilling sites. Another system gives underwriting advice to insurers of commercial property. There is even an expert system to teach personnel how to repair and maintain semiconductor production machines for microcomputers. Ion Technology in Gloucester, Massachusetts, used this repair system because training for its maintenance personnel takes about four or five months and the repairs were backlogged.

Expert systems are just beginning to penetrate some areas:

☐ To automate its analysis and indexing of financial information, the Securities and Exchange Commission is developing an expert system using natural language that can read financial statements.

☐ The New York Stock Exchange (NYSE) would like to see an expert system that will enable NYSE computer surveillance systems to read and take into account news reports when watching for unusual trading activity.

☐ E. F. Hutton is working on a shell to use with their existing data. It would allow their own 6,500 brokers access to the insights of the firm's top analysts and investment advisers and to use their data more effectively when searching for sales opportunities or answering clients' queries.

The U.S. Government has poured millions of dollars into AI research. It is presently examining the potential of expert systems and is sponsoring prototypes that may change the way government handles public administrative tasks such as processing welfare claims or responding to nuclear power-plant emergencies. Researchers who met at the Expert Systems in Government Conference in late 1986 described several of the systems planned. Here are two examples:

☐ The U.S. Nuclear Regulatory Commission (NRC) is funding the development of an expert system to help its emergency response team analyze data during a nuclear power plant meltdown. The commission believes that the complexity of determining the right strategies for handling severe accidents requires them to consider the use of expert systems.

☐ The U.S. Department of Energy is spending money to design an alarm filtering system for nuclear power plants. When completed, the system will indicate to operators which of the hundreds of alarms need top-priority attention.

Expert systems are barely out of their infancy. Those people who are already using them see the advantages. In some cases, expert systems perform as well as or better than humans. Most people agree that it is a great advantage to accumulate the experience and knowledge of experts so that this information can be transferred to future generations.

However, expert systems do have their limitations. They can give the user only what is programmed in the system. In addition, they are expensive and work well only on problems that are specifically defined and in very specific fields.

Because users usually communicate with the expert system by keyboard or CRT, the system can make recommendations based only on the information the user enters. One critic made the analogy that this process is equivalent to communicating with a human expert by electronic mail. Other, perhaps significant, evidence cannot be collected. For example, a medical diagnostic system cannot get any clues from the patient's physical appearance, thereby identifying how poorly or well the patient looks.

Regardless of the advantages and limitations, expert systems are the focus of a lot of attention among people who want to extend the application and power of computers. There are those who think that the future of computers and their impact on society will be largely dependent on continuing to develop practical applications such as the expert system.

KEY TERMS

artificial intelligence (AI) (p. 309)

expert system (p. 309)

heuristic programming (p. 309)

inference engine (p. 312)

knowledge base (p. 312)

knowledge engineer (p. 312)

shell (p. 312)

QUESTIONS

1. How does an expert system relate to the field of artificial intelligence?
2. Describe the difference between traditional software for problem solving and expert systems used for problem solving.
3. Describe the basic premise on which early researchers based their first work on expert systems.
4. What are the two main components of an expert system? Briefly describe what each does.
5. What is heuristic programming?

OBJECTIVES

- ☐ Define the purpose of a programming language
- ☐ Identify the basic instructions performed by any programming language
- ☐ Discuss the four categories of programming languages
- ☐ List several major high-level programming languages
- ☐ Discuss some considerations involved when choosing a programming language
- ☐ Describe an operating system and list several different types

OUTLINE

PROGRAMMING LANGUAGES
    Basic Instructions of a Programming Language
    Categories of Programming Languages
    Procedural versus Nonprocedural Languages
    Major High-level Languages
    Choosing a Programming Language

OPERATING SYSTEMS
    Control and Service Programs
    Types of Operating Systems
    Popular Microcomputer Operating Systems

INFOMODULE: Careers in an Information Age

SYSTEM ANALYST

PROGRAMMER

COMPUTER OPERATOR

DATA-ENTRY OPERATOR

COMPUTER SERVICE TECHNICIAN

DATA-BASE ADMINISTRATOR

INFORMATION SYSTEM MANAGER

OTHER COMPUTER-RELATED CAREERS

HOW COMPUTERS AFFECT OTHER JOBS

11

Programming Languages and Operating Systems

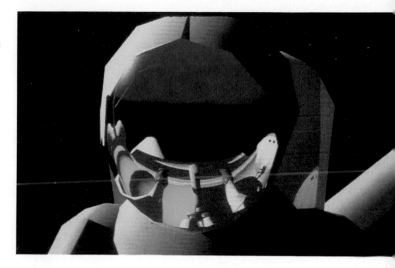

PROFILE: William H. Gates

At the age when boys are trying to find ways to impress girls, thirteen-year-old Bill Gates was losing his heart to computers. An extraordinarily bright student in mathematics, Gates became fascinated with computer programming. In the late 1960s, while he was in high school, Gates and some friends volunteered to work evenings for no salary at Computer Center Corporation in Seattle. Their job was to find bugs in the elaborate programs provided to the Center by Digital Equipment Corporation for its DEC computer. While several teenagers took part in this operation, the clear leaders were Gates and his friend, Paul Allen, who was two years older.

Computer Center didn't turn over its computer to the youngsters simply as an act of community good will. According to its contract with DEC, as long as it was able to uncover bugs in DEC's programs, the company did not have to pay for the use of the DEC computer. Of the original team, only Gates and Allen stayed on long enough to get paying jobs with Computer Center.

By the time Gates was fifteen, he and Allen had formed Traf-O-Data, a company that sold computer analyses of traffic patterns. The effort grossed them around $20,000 a year.

Then, in 1974, they developed Microsoft BASIC, the first high-level language for microcomputers. Later, in 1975, the language became part of the MITS Altair, the first personal computer.

Subsequently, Gates and Allen founded a second company, Microsoft, to market Microsoft BASIC and create other software for microcomputers. Gates, however, had to leave Harvard to find the time to manage the daily operations of their new company. In 1981, IBM adopted Microsoft BASIC for its personal computer line, a move that turned Microsoft into a thriving company.

Allen left Microsoft before it really started to bloom financially. Gates stayed on, however, serving not only as a developer of ideas, but also as an effective salesman. He also saw PC-DOS and MS-DOS, the company's biggest successes, become the operating software that runs millions of personal computers.

By the time Gates was thirty years old, Microsoft went public in search of investors. Gates' share of the stock was worth more than $300 million—enough to compensate for the work he did as an unpaid whiz kid.

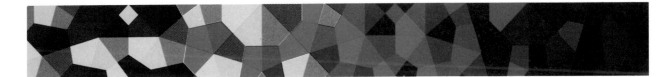

To take advantage of the capabilities of the computer hardware, people need some means of communicating exactly what they want it to do. The computer must be instructed through each detail of an operation. For example, if a user wants to print a document, the computer must be given detailed instructions on how to access the file, initialize the printer, send the data to the printer, and so on.

This chapter looks at programming languages that provide instructions for a computer to perform specific operations. It also describes operating systems, which provide: (a) instructions to manage the details of a computer's operation; and (b) services to the user.

PROGRAMMING LANGUAGES

To some extent, we are all familiar with languages such as English, French, German, and Spanish. People use language to communicate with one another. Each language consists of sounds and symbols and contains grammatical rules that govern its use. Programming languages are similar. A **programming language** is a set of written symbols that instruct the computer hardware to perform specified tasks. Use of these symbols is governed by a set of rules called **syntax.**

Basic Instructions of a Programming Language

Several hundred programming languages are used for computers today. While the specifics of each language may vary, certain basic instructions are performed by all programming languages. These instructions are divided as follows:

☐ Input/output instructions—transfer instructions and data between the central processing unit and input and output devices
☐ Arithmetic instructions—perform mathematical operations such as addition, subtraction, multiplication, and division
☐ Logic instructions—perform comparisons such as equal to, not equal to, less than, greater than, greater than or equal to, and less

Types of Programming Language Instructions

- Input/output
- Arithmetic
- Logic
- Control
- Data movement
- Specification

than or equal to, and test certain conditions. Testing a condition involves evaluating the values or logical relationships of one or more data items. For example, in the statement, "If x > 10, then y = 1, else y = 2", x > 10 is the condition being tested. If x is greater than 10, then the value of y will be set to 1. If it is not greater than 10, the value of y is set to 2.

☐ Control instructions—alter the order in which the program instructions are to be executed

☐ Data movement instructions—copy and move data within primary storage

☐ Specification instructions—specify various parameters such as constants, what portions of memory will be used, file access method, and so on

While every programming language is capable of these basic functions, the methods used to accomplish them vary widely.

Categories of Programming Languages

Of the hundreds of different programming languages available, all fit into one of four general categories: machine language; assembly language; high-level language; and fourth-generation language.

Machine Language **Machine language** is the only programming language that the computer can understand. It is a language made up entirely of 1s and 0s. There is not, however, one universal machine language. The arrangement of 1s and 0s to represent similar instructions, data, and memory locations differs among computers because of different hardware designs.

Machine language programs have the advantage of very fast execution speeds and efficient use of primary memory. Use of machine language is a very tedious, difficult, and time-consuming method of programming. Machine language is a low-level language. Since every detail of an operation must be specified by the programmer, a **low-level language** requires that the programmer have detailed knowledge of how the computer works. As you might imagine, it is easy to make an error and very difficult to debug a machine-language program.

If machine language were the only means of programming a computer, there probably wouldn't be many programmers, and there certainly wouldn't be the vast number of application programs available for our use. To make programming simpler, other easier-to-use programming languages have been developed. These languages, however, must ultimately be translated into machine language before the computer can understand and use them.

Assembly Language The next higher level of programming languages is **assembly languages.** They are also classified as low-level languages because detailed knowledge of hardware specifics is still required.

Assembly languages use mnemonics in place of 1s and 0s to represent the operation codes (Figure 11–1). A **mnemonic** is an alphabetical abbreviation used as a memory aid. For example, instead of using a combination of 1s and 0s to represent an addition operation, the mnemonic *AD* might be used.

Assembly language uses symbolic addressing capabilities that simplify the programming process because the programmer does not need to know or remember the exact storage locations of instructions or data. Symbolic addressing is the ability to express an address in terms of symbols chosen by the programmer rather than in terms of the absolute numerical location. Therefore, it is not necessary to assign and remember a number that identifies the address of a piece of data. Instead, a programmer can assign data to a symbolic name such as TOTAL. The assembly language will automatically assign an address when first encountering the symbolic

Assembler code (mnemonics)

```
sseg                    segment stack
                        db 256  dup (?)
sseg                    ends
dseg          segment
data                    db "2 x 4 =  "
dseg          ends
cseg          segment
assume        cs:cseg,ds:dseg,ss:sseg,es:nothing
start         proc far
                        push ds
                        mov ax,0
                        push ax
                        call main
start         endp

main                    proc near
                        cld
                        mov ax, dseg
                        mov ds, ax
                        mov ax, 0b000h
                        mov es, ax
                        mov dx, 0
                        mov bx, 0
                        lea si, data
                        mov di, 32848
                        mov al, 02h
                        mov bl, 04h
                        mul bl
                        or al, 30h
                        mov al, data+9
    msgsb:    mov cx,9
    lbl:                movsb
                        inc di
                        mov al, 135
                        mov [di], al
                        loop lbl
main                    endp
cseg                    ends
                        endstart
```

Machine-language instructions

```
0100
110010  100000  1111000  100000  110100  100000
111101  100000  100000
11110
10111000
1010000
11101000
11111100
10111000
10001110  11011000
10111000
10001110  11000000
10111010
10111011
10001101  110110
10111111
10110000  00000010
10110011  00000100
11110110  11100011
00001100  110000
10100000
10111001
10100100
1000111
10110000  10000111
10001000  00000101
11100010  1111000
```

FIGURE 11–1

A comparison of assembler codes (mnemonics) and machine-language instructions for a program that computes and prints out the result of 2 × 4.

Categories of Programming Languages

- Machine
- Assembly
- High-level
- Fourth-generation

name and then remember the address each time the symbolic name is encountered.

Before they can be used by the computer, assembly languages must be translated into machine language. This conversion is done by a language-translator program called an **assembler.** Assembly languages provide an easier and more efficient way to program than machine languages while still maintaining control over the internal functions of a computer at the most basic level. The advantages of programming with assembly languages are that they produce programs that are efficient, use less storage, and execute much faster than programs designed using high-level languages. However, assembly languages are still machine-oriented and require a thorough knowledge of the computer hardware. Compared to the high-level languages, they are tedious and prone to errors. Let's take a look at high-level languages.

High-level Language **High-level languages** are languages whose instructions closely resemble human language and mathematical notation. High-level languages do not require that the programmer have detailed knowledge about the internal operations of a computer.

Because of the close resemblance to human language, high-level languages are also much easier to learn and use than either machine or assembly languages. Typically, less time and effort are required to program in a high-level language because programming errors are easier to avoid and correct.

Many high-level languages are also designed to be machine-independent. They can be transported from computer to computer and executed with few changes. As a result, high-level languages are used more often than machine or assembly languages.

Sometimes, portions of a program may require more speed or efficiency than can be achieved with the high-level programming language being used. Most high-level languages allow assembly language programs to be used by a program to supply the needed boost in capabilities.

High-level languages must also be translated into machine language before they can be used by a computer. One of two different language-translator programs is used to translate high-level languages: a compiler or an interpreter. A **compiler** translates a whole program, called the source code, at once into machine language before the program is executed. Once converted, the program is stored in machine-readable form, called the object code. The object code can be immediately executed anytime thereafter. The source code remains intact after the conversion and can be updated and changed as required, and then recompiled into object code.

An **interpreter** translates a program into machine language one line at a time, executing each line of the program after it is translated. With most interpreters, the machine-readable form is not stored in primary storage or on a secondary-storage media. Therefore, the program must be interpreted each time before it is executed.

Fourth-generation Language The different categories of languages are sometimes labeled by generations—from lowest to highest. Machine lan-

Types of Language-translator Programs

- Assemblers
- Compilers
- Interpreters

guages are considered first generation; assembly languages are second generation; and high-level languages are third generation. **Fourth-generation language** is a term that describes a variety of programming languages that allow users to create programs with much less effort than is required by high-level languages. The objectives of a fourth-generation language include

☐ Increasing the speed of developing programs
☐ Minimizing user effort to obtain information from a computer
☐ Decreasing the skill level required of users so that they can concentrate on the application rather than the intricacies of coding, and thus solve their own problems without the aid of a professional programmer
☐ Minimizing maintenance by reducing errors and making programs that are easy to change

Depending on the language, the sophistication of fourth-generation languages varies widely. These languages are usually used in conjunction with a data base and its data dictionary and are often found as part of an MIS or DSS. Fourth-generation languages include: data-base query languages; report generators; and application generators.

A **data-base query language** permits formulation of queries that may relate to several records from one or more files. The appropriate records can then be printed or displayed in a suitable format. Examples include IBM's SQL and Artificial Intelligence's INTELLECT.

A **report generator** allows data from a data base to be extracted and formatted into reports. It also allows substantial arithmetic and logic operations to be performed on the data before they are displayed or printed. FOCUS, by Application Builders, Inc., and RAMIS II, by Mathematica Products Group, are two examples of fourth-generation languages that incorporate report generators.

An **application generator** allows data entry and permits the user to specify how the data base will be updated, what calculations or logic operations will be performed, and what output will be created. Examples include MANTIS, by Cincom Systems, Inc., and NOMAD2, by D & B Computing Services.

Procedural versus Nonprocedural Languages

Programming languages are classified into two different types: procedural languages and nonprocedural languages. **Procedural languages** specify *how* something is accomplished. Common procedural languages include BASIC, Pascal, C, Ada, COBOL, and FORTRAN. **Nonprocedural languages** specify *what* is accomplished without going into the details of *how*. Data-base query languages and report generators are examples of nonprocedural languages.

The difference between procedural and nonprocedural languages can be illustrated with the analogy of giving directions to a taxi driver. Directions given using a procedural language approach might go as follows: "Drive 600 yards forward. Turn right. Drive 350 yards forward. Turn left.

Drive 500 yards forward. Stop." Using a nonprocedural language approach, you would simply tell the driver what you want: "Take me to the Fairview Hotel."

Major High-level Languages

FORTRAN FORTRAN (FORmula TRANslator) was introduced in 1957 and is the oldest high-level programming language. It was designed primarily for use by scientists, engineers, and mathematicians to solve mathematical problems. FORTRAN is well-suited for complex numerical calculations, but because it lacks certain input/output and nonnumeric operations, it is not very useful for manipulation of large data files. Figure 11–2 is a brief example of a FORTRAN program.

COBOL COBOL (COmmon Business Oriented Language) is a widely used programming language for business data processing. It was developed in the late 1950s by the Conference on Data Systems Languages (CODASYL) committee that consisted of manufacturers, users, and government agencies. It was specifically designed to manipulate the large data files typically encountered in business.

COBOL uses descriptive English-like statements that offer a self-documenting quality. This feature makes it easy to understand and follow the logic of a program. However, COBOL is a wordy language, and it is more difficult and tedious to use than other high-level languages that are more compact. A COBOL program is generally much longer than other high-level language programs that accomplish the same task.

Although other programming languages perform the same operations as COBOL more efficiently, COBOL is likely to be the predominant

FIGURE 11–2

A FORTRAN program that computes the sum and average of ten numbers

```
C     COMPUTE THE SUM AND AVERAGE OF 10 NUMBERS
C
         REAL NUM, SUM, AVG
         INTEGER TOTNUM, COUNTR
C
         SUM = 0.0
C     INITIALIZE LOOP CONTROL VARIABLE
         COUNTR = 0
         TOTNUM = 10
C
C     LOOP TO READ DATA AND ACCUMULATE SUM
20 IF (COUNTR .GE. TOTNUM) GO TO 30
         READ, NUM
         SUM = SUM + NUM
C         UPDATE LOOP CONTROL VARIABLE
         COUNTR = COUNTR + 1
         GO TO 20
C     END OF LOOP - COMPUTE AVERAGE
30 AVG = SUM / TOTNUM
C     PRINT RESULTS
         PRINT, SUM
         PRINT, AVG
         STOP
         END
```

FIGURE 11–3

A COBOL program that computes the sum and average of ten numbers

```
IDENTIFICATION DIVISION.
PROGRAM-ID.        AVERAGES.
AUTHOR.            DEB KNUDSEN.
DATE-COMPILED.
ENVIRONMENT DIVISION.
CONFIGURATION SECTION.
    SOURCE-COMPUTER. HP-3000.
    OBJECT-COMPUTER. HP-3000.
INPUT-OUTPUT SECTION.
FILE-CONTROL.
    SELECT NUMBER-FILE ASSIGN TO "NUMFILE".
    SELECT REPORT-FILE ASSIGN TO "PRINT,UR,A,LP(CCTL)".
DATA DIVISION.
FILE SECTION.
FD   NUMBER-FILE
     LABEL RECORDS ARE STANDARD
     DATA RECORD IS NUMBER-REC.
01   NUMBER-REC                      PIC S9(7)V99.
FD   REPORT-FILE
     LABEL RECORDS ARE STANDARD
     DATA RECORD IS REPORT-REC.
01   REPORT-REC                      PIC X(100).

WORKING-STORAGE SECTION.
01   END-OF-NUMBER-FILE-FLAG         PIC X(3) VALUE SPACES.
     88   END-OF-NUMBER-FILE                  VALUE "YES".
01   SUM-OF-NUMBERS                  PIC S9(7)V99.
01   AVERAGE-OF-NUMBERS              PIC S9(7)V99.
01   NUMBER-OF-NUMBERS               PIC 9(5).

01   WS-REPORT-REC.
     05   FILLER                     PIC X(2)    VALUE SPACES.
     05   FILLER                     PIC X(17)   VALUE
                                     "Sum of Numbers = ".
     05   WS-SUM-OF-NUMBERS          PIC Z,ZZZ,ZZZ.99-.
     05   FILLER                     PIC X(3)    VALUE SPACES.
     05   FILLER                     PIC X(15)   VALUE
                                     "# of Numbers = ".
     05   WS-NUMBER-OF-NUMBERS       PIC ZZZZ9.
     05   FILLER                     PIC X(3)    VALUE SPACES.
     05   FILLER                     PIC X(21)   VALUE
                                     "Average of Numbers = ".
     05   WS-AVERAGE-OF-NUMBERS      PIC Z,ZZZ,ZZZ.99-.
     05   FILLER                     PIC X(8)    VALUE SPACES.
```

language in business for some time to come because the expense in time and money to convert existing programs and retrain programmers and users would be prohibitive to many companies. Since many COBOL programs are already in place and operating satisfactorily, the attitude of many people in the business environment is, "If it isn't broken, don't fix it." Figure 11–3 is a brief example of a COBOL program.

BASIC BASIC (Beginner's All-purpose Symbolic Instruction Code) was developed at Dartmouth College in the mid-1960s to provide students with an easy-to-learn, interactive language on a time-sharing computer system. In an interactive language, each statement is translated into machine language and executed as soon as it is typed and entered into the computer. If

FIGURE 11–3
(continued)

```
PROCEDURE DIVISION.

100-MAIN-PROGRAM.
    OPEN INPUT  NUMBER-FILE
         OUTPUT REPORT-FILE.
    MOVE SPACES TO REPORT-REC.
    MOVE ZEROS TO SUM-OF-NUMBERS.
    MOVE ZEROS TO AVERAGE-OF-NUMBERS.
    MOVE ZEROS TO NUMBER-OF-NUMBERS.

    READ NUMBER-FILE
      AT END MOVE "YES" TO END-OF-NUMBER-FILE-FLAG.

    IF END-OF-NUMBER-FILE
      NEXT SENTENCE
    ELSE
      PERFORM 200-PROCESS-NUMBER-FILE
        UNTIL END-OF-NUMBER-FILE.

    PERFORM 300-COMPUTE-AVERAGE.

    PERFORM 400-PRINT-RESULTS.

    CLOSE NUMBER-FILE
          REPORT-FILE.

    STOP RUN.

200-PROCESS-NUMBER-FILE.
    ADD 1 TO NUMBER-OF-NUMBERS.
    ADD NUMBER-REC TO SUM-OF-NUMBERS.

    READ NUMBER-FILE
      AT END MOVE "YES" TO END-OF-NUMBER-FILE-FLAG.

300-COMPUTE-AVERAGE.
    DIVIDE SUM-OF-NUMBERS BY NUMBER-OF-NUMBERS
      GIVING AVERAGE-OF-NUMBERS.

400-PRINT-RESULTS.
    MOVE SUM-OF-NUMBERS TO WS-SUM-OF-NUMBERS.
    MOVE NUMBER-OF-NUMBERS TO WS-NUMBER-OF-NUMBERS.
    MOVE AVERAGE-OF-NUMBERS TO WS-AVERAGE-OF-NUMBERS.

WRITE REPORT-REC FROM WS-REPORT-REC.
```

there is an error in the statement entered, BASIC also provides error messages immediately.

BASIC was developed as a shortened and simplified version of FORTRAN. It allowed novice programmers to learn and begin programming in a matter of a few hours. Because it is easy to learn and use, BASIC became the most popular language for microcomputers and is available for most microcomputers in use today.

Since BASIC's inception, many extensions to the language have been developed to take advantage of specific hardware. This development has resulted in the emergence of many different, nonstandardized versions of BASIC. The American National Standards Institute (ANSI) set standards for the most essential portion of the BASIC language, called Minimal

HIGHLIGHT

CHOPSTICKS BY COMPUTER

One of the ironies of our age is that the most modern machines are being used to help manufacture one of the world's oldest eating implements.

Lakewood Industries, in Hibbing, Minnesota, uses a Danish-designed computer system to turn out 132,000 pairs of chopsticks an hour. This manufacturing process is seven times faster than the traditional Japanese methods. Lakewood's designer estimates that the computerized system will produce seven million pairs of chopsticks a day when the plant reaches full production.

Lakewood makes its chopsticks from aspen trees, which are cut into cordwood. Then the wood is cut into short lengths, scraped of its bark, and cut into ribbons. These wooden ribbons are fed into machines that stamp out the chopsticks. The computer dictates the cutting, making sure the maximum number is stamped from the wood.

Most of the chopsticks will be sold in the Far East.

BASIC, in 1978. Minimal BASIC and its various extensions were not well-suited to structured programming methods. In answer to the demand for structured languages, structured versions of BASIC, such as True BASIC, have emerged. Figure 11–4 shows a BASIC program for the Microsoft BASIC language.

Pascal and Modula–2 Niklaus Wirth of Zurich developed **Pascal** in the late 1960s and named it after Blaise Pascal, the French mathematician and philosopher who invented the first practical mechanical adding machine. It is suited for both scientific and file-processing applications.

Pascal was originally designed to teach the concepts of structured programming and top-down design to students. Because of its structured nature, some schools have replaced BASIC with Pascal in introductory programming classes. Like BASIC, Pascal is not standardized and has many

FIGURE 11–4

A BASIC program that computes the sum and average of ten numbers

```
10    REM COMPUTE SUM AND AVERAGE OF 10 NUMBERS
20    LET SUM = 0
30    FOR I = 1 TO 10
40       INPUT N(I)
50       LET SUM = SUM + N(I)
60    NEXT I
70    LET AVG = SUM / 10
80    PRINT "SUM = ",SUM
90    PRINT "AVERAGE = ",AVG
999   END
```

different versions. An example of a short Pascal program is shown in Figure 11–5.

Because Pascal was originally designed as a teaching tool, it lacked some features to make it a good application-software development tool. To add the required additional features and to correct the existing problems of Pascal, Niklaus Wirth redesigned Pascal and called it **Modula–2.** Figure 11–6 shows an example of a short Modula–2 program. Modula–2 improves the modularity, the input and output capabilities, and the file-

FIGURE 11–5

A PASCAL program that computes the sum and average of ten numbers

```
PROGRAM average(input, output);
{ Compute the sum and average of ten numbers }
VAR num, sum, avg : real;
    i : integer;

BEGIN
    sum:=0.0;
    FOR i := 1 TO 10 DO
    BEGIN
      read(num);
      sum:=sum + num;
    END;
    avg:=sum/10;
    writeln('Sum =',sum);
    writeln('Average =',avg);
END.
```

FIGURE 11–6

A Modula–2 program that computes the sum and average of ten numbers

```
MODULE averageNum;
FROM InOut IMPORT WriteLn, WriteString, ReadCard;
FROM RealLnOut IMPORT WriteReal;

VAR
    i:CARDINAL;
    sum, average:REAL;
    Nmbs:Array[1..10] OF CARDINAL;

BEGIN
    WriteLn;
    WriteString("Enter number: ");
    WriteLn;
    FOR i := 1 TO 10 BY 1 DO
      ReadCard(Nmbs[i]);  (* get numbers from keyboard *)
      WriteLn;
    END;
    sum := 0.0;
    FOR i := 1 TO 10 BY 1 DO (* sum numbers *)
      sum := sum + FLOAT(Nmbs[i]);
    END;
    average := sum / 10.0;  (* calculate average *)
    WriteLn;
    WriteString("Sum = ");
    WriteReal(sum,10);
    WriteLn;
    WriteString("Average = ");
    WriteReal(average,10);
END AverageNum.
```

FIGURE 11–7

RPG coding sheets (Courtesy of International Business Machines Corp.)

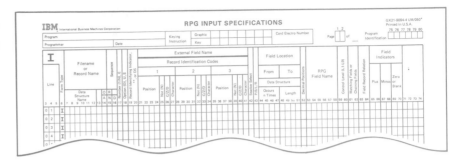

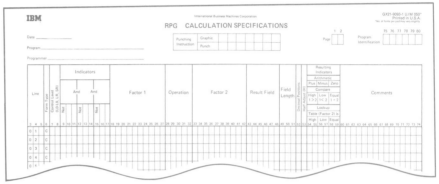

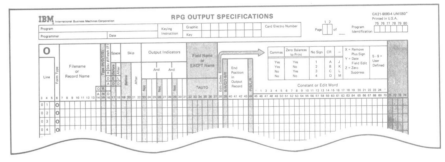

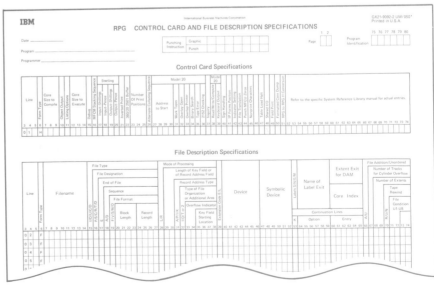

handling capabilities of the language. The original version is also still in use.

RPG RPG (Report Program Generator) was developed in the mid-1960s. Since most people at that time had no programming experience, RPG was designed to be especially easy to learn and use. A programmer uses coding sheets (Figure 11–7) to specify input, output, processing operations, and file specifications which are then entered into the computer for processing. Although it is easy to learn, RPG is limited in capabilities. It can be used for producing reports and processing files on tape or disk, but it is not well-suited for mathematical or scientific applications.

C The **C** programming language, developed at Bell Laboratories, incorporates many advantages of both low-level and high-level languages. Like assembly language, it enables the programmer to have extensive control over the computer hardware. But because it uses English-like statements, which make it easy to read, it is often classified as a high-level language. C also incorporates sophisticated control and data structures, which make it a powerful, but concise language.

It is well-suited for the development of system software, because that was its original purpose in design. However, C is becoming a popular choice in developing application programs because of its power and structured nature. Figure 11–8 is an example of a brief C program.

Ada The **Ada** programming language was developed in the late 1970s with the support of the U.S. Department of Defense. It was named for Augusta Ada, Countess of Lovelace, who is considered by many to be the world's first programmer. The goal was to build a very powerful, complete, and yet efficient, structured language to be used in military applications, such as controlling weapon systems.

To accomplish this goal, the language was designed with powerful control and data structures and with a set of commands that allowed it to control hardware devices directly. Currently, Ada is used primarily by the

FIGURE 11–8

A C program that computes the sum and average of ten numbers

```
#include <stdio.h>

main ()
    {
        int i, num;
        float sum;

        printf("Enter numbers \n");
        sum = 0;
        for (i = 0; i < 10; i++)
          {
            scanf("%d",&num);
            sum = sum + num;
          }
        printf("Sum = %3.1f\n",sum);
        printf("Average = %3.1f\n",sum / 10.0);
    }
```

U.S. Department of Defense, but the powerful and efficient nature of the language suggests that it may see greater use in other applications in the future. Figure 11–9 is an example of a brief Ada program.

Choosing a Programming Language

With so many programming languages to choose from, how does a programmer select one? Several factors should be considered.

- ☐ The nature of the problem—Is the programming language designed for this type of problem?
- ☐ The speed at which the program needs to execute—If the program will be used frequently, a programming language, such as assembly, may be necessary to reduce execution time.
- ☐ The expertise of the programming staff—Do the programmers already know the language under consideration? If not, can they learn it in the required time period, and is the additional cost of training justifiable?
- ☐ The portability of the language—Will the program have to run on more than one type of computer? Machine and assembly languages are machine-specific and require extensive changes or complete rewrites if new hardware is used. High-level languages are more portable and usually can be run on different computers with little or no changes.
- ☐ The amount of program maintenance expected—Will the program be subject to periodic updates and revisions? If so, a structured, high-level language may be the best choice.

Major High-level Languages
■ FORTRAN
■ COBOL
■ BASIC
■ Pascal
■ Modula–2
■ RPG
■ C
■ Ada

OPERATING SYSTEMS

When computers were first invented, every detail of how the hardware operated had to be programmed into the computer manually by setting switches or hand wiring circuits. This was a long, tedious process that had to be repeated for each program executed. The programmer required specific and detailed knowledge about how a particular computer system operated. The CPU was inactive most of the time while these details were being programmed. Because hardware costs for the early computers were

FIGURE 11–9

An Ada program that computes the sum and average of ten numbers

```
PROCEDURE average number IS
    USE simple io;
    num, sum, avg: REAL;

BEGIN
    sum := 0;
    FORiIN 1...10 LOOP
      GET(num);
      sum:=sum + num;
    END LOOP;
    avg:=sum / 10;
    PUT("Sum ="); PUT(sum);
    PUT("Average ="); PUT(avg);
END average number;
```

HIGHLIGHT

ADA JOINS THE ARMY

If America's Strategic Defense Initiative (also known as Star Wars) ever goes into effect fully, it will be regulated by the computer language called Ada. The complexity of such a system demands a precise and far-reaching language. Indeed, in 1983, the U.S. Department of Defense ordered that all its subsequent "mission critical" undertakings be written in Ada.

Named for Augusta Ada, Countess of Lovelace, the 19th century mathematician, Ada was developed in the late 1970s by a team of international program designers, headed by Paris-born Jean Ichbiah.

Among the language's many virtues is that it lends itself to structured programming. Component programs can be written in self-contained packages, or modules, by separate programmers and then fit together as an integrated whole. Such step-by-step building allows each module to be designed, tested, and debugged without affecting the integrity of the rest of the system. It is the closest thing yet to true portability, because a program can be written in Ada for one computer yet recompiled and run properly on other computers.

The jobs Ada is asked to do are incredibly complex. According to one estimate, the Star Wars operation will demand from 25 million to 100 million lines of code. The space shuttle program requires one million lines, 250,000 of which are devoted just to ascent and descent operations.

The main problem with Ada is that it is an extremely difficult language to learn. Some critics say that this difficulty can lead to programming errors that can destroy a space mission—or perhaps the world, for that matter.

But the Defense Department has insisted that Ada not be compromised by computer dialects, subsets, or extensions. Thus any company that wishes to manufacture an Ada compiler (translator) must pass a battery of nearly 2,000 tests. With such stringent standards, the Defense Department expects Ada to maintain its precision and reliability.

Besides its space and defense uses, Ada has been adopted as the standard programming language for the North Atlantic Treaty Organization (NATO) and is used to monitor hospital patients who are using kidney dialysis machines.

so high, users wanted to increase the efficiency of the CPU. To accomplish this, a program, called an operating system, was created.

An **operating system** is a set of programs that controls and supervises a computer system's hardware and provides services to programmers and users of a computer system. Its purpose is to manage the hardware for the most efficient use of computer resources and to provide an interface between a user or an application program and the hardware. The operating system dramatically increased the efficiency of the CPU, because it took the burden of programming every detail of an operation off the programmer.

The operating system resides in primary storage, so the details of an operation are received and executed by the computer at computer speeds, thus eliminating the long delays present when humans had to intervene. An operating system can also execute another program immediately without human involvement.

Control and Service Programs

The programs that make up an operating system are generally divided into two categories: control programs and service programs.

Control programs manage the computer hardware and resources. Three of the major functions of control programs are: resource allocation; job management; and data management. Computer resources, such as CPU time, primary storage, and input and output devices, are allocated for use by control programs. Programs that are being submitted for execution are scheduled, controlled, and monitored by control programs to ensure the most efficient processing. Input and output data are also managed by the control programs.

The main program in most operating systems is the supervisor program. The **supervisor program** is a control program that is also known in some operating systems as the monitor, executive, or kernel. It is responsible for controlling all the other operating system programs as well as other system and application programs. The activities of all the hardware components of the computer system are controlled by the supervisor program.

Service programs are programs in the operating system that provide a service to the user or programmer of the computer system. Examples include language-translator programs and utility programs. **Language-translator programs** convert other programs into machine-language instructions that can be executed by the computer. For example, assemblers, compilers, and interpreters are language-translator programs. **Utility programs** perform common or routine functions, such as loading, saving, or copying a program, keeping track of the files stored on a disk, and preparing a disk for use.

Control and service programs are stored on a **system resident device.** Depending on the system, the system resident device may be a hard disk, floppy diskette, or tape. When the computer is turned on, essential portions of the supervisor program are loaded into primary storage from the system resident device; they reside there throughout the computer's operation. Other portions of the supervisor and the rest of the operating system programs are loaded into primary storage as needed and removed when they have completed their task.

Types of Operating Systems

There are several types of operating systems, including single-program operating systems, concurrent operating systems, time-sharing operating

A Cray supercomputer produced this three-dimensional schematic simulation of a thunderstorm. The position of the arrows indicates that the low-level rotation is intensifying. This type of simulation helps meteorologists to predict the paths and intensities of severe storms. (Gene Moore/Phototake/NYC. Inset: Joseph Klemp and Richard Rotunno/National Center for Atmospheric Research)

systems, multiprocessing operating systems, virtual-storage operating systems, real-time operating systems, and virtual-machine operating systems.

Single-program Operating System A **single-program operating system** allows one program to execute at a time. The program must completely finish executing before the next can begin.

Concurrent Operating System A **concurrent operating system** allows a single CPU to execute what appears to be more than one program at the same time when, in fact, only one program is being executed. The CPU switches its attention between programs as it receives requests for processing, executing statements from one program, and then from another. This processing happens so fast that it appears that the programs are being executed simultaneously.

Time-sharing Operating System A **time-sharing operating system** allows multiple users to access a single computer system. The attention of the CPU is switched among users on a timed basis, which is controlled by the operating system. As long as the computer system does not have more

335

Types of Operating Systems

- Single-program
- Concurrent
- Time-sharing
- Multiprocessing
- Virtual-storage
- Real-time
- Virtual-machine (VM)

---

users than the operating system can handle, it will appear as if each user has uninterrupted access to the CPU. If the number of users exceeds the operating system's capability, noticeable delays in processing will result.

Multiprocessing Operating System A **multiprocessing operating system** allows the simultaneous execution of programs on a computer that has several CPUs. Many computer systems such as mainframes and supercomputers have more than one CPU.

Virtual-storage Operating System A **virtual-storage operating system** allows the use of a secondary-storage device as an extension of primary storage. A problem experienced by some computer users is a lack of sufficient primary storage to meet processing needs. A virtual-storage operating system can resolve this problem. The storage device can be accessed rapidly, e.g., using a hard-disk drive. Portions of a program are swapped between the secondary-storage device and primary storage as needed; this gives the illusion of having the maximum amount of primary storage in the CPU available to each user. With this type of operating system, the user need not worry about how much primary storage is available.

Real-time Operating System A **real-time operating system** allows a computer to control or monitor tasks performed by other machines and people by responding to the input data in the required amount of time. For controlling processes, immediate response is usually necessary; for simply monitoring processors, periodic response is generally adequate.

Virtual-machine (VM) Operating System A **virtual-machine (VM) operating system** is a very powerful program that can run several different operating systems at a time. It allows several users of a computer system to operate as if each had the only terminal attached to the computer. To users it appears as if each one were on a dedicated system and had sole use of the CPU and input and output devices.

After the VM operating system is loaded, the user chooses the operating system that is compatible with the application he or she plans to run or is familiar with and wants to develop applications for. Other operating systems, such as the virtual-storage operating system, appear as just another application program to the VM operating system. The VM operating system gives users flexibility and allows them to choose an operating system that best suits the needs of a particular application.

Popular Microcomputer Operating Systems

Probably the most familiar operating systems are those found on microcomputers. All or part of these operating systems usually reside on a disk and are referred to as a **disk operating system (DOS).** Several of the most common systems include MS-DOS (Microsoft Disk Operating System), various versions of the UNIX operating system, CP/M (Control Program for Microcomputers), Apple PRODOS, and the Apple Macintosh operating system. Multitasking operating systems for microcomputers, such as OS/2 designed by IBM and Microsoft, have been announced.

Current operating systems allow users to develop and run programs on the 32-bit microprocessors, such as the Intel 80386, but they are not designed to take advantage of the full power of these chips. Newer, more powerful microcomputer operating systems are expected shortly that will be able to take full advantage of the capabilities offered by the 32-bit microprocessors.

SUMMARY

In order to instruct a computer to perform specific tasks, a set of written symbols called a programming language is used to construct a program. Each programming language has a set of rules, or syntax, governing the use of the symbols. There are many programming languages, but each performs the following basic instructions: input/output; arithmetic; logic; control; data movement; and specifications. Programming languages are divided into four categories: machine language; assembly language; high-level language; and fourth-generation language.

Common high-level languages include FORTRAN, COBOL, BASIC, Pascal, Modula–2, RPG, C, and Ada.

When choosing a programming language, the following items should be considered: the nature of the problem; the speed at which the program needs to execute; the expertise of the programming staff; the portability of the language; and the amount of program maintenance expected.

The set of programs that controls a computer system's hardware and provides services to users of the system is called an operating system. An operating system is composed of two types of programs: control programs and service programs. Control programs manage the computer hardware and resources. Service programs provide a service to the user or programmer of a computer system. There are several different types of operating systems, including single-program operating systems, concurrent operating systems, time-sharing operating systems, multiprocessing operating systems, virtual-storage operating systems, real-time operating systems, and virtual-machine (VM) operating systems.

An operating system for a microcomputer is called a disk operating system (DOS).

Popular microcomputer operating systems include MS-DOS, UNIX, CP/M, Apple PRODOS, and the Apple Macintosh operating system.

Key Terms

Ada (p. 331)

application generator (p. 324)

assembler (p. 323)

assembly language (p. 321)

BASIC (p. 326)

C (p. 331)

COBOL (p. 325)

compiler (p. 323)

concurrent operating system (p. 335)

control program (p. 334)

data-base query language (p. 324)

disk operating system (DOS) (p. 336)

FORTRAN (p. 325)

fourth-generation language (p. 324)

high-level language (p. 323)

interpreter (p. 323)

language-translator program (p. 334)

low-level language (p. 321)

machine language (p. 321)

mnemonic (p. 322)

Modula-2 (p. 329)

multiprocessing operating system (p. 336)

nonprocedural language (p. 324)

operating system (p. 333)

Pascal (p. 328)

procedural language (p. 324)

programming language (p. 320)

real-time operating system (p. 336)

report generator (p. 324)

RPG (p. 331)

service program (p. 334)

single-program operating system (p. 335)

supervisor program (p. 334)

syntax (p. 320)

system resident device (p. 334)

time-sharing operating system (p. 335)

utility program (p. 334)

virtual-machine (VM) operating system (p. 336)

virtual-storage operating system (p. 336)

Review Questions

1. Describe a programming language.

2. _____ is the set of rules that governs the use of a programming language.

3. What is the function of control instructions in a programming language?

4. Compare machine language and assembly language.

5. What characterizes a low-level programming language?

6. What is the purpose of a mnemonic?

7. The language-translator program that converts assembly language into machine language is called a(n) _____.

8. Describe in general a high-level language.

9. What is the difference between a procedural and nonprocedural programming language?

10. Why must a high-level language be converted to machine language?

11. What is the function of a compiler?

12. A program that translates a program into machine language one line at a time and executes each line after it is translated is called a(n) _____.

13. A(n) _____ allows a programmer to simply specify what is accomplished without going into the details of how it is to be done.

14. Describe three types of fourth-generation languages.

15. Discuss some of the characteristics of the major high-level programming languages.

16. What is the function of control programs?
17. The main program in an operating system responsible for controlling all other programs is the _____.
18. Describe the purpose of service programs.
19. In a large computer system, the operating system programs are stored on a(n) _____.
20. List six basic types of instructions found in a programming language.
21. List and define the four general categories of programming languages.
22. Discuss some of the factors to consider when choosing a programming language.
23. Discuss the purpose of an operating system. Why is it needed? Define an operating system.
24. List and briefly define the seven types of operating systems discussed.
25. Explain the objectives of a fourth-generation language.

INFOMODULE
Careers in an Information Age

There was no such thing as a career in computers until the late 1940s. However, according to the U.S. Bureau of Labor Statistics, by 1961 there were about 8,500 computer specialists, and today there are almost 1.5 million people working in computer jobs. Another 2 million people are employed in related fields—people working in the computer industry itself, in business, and in all the other professions that rely on the use of computers. Studies project the number will increase by about 47 percent by 1990.

All this means that the job market for computer professionals is booming. Even if you are not a system analyst, programmer, or other computer specialist, the likelihood is great that your job will require using computers. Computers and information handling will be essential parts of the work of travel agents, news reporters, law enforcers, fire fighters, editors, engineers, lawyers, teachers, scientists, and many other professionals. Computers have already become a major tool in many of these occupations.

After a period of tremendous growth and readjustment, the dust is beginning to settle in the computer industry. Growth was extremely rapid in the early 1980s. But as the decade wore on, some companies crumbled in the face of the highly competitive environment; some models of computers were discontinued, and some software companies fell by the wayside.

Although the growth of some areas in computers may not be quite as rapid today, the outlook for the job market for computer professionals is still among the best in the nation. The Bureau of Labor Statistics says that positions for computer operators, programmers, and system analysts are still among the fastest growing fields in the U.S.

In this section, you will find descriptions of these occupations and some of the other professions in computers. Other professions in which the computer will play an important role will also be discussed.

SYSTEM ANALYST

System analysts are strategists and planners who improve and design information systems. They analyze the problems of the current information system, decide how to solve them, decide which data to collect, and determine the processing steps needed to get the information to the user.

Candidates for this position should realize that most companies require at least a bachelor's degree in business with knowledge or experience in software and hardware. Some background or courses in management are helpful. Often, these positions are filled by programmers moving up the corporate ladder.

Substantial growth is predicted for this field. In 1970, there were only 93,000 system analysts; studies project that by 1990 there will be more than 400,000.

PROGRAMMER

A **programmer** is the person who codes the instructions that tell the computer how to solve a problem. Programmers code the algorithm, designed by a system analyst to solve a problem, into a programming language and make sure it all works. In a small organization, the jobs of programmer and system analyst are sometimes combined into a position called programmer/analyst.

Application programmers write programs for users to solve problems; system programmers write programs that run the computer.

Most programmers are required to have a bachelor's degree in computer science.

The need for programmers is steadily increasing; the number is expected to rise from 170,000 in 1970 to 500,000 in 1990.

COMPUTER OPERATOR

A **computer operator** is responsible for starting and running the equipment—computer, disk drives, tape drives, printers, or any other peripherals. Computer operators schedule the equipment's time for data-processing jobs, test the equipment, maintain the equipment, load the tapes and disks onto the drives, and prepare the printers. While programs are running, they constantly monitor not only the equipment for mechanical failures, but also the environment for proper temperature and ventilation.

Formal educational requirements are not as stringent as for programmers, but because logs of activity in the computer room are usually required, operators must be able to write clear and accurate reports. Some companies do require formal training, but others will provide on-the-job training. Most computer operators have some college education, but it may not be necessary.

DATA-ENTRY OPERATOR

In the early days of computers, keypunch operators entered data into the computer by typing them onto punched cards at a keypunch machine. Today, a **data-entry operator** usually enters the data at a keyboard and video display terminal.

Good keyboarding (typing) skills with a high degree of accuracy are required. Data-entry personnel are usually not required to have training in data processing. A high school diploma is usually sufficient.

According to the Bureau of Labor Statistics, the demand for data-entry operators will begin to decline. This reduction in personnel is due to the growing number of on-line applications in which users enter their own data and because of technology such as optical scanners where data entry occurs electronically.

COMPUTER SERVICE TECHNICIAN

Computers, like any other machines, break down and need maintenance. With more than the 30 million personal computers in the United States and more computers being purchased by businesses, there is a high demand for computer service technicians. The job of **computer service technician** is to install and repair computer equipment, such as broken computers, damaged disk drives, tape drives, keyboards, circuit boards.

In large companies, a computer service technician's job is to keep computer downtime to a minimum. Many stores that sell personal computers hire computer service technicians to repair and service the equipment they sell.

Service technicians are usually experts at using the latest testing and diagnostic devices. Training in electronics is essential, and some background in programming is an asset.

The demand for computer service technicians will continue to grow for some time.

DATA-BASE ADMINISTRATOR

With the increase in the number and size of current data bases in government and businesses, there is a need for someone to coordinate all the elements. **Data-base administrators** are in charge of designing, implementing, and maintaining the data base. They are responsible for monitoring who uses the data bases and for data security; and they direct and plan for all the elements that are required to maintain a data base. Data-base administrators consult with other people in the organization regarding their information needs and the best ways for them to access the information. They also help other managers in the organization plan the collection, storage, and organization of the data.

The nature of this job is very technical, so at least a bachelor's degree in computer science or data processing is required.

INFORMATION SYSTEM MANAGER

The **information system manager** is the person who plans and oversees all the information resources in an organization. The job is one of the higher level computer positions, although the title may vary depending on an organization's size and structure. The title might be Management Information System (MIS) Director, Information System Manager, or Data Processing Manager. A person in this position needs technical knowledge about the system development process and must also have managerial and leadership skills in order to oversee and motivate the programmers, system analysts, and computer operators in a data processing or MIS department. This person must also be familiar with the organization's overall goals and information needs.

A degree in business with information system courses is generally required. Many people who hold this position are required to have a master's degree in business. Some firms, however, place less emphasis on formal business education and take their managers from the ranks of those who have worked as programmers and system analysts.

OTHER COMPUTER-RELATED CAREERS

Many other jobs have developed directly from the computer industry. Here are just a few:

- ☐ Sales representatives—People who sell the computer equipment and software
- ☐ Technical writers—Writers with experience in a particular technical area who can explain in nontechnical terms how to use the equipment and software. They write user manuals, operator manuals, and software documentation.
- ☐ Security personnel—People who specialize in techniques to protect the computer room, hardware, programs, and the data and information stored
- ☐ Electronic data-processing (EDP) auditors—Accounting and business experts who monitor and evaluate computer operations to assure that there are no incidents of fraud or misuse of the system's capabilities
- ☐ Hardware developers—Creators of new ideas using the latest technology to design computer hardware and chip circuitry

- ☐ Software engineers—People who create and write new system programs (e.g., operating systems) and new application programs for business (e.g., word processors, spreadsheets, data-base management software) or for entertainment (e.g., video games)
- ☐ Network designers—Telecommunication specialists who design and improve computer networks

HOW COMPUTERS AFFECT OTHER JOBS

No matter what career you choose, it is likely that computers or information handling will be a major tool in performing your job. You are quite likely to be an important part of the entire computerized system on which the company bases its operations.

Here is a list of some of the ways computers have affected noncomputer careers.

- ☐ A graphic artist designs logos for television programs and for the art in music videos with computers and graphics software.
- ☐ Movie and television producers and special-effects creators produce unusual scenes with computer images and simulations.
- ☐ Journalists enter news stories directly from computer terminals or personal computers. Copy editors revise text on the computer, then electronically send it to electronic typesetting equipment and print the final story on computer-controlled presses.
- ☐ Technicians in hospital laboratories operate computerized testing equipment, store the results in a computer, and retrieve them upon request.
- ☐ Secretaries in offices use computers for word processing; some also implement financial applications, such as handling budgets and keeping expense records.
- ☐ Automobile mechanics use computer diagnostics to pinpoint engine troubles.
- ☐ Physicians prescribe diagnostic testing on their patients by computer-controlled tools, and they coordinate all phases of their office management by computer.

☐ Teachers use computers to expedite research, design learning materials, keep student records, and also teach their students how to use computers as study aids.

☐ Managers retrieve information from the company's data bases via computers in the form of reports; they also send messages and schedule their week's appointments using computers.

Even though your chosen profession may not be that of a computer professional or specialist, you will more than likely be using a computer in some aspect of any career choice. For example, if you are a teacher, you might become the expert in computer-aided instruction (CAI) in your school; in the textile and fashion industry, you might not only be a designer, but also the expert in the company's CAD system used for designing, sizing, cutting, and manufacturing clothing. Almost every field will have specialists who have not only the knowledge of that field, but also the skills and knowledge about how computers can enhance their positions.

A familiarity with computers will be valuable to you in almost any job coming up in the Information Age.

KEY TERMS

computer operator (p. 340)

computer service technician (p. 341)

data-base administrator (p. 341)

data-entry operator (p. 341)

information system manager (p. 341)

programmer (p. 340)

system analyst (p. 340)

QUESTIONS

1. Describe the role of a system analyst.
2. Discuss the roles of a computer operator, data-entry operator, and computer service technician.
3. Describe the basic responsibilities of a data-base administrator.
4. Describe the role of an information system manager.
5. Describe some ways in which computers have affected jobs that traditionally were not computer-oriented.

PART FOUR
Application Packages

Rather than radically changing social patterns they [computers] are likely to be folded into the fabric of society, altering daily life in small but cumulative ways . . . . nearly all of us will become familiar with their operation, unintimidated, and therefore easily able to appreciate and take advantage of them.

John Case, author and senior editor of Inc. *magazine*

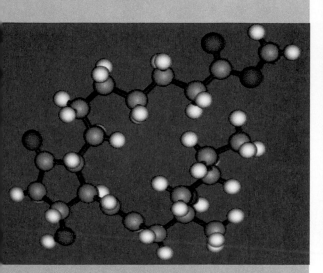

OBJECTIVES

☐ Define application packages and describe how they might be used

☐ Describe the difference between user-written and prewritten application packages

☐ Describe the differences between specialized and generalized application packages

☐ List the five application packages most in demand for microcomputers

☐ Discuss integrated application packages

12

Introduction to Application Packages

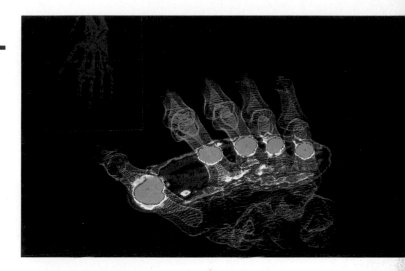

PROFILE: Dan Bricklin and Bob Frankston

Dan Bricklin, like many other students, was not fond of the tedious mathematical calculations that were required when he attended the Harvard Business School in 1978. Many of his assignments involved preparation of financial planning sheets for mock organizations. The work was repetitive and required numerous hand calculations to obtain meaningful results. At times Bricklin would discover that a calculation he had made in the middle of the worksheet was wrong. To correct the error, that and all dependent calculations had to be redone. This process was very time-consuming and frustrating. Unlike most students, however, Dan Bricklin did not just wish for a better way, he eventually did something about it.

At about that same time, microcomputers were starting to enter the marketplace. Initially, they were hardly more than high-tech toys for hobbyists and game players. But Bricklin saw a more practical and productive use for them. From his past computer experience, Bricklin thought that an electronic spreadsheet would be a practical idea for small computers. He teamed up with his friend, Bob Frankston, and they began to develop an electronic spreadsheet. The product was called VisiCalc and was the first spreadsheet of its kind.

The two partners literally worked around the clock to get their programming idea off the drawing board. Recalling those early days (and late nights) in *Datamation* magazine, Bricklin said, "We settled into a routine that would carry us through the end of my term at Harvard. I would go to school during the day and Bob would sleep. We would meet in the evenings to discuss progress and problems. Then Bob would go to work on the computer for the rest of the night, when the time-sharing rates were cheaper."

In January 1979, Bricklin and Frankston incorporated as Software Arts, Inc., and soon after, in conjunction with Personal Software (later to become VisiCorp), began marketing VisiCalc. It was truly a revolutionary product, changing the microcomputer into a useful business tool. This was the beginning of the microcomputer application software industry.

VisiCalc went on to become the best-selling software package. In 1983, however, problems between Software Arts, Inc., and VisiCorp led to lawsuits between the two companies over the rights of VisiCalc. The lawsuits left the company in limbo in terms of the software's further development and upgrades. Bricklin and Software Arts, Inc., were eventually awarded the rights to VisiCalc; but because they had failed to react quickly to the new 16-bit technology while other companies developed new products for it, they lost their number one position in the marketplace.

Eventually, Bricklin sold the company and the rights to VisiCalc to Lotus, Inc., where Frankston is employed. Bricklin reentered the software business with a new product and a new company called Software Garden, Inc. Without his vision of the electronic spreadsheet and his commitment to make it a reality, the application software industry might not be where it is today.

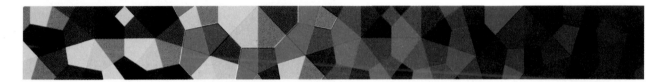

U p to this point, this text has focused on computer hardware and programming. That's all well and good, but perhaps your job is *not* as a hardware specialist or a programmer. Or perhaps you have no desire to become a technical whiz kid. What if your job is to get a specific task done or solve a problem *using* a computer? The chapters in Part Four present several major application packages used by people and businesses to solve problems and perform the kinds of tasks that you are likely to be confronted with in your life and work.

This chapter introduces basic concepts of application packages, which are used on both large computer systems and microcomputer systems. However, because microcomputers are a productivity tool in *both* businesses and in homes, and because most people are likely to come into direct contact with them rather than large computer systems, the discussion on application packages in the text focuses on those used with microcomputers. The InfoModules in Part Four, however, show the widening variety of applications for which computers of all sizes are used.

Chapters 13, 14, 15, and 16 describe the five most popular types of application packages for microcomputers in more detail.

APPLICATION PACKAGES DEFINED

The key to making the computer useful is to combine it with software in a particular application. An **application** is the job or task a user wants the computer to do. For example, word processing text or calculating statistics are applications. An **application package** is software that, in conjunction with the system software, instructs the computer how to do the job. Application software helps the user work faster, more efficiently, and thus more productively than if the job were done manually.

Dan Bricklin and Bob Frankston designed the first electronic spreadsheet, VisiCalc, to increase the speed and ease of calculating financial planning sheets. Many other tasks have also benefited from computerization. Other application packages are word processors, data managers, payroll programs, personal financial-analysis programs, and many more. In fact, all of the applications of computers described in this book solve problems or perform tasks, and therefore, require application software.

Application packages come in varying levels of sophistication and complexity. The demand for user-friendly software has made software developers more sensitive to the needs of the novice and nontechnical user.

User-friendly has come to mean that something is "easy to learn and use." But whether software is "easy to learn and use" is really dependent on the skills, sophistication, and needs of the user. What may be easy to use for the novice may be so simple that it's not useful to the more experienced user who needs more features and sophistication. The market has seen the development of some powerful and complex packages that are also user-friendly. So, no matter what the user's technical level, there should be an application package to match those needs and abilities.

PREWRITTEN AND USER-WRITTEN APPLICATION PACKAGES

Application software is developed from two main sources: (a) the users themselves; or (b) another person or group (then sold to the user). **Prewritten application packages** are those packages that have been written by another person or group and made available to computer users. Generally, prewritten software is available for purchase through a vendor, distributor, or directly from the author.

The use of prewritten software packages has several advantages. First, prewritten software packages can be set up and running quickly; they are ready for immediate use. If you need application software now, it is probably available. Once purchased, it is ready to put into the computer to use.

Another advantage is that they are usually less expensive than those produced in-house by the user company or an individual. In-house developmental costs for software are high because development is time-consuming and takes skilled personnel to accomplish.

Third, prewritten software is already available for almost any task required. If the need is for one of the more popular types of application packages, such as word processors, spreadsheets, or data managers, at least one of the hundreds available for purchase will probably work for most users. However, the more specialized the task, the more difficult it is to find a package that meets a user's exact needs because most software is written in a very general manner to allow the largest number of users to take advantage of it.

A fourth advantage is that prewritten software has already been tested. Any new software requires a great deal of testing before it is ready to use.

Finally, some prewritten application packages can be customized or modified by the user to meet the user's requirements more exactly. However, this can sometimes be complicated and may still not meet the user's needs.

An alternative to prewritten software is for users to write their own application packages. **User-written application packages** are those that are designed and coded by the user of the package. A user can be either an individual, such as yourself, or an organization, such as a business.

Prewritten Application Packages

Advantages
- Can be purchased for immediate use
- Are relatively inexpensive
- Are available for many varieties of tasks
- Have already been tested
- Can sometimes be customized or modified by user

Disadvantage
- May be too general to meet exact needs

Users write their own software because their specific needs do not match the capabilities of any of the packages already on the market. The main advantage to user-written application packages is that they can be tailored to the user's exact specifications.

An added advantage to writing one's own software is that the creator may, in turn, be able to market and sell it to others. The whole application software industry for microcomputers got its start when Bricklin and Frankston created and sold the first electronic spreadsheet. What was user-written software to them quickly became prewritten software to us.

Whether for an individual user or a business, writing one's own software requires attention to a number of factors. First, the user must have the skill to design an application package that will accomplish the desired task. Second, the user must know a programming language well enough to code the program. Third, the user must have enough time; it could take months to complete the project. Finally, costs to design and write a program can be high and difficult to predict in advance.

In some cases, the wise decision might be to select a prewritten package that is close but doesn't precisely meet the user's needs rather than spend the time and money developing software. Users must balance the *need* for writing their own software against the *costs* involved.

SPECIALIZED AND GENERALIZED APPLICATION PACKAGES

Application packages can be grouped into two broad categories: specialized and generalized. A **specialized application package** performs a specific task and cannot be changed or programmed to perform a different task. For example, a payroll package is designed to be used exclusively for payroll functions. Another specialized package might be designed to choreograph musical productions. It cannot be used or programmed to do other tasks such as cost analysis.

A **generalized application package** is one that can be applied to a wide variety of tasks. A spreadsheet has features and capabilities to create one worksheet to calculate a payroll and another worksheet to monitor personal investments.

TYPES OF APPLICATION PACKAGES

There are many types of application packages for the microcomputer on the market today. New ones are being developed as microcomputers become faster and more powerful. Applications that were traditionally large-system applications, such as CAD systems and expert systems, are now available for microcomputers.

The applications themselves have grown in number, size, speed, power, and capabilities. For example, when Dan Bricklin first conceived the electronic spreadsheet, most microcomputers had 48K or less of RAM to work with. This capacity severely limited the size and capabilities of the software that would run on them. Today, however, most microcomputers have at least 256K of RAM and most can add more. Obviously, today's spreadsheets can be a lot more powerful than the first one.

Application packages, such as accounting and financial packages (including payroll, accounts receivable, accounts payable, general ledger,

Computers enhance the creative processes in many facets of entertainment. For example, the music at a dance presentation you attend might be generated at a computer keyboard, and the dancers' moves might be choreographed with the help of a computer.

budgeting, financial planning), are used in almost every kind of business. Vertical-market packages, software designed to handle the unique needs of specific markets (businesses) such as medical offices, law firms, car dealerships, and hotel management, are also being sold. It would be impossible to detail all the types of application software in this section.

Five application packages have emerged as the most popular and widely used with microcomputers: word processor; data manager; electronic spreadsheet; graphics; and electronic communication.

Word Processors

At some time you probably have been required to handwrite or type a long term paper or similar document; you know just how time-consuming editing and rewriting the text can be. A word processor can make the job much

351

HIGHLIGHT

USING "USER-FRIENDLY"

Of all the terms spun out by the computer revolution, none has become more popular than "user-friendly." In fact, advertisers and salespeople now apply it indiscriminately to any product that has any interaction with human beings—which is to say, all products. Consequently, a car with power steering becomes "user-friendly" because it is easier to drive than a car without it. (Does that make other cars "user hostile"?) Conceivably, a book with large type and widely spaced lines is more "user-friendly" than a telephone directory with small type.

Even when the term is applied to computers, software, and accessories, use of the term "user-friendly" is commonly overdone to the point that it can mean anything. Does the computer use a mouse instead of a stylus for interaction? Does the system support color graphics? Does it use icons instead of text? If the answer is "yes" to each of these questions, then there are plenty of computer salespeople and advertisers ready to assure you that you are in the friendliest of territories.

However, those people who are more concerned with precise description than with sales slogans say that "user-friendly" can still be a valuable phrase when it applies to the real world and not the sales-driven imaginary one.

For a computer or its software to be truly user-friendly, it has to be considered in relation to the work being done, as well as to the skills and demands of the operator. The term is relative, not absolute. One user-friendly quality is the group of features that actively assists the particular user in the execution of a task by anticipating potential mistakes and keeping them from being catastrophic. The term should mean that a system is designed to encourage rather than discourage use. Capability is a big factor, too, since ease of use and error compensation mean little if the system can't do the job that is assigned to it.

Until speakers and writers concede to use it precisely, "user-friendly" remains too user-friendly.

simpler, easier, and faster. A **word processor** is software that edits, manipulates, and prints text (Figure 12–1). It automates many manual tasks associated with writing in longhand or typing, such as cutting and pasting, centering, and setting margins. WordStar, MultiMate Advantage, and WordPerfect are three of the most popular word processors. (Word processors are discussed in detail in Chapter 13.)

FIGURE 12–1

(a) WordPerfect and (b) Multi-Mate Advantage are word processors. Shown here are the areas where the user enters and edits a document.

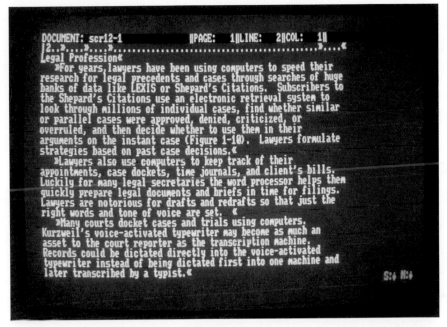

(a)

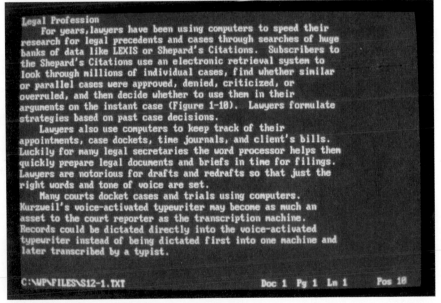

(b)

Data Managers

The demand that data and information be organized and accessible in different formats has exceeded what can be done manually in a reasonable amount of time. Data managers were developed in answer to this demand. **Data managers** store, organize, manipulate, retrieve, display, and print data (Figure 12–2). The term "data manager" describes file managers and data-base managers, both of which are described in Chapter 14. Data managers are important to corporations and federal and state governments because they can keep track of the vast amounts of data that these organizations have to gather and store.

You might use a data manager at home to itemize valuable personal items or to list addresses and phone numbers of friends, relatives, or business contacts. A fund-raising campaign might use a data manager to keep track of the thousands of businesses that have to be contacted and other related information. When a fund-raiser makes a contact for a donation or receives a pledge, all the pertinent data are available on the computer. PFS:File, dBASE III, and RBASE 5000 are popular data managers.

Electronic Spreadsheets

Spreadsheet users can now benefit from an **electronic spreadsheet**, the software that displays, manipulates, and prints rows and columns of data. It is similar to the paper spreadsheet in that both have columns and rows in which data and labels are entered. The difference lies in the fact that data in an electronic spreadsheet can be easily edited by the user, and all other dependent figures in the spreadsheet are then recalculated automatically and the results stored.

Electronic spreadsheets can perform a wide variety of tasks from budgeting personal income to financial planning for a corporation (Figure 12–3). Lotus 1-2-3 and SuperCalc are two popular spreadsheets. (You'll get a closer look at electronic spreadsheets in Chapter 15.)

FIGURE 12–2
The data manager in PFS:First Choice can organize different types of data. For example, as shown on this input screen, data for a personal inventory system can be entered. Depending on the user's needs, the data can be manipulated into different formats.

FIGURE 12–3
A spreadsheet can be used for a variety of tasks. This user is preparing for income tax filing.

Graphics Packages

Graphics packages display data visually in the form of graphics images. For example, even after using a spreadsheet or data manager to manipulate and organize data, it can sometimes be difficult to see relationships or interpret that information. Presenting the information visually (graphically) is one way to make this easier. One type of graphics package can extract and display data graphically in line, pie, or bar charts (Figure 12–4). Business managers use graphics packages to present statistics and other data and their relationships to staff or to clients. At home, you could use graphics to create a bar graph to show if your monthly spending varied from your budget. A popular independent, or stand-alone, graphics package is PFS:Graph. Graphics software may also be part of a larger package, such as the one in Lotus 1-2-3. Graphics packages are available that enable artists to create pictures and engineers to create designs. (Chapter 16 looks at graphics in more detail.)

Communication Packages

As more individuals and organizations use computers, the need to transfer data from one computer to another has increased. Law enforcement agencies exchange information on criminals, home users access information services such as CompuServe, and some individuals and businesses send electronic mail. To facilitate this communication between computers, **communication packages**, such as the popular PC-Talk, are used. (A closer look at communication packages and how to use them appears in Chapter 16.)

Five Most Popular Application Packages

- Word processors
- Data managers
- Spreadsheets
- Graphics
- Communication

FIGURE 12-4
The Smart Software System, by Innovative Software, Inc., allows data from a spreadsheet file to be used directly by a graphics program. Here, a three-dimensional bar chart that shows sales of ice cream by flavor and gallon is created from data in a spreadsheet file. (Courtesy of Innovative Software, Inc.)

TYPES OF INTEGRATED PACKAGES

The data files of many of the early programs designed for microcomputers were not always compatible with each other. The programs were not integrated, i.e., data could not be electronically moved from one program to the other. Transferring data from one program to another was either impossible or complex and tedious. Typically, the user's only recourse was to rekey all the data into the receiving program.

The cover art for this textbook was prepared by ICOM, Inc., a company known for producing audio-visual presentations. Here, Patrick Baum and Anne Miller are at the Genigraphics computer facility where they created the image, manipulated the shapes, changed the colors, and produced a transparency suitable for the publisher to use. (Courtesy of ICOM, Inc., Columbus, Ohio)

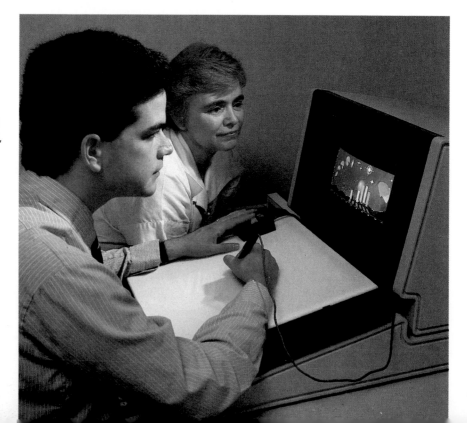

For example, if you were asked to analyze and make a presentation of the sales performance of all thirty-six sales regions for company X, you could purchase a spreadsheet for all the necessary calculations and a separate graphics package to produce the graphs. Although it takes five hours to enter data and formulas into the spreadsheet, the results are impressive. But now you need bar graphs for the presentation. You spend the next hour poring over the manuals to find a way to transfer the data from the spreadsheet to the graphics program. No luck! Your only option is to spend another several hours reentering the spreadsheet figures into the graphics program. This duplication could easily have been avoided if the data in the spreadsheet could have been electronically transferred to the graphics program, i.e., if the two programs had been integrated.

Integrated software allows several programs to share the same data. For example, a graphics package can use data directly from the spreadsheet file to draw a graph. Integration also implies the use of familiar functions and a common set of commands and keystrokes among programs. However, in reality, this happens in varying degrees. The result of integration is the user can work faster, more efficiently, and thus, more productively than if nonintegrated programs were used (Figure 12–5).

The demand for integrated software has led to the development of four distinct approaches to integration: the integrated family of programs;

FIGURE 12–5
Open Access II contains spreadsheet, graphics, word processor, data-base management, and communication programs that can share data.

HIGHLIGHT

COMPUTERS IN THE COURTROOM

Everyday, it seems, someone has thought of a new way to integrate computers into our lives and work. One way is computer-aided transcription (CAT) for court stenographers. A common delay in court is due to the stenographer having to search through notes to reread testimony. Usually, there are also substantial delays in obtaining typed transcripts of the stenographer's notes.

With CAT, the stenographer uses the same technique as before to record the testimony on a 22-button stenotype machine. However, the stenotype machine is now wired directly to a computer that transcribes the stenographic shorthand into English and sends the output almost immediately to monitors on the judge's and each of the lawyers' tables. The judge and attorneys can easily scroll through the transcript displayed on the monitors to review earlier testimony. Edited and typed transcripts are available in a matter of hours. It also reduces the waste of time and redundancy of having the stenographer dictate notes to a typist.

the all-in-one integrated package; the integrated operating environment; and background integration.

Integrated Family of Programs

An **integrated family of programs** is a group of independent application programs that can share data and use common commands and keystrokes. For example, if one program in the set uses the function key F10 to save (store), then all the other programs will also use F10 to save. It is faster and easier to learn each program if they all have the same commands and keystrokes for the same operation.

Each program works independently. Because only one application program is loaded into the computer at a time, more memory is available for it. Thus, the integrated family can be more powerful and have more features than its counterpart, the all-in-one integrated package. One disadvantage is that merging data into one application or sharing data between applications can be slower and more awkward than an all-in-one integrated package.

The PFS family of programs is one popular integrated family of programs. It uses a common set of function keys, commands, and keystrokes.

All in-one Integrated Packages

The **all-in-one integrated package** combines several types of applications into one single program. Most of these packages combine some or all of the word processor, spreadsheet, data manager, graphics, and communication programs. The user can conveniently switch between applications and use a common set of commands. With this kind of integrated package, the user can also:

☐ Transfer data from one application to another
☐ Combine data from several applications and transfer that collection of data to another
☐ Set up individual fields within an application that automatically update related fields in other applications

A limitation of an all-in-one package, however, is that it requires large amounts of the computer's primary storage capacity; many require well over 256K because the single program contains all the applications and is, therefore, very large. Because of this large memory requirement, some of the individual applications in an all-in-one package do not have as many features as their stand-alone equivalents. Some developers have eliminated this problem by including some special functions that conserve memory and allow individual applications to retain their power.

Some programs, such as Open Access II and The Smart Software System, are designed so they can function either as an integrated family or be combined as an all-in-one integrated package. Popular all-in-one integrated packages include Enable, Framework, and Symphony.

Integrated Operating Environment

The **integrated operating environment** uses a program called a window manager, or integrator, permitting independent applications, such as WordStar (a word processor), Lotus 1-2-3 (a spreadsheet), and dBASE (a data-base manager), to work concurrently in an integrated way. With this combination, a user can retain the power and capabilities of these separate packages and yet be able to share and merge data between them.

These programs work by using **windows**, separate areas or boxes, on the screen that enclose independent applications. Several applications or documents can then be displayed on the screen concurrently, and data can be transferred among them. DesQ and Windows are popular integrated operating environment packages.

Background Integration

Utility programs assist the user in various administrative tasks. **Background integration** places these utilities in memory so that they are available instantly at the touch of a key while other software is still running. Typical utilities in background integration are a calculator, calendar, appointment book, notepad, and telephone directory and dialer. These utilities can be useful additions to any software. For example, the user could access a calculator while word processing a document, or use a notepad to take notes while working in a data base. SideKick is a popular example (Figure 12–6).

Four Approaches to Integration

- Integrated family of programs
- All-in-one integration
- Integrated operating environment
- Background integration

FIGURE 12–6
SideKick, a utilities program, is shown here with MultiMate Advantage, a word processor. The user can call up the SideKick calculator to add a column of figures; then the total can be entered in the document.

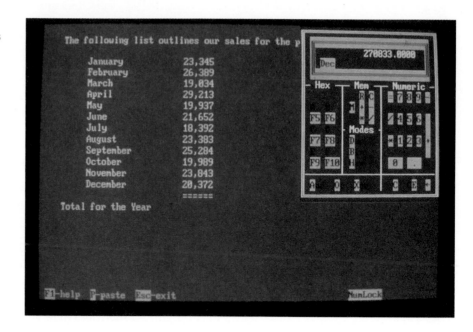

SUMMARY

Many tasks that people perform manually can be done faster and more efficiently with a computer. An application package is a program that interacts with the system software to direct the computer to complete a task for the user. The five most popular application packages for microcomputers are word processors, data managers, spreadsheets, graphics, and communication packages. A user-friendly application package is one that is easy to learn and use.

Application packages can be purchased (prewritten application package) or designed by the user (user-written application package). A specialized application package performs a specific task and cannot be used to perform other tasks. A generalized application package can be applied to a variety of tasks.

Software developers have found a way to integrate several application packages. Integrated software is designed so that data can be easily shared among the packages. Ideally, integrated applications have a familiar set of functions, a common command set, and common keystrokes. Several approaches have been taken to integrate application packages. These include the integrated family of programs, the all-in-one integrated package, the integrated operating environment, and background integration.

Key Terms

all-in-one integrated package (p. 358)

application (p. 348)

application package (p. 348)

background integration (p. 359)

communication package (p. 355)

data manager (p. 353)

electronic spreadsheet (p. 354)

generalized application package (p. 350)

graphics package (p. 355)

integrated family of programs (p. 358)

integrated operating environment (p. 359)

integrated software (p. 357)

prewritten application package (p. 349)

specialized application package (p. 350)

user-friendly (p. 349)

user-written application package (p. 349)

utility program (p. 359)

windows (p. 359)

word processor (p. 352)

Review Questions

1. A program that helps a user accomplish a task using a computer is called a(n) _____.

2. What does the phrase "user-friendly software" generally mean?

3. An application program that can be purchased ready-to-use is a(n) _____ application package.

4. Application software is developed from two main sources. What are they?

5. Compare the costs involved in purchasing ready-to-use, prewritten application software to the costs of writing software in-house.

6. _____ application packages are those that are designed to meet a user's exact specifications.

7. What is a specialized application package?

8. Give some examples of specialized application packages.

9. A(n) _____ application package is designed so that its capabilities can be applied to a wide variety of tasks.

10. Describe the functions of a word processor.

11. Describe the functions of a data manager.

12. Describe the functions of a spreadsheet.

13. A(n) _____ allows the user to display data in graphic form.

14. Which type of application package facilitates sending data from one computer to another?

15. What are the main features of integrated software?

16. A group of independent application packages that are designed to share data and use common commands and keystrokes is a(n) _____.

17. List several features of all-in-one integrated packages.

18. The use of which kind of integrated package allows independent, nonrelated applications to work concurrently in an integrated environment?

19. Give some examples of utility programs.

20. With regard to use, what are the two broad categories of application software?

21. _____ integrates utility programs with application software packages.

22. Discuss the advantages and disadvantages of using user-written and prewritten applications.

23. Why is a spreadsheet considered a generalized application package?

24. What are the five most popular microcomputer applications? Give examples of how you might use each of them.

25. Describe the four different approaches to integration.

INFOMODULE
The Expanding World of Computers

Computers are the magic carpets we read about in fairy tales—they give us power, speed, and perspective that are miraculous by the standards of an earlier generation. Their shrinking size and growing applications have made these devices life-simplifying, life-enhancing, and life-saving.

COMPUTERS FOR PERSONAL USE

Once the pride of data-processing departments and offices, personal computers have also found a home—in the home. They are the ultimate home office assistants, making up with speed and versatility what they lack in the personal touch.

Home Finance, Business, and Management

Although using a home computer to balance a personal checkbook may be more trouble than it's worth, computerizing financial records can help users to prepare for filing their income tax returns. For a more extensive handling of personal finances, an electronic spreadsheet package can be invaluable. Besides keeping financial records, a spreadsheet helps to analyze data and prepare plans by allowing "what if" questions to be posed and gives instantaneous answers.

Other prepackaged software is also available to home users. For example, the Economics Investor (developed by Econ) is an investment-analysis package just for the small investor. The program includes equations for each of 1,200 stocks, based on how well they performed during the last ten years in relation to variables such as inflation and value of the dollar.

For the person who sells cosmetics, household goods, health products, or cleaning supplies (popular home-based businesses), a computer is an ideal partner. It can help a business with little or no staff with bookkeeping, inventory control, and ordering supplies. It is also useful for calculating sales taxes, income taxes, and evaluating possibilities for business expansion.

With the proper software and hardware, computers can help physically manage our homes. Sensors and hookups with built-in timers that are controlled by a personal computer can regulate home lighting and heating and, thus, conserve energy. In some systems, sensors turn lights on and off as people enter and leave a room, or timers activate appliances, such as coffee makers, at preset times. Computerized home security and fire-alarm systems can alert the home owner, the police, and the fire department automatically. By controlling water-sprinkling systems, computers can also aid in the creation of a green lawn or a productive garden.

Personal Development and Access to Information

Computer programs can determine the most efficient exercise and fitness plan for an individual, taking into account such factors as age, weight, current level of activity, medical considerations, physical limitations, and personal goals. Sports physicians use computers to plan individualized programs for professional athletes to ensure development of all the appropriate muscle systems.

Some exercise devices, including bicycles and rowing machines, contain microprocessors or small computers that monitor oxygen consumption, blood pressure, heart rate, and other metabolic functions to pinpoint the most effective and efficient kinds of exercise. Daily training calendars and progress charts can also be created, modified, and maintained with a computer.

For self-improvement or knowledge, a personal computer owner can choose to subscribe from a broad selection of information services, such as news, sports, weather, stock quotations, bibliographies, electronic mail, and bulletin boards.

Home computer owners in Lawrenceburg, Tennessee, will soon be able to view current weather radar on their video display terminals by tuning in WLLX-FM 92. The viewers' computers must be equipped with enhanced graphics and a special inexpensive receiver to pick up the transmission, however.

Completing a search for particular facts using an information network service can save hours of tiresome library work. For example, the world's largest genealogical library, operated by the Church of Jesus Christ of Latter Day Saints (Mormon Church in Salt Lake City, Utah), has developed software for storing and sharing information on family histories. Soon it will go on-line with its files of the lineage of about one billion families dating from the 1500s.

Entertainment and Amusement

A computer can be the core of home entertainment, running games for all ages and interests, activating toys for youngsters, as well as providing hobbyists with new methods of approaching their hobbies.

Computer games generally take one of two forms: (a) graphic, action-oriented games; or (b) interactive, thought-provoking games. Pac-Man, pinball, and the "shoot 'em up" variety develop such motor skills as eye–hand coordination and

require more player action. Computer checkers, chess, and some adventure games require the player to respond thoughtfully rather than instinctively to moves or questions that appear on the screen. Some game software combine colorful graphics, realistic sound effects, and a written script to make playing them more exciting. Computer games have come a long way since Pong, the first mass-produced video game, invented by Nolan Bushell, was popular.

Computers have even advanced ever-popular toys such as Etch-A-Sketch, which allowed the user to draw by using a dial-directed stylus. Etch-A-Sketch was pretty advanced for its time, but now it is old hat compared to its successor, the Animator. Instead of allowing only one drawing, as Etch-A-Sketch did, the Animator, with its 18K computer and liquid crystal display, enables the user to create and store a dozen different drawings, which can then be played back to simulate movement.

The doll that once amazed children by saying "mama" has been upstaged by JILL, a 34-inch talking doll with a tape recorder and a voice-recognition chip that enables her to interact with her owner. The high-tech doll's arms, head, mouth, and eyes are synchronized to move as she tells stories. Each taped story contains plots with different choices. The doll prompts the child to make a decision, the storyline is ad-

Summer vacation may mean summer camp—learning to swim, pitch tents, and build bonfires—but youngsters who attend National Computer Camps learn to program computers in addition to their other recreational pursuits. (Courtesy of National Computer Camps)

In the computerized game, Photon, the player dodges through the futuristic environment of passageways, mazes, and catwalks. The object of the game is to reach the enemy team's goal, somewhere beyond the fog and past the enemy's lasers, without being "disrupted." Points are automatically racked up on the central computer. (Courtesy of Photon Entertainment, Inc.)

justed, and the tape continues. In this way, the doll can tell a different story each time.

COMPUTERS IN EDUCATION

Now that computers are in 97 percent of public schools in the United States, they are becoming valuable and versatile classroom fixtures (Figure 1). Students can learn at their own pace through **computer-aided instruction (CAI)**, a method of teaching or training individuals or groups where a computer program instructs students through an interactive dialogue. These dialogues usually take the form of drills, tutorials, or simulations.

Most educational application packages incorporate interesting and colorful graphics to hold the student's attention and include programs to increase reading comprehension, improve spelling, build vocabulary, and develop thinking and other special skills.

Drills

A computer **drill,** or practice session, lets the student learn at an individual pace by repeating an idea or concept in order for the student to *memorize* it. The program asks (and, if necessary, re-asks) questions, quizzing the student on a particular subject until the student has memorized the material. Packages for drilling students on multiplication and division or on English grammar rules are typical examples (Figure 2).

Tutorials

A **tutorial** is a teaching method by which a concept is explained to the student, and then ques-

FIGURE 1

Logo, a programming language, teaches programming fundamentals to youngsters. (Courtesy of Apple Computer, Inc.)

tions are asked about it, testing the student's *understanding*. The student's progress can be automatically monitored as the answers are given and checked for accuracy. The computer is programmed to explain, in detail, the errors in incorrect answers to further help students understand the material.

Computerized tutorials have proven especially helpful in adult literacy education. Adult students are usually eager to use the computer; some students in these sessions have been able to improve their reading and comprehension skills by two and one-half years in approximately twenty weeks.

Simulations

Simulations provide learning situations to challenge a student's thinking skills; they are used to teach students *how* things work. Simulations use computer modeling to create real-life situa-

tions. By creating a model of how something works or behaves, students can change the variables of the program to see how the subject might act. For example, students might do a chemistry experiment with a computer model instead of using real compounds, which could be dangerous, to observe the reactions.

Some large companies use all three types of CAI and find them useful to teach new employees their jobs, especially when they involve technical information. Because individual training time can be self-paced and neither a central place nor a time for sessions is necessary, companies save money when training a large number of employees. It is reported that, on the average, computer-aided instruction cuts a company's training cost by approximately 30 percent.

Teachers, too, use the computers in their classrooms. There are programs such as Archive, which lets the teacher design tests, and Report Card, which helps the teacher keep track of up to 300 students.

COMPUTERS IN THE ARTS

There are many tools of the trade for persons involved in "the arts"—painting, music, and dance. Today, one tool common to all is the computer.

Art

Using a drawing tool, such as a digitizer or a light pen, and the graphics capabilities in a variety of application packages, an artist can create images on a computer display screen to produce an entirely new form of art. Laser printers can transfer these images to paper with high-quality resolution and a great clarity of line and color.

Art historians are using the computer to restore old masterpieces, such as the Mona Lisa and the frescoes in the Sistine Chapel, by scanning the pictures one dot at a time, digitizing the work, and taking measurements of the intensity of the red, blue, or green color found at each dot. These data are then converted into digital form to be read and analyzed through

FIGURE 2
This youth is using a math drill that requires him to determine if the addition and subtraction problems presented on the screen are correct or incorrect.

computer enhancement, thus providing information about techniques that could be safely used to clean dirt and remove the discoloration that comes with time.

Film production studios create and animate characters with computerized techniques.

Three-dimensional and real-life animation are seen in displays at many amusement parks. For example, the Hall of Presidents, an attraction at Walt Disney World, shows animated, speaking figures representing the presidents of the United States.

This student is learning to tell time with an easy-to-operate program called Timekeeper. By touching the screen or typing in the time on the keyboard, the student can move the clock's hands to match digital time or time displayed in words.

Music

At the Center for Computer Research in Music and Acoustics (CCRMA) at Stanford University, composers, physicists, engineers, acousticians, and programmers work together to create new kinds of music. The founder of CCRMA, John Chowning, says that it will be a long time before computers compose music on their own because artificial intelligence cannot yet simulate the creativity of a musician's mind.

Nonetheless, the computer has found its way into music to perform such functions as:

☐ Creating music and sampling real sounds (Through a musical instrument digital interface [MIDI], computers connected to musical instruments create music by synthesizing new sounds and setting and maintaining rhythms [Figure 3].)

☐ Storing and recording (Sounds and music in their digital form can now be easily stored on various kinds of storage media. Once the music is stored, it can be arranged or changed at the computer keyboard.)

☐ Controlling sounds (Computerized musical devices allow a musician to control the timbre and depth of various sounds precisely and without loss of clarity.)

☐ Editing musical passages (Many musicians, including Stevie Wonder, Bruce Springsteen, and Wang Chung, create and edit their musical scores with personal computers and synthesizers. Computer editing saves hours of studio recording time.)

Dance

Dance routines are often written in instructions called "dance notation." This notation can be created with a computer by attaching sensors to a dancer. Another technique is to videotape specific movements. The dancer's moves are transmitted to a computer where they are digitized and stored. The choreographer or an instructor can retrieve these movements on a video display screen, arranging them into the various combinations that comprise a dance routine.

FIGURE 3
A musician creates musical scores on various keyboards, and because he is using a MIDI, the scores are entered into the computer. The digitized music can be saved and played back later, and it can be edited any time—or many times—to achieve just the right sound.

COMPUTERS IN MEDICINE AND HEALTH CARE

Many physicians and medical researchers enter their fields of specialty not only with a knowledge of physical science, but also with skills in using computers. Besides the usual recordkeeping and administrative types of tasks in pharmacies, doctors' offices, and hospitals, this combination of knowledge and technology enables doctors and other health-care technicians to: (a) test for and diagnose diseases and illnesses faster and more accurately; (b) design prostheses and reconstruction models; (c) build and use devices to monitor vital signs and other bodily functions; (d) design and test pharmaceuticals; and (e) offer choices in life-style and job selection for people who are physically challenged.

Diagnosis

Some computerized methods that aid the physician in diagnosing diseases and illnesses include digital subtraction angiography, sonography, computed tomography, and computerized lab testing.

Digital subtraction angiography (DSA) creates a clear view of the flow or blockage of blood. Pictures are first made by a digital X-ray scanner. Then, an injection of a contrasting agent (iodine) is introduced into the body, and a second image is made. The computer subtracts the first image from the second, which leaves an image that shows what has changed.

In sonography, beams of high-frequency sound waves penetrate the patient's body, and the computer translates the echoes that are bounced back into an image that the doctor can read. Sonograms view internal organs, such as the heart, liver, and gall bladder, and help monitor the growth and condition of the developing fetus.

Computed tomography (CT) scanners can view different sections (or slices) of the body from many angles by moving X-ray tubes around the body. The scanner converts the X-ray pictures into digital code to create high-resolution images. It is possible to create three-dimensional pictures by combining the cross sections,

thus giving surgeons a total picture when planning reconstructive surgery (Figure 4).

Computerization of laboratory tests, such as typing blood and testing sugar levels, leads to faster and more accurate reporting of test results and, therefore, more accurate diagnoses. During biopsy procedures, surgeons require reports rapidly to determine if further surgery is called for. If these processes are computerized, the results can be automatically sent to the operating room, printed and returned to the patient's physician, placed in the main file, and updated in the billing files.

Prostheses Design and Reconstruction

Programmers and engineers work closely with physicians using computers to design prostheses and to create models for reconstructive surgery.

Some orthopedic surgery requires the creation and implantation of artificial limbs and other

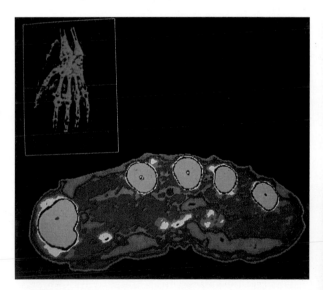

FIGURE 4

The National Hansen's Disease Center/Louisiana State University Center for Biomedical Research has developed an interactive kinematic simulation of a human hand so that simulated experimental surgical procedures can be performed and resulting mobility evaluated. Initial data are extracted from computer tomogram scans. (Courtesy of National Hansen's Disease Center and Evans & Sutherland)

replacement parts, such as hip joints. By using diagnostic scanning procedures, technicians can digitize an accurate picture of the damaged bone and visually compare it for fit and function. Then the prosthesis is built, usually with the help of computer-aided manufacturing machinery, to ensure the precise measurements are met.

Tooth crowns can be created in the dentist's office while the patient waits. After the natural tooth has been trimmed, the dentist can use a pen-sized laser probe to measure that tooth and the adjacent teeth, and feed the dimensions into a computer. A computer-controlled milling machine, maintaining those exact specifications, creates the crown from metal and porcelain. The dentist then cements the finished crown in place.

Monitoring Equipment

Computer-controlled devices are used where patients need constant monitoring, such as in intensive care units, post-operative recovery rooms, and premature-baby nurseries.

Premature infants, especially babies whose birth weight is under three pounds, are at high risk of death from strokes that can be caused by high blood pressure. These babies' vital signs, blood gases, and head movements can be computer monitored, with measurements being taken up to 32 times per minute. It would be physically impossible for nurses to obtain the same volume of data; and it could be hazardous for the infant to undergo the amount of physical contact that such data gathering would require. Researchers are hopeful that causes and prevention of Sudden Infant Death Syndrome (SIDS) can be learned from these computer-monitoring tactics.

Other computer-controlled medical devices have been developed (Figure 5). One such device frees diabetics from hypodermic needles by automatically dispensing the proper doses of insulin from a reservoir implanted in the patient's body.

Pharmaceutical Design and Testing

Developing a new drug is time-consuming and costly, involving years of research and experimentation and costing millions of dollars. Thousands of compounds have to be made and tested before a new drug can be released for production and human use.

However, computer graphics techniques save drug researchers time by simulating, in 3-D, the shapes of molecules. Because the shape of a molecule usually determines its behavior, biochemists can accurately predict how various

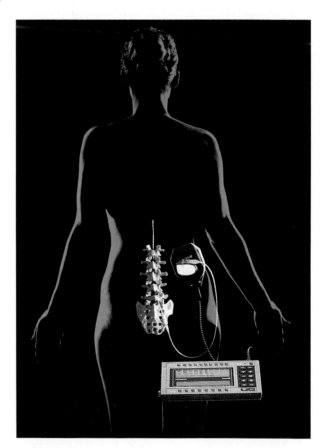

FIGURE 5
This photo illustrates placement of Medtronic's Itrel Spinal Cord Stimulation System's pulse generator, lead, and external programmer unit. The implantable, computerized pulse generator produces electrical signals that block pain messages traveling to the brain. (Reprinted with permission of Medtronic, Inc. © 1987.)

molecules should be combined. Some computers are programmed to simulate various attributes of test animals so that checking for toxicity or verifying the safety of certain procedures can be done by computer simulation without endangering human or animal life.

Help for the Physically Challenged

Devices that stimulate muscles to move (patterned electrical stimulation) continue to be improved. The computer stores a signal of brainwave muscle patterns, reads the signal, and then gives an electrical stimulation to the appropriate muscle group to cause movement. Tendon injuries are being treated this way, and improvement has been shown in patients paralyzed by strokes, accidents, or cerebral palsy.

Dr. Jerrold Petrofsky at Wright State University in Dayton, Ohio, is one of the most widely recognized researchers using this type of computer technology. His patients, with damaged spinal nerves causing paralyzed limbs, are able to walk and ride bicycles by using attached electrodes and adapted equipment (Figure 6).

Other requirements of physically challenged individuals are being addressed in computer design. The Kurzweil Reading Machine scans printed words and then speaks them aloud through a speech synthesizer. The Versabraille is a laptop computer that some blind people use to write letters or take notes. There are also braille keyboards, keyboards adapted for those with limited muscle control, and keyboards that can be activated merely by eye movement.

KEY TERMS

computer-aided
instruction (CAI) (p.
365)

drill (p. 365)

simulation (p. 366)

tutorial (p. 365)

QUESTIONS

1. How might a personal computer benefit you at home?

FIGURE 6
This demonstration of an outdoor tricycle for the physically challenged shows how a computerized electrical stimulation-feedback system stimulates paralyzed muscles to pedal the tricycle. (Courtesy of Wright State University)

2. Describe three techniques used in computer-aided instruction.
3. Describe the new types of technology and devices that allow computers to be applied in the arts.
4. List several ways that computers are improving health care.
5. Describe two ways that computers or computerized devices are assisting people who are physically challenged. Have you seen other ways that were not mentioned?

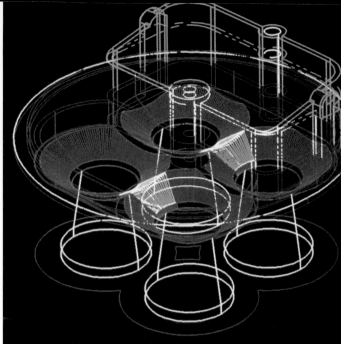

OBJECTIVES

- [ ] Distinguish between a word processor, a word-processing system, and word processing
- [ ] List the components in a typical word-processing system
- [ ] List some uses for a word processor
- [ ] Describe the two basic functions of a word processor
- [ ] Name and describe some features of a typical word processor

OUTLINE

13

Word Processors

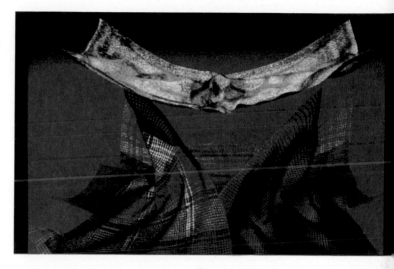

PROFILE: An Wang

One of life's little ironies is that the man who did the most to bring computerized word processing to American homes and offices could barely speak a coherent sentence of English when he came to this country. An Wang already had a degree in engineering from a Shanghai university when he ventured to the United States to continue his education. When he landed in Newport News, Virginia, however, he was far from comfortable with the English language.

Wang's government sent him to the U.S. to continue his scientific education. However, when the civil war in China intensified, Wang decided to live in the United States. Eventually, he enrolled at Harvard, where in 1948 he completed his doctorate in applied physics.

By successfully combining his theoretical and practical work, Wang developed the magnetic-core memory for computers. He acquired a patent for his invention and ultimately sold it to IBM for $500,000. Using this capital, Wang started his own electronics company in 1951. At first, his company concentrated on producing calculators. But when

the market for them began to shrink, he gradually switched to manufacturing word-processing machines. Beginning in 1972, Wang Laboratories started selling these machines which were made from the outer shells of IBM Selectric typewriters, with memory functions handled by magnetic-tape cassettes. Within a few years, the Wang Word-Processing System had grown into an assembly of elements that included a CRT screen, multiple workstations, and programs that could be modified to process words in languages besides English. However, the system's major selling point was the fact that it could be learned and used quickly by anyone who knew how to type.

In 1984, Wang Laboratories reported sales amounting to $2.4 billion, and An Wang was listed among the ten richest men in the U.S. In spite of his riches, he lives simply. One magazine reported that while Wang had given a $4 million grant to his alma mater, Harvard, and an additional $4 million to help rebuild Boston's performing arts center, he owned only four suits—all identical.

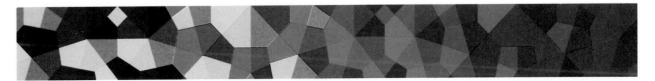

Word-processing equipment is to the typewriter what the typewriter was to the pen and pencil. Since amateur inventor Christopher Sholes of Milwaukee created the typewriter in 1873, people have been finding better ways of putting words on paper—ways that were faster and more efficient. The manual typewriter evolved into the electric typewriter, and that evolved into the electronic typewriter. Now, computers and their word-processing software are the foundation for today's office automation.

Students and professionals also routinely use word-processing software and computers instead of typewriters in their classrooms, offices, and homes.

This chapter looks at the uses of word processors, the kinds of tasks they can accomplish, and some of the features that are common to most packages.

DEFINITION

Several distinctions should be made before proceeding with this discussion. They involve terms that are very similar but which have different meanings: word processor, word processing, and word-processing system.

A **word processor** is the software, or program, that manipulates the text. Word processors for microcomputers are packaged in diskette form. You may have seen them on the shelves in computer stores (Figure 13–1).

Word processing is the *activity* of entering, viewing, storing, retrieving, editing, rearranging, and printing text material using a computer and appropriate software.

A **word-processing system** is the combination of hardware and software used for word processing. Usually this consists of a general-purpose computer and software.

However, some businesses use a **dedicated word-processing system,** a type of computer made mainly for the purpose of word processing. A few years ago, this system was the dominant one. Dedicated word-

FIGURE 13-1
A wide variety of word processors are available to suit many word-processing needs.

processing systems are still used by many companies despite the advent of inexpensive and powerful word processors for microcomputers.

For example, the IBM Displaywriter is a dedicated word-processing system, whose main purpose is for word-processing tasks. But the IBM PC, a general-purpose microcomputer, can be programmed for many tasks including both data processing and word processing.

Most word-processing systems today, however, are computers into which the appropriate software is loaded. When a WordPerfect diskette (a popular word processor) is loaded into an IBM PC (a microcomputer), you have a word-processing system.

Most word processors perform similar tasks. The minimal features on this software enable users to write, edit, and print text easily and efficiently.

However, some word processors are more versatile than others. Some are difficult to learn, but easy to use; others are easy to learn, but not as efficient to use. Some are capable of very complex tasks, such as indexing, sorting lists, and preparing form letters. These extra features are needed for many jobs, but they cost more and take more time to learn.

At the other end of the spectrum are the very simple and inexpensive programs for people who just want to type letters, short reports, and memos, and print them on $8\frac{1}{2}'' \times 11''$ paper.

The important thing in choosing a word processor is to make sure that it has the features that you require. What might seem frivolous to one person may be important to another. One program may include a large dictionary to check for spelling errors, but no feature to create personalized letters. Another program may have capabilities for creating personalized letters, but a very small dictionary—or none at all.

Word processing is a popular application of computers, and word processors are available for almost every computer, large and small, on the market.

COMPONENTS OF A WORD-PROCESSING SYSTEM

Because the purpose of a word processor is to accomplish a specific task— i.e., to produce a written communication—specific pieces of equipment and software are required.

☐ A computer with sufficient RAM in primary storage is required in order to run a word processor. These specifications are listed on the word-processor packaging. So, a buyer must make sure that his or her computer has enough memory to accommodate the software. Some word processors require more memory than others.

☐ A video display screen, or monitor, to view the document as it is typed and edited is needed. A high-resolution, monochrome monitor usually gives better results for word processing than a color monitor. If a word processor is being used that incorporates graphics images, a high-resolution monitor is even more important.

☐ Usually, two floppy-diskette drives (or one floppy-diskette drive and a hard-disk drive) are needed. Some word processors require only one drive. Having two drives, however, makes it much easier to load files and programs. A hard-disk drive is helpful if the user is creating large numbers of documents or very long documents. Such a drive has a larger storage capacity, reduces the need to change diskettes frequently, and speeds up the transfer of data between the computer's memory and the hard disk.

☐ A printer is needed to receive the text from the computer and print it on paper. Many dot-matrix printers provide near letter-quality print at affordable prices. Letter-quality (daisy-wheel) printers are more expensive, but they produce excellent type. Laser printers offer near-typeset quality and print text and graphics in the same document. An appropriate interface card is also needed.

☐ A word processor (the software) to load into the computer is the final essential item. WordPerfect, Microsoft Word, WordStar, MultiMate Advantage, and PFS:Write are typical word processors. They are available for many brands of computers.

Once all these components are assembled, it is important to coordinate them into a work environment that offers comfort for the user and promotes productivity. The InfoModule on page 391 describes some factors that make a workstation comfortable and efficient.

A COMMUNICATION TOOL FOR EVERYONE

Do not think that word processors are high-tech tools useful only to highly trained people in automated offices. They are, of course, used by large corporations, but they are also put to work in small businesses, schools, and homes. They are useful to anyone who wants to write a report, a novel, a memo, a letter, a term paper, or any other kind of written communication.

In business, word processors are often used to create individualized form letters, daily correspondence, and reports that may require revisions. Secretaries, salespeople, and managers alike create documents using word processors.

In schools, word processors are sometimes used in keyboarding classes to teach students to type. Teachers use them to type lesson plans and tests. School secretaries prepare school-board minutes and reports, cafeteria menus, letters to parents, and activity lists with word processors.

Users of Word Processors

- Businesses
- Homes
- Schools
- Professionals

Design engineers work with scale models to determine an office environment that offers optimal working conditions and comfort for the user. Those designs have been incorporated into this office setting. (Courtesy TRW Inc. Inset: Courtesy of Hewlett-Packard Co.)

At home, family members type personal and household correspondence, reports, and lists. Students produce neater term papers and homework assignments, and professionals, such as writers and journalists use word processors to compose their books, articles, and newsletters (Figure 13–2).

There are many reasons to use word processors. They help the writers generate documents faster than traditional typewriters because there is no need to retype pages or "white-out" words and lines. Typographical errors can be corrected and editing changes can be made on the screen before the text is actually printed. Words and paragraphs can be moved to any place in the text, and characters can be changed, inserted, or deleted with a few keystrokes. If there is a "dictionary" feature in the software, even spelling can be automatically checked.

Revisions can be made in the document until it is exactly right. Then the final printed document is clean and neat, and there are no smudges where corrections have been made.

Another tremendous benefit of using a word processor to generate a written document is that it relieves the pressure of making errors. A word processor cannot generate ideas for writers, but it can give them the freedom to concentrate on the creative aspect of their work—developing ideas. They do not have to be concerned with, "How long will it take me to retype this manuscript if I change it?"

Reasons to Use Word Processors

- Text prepared faster
- Typos corrected easier
- Revisions made faster
- Drafts not retyped
- Final copy clean

HOW WORD PROCESSORS WORK

Word processors have many features and functions to help manipulate text, but the basic functions common to all of them are: (a) text editing; and (b) formatting.

Text editing activities include entering the words that make up the text, making deletions or insertions, and moving words, phrases, or blocks of text from one place to another. When text is entered, it is displayed on the screen and stored in the computer as a document (also called a file); then revisions can be made to it until it is exactly the way the writer wants.

Formatting a document refers to establishing the way the document looks on the screen and when it is printed, such as setting left and right margins, tabs, and line spaces. Margins can be justified (made to appear even) left or right; headings can be centered; words can be underlined, boldfaced, and italicized; headers can be placed at the top of a page and footers at the bottom. Automatic page numbering is also a feature of the formatting capability.

These formatting specifications and parameters are communicated from the computer to the printer before printing starts.

The way in which a word processor is controlled is described as being either **menu-driven** or **command-driven**. Menu-driven means that the choices available during operation are made from a menu, or list, shown on the screen. Choices are usually made either by moving a cursor to the selection and highlighting it, or by typing the number of the selection.

Command-driven word processors require that a command be entered, e.g., <Ctrl-L > to "load" a file. Some programs use a combination

---

Functions of a Word Processor

- Text editing
- Formatting

FIGURE 13–2
This writer revises text on the screen prior to printing a hard copy. The word-processing system is composed of a micro-computer and word processor.

of both methods. Command-driven programs can become quite cumbersome to use. Sometimes, the command list is very long and difficult to remember. Menu-driven word processors are becoming the most popular because people say they are easier to use.

Word processors handle files (documents) in different ways. A **page-oriented** word processor brings only one page of a document from the disk into primary storage at a time. Pages are swapped between disk and primary storage as the user makes corrections on the pages.

On the other hand, a **document-oriented** word processor brings the entire document from the disk into primary storage. Since the entire document resides in primary storage, changes are not saved until a save command is given. Remember that the text stored in primary storage is volatile. If substantial changes are being made, it is advisable to save the document to disk every fifteen minutes so the changes are not lost in the event that power to the computer is interrupted.

Some word processors employ a **virtual memory** scheme that swaps portions of the document between primary storage and disk as the primary storage is filled. This swapping happens automatically, and it gives the illusion that an unlimited amount of primary storage is available.

Within the two main activities of the word processor—text editing and formatting—there are many specific features at work to help accomplish them. Although different word processors have different combinations of features, those that are common to most of them are discussed next.

Ways Word Processors Are Controlled

- Menu-driven
- Command-driven

HIGHLIGHT

COMPUTERS AND CREATIVITY

Few people in science and business need to be convinced that computers are essential to their profession. But what about writers? To what degree has custom, poetic stereotypes, and fear of hardware kept them limited to pen or typewriter? Not much, it seems. *Writer's Digest*, a major trade magazine for writers, now routinely carries articles and columns about computers and the creative process. Younger writers, who learned their craft during the period when computers were first introduced into the classroom, look upon the devices as regular tools of the trade. Journalism schools and newspapers have long since assimilated computers into their instructional and operational schemes.

But the unarguable merits of computerized word processing have also convinced veteran writers to take a chance with the "new" technology. Some have become almost evangelistic about it. Author/columnist William F. Buckley, Jr., for example, was instantly converted to computerized composition after seeing a primitive word processor at work when he was visiting literary critic Hugh Kenner. Gene Perret, a veteran member of Bob Hope's comedy writing team, became so impressed with computer capabilities that he carries one with him, even when he's not on a specific writing assignment. Since becoming a convert, Perret has spent a good deal of time trying to convince other team members to forsake their typewriters.

Best-selling author David Halberstam is another computer enthusiast, as is *New York Times* book reviewer Christopher Lehmann-Haupt.

What all these writers have in common is the need to produce a lot of work in a relatively short amount of time and with the least distraction possible. (Buckley reportedly dashed off a 7,500-word children's book in two hours on his Epson PX–8). For writers, computing and creativity are almost synonymous terms.

TEXT EDITING FEATURES

Cursor Movement

The **cursor** is the box or line (sometimes blinking) that marks the user's present location on the screen. This location is the place where the next character will be entered or the next operation begins. The cursor is controlled by the arrow keys, other named keys, or brief commands that make the cursor quickly move or jump to the right place.

Some commands cause the cursor to jump to the first or last character on the display screen, or to the start or the end of a line. These shortcuts speed editing. They are there so that the user does not have to move the cursor one character at a time to get it to its destination.

Status Line

The **status line** at the top or bottom of a display screen provides information about the current document and the system. It may include: the name of the document (also called the file name), page, line, and column number on which you are working; the amount of available memory, and current mode of operation; and the designation of disk drive being used.

Windows

A **window** is a section of the display screen, usually with a border around it. Many word processors allow more than two to be displayed. Windows let the user see two portions of a particular document at the same time, or to see portions of two separate documents. Windows can display not only portions of specific documents, but also menus, option lists, or specific messages for the user.

A window can be displayed on top of another window, or the two can be displayed side by side. The window feature is sometimes referred to as a split screen (Figure 13–3). The main window in a word processor is the edit window—the work area for entering and editing a document.

Modes

Text is entered in either the **insert mode** or the **exchange mode.** When additional text is added in the insert mode, all text to the right of the addition shifts to make room for the new material.

However, in the exchange mode, the newly inserted characters replace, or strike over, existing ones.

FIGURE 13–3
Many word processors offer a split-screen function so that a user can see and edit two different parts of the same document or two different documents at the same time.

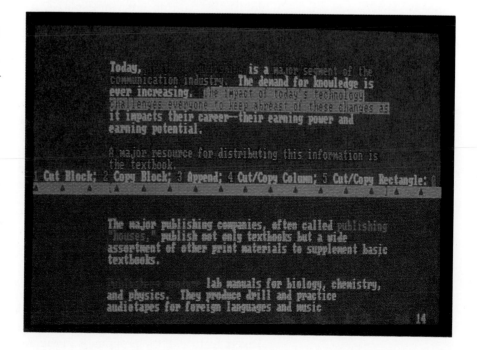

Wordwrap

A feature common to most word processors is **wordwrap.** When this feature is activated, the user does not need to press the return key at the end of a line of text as you do on a typewriter. The user just continues entering, and the program "wraps the type around" past the margin and puts the words on the next line. This process continues to the end of the paragraph. At this point, pressing the return key moves the cursor down to the next line to begin a new paragraph. Some word processors offer the option of disengaging this feature.

If the text is not supposed to go to the end of the line—e.g., in a typed column of names—the return key is pressed after each item in the list.

Hyphenation

The wordwrap function automatically takes the entire word to the next line; however, this often leaves a large blank space at the end of a line, giving an awkward appearance to the page. This problem can be solved by a **hyphenation** feature. There are three different types of hyphen: (a) a hard hyphen; (b) a soft hyphen; and (c) a nonbreaking hyphen. A hard hyphen is inserted by the user with a hyphen key. The hard hyphen stays with the word even if it is wordwrapped to the middle of a line after editing occurs. If the word no longer requires hyphenation the user must delete it. Soft hyphens are inserted by an automatic hyphen feature. If the position of the word changes during reformatting, causing the hyphen to be unnecessary, the automatic hyphen feature removes the hyphen. A nonbreaking hyphen insures that the word will not be broken at the end of a line. For example, there may be a phrase that contains a hyphen such as "24-carat gold," that you do not want split. A nonbreaking hyphen prevents the characters "24-" from appearing at the end of one line and the words "carat gold" at the beginning of the next line.

Scroll

Screen size does not affect the size of a document. Most computer screens display twenty-five lines of eighty characters each (sometimes referred to as being "eighty-columns wide").

If a document is too long or too wide to be created or viewed totally on the display screen, the **scroll** feature gives the user the ability to move the edit window to create or see text that is outside the display screen.

Most word processors scroll the text both vertically (top to bottom or the reverse) and horizontally (left and right movement). If the user scrolls the text vertically from top to bottom, the copy at the top of the screen will move out of sight off the top edge of the screen, leaving a blank area at the bottom for the user to continue typing.

Insert

Adding a character, phrase, or block of copy to the existing text employs an **insert** feature. If the program is in the insert mode, the existing text automatically shifts to make room for the new text. If it is in the exchange mode, entries will strike over and replace the existing text.

Delete

The **delete** feature allows a character, phrase, or a block of text to be removed. The remaining text automatically shifts to fill the space left by the deleted text.

Search and Replace

Search and replace is a feature especially helpful when you have just finished a report and discovered, for example, that a person's name was misspelled throughout. The program searches for all occurrences of that string of characters (word or phrase) and automatically replaces it with the correction. This "global" search and replace means that an entire document is searched so that each instance of a specified error is found and changed. A variation of this feature simply locates a particular word and asks the user at each instance if the string should be replaced.

Undo

If a writer takes an action too hastily during the editing process, it can usually be retracted with the **undo** feature—retracting the entry and restoring the text back to its original form. For example, if a paragraph that should not have been removed is deleted, the undo feature recalls the deleted paragraph back to the screen. It can still be retrieved because the deleted text had not yet been destroyed; it was stored in a buffer. Usually, a keystroke or two will undo the action.

Block Edit

Block editing permits large units of text—paragraphs or even pages—to be moved, copied, deleted, saved, or altered as a unit. It is more efficient to move an entire page or paragraph at one time than it is to move it a character at a time.

The feature first requires that the user mark both the beginning and the end of the text being changed. Then the whole block of text is manipulated according to further instructions. Block editing commands typically include delete, copy, move, save, boldface, underline, and italicize.

FORMATTING FEATURES

The format of a document refers to the way it will look on the screen or when it is printed. Some features are specified before the user begins keying in the document, some during entering and editing, and others at the time when the document is being prepared to print.

But not all format characteristics appear on the screen the same way they will when they are printed. For example, most word processors display text single-spaced, but give the option of printing a double-spaced document.

Character Enhancements

Most word processors permit the user to specify special enhancements to the text style when it is printed. Typical **character enhancements** are creating boldface type or italics, underlining, or a combination of these features. Some word processors indicate boldface by placing markers before and after the text on the screen, and that text appears boldface when printed. Even though a word processor may permit these enhancements, some printers are not capable of handling all of them.

Margin Settings

The specifications allocating space on the left, right, top, and bottom of a printed document are the **margin settings.** Some word processors set the margin specifications, and they cannot be changed. Although most word processors allow the user to specify all four margins, others preset the top and bottom margins, but allow the left and right margins to be adjusted.

Default Settings

Word processors that allow the user to specify margins, line spacing, tab settings, page length, or other parameters also incorporate **default settings.** These settings are parameters or specifications the system uses automatically when the user does *not* specify a particular setting.

Justification

The feature that aligns the text flush with the margin is called **justification.** It can be used to make the right margin even, the left margin even, or both. This style of blocking text can be seen in commercially generated books and magazines.

Centering

Centering, placing a heading in the center of a blank line, can be easily done with one or two keystrokes with a word processor. This task is more complex and time-consuming on a standard typewriter.

Tab Settings

Just as a traditional typewriter permits indention, a word processor also provides **tab settings** to make indentions. The tab on a word processor works basically the same way. However, many word processors have a sophisticated tab feature that simplifies typing columns of text or columns of numbers with decimal points. The feature can automatically align columns and decimal points.

HIGHLIGHT

THE MYTH OF THE PAPERLESS OFFICE

Where did we ever get the idea that computers would eliminate the piles of paper in offices? Well, once upon a time, much of the computer advertising suggested that computerization would eliminate the need for so many paper files. It does seem to make sense that by writing and editing on computers and by storing all the information in files on small disks, the reams of paper copies of drafts and files would be eliminated.

Instead, it appears that computerization may be accelerating the paper chase. Despite the popularity of word processors, electronic mail, videotext, and computerized business accounts, an estimated 21 trillion pages of paper are stored in offices in the U.S., and that number is growing. U.S. businesses still turn out enormous amounts of paper. In 1985, they used approximately 2.8 million tons of computer paper alone.

Some people speculate that computerization is generating more paper because some kinds of communication are just not possible electronically. For example, communication between some businesses or between a business and some clients is impossible because their computer systems are not compatible. Another reason is that some people still do not trust computers and electronic storage. They want to see hard copy.

Line Spacing

A word processor usually displays the text entered in single-spaced format. However, many word processors permit the user to change to double- or triple-line spacing when the document is printed. This selection is usually apparent on the screen in a status line, even though the text still appears single-spaced on the screen.

Page Breaks

After a user has entered the text, the program indicates the **page breaks,** i.e., where the text will begin and end on each page when it is actually printed. The user can override the automatic page break to change where the text should stop on one page and begin on another. According to rules of proper typing, a single line of a paragraph should not be left alone at the bottom or top of a page. This problem often occurs with automatic page breaks. A widow line occurs when the last line of a paragraph at the bottom of a page is placed at the top of the next page. An orphan line is found when the first line of a paragraph at the top of the page is placed at the bottom of the previous page. Many word processors have an option that allows you to choose whether widow and orphan lines will be allowed, then the word processor automatically adjusts the text during formatting so they will not occur.

Automatic Page Numbering

The page number is automatically printed on each page with the **automatic page numbering** feature. Some programs provide the option of removing the page number from certain pages or choosing the placement of the number on the paper—top, bottom, left, or right.

Headers and Footers

A **header** is a line (or lines) of text at the top of each page. A **footer** is text that appears at the bottom of each page. For example, the report's title and page number could be printed at the top or bottom of every page. Generally, this information is entered after the rest of the document is keyed. It is usually keyed in one time for the entire document rather than page by page; this feature is usually designated when the printing specifications are entered.

SPECIAL FEATURES

In the early days of word processors, many features were available only as separate programs to use in conjunction with a word processor. Now, they are frequently offered as standard word processor features.

Mail Merge

Sometimes the same letter needs to be sent to a number of individuals. Instead of retyping the letter for each person, a word processor creates multiple "originals," each of which *appears* to have been retyped.

With the mail-merge feature, a form letter is created that contains specially coded characters that tell the word processor where each variable should be inserted. A variable is a word or phrase that changes from letter to letter, e.g., the recipients' names and addresses. Then the user compiles the list of names and addresses. The **mail merge** function actually inserts the variable-list information into the previously designated spaces on the form letter, thereby creating personalized letters as final documents.

Some word processors let the user create the variable list (for example, the address list) within the word processor itself. Others require the list be created in a separate data-manager program (which will be discussed in the next chapter). Still others let the users choose between the two.

Glossary

The **glossary** feature lets the user automate some word-processing tasks. With this feature, typing a normally time-consuming phrase can be reduced to one or two keystrokes.

For example, the name "S. J. Perelman" may be used frequently in a term paper about American humor. The name or phrase can be stored and labeled with an abbreviation; for example, SP could be the label for S. J. Perelman. When the user keys in the document, only the label is typed, but the full phrase appears on the screen.

Help Window

Most word processors include a **help window** that can be called up any time during entering and editing phases. A help window will list the keys and commands that are available to the user at that time or describe the steps for a particular function. It is a handy reference and reminder of the various commands or procedures.

Spelling Checker

A **spelling checker,** or dictionary, locates misspelled words and typographical errors in a document. The checker compares words in a document with its dictionary of 15,000 to 100,000 correctly spelled words. It highlights on the screen the words that are not in its dictionary and the words that are misspelled. Most spelling checkers present options for the correct spelling. Then, the user can choose to replace the word with the correct spelling or leave it as it is.

A spelling checker cannot detect misuse of correctly spelled words. For example, in the sentence "I red the book," the spelling checker will not know that "red" is not the correct word; "red" is a correctly spelled word. The writer used the wrong "read."

Some spelling checkers accept additional words to an auxiliary dictionary. This feature is helpful if the program's dictionary is small or if the user is writing a paper using technical terms that wouldn't ordinarily appear in the dictionary. The checker will then use those added terms as part of its own dictionary. If a writer's use of technical terms (in medical or legal papers, for example) is extensive, special spelling checker programs devoted just to words in a particular field are available.

Outliner

A feature called an **outliner** helps organize the writer's thoughts and writing. Ideas can be entered as they occur. Then they can be easily organized and reorganized as headings and subheadings until the outline flows the way the writer wants it.

Grammar Checker and Thesaurus

A grammar checker and thesaurus are two other helpful tools to use with a word processor. These features are either available as separate programs or as part of the word processors themselves. Using one of these independent programs means that it will have to be loaded into the computer for each use.

Grammar Checker A **grammar checker** points out possible problems with punctuation, grammar, sentence structure, and writing style. Most grammar checkers for microcomputers are still fairly elementary and are no replacement for good editing. Because English grammar consists of so many rules and exceptions, grammar checking demands more "comprehension" capabilities than most microcomputers can handle.

But a grammar checker can examine writing in two ways:

1. It uses a few simple rules and can find some errors. For example, it can locate a period followed by two spaces and then a lowercase letter and recognize this as a capitalization error.
2. Another method compares words and phrases in the document with those in its file. It might locate "would of" in the document and suggest that "would have" is correct grammar.

Thesaurus A **thesaurus** suggests synonyms for words. When the writer is stumped for just the right word, the computerized thesaurus can help. The thesaurus is usually accessed by placing the cursor on the word to be replaced. With one or two keystrokes, a list of synonyms is presented on the display screen. Sometimes, even the synonyms have lists of synonyms.

SUMMARY

Word processors were developed to speed up the process of written communication and are now the foundation for today's office automation.

Word processing is the activity of entering, viewing, storing, retrieving, editing, rearranging, and printing text using a computer. The software that facilitates word processing is called the word processor.

A word-processing system is composed of a computer, a monitor, a disk drive, a printer, and the word processor (software). A word processing system usually requires two diskette drives; a hard-disk drive is helpful to people who are working with many documents or very long documents. Some businesses use a dedicated word-processing system, a special computer designed for the purpose of word processing.

Word processors are used in business, in homes, in schools, and in many professions to generate letters, memos, formal reports, and manuscripts among many other types of documents. There are several reasons why one might use a word processor: (a) to prepare documents faster; (b) to correct typographical errors and make revisions easily; (c) to eliminate typing drafts; and (d) to produce clean copy.

Two basic functions common to all word processors are: (a) text editing; and (b) formatting.

Text editing involves entering the text and making revisions and changes to it. Formatting refers to how the document is to look either on the screen or in its final printed form.

Word processors are either menu-driven or command-driven. Menu-driven word processors are the most popular because they are easier for many people to use; the choices made during operation are selected from a menu, or list, of options on the screen. Command-driven word processors require the user to type a command when selecting operations.

A page-oriented word processor brings only one page of a document into primary storage at a time. A document-oriented word processor brings in an entire document. A virtual memory scheme swaps portions of the document between primary storage and disk as memory becomes full, which gives the illusion of unlimited primary storage.

Some of the text-editing features of a typical word processor are: cursor movement; insert mode; exchange mode; wordwrap; hyphenation; scroll; insert and delete; search and replace; undo; and block edit. A status line provides information about the document and the system. Windows are bordered areas containing portions of a document, menus, options, or help messages. The main window is the work area where text is entered. More than one window can be displayed at a time on the screen.

Formatting features include character enhancements, margin settings, default settings, justification, centering, tab settings, line spacing, page breaks, automatic page numbering, headers, and footers.

Features that at one time were not available on word processors, but are appearing on newer models, include mail merge, glossary, help windows, spelling checkers, outliners, grammar checkers, and thesauruses.

Key Terms

Review Questions

1. Briefly trace the evolution of word processing.

2. What is the difference between a typical word-processing system and a dedicated word-processing system?

3. A(n) _____ is the software that allows the entering and manipulation of text on a display screen and then communicates that text to a printer to be printed.

4. How do you determine if your computer has enough primary storage to accommodate a specific word processor?

5. List the items that comprise a typical word-processing system.

6. Why might one want to use a hard-disk drive in a word-processing system?

7. Which kind of monitor is usually recommended for word processing?

8. Explain the advantage of using more than one disk drive with a word processor.

9. List some of the places where you would find word processors used.

10. List some of the tasks for which people use word processors.

11. What are some of the advantages of using a word processor over a standard typewriter?

12. The two basic functions common to all word processors are _____ and _____.

13. Describe the difference between a menu-driven and a command-driven word processor.

14. _____ refers to entering the text and making revisions.

15. Give an example of block editing. Tell why this type of edit is important.

16. What is the difference between a page-oriented word processor and a document-oriented processor?

17. Compare the insert and exchange modes of entry.

18. Explain the scroll feature. Why would it be used?

19. What are the dimensions of a typical display screen?

20. Describe an instance in which the search-and-replace feature would be used in creating a document.

21. List some of the items of information one might find in a typical status line on a word processor.

22. Describe the mail merge capability.

23. Why might one use the glossary feature?

24. Which feature allows the user to view more than one document on the display screen at a time?

25. Describe the spelling checker, outliner, grammar checker, and thesaurus features.

INFOMODULE
The Automated Office

In the late 1800s, the invention of the type-writer brought automation and increased productivity to the typical office. Later, accounting machines and calculators added to office speed and efficiency. In a modern office of a large company before the 1960s, you probably would have seen a large, open space with rows of secretarial desks topped with typewriters and adding machines, lines of filing cabinets, and bubbling water coolers.

Here, letters, reports, and memos were typed. Data were written or typed and sorted manually. The original was sent via the U.S. Postal Service, and a carbon copy was filed in the filing cabinet.

Recordkeeping was usually handled right in the business office by clerks and accountants who processed the company's data and oversaw the office's information needs.

MODERN AUTOMATION

Computers have had a powerful impact on the office environment and the way offices are operated. In fact, following the acceptance of computer technology, the whole concept of general office work and the business workplace changed in the 1970s and 1980s. The **automated office** is no longer a vision of the future; for many companies, it is a reality.

Automated offices combine traditional office procedures, computers, and communication technology. This automation includes the way documents are generated, reproduced, copied, and filed. The term "office automation" refers to the way information is generated and communicated within an organization. It also covers the way messages are transmitted. Office automation affects every department in an organization—from the switchboard to the secretary's desk, from the accounting department to the chief executive's office.

There are several reasons why many offices have turned to automation. The main reason is to increase productivity—to make the flow and production of documents and information more efficient, cheaper, and faster.

The two main innovations toward office automation were: (a) the introduction of word-processing equipment; and (b) new computerized, data-processing techniques, beginning with punched cards and computers. The concept of an automated office incorporates more than just these technologies, however. Let's look at some of these technologies (Figure 1).

WORD PROCESSING

It is generally agreed that the introduction of word-processing machines in the 1960s is the pivotal factor in changing the way offices were operated. Today, word processing is the most widely adopted of all the new office technologies.

At first, the IBM magnetic-card memory type-writers were added to the office environment. These were followed by dedicated word-processing machines, the small computers that handled only text material. But as general-purpose microcomputers and easy-to-use software became available, more offices began to use them for word processing.

DATA PROCESSING AND RETRIEVAL

New and faster ways to handle the office's information needs came with the arrival of computers and punched cards. The introduction of computerized equipment separated data-processing activity from general office activities and placed it in its own department.

Most of a company's files are now stored electronically in these data-processing departments. Some files need to be stored for many years, and electronic media, such as tapes and disks, take up much less space than filing cabinets.

FIGURE 1

Computer systems in auto-
mated offices have a variety of
functions. Some are used for
word processing, others for
data processing, and still others
for sending and receiving electronic mail. The individual system's application functions can
change from time-to-time depending on the program being
implemented. (Courtesy of Honeywell, Inc.)

Although much of an organization's data and
information have been relegated to separate
quarters, truly automated offices link this department electronically to other departments. From
their desks, secretaries, managers, executives,
or others can access data and information relevant to their jobs.

ELECTRONIC MAIL

One could say that an early form of **electronic
mail,** or "E-mail," was the telegram, which sent
coded signals by electric transmission over wire.
Now, letters, memos, and other forms of correspondence can be sent electronically, in streams
of 0s and 1s, directly to the recipient's personal
computer or terminal. This process is faster and
usually cheaper than overnight mail delivery.

Mail can be sent short distances, between
offices, or long distances—even around the
world—by satellite. At its destination, the communication is placed in a file inside the recipient's computer to be read immediately or stored
for later use.

The Radisson Hotel in Nashville, Tennessee,
is the first major hotel to offer electronic mail
service to its guests. The service, Hotelcopy
Inc., allows the Radisson's guests, a large portion of whom are business people, to send up

to ten pages worldwide to other users in less
than a minute.

Facsimile transmission, sometimes referred
to as FAX, is another form of electronic mail. To
send a copy, the FAX machine optically scans it,
then sends it, including text, pictures, even
handwriting, long distances using telephone
lines (Figure 2). Another FAX machine at the

FIGURE 2

A FAX machine electronically sends a document to a
branch office in another city.

receiving end converts the document into original form.

Voice mail is sent as the human voice. The message is stored in the computer, and the computer sends the message to the recipient's voice "mailbox" where the message can be heard when it is convenient.

A freight trucking company in Joplin, Missouri, gets about 6,000 calls a day from its truck drivers and clients. With voice mail and a telephone management system, the company saves telephone time and money by not having to put callers on hold.

ELECTRONIC CALENDARS

An **electronic calendar** is an electronic scheduling system used in automated offices. It is used like an ordinary appointment book, to schedule appointments and events, or to log activities. But it has more flexibility because it can be available to several people through a computer. This way prior to scheduling a meeting, participants' calendars can be checked to find the best available times.

Electronic calendars are also used as a log of activities by engineers, lawyers, and other professionals for their time-billing systems. For example, a psychologist can effectively use an electronic calendar to log time spent with each patient and use it later for precise billing.

ELECTRONIC TELECONFERENCING

Computerized conferences enable people in different places to talk to each other. **Electronic teleconferencing** electronically links participants through their computers. A variation also allows people to confer by leaving messages for conferees at different times.

Similar to electronic teleconferencing is the **electronic blackboard.** The user writes on a pressure-sensitive chalkboard with ordinary chalk. The image is digitized and electronically transmitted by telephone lines to one or more other conference locations and displayed on a monitor. The image gradually appears on the monitor at the destination as if an invisible hand were writing it.

TELECOMMUTING

Telecommuting allows people to work at home by connecting home and office through communication channels. The benefits of this approach are still being argued, but the trend is growing. According to the New York research firm Electronic Services Unlimited, in 1985 approximately 100,000 people telecommuted to work. The firm predicts that by 1990 as many as 10 million people (including those who use this method for overtime work) will be involved in telecommuting.

DESKTOP PUBLISHING

Desktop publishing is a concept that combines the use of a microcomputer with page-composition (graphics-oriented) software and high-quality laser printers. Anyone can use such a system to create and publish documents—among others, departments within corporations that want to publish in-house, small businesses, and writers who like the idea of self-publishing.

Booklets, brochures, newsletters, and annual reports can be produced with desktop-publishing software (Figure 3). Even a fifty-page magazine can be designed, and its pages made-up and printed. The uniqueness of a desktop-publishing system lies in the page-design and composition software. It is basically a graphics-oriented software because it involves positioning and repositioning graphics and other elements of a page on the screen. An important feature of this software is that it enables the user to see on the screen what the entire page will look like when it is printed, a factor referred to as "what you see is what you get," or WYSIWYG.

Most page-composition software has some word processing capabilities. Sometimes the text is created and formatted with a word processor first and then transferred to the page-composition software to be manipulated.

Some of the art is also created with separate graphics software and then transferred to the page-composition software to be positioned on the particular page being "pasted up."

The final product can be printed either as camera-ready copy for mass printing, or copies

FIGURE 3
This hobbyist creates a news-letter for a model-airplane club with his microcomputer and a desktop-publishing software package.

can be printed for distribution directly from the computer. Laser printers produce type and graphics as crisp and detailed as those in pro-fessionally published magazines and textbooks.

So far, most page-composition software has been developed for the Apple Macintosh; how-ever, programs have subsequently been devel-oped for the IBM PC and compatible microcom-puters. The term ''desktop publishing'' was coined by Paul Brainard of Aldus Corporation when that company's software, PageMaker, was introduced. With the combination of the Apple Macintosh microcomputer, Apple LaserWriter (a laser printer), and the Aldus PageMaker, the concept of desktop publishing took off.

Today, other software developers, such as Graphics Corporation and Xerox Corporation, offer desktop-publishing packages such as Ready, Set, Go and Ventura Publisher, respec-tively, for microcomputers.

INTEGRATION

An office is not really fully automated until all the electronic elements are linked. Automated offices are linked, or integrated, so that all the

equipment and people can communicate elec-tronically through the network using all the elec-tronic files and other data and hardware re-sources within an organization. Departments thus share company data and equipment, such as laser printers and large computers.

Ultimately, as offices become more heavily automated, every office worker will have a workstation that will communicate with any other electronic resource in the company.

Total office automation and integration is a gradual occurrence in most offices. Little by lit-tle, new technology is introduced, and finally the entire system is integrated within the organiza-tion.

Everyone in an office is affected by office automation—salespeople, order-entry clerks, typists, accountants, managers, and executives. Office automation can change a company's op-eration and make it more productive, efficient, and competitive.

ERGONOMICS AND THE HUMAN TOUCH

All the benefits of speed and efficiency and all the productivity gains of office automation can be lost if the high-tech physical environment doesn't meet the emotional and physical needs of the people who work in it. The desire for workers' comfort has brought forth a concern for **ergonomics,** or human engineering, the science of designing the workplace for the comfort and safety of the worker.

Office-equipment and furniture manufacturers design their products according to the needs of people who will use them. Chairs are constructed to prevent backaches, and computer screens have special shields to prevent eye strain.

Some of the generally agreed upon standards for preventing discomfort or pain at a modern electronic workstation include

- ☐ Placing the keyboard at a height of 24–27 inches
- ☐ Keeping the computer screen about 18–24 inches from the eyes
- ☐ Positioning the computer screen to avoid glare from lamps or windows
- ☐ Covering windows to diffuse the light coming through
- ☐ Installing wood floors or antistatic fiber carpet
- ☐ Using a posture chair where the seat height and back tilt are adjustable
- ☐ Using a glare-free desktop
- ☐ Using a stable computer stand
- ☐ Arranging a handy storage area
- ☐ Placing feet flat on floor
- ☐ Maintaining a horizontal arm position

Figure 4 is a diagram of a workstation that has taken these ergonomic features into consideration.

Office designers are also trying to combat the coldness and impersonal feel of the plastic and metal high-tech environment. Decorators suggest sound-absorbing materials and softer lighting (fewer overhead lights and more area lighting). They are also using colors and materials—fabric and wood—that resemble more of a home environment.

Studies show that people are more productive in well-designed work areas; therefore,

FIGURE 4

A design for an ergonomically sound work area

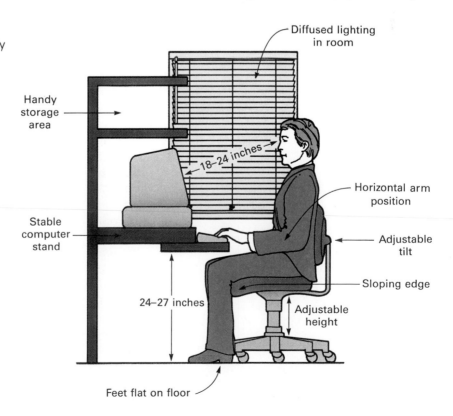

some companies are willing to spend a lot of money to make their workers comfortable. Pacific Bell's experiment in using office design to improve performance in their El Segundo, California, office cost them approximately $11 million. Before the money was spent, however, employees were polled about their preferences on everything from color combinations to ventilation. According to the company spokesperson, the extra attention paid off; workers are pleased and productivity increased.

KEY TERMS

automated office (p. 391)

desktop publishing (p. 393)

electronic blackboard (p. 393)

electronic calendar (p. 393)

electronic mail (p. 392)

electronic teleconferencing (p. 393)

ergonomics (p. 395)

facsimile (p. 392)

telecommuting (p. 393)

voice mail (p. 393)

QUESTIONS

1. Describe some of the elements of an automated office.
2. Why have some companies turned to office automation?
3. Explain integration in an automated office.
4. What is the most widely adopted of the computerized technologies?
5. What are some considerations when a company is planning an ergonomically appropriate office?

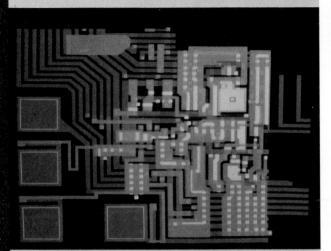

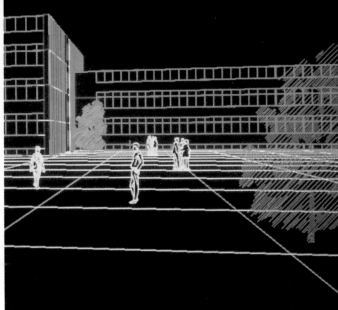

OBJECTIVES

- ☐ Describe the two types of data managers—file-management systems and data-base management systems

- ☐ Identify appropriate applications for file-management systems and for data-base management systems

- ☐ List and describe several common features of data managers

OUTLINE

FILE-MANAGEMENT VERSUS DATA-BASE MANAGEMENT SYSTEMS

COMPONENTS OF A COMPUTER SYSTEM USING DATA MANAGERS

USES OF DATA MANAGERS

FEATURES OF DATA MANAGERS

INFOMODULE: Computers in Government

FEDERAL GOVERNMENT

STATE GOVERNMENT

LOCAL GOVERNMENT

14

Data Managers

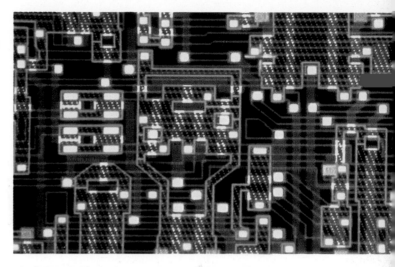

PROFILE: Jonathan Rotenberg

Jonathan Rotenberg knows his computer users. In 1975, when he was just thirteen years old, Rotenberg founded the Boston Computer Society as a way of bringing together the people in his area who were excited about the computer's scientific and business prospects and who were practicing enthusiasts. By the time the organization was ten years old, it had more than 7,000 members, and observers were calling it "the most influential computer group in the world." Today, with Rotenberg still at its helm, it has about 23,000 members and the Boston Computer Society is still the largest and most influential user group in the world.

While still in prep school, Rotenberg became fascinated with the school's new Altair computer. He even helped assemble it from the kit. Because virtually no one knew what to do with the new device, Rotenberg got the idea of forming a club, the Boston Computer Society, where people could discuss and demonstrate computer uses and problems. Only Rotenberg and a friend showed up for

the group's first scheduled meeting. Undaunted by the failure, Rotenberg and his father began publishing a newsletter about computer uses that listed computer shows being staged in Boston. The two hand-delivered the newsletters to computer shops all around town. When Rotenberg called the next meeting, more than fifty people attended.

In its current form, the Society holds meetings, entertains visitors, answers calls about computer problems, publishes the magazine *Computer Update,* and generally acts as an advocate for the computer industry.

In addition to his Society duties, Rotenberg organizes computer shows and serves as a consultant to some of the top manufacturing firms.

His chief aim, however, is to develop the Boston Computer Society into a national organization with chapters all over the country. Experience suggests he's the ideal man for the job.

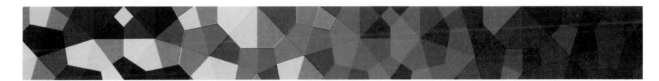

Today's society thrives on information. To meet our ever-increasing demand for information, we require more and more data to be gathered, stored, and manipulated. In fact, many of us require so much data that it has become impossible to manage and extract the information we need in a timely fashion. To solve this problem, computers are being called upon to help manage and store the data we gather.

In the early days of microcomputers, only large computers had the capabilities and software (required by many applications) to store and manage large amounts of data efficiently. Today, however, microcomputers have the capability and software to store and manage the data requirements of many businesses. This chapter examines the types of software available for data management on a microcomputer and the major features found in these packages.

FILE-MANAGEMENT VERSUS DATA-BASE MANAGEMENT SYSTEMS

A **data manager** can be one of two general types of programs used to manage data: (a) file-management systems; and (b) data-base management systems.

A **file-management system** is a program that stores, manipulates, and prints data stored in separate files. Only one file can be accessed and manipulated at a time (Figure 14–1a). Usually these files are stored and used in their respective department locations. For example, if a person wants to use a file-management system to store the data for the personnel and payroll departments in a company, separate files containing data about each employee would have to be created.

Using a file-management system has its limitations. One limitation is that it makes locating and manipulating data from files in different departments difficult and time-consuming.

Another limitation is that data are unnecessarily duplicated. Because files are often widely distributed, any data that are the same, such as the employee name and number, would have to be entered and stored in each file.

Types of Data Managers

- File-management system
- Data-base management system

400

FIGURE 14–1
(a) A file-management system can access only one file at a time. (b) A data-base management system can access more than one file at a time.

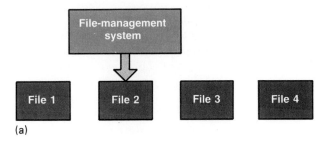

(a)

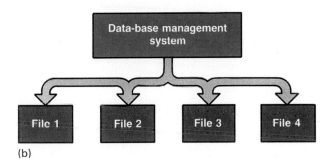

(b)

A third limitation is poor data reliability. When data are updated, each file must be individually accessed and the changes made to it. You can imagine how difficult it is for a business which maintains many files in separate locations to ensure that when data are updated in one file, all other files containing that data are also updated. Therefore, using a file-management system has the major limitations of being unable to distribute data widely in an efficient manner, data duplication, and poor data reliability.

The data-base concept was developed to solve the problems associated with a file-management system. A **data base** is a collection of related files stored together in a logical fashion.

A **data-base management system (DBMS)** is the program that stores, manipulates, and prints data in a data base. In a data base, data from more than one file can be accessed at the same time (Figure 14–1b).

DBMSs have certain advantages over file-management systems. First, they usually require most data to be entered only once. Once a data item is entered, it can be used by any file in combination with any other data in the data base. This feature eliminates excessive data duplication. Second, because the data are generally stored only once, updates have to be entered only once. Finally, a data base also centralizes storage making it easier to find and manipulate the desired data.

COMPONENTS OF A COMPUTER SYSTEM USING DATA MANAGERS

Certain hardware requirements and software are needed to run a data manager.

☐ The computer must have sufficient RAM in primary storage to run the data manager. The required memory is usually listed on the software package. A DBMS usually requires more memory than a file-management system because it is generally a larger program with more capabilities.

☐ A monochrome monitor is sufficient for most applications. However, some data managers allow color to be displayed and some allow the incorporation of graphics in the data base. If this is the case, a color/graphics monitor and the appropriate color/graphics circuitry are needed.

☐ Most data managers require two floppy-diskette drives—one for the program and another for the data. If the program can be completely loaded into the computer's memory, then one diskette drive is sufficient. In this case, the program diskette is first inserted into the drive; the program is loaded, and then the diskette is removed and the data diskette is inserted. However, because of faster access speeds and greater data capacity, a hard-disk drive is usually recommended in addition to a single floppy-diskette drive.

☐ A printer is needed if hard copy of the data is required. A printer interface card is also needed.

☐ The appropriate data-manager software is the final item. PFS:File and Framework are examples of file-management systems; dBase III and Open Access II are popular data-base programs.

USES OF DATA MANAGERS

A file-management system is not as powerful or sophisticated as a DBMS, and hence, the types of applications it is suited for are also less sophisticated. Examples of applications for which a file-management system is well-suited include maintaining the following types of data: a mailing list;

FIGURE 14–2
A file-management system is adequate for many uses such as managing a home budget.

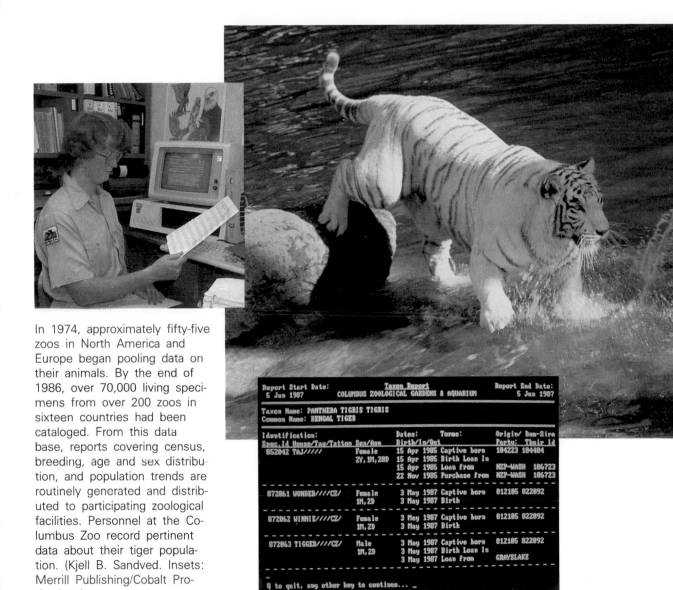

In 1974, approximately fifty-five zoos in North America and Europe began pooling data on their animals. By the end of 1986, over 70,000 living specimens from over 200 zoos in sixteen countries had been cataloged. From this data base, reports covering census, breeding, age and sex distribution, and population trends are routinely generated and distributed to participating zoological facilities. Personnel at the Columbus Zoo record pertinent data about their tiger population. (Kjell B. Sandved. Insets: Merrill Publishing/Cobalt Productions)

a file of names, addresses, and phone numbers; an inventory list or list of any items; and a home budget (Figure 14–2).

A San Francisco disk jockey, "Doctor Don" Rose, has created an unusual data base consisting of material from almost three years of old shows. Now, he can assemble jokes on a particular subject, make selections for the current show, and print them out to create a new show's script. He can even match past years' shows for compiling historical trivia, making sure he doesn't duplicate material from year to year. Additionally, he has computerized files on financial records, real estate investments, and a 1,200-bottle wine cellar.

Because a DBMS allows its user to create and access multiple files, it lends itself to more complex applications. One of the most popular applications is for accounting systems. Creating an accounting system involves the integration of several different files including general ledger, accounts receivable, accounts payable, and payroll. Other applications that require the integration of several files and that are well-suited to a DBMS include financial management, travel-agency management, medical-office management, and real-estate management.

FEATURES OF DATA MANAGERS

This section describes the basic features of file-management systems and data-base management systems which allow the user to create, maintain, and manipulate the information stored within a file. These features are common to almost all data managers, but depending on the software package, the actual commands used to execute them vary.

File-management systems are generally easier to learn and use because the user is manipulating the data in only one file. But with a DBMS, it is possible to manipulate multiple files simultaneously. For this reason, a DBMS is harder to learn but it is a more powerful system.

You may assume that the following features apply to both systems unless otherwise indicated.

Help Windows

Most data managers include a **help window** that can be called up any time. A help window will list the keys and commands that are available to the user at that time or describe the steps for a particular function. It is a handy reference and reminder of the various commands or procedures.

Searching

Searching a file means to look through a file and to locate data. Searching for data may also be called "finding" or "retrieving" by some systems. Only one file at a time is searched with a file-management system, but a multiple file search is possible with a DBMS.

If a user is uncertain as to exactly what data he or she is looking for, an entire file can be searched one record at a time. Listing each record in the file allows the user to visually search, sometimes called "browsing," the file until the right one is located.

More often, however, the user knows what data are needed. With most data managers, the user can enter the search parameters to locate the specific records containing those data. Those records will be found and displayed.

Updating

Updating is the process of changing the content of a record or records in a file. This updating may be adding, deleting, or changing the contents of a record. By accessing records and changing the field contents, the user can keep all the records current.

HIGHLIGHT

A REAL LABOR-SAVING DEVICE

How do you agree on figures when your opponent is using a mainframe computer and you're stuck with a handheld calculator? For a long time, that has been the situation in contract negotiations between corporations and labor unions.

But contracts are a lot more complicated than simply stating how many workers get how much an hour for how many hours a week. Today, negotiators have to figure in benefits of all sorts, varying pay scales, payroll deductions, company contributions, and a dizzying variety of other financial variables. Previously, with access to their large computer systems, company representatives got a far more accurate picture of life under a new contract than union negotiators could.

To remedy this imbalance, labor lawyer Jerome Tauber has created a computer program that runs on an IBM PC. It combines database information with a spreadsheet so that union representatives can tell what each item in a proposed contract will mean in the long term.

Tauber's program makes for a fairer ''fight.''

Adding

Adding to a file means to add an additional record or records to an existing file, e.g., adding a new person to a customer file or a new product to an inventory file.

Some data managers put the added records at the end of the file, but others place them in a spot vacated by previously deleted records. In some data managers, it is possible to insert a new record at any point in the file.

Sorting

Usually, it is easier to read data if they are arranged in some predesigned order. **Sorting** records means to arrange them in order. The sort can be numerical or alphabetical, and the data can be arranged in ascending or descending order.

The fields used in the sorting process are the **key fields.** Most data managers allow sorting by more than one key field. This would be used, for example, when sorting names. If the last names are the same, the name might be further sorted by first names. The first key field in the sort is called the primary key, while subsequent fields are the secondary key fields.

Deleting

Removing records from a file is called **deleting.** Individual fields within a record can also be deleted. After the data are deleted, those data items are no longer available. Extra care should be taken when deleting to avoid removing a field or record unintentionally. It is wise for the user to keep a backup copy of the file to have in case of accidental deletion.

Screen Forms

A **screen form** is created to define the layout for entering data into a record. The screen form allows the fields to be positioned according to the user's preference (Figure 14–3). More than one screen form can be created for each record so the user can choose how the data will be displayed.

A screen form can serve more than one function. First, it provides data entry points to define records or a data dictionary where the attributes are defined. These attributes include the field name, the field type (text, numeric, key, nonkey, decimal, date, time, or others), the length of the field, and any validity checks to verify that data are entered properly. Sec-

FIGURE 14–3
More than one screen form may be created to display the field names and data. The user selects which screen form will be used.

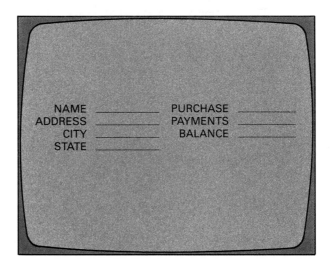

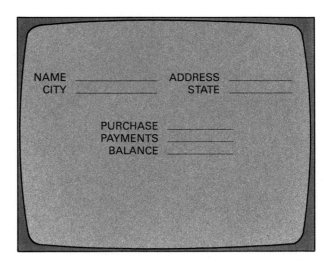

ond, it can serve as an output screen form in which field alignment is determined for printing.

Screen forms are designed from a blank screen by using the cursor to indicate the placement of the fields and their lengths, and by typing identifying labels for each field. With some data managers, this is done in response to on-screen prompts.

Report Generators

All data managers allow the user to print files, and many allow the user to customize the way output will look. This customizing is possible with those data managers that contain a report generator. With a **report generator,** the user defines how the report will appear when printed. Most report generators have these four features: headers; footers; formatting; and statistics.

Headers   The header section of a report is located at the top of the report page and contains items such as the date, page number, column headings, or even a company logo.

Footers   The footer, like the header, is a separate section of the report, but it is located at the bottom of the page. The footer may contain page numbers, the user's name, or other relevant information.

Formatting   Formatting features let the user control the way a report looks by setting margins, justifying text, and indicating page lengths and line spacing.

Statistics   Many report generators can perform some simple mathematical functions. Some can provide basic statistical information such as calculating column subtotals, grand totals, averages, and counting.

Manipulating a Relational Data Base

Because the relational data-base structure is the most commonly used structure in the design of most of today's powerful data bases, we'll examine three common ways in which they can be manipulated. Recall from Chapter 9 that in a relational data base, data are organized into tables (files) by rows (records) and columns (fields). Relational data bases can be manipulated by using selecting, joining, and projecting operations. They may incorporate one, two, or all three options. The actual command names may vary among the various relational data bases, but the basic operation is the same.

Selecting   Choosing the records to be displayed from a table is called **selecting.** It is used to limit the records which are retrieved. When selecting a record, the entire record is retrieved. For example, Figure 14–4 shows the result of a selecting operation where all the records were selected in

Common Operations for Manipulating Relational Data Bases

- Selecting
- Joining
- Projecting

FIGURE 14–4
The selecting feature allows a new table to be created using only the rows (records) desired. Here, the records of the second-shift workers are selected and placed in a new table.

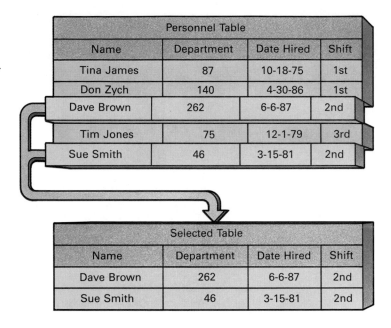

which the "Shift" field contained the value "2nd." The selected table now lists all the second-shift employees' records.

Joining Sometimes called merging, **joining** files is combining records from two or more tables into a new table. The tables can be joined only if they contain a common key field. For example, in Figure 14–5 the customer table and the product table are joined using the common field "ItemNumber."

Projecting Sometimes a table contains more records and fields than are needed by a user. The **projecting** feature can be used to create a table that is a subset of the larger table by combining only the needed rows and columns to form a new table (Figure 14–6).

Transferring

Some software packages are integrated, meaning they can share data and they contain a data manager and one or more of the following—a spreadsheet, graphics program, communication program, or a word processor. With the capability of **transferring,** a data file created in a data manager, for example, can be sent to and incorporated as part of a spreadsheet program.

Converting

Programs sometimes use different formats for storing data on disk. When this occurs, one data manager will not be able to interpret a file created by another data manager. **Converting** data is taking the form in which data are stored in one data manager and changing them so they can be used by

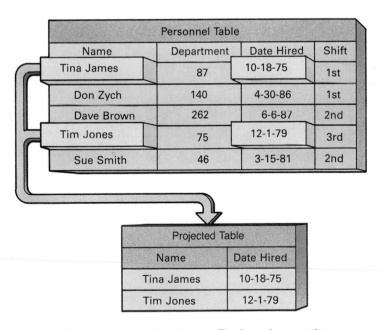

Customer Table

Name	Current Balance	Item Number
Mike Toony	60.00	100038
Jerry Layman	278.37	14066
Robert Steele	47.95	21373

Product Table

Item Number	Description	Price/Unit
100038	Band saw	300.00
14066	Shelving	37.95
21373	Hammer	9.50

Joined Table

Name	Current Balance	Item Number	Description	Price/Unit
Mike Toony	60.00	100038	Band saw	300.00
Jerry Layman	278.37	14066	Shelving	37.95
Robert Steele	47.95	21373	Hammer	9.50

FIGURE 14–5
The joining feature allows tables to be combined through a key field.
ItemNumber is the key field above.

FIGURE 14–6
By using the projecting feature, a new table can be created containing only the needed records and fields.

Personnel Table

Name	Department	Date Hired	Shift
Tina James	87	10-18-75	1st
Don Zych	140	4-30-86	1st
Dave Brown	262	6-6-87	2nd
Tim Jones	75	12-1-79	3rd
Sue Smith	46	3-15-81	2nd

Projected Table

Name	Date Hired
Tina James	10-18-75
Tim Jones	12-1-79

another data manager. This is usually done by a utility program that converts a file from its current format to the desired format.

Copying

The **copying** feature allows a user to make duplicate files to store in another location. For example, a temporary file created from the joining of two other files may be copied into a new permanent data-base file.

HIGHLIGHT

IT'S WORKING!

You've probably seen their pictures displayed on milk cartons and in newspaper advertisements. The faces are of missing children from all over the United States. Advo-System, Inc., the largest direct-mail house in the United States, has been responsible for sending photos of these missing children right to our homes.

Because of the Advo-System mailings, a three-year-old girl who had been missing from her home in North Carolina was found. Perhaps not an outstanding accomplishment for the authorities, but consider the fact that the girl had been missing for ten years. Imagine the changes that occur in a child between the ages of three to thirteen. A child loses the "babyish" look of a preschooler and becomes an adolescent. How would a person recognize a child after all those years?

A baby photo of the missing girl was "aged" through a computer process, and a new photo was generated to give an image of how the baby would have matured and what she would look like as a teenager. The girl's "aged" photo was sent on an updated flyer to over 50 million homes; someone in New Mexico recognized the girl, and the girl was ultimately reunited with her mother.

Although only several dozen children have been found since Advo-System, Inc., began sending their mailings, perhaps by the computer-aging techniques, those who have been missing for longer periods of time may have a better chance of being found.

Printing

Sometimes it is necessary to print only the raw data rather than use a report generator to print a more formal report. The **printing** feature allows the user to print the contents of the screen at any time.

Graphics

Some data managers include **graphics** capabilities. Reports with data and graphics, such as charts or graphs, can be generated, stored, and printed without first transferring the data files to a separate graphics program.

Data Security

Data stored in a file are often of a sensitive or confidential nature. Therefore, a user may want to restrict access to the computer and data except by authorized personnel. This restriction can be done mechanically, e.g., by building a lock that requires a key to turn on the computer. Data managers also provide features built into the software itself that will either prevent access or make it easy to track down the intruder. Three methods used to accomplish this are: data encryption; passwords; and audit trails.

Data Encryption   Data **encryption** is a way to code data so that they will appear as a scrambled display of alphanumeric characters if they are retrieved by unauthorized persons. A utility program would also be available to decrypt a file so that it could be read again.

Passwords   A **password** may be a letter, number, or a combination of both designed to prevent access unless the exact entry code is used. A data manager can be designed so that a password permits access to the entire data manager or to only certain files. It can also be designed so that the user needs one password to view the file, and another password to change, add, or delete anything in the file.

Audit Trails   **Audit trails** show any activity in a file. For example, a typical audit trail shows what was done (deleted, changed, added), what was affected (a specific field, record, or file), when it was done (time, date), and by whom (employee identification or password).

Data Security

- Locks
- Encryption
- Passwords
- Audit trails

Validating

Data-entry checks can be built into the data manager to prevent invalid data from being entered. Checking data for appropriateness and accuracy is called **validating.** Validity checks may be accomplished in the data manager by:

- ☐ Format checking—determining if data are in the correct format, e.g., numeric or text
- ☐ Range checking—determining if the data fall within an acceptable range, e.g., greater than 100 but less than 500
- ☐ Accuracy checking—making sure that an entry is possible, e.g., cross-checking a product number with the product numbers in an inventory file

Backup Files

A **backup file** feature of a data manager will make a copy of an existing file. The user generally is given the option to make a backup when a file is saved. If the user elects to make a backup file, it is created automatically when the current file is saved.

Macros

When using a data manager, the same sequence of keystrokes or commands may be used often. To automatically execute the repeated commands, many data-manager programs use a macro. A **macro** is a file that contains information that tells the program that a previously created series of keystrokes or commands are to be executed again.

Two common ways of creating macros are: (a) by using a macro editor to type a file that contains the keystrokes and commands to be executed; or (b) by using a macro recording function that automatically creates a macro file at the same time as a series of keystrokes and commands that are to be repeated are entered in the data manager. Both methods require that the macro file be given a separate name so that it can be accessed. To run the macro, the user selects the macro command and supplies the macro name.

Using macros can increase the speed and efficiency of manipulating data with a data manager. Some data-manager programs also incorporate a powerful programming language that increases a macro's power and capabilities.

Multiuser Data Manager

A **multiuser data manager** is one that can be used on a multiuser computer system where more than one person has access to the files in a data manager at the same time. Sometimes, however, unintended deletions, additions, or changes occur when two people work with the same file in a data manager. Errors occur because one person does not know what the other is doing; therefore, one person's update may be accidentally deleted by the other person.

To prevent this from happening, a data manager can restrict access or lock the file. **File-locking** is a procedure that permits only one user to access a file at a time. The file is not free to be manipulated by another person until it is released by the first person.

SUMMARY

Many data manager applications that were once possible only on large computers are now possible with microcomputers because of their expanding power and the availability of more sophisticated programs.

A microcomputer uses two main types of programs to manage data: file-management systems; and data-base management systems. These are commonly referred to as data managers. The file-management system and the data-base management system (DBMS) are both programs that can store, manipulate, and print files. The main difference between the two is that a file-management system can access only one file at a time, while a DBMS can access multiple files simultaneously.

A file-management system, because of its structure, has limitations: (a) because data are widely distributed, they are difficult to locate and manipulate efficiently; (b) data are duplicated; and (c) data may be unreliable.

The data-base concept was developed to help overcome these problems. A data base is a collection of related files stored in a logical way. With a data-base design, data are stored in a centralized location which makes them easier to locate.

In order to use a data manager, a computer system needs certain hardware: (a) sufficient RAM in primary storage to support the data manager; (b) an appropriate monitor; (c) a printer, if hard copy is needed; and (d) usually two floppy-diskette drives, or one floppy-diskette drive and a hard-disk drive.

File-management systems are suited to applications, such as mailing lists, name files, home budgets, and inventory lists.

DBMSs are suited to more complex uses, such as accounting, financial management, and other multiple-file applications.

Microcomputer data managers have the following features:

☐ Commands for manipulating data, such as searching, updating, adding, sorting, and deleting

☐ Screen forms in which to lay out the data fields and report generators to provide customized output

☐ Methods for combining data-base files such as joining, selecting, and projecting

☐ Ability to transfer data from one integrated program to another, or to convert the files to a usable form for another software package

☐ Methods for maintaining data security—data encryption, passwords, and audit trails

☐ Commands that enable the data manager to copy, print, validate, provide backup files, produce graphics, and execute a macro file

Problems can arise with multiuser data managers if two users try to access the same file at the same time. One way to overcome this potential problem is to restrict file use by file-locking, which limits access to a file at any one time to only one user.

Key Terms

adding (p. 405)

audit trail (p. 411)

backup file (p. 411)

converting (p. 408)

copying (p. 409)

data base (p. 401)

data-base management system (DBMS) (p. 401)

data manager (p. 400)

deleting (p. 405)

encryption (p. 411)

file-locking (p. 412)

file-management system (p. 400)

graphics (p. 410)

help window (p. 404)

joining (p. 408)

key field (p. 405)

macro (p. 411)

multiuser data manager (p. 412)

password (p. 411)

printing (p. 410)

projecting (p. 408)

report generator (p. 407)

screen form (p. 406)

searching (p. 404)

selecting (p. 407)

sorting (p. 405)

transferring (p. 408)

updating (p. 404)

validating (p. 411)

Review Questions

1. Describe a file-management system.
2. Describe a data-base management system (DBMS).
3. Name several types of applications where a DBMS would be more efficient than a file-management system.
4. List the components of a computer system using data managers.
5. Why does a DBMS usually require more memory than a file-management system?
6. Name three applications that are well-suited for a file-management system.
7. The process of locating data within a file is called _____.
8. What is the purpose of a help window?
9. The process of accessing a record and changing its field contents is called _____.
10. Explain the process of sorting a group of records.
11. Describe the purpose of a screen form.
12. Describe the purpose of a report generator.
13. How does transferring a file differ from converting a file?
14. The _____ feature of a data manager allows a duplicate file to be created.
15. The process of coding data so that they cannot be read by unauthorized persons is called _____.
16. What is the function of a password in a data manager?
17. How can an audit trail feature help ensure data security?
18. What does it mean to validate data?
19. Describe the function of a macro.
20. Why is it important to maintain a backup file?
21. Describe a multiuser data manager.
22. Describe one type of problem that can occur in a multiuser data manager when more than one person accesses a file at the same time.
23. Describe file locking and the reason it is used.
24. What does a key field have to do with sorting in a data manager?
25. Describe the relational data-base features of joining, selecting, and projecting.

INFOMODULE
Computers in Government

Some people still think of the computer as a recent phenomenon, but it has actually been in productive use for almost four decades. The first large-scale uses of computer systems were by government organizations. The U.S. Bureau of the Census began using the UNIVAC I for general data processing in 1951. Today, the federal government is still the largest user of computers and one of the largest funders of computer research.

By one estimate, the federal government holds over 4 billion personal files on U.S. citizens in computerized files in their various departments and agencies. The U.S. Patent and Trademark Office alone receives about 20,000 documents every day. The Securities and Exchange Commission (SEC) receives 6 million pages of documents and reports a year. Imagine the volume of data held by the Internal Revenue Service, the Census Bureau, and the Social Security Administration, all of which collect information on most of the U.S. population.

With this massive job of collecting, organizing, and analyzing data, it's easy to see why computers are needed throughout the government.

All this stored information is valuable to those governmental departments, such as the Department of Health and Human Services, that provide the benefits in social programs and to law enforcement agencies that combine to form a powerful information exchange network. This information is necessary to agencies that plan the country's space and defense programs, and to departments that monitor the weather and environment, among many others.

FEDERAL GOVERNMENT

Much of the government's use of computers is for typical administrative and businesslike applications, such as generating reports, data processing, calculating payrolls, auditing, planning, and other financial and management functions. The government became heavily dependent on mainframe computers for these daily administrative operations during the 1960s and 1970s. As the 1980s approached, personal computers were integrated with the large systems to help distribute the work load. Today, there are over 140,000 microcomputers scattered throughout various government offices, with plans to install many more.

More efficient and effective use of data and information was one reason behind The Paperwork Reduction Act of 1980. Another goal of this legislation was to reduce the paperwork burden and encourage a paperless operation. While the paperless office is not a reality, the legislation has encouraged the use of computers by the various government agencies.

Internal Revenue Service

The Internal Revenue Service (IRS) has used computers since the 1950s to process tax returns; today, it processes 100 million tax returns a year. This massive task makes the IRS the federal government's largest computer user. Computers are involved throughout the routing that your tax return follows—from the time you mail it, until your refund check arrives. The returns are first handled at a regional office where clerks key the data into a computer through terminals. (In addition to the standard paper form, the IRS also permits returns to be sent on floppy diskettes.) The returns are stored on diskettes to be processed by a computer that checks arithmetic accuracy. The results of this processing are stored on magnetic tapes that are then sent to the National Computer Center in Martinsburg, West Virginia. There, the return is subject to additional computer verification, such as comparing it to information supplied by banks and employers, and W-4 forms. Mathematical formulas are applied to the returns, e.g., comparing the amount of charitable contributions to income. An extremely high percentage of contributions could signal that an audit should be conducted. The computers also verify whether a refund is due or if the amount of the payment check sent corresponds to the amount of tax actually due (Figure 1).

IRS auditors even take laptop computers on location to make business and personal income tax audits.

Politics

Computers have been used to tally national election votes since 1952 when the UNIVAC I first attracted worldwide attention. In the national presidential election that year, it correctly predicted Dwight Eisenhower's victory over Adlai Stevenson after only 5 percent of the votes were counted. CBS News, with Walter Cronkite anchoring the 17-hour coverage and Charles Collingwood at the UNIVAC computer room, were skeptical and did not announce the prediction until it proved to be correct. Since then computers have become permanent fixtures in Presidential elections. But the trend in using computers for predictions has caused national controversy over the fairness of predicting

FIGURE 1
This clerk is entering information from income tax forms to be verified by a computer.

the results on the East Coast count before the polls are even closed on the West Coast. Because of this controversy, most responsible organizations have agreed to discontinue its use publicly.

Political parties maintain data bases of voter registration and past election results. Potential candidates use computers to analyze opinion polls and to draw a list of names of people who might volunteer their services or make monetary contributions. The selected names can then be merged by a computer program with a form to create a "personalized" letter to be mailed. Other software is used to organize a candidate's schedule of activities, to control the campaign budget, and to write and revise speeches.

Once candidates have been elected to the legislature, they have access to other computer data-base services. The House Information System contains data on federal grants, pending legislation, and U.S. Supreme Court decisions, among other topics. The LEGIS system provides information on the status of all bills currently under discussion. Again, word processing speeches and preparing computerized mailings are two ways that the computer keeps the legislators in contact with the constituents at home.

A computerized tally board that displays the result of members' votes is located above the Speaker's chair in the U.S. House of Representatives. To vote, members insert an identification card, similar to a credit card, into a terminal and then press the appropriate button to match their choice. These devices are also used to record roll call.

The White House has its own state-of-the-art mainframes and microcomputers that help with the daily tasks of speech writing, appointment scheduling, and report generating. Thousands of letters are produced daily, and many are sent on their way to other offices through an electronic-mail system.

Defense

The U.S. defense system relies heavily on computers to alert citizens in case of an emergency. Agencies such as NORAD (North America Aerospace Defense) use computers to detect missiles that might be headed toward the United States. Computers are part of the early warning systems in satellites and AWACS (Airborne Warning and Control System) aircraft. Computers also compile data from surveillance and intelligence operations. All these operations are linked by computers to give the President and others in the chain of command a means to control the many components of the defense system in case of national emergency. Decisions can be made quickly based on the most up-to-date intelligence information available.

Computers are intrinsic to some of the weapons used to maintain the nation's defense. Computers inside weapons such as the Cruise missile can guide it to the intended target. Sophisticated computer guidance systems contained in jet fighters and ground vehicles such as tanks not only provide weapon guidance, but also provide the operators with navigational directions even in total darkness.

The Defense Advanced Research Projects Agency (DARPA) contributes funds for research in areas that eventually are applied to defense systems, such as chip design, artificial intelligence, and robotics.

Other Federal Government Agencies

Although the IRS may be the largest agency using computers, other agencies maintain huge data bases. The Social Security Administration contains data on more than 200 million applicants and 40 million retirees, the Library of Congress catalogs books, and the U.S. Office of Personnel Management handles records for all civilian federal employees. The Veteran's Administration answers questions and processes benefits with computers. The National Weather Service monitors weather conditions around the world. Most of the statistics on atmospheric conditions are gathered by satellites and analyzed by computers.

The Central Intelligence Agency (CIA) installed its first mainframe in the 1960s for typical administrative tasks such as payroll and inventory. Today, computers have become an important tool, assisting in the CIA's primary job of collecting and processing intelligence information. For example, here are some of their applications of computers:

☐ Screening and routing thousands of cabled messages every hour. The messages are read, routed, and saved in electronic form

☐ Designing and producing maps and charts by their cartographers

☐ Analyzing terrorists' activities, narcotics trafficking, and the political stability of various countries

The FBI has a new weapon to use against violent criminals—the National Center for the Analysis of Violent Crime. The center's main feature is a computer system that analyzes the information on unsolved homicides by searching through all the collected information and looking for patterns or similarities among the different cases. The FBI plans to expand this sophisticated information system to include data on rapes, child molesting, and arson cases.

Since the first use of the computer in 1951 by the U.S. Bureau of the Census, the U.S. population has drastically increased. In 1980, the agency collected and analyzed data on the country's 226 million people with a much more sophisticated computer system than its first one. Without computers, the project would have taken years to complete. Even so, compilation took nearly a year. Additional demands continue to be placed on that agency from a society that is hungry for information about its population. The Census Bureau provides not only a count of people, but also statistics by age, level of income, race, sex, geographic areas, and other data and projections. To acquire and analyze the data that will eventually be used by many businesses and agencies, more automation than ever before is planned for the 1990 census.

In 1987, the Federal Aviation Administration (FAA) installed a new computer system to help air traffic delays and improve safety. On a single screen, the new system provides a radar display of every airplane across the United States flying under jurisdiction of the control system. With this system, FAA traffic managers in the Washington, D.C., command center can see air travel in the entire country and focus on areas where the traffic is dangerously heavy.

FIGURE 2
A governor's assistant gathers and enters data concerning state issues into a data base. The data can later be manipulated and statistical analyses can be performed.

STATE GOVERNMENT

State governments have computers and information systems, too. Data bases, word processors, and spreadsheet programs help control and manage the state's taxes and finances, general record keeping, statistics, and payrolls (Figure 2). In some states, computers in the Division of Motor Vehicles process driver's license applications, check titles, and print the registration form.

In recent years, many government services have been delegated from the federal to the state level of government, increasing the state government's work load. Some states, such as California and South Carolina, have linked, or are planning to link, various local government bodies together in a network. Others, such as Michigan, provide a terminal for all state senators' and representatives' offices. States such as Alaska, where travel is often difficult, have networked various information offices and have linked sites across the state with audio conferencing capabilities.

Because of his proficiency with computers, New Hampshire's governor, John Sununu, bal-

FIGURE 3
With the help of a robot, a police officer in Orlando, Florida, gives students instructions on safety topics. (Courtesy of Orlando Police Department)

anced the state budget without raising taxes. By using various software packages and spreadsheets, he was able to access, analyze, and control the state's finances, thereby changing a $41 million deficit in 1982 to a $48 million surplus in 1985.

Some states have initiated lotteries as alternative ways to raise capital for education and other needs. While the winning numbers are not picked by the computer, most other phases of the operation are under computer control.

LOCAL GOVERNMENT

There are approximately 80,000 various local government units in the United States, including county and city governments, townships, and school districts. Many are quite small with limited funds; consequently, computers may not be used to the same extent as their larger counterparts. However, most local governments use computers for routine payroll, budgeting, utility billing, and word-processing functions. Some police departments use computerized robots as part of an educational and safety training program (Figure 3).

Two especially important areas of computer use in local governments are in fire and police protection. One of the first cities to computerize its fire response systems was San Francisco. SAFER (System for Assigning of Fire Equipment and Resources) was implemented to assign

FIGURE 4
Many police departments are linked to the FBI's National Crime Information Center (NCIC) computers where they have access to thousands of criminal records maintained by the FBI. This additional information is often required to solve local criminal investigations.

available fire-fighting equipment efficiently to handle approximately 30,000 calls a year. The computer also maintained a historical record that provided data for future analysis of the system. Many other cities have adopted similar programs to make fire fighting more efficient.

Some large cities have installed computers in police patrol cars. The officer enters the license number of a vehicle and immediately checks the registration of the car to learn if the driver has any previous arrests or outstanding warrants. If these data indicate that the vehicle is stolen, the officer approaches the driver with extreme caution.

The Federal Bureau of Investigation (FBI) has established the National Crime Information Center (NCIC) as a common storage place for over 8 million records (Figure 4, p. 419). These criminal records are accessed many thousands of times a day, and information is available to local police in about two seconds. This information can help track criminals by their behavior, locate stolen goods, and trace criminals who have left town.

The larger cities also use computers in traffic control. For example, San Francisco uses computers to control its public transportation system, the Bay Area Transit System (BART).

Since the funding of the ENIAC in the 1940s, the government has been one of the largest funders of computer research. Many advances in today's computers perhaps would have been delayed or would not have occurred without the federal government's eagerness to have the latest technology.

QUESTIONS

1. Why is the federal government the largest user of computers in the U.S.?
2. How does the federal government use computers in processing income tax returns?
3. Why don't all city governments use computers to the same extent?
4. Describe how computers are used in defense systems.
5. Briefly describe how a national network of computers is used to help trace criminals.

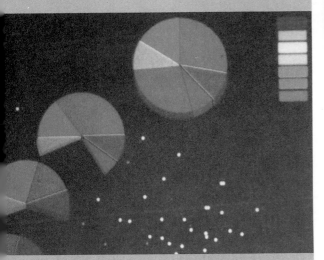

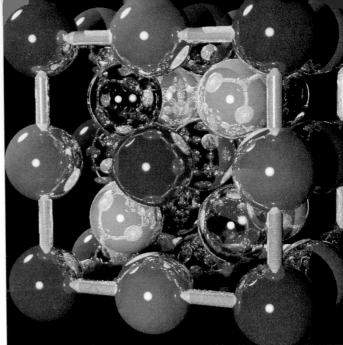

OBJECTIVES

☐ Identify the parts of a spreadsheet

☐ Recognize areas where businesses and individuals could use a spreadsheet

☐ List common features and functions of a spreadsheet

OUTLINE

15

Spreadsheets

PROFILE: Mitchell Kapor

How does a self-described "nerd" make it big in the world of entrepreneurship and business? Mitchell Kapor did it by combining an interest in personal consciousness, antiwar activism, and interdisciplinary study of linguistics, psychology, and computer science at Yale University.

After college, Kapor entered the working world as a stand-up comic, disk jockey, and teacher of transcendental meditation. Instead of following the usual path toward corporate success by earning an MBA degree, he took his master's in psychology and became a counselor in the psychiatric unit of a small hospital.

Still, Kapor, who grew up in a Brooklyn middle-class family, was on his way to becoming a multimillionaire. Kapor first veered toward computer entrepreneurship when he came across an Apple II. While still at Yale, he had found that working with mainframes was extremely frustrating. On campus, mainframes were often inaccessible and required special programming skills and punched cards for both the instructions and data. This was not so with microcomputers; they were easy to use and program. Kapor was captivated.

The microcomputer was the perfect tool for turning his creative instincts loose. He began doing freelance programming in the BASIC language for other new owners of microcomputers. His first programming job was to create a small data base of patient information for a doctor.

This simple beginning led Kapor to an alliance with Jonathan Sachs, a former Data General Cor-

poration programmer. The two men devised an electronic spreadsheet that was sophisticated enough to appeal to the business world, yet could be run on a microcomputer. (A spreadsheet, as you will learn in this chapter, is a device for keeping track of and manipulating rows and columns of numbers.) The two developers called their program Lotus 1-2-3. Their spreadsheet was designed for use with the IBM Personal Computer and compatibles; it made projections, displayed results, and sorted data. The documentation for Lotus was clear and concise, and the program did what it promised. Moreover, it was fast.

Lotus 1-2-3 revolutionized accounting on small computers in much the same way word processors changed writing with typewriters. This program convinced the business community of the value of the relatively new microcomputer. It was the impetus that sent IBM PC sales soaring. With an alluring product, the additional thrust of IBM's sales, and Kapor's expertise, all the elements for success were in place. First-year-sales projections for Lotus were $3 million, but actual sales were $53 million. Kapor proved to be a master of marketing and a genius at advertising.

Kapor resigned as chief executive officer of Lotus in 1986 to spend time with his family, to study linguistics at MIT, and to consult at Lotus. Incidentally, Kapor chose the name "lotus" not only for its association with a dream-inducing flower and an expensive sports car, but also because it symbolizes inner peace.

The earliest methods that humans used to keep track of items included tying ropes in knots, marking notches on sticks, and other crude devices. Then came the abacus, a wooden frame with wires and beads for calculating. Gradually, as numbering systems were developed, the paper and pencil approach started. Each item to be counted was assigned a number, and the numbers could be added, subtracted, multiplied, and divided.

As time went on, a sophisticated means of keeping track of and manipulating these numbers was devised. For ease in manipulating, the numbers and dollar amounts were written on paper that had been divided into rows and columns; the paper was called a spreadsheet.

DEFINITION

A **spreadsheet** is little more than a means of keeping track of and manipulating numbers—separating them into rows and columns. Paper spreadsheets are forms with horizontal and vertical lines that separate each row and column of numbers. You may have seen paper spreadsheets similar to the one in Figure 15–1. A spreadsheet can take other forms, too; each user can adapt a spreadsheet to various applications and formats.

With the development of the computer, the paper spreadsheet was converted to a computerized format called an **electronic spreadsheet;** it could manipulate rows and columns of numbers, make calculations, and actually evaluate formulas.

The first electronic spreadsheets operated only on large computer systems, and because of their limited availability, most businesses and individuals still used paper spreadsheets. The development of VisiCalc in 1979, the first electronic spreadsheet for microcomputers, gave everyone easy and affordable access to this powerful tool.

VisiCalc was rather crude compared to today's standards, because it was severely limited in the volume and size of jobs it could handle. But with the continuing development of more sophisticated hardware and software, programs improved to such an extent that most of today's computer spreadsheets allow at least 65 columns and 254 rows for a total of 15,000

FIGURE 15–1

A paper spreadsheet

Corsican Bros. Car Wash
Sales / Profit
Second Quarter

		A April	B May	C June
1	Units Washed	850	986	1044
2	Price	5 50	5 50	5 50
3	Revenue	4675 00	5423 00	5742 00
4	Less: 40% Costs	1870 00	2169 20	2296 80
5	Less: Supplies .50	425 00	493 00	522 00
6	Profit	2380 00	2760 80	2923 20
7				

spaces for entries. If a paper spreadsheet that size were stretched out, it would be over three and one-half feet long and more than five feet wide. Imagine how cumbersome a 65-column paper document would be? Then, consider that some spreadsheets allow as many as 256 columns and 2,048 rows—over one-half million cells!

Today, instead of writing and calculating each entry by hand, a person can sit at a computer keyboard and use an electronic-spreadsheet program to make the necessary entries; the computer then makes all the calculations. Not only that, but the spreadsheet program can accept a correction in one item and then recalculate any of the affected numbers throughout the document. Corrections and recalculations are made by the computer.

Additionally, if the user wonders just how an increase or decrease in one particular entry might affect the end result, the program allows the user to pose various "what if" questions. Changes are made in the entries on the spreadsheet, but a copy of the original plan is maintained for comparison. For example, what if a person decided to buy a used car at a certain price; how would that choice affect other areas of the budget, such as car insurance, loan payments, automobile repair expenses, and other living expenses? What if the person bought this year's model instead, and

FIGURE 15–2

This woman analyzes long-range effects before making important business decisions. The spreadsheet capability of analyzing many different situations will show ramifications of each choice so that the most profitable course of action can be taken.

the payments are higher? A spreadsheet can analyze the affects on all these areas so that the purchase can be more closely evaluated (Figure 15–2).

The shortcuts and speed of the electronic spreadsheet certainly explain their popularity. There are hundreds of spreadsheet programs available for almost any brand of computer. Figure 15–3 illustrates an electronic version of the same paper spreadsheet in Figure 15–1.

Throughout the remainder of the chapter, the term "spreadsheet" refers to an electronic spreadsheet, unless otherwise indicated. Spreadsheet processing is one of the most popular computer applications; it brings to accounting functions the shortcuts, speed, and accuracy that word processors bring to writing.

COMPONENTS OF A COMPUTER SYSTEM USING A SPREADSHEET

Before a spreadsheet can be used, the following computer components must be assembled:

☐ A microcomputer with sufficient RAM in primary storage (The more powerful spreadsheets require more storage space than others. Specific information is provided on the spreadsheet package. The computer must have enough memory to accommodate the software chosen.)

☐ Spreadsheet software (The TWIN, VP Planner, MultiPlan, PFS:Plan, and Lotus 1-2-3 are typical spreadsheet programs. They are available for many brands of computers.)

☐ Storage in the form of a floppy-diskette drive (two drives are preferable so switching diskettes is not necessary) or a hard-disk drive and one floppy-diskette drive (The hard disk provides greater storage capacities.)

FIGURE 15–3
A screen of the paper spreadsheet as it would appear if created electronically

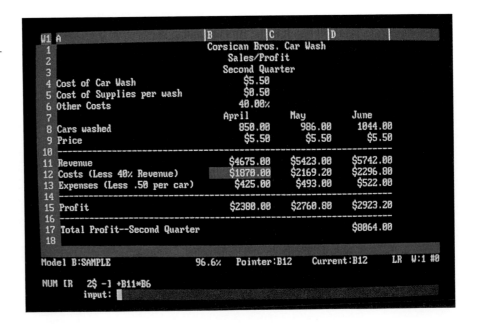

HIGHLIGHT

HIGH TECH ON THE FARM

In Yuma, Colorado, computers may prevent some farmers from losing their farms. Since the early '80s, when crop and land values started to decline, farmers have had trouble getting loans. Consequently, many farmers across the country have lost their property.

To help farmers cope with their financial situations, the Farmer's State Bank brought in a microcomputer and an expert to teach farmers about asset-to-revenue ratios and other equations to make them better financial managers.

When a farmer approaches the bank for a loan, the bank officers, the computer expert, and the farmer look at the farmer's entire financial situation. By entering all the financial and crop-growing and sales data, the expert can run a simulation that shows the farmer how to make better use of available assets.

For example, if the farmer is using too much fertilizer per acre, the program shows the direct financial gains of cutting back; or perhaps there are some assets the farmer can sell that will not influence revenue. Together, the bank and the farmer try several different "what if" situations, projecting operations for the next five years and seeing what the outcomes will be for each.

Then, the team can select the best possible solution and restructure the operation to try to make the farm more productive, avoid the need for another loan, or delay the prospect of foreclosure. The bank can see if it is even feasible to make a loan to the farmer.

Many farmers were initially resistant and skeptical; but the program definitely helped some of them save their farms.

☐ A printer is helpful, and if paper copies of the spreadsheet are necessary, a printer that can print wider than the $8\frac{1}{2}''$ standard paper is needed.

APPLICATIONS OF A SPREADSHEET

Any application where the problem can be written in mathematical terms is a candidate for electronic spreadsheet use. There are several other factors to look for when considering the possibility of using a spreadsheet to solve a problem. A spreadsheet should be considered for any reports that are

☐ Repeated regularly
☐ Edited
☐ Revised
☐ Made up of both variable and fixed data
☐ Required to be neat and legible

When even relatively simple paper spreadsheets are recreated monthly, it can take many hours to prepare the paper forms and make the entries by hand. Valuable time is wasted in rewriting the columnar headings that are the same from month to month on blank paper forms. With an electronic spreadsheet, a **template,** or blank form, of the required report can be created. The template contains any standard information or formulas that don't change; that form can be called to the screen, and the new data for the particular time period can be inserted.

For example, a clerk who prepares monthly reports for the company president could create a template that would include headings for all the standard expenses of the company, such as rent, utilities, insurance, and payroll. When the report is due, the clerk simply calls up the template form and enters the name of the new month and the amounts of expenses incurred for that month. Even a small company could save time by not having to handwrite all the standard parts of these reports each time.

Editing a paper spreadsheet can be an involved process. When mathematical calculations are made by calculators and entered by hand, transpositions in numbers and erroneous entries may occur. A correction that is made in one cell generally necessitates a corresponding change in the total of that particular column, and additionally, may affect other cells or totals. Therefore, making corrections by hand involves erasures. If many mistakes are found, a paper spreadsheet could be erased to shreds before the final entries are approved.

Revising on a paper spreadsheet can also cause problems, because in addition to erasures, the entire spreadsheet may have to be rewritten. For example, if the president of a small company wants to know the effects on profits of manufacturing and selling 500 more bookcases each month, a new spreadsheet must be created. In a company that uses paper spreadsheets, the clerk would have to make the necessary calculations, handwrite the entries, check and cross-check the totals, possibly make erasures, and then recheck the entries. Then, what if production were increased by 850? Another spreadsheet would have to be started.

However, the clerk at the company that uses electronic spreadsheets just copies the existing spreadsheet, enters the changes, and lets the computer recalculate all the figures, creating a new spreadsheet to answer the "what if" questions posed by the president.

Spreadsheets contain both fixed and variable data. When variable data changes in a paper spreadsheet, the erasure-and-recalculate procedure begins again; in an electronic spreadsheet, the speed, power, and accuracy of the computer makes calculations in fractions of a second.

Finally, it is important that a spreadsheet be neat and legible for those who need to read it. A paper spreadsheet is only as neat and legible as the handwriting of the person creating it. Even extremely legible entries may lose clarity if there are many erasures; the electronic spreadsheet can simply be revised and reprinted. Not only is the computer-generated spreadsheet neater, but data in the spreadsheet can also be used to create graphs and charts to represent the data visually. (Business and analytical graphics are discussed in Chapter 16.)

FIGURE 15–4
An interior designer uses voice
input to enter data into a
spreadsheet program that analyzes them prior to preparing a
client's estimate. (Courtesy of
Texas Instruments)

Accountants and business people use spreadsheets to maintain important data, such as sales, expenses incurred, costs of doing business,
inventory control, and projections of profits or losses (Figure 15–4). With
spreadsheet data easily accessible, the most comprehensive information is
available for managers to make decisions about future expenditures, or
plans for expansion of products or services, or to formulate pricing strategies.

Personal uses of spreadsheets include keeping track of cash flow, preparing household budgets and personal financial statements, and figuring
annual income taxes, among others (Figure 15–5). People who sell items

FIGURE 15–5
An accounting student uses a
laptop computer and a spreadsheet software package to
complete his assignments at
home.

such as household products, beauty aids, and cleaning supplies from their homes, could use a spreadsheet program for orders, inventory, and accounts payable and receivable.

A spreadsheet program can be used for any application where rows and columns of numbers are involved. A spreadsheet could be created in table format to help young students learn mathematical facts.

PARTS OF A SPREADSHEET DISPLAY

Figure 15–6 shows a blank spreadsheet, or **worksheet.** The empty space is hardly impressive; it's hard to imagine that anything useful could be derived from this simple format. However, you will see that looks can be deceiving.

Each spreadsheet is assigned a **modelname** by the user so that it can be easily identified. The modelname is comparable to the file name that identifies a file.

The spreadsheet display is composed of two main parts: (a) the **window,** the area on the screen where the entries are visually displayed; and (b) a **control panel,** the area that gives the user valuable information about the activity on the spreadsheet.

The various parts of a spreadsheet are shown in Figure 15–7. The numbers down the left side of the screen constitute the **row** grid, and the alphabetic characters at the top of the screen are the **column** grid. Using a combination of these labels identifies specific points on a spreadsheet.

Windows

Other windows can be superimposed over the main spreadsheet display window, including various menus with options for making and manipulating the entries on the spreadsheet.

Some display screens can be divided into several windows, where different spreadsheets can be viewed simultaneously, or several parts of a complex spreadsheet can be seen at the same time. Each window typically has an identification name or number so that the user can tell which spreadsheet is being viewed.

Coordinates The point where imaginary row and column grid lines intersect is the **coordinate,** or the address of that particular point. In Figure 15–7, Coordinate A1 is the point where a line from Column A intersects a line under Row 1. The box formed by the imaginary lines at each coordinate is the **cell.** (Later discussions will explain what kinds of data are entered and how the data get into each cell.)

Cursor The **cursor** is a symbol, usually a box or line, that marks the place on the screen where the next character typed will appear or the next entry will occur. The spreadsheet cursor is often referred to as a pointer. It can take one of several different forms: a shaded block or brackets; inverse video, where the background is light instead of dark; or underlined characters, among others. The cursor indicates the cell that is available for use,

FIGURE 15–6
A blank spreadsheet, or work-sheet

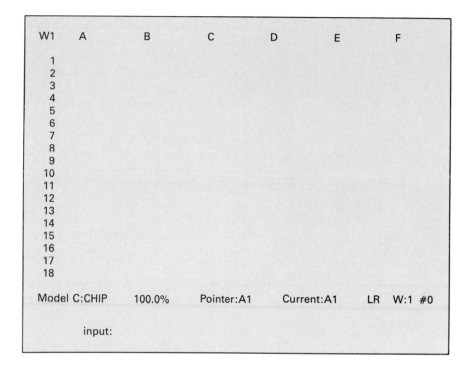

FIGURE 15–7
The parts of a spreadsheet

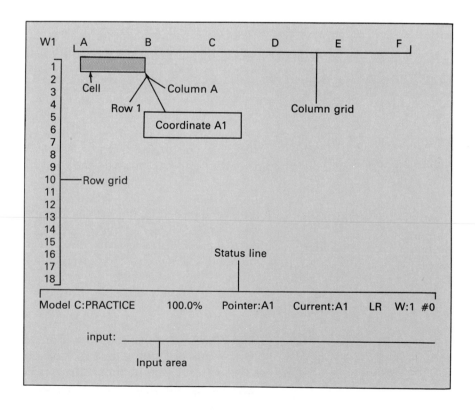

sometimes called the **active cell,** or the current cell. The cursor's size can change to reflect the width of the column it is marking.

Cursor movement is usually controlled by the arrow keys on the numeric keypad that is often located at the right-hand side of the keyboard. The cursor moves in the same direction as the arrow points. Faster movement can be accomplished by **scrolling,** a method of moving rapidly about the spreadsheet. By using various keys and key combinations, such as the Home, End, PgUp, PgDn, the user moves the cursor over larger distances quickly instead of one cell or row at a time. Another method of moving rapidly is **jumping,** where the user designates which cell is needed, and the cursor moves automatically to that page or cell coordinate.

Menus Lists of the actions or options from which the user can choose are called **menus.** Often, there are menus listed under menus because some spreadsheets have as many as two hundred or more commands from which to choose. Categories of commands are grouped together, and subcategories of similar commands are grouped under them. For example, a spreadsheet program may have a menu that contains a ''format'' command that, when selected, presents another menu that contains more explicit choices that can change how the contents of a cell are displayed.

Sometimes, menus are presented in windows that overlap the display screen; other times, menus are set up so the user makes a selection from a first menu found at the top of the screen, and another menu is ''pulled down'' over part of the display screen.

There are two major formats for menus: the one-letter menu and the keyword menu. The **one-letter menu** lists only the beginning letter of each command. This menu takes less space in the spreadsheet window; however, the user has to remember not only the word command that each abbreviation stands for, but also the action of each command (Figure 15–8a).

Another type of menu is the **keyword menu** where the whole word that represents the command is listed (Figure 15–8b). If the user doesn't remember that ''C'' means ''copy,'' seeing the word may be a prompt of the particular action represented.

The procedure for accessing and activating menus is different from program to program, but usually one of the function keys will display the various menus. Users generally select commands from menus by one of three methods: (a) using the arrow keys or mouse to move the cursor so that it highlights the desired command, then executing the command; (b) typing the first letter (or letters) of the command; or (c) pressing the appropriate function key or key combination.

Help Windows Most spreadsheet programs include **help windows** that contain lists of the keys and commands available at the time. Help windows are usually superimposed over the display screen and offer handy reminders of the steps required to perform particular operations.

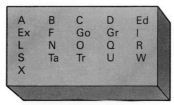

(a) One-letter menu

Spreadsheet Command Selection Menu

Auto	Blank	Copy	Delete	Edit	Exit/Save	Format
Goal_Seek	Graph	Insert	Locate	Name	Order	Query
Recalc	Setup	Table	Transfer	Update	Window	Xternal

⟨move keys⟩   ⟨edit⟩   ⟨print⟩   ⟨graph#⟩   ⟨query⟩   ⟨change⟩

(h) Keyword menu

FIGURE 15-8
(a) One-letter menu. (b) Keyword menu

Control Panel

The control panel is the area at the top or bottom of the screen that contains information about what is happening on the particular spreadsheet being worked on. A typical control panel includes a status line, a prompt line, and an entry line.

Status Line A **status line** may include information such as the spreadsheet modelname, the amount of available memory remaining, the position of the cursor, and the window name or number designation (Figure 15–9).

Prompt Line A **prompt line** generally has two major functions. The prompt may be posed as a question that requires a reply from the user, such as ''Do you want to quit without saving (Yes/No)?'' It could also be a line that describes a command or tells what options are available when using that command.

Input Line The **input line,** or entry line, is the place where data are keyed and held before they are recorded in a specific cell. The data can be edited before they are entered into the actual spreadsheet. Usually, a single keystroke moves the numbers from the input line to the spreadsheet.

Parts of a Spreadsheet Display

- Window/Screen
  - □ Coordinates
  - □ Cursor
  - □ Menus
  - □ Help windows
- Control Panel
  - □ Status line
  - □ Prompt line
  - □ Input/entry line

FEATURES OF A SPREADSHEET

Electronic spreadsheets have many features that make them more efficient and effective than paper spreadsheets. For example, portions of a spreadsheet can be quickly and easily moved or copied; mathematical formulas that are entered are calculated by the computer. Spreadsheet features allow

FIGURE 15–9
Some items that may be found on a status line

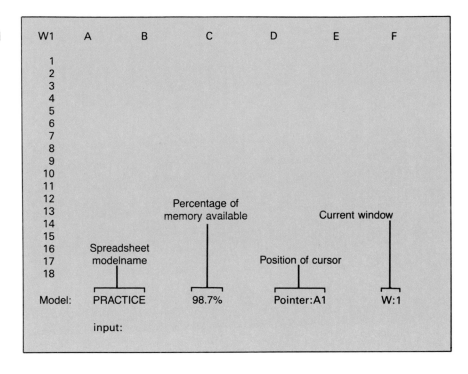

the user to present and manipulate values in many ways. Some common features found in spreadsheet programs are discussed in this section.

Loading, Saving, and Exiting a Spreadsheet

The load feature of a spreadsheet accesses an existing spreadsheet (file) that has been saved on a disk. The usual method is to activate the load command or its equivalent, and enter the desired spreadsheet modelname.

The save feature stores a spreadsheet that the user creates on a disk. The user can then recall the file back into computer memory at a later time and continue working or editing that particular spreadsheet.

The exit feature allows the user to quit working on a particular spreadsheet without saving it. An existing spreadsheet can be loaded and changed to answer various "what if" questions and then exited without overriding the original data that were stored on the spreadsheet. However, some programs automatically save programs as they exit. If this happens, the changes that are made to answer the "what if" questions are saved, and the original spreadsheet is permanently altered.

Password Protection

Unless the exact **password**—a letter, number, or combination of both—is used, access to a password-protected spreadsheet is not possible.

Modes

Spreadsheet programs have two modes of operation: (a) a command (or menu) mode; or (b) a ready/entry mode.

Command Mode   When the spreadsheet is in the **command mode,** the user is offered menus from which to make command selections. Usually, this is done by moving the cursor to the selection and highlighting it. Some commands may be invoked by various keys or key combinations.

Most spreadsheets offer multiple levels of command menus to accommodate the wide variety of selections. Many keys have more than one function assigned to them. A key used alone accesses one function, e.g., making a copy. But the same key, used in conjunction with the <SHIFT> key, offers a second function, perhaps creating a new window; and used with still another key, such as the <CTRL> key, it provides even a third function, perhaps editing the spreadsheet.

Ready/Entry Mode   The **ready/entry mode** indicates that the program is ready for the user to enter data. The program automatically shifts from the ready mode to the entry mode as soon as the first character is typed.

There are different types of data that can be entered into the cells; the user may have to specify what type of data is being entered, because the computer views entries based on identifying characteristics. The two types of entries are: (a) labels, which are nonnumeric data; and (b) values, which are numeric data and can include both constants and formulas.

Labels   A **label** is typed text used to identify various aspects of the spreadsheet. For example, a label placed at the top identifying the contents of a spreadsheet might appear like this:

Bookcase Company
Profit and Loss Statement
for the period January to March

Other entries that would need labels include the columnar or row headings and any other words or text necessary to identify or clarify the spreadsheet information. Some programs automatically recognize as a label any entry that begins with an alphabetic character or certain special characters. If a label is to begin with numbers or other special characters that normally indicate a value, specific keystrokes are required to tell the computer that the entry is a label. Lotus 1-2-3, the popular spreadsheet program developed by Lotus Development Corporation, uses an apostrophe (') to identify an entry as a label.

Many programs include an **automatic spillover** option so that if the cell label is too long and does not fit the column width, the text continues on, or spills over, into the next cell.

Spreadsheet Entries

- Labels
- Values
  - ☐ Constants
  - ☐ Formulas

Values After the spreadsheet labels are entered, the **values,** both constants and formulas, are inserted. **Formulas** are the mathematical equations for the spreadsheet program to add, subtract, multiply, and divide combinations of cells. Built-in functions, such as SUM, SIN, and MAX, can also be used in formulas, i.e., the program can automatically total, find the sine, and determine the maximum value in a list of numbers. (More discussion on built-in functions appears later in the chapter.)

Formulas must be defined as value cells only; any cell with a label designation cannot be used for a formula. Some formulas may begin with a function, such as the word SUM, or with a cell reference, such as D6. In order to identify them as values and not as labels, a special character entry is usually required. The plus (+) sign character is a common example used to indicate that the entry that follows is a value and not a label. The spreadsheet in Figure 15–10 has the individual entries identified.

The basic mathematical operators used by most spreadsheets are represented as follows: * indicates multiplication; / indicates division; + indicates addition; − indicates subtraction.

Most spreadsheet programs solve the formulas that are entered using the normal order of mathematical operations. That is, they assume that multiplication and division are to be done before addition and subtraction, and that operations enclosed in parentheses are done first.

Some spreadsheets may be programmed to read and solve equations left to right. This procedure would affect how formulas are entered. Therefore, it is important to know which method your program uses, because answers can vary drastically depending on the method of solution.

As an example, use the simple formula $10 + 10/2$. If the rules of the normal order of operation were followed, the division operation would be performed first, then the addition; the answer would be 15. But, if this equation were solved from left to right, the addition operation would be performed first, then the division; the answer would be 10.

In Figure 15–10c, the formula $+B15 + C15 + D15$ is shown for cell D17. The computer understands that the entry in that cell is the sum total of those cells. Therefore, $8,064.00 appears in the cell, but the formula (not the total) for the cell entry is shown above the input line. The computer completes the calculation and enters the result where specified. Remember, formulas cannot include cell references that contain labels. Also, it is necessary to indicate that the entry in Cell D17 is a formula by preceding it with the appropriate keystrokes (in this case a + sign).

Some programs will allow the user to toggle, or switch, between label and value entries just by using certain keys. This option is handy when a number such as a date or address needs to be entered and recognized as a label. For instance, the numbers in the year 1990, street addresses, and zip codes would ordinarily be construed as values because they begin with numbers. These entries would have to be specifically identified as labels, or the computer would recognize them as values.

Built-in Functions

Most spreadsheets have **built-in functions** where formulas to certain problems have already been created and stored in the program. These

FIGURE 15–10
The cursor on the screen is positioned to show: (a) an example of a text entry; (b) an example of a number entry; and (c) an example of a formula entry.

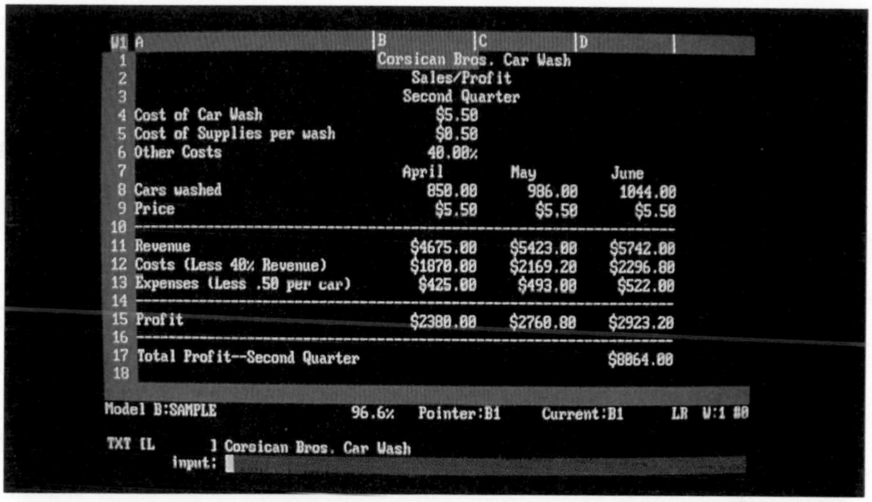

(a)

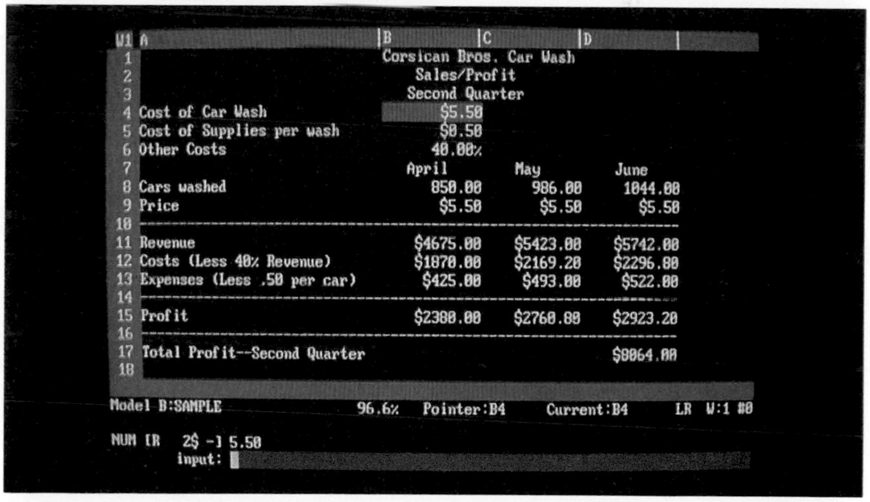

(b)

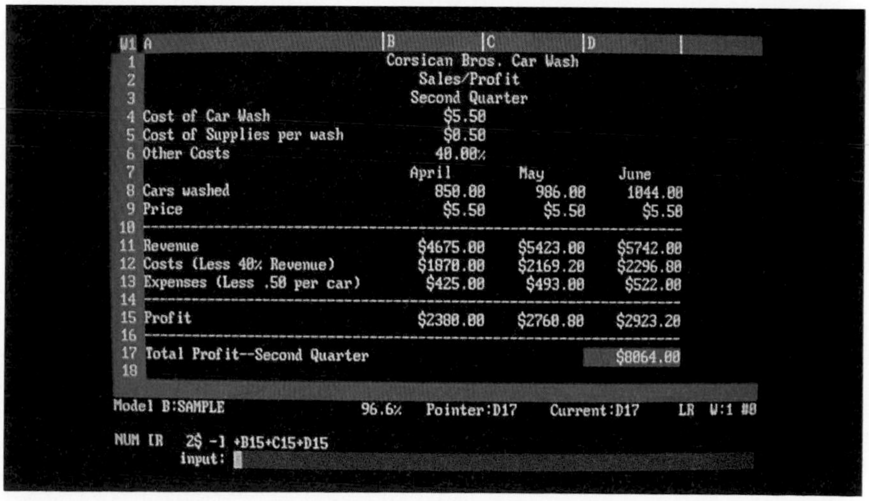

(c)

functions provide shortcuts for many common tasks. Typically they include

☐ Mathematical function—performs a mathematical transformation on a single value and returns a single value (For example, a SQRT(x) determines the square root of a value.)

☐ Statistical function—accepts a list of values and provides summary statistics about those values (For example, an average function returns the average value from a list.)

☐ Financial function—calculates the effect of interest rates on sums of money over time (For example, a payment function calculates the payment that will pay off the principal of a loan borrowed at the specified interest rate after the specified number of payments have been made.)

☐ Date function—calculates with dates and times (For example, it can automatically enter the date and time in a report.)

☐ String function—performs operations on text (For example, a length function indicates the number of characters in a string.)

☐ Logical function—tests the condition of cells or performs comparisons to determine what value should be entered in a cell (For example, an IF function enters one value in the cell if the condition is true and another value in the cell if the condition is false.)

☐ Table function—retrieves an entry from a table (For example, a "value look-up" function can search an income tax table that has been entered into the spreadsheet to find a specific number.)

Most spreadsheets have dozens of built-in functions. The actual name of a particular function varies from program to program. The spreadsheet reference manual provides details of the functions offered by that spreadsheet.

Editing

Editing is the means by which typographical errors, wrong values, or erroneous formulas can be corrected. It is just such editing chores done on a paper spreadsheet that can cause the accountant headaches. Errors found before they have been entered to the spreadsheet can be edited first on the screen simply by making the corrections on the input/entry line. But, if the entry has already been recorded on the spreadsheet, most programs offer an "Edit" command menu choice so that corrections can be made.

Designating a Range of Cells

Designating a **range of cells** is a method of selecting specific cells. The range can consist of one cell or a large portion of the spreadsheet; that cell, or cells, can be copied, moved, deleted, saved, printed, or otherwise treated as a unit. This feature is a time-saving device when the spreadsheet is large.

Although programs vary, the usual way to identify a range of cells is to type the coordinates of the upper-left cell first; then a delimiter (usually two periods or a colon), followed by the coordinates of the lower-right cell. For example, if a column of numbers starting at C1 and continuing through to C200 needs to be added, entering the range of cells saves the drudgery of keying each separate row's cell label under column C. Merely keying SUM C1..C200 (or a similar formula, in most cases) tells the computer to give the total of the entries in that column.

Naming Cells

A single cell, or even a range of cells, can be named for ease in identification. Going back to Figure 15–10b, the cell containing the cost of the car wash could be named COST. Then, the formula at Cell C11 for finding how much revenue was made could be stated as +350 * COST.

Names can be added, revised, and even deleted if they are no longer useful. In large spreadsheets, identifying various ranges by name can speed up the process of moving from one portion of the spreadsheet to another. The user specifies the name of the cell or range of cells, and the program jumps directly to that area. Most programs require special keystrokes before accepting the typed name.

Moving

The move feature allows the user to reposition the contents of individual cells or ranges of cells from one location to another. With this feature, the appearance or layout of the spreadsheet can be redesigned. When a range of cells is moved, any formula in the spreadsheet that will be affected by the move must be corrected. For example, if the contents of Cell B2 is moved to Cell B10, and the formula in Cell E2 is 2 * B2, then the formula in Cell E2 will have to be edited to be 2 * B10 to obtain the same results.

Copying

The copy feature selects an existing cell or range of cells and replicates them in other cells of the worksheet. To copy labels or numbers, the user simply identifies both the range of cells to be copied and the range of cells into which they are to be copied.

Copying formulas is a bit more involved. Sometimes, a user wants exactly the same formula using exactly the same cell references in both places. In this case, the computer must be instructed to copy the formula using **absolute cell reference.** For example, if the formula in Cell D1 (Figure 15–11a) is copied to Cell D2 using absolute cell reference, it will appear exactly the same and will evaluate in both cases to 10.

Usually, however, the user wants a similar calculation, but different cell references. Then, the computer is instructed to copy the formula using relative cell references. For example, if the formula in Cell D1 (Figure 15–11b) is copied to Cell D2 using **relative cell reference,** it would change to B2 + C2 and evaluate to 6.

There may also be times when a user wants some references in the same formula to be relative and others to be absolute. In this case, the

FIGURE 15-11
Cell references: (a) absolute; (b) relative; and (c) mixed.

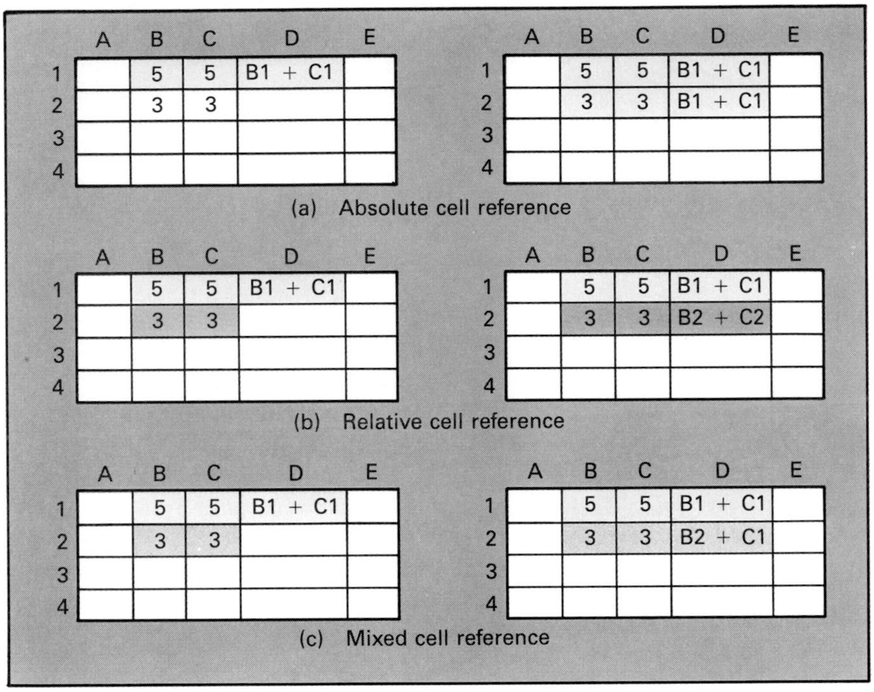

(a) Absolute cell reference

(b) Relative cell reference

(c) Mixed cell reference

computer is instructed to copy the formula using **mixed cell reference.** Either absolute or relative is specified for each cell reference. For example, if the formula in Cell D1 (Figure 15–11c) is copied to Cell D2 using relative cell reference for Cell B1 and absolute cell reference for Cell C1, the formula in Cell D2 will be B2 + C1 and evaluate to 8.

Formatting

The **formatting** process includes various instructions and techniques that change how the contents of a cell are displayed. Format changes can be made in one of two ways: (a) globally, which affects the entire worksheet; or (b) individually, which affects an individual cell or range of cells.

Attributes The characteristics or formatting commands that are available in most spreadsheets are called **attributes.** Attribute commands can

☐ Change column widths
☐ Set precision of numbers (the number of decimal places)
☐ Set justification (usually left, centered, or right)
☐ Determine number formats (how the number will appear). Some common number format choices are shown in Table 15–1.
☐ Establish character attributes (boldface, underline, italics)
☐ Set data types (text or value)
☐ Change appearance of negative values (appear in parentheses; preceded by DB (debit) or preceded by CR (credit); or appear in red)

TABLE 15–1
Common number format
choices

Integer—whole number
Dollar—dollar ($) sign and two decimal places
Floating point—decimal point followed by specified number of places
Exponential—scientific notation
Commas—numbers displayed with commas
Leading $—leading dollar ($) sign placed before any other format
Percent—displayed using a percent (%) sign
Foreign currency—displayed using foreign currency symbol, such as DM for deutsch marks (German money)

- ☐ Lock cells (prevent cell entries from being changed)
- ☐ Hide cells (the contents of the cell are not displayed on screen)

There are many other formatting features. One is the insertion of blank rows and columns creating readability. They can be used to separate headings from numbers in the spreadsheet. Underlines or other characters can also be inserted by creating a blank row and using a repeating label to insert a line or column width of a specified character.

Figure 15–12 shows how a spreadsheet can look before formatting. Figure 15–13 shows that the same spreadsheet is more readable and easier to interpret after formatting.

Titles   The **titles** feature freezes row or column headings so that they stay in the window when the rest of the worksheet is scrolled. This feature is especially helpful when there are many rows and columns of numbers that the user must scroll through and review. If the titles scroll off the window, it is difficult to remember what the numbers represent. However, the titles command freezes the titles and they remain on the screen so the data can be identified no matter what row or column of the worksheet you are in.

Revising

Once the spreadsheet has been formatted properly and meets the approval of the user, no doubt someone will pose some interesting, thought-provoking questions, such as: What if we don't wash that many cars? Or, what if the price of car wax increases? Or, what if we give all the employees a bonus? So, is it back to square 1, or is that Cell A1? No, the spreadsheet includes the capability of **spreadsheet analysis,** a process whereby these "what if" questions can be answered relatively simply. The existing spreadsheet is copied with the necessary cells being revised to answer the queries; then the calculations are made on the newly copied spreadsheet. The questions are answered in minutes instead of days.

Recalculating

Some spreadsheets automatically recalculate the totals over the entire worksheet after a new figure is entered; others require a special menu selection (sometimes called manual recalculation) where the user is given the choice of recalculating the entire spreadsheet or only the affected row or column.

Backup

It's always wise to have a backup copy of a spreadsheet made so that a day's input of valuable data is not lost. The purpose of the backup func-

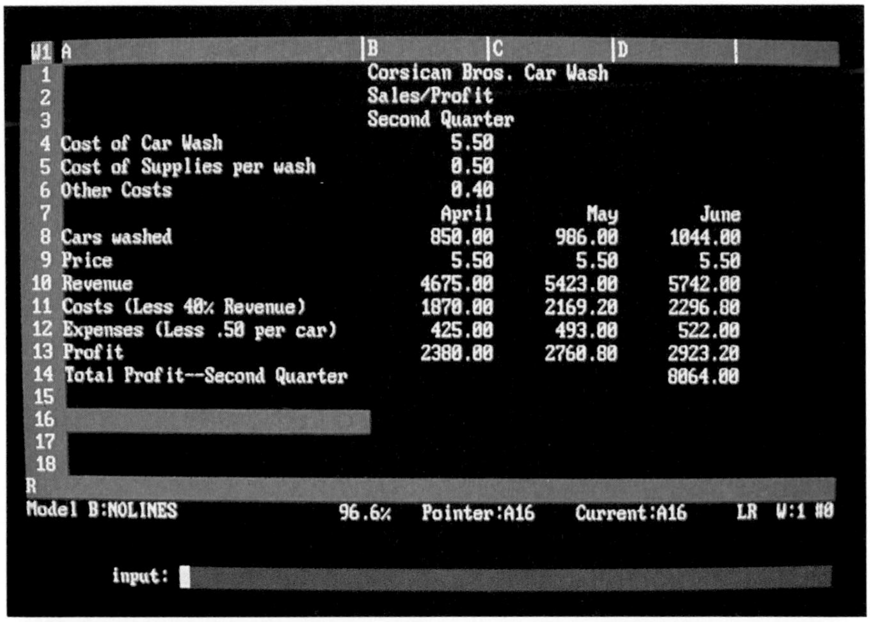

FIGURE 15–12

A spreadsheet before formatting

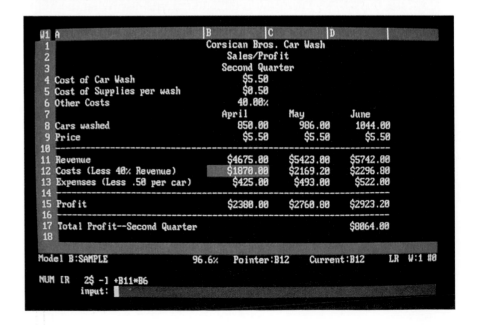

FIGURE 15–13

A spreadsheet after formatting

HIGHLIGHT

COMPUTING INCOME TAXES

Those who look for a bright spot when it comes time to prepare their income tax forms may find one in the wide variety of tax-calculation computer programs available. While the costs can run from $80 to $350 or more for the programs, users find them preferable and safer than the tax-preparation guides in book form.

A big boost for these programs came as the result of the much-revised federal tax law that went into effect in 1987. Supporters of the law argued that it would simplify computing one's own tax returns, but it did quite the reverse for most people.

One popular program, the HowardSoft Tax Preparer, allows for the insertion of new numbers during the calculation's final stages and can automatically print twenty-two forms and schedules that are acceptable to the Internal Revenue Service.

tion is to make a copy of the existing model. However, in some spreadsheets, a backup is saved on the disk in a condensed form and cannot be directly reloaded into memory as a working copy. In this case, there is a utility program available that expands the condensed backup file so that it can be used if needed.

Macros

The user may need to execute the same sequence of keystrokes or commands repeatedly throughout work on a spreadsheet. To automatically repeat the commands, most spreadsheet programs use a macro. A **macro** is a file that contains a group of commands; it tells the program that a previously created series of keystrokes or commands are to be executed. Using macros can increase the speed and efficiency of making entries on a spreadsheet.

Two common ways for users to create macros are: (a) using a macro "editor;" or (b) using a macro "recording function." With a macro editor, the user types the instructions, keystrokes, and commands into a file, names the file, and later accesses that file to repeat those commands whenever they are required. With the recording function, a macro can be created and saved by recording the user's keystrokes and commands as the actions are actually performed. This macro is also identified with a name and can later be accessed so the saved actions can be executed.

Printing

Printing the spreadsheet produces a hard, or paper, copy. Usually a special print menu is accessed and the size of paper, number of copies, and margin parameters are designated. The row and column grid designations can be deleted at this point to give the printed spreadsheet a more formal appearance. Some programs can show more columns by printing the spreadsheet sideways.

Sorting

Many spreadsheets can sort data by rows or columns, alphabetically or numerically. This feature usually gives many choices, allowing the user to search for specific numbers or labels, and also arranging the spreadsheet in date order or ascending or descending dollar amounts.

Graphing

The data entered and saved in a spreadsheet can serve as the basis for generating graphics, pictorial representations such as pie charts, line charts and bar charts, of data in the spreadsheet. (Chapter 16 contains more information on graphics.)

SUMMARY

A spreadsheet is a paper tool on which to keep track of and manipulate numbers. An electronic spreadsheet uses a computer and special software to do the same manipulations. A blank spreadsheet is called a worksheet.

Businesses use spreadsheets to keep track of information including sales, expenses, costs, inventory, and profits or losses. Home uses of spreadsheets include: tracking cash flow; preparing budgets; and figuring taxes.

A spreadsheet application is appropriate if the problem can be stated in a mathematical format, and if the problem is to be repeated, edited, revised, made up of both variable and fixed data, and required to be neat and legible.

Creating a template, or blank form, that contains repetitious formats can save time for the user.

The spreadsheet display on a computer monitor includes: the window, where the entries are displayed; and the control panel, where miscellaneous information about the spreadsheet is displayed. The control panel visually reports what is happening on a given spreadsheet. It contains the status line, prompt line, and an input or entry line.

The numbers down the left side are the row grid and the alphabetic characters across the top are the column grid. At the intersection of an imaginary line drawn from these grids lies the coordinate, or the address of a point on the spreadsheet. The box formed is called a cell, the place where information is entered. The cursor is a designation on the screen that identifies the cell that is available for use. That cell is called the active cell, or the current cell.

Scrolling either from top to bottom or left to right is a way to rapidly move the cursor around the spreadsheet.

Menus are presented on the screen as ''pull-down'' menus or windows with one-letter menus or keyword menus.

A spreadsheet has two modes of operation: command mode, where the action choices are listed; and the ready/entry mode, where the program is ready for the user to move the cursor and begin making entries.

There are two types of entries from which to choose: (a) labels are nonnumeric, or typed text; and (b) values are numeric data and include constants and formulas. Spreadsheets can complete mathematical equations using the values from various value cells.

Formulas that are created can be copied to other cells, but then they must be referenced in one of three ways: absolute cell reference; relative cell reference; or mixed cell reference. Spreadsheets contain built-in functions where formulas have been stored in the program; these include mathematical, statistical, financial, date, string, logical, and table functions. Most spreadsheets have dozens of built-in functions that offer shortcuts; users do not have to write formulas for these built-in functions.

Spreadsheets can be edited, thereby correcting typographical errors and wrong values. A range of cells can be selected to be edited or acted upon; it may be one cell or an entire portion of the spreadsheet. A cell or a range of cells can be named for ease in identification, moved from one place on the spreadsheet to another, or even copied.

Spreadsheets can be formatted to create a pleasing appearance, revised to analyze "what if" questions, copied for backup or other uses, recalculated when new values are inserted, and printed.

Spreadsheet data are used with graphics software to create pie, line, and bar charts for visual displays.

Key Terms

absolute cell reference (p. 439)

active cell (p. 432)

attributes (p. 440)

automatic spillover (p. 435)

built-in functions (p. 436)

cell (p. 430)

column (p. 430)

command mode (p. 435)

control panel (p. 430)

coordinate (p. 430)

cursor (p. 430)

editing (p. 438)

electronic spreadsheet (p. 424)

formatting (p. 440)

formulas (p. 436)

help window (p. 432)

input line (p. 433)

jumping (p. 432)

keyword menu (p. 432)

label (p. 435)

macro (p. 443)

menu (p. 432)

mixed cell reference (p. 440)

modelname (p. 430)

one-letter menu (p. 432)

password (p. 434)

prompt line (p. 433)

range of cells (p. 438)

ready/entry mode (p. 435)

relative cell reference (p. 439)

row (p. 430)

scrolling (p. 432)

spreadsheet (p. 424)

spreadsheet analysis (p. 441)

status line (p. 433)

template (p. 428)

titles (p. 441)

values (p. 436)

window (p. 430)

worksheet (p. 430)

Review Questions

1. Define the terms worksheet and modelname.
2. What are the advantages of an electronic spreadsheet?
3. Describe the spreadsheet grid.
4. How are a cell's coordinates derived?
5. What is an active cell?
6. Describe the differences between one-letter and keyword menus.
7. What information might be contained in a control panel?
8. What is a template and how might it be used?
9. Describe the advantages of being able to pose "what if" questions within an electronic spreadsheet.
10. Describe the two modes of operation in a spreadsheet.
11. What types of entries can be made in a spreadsheet?
12. What is the order of mathematical operations?
13. Explain why knowing the order of operations is critical.
14. Give examples of built-in functions.
15. What is meant by the term "range of cells"?
16. List some of the formatting attributes.
17. Tell why a spreadsheet would be formatted.
18. What is a window and what information might be found there?
19. Explain the different ways that a cursor can be moved around the screen.
20. Explain the function of the titles feature.
21. Describe the three types of cell references that can be used when copying formulas.
22. Name the three ways commands can be selected from menus.
23. What is the purpose of a help window?
24. List ways that businesses use spreadsheets.
25. Give examples of ways that spreadsheet packages could help an individual.

INFOMODULE
Computers in Business

Business applications for computers continue to proliferate as more and more business people recognize the advantages of having computers do a wide variety of tasks for them. Historically, computerization for most businesses has meant the purchase of a mainframe or minicomputer and expensive application software. However, as microcomputer prices go lower, their power increases, and more and better software packages become available, even small businesses can afford to computerize their operations. Special packages have been created for groups with large and complex requirements, such as the federal government's Internal Revenue Service. But the local department store can also purchase an accounting package to organize accounts, run the payroll, control inventory, and act as a sales representative.

As computers become increasingly prevalent, people in all areas of business are learning how to use them. This section describes some of the business applications for which computers are used.

ACCOUNTING

Accounting lends itself to computerization readily because many of the functions are repetitive and require the accuracy and speed that the computer gives.

Spreadsheets

Spreadsheets are one of the best known business uses for a computer, and the computer can easily manipulate and keep track of the entries. The electronic spreadsheet has replaced the cumbersome paper spreadsheet in many businesses.

Payroll

Payroll applications are an efficient use of the computer's ability to accomplish repetitive tasks

quickly. A payroll package automatically calculates gross pay, adds any bonuses, subtracts the necessary deductions, totals the net pay, and even prepares the paycheck for each employee.

According to the Charles Babbage Institute at the University of Minnesota, the first computerized payroll was processed in 1954 for the General Electric Company in Louisville, Kentucky, by a UNIVAC computer. Today, payroll processing has become a separate industry, growing at an annual rate of 25 percent. In 1985 alone, one large payroll company, Automatic Data Processing, Inc., processed one in every twelve paychecks issued in the United States—a total of 378 million paychecks.

Job-cost Analysis

Some payroll packages offer a job-cost analysis capability. This function allocates payroll costs to specific projects and helps keep a close watch on how much time and money are being spent on each project.

General Ledger

A general ledger contains a set of all the accounts for a particular business. These may include

- [ ] Accounts payable—the amounts that must be paid to creditors for items purchased
- [ ] Accounts receivable—the amounts that are owed by customers from credit transactions
- [ ] Expense accounts—the amounts that are owed for other expenses, including utilities, loans, and bad debts (those that will never be paid)

General-ledger software can usually generate bills or statements of accounts from the data contained in the accounts-payable files. All the expenses of the company can be accumulated from the individual accounts, and the income totalled from all the revenue accounts to give

Individual service station managers send day-to-day operating data directly to Shell Oil data processing headquarters.

the overall income picture—profit or loss—for the company.

Reporting

Tax-reporting regulations specify different reports and different filing dates for businesses, depending on the amount of the total payroll. Monthly, weekly, or less frequent tax deposits may be required. The government also requires

that the employer accumulate and pay Social Security, federal, state, and local taxes quarterly. All in all, it can be a complicated procedure to record and report all this information to the proper agencies at the appropriate times.

One of the benefits of a payroll accounting package is the ability of the software to accumulate the various tax totals. Some even provide copies of the reports that various government agencies require. Comprehensive periodic,

FIGURE 1
A bank teller's computer terminal and printer are linked to the bank's mainframe computer to process customer transactions.

Computerized Accounting Functions

- Spreadsheet
- Payroll
- Job-cost analysis
- General ledger
- Other reports and filings

---

quarterly, or year-end reports can be generated to advise management of payroll expenses and tax consequences on a regular basis.

BANKING

Banking is yet another type of business application that benefits from computerization because of the repetitiveness of the transactions, the accuracy required, and the speed required to handle the great volume of daily transactions. Each teller station has a terminal and operates on-line when accessing accounts to cash checks or make deposits (Figure 1).

Most banks and branch offices also have installed automated teller machines that dispense set amounts of cash (Figure 2).

Home banking is an option provided by some banks for customers who have personal computers with modems or touch-tone telephones and special home-banking devices. Banking transactions are entered through the microcomputer or telephone keypad by pressing keys for the account number, choosing the appropriate function, and receiving confirmation of the process.

There are those who suggest that **electronic funds transfer (EFT)** is the ultimate solution to fast money transactions. EFT is a computerized method of transferring funds from one account to another. SmartCard International, Casio Microcard Corporation, and Micro Card Technologies, Inc., have designed microchip credit cards that resemble a conventional plastic credit card. These "smart" cards contain microprocessors with programmable functions. They even have a memory capability, so that as purchases are made, the appropriate deductions are also

FIGURE 2
Automated teller machines are linked to the bank's mainframes and offer individuals easy and convenient access to their bank accounts. (Courtesy of Diebold, Inc.)

made. No money is physically involved, and no checks are used. The funds are electronically deducted from the purchaser's bank account and added to the merchant's account.

INVESTING

People who invest in the stock market need current information about the financial condition of their investments. The Dow Jones News Retrieval is one of many electronic information services offered to give traders the instant financial data they need for making decisions on stock trading. Other services include Standard and Poor's Compustat, Wharton's Econometric, and Data Resources, Inc., (DRI).

Computers keep track of the stocks being traded on the floor of the New York Stock Exchange. The average volume of shares traded daily is 140 million. The older ticker-tape machines would be hard-pressed to keep up with the hundreds of thousands of trades handled daily. In 1975, the Designated Order Turnaround (DOT) system was implemented to handle orders. Although some transactions are still completed by specialists, the turnaround time for a market order processed by a computer is approximately 75 seconds. Many brokers keep their clients' portfolios up-to-date with computers.

SALES

The area of retail sales includes many repetitive transactions that lend themselves to computer technology. Although each sale is different, the basic recording process remains the same.

Remember learning about source data and scanners in Chapter 3. You have no doubt seen source-data input in action in a supermarket where a POS terminal is used. Scanners were first used in Kroger supermarkets in Cincinnati, Ohio, in the early 1970s. The A. C. Nielsen polls predict that by 1989, scanner-equipped stores will account for 62 percent of commodity sales (Figure 3).

FIGURE 3
Many businesses, including grocery stores, are automating inventory using handheld computerized input devices. These devices store information read from the bar codes on each product. These data can later be entered directly into the main computer system. (Courtesy of Albertson's, Inc.)

Handheld computers are used by salespeople who are frequently on the road. As each order is solicited, the salesperson enters the pertinent data concerning the sale, checks available inventory, specifies an expected delivery date, and at the same time updates the sales manager's weekly report.

Other computer sales terminals include such one-stop shopping marvels as The Shopping Machine ™ and Touch 'n' Save ™. These devices, sometimes called transaction terminals, are usually placed in a kiosk in a mall or other store. They contain electronic catalogs where as many as 54,000 frames of merchandise can be viewed. Some terminals use touch screens to help shoppers search the on-line data base for a specific product. Credit-card customers place orders at machines that are equipped with readers that scan the metallic strip on the back of the card gleaning information about the card holder.

Computers also spur sales by simulating products and services. In L. S. Ayres & Company's department stores in the midwest, customers can try on ten different clothing ensembles a minute. A leased system called a Magic Mirror ™ programmed with the Liz Claiborne spring collection was tried at three Ayres stores. While standing in front of the mirror, the customer sees her face, but the computer projects a comparable body image with as many different outfits as the customer wants to try. The simulation concept proved to be quite a sales representative, because Claiborne's sales increased over 700 percent in one week.

Customers can also try new hair colors and styles without worrying about how long it will take for hair length or color to grow back (Figure 4).

INVENTORY AND QUALITY CONTROL

One of the benefits of using a computer is to generate reports quickly and easily, giving the merchant the most up-to-date picture of sales (Figure 5).

Many inventory-control programs used in retailing automatically generate purchase orders to

The New York Stock Exchange is a busy place where trade decisions must be based on the most current data available. Computers play an important part in furnishing stock brokers with the latest stock prices. This broker informs his client of late-breaking developments from data displayed on the screen in his office. (Preston Lyon/Index Stock, Inc. Inset: Merrill Publishing/Cobalt Productions)

FIGURE 4
Representatives of Clairol use a computerized system that produces an image of the client. This image can then be modified to show the client how she would look with different combinations of makeup or hairstyles and colors without actually having to try them. The consumer can then use this information to choose the style she prefers. (Courtesy of Clairol, Inc.)

FIGURE 5

This waitress entered her customer's order at a central computer terminal that directed the order to one of three kitchens. Here, she picks up a meal while the cook checks an incoming order. The data stored in the computer are used to monitor and control inventory.

At Burlington Industries, Inc., computers help create textile designs and control the equipment that produces the textiles. Here, engineers design new textile plants. (Courtesy of Burlington Industries, Inc.)

reorder stock as soon as the supply on hand is reduced below a specified level. The supplier's computerized system takes the order, prepares an invoice and shipping label, and appropriately reduces the inventory record of the products shipped.

At J. P. Stevens, a large textile company, microcomputers are used for quality control. Handheld computers check for inferior quality by grading the cloth as it comes off the weaving looms. This type of product control means that substandard goods can be identified. The company also uses computers to create the textile designs and graphics, schedule maintenance of the plant and equipment, and function in the more traditional budgeting and planning areas.

PROJECT MANAGEMENT

Project management software is used with computers to plan, track, and analyze complex projects in professions as diversified as marketing, construction, or running a bakery. Project management software can coordinate all the timing and resources of a variety of projects. The project manager, or person in charge of coordinating the entire project, can establish budgets, arrange schedules, and plan pricing strategy by accumulating data and having all the facts on which to base the total project's plans. Some programs are similar to spreadsheets in that changing delivery dates and times in one column will also change the dates and times of scheduled activities in the other affected columns. In the construction industry, for example, painters can't begin until plumbers, electricians, finish carpenters, and masons have completed their work. Therefore, scheduling painters would be one of the last items on the lists of things to be done.

Like many small businesses, Beth's Bakery uses a microcomputer and project management software to plan production of baked goods and to track sales. By graphing sales of previous weeks, decisions are made on the volume of any baked goods needed for a particular day of the week. A printout tells Beth how many batches to make, how many people should be scheduled to work, and how long it will take the

crew to meet the day's quota. After sales due to a special promotion, a graph showed an increase in sales volume, but then sales dropped dramatically; people were buying a lot of items on the sale day and apparently not coming back until the next sale day. Beth's Bakery developed a new pricing strategy that reduced prices and spread sales more evenly. Many businesses are using microcomputers for managing their operations (Figure 6).

MARKETING

Computers are widely used in marketing operations where they create form letters, generate and analyze market surveys, prepare invoices, process mail orders, and verify status of orders. Computers can also help managers analyze markets and sales and plan marketing strategies. Sales people can be provided with computer-analyzed information about their customers, such as what kinds of products they buy, when they tend to place their largest orders, and

FIGURE 6
Many small businesses such as this veterinarian's office use a computer to manage an otherwise overwhelming amount of records.

FIGURE 7
Advertising executives use a microcomputer to help them write copy for advertisements and to analyze the effectiveness of an advertising campaign. (Courtesy of Hewlett-Packard Co.)

whether orders are influenced by sale price promotions. Reports can also be created that indicate exactly how well or poorly specific products sell in certain areas; other reports can show each salesperson's bottom-line totals.

Advertising

The purpose of advertising is to sell a product or service. With computers, advertising professionals create art and graphics displays, write and revise copy, and print and disseminate ads with the goal of selling more products (Figure 7).

Telemarketing

Telemarketing involves ways to reach previously untapped markets, and it has proved to be very successful. Sales calls to new customers can cost anywhere from $100 to $200 per visit, depending on the product, company, travel time, and other variables. More recently, telemarketing personnel use the telephone and a computer system to make initial contacts. You may have received computerized sales calls on the telephone. In this kind of call, a computer and modem work together, dialing a series of telephone numbers. When the person answers the phone, a prerecorded message plays. The person may be asked to respond to a questionnaire or sign up for the particular service.

We've seen that computers have become an integral part of most businesses today. As old software is improved and new packages are developed, it's pretty safe to assume that making a computer a business partner is a pretty smart decision.

KEY TERMS

electronic funds transfer (EFT) (p. 449)

telemarketing (p. 454)

QUESTIONS

1. List three accounting functions and explain the benefits of computerizing them.
2. Describe several ways in which computers are used in banking.
3. Explain some ways in which computers are used in sales.
4. Describe how computers are being used to control inventory or monitor quality control.
5. Describe how advertising and marketing departments could use computers.

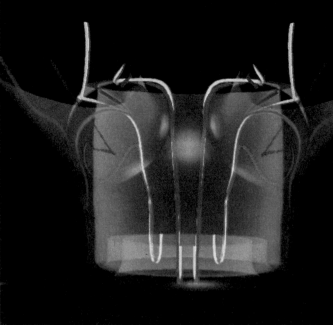

OBJECTIVES

☐ Explain the purpose of a graphics package and distinguish between text and high-resolution graphics

☐ List three basic types of graphics packages and where each might be used

☐ Identify and discuss some common features of graphics packages

☐ List several factors involved in creating presentation-quality business and analytical graphs

☐ Define the purpose of a communication package

☐ Identify several uses of communication packages

☐ List and define several common features of communication packages

OUTLINE

GRAPHICS PACKAGES

COMPONENTS OF A COMPUTER SYSTEM USING GRAPHICS

APPLICATIONS OF GRAPHICS PACKAGES

GRAPHICS PACKAGE FEATURES

CREATING BUSINESS AND ANALYTICAL GRAPHS

COMMUNICATION PACKAGES

COMPONENTS OF A COMPUTER SYSTEM USING A COMMUNICATION PACKAGE

APPLICATIONS OF COMMUNICATION PACKAGES

FEATURES OF COMMUNICATION PACKAGES

INFOMODULE: Electronic Networks

BULLETIN BOARDS

ELECTRONIC MAIL

TELECONFERENCING

INFORMATION SERVICES

COMMERCIAL DATA-BASE SERVICES

GATEWAY SERVICES

VIDEOTEXT

16

Graphics and Communication Packages

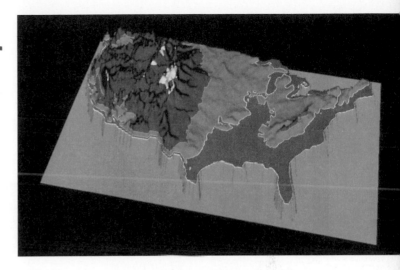

PROFILE:

Augusta Ada, Countess of Lovelace

She was the daughter of an immortal poet who found her own immortality in the precise beauty of mathematics. While it was a long time before she was suitably recognized, her effect on the world has been as profound as that of her famous father, the dashing poet, Lord Byron. Augusta was born to Lord Byron and Annabella Milbanke in 1815. Within weeks after her birth, Byron left his family, never to see his daughter again. He died when she was eight years old.

Augusta Ada—later the Countess of Lovelace—showed an early talent and inclination toward mathematics, traits her mother encouraged and supported. She also became, while still quite young, an accomplished linguist and musician.

Because of her facility with languages, Augusta took the job of translating, from Italian into English, Count Luigi Frederico Menabrea's article on an "analytical engine," a forerunner of the computer, developed by Englishman Charles Babbage. But she did more than translate the treatise; she added her own notes and observations about the device and the theories behind them. She actually worked out most of the theoretical principles and the programming behind Babbage's analytical engine.

No doubt, her commentaries on the Menabrea article were enlivened by the fact that Babbage had once invited Augusta and her mother to see his invention. Augusta was wholly impressed by the device, and subsequently she and Babbage became friends.

In 1852, the Countess died. By then she had established her name as a mathematical scholar, and one who at least glimpsed the horizons her studies had pointed toward. She has since been given the title of the "first programmer;" and as recognition of her efforts and insights, the United States Department of Defense has named its most complex and far-reaching computer language "Ada."

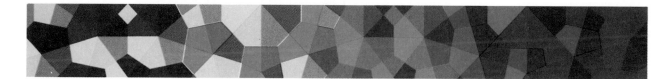

G raphics and communications are two of the fastest growing areas of microcomputer applications. Artists and graphic designers use microcomputers to create graphic images and pictures; engineers and architects use them to design products and structures; and business executives use them to prepare graphs and charts for business meetings.

Because of its ability to communicate and share data with other computers, the microcomputer has become an important tool for research, data gathering, and information exchange. This chapter examines aspects of both graphics packages and communication packages for microcomputers.

GRAPHICS PACKAGES

Artists and graphic designers have traditionally used brushes, paints, pens, ink, and drawing boards to produce images. The process of creating even a simple business chart suitable for presentation required skill and a great deal of time. However, now computers and graphics software can be used to complete complex art and graphs simply and easily. **Graphics packages** are those programs that allow artists and other people to use a computer to create, edit, display, and print graphic images. These graphic images can range from simple bar charts to very complex designs and pictures.

Graphics packages create the images with one of two types of graphics:

1. **Text graphics**—where any character the keyboard generates is used to create shapes and lines. The extended ASCII character set for the IBM PC and most compatibles contains a number of special characters designed just for graphics. Some of these are shown in Table 16–1.
2. **High-resolution graphics**—where the individual dots, called **pixels,** that make up a display screen are turned on and off to form various shapes. **Resolution** refers to how sharp or clear an image is. All display screens do not contain the same number of pixels. The more pixels a display screen has, the higher the resolution, or quality, of the image.

Types of Graphics

- Text graphics
- High-resolution graphics

TABLE 16–1
Extended ASCII character set

ASCII Value	Character	ASCII Value	Character	ASCII Value	Character	ASCII Value	Character
128	Ç	160	á	192	∟	224	α
129	ü	161	í	193	⊥	225	β
130	é	162	ó	194	⊤	226	Γ
131	â	163	ú	195	├	227	π
132	ä	164	ñ	196	—	228	Σ
133	à	165	Ñ	197	+	229	σ
134	å	166	ª	198	╞	230	μ
135	ç	167	º	199	╟	231	τ
136	ê	168	¿	200	╚	232	Φ
137	ë	169	⌐	201	╔	233	Θ
138	è	170	¬	202	╩	234	Ω
139	ï	171	½	203	╦	235	δ
140	î	172	¼	204	╠	236	∞
141	ì	173	¡	205	═	237	Ø
142	Ä	174	«	206	╬	238	ε
143	Å	175	»	207	⊥	239	∩
144	É	176	░	208	⊥	240	≡
145	æ	177	▒	209	╤	241	±
146	Æ	178	▓	210	╥	242	≥
147	ô	179	│	211	╙	243	≤
148	ö	180	┤	212	╘	244	⌠
149	ò	181	╡	213	╒	245	⌡
150	û	182	╢	214	╓	246	÷
151	ù	183	╖	215	╫	247	≈
152	ÿ	184	╕	216	╪	248	°
153	Ö	185	╣	217	┘	249	•
154	Ü	186	║	218	┌	250	•
155	¢	187	╗	219	█	251	√
156	£	188	╝	220	▄	252	ⁿ
157	¥	189	╜	221	▌	253	²
158	Pt	190	╛	222	▐	254	■
159	ƒ	191	┐	223	▀	255	(blank 'FF')

COMPONENTS OF A COMPUTER SYSTEM USING GRAPHICS

In order to produce graphics, a computer system must have the appropriate components. It is a good idea to know what hardware is required before purchasing a graphics package. Here are some general considerations:

☐ A computer with a sufficient amount of RAM in primary storage to run the graphics program is required. This information is provided on the program packaging. Some graphics programs are incorporated into spreadsheets, in which case sufficient memory to run the spreadsheet will also be needed.

☐ To produce high-resolution graphics and color, a high-resolution monitor is needed that can display color and the appropriate circuitry (usually in the form of a plug-in graphics card) to drive the monitor.

□ Two floppy-diskette drives (or one floppy-diskette drive and one hard-disk drive) are needed. Some graphics programs only require one floppy-diskette drive, although in most cases having two floppy-diskette drives, or a floppy-diskette drive and a hard-disk drive, makes working with the programs easier and faster.

□ A printer or plotter is needed to create hard copy of a graphic. Most programs have a designated set of printers and plotters with which they are compatible. Others, however, can be customized to operate with any printer or plotter. An appropriate interface card is also needed.

□ The appropriate graphics software is the final component. It may be a stand-alone package or incorporated as part of another program. Print Shop, MacPaint, PC Storyboard, and dGraph III are typical examples of graphics programs. Many spreadsheet and integrated programs such as Lotus 1-2-3, Excel, Enable, and Framework incorporate graphics programs.

APPLICATIONS OF GRAPHICS PACKAGES

Graphics packages for microcomputers can be divided into three basic types: painting and drawing programs; design programs; and business and analytical programs.

Painting and drawing programs let the user become an artist without the paint, canvas, or brushes; however, the creativity still must come from the person using them. This type of package is used by individuals for amusement or by small businesses to create forms, logos, and letterheads. With input devices such as a mouse, light pen, and graphics tablet, these programs let users choose from many different pointer, or "brush," sizes and shapes to paint an image, draw and fill shapes, and change color and texture. MacPaint is an example of a paint and draw program (Figure 16–1). Because of the availability of very high-resolution screens and sophisticated graphics programs, computer images are now rivaling those of canvas or film in clarity and crispness.

Design programs help designers complete the tasks associated with hand drafting of designs easier and more efficiently. They eliminate the need to manually erase or redraw a design. They may go further than two-dimensional drawings by creating three-dimensional objects that can be rotated and viewed from any angle. Some packages also provide simulation capabilities. For example, a skyscraper design might be mathematically tested with a program to see if it would withstand the forces of an earthquake. Design programs are used primarily by engineers and architects. Figure 16–2 shows an example of what can be done using a computer-aided design (CAD) program.

The **business and analytical program** transforms numerical data into pictorial representations—charts and graphs—that show the relationships among the data. Typical graphs that can be produced include bar, line, pie, scatter, stacked-bar, three-dimensional, and surface graphs. These are sometimes referred to as presentation-graphics programs, although strictly speaking they do not all provide high-quality presentation graphics.

Types of Graphics Programs

- Painting and drawing
- Design
- Business and analytical

FIGURE 16–1

This graphic was created on a Macintosh microcomputer using MacPaint, a paint and draw program. (Courtesy of Apple Computer, Inc.)

Presentation graphics are graphics that are suitable for a formal presentation.

This type of graphics program may be a stand-alone package or incorporated as part of a spreadsheet or integrated package. A spreadsheet program that incorporates business and analytical graphics was used to produce the graph in Figure 16–3. Many of the graphics programs incorporated in spreadsheets are adequate for informal uses, but they are not appropriate in a formal presentation. Many of the stand-alone programs, such as Grafix Partner and PC Storyboard, can enhance charts and graphs generated by other programs.

GRAPHICS PACKAGE FEATURES

The following discussion will familiarize you with some of the major features and terminology associated with graphics packages. They differ in the number and types of features offered. Some programs are easier to use. Some graphics packages combine elements of all three types of programs—paint and draw, design, and business and analytical—into one program. More graphics programs will accommodate the functions of all three program types as hardware capabilities and software sophistication increase.

Graph Types

Most business and analytical graphics programs display at least bar, pie, and line graphs. Probably the most popular is the bar graph. **Bar graphs** use a fixed scale to compare data in simple and compound relationships. There are many variations. Figure 16–4 shows several popular types of bar graphs.

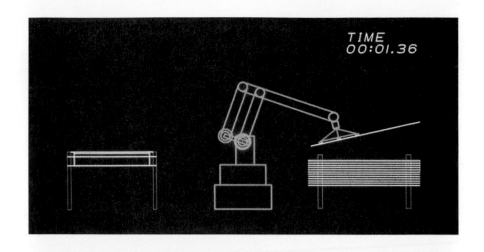

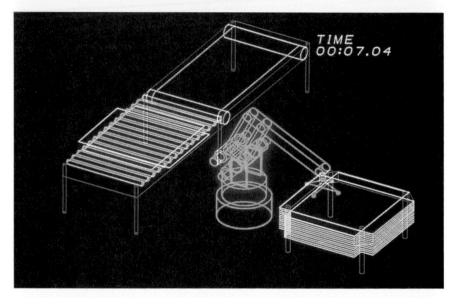

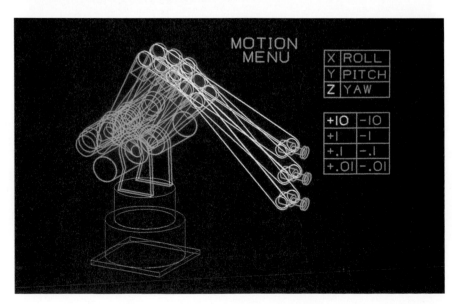

FIGURE 16–2
Computer-aided design software can be used to analyze and simulate how a robot will move in its factory-floor environment. The operator can check work-cell design elements, such as interference in the motion of the robot or "hand," with other work-cell components. (Reprinted with permission from Calma Co., a wholly-owned subsidiary of the General Electric Co., U.S.A.)

FIGURE 16–3
A business and analytical graph created with a spreadsheet package

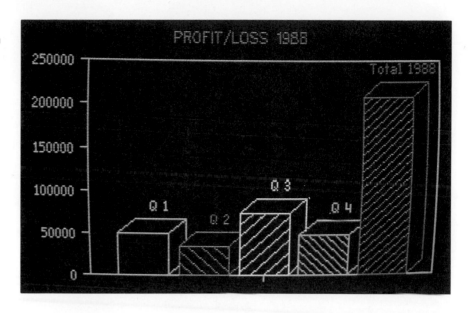

A **pie graph** shows the relationship of parts to a whole. The pie, or circle, represents the whole amount, and the segments represent proportional quantities or percentages of the whole. Some programs allow the user to emphasize individual segments by pulling them away from the whole (exploding them), changing color, or shading them. Figure 16–5 shows a pie graph.

Line graphs show trends and emphasize movement and direction of change over a period of time. Points are plotted on the graph and then connected by straight or curved lines (Figure 16–6). Line graphs are more appropriate than bar or pie graphs when many data points must be graphed. Line graphs that have the area between the lines or curves shaded or filled-in are called stacked-line graphs (Figure 16–7).

A **scatter graph** shows the correlation between two sets of data. If both sets of data increase at the same rate, the correlation is positive (Figure 16–8a). If both sets of data decrease at the same rate, then the correlation is negative (Figure 16–8b). If there is no relationship between the two sets of data, the correlation is zero (Figure 16–8c).

Input Options

A graphics program may offer different input options. Some of these include a keyboard, light pen, mouse, and digitizing tablets. (These devices were discussed in Chapter 3.) Other input options include scanners, which digitize two-dimensional printed images, and video cameras, which digitize two- and three-dimensional images (Figure 16–9).

Output Options

Several output options are usually available with each program. All packages display the graph on the screen for viewing. Most will show the effect of changes to various parameters before saving the graph or printing it.

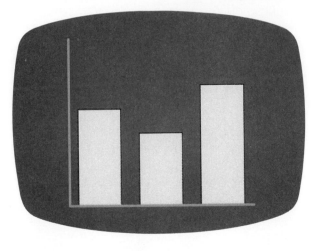

Single bar

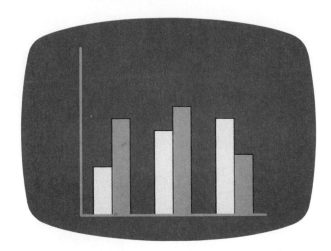

Two bars

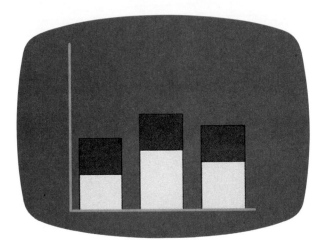

Stacked bars

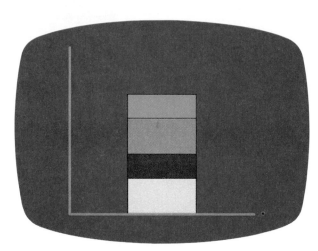

100 percent bar

FIGURE 16–4
Several bar-graph variations

FIGURE 16–5
Pie graph

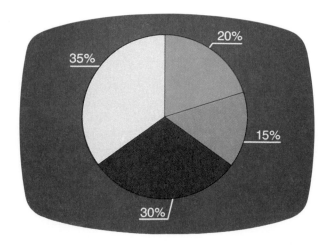

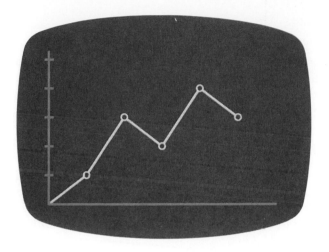 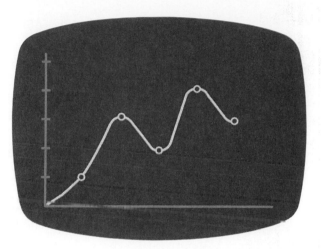

Plot points connected
by straight lines

Plot points connected
by curved lines

FIGURE 16–6
Line graph connected by both straight and curved lines

Other output options include printing the graph on a printer or plotter, altering the size of the graph and its position on the paper, and revising the **aspect ratio**—the relationship between the width and the height of an image. Many printers have a different aspect ratio than the computer screen on which the graphic was created. For example, there may be 20 pixels to one-half inch on the screen, but the printer may print 40 dots per one-half inch. A circle on the display screen is printed as an ellipse if the aspect ratio is not appropriately adapted (Figure 16–10). The aspect ratio can be modified to correct the appearance of the graphic when printed.

Graphics can be saved on a disk in several formats: (a) one that will use them in the graphics program again; (b) one that incorporates them into a document; or (c) one to be used by a slide show feature. A **slide show** feature displays a number of graphics on the monitor in a predetermined order, for a predetermined time period. This produces the same effect you would get by using photographic slides and a slide projector.

FIGURE 16–7
Stacked-line graph

Many graphics programs will also produce presentation slides and transparencies to be used with standard slide and overhead projectors. However, a system must be equipped with the appropriate slide-making supplies and equipment in addition to the software.

Modes of Resolution

Most graphics programs include the option of either text or high-resolution graphics. Certain graphs such as pie graphs and three-dimensional graphs require high-resolution capabilities. Remember that a system must include the appropriate hardware to take advantage of high-resolution graphics.

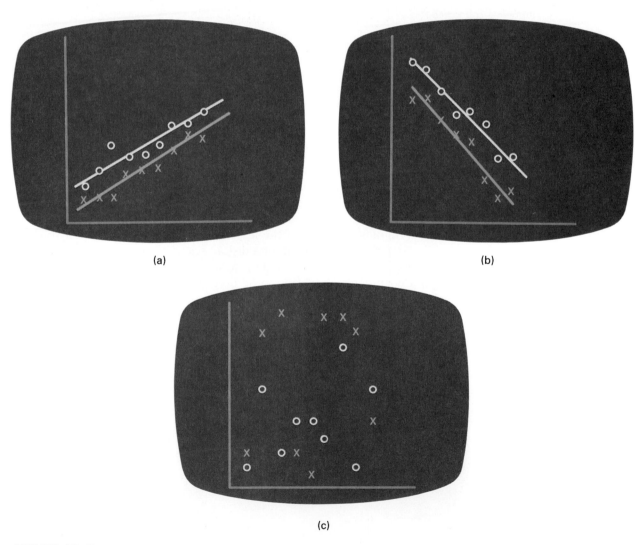

FIGURE 16–8
Scatter graphs. (a) Positive correlation. (b) Negative correlation. (c) Zero correlation.

FIGURE 16–9
Video cameras can be used to digitize an image and send it to a computer
where it is stored and can later be manipulated and printed. (Courtesy of New
Image Technology, Inc.)

Some programs permit several degrees of resolution for pixel-
oriented graphics. For example, a user may be able to choose a 320-by-200
pixel display or a 640-by-200 pixel display. The exact number of choices
and the pixel number for each depends on the system's capabilities as well
as the software.

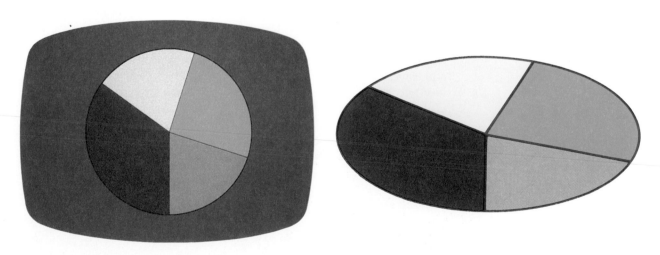

Normal circle as
drawn on screen

Distorted circle is
printed when incorrect
aspect ratio is used.

FIGURE 16–10
Aspect ratio effects

Help Window

Like any other program, good assist tools such as reference manuals, tutorials, and help windows make the learning process and use of the program easier. Usually, with a single keystroke, a **help window** can be displayed on the monitor. It is an easy reference to the available commands and features that can be used. A good program lets the user access the help window without disrupting the program and returns the user to the window where help was originally requested.

Undo

An **undo** feature cancels the changes the user just made and returns the graphic to its previous state. However, most undo features work only if no other action has been taken.

Image Manipulation

Some of the features that allow a user to manipulate a graphic include the ability to: (a) identify the object to be manipulated; (b) copy; (c) cut and paste; (d) reduce and expand; (e) drag; (f) rotate; (g) superimpose; (h) change line thickness; and (i) change dimensions. More options create more flexibility.

Identify the Object to Be Manipulated There are two basic ways to identify the object to be manipulated. The first is to **select** the object, usually by using a pointer device to draw a rectangle around the object. This selected area includes both the object and the background. The second way is to **lasso** the object, also by using a pointer to identify the object. However, only the object is lassoed—not the background.

Copy The **copy** feature duplicates an identified portion of the graphic and leaves the original intact. For example, to create a repeating shape, the user needs only to draw it once and then use the copy feature to duplicate it as many times as needed.

Cut and Paste The **cut and paste** feature cuts (erases) an object from the graphic and places it in a buffer so that it can be pasted (inserted) in another portion of the graphic.

Reduce and Expand Some programs have a **reduce and expand** feature that shrinks and enlarges objects. Reducing and expanding the object are sometimes referred to as "rubberbanding."

Drag The **drag** feature identifies an object to be moved, or "dragged," to a new position.

Rotate The **rotate** feature turns an object to view it from other angles. Some rotate only by 90-degree increments; others rotate an object to any degree specified.

Superimpose The **superimpose** feature moves an object over another object, or portion of that object, without erasing either one. When separated, both images remain intact.

Change Line Thickness This feature changes the line thickness of a selected object.

Automatic Dimensioning The **automatic dimensioning** feature changes the dimensions of an image by simply telling the computer what size the image should be. Some programs may be limited to certain ratios; others may be more flexible, allowing the user to choose specific dimensions.

Supercomputers analyzed millions of pieces of data before coming up with the optimum design for the hull of the Stars and Stripes, the 12-meter sailing yacht that won the America's Cup race held in Australia in 1987. Plausible designs were suggested and tested (by simulation) for seaworthiness and speed until the winning hull was identified. Onboard computers charted the best course and suggested sail trims. (Leo Mason/ Image Bank. Inset: Courtesy of Cray Research, Inc.)

Grid

A **grid** is a pattern of horizontal and vertical lines that helps a user visualize, pinpoint, and enter specific coordinates for the data. Many programs have the option of turning grid lines on or off, i.e., making them visible or invisible. When turned off, grid marks or hash marks remain on the horizontal and vertical axes to identify the scale. A scale shows the increments between the grid marks. For example, a scale may be incremented by 5, 10, or any other quantity.

Color

Most graphics programs permit the colors of the background, labels, and the graph itself to be changed. Color is an important factor in graphics presentation. It can highlight a portion of a graph to emphasize it or give it meaning, or enhance images created with both paint-and-draw and design programs.

Titles

The **titles** feature lets the user enter labels on graphic displays. However, the flexibility of entering text varies widely among programs. Some allow the user to enter titles but force them into predefined positions; others allow the user to place text anywhere. Also, the number of available type fonts and sizes varies among graphic programs.

Zoom

The **zoom** feature moves the window either closer to view an enlargement of a portion of a graphic image or away to view the entire scene.

Pan

The **pan** feature moves the window from side to side so the user can create and view a graphic that is wider than the computer screen.

Mirror

The **mirror** feature automatically draws a mirror image of the object at the same time the user draws the original. For example, if the user draws a line upwards, an identical downward line will be drawn automatically.

Animation

Animation is the ability to simulate motion. Design and paint-and-draw programs with this feature can create images that move so engineers can see how various parts will interact. Animation can also serve as a teaching tool. For example, a graphics animation shows students how the moving parts of an internal combustion engine operate.

Picture Libraries

Many graphics programs include a **picture library** of shapes and images to use. The shapes may include rectangles, circles, triangles, ellipses, parallelograms, or others. In addition, some programs offer a selection of images such as trees, animals, and houses that can be incorporated into the user's graphic creations. Separate disks with hundreds of different images are available for some programs.

CREATING BUSINESS AND ANALYTICAL GRAPHS

Many of you who are taking this course are headed into managerial positions. A study by the Wharton Business School's Applied Research Center found that people who created and used visuals in their business and analytical presentations were perceived to be more professional and more interesting than those who did not. Because of their importance in the business environment, some basic concepts of business and analytical graphs will be examined in this section.

The use of pictorial representations of data makes it easy to compare data or to spot trends that might otherwise be difficult to determine from just numerical data. Business and analytical graphics programs provide the tools to create a graph. Numerous design options are available and vary from program to program. Sometimes, a basic graph with no frills will suffice. But, to be the most effective in a formal presentation, the user should design a dynamic graph that will impress the point needed to be made upon an audience. Attention to proper design is important. A poorly designed chart or graph can be very misleading.

In general, a good presentation graph should

☐ Be simple
☐ Be accurate and easy to interpret
☐ Make an impact on the intended audience

Keep the graph simple. Too much information can make it difficult to grasp the meaning of the graph. A graph should not show finite details or figures, but rather should focus on general ideas such as trends, comparisons, and movement. Keeping a graph simple increases its clarity and effectiveness.

The information used to create the graph must be accurate or else the graph may not have the intended meaning.

In addition, the use of appropriate scales makes it easier to eventually interpret a graph. Poorly designed scales on the horizontal or vertical axis may cause a curve to appear more or less curved than it really is. When two graphs are to be compared, the increments between grid marks should be the same on the horizontal and vertical axes of both. Changing the distance between grid lines for a portion of a graph may cause identical data to appear different or vice versa (Figure 16–11).

To make a favorable impact on the intended audience, several factors should be considered. Maintain proper balance and spacing of the elements. Elements in a graph should fill the available space and balance with

Business and Analytical Graph Design

- Simple
- Accurate and easy to interpret
- Have impact

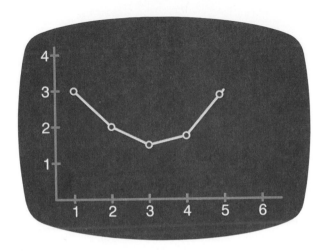
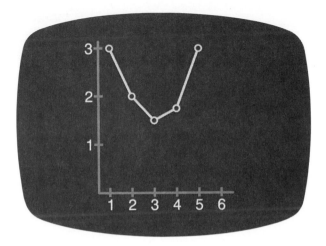

Equal distance between grid marks on horizontal and vertical axes gives the graph a smoother, more realistic appearance.

Contracted and uneven grid marks make the curve appear to have a severe dip.

FIGURE 16–11
Correct versus distorted scale

the other dimensions. Bars and columns should be wider than the space between them (Figure 16–12).

Choose design elements such as color, shape, and texture carefully. They can alter the visual effect of a graph. Emphasize important elements of a graph. For example, a segment of a pie chart can be exploded, or a bar might be colored or shaded differently from other bars to make it stand out (Figure 16–13).

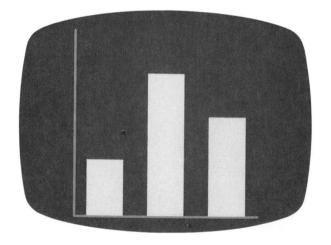
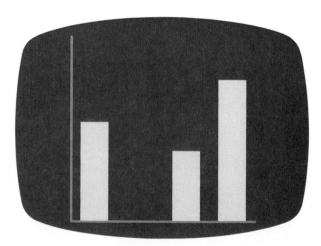

Balanced graph

Unbalanced graph

FIGURE 16–12
Balanced versus unbalanced bar graph

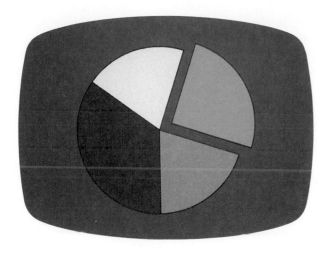

Exploded pie chart

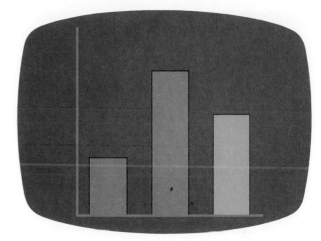

Colored bar for emphasis

FIGURE 16–13
Exploded pie and colored bar charts

When shades of colors and textured patterns are used, they should move from darker in the foreground to lighter in the background because lighter colors tend to "jump" forward. Blues and greens are generally considered good background colors for graphs. In business situations, it is usually recommended to avoid red (it suggests failure to most business people) unless failure is what is being conveyed. Also, if the colors red and green appear next to each other a person with red-green color blindness will see only brown. This affliction affects approximately 4 percent of males in the U.S.

Avoid using textures or patterns that can cause distortion. For example, solid bars stand out more than outlined bars and vertical lines in a horizontal plane make the surface appear higher.

Plot lines, the lines that connect the data points in a graph, should be of different thicknesses, or weight. The plot lines should be the heaviest, grid lines the lightest. Use color shades or textures to differentiate between plot lines. Grid lines should not overlay solid areas on the charts.

Numbers and titles should be large enough to read. Titles should be horizontal whenever possible for easier reading.

The design elements may influence where the viewer's attention will be focused and what part of the graph will be perceived as the most important. Not all programs give the user control over every aspect of creating a graph. Some allow more flexibility in graph designs than others.

COMMUNICATION PACKAGES

Communication packages are programs designed to control communication between two computers. It is the purpose of the communication software to:

☐ Establish and maintain communication with another computer

Purposes of a Communication Package

- Establish and maintain communication
- Set communication parameters
- Direct outgoing and incoming data

☐ Tell the computer how to send data (i.e., determine the communication parameters)

☐ Direct outgoing data from the keyboard or disks through the communication port and into a modem, and direct incoming data from the communication port to the screen or disk

There are many communication packages with a wide variety of options. But no matter how sophisticated or how basic a communication program is, all must be able to perform two general functions: (a) set essential communication parameters; and (b) emulate a dumb terminal. The four essential **communication parameters** are the:

☐ Baud rate of the transmission

☐ Number of data bits used to create each character

☐ Number of stop bits

☐ Type of parity checking used for error checking during transmission

The baud rate is the number of times per second that the signal being transmitted changes (modulates or demodulates). The number of bits that make up a character is specified by the user. In microcomputer communication, characters are made up of either seven or eight bits. Each character is surrounded by start and stop bits. These bits allow the receiving terminal to synchronize itself with the incoming data on a character-by-character basis. The start bit is always a zero bit. Depending on what the receiving computer expects, there are usually one or two stop bits. The user enters the appropriate number of stop bits. The parity bit is used to check for transmission errors. Three parity-checking options are generally used with microcomputer communication: even; odd; or none.

In order to specify odd or even parity, the number of data bits that make up a character must be seven so that the eighth bit can be used for the parity setting. When the number of data bits is set at eight, the parity setting is always none because all the bits are used to make up the character. The none option can also be chosen for 7-bit characters.

The computer receiving the data adds all the one bits to see if they total an odd or even number. If the parity setting is odd and the bit total is odd, or the setting is even and the bit total is even, the computer assumes the data were sent correctly. If the parity setting is odd and the bit total is even, or the setting is even and the bit total is odd, the computer is alerted that an error in data transmission has occurred. Many programs allow the user to choose how a parity error is handled. For example, the user may set the program to signal that an error has occurred or to ignore the error.

Parity checking is only an elementary form of error checking. It cannot detect errors such as the loss of an entire character or larger block of data. Both for sending and receiving, computers must use the same values for each parameter for the communication to be successful.

A communication package also must cause the user's microcomputer to emulate a dumb terminal—to operate in what is called, in most programs, the terminal mode. A **dumb terminal** is a stand-alone keyboard and display screen unit that can only send data to or receive data from a

Essentials of a Communication Program

- Ability to set basic communication parameters
  ☐ Baud rate
  ☐ Number of data bits
  ☐ Number of stop bits
  ☐ Type of parity checking
- Ability to emulate a dumb terminal

computer to which it is connected. A dumb terminal cannot function as a stand-alone computer. It is essential that the microcomputer emulate a dumb terminal because most minicomputers and mainframes used in business or information services will only communicate with this kind of terminal.

COMPONENTS OF A COMPUTER SYSTEM USING A COMMUNICATION PACKAGE

In order for one computer system to communicate with another computer system, it must have the following equipment:

☐ A computer with a sufficient amount of RAM in primary storage to run the communication program (This information is provided on the program packaging.)

☐ A modem, serial interface (built-in or plug-in-card), telephone, and the appropriate cables

☐ One floppy diskette drive (If the communication program is part of a larger integrated program, however, two floppy-diskette drives, or one floppy-diskette drive and a hard-disk drive, are usually needed.)

☐ The appropriate communication software (This may be a stand-alone package or incorporated as part of another program. Crosstalk XVI, Hostcomm, PC-TALK III, and SmartCom II are some popular examples of stand-alone communication programs. Some integrated packages, such as Open Access II, also contain communication programs.)

APPLICATIONS OF COMMUNICATION PACKAGES

Much of our society is built around the acquisition, manipulation, and use of information. The traditional approach to gathering information often meant long hours of research to find the appropriate sources of data and then more time to pore over the vast amounts of data to extract what was pertinent to the search. Today, however, many computerized information services have large data bases that can provide the needed data, in a usable form, and in a fraction of the time it takes to research by hand. There are data bases for practically any topic, including medical, scientific, financial, weather, and sports. Communication programs establish the necessary link between a microcomputer and the computers that run these data bases.

In addition to providing information, services such as shopping and banking can be accomplished using communication programs.

Communication software lets a person keep in touch and exchange ideas with other professionals or with users of the same type of computer equipment through bulletin boards and electronic mail. (Bulletin boards and electronic mail are covered in the InfoModule on page 484.)

Now let's examine some typical features of communication packages.

FEATURES OF COMMUNICATION PACKAGES

Once the four basic parameters are set and the ability to emulate a dumb terminal is established, a basic communication link is possible. A number of other features increase the usefulness of a communication program.

Uploading and Downloading

Two features that make the link more useful are uploading and downloading. **Uploading** occurs when data from the user's disk are sent to another computer, and **downloading** occurs when data are received from another computer and saved on the user's disk. Almost all communication programs will upload and download data; otherwise, the program's usefulness is very limited.

On-line refers to the condition when the user's computer is linked to, and communicating with, another computer. **Off-line** refers to the condition when no communication link is established.

The user can create a file on a disk before going on-line, which can then be uploaded from that disk and sent. This procedure significantly reduces the time spent on-line and, thus, lowers costs for a communication session. Downloading lets the user capture (receive) data on a disk from a communication session with another computer. The data can then be read or edited off-line any time after the session. This process can dramatically reduce the cost of using information services such as CompuServe and The Source, where charges are based on the length of on-line time.

Data-capturing Options

A data **buffer** is an area set aside in the microcomputer's primary storage to temporarily store data. Many communication programs provide a data buffer that allows the user to capture data and review, search, and edit the data before saving them on a disk. Or, it gives the option to discard the contents of the buffer without ever saving it on a disk. A data buffer conserves disk space by allowing the user to select and save only the data needed.

Data received after a disk is full may be saved in a buffer or may be lost, depending on the program. Some communication programs provide a status indicator telling how much buffer space is left. If this status indicator is ignored, however, the buffer may become full and any data that overflows the buffer will be lost. With more preferable programs, when the buffer becomes full, the overflow data are automatically saved on a disk. Others issue a warning when the disk is full so that the user can change disks or erase files from the current disk to make room. Data stored in the buffer are volatile. If the computer is turned off or data are erased before storing them on a disk, they are lost.

Another data-capturing capability in some programs is the option to send data directly to a printer as they are received. The data are usually simultaneously displayed on the screen. The printer must be able to print at the same rate that data are being sent, or data will be lost. However, the use of a buffer allows communication at higher baud rates than the user's printer would normally handle. Print spoolers (a type of buffer) are available that allow the data to be temporarily stored and sent to the printer at the proper rate.

Mode Switching

Most communication programs have at least two modes: a command mode; and a data transfer (or conversation) mode. The **command mode** is the one in which whatever is typed at the keyboard is interpreted as a command. The **data-transfer mode** is the mode in which communication actually takes place. Some programs allow the user to easily switch between these two modes without disconnecting the communication link. The mode-switching feature allows the user to temporarily leave the data-transfer mode and enter the command mode (e.g., to access commands to display a disk directory, delete a file, activate a printer, and so on) and then to reenter the data-transfer mode.

The ability to operate in both full-duplex and half-duplex modes is another feature of some programs. Communication between microcomputers and between microcomputers and mainframes usually takes place in full-duplex mode; however, many information services and bulletin boards operate only in half-duplex mode.

File-transfer Protocols

File-transfer protocols are sets of rules for the transfer of data. Protocols ensure the error-free transfer of data. They are usually supplied as built-in options that can be selected as the user needs them. Some programs also allow the user to define a specific protocol.

Both computers in the link must use the same protocol for the data transfer to take place. Because of the amount of error checking that takes place with some protocols, their use can increase the time it takes to complete a transfer of data. Some common protocols offered by communication programs include XON/XOFF, Xmodem, and Kermit.

The **XON/XOFF protocol** controls the transfer of text data. An XOFF signal tells the transmitting computer to stop sending data until it receives a signal to start again. The XON signal tells the computer that it can begin sending data. In some programs, this protocol is invoked directly from the keyboard to stop data transmission temporarily. In others, it is done automatically. This procedure prevents overflowing the data buffer.

The **Xmodem protocol** is a public domain protocol developed by Ward Christensen that is widely used within the microcomputer industry for sending and receiving nontext (binary) files. Files are sent in 128-byte blocks. If the protocol detects an error, the entire block is resent. If the block cannot be sent successfully, the Xmodem protocol terminates the transfer rather than send erroneous data. This termination indicates to the user that problems exist in either the data or communication link.

The **Kermit protocol** is also used for sending and receiving nontext files and is popular on larger computers.

A flexible communication program for a user would be one that allows both text and nontext files to be sent and gives the choice of several available protocols.

THE COMPUTER THAT SPILLED ITS GUTS

In 1986, the American press revealed that members of President Ronald Reagan's administration had secretly sold military goods to Iran and used the profits to finance the unofficial army that was trying to overthrow the government in Nicaragua. The commissions called in to investigate these apparent violations of law were faced with the problem of trying to find out who did what and when long after the events in question had occurred. Most of the blame was being laid at the door of the National Security Council.

The investigators discovered that the council offices were connected to a computer system that handled electronic mail transmissions. Because the council was dealing in delicate and secretive matters, the system would remind the user each time a message was put into it that the message was ''classified.''

What the system failed to indicate was that it also automatically stored a copy of every message in a permanent electronic file. When the investigators discovered this, it became merely a matter of searching through the files for detailed notes on the entire arms scandal.

Ironically, the National Security Council had kept its paper shredders busy throughout the affair in the belief that it was maintaining tight security.

Pacing Option

Sometimes the rate at which one computer can send data and the rate that the other computer can receive data are not the same. Some computers also require that the transmitting computer wait for a special prompt before sending data. These situations are often found in microcomputer-to-mainframe communications. The **pacing** feature allows the user to determine a specified time to wait between sending instructions. It also can instruct a program to wait for a specified character that prompts the transmitting computer to begin sending data.

Character Stripping and Conversion

This feature allows the user to inspect, change, or delete any character as it leaves or enters the computer. For example, if an incoming text file contains special control characters for formatting or printing instructions that are not compatible with the user's word processor, the program can delete those characters or change them to match the appropriate codes.

Break Signal

The **break signal** tells the computer receiving data to stop or interrupt the current operation without disconnecting the communication link. However, if the standard DOS-break sequence (the Ctrl-Break sequence on IBM PC's and compatibles) were used, the danger of terminating the operation of the communication program, the communication link, or both would be extremely high.

Time On-line Status

Some programs keep track of and display the time spent on-line during a particular communication session. This feature can help the user track and budget the costs incurred for each communication session.

Directory Storage and Automatic Dialing

Directory storage is a feature that lets the user store in a directory on disk all the pertinent information required to complete a connection to another computer. **Automatic dialing** is a feature that automatically dials the phone number of another computer using the information stored in a directory.

A directory can contain information such as names, telephone numbers, and communication parameters. It can also hold the **log-on sequence**, which is the series of keystrokes, account numbers, and passwords needed to access a computer or information service. With one or more keystrokes, the program automatically dials and connects to the specified computer using the information stored in the directory. To store that information, a particular communication session needs to be described only once. It is then saved and easily accessed over and over again.

Programs differ in the amount of space available for each directory entry and for the total number of directory entries. Some, such as PC-Talk III, provide enough space for access numbers, account numbers, and passwords. In addition, they let the user program the function keys to enter a particular log-on sequence automatically. SmartCom II, among others, has the log-on sequences for some of the popular information services already programmed. The user simply supplies the account number and password to the file to make it usable.

Autoanswer

When the computer is on, the **autoanswer** feature, in conjunction with the appropriate modem, automatically answers calls from other computers. It creates a bulletin board file and receives electronic mail even when the user is not present.

Automatic Message Transfer

The **automatic message transfer** feature automatically dials a specified computer and leaves a message at a preset time.

Error Handling

There are many different ways a program can alert the user to errors he or she makes. The ways vary among programs, but a good program should indicate what the error is and, if possible, suggest steps to recover from the error.

Password Protection

A **password** feature allows the user to create passwords that give protection to files, dialing directories, and other portions of the communication program so that unauthorized people cannot access them. This feature is valuable if sensitive data are involved, or if several people have access to the communication program.

Encryption

The **encryption** feature creates an unreadable version of a file before it is transmitted. A decrypt feature recreates the readable version of an encrypted file after it is received. This feature can ensure the confidentiality of a file as it is sent over communication lines.

FIGURE 16–14

PC-TALK III command summary help window

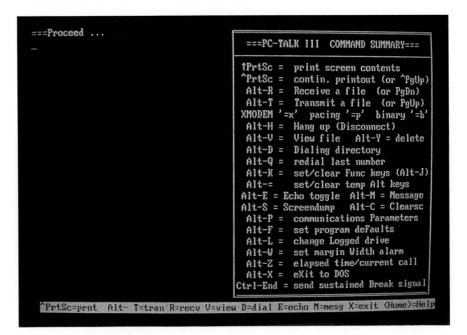

Help Window

Reference manuals, tutorials, and help windows supply references to the available commands and features. Help windows can usually be accessed any time during the operation of a program and will return the user to the window where help was originally requested. A good help window lists the keys and commands that are available to use at that time, or it describes the steps for a particular function. The PC-TALK III command summary window is shown in Figure 16–14.

SUMMARY

Graphics packages use the power and speed of the microcomputer to create, edit, display, and print graphic images. Text graphics is the creation of graphics with text characters. High-resolution graphics is the creation of graphics by turning the pixels on and off. Pixels are the individual dots that make up the display screen. The sharpness or clarity of an image is referred to as its resolution. The more pixels a display screen has, the higher the resolution, or quality, of the graphic image.

There are three basic types of graphics programs: painting and drawing programs; design programs; and business and analytical programs. Graphics packages contain a variety of features, including different graph types, several options for input and output, operations in text or high-resolution mode, numerous image manipulation options, color, and many more.

Presentation graphics are graphics that have been prepared for use in a formal presentation. Business and analytical graphics have become an important aspect of business presentations. A graph for presentation should be simple, accurate, easy to interpret, and make the desired impact on the audience.

Communication packages are programs that control the communication process between two computers. As well as being able to emulate a dumb terminal, it is essential that all communication programs be able to set the following communication parameters: baud rate; number of data bits used to create each character; number of stop bits; and type of parity checking. A dumb terminal is a keyboard and display screen that can only send data to or receive data from another computer.

Communication programs can link computers to information services, bulletin boards, and electronic mail systems.

Two powerful features of a communication package are the abilities to upload (send data from the user's disk to another computer) and to download (receive data from another computer and save them on the user's disk). Other features include multiple data-capturing options, switching between program modes, and multiple file-transfer protocols (the rules for the transfer of data).

Key Terms

animation (p. 470)

aspect ratio (p. 465)

autoanswer (p. 479)

automatic dialing (p. 479)

automatic dimensioning (p. 469)

automatic message transfer (p. 480)

bar graph (p. 461)

break signal (p. 479)

buffer (p. 476)

business and analytical program (p. 460)

command mode (p. 477)

communication package (p. 473)

communication parameters (p. 474)

copy (p. 468)

cut and paste (p. 468)

data-transfer mode (p. 477)

design program (p. 460)

directory storage (p. 479)

downloading (p. 476)

drag (p. 468)

dumb terminal (p. 474)

encryption (p. 480)

file-transfer protocols (p. 477)

graphics package (p. 458)

grid (p. 470)

help window (p. 468 and 481)

high-resolution graphics (p. 458)

Kermit protocol (p. 477)

lasso (p. 468)

line graph (p. 463)

log-on sequence (p. 479)

mirror (p. 470)

off-line (p. 476)

on-line (p. 476)

pacing (p. 478)

painting and drawing programs (p. 460)

pan (p. 470)

password (p. 480)

picture library (p. 471)

pie graph (p. 463)

pixel (p. 458)

presentation graphics (p. 461)

reduce and expand (p. 468)

resolution (p. 458)

rotate (p. 468)

scatter graph (p. 463)

select (p. 468)

slide show (p. 465)

superimpose (p. 469)

text graphics (p. 458)

titles (p. 470)

undo (p. 468)

uploading (p. 476)

Xmodem protocol (p. 477)

XON/XOFF protocol (p. 477)

zoom (p. 470)

Review Questions

1. _____ allow people to use microcomputers to create, edit, display, and print graphic images.

2. What is text graphics?

3. The sharpness or clarity of an image is referred to as its _____.

4. What are pixels?

5. Graphics that turn pixels on and off to create an image are referred to as _____.

6. Name three basic types of graphics programs.

7. True or False: Spreadsheet programs can create presentation graphics.

8. A(n) _____ graph shows the relationship of the parts to a whole.

9. The _____ is the relationship of the width to the height of an image.

10. _____ are patterns of horizontal and vertical lines that aid the user in entering, visualizing, and pinpointing data.

11. The ability to simulate motion is called _____.

12. List three features of a good presentation graph.

13. What type of graph—bar, pie, or line—would best show how much money from your total budget was spent on entertainment? Why?

14. What is the purpose of a communication package?

15. What two general functions are all communication programs capable of?

16. Name the four basic parameters that a communication program establishes.

17. A(n) _____ is a keyboard and display screen that can only send data to and receive data from another computer.

18. For what purposes can people use communication programs?

19. _____ is the process of sending data from the user's disk to another computer via a communication link.

20. Receiving data from a computer via a communication link and saving them on a disk on the user's computer is called _____.

21. Define on-line and off-line as they relate to the communication process.

22. A(n) _____ is an area set aside in primary storage to temporarily store data.

23. The mode in which communication actually takes place is called the _____ mode.

24. The sets of rules for the transfer of data are called _____.

25. Name some features of communication programs, and describe how they are used.

INFOMODULE

Electronic Networks

Equipping a personal computer with communication hardware and software can open a whole new world of information resources. In this section, some of the types of electronic networks available to people, including bulletin boards, electronic mail, teleconferencing, information services, commercial data-base services, gateway services, and videotext, will be discussed.

BULLETIN BOARDS

One of the easiest and least expensive ways to begin exploring communication capabilities is by using a bulletin board system (Table 1). A **bulletin board system (BBS)** is essentially an electronic equivalent of a conventional bulletin board. Many BBSs are established as a way for users to exchange information about any topic; others are set up for people who own a specific brand or model of computer.

How They Work

Although features vary among BBSs, most provide the user with the ability to:

☐ Post messages for other users to read
☐ Read messages posted by other callers
☐ Communicate with the **system operator (sysop),** the person who operates the bulletin board, to ask questions about the BBS's operation, report problems, or make suggestions
☐ Post notices of equipment or services for sale
☐ Upload and download programs

Most BBSs currently in operation are noncommercial and free of charge. The telephone company, however, charges for long distance phone time that may be used when communicating with a BBS.

There are two basic types of BBSs: message-only; and file transfer. Message-only systems allow public or private messages to be sent and received and public bulletin boards to be viewed.

BBSs with file-transfer capabilities also allow files to be uploaded and downloaded. These are the most popular because a vast array of free, public-domain software can be downloaded including games, application software, and system utilities.

The first electronic bulletin board system was created in 1978 by Ward Christensen and Randy Suess to help the members of the Chicago Area Computer Hobbyists Exchange trade information.

Most BBSs are operated by individuals who have an interest in computers and communication and who have a desire to share information with others. But hardware manufacturers, software publishers, and other businesses have also started bulletin boards. A business might use a service for customers or clients to place orders, ask questions, and solve problems relating to the company's product. Parker Brothers, a game company, set up such a bulletin board for its customers to order replacement parts for games such as Monopoly.

Benefits and Drawbacks

The benefit of using a BBS is that it provides an easy and inexpensive way to share information; however, there are some drawbacks. Sysops for the private, individual BBSs donate their own equipment (computers and modem) and software. Because they donate their time as well, the hours of operation vary. Many BBSs handle only one call at a time. Limits are often imposed so one caller does not tie up the bulletin board for long periods of time.

ELECTRONIC MAIL

Electronic mail refers to the variety of methods used to electronically transmit mail and messages almost anywhere in the world. To send

TABLE 1

Hints on using a bulletin board system (BBS)

☐ Keep pencil and paper near your computer to write down names of files, list commands and other instructions, or note names of people or messages that are of interest.

☐ Write down the password, if there is one, and keep it handy.

☐ Ask questions of the system operators (sysops) and BBS users. These are usually people who like to share their thoughts and experiences with others.

☐ If the BBS line is always busy, try early morning hours.

☐ If calling long distance, prepare messages before going on-line to save on phone charges.

☐ Most BBSs use the remote bulletin board system (RBBS) or Hostcomm bulletin board system program. If the BBS you use requires a long-distance call, try to find out what program that BBS uses. Then find a local bulletin board that uses the same program to familiarize yourself with the operating environment. This saves money because time is not spent on a long-distance phone connection to learn how that BBS operates.

☐ For public domain software, try local BBSs. If the software is not available locally, then try long-distance BBSs.

and receive electronic mail with a personal computer, the computer must be equipped for communication.

How It Works

There are two ways to create the messages to be sent: (a) use a microcomputer and an on-line editor available in the electronic mail system; or (b) use a microcomputer and a word processor, and then upload to the electronic-mail service.

A typical transmission might proceed as follows:

1. The sender accesses an electronic-mail system.
2. The sender keys or uploads the message into the computer.
3. The sender tells the computer where to send message.
4. The sender issues the command to "mail" the message.
5. The message is transmitted to the specified destination.
6. The message is received and can be read immediately at the terminal or placed in the recipient's file space ("mailbox") where it can be retrieved and displayed or printed at any time.

There are two general types of electronic mail: (a) an in-house network, which connects all or some of the employees within a business; and (b) an external network connecting people at different locations around the world.

In-house systems are generally configured in one of three ways:

1. As a local-area network (LAN) where the personal computers don't need to be equipped for telecommunications to be included in the network (The LAN typically is located in a single building with each computer linked by a direct cable. Messages can be sent and received anywhere in the building.)

2. As an internal communication system where each personal computer uses a modem and telephone lines instead of LANs (This arrangement is useful if different brands of computers are used.)
3. As a dedicated system, where special devices are used exclusively for the transfer of electronic mail and voice transmissions

External systems take one of two different forms:

1. As Telex and TWX printing machines (Messages are received and then printed.)
2. As part of a commercial information service (For example, SourceMail is available from The Source and EMAIL from CompuServe. Electronic mail can be sent between subscribers of the same service and some between subscribers of different services.) ·

Benefits and Drawbacks

Electronic mail has several notable benefits:

☐ It is faster than traditional mail and less expensive to prepare and send.
☐ A single message can be sent simultaneously to multiple addresses.
☐ Unlike a telephone call, the receiver of the message doesn't need to be on the line at the same time as the sender.

☐ A busy person doesn't need to be interrupted to receive the message.
☐ The message can be printed on paper.

However, electronic mail does have some drawbacks:

☐ It is expensive to set up, and if used indiscriminantly, it can be expensive to operate.
☐ There is no guarantee that electronic-mail systems will be compatible.
☐ There is also the problem of privacy and security of electronic mail. It is difficult to ensure that only the recipient reads the mail.
☐ Electronic "junk mail" has emerged.

TELECONFERENCING

Voice teleconferencing, where three or more people could talk to each other on the phone simultaneously, was an early form of teleconferencing. This method, however, does not convey charts and graphs and requires all participants to be present at the same time.

Then video teleconferencing became possible; voices and images can be combined and transmitted to different locations (Figure 1). However, equipment is expensive, difficulties arise in arranging participants' schedules, and

FIGURE 1
Employees at different locations use video teleconferencing to hold a business meeting where the participants can see and converse with each other. (Courtesy of American Satellite Co.)

FIGURE 2
The Source information service main menu screen (Courtesy of The Source)

there is a problem of the perception people get of those appearing on video.

The latest and most promising technology is **electronic teleconferencing,** where computer systems are connected by the telephone system, and participants key in their conversations. Teleconferencing systems are similar to BBSs, but they are much larger and require large computer systems to run them and store the data. Most BBSs are operated on microcomputer systems.

To have a successful conference, participants do not need to be at their computers at the same time. A question might be asked of a participant and sent to that individual's "mailbox." The recipient can then access and read the message at a convenient time and send an answer back.

Members of the teleconference can be anywhere in the world. Teleconferencing won't replace business travel; however, it can replace nonessential trips.

INFORMATION SERVICES

An **information service** is a business that supplies information to subscribers on numerous general interest topics by using powerful large computer systems that store millions of pieces of data. In some ways, information services are similar to BBSs; however, they are run on a much larger scale, supply much more information, and operate as businesses for profit.

How They Work

Information services require a subscription and payment of hourly access charges. Some may also require an initial sign-on fee.

Although some have limited hours, these services usually operate twenty-four hours a day, seven days a week. Charges are usually higher for daytime access than for evening or weekend access.

New subscribers are usually issued a user number and a password, which are required to access the service and retrieve information from it.

The topics covered vary among the information services. Typical information offered by most of these services include news, sports, weather, business, finance, and investment. They also offer: computerized shopping; games; teleconferencing facilities; forums on computers and computing; airline information; theater, restaurant, and hotel guides; on-line encyclopedias; editing capabilities to write letters; and computer programs. An information service can supply not only information on many subjects, but also can provide many services (Figure 2).

Several popular information services are The Source, CompuServe, Delphi, and Dow Jones News Retrieval.

COMMERCIAL DATA-BASE SERVICES

In addition to information about general topics, commercial **data-base services** offer information on highly specialized topics.

They are collections of large-scale data bases that contain millions of articles, abstracts, and bibliographic citations from thousands of books, periodicals, reports, and theses. A subscriber is permitted to electronically search these collections for needed information.

Several popular commercial data base services are Dialog, Bibliographic Retrieval System (BRS), and NewsNet. The largest commercial data-base service is Dialog, a subsidiary of Lockheed Corporation, which offers approximately 200 data bases. It covers topics such as agriculture, business and economics, chemistry, current events, education, energy and environment, law and government, medicine and biosciences, science and technology, social sciences and humanities, and many more.

Some of the large data bases also offer scaled-down versions of their services. For example, Dialog offers Knowledge Index, which is designed so that people who have little or no experience searching commercial data bases find them easy to use. It has fewer features and simpler commands than Dialog and offers approximately twenty-five of Dialog's most widely used data bases. Knowledge Index costs less to use, but is available only during evenings and on weekends. BRS also offers a low-cost alternative for evening and weekend service, called After Dark, with about forty data bases.

In addition to commercial data-base services, some commercial data bases are totally dedicated to special interests and can be subscribed to individually. For example, LEXIS, a specialized data base of legal information, is offered by Mead Data Central. Many data bases found in major commercial services also exist as stand-alone data bases and can be subscribed to individually.

How They Work

Most services have aids such as printed catalogs and on-line indexes to help you select the appropriate data base. The next step is to access the chosen data base, and enter the specific commands and search terms. Search terms are the words or phrases actually searched for in a data base to help identify pertinent information.

A good way to begin a search is with general terms or topics, and move toward more specific topics to retrieve pertinent records that might have been originally excluded if a narrow scope was used.

Most services use Boolean operators to eliminate specific terms or topics and combine search terms. The Boolean operators AND, OR, and NOT indicate the logical relationships among various search terms. For example, to search for information on software copyright laws, you might use the search terms ''software and copyright.'' A search of ''software OR copyright'' would find all references that contain the word ''software,'' all that contain the word ''copyright,'' and all that contain both words. The search would find a lot of irrelevant information using the OR operator. A search of ''software NOT copyright'' would locate all references containing the word ''software.'' In this case, you would also find a lot of very general software information. By searching ''software AND copyright,'' only references containing both search terms, are located. This search would be the best choice in this case.

The data base will then be searched, and the names of the located records will be displayed. Usually, you can preview records so you can eliminate those you don't need.

GATEWAY SERVICES

A **gateway service** buys large quantities of connect time from each member of an information or a commercial data-base service at wholesale rates and then resells the time to its subscribers at retail rates.

With one call to the gateway service, the subscriber can connect to one of several different services. By subscribing to a gateway service, the sign up fees or monthly minimum fees charged by individual services are waived. Charges are made for only the actual connect time to each service at the service's regular rates. The Business Computer Network (BCN) is one popular gateway service; Searchlink is another.

VIDEOTEXT

Videotext is an interactive information service similar to the other information services, but it uses color displays and graphics. The services we have discussed thus far transmit and receive data as monochrome text and have no graphic capabilities. Videotext is designed to heighten the appeal and interest level of the information consumer with color and graphics. This is both an advantage and a disadvantage because users are required to have computer systems that display color and graphics.

France has had particular success with videotext systems. Unlike in the U.S., however, the government-controlled telephone system in France funded the cost of the color/graphics terminals for those who wanted the system and met certain requirements. The telephone company did this primarily to help increase telephone usage. Although many other services such as banking and shopping are available, the most popular use for the system in France today is to chat with other people through one of the many privately run services.

KEY TERMS

bulletin board system (BBS) (p. 484)

data-base service (p. 488)

electronic mail (p. 484)

electronic teleconferencing (p. 487)

gateway service (p. 488)

information service (p. 487)

system operator (sysop) (p. 484)

videotext (p. 489)

QUESTIONS

1. Describe a bulletin board system and give some advantages and disadvantages.
2. Discuss some advantages and disadvantages of electronic mail.
3. Discuss the evolution of teleconferencing.
4. Explain the differences between an information service and a commercial data-base service. Give examples of each.
5. Define videotext and suggest possible uses.

PART FIVE
Implications of the Information Age

The revolution manifest in this new age—
this age of intelligent machines—is in its
earliest stages. The impact of these new
machines that augment our mental resources
will be greater than the radical technological
and social changes that have come before. It
cannot be stopped. Today's challenges are to
be found in our need to understand it, to
learn to live creatively and harmoniously
with it, and to harness it to constructive
uses.

Raymond Kurzweil, researcher in artificial
intelligence and chairman of Kurzweil
Applied Intelligence, Inc.

OBJECTIVES

☐ Describe the new kinds of crimes that have been created or accelerated by computerization

☐ Discuss how computers have shifted traditional labor and employment patterns in the United States

☐ Discuss people's concerns about privacy, electronic work monitoring, VDTs and health hazards, and computer ethics

17

Social Concerns

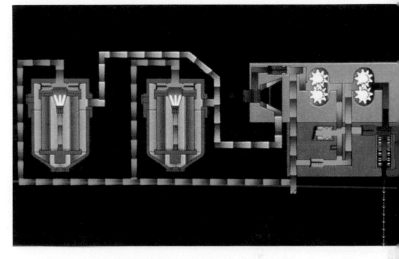

PROFILE: Antonia Stone

Antonia Stone thinks computers should not be tools just for the privileged, but lifelines for the uneducated, the unwanted, and the poor. Computers should provide an opportunity for upward mobility. A teacher by profession, in 1980 Stone founded Playing to Win, a nonprofit organization to make computers and computer training available to people who are economically, mentally, and socially handicapped.

Originally, Stone wanted to take her computer literacy concept into the geographically remote regions of Appalachia. Instead, she discovered there were plenty of similar needs to fill nearer her own New York City home. Soon she was setting up and supervising programs in public libraries, low-income housing projects, prisons, and juvenile detention centers. Her aims in each program were to use computers to teach, in video-game format, basic reading, writing, and math, and then to develop these computer-taught abilities into salable job skills.

Sometimes people were skeptical of Stone's approach, but they couldn't deny the positive results. They couldn't help but see that the students were responding to the one-to-one tutoring and the human attention they were getting. An interesting phenomenon occurred. It seemed that most of the children who couldn't read, count, or write appeared to have no innate fear of the computer—computerphobia.

Stone has come to accept the accomplishments that her computer-use concepts have created. One observer of a 19-year-old mentally retarded student who learned to read and do arithmetic through Playing to Win noted that, "Working the computer gives him a sense of accomplishment and power over at least one part of his environment."

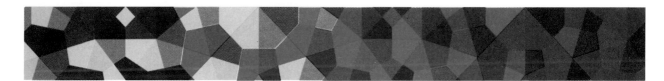

Significant inventions, such as the computer, always crinkle the social fabric into dramatic new patterns that alter how things are produced, how they are protected by law, and how they are used. Very often, these inventions cause society to revise its ethical values, too.

Society never fully adjusts to new inventions. The appearance of the automobile still haunts us by raising arguments about the need for drunk-driving, seat-belt, and airbag legislation, about destruction of farmlands by interstate highways, and about the legality of radar detectors. Society is now experiencing just the first big wave of change and controversy as a result of computers.

In this chapter, you'll look at computer-related crimes, society's concerns about privacy, and the existence and security of huge data banks of personal data. You'll read about the effects of computers on the job market and about issues in the workplace, including health, safety, and electronic work monitoring. Finally, you'll see how the emergence of computers has created some ethical questions for today's computer users.

COMPUTER CRIME

A **computer crime** is generally defined as one that involves the use of computers and software for illegal purposes. This doesn't mean that all the crimes are new types of crime. On the contrary, many of these crimes, such as embezzlement of funds, the alteration of records, theft, vandalism, sabotage, and terrorism, can be committed without a computer. But with a computer, these offenses can be carried out more quickly and with less chance that the person responsible for the crime will be discovered.

Computer crimes are on the rise and have been for the last twelve years. Just how much these computer crimes cost the American public is in dispute, but estimates range from $3 billion to $5 billion annually. Even the FBI, which attempts to keep track of the growth or decline of all kinds of crimes, is unable to say precisely how large a loss is involved; however, it estimates that the average take from a company hit by computer crime is $600,000.

494

A number of reasons are given for the increase in computer crime: (a) more computers in use and, thus, more people who are familiar with basic computer operation; (b) more computers tied together in satellite and other data-transmission networks; and (c) the easy access of microcomputers to huge mainframe data bases.

The Criminal

Movies and newspaper stories might lead us to believe that most computer crimes are committed by teenage "hackers"—brilliant and basically good

Jails and prisons are overcrowded, and incarceration is expensive. An alternative to imprisonment for some criminals is found in an electronic monitoring system. A tamper-resistant transmitter is attached to the offender's ankle. It sends digital signals to the receiver, a microcomputer (on the table). The microcomputer sends the signals over the telephone lines to a host computer that is located at the correctional institution. By verifying that the offender stays within range of the receiver (approximately 150 feet), or checks in at preset times, it is possible to maintain accurate records of the prisoner's whereabouts. This punishment would be ironic if a person was convicted of committing a computer crime.

children who let their imagination and technical genius get them into trouble. But a realistic look at the crimes reveals that the offender is likely to be an employee of the firm against which the crime has been committed, i.e., an "insider."

Difficulty of Detection and Prevention

Given the kind of person who commits a computer crime and the environment in which the crime occurs, it is often difficult to detect who the criminal is. First of all, the crime may be so complex that months or years go by before anyone discovers it.

Second, once the crime has been revealed, it is not easy to find a clear trail of evidence that leads back to the guilty party. After all, looking for "weapons" or fingerprints does not occur as it might in the investigation of more conventional crimes.

Third, there are usually no witnesses to the computer crime, even though it may be taking place in a room filled with people. Who is to say if the person at the next terminal, calmly keying in data, is doing the company's work or committing a criminal act (Figure 17–1)?

Fourth, not enough people in management and law enforcement know enough about computer technology to prevent the crimes. Authorities have to be familiar with the computer's capabilities within a given situation to guard against its misuses. In some large cities, such as Los Angeles, police departments have set up specially trained computer crime units.

FIGURE 17–1

Large computer rooms with many terminals make it difficult to prevent or detect an individual who is fraudulently using the system. (Courtesy of Honeywell, Inc.)

Difficulty of Detection

■ Crime is too complex
■ Too much time elapses
■ No witnesses
■ Complex technology

But even when an offender is caught, the investigators, attorneys, judges, or juries may find the alleged crime too complicated and perplexing to handle. More attorneys are specializing in computer law and studying the computer's potential for misuse.

After a computer crime has been discovered, many companies do not report it or prosecute the person responsible. A company may not announce the crime out of fear that the public will find out the weaknesses of its computer system and lose confidence in its organization. Banks, credit card companies, and investment firms are especially sensitive about revealing their vulnerabilities because they rely heavily on customer trust.

To avoid public attention, cautious companies will often settle cases of computer tampering out of court. And if cases do go to trial and the offenders are convicted, they may be punished only by a fine or light sentence because the judge or jury isn't fully trained to understand the nature and seriousness of the crime.

Not all companies are timid in apprehending computer criminals. For example, Connecticut General Life Insurance Company decided it had to get tough on violators. So when the company discovered that one of its computer technicians had embezzled $200,000 by entering false benefit claims, it presented its findings to the state's attorney and aided in the prosecution of the technician. The technician was found guilty and sentenced to prison, not just for the computer misuse, but also for grand theft and insurance fraud. Connecticut General now has a policy of reporting all incidents of theft or fraud, no matter how small.

An employee uses a passkey and enters an access code before entering a high-security computer facility.

Types of Computer Crimes

Data Manipulation   Altering the data that enters or exits the computer is generally called **data manipulation** (sometimes called ''data diddling''). Some examples are: changing school grades by putting false data into a school's computer system; changing credit standing by accessing credit-bureau computer files; and entering or deleting information. Another type of data manipulation is **salami slicing**, i.e., skimming off a tiny bit of money from a number of accounts and diverting it into the manipulator's own account.

Time Bomb   Coding a computer program to destroy itself after it has been run a certain number of times is called a **time bomb**. This method of sabotage is sometimes used by disgruntled employees. It is also used, however, by software developers against companies that buy the software on credit. If the buyer doesn't pay for the software by the time agreed upon, then the program self-destructs. When the bill is paid, the developer tells the buyer how to ''defuse the bomb.''

   Another type of time bomb is the Trojan horse. Vandal hackers create programs to post on bulletin board systems. Although the program seems to be legitimate software (e.g., word processor or computer game), when the unsuspecting user downloads and uses the program, the Trojan horse has been programmed to scramble data, erase the hard-disk index, or even erase all the data on a hard-disk drive. If the user does not have backup copies, the contents of the disk may be irretrievably lost.

Trap Door   Creating a special password that, once keyed in, gives that person access to the system is called a **trap door**. The programmer can then get back into a program. No one else knows about it, and the entry is not documented.

Many computer facilities are protected by closed-circuit television.

HIGHLIGHT

SAFE DEPOSITS FOR DATA

In the last few years, a new type of business has emerged—the safekeeping of valuable data for other people. These data safe deposits have been cropping up all over the country—more than 200 of them, in fact.

Businesses that fear something will happen to their data, causing a business interruption, contract with a company such as Dataport. Backup copies of valuable data are made and placed in Dataport's vaults.

Dataport, one of the largest data deposit companies in the United States, built their vaults 100 feet below the World Trade Center in New York. The walls are thirty feet thick, the glass inside the building is bulletproof, and guards are at their stations twenty-four hours a day.

Paychex, Inc., was glad they were using a company like Dataport when an intruder at one of their processing centers destroyed a week's worth of payroll and tax data. With the backup tapes stored at Dataport, Paychex was able to recreate the lost files—but not without a cost of over $25,000.

Data Stealing   Using a computer to steal information that has been gathered for an organization's legitimate purposes and using it for one's own purposes is called **data stealing**. An example is taking a client list from one company and selling it to a competitor.

Time Stealing   **Time stealing** is using a computer without authorization and thus "stealing" the amount of money that would have been paid in "rent" for the time used, or "stealing" the money it takes to keep that computer in operation for its *intended* purpose.

Electronic Eavesdropping   Tapping, without authorization, into communication lines over which computer data and messages are sent is called **electronic eavesdropping**.

Industrial Espionage   Stealing designs, marketing plans, or other trade secrets by computer from one company and selling the information to another is a form of **industrial espionage**.

Piracy

As more people learn to use computers and as more uses are found for them, there is a corresponding growth in software piracy. In this case, **piracy** is making unauthorized copies of copyrighted computer programs. It's something like buying a popular record and taping copies of it for sale (an act which is also illegal).

COMPUTERS AND THE RIGHT TO PRIVACY

Amendment IV of the Bill of Rights guarantees United States citizens that the right to be secure in "their persons, houses, papers, and effects against unreasonable searches and seizures, shall not be violated."

Privacy of personal data stored in computers, of course, is not mentioned in the Bill of Rights. So the issue has naturally arisen as to exactly how much **privacy** citizens have a right to. For the discussion in this text, privacy means the right of control over one's personal data.

Privacy is a much easier issue to deal with if you conduct your life within the walls of your home and beyond the eyes and ears of passersby. But once you breach those walls by installing and using a telephone, setting up a bank account, filing an insurance claim, applying for a loan, enrolling in school, admitting yourself to a hospital, or any one of hundreds of other such actions, your privacy is endangered.

How Computers Increase the Danger

Computers alone don't invade our privacy, but they enable people to do it with greater ease and frequency than ever before. Primarily, computers assist in the invasion of privacy in two ways: (a) they enable the user to stockpile and categorize a lot of information about us in a very small space; and (b) they allow other users quick access to anything and everything that is in the stockpile.

The federal government is the biggest stockpiler. Its various departments, bureaus, and offices have more than three and one-half billion files about its citizens. When you add the computerized files of all the state agencies (health, welfare, education, law enforcement, etc.) and such private institutions as banks, hospitals, insurance companies, and credit bureaus, then it is clear that none of us has a lot of privacy left if someone wants to poke about in our lives.

Information on what we buy, how we pay for it, what we read, what we watch on television, what our sicknesses are, and how much we earn is valuable information for those who want to sell us things—whether it be eggbeaters or ideas. If there is money to be made, some people will proceed without regard to the laws or ethics involved. Invasion of privacy is dangerous because it means people can use our preferences, weaknesses, and habits to their own advantage.

Still, there are organizations and institutions that need to know something about us if they are going to work toward our own good. Often, doctors must have quick access to our complete medical history to cure us or save our lives. Banks need proof that our credit record is good so they can loan us the money for a new car or house. Basically, the question of privacy boils down to the fair collection and use of personal data.

What Society Is Afraid Of

Here are some of the specific dangers that society sees in the huge personal data banks that are stored by government agencies and large private organizations:

☐ To begin with, the data collected may be inaccurate. The computer doesn't know which information is true and which is false. All it tells is what is in the file. The data may be wrong for any number of reasons: (a) a mistake on the part of the person who gathered it originally or the one who keyed it into the computer; (b) a mismatch of the right information and the wrong name; or (c) information that was once correct, but which is now out of date.

☐ People are concerned that the personal data collected about them may not be secure from illegal access and use. They also fear that private data sent over communication lines may be illegally intercepted. Although many organizations do establish elaborate security systems, computer-related crimes and theft have increased in the last few years.

☐ There is fear that one giant data base with all personal information about every member of our society in it will be compiled. If all the agencies put all their data banks together into one, for example, it would include almost everything about us anyone would ever want to know.

☐ The computer's great ability to store and classify vast amounts of data also leads to the tendency to collect and keep more information about people than is actually needed to fulfill the function for which it was being collected. Because information about us is often very useful, and sometimes very profitable, the temptation is to amass as much of it as possible.

Adequate security is needed to protect the large amounts of data stored on disk or tape by an organization.

Privacy Concerns

- Inaccurate data
- Illegal access and use of data
- One huge data base
- Collection of more data than needed
- Exchange of data between organizations

☐ To compound the danger of too much personal data being too easily accessible in one place, there is the even more ominous fact that data collection agencies commonly combine and exchange their information. This enables anyone with access to get not only an individual's credit records, for example, but also health, insurance, and employment records.

Even though there is legislation against federal agencies using the information for a purpose other than it was intended, there is a system called **matching**. In matching, one agency compares its data with another's for a specific purpose. For example, the Internal Revenue Service files are being matched against the welfare rolls to catch welfare cheaters. There are advantages to this system as well as a potential for misuse.

The fact that an individual, business, or agency has these records may cause no particular harm to you, but their interpretation of the data to make decisions about you could be hazardous. The combination of potentially inaccurate, out-of-date, and irrelevant information is dangerous.

JOB SECURITY

One of the most apparent social effects of the computer is the way it has altered the United States job market, a fact that Antonia Stone was aware of when she decided to promote computer literacy to the underprivileged. It has changed the way work traditionally has been done at every level of production—from design, to manufacture, to distribution. When computers were still in their infancy, labor union leaders predicted they would take jobs away from people. To some degree, their predictions have been correct.

As of 1986, there were over 100,000 industrial robots used throughout the noncommunist countries of the world. There are more robots and fewer people on auto assembly lines now (Figure 17–2). General Motors (GM) alone has over 40,000 programmable devices, 4,000 of which are robots. GM plans about 200,000 programmable devices (14,000 are robots) for the two new plants it expects to open in 1989.

Office jobs have been eliminated because a few workers using word processors are now able to turn out more letters and reports than a roomful of secretaries, laboring away at "old-fashioned" typewriters. For example, a few years ago, a large law firm would have a staff of several people typing

FIGURE 17–2
Many automobile assembly line jobs, such as painting and welding, are being automated through the use of robotics. Here, the chassis are spray painted as they roll down the assembly lines. (Courtesy of Honda of America, Marysville, Ohio)

FIGURE 17–3
News stories can be entered and stored directly in the computer. The files can then be transmitted electronically to a typesetting machine, eliminating the need for a linotypist. (Courtesy of *Chicago Tribune*)

briefs and other legal documents. Now, this might be done by only one person with a word processor.

Today, newspaper reporters can prepare their articles to be set in type as they are being composed on a computer terminal. Just a few years ago, typesetting was done by skillful and well-paid linotypists who are no longer needed (Figure 17–3).

In a report to Congress, the W. E. Upjohn Institute predicted that 200,000 workers could be displaced by robots and computers by 1990. As many as 50,000 of those lost jobs could be among auto workers.

Others think the threats of unemployment are overstated. In its report to Congress, the Office of Technology Assessment indicated that programmable automation probably won't create massive nationwide unemployment in this decade.

Obviously, there is a "pro" side to robots. They can do some jobs faster and cheaper than human beings. Better still, robots never become ill, never need breaks, and can work twenty-four hours a day. These facts not only mean economy for the manufacturer, but also lower prices for the consumers. Not being susceptible to human ills and not being inclined to sue for any physical injuries, robots are especially valuable in performing high-risk and monotonous jobs, such as mining, diving, painting, working with toxic chemicals, and assembling parts.

Robots do create some jobs. After all, someone has to design, build, sell, and maintain them. Some newer industries would never have been possible without them. Although predictions of the disastrous effects of computers on employment have not yet come to pass, many jobs, especially in manufacturing and the auto industry, are being eliminated.

Thus far, the effect of these job shifts has been to weaken the labor union—not just because machines can do the work of people, but also because computers enable one worker to do a variety of related jobs well instead of specializing in one task. Unions were organized on the principle that a worker had a specific job and was protected in keeping it.

In response to union and societal concerns, heavily computerized companies often try to soften this reality by waiting for workers to retire or not replacing workers who resign. Some companies offer retraining and job-placement help for those who have been nudged out by computers.

ELECTRONIC WORK MONITORING

The National Institute of Occupational Safety and Health (NIOSH) estimates that more than eight million video display terminal (VDT) operators are being watched by their own computers. The term for this new way of supervising workers is **electronic work monitoring**.

How can computers monitor workers? They can count keystrokes, track data-entry errors, record the length and frequency of breaks, and measure the time it takes the operator to handle a customer-service transaction. In short, the computer can measure the quantity and, in some ways, the quality of an employee's work.

It used to be that this kind of monitoring was found only on the factory assembly line as a way of calculating each worker's productivity. Or, it might be simply a supervisor looking over a worker's shoulder to see if the job is being done. With electronic work monitoring, the white-collar worker is now faced with the same situation as the assembly-line worker always has been.

A Tool for Productivity

Is there anything wrong with electronic work monitoring? Surely the employer has a right to know who is producing and how well. How else, employers argue, can they decide who to promote, who to reprimand, and who to fire? They claim that this system is fair and objective. With electronic work monitoring, each employee can have a detailed, electronic record of productivity right there in his or her permanent file.

Companies see this as a cost-effective way to measure job performance, to provide incentive pay to workers who perform more than the minimum requirements, and to make the most of the new technology to bring their costs down.

The Potential for Probing

Many workers see the work-monitoring issue as an invasion of their privacy and as a not-very-subtle way of speeding up their work. But the companies say that workers who use company equipment necessarily give up some privacy rights. So the arguments continue.

There is room in this practice for company misuse if, for instance, company managers take note only of the operator's speed in completing a transaction and give no weight to the quality of the work. Furthermore, employees may never get the chance to see the data compiled about them and, thus, have no chance to correct any inaccuracy. Electronic work mon-

HIGHLIGHT

FREEDOM OF INFORMATION: THE GOOD NEWS AND THE BAD NEWS

First the good news: When the British magazine *Computing* decided to test the United States' Freedom of Information Act, it had one of its U.S. correspondents ask for copies of all reports compiled by the United States General Accounting Office on government computer systems and government contracts. The reporter received over 100 pounds of files. It works!

Now the bad news: After reading through all the documents, the magazine reported discovering several "incidents." One file indicated that the Nuclear Materials Management and Safeguards System didn't hold accurate data, which means that the U.S. Government doesn't really know how much of which material (for making atom bombs) has been sent where.

Another shocking document revealed the Pentagon had once been caught using a computer to monitor voting records of representatives to see which ones were sympathetic to its spending plan. Another file revealed inefficient use and mismanagement of computer systems at NASA and the North American Strategic Defense Command.

It appears that the Freedom of Information Act guarantees some interesting and sometimes frightening reading.

itoring, since it is easy and automatic, may also tend to substitute machine measure for human evaluation of job performance. Finally, some employees say, this kind of measuring could allow the company to fire employees with information that only appears to be objective.

Companies using electronic work monitoring say that the computer *is* objective. When it registers an employee's performance and puts the record in an electronic file, the company is really protecting the individual's privacy, not violating it.

This productivity versus privacy argument may never be settled without laws to govern the monitoring or an agreement on the practice between the company's management and worker representatives.

HEALTH AND SAFETY

Are computers hazardous to your health? Well, the jury is still out on this question. Some people are worried that the radiation coming from video display terminals may cause cataracts, cancer, miscarriages, visual problems, stress, and sterility. These charges have been researched by such agencies as the Food and Drug Administration's Bureau of Radiological Health, the Occupational Safety and Health Administration, the National Institute of Occupational Safety and Health, and the Canadian Radiation

Protection Bureau. One Japanese report recommends that pregnant workers not use VDTs until more conclusive studies can be made.

The American and Canadian studies have failed to demonstrate any connection between VDT radiation and disease. The House Education and Labor Subcommittee on Health and Safety reported to Congress that it found no connection either. But it did suggest that employers and employees work together to set up satisfactory operation and work guidelines.

Still, workers' fears continue, and other private and government studies are underway. Among the other common complaints of VDT operators are these:

☐ Eye strain, neck strain, backache, and fatigue (Studies confirm that these ailments can result if users aren't provided comfortable workstations with proper lighting, adjustable chairs, and frequent breaks from the terminals.)

☐ Mental stress (Many people who work at terminals feel that they are expected to produce more and do it faster because computers themselves are so fast. In fact, workers who are aware of being monitored by the computer frequently feel additional pressure.)

Some people are concerned about the emotional and personality changes that could occur from being isolated from other workers and the social aspects of human interaction. In today's high-tech, automated society, people can conduct business and communicate without ever coming face to face. Computer operators can work an entire shift, taking their instructions from a terminal screen. Employees can send and receive memos to each other electronically, seldom engaging in personal conversation.

In 1985, the National Association of Working Women and the Service Employees International Union campaigned strongly on behalf of VDT safety. To date, Washington, California, New Mexico, Rhode Island, Wisconsin, and Massachusetts have passed VDT-safety laws. While all the laws are slightly different, they generally deal with creating more comfortable workstations, medical checkups, and employer/employee discussions.

In the meantime, **ergonomics**, the study of adjusting the machine and the workplace to the worker, has been applied to the electronic office. Efforts are continually being made by ergonomic specialists and furniture and equipment designers to design the workplace to be safe and comfortable.

COMPUTER ETHICS

It may not be immediately apparent that computers pose any particular ethical problems. But **computer ethics**, a standard of behavior regarding the use of computers for individuals and organizations, is needed in addition to any laws that exist.

As long ago as 1970, the American Federation of Information Processing Societies (AFIPS) saw the need for standards and, thus, established a code of computer ethics for its members. And the Institute for Certification of Computer Professionals (ICCP) requires that an applicant for a certificate must meet ethical standards as well as fulfill education and experience criteria.

The observance of ethics is a way of self-regulating conduct when the law or situation doesn't indicate a clear course of action. Here are some persistent ethical questions regarding computers:

☐ Is it an invasion of privacy to monitor an employee through his or her own computer?

☐ Is it fair for an employer to use the data collected from electronic work monitoring as the only evidence for evaluating an employee?

☐ Does a company owe a worker who has been replaced by a computer any consideration other than that prescribed by labor law or contract?

☐ Is it right for someone who buys a software program to make a copy for a friend?

☐ Should computer operators regard all data they process as completely confidential?

☐ Is it fair to tap into someone else's computer data files?

SUMMARY

The advent of computers has also brought about computer crime. Computer crimes, most often committed by an "insider," are usually difficult to detect. Many of these crimes are not reported because businesses fear that the weaknesses in their computer systems will be made public. When the crimes are brought to court, the criminal is sometimes given just a light sentence.

Computer crime takes several forms: data manipulation; time bomb; trap door; data stealing; time stealing; electronic eavesdropping; and industrial espionage.

Piracy is making unauthorized copies of programs under copyright.

The issue of privacy has emerged since the appearance of huge data banks and reported incidents of misuse of personal information. Some people think that computers increase the danger to our privacy because: (a) they permit the stockpiling of a lot of information in one place; and (b) they allow users to access everything in the stockpile.

Society's concerns are that: (a) the data may be incorrect; (b) the data may not be secure from illegal access; (c) there will be one giant data bank where all information about them is stored; (d) more information will be collected and kept than is needed; and (e) information may be exchanged between organizations.

The concern for unemployment from use of computers and robots in the workplace has workers and managers trying to find ways to handle displaced workers. They are also debating the issue of electronic work monitoring. Managers say they need this efficient measurement tool, but workers feel it's an invasion of privacy.

The reports that VDT radiation causes disease has not yet been confirmed; but people are still worried. Other concerns about the use of computers include physical stress, mental stress, and worker isolation.

A firmly established code of computer ethics is needed in addition to current legislation to assure data are handled in a way that will not deprive citizens of their right to privacy.

Key Terms

computer crime (p. 494)

computer ethics (p. 506)

data manipulation (p. 498)

data stealing (p. 499)

electronic eavesdropping (p. 499)

electronic work monitoring (p. 504)

ergonomics (p. 506)

industrial espionage (p. 499)

matching (p. 502)

piracy (p. 499)

privacy (p. 500)

salami slicing (p. 498)

time bomb (p. 498)

time stealing (p. 499)

trap door (p. 498)

Review Questions

1. Why is computer crime on the increase?
2. Most computer crimes are perpetrated by people who are _____.
3. Give three reasons why computer crime is difficult to detect.
4. Why are some companies reluctant to report incidents of computer crime?
5. Briefly describe electronic eavesdropping.
6. _____ is the act of making illegal copies of someone else's software.
7. Describe data manipulation with regard to computer crime.
8. Explain the difference between data stealing and time stealing.
9. Stealing trade secrets with the use of a computer is a form of _____.
10. What does privacy refer to in regard to computers and data?
11. What factors can cause the inaccuracy of data collected by an organization?
12. Which technological advance has changed the workplace in the automobile industry?
13. How does computer technology increase the danger to individual privacy?
14. Name the biggest stockpiler of data in the United States.
15. What kinds of personal data are collected and stored about individuals and by whom?
16. How can a computer monitor a worker's productivity?
17. What are some complaints of VDT users?

18. What are computer ethics?

19. What are some of the ethical questions surrounding computers?

20. Why does the concept of agencies matching files concern some people?

21. Explain why computer criminals are seldom brought to justice.

22. How does the commission of crimes such as computer fraud and theft differ from the traditional crimes of fraud and theft?

23. What specifically are people afraid of in regard to privacy and the huge data banks?

24. Discuss the impact of computerization on the work force.

25. Why do some people object to electronic work monitoring?

INFOMODULE

Legal Issues and Legislation

Because information is often randomly gathered, carelessly guarded, and easily accessible via computer technology, the assaults on personal and corporate privacy are difficult to detect and legislate against. Much of our safety under present conditions will depend on the thoroughness and ethics of those who compile the data in the first place. New laws are being made. Of the 400 laws passed by the 98th Congress, fifty-eight were related to information technology. Most states have also passed laws to discourage computer crime or privacy invasion.

PRIVACY AND ELECTRONIC EAVESDROPPING

One difficulty arising from this phase of social change is that the laws have to take into account the rights of all the people who might be affected.

For example, is information about *you* the property of the person or company that gathers it, or do you have some right to or ownership of it? If someone gains access to information you have freely provided to someone else, does that constitute theft or ethical misuse? Questions such as these keep the legislatures and courts busy, balancing conflicting interests.

In the 1960s and 1970s, some federal agencies and Congress became aware of the seriousness of the problem. Congress passed the **Freedom of Information Act of 1970** to allow citizens to find out which federal agencies are keeping records on them and to secure copies of the records to see if they are correct.

TABLE 1
Key federal privacy and other computer-related legislation

PRIVACY
Freedom of Information Act of 1970
Allows citizens to find out which federal agencies are collecting and storing data about them and to secure copies of the records to see if they are correct.
Fair Credit Reporting Act of 1970
Provides that people have the right to inspect their credit records. If a citizen challenges data in the record, the credit agency is legally required to investigate the accuracy of that data.
Crime Control Act of 1973
Stipulates that those responsible for maintaining state criminal records that were developed with federal funds must ensure the security and privacy of the data in those records.
Privacy Act of 1974
Establishes laws to prevent federal government abuses against an individual's privacy: forbids data on individuals to be collected for one purpose and used for another without the individual's consent; gives individuals the right to find out what information the government has collected about them; allows individuals to have copies of these files and have a way to correct wrong data; requires the government agency involved to ensure that the records are up-to-date and correct and must protect them from misuse; among other provisions.
Education Privacy Act of 1974
Restricts access to computer records of grades and behavior evaluations in private and public schools. Students have the right to examine and challenge the data in their records.
Tax Reform Act of 1976
Puts limitations on the IRS in its access to personal information in bank records and on its providing other agencies with that information.
Right to Financial Privacy Act of 1978
Establishes restrictions on government access to customer files in financial institutions, and it gives citizens the right to examine data about themselves in those files.

This legislation was the forerunner of a series of acts to stop unnecessary and unauthorized snooping into credit ratings (the Fair Credit Reporting Act of 1970), educational records (the Education Privacy Act of 1974), and personal finance (the Right to Financial Privacy Act of 1978). Most federal privacy legislation until the mid-1980s related to the behavior of the federal government and the organizations to which it supplied funds. Now, legislation is appearing that reaches into the private sector.

To establish the position that the federal government has no right to keep secret records about any citizen and to protect citizens from privacy abuses by the federal government, Congress enacted the **Privacy Act of 1974**.

Some of the provisions of this act are:

☐ It allows individuals to find out what data about them have been collected, filed, and used by government agencies.

☐ It forbids data on individuals collected for one purpose to be used for another purpose without their consent. However, the government's more frequent use of "matching" decreases the power of this provision.

☐ It specifies that individuals must be allowed to have a copy of all records pertaining to them and have a way to correct incorrect data.

☐ It says the government agency involved must ensure that the records are up-to-date and accurate and must protect them from misuse.

Privacy Protection Act of 1980
Prohibits government agents from making unwarranted searches of press offices and files.

Electronic Funds Transfer Act of 1980
Stipulates that those who offer the electronic funds transfer (EFT) check service must tell customers about third-party access to the customers' accounts.

Debt Collection Act of 1982
Sets up due-process conditions federal agencies must follow before releasing any information about bad debts to credit bureaus.

Cable Communications Policy Act of 1984
Requires cable television services to tell their subscribers if any personal information about them is being collected, used, or disclosed.

Electronic Communications Privacy Act of 1986
Makes it illegal to intercept data communication, such as electronic mail.

Computer Fraud and Abuse Act of 1986
Gives federal jurisdiction over interstate computer crimes in the private sector. Applies to computers used by the federal government and federally insured financial institutions.

COPYRIGHT PROTECTION

Copyright Act of 1976
Protects creative and intellectual property, such as books, plays, songs, photographs, and computer programs from the moment of creation.

Semiconductor Chip Protection Act of 1984
Intended to prevent one company from reproducing the chip pattern of another. The act gives original developer a ten-year period of exclusive rights.

The refinement of computer technology in the 1980s led to the passage of other federal laws to protect privacy. You can see some of them cited in Table 1 (p. 510).

Computer-related areas that may require better protective laws include electronic mailboxes and bulletin boards, data-communication lines, and unattended computer terminals. The Electronic Communications Privacy Act of 1986 made the interception of data communication illegal. Another related law is the Computer Fraud and Abuse Act of 1986, which gives the federal government jurisdiction over interstate computer crimes and crimes involving computers used by the federal government.

LIABILITY FOR INCORRECT INFORMATION AND SOFTWARE WORKABILITY

Have you ever been the victim of a "computer error"? Perhaps you have been sent a check with the wrong amount printed on it, or received your class-registration form with the wrong classes listed. These errors result more in inconvenience than anything else. But some errors and losses are so great that the courts are trying to discover just who is legally responsible for them—whether the faults are in the information, system designs, or expert systems that are used. (Expert systems are described in more detail in the InfoModule on page 309.)

Incorrect Information

Although the extent to which any agency or company can be held accountable for the accuracy of information it gives out is not clear, these organizations are becoming more vulnerable to large claims.

The question of blame is quite complex, as shown by these two examples of litigation:

☐ The family of victims in an airplane crash in Alaska sued the airline and its chartmaker. The pilot had relied on graphically drawn charts that include faulty government data. The family won and collected damages.

☐ A federal court in Boston ruled that the U.S. Weather Service was not liable for an erroneous forecast that resulted in the deaths of four lobster fishermen.

Society is becoming aware of just how deeply wrong information can affect us. For example, incorrect data provided to air traffic controllers or drug manufacturers can have life or death consequences for hundreds or thousands of people. Some providers of information and expert-system software are working within their own companies and trade organizations to prevent both potential tragedies and lawsuits. They are using two basic approaches: (a) testing and verification of data to create a more reliable product or service; and (b) limiting their liability in advance through contract provisions and disclaimer statements on their packages.

Software Workability

There is an ongoing battle between software manufacturers and the people who buy the software as to who must bear the cost of damages if the software doesn't work. Currently, software suppliers give no performance guarantee. Manufacturers say they can't possibly anticipate all the software applications and ensure its usefulness. Consumers argue that the software should do what it says it will.

The question of responsibility becomes even more acute in the matter of expert systems. Because they are designed for specific and complex uses (such as medical diagnosis), and because the results of any defects would be more catastrophic, the legal implications are potentially more serious. In fact, when there is an accident or financial loss arising from the system, it might be blamed on the manufacturers of the hardware, the data base, the software, or on its user—each of which might be charged with liability. It is not surprising, then, that the laws applying to responsibility here are in the very early stages of evolution.

COPYRIGHT AND INFRINGEMENT

Computer software is protected by federal copyright law, and many of the ethical and legal problems surrounding computer technology today are perceived to arise from copyright violations.

The only way software manufacturers can recover their expenses in developing programs and make a profit is to sell the program in large numbers. Naturally, each pirated copy sold reduces the number the developers can sell. Since pirates have to pay only the copying costs—and none of the research and development expenses—they sell the programs cheaper than the developer.

To discourage unauthorized copying, software developers use such methods as:

☐ Licensing one or several manufacturers to produce the programs and pay the developer a royalty fee on each program produced

☐ Putting a seal on the software package and stating that when the seal is broken, the buyer is automatically agreeing that, among other things, only he or she will use the software [The assumption here is that breaking the seal is the same thing as signing an agreement (Figure 1).]

☐ Building "locks" into the programs to prevent them from being copied or permitting only a limited number of backup copies to be made (Unfortunately for the program developers, these locks are not unbreakable.)

FIGURE 1
The software license agreement outlines the terms and conditions that the buyer automatically agrees to upon acceptance and opening of the software package.

In the United States, the **Copyright Act of 1976**, which went into effect January 1, 1978, specifically lists computer programs among the works protected from the moment of their creation—instead of from the time they are officially registered.

The standard notice includes the copyright symbol ©, the date of the program's creation, and the name of the author or copyright owner. Here's an example: © 1988 XYZ Software Co. The copyright notice appears on the computer monitor when the computer is turned on and the software is installed (Figure 2).

Some espionage incidents involving chip design led Congress to pass legislation, the Semiconductor Chip Protection Act of 1984, to prevent one company from reproducing the chip pattern of another. The act gives the original developer a ten-year period of exclusive rights.

The more effective software manufacturers became in thwarting copying, however, the more complaints they got from customers who had legitimate need for extra copies of the program. Some needed the copies for backup. Others needed to load the programs on large-capacity disk drives. The result was that some customers, including the U.S. Department of Defense, quit buying copy-protected software. As a consequence, manufacturers began dropping the anticopy features in their software

---

Copyright

■ © symbol
■ Date of creation
■ Name of author or copyright owner

---

packages. To compensate for this setback, the manufacturers stepped up their prosecution of those suspected of copying and selling the software.

People familiar with the variety and cleverness of computer criminals agree that there needs to be more specific legislation. The present laws cannot be stretched to cover all the criminal opportunities that a new technology creates.

ISSUES ON THE HORIZON

But as a solution or response is found for one set of computer-related concerns, other problems pop up. Here are some recent ones:

☐ Digital audio tape (DAT) recorders can make copies of music on compact disks that are as good as the original. This is bound to cut down on the number of compact disks sold

---

FIGURE 2
Copyright notices inform a user that the program is protected by the Copyright Act of 1976 and cannot be duplicated.

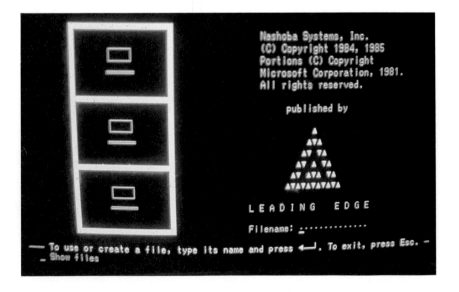

and on the amount of royalties paid to the songwriters whose songs are on the disks. Should DAT records be legal only if they have a built-in chip which prevents buyers from copying? Or, should a buyer have the right to record anything that the DAT recorder is capable of duplicating? What role, if any, should the government have in settling this problem?

☐ In its effort to ensure that all income is reported, should the Internal Revenue Service have the right to use its computers to match its own list against commercially available lists of people judged to have high income? Under such a matching scheme, if a person on the commercial list does not show up on the IRS list, or if there seems to be a big difference between the level of income reported and the level suspected, the IRS would launch an investigation. Until the computer came along, such investigations could never have been started. Are laws needed to keep them from being started now? Or, should laws be passed to give the IRS the right to use any information it can?

☐ As it becomes easier for people to "eavesdrop" on electronic communication (data banks, message systems, communication networks), how can our old privacy and theft laws be stretched or updated to cover offenses that were unimaginable just a few years ago?

State and federal lawmakers are finding computer-related questions a regular part of their legislative sessions. In 1986, the U.S. Congress passed the Computer Fraud and Abuse Act giving jurisdiction to the federal government over interstate crimes in the private sector. Among its several provisions, the act makes it a federal misdemeanor to use stolen passwords to defraud or gain entry to a "federal-interest computer" to inspect or obtain data. It makes the accessing of such a computer a felony if: (a) the aim is to steal by computer; (b) computer data are changed or destroyed; (c) the loss is at least $1,000; or (d) the data involved are medical records.

It hardly requires a crystal ball to see more legal issues being raised and more legislation being passed as the computer continues to imbed itself into the business, social, political, and personal fabrics of our lives.

KEY TERMS

Copyright Act of 1976 (p. 514)

Freedom of Information Act of 1970 (p. 510)

Privacy Act of 1974 (p. 511)

QUESTIONS

1. What landmark legislation in 1970 allowed citizens to find out which federal agencies are keeping records on them and to get copies of the records?
2. Of what significance is the Privacy Act of 1974?
3. How is the issue of who is responsible for computer "mistakes" being resolved?
4. How does U.S. copyright law protect computer software against piracy?
5. Suggest possible solutions or legislation for the copyright and privacy issues on the horizon.

OBJECTIVES

☐ Describe some of the ways people are trying to make faster and more powerful computers

☐ Discuss some of the areas of artificial intelligence that are being explored

☐ Name and describe several new chip technologies being considered

☐ Discuss some of the trends and changes occurring in our society as a result of the Information Revolution

18

A Future With Computers

PROFILE: Alan M. Turing

It wasn't the only question in Alan M. Turing's short life, but it seems to have been the most insistent one: Can machines think? He spent much of his time in pursuit of the answer. Turing was born in London in 1912 and showed a talent for mathematics at an early age. In 1931, he enrolled at Cambridge University. Subsequently, he came to the United States and continued his studies at Princeton, where he worked with the distinguished scientist John von Neumann.

By 1937, Turing had drawn up plans for a machine that could assess encoded data and draw conclusions from it. When Germany went to war with England a few years later, the British government approached Turing to help construct a method for breaking German codes. The resulting machine, which bore the unofficial name of "Eastern Goddess," worked and was crucial in keeping Turing's country abreast of Nazi plans. So secret were the details of Turing's code-breaking method that they have never been publicly revealed.

Following the war, Turing went to work at Britain's National Physical Laboratory, where he labored on a machine called the "Automatic Computing Engine." During this immediate postwar period, he wrote a paper on "Intelligent Machinery," in which he equated the human brain to a machine. Some were enchanted with Turing's notions; others thought them more science fiction (or heresy) than science.

To answer the question of whether a machine can think, at least to his own satisfaction, Turing devised a test. It basically boiled down to this point: If, after a series of query-and-response exchanges between a human being and a machine that can make responses (via print, terminal, etc.), the human is convinced that the machine's behavior is intelligent, then it *is* intelligent. To Turing, the manifestation of intelligence in a machine was its ability to store and sift through a lot of data to arrive at "reasonable" conclusions. He ultimately concluded that, within the definitions of his test, a machine can think.

His obsession with thinking machines and his belief that they could be constructed made Turing a significant pioneer in the field of what is now called artificial intelligence (AI).

In spite of his scientific successes, Turing was not a happy man. Friends said he exhibited whimsical, childlike qualities throughout his life. Turing was found dead at his home in 1954, a cyanide-covered spoon nearby. Officials concluded that the 41-year-old genius had taken his own life.

Some people suggest that the computer advances of the last forty years are only the beginning—that even more dramatic breakthroughs in electronics and computers are looming on the horizon.

About 100 years ago, the United States had progressed from an agricultural society and economy to an industrial one. The Industrial Revolution centered on the steam engine and similar technologies, and resulted in a dramatic change in methods of factory production that led to an urbanization of population patterns and major changes in American lifestyles.

Now, according to those experts who study trends, we are seeing an Information Revolution, one that affects economic and societal patterns via the transfer of information. Starting in about 1947 with the ENIAC (one of the first general-purpose, electronic digital computers), the U.S. began to experience a tremendous increase in its ability to collect and store information; and Americans began to develop new technologies to manipulate and communicate that information.

Some people suggest that the "revolution" is actually over. They say that the most important discoveries have been made (computers and communication technology) and that we're now in a stage of evolving or refining those technologies and adjusting to the changes occurring in our personal lives, our economy, and our work. Whatever the stage, we are clearly in the midst of the Information Age, living in an information-centered economy with all its rewards and problems.

Although some changes have occurred relatively fast, progress has been very slow in giving computers "intelligence," and no major breakthrough, or "intelligence revolution," has occurred yet. This chapter looks at some of the areas to watch closely and at some of the forecasts for our society.

Information Revolution

- Massive amounts of information collected and stored
- Technology to manipulate and communicate that information

NEW DIRECTIONS IN TECHNOLOGY

The discovery and harnessing of electricity, coupled with the development of vacuum tubes, brought us to the first generation of computers. Then semiconductors (transistors) brought in the second generation. Integrated circuits, containing thousands of switches on a chip, were key to the third. Finally, microscopic-sized circuits on a chip (LSI and VLSI) were the elements of the fourth generation. Now, scientists are looking for that technological breakthrough to propel us into the **fifth generation** of computers. Many people argue that the development of artificial intelligence will mark the beginning of a fifth generation of computers.

Meanwhile, scientific research is being done on several fronts, all with the purpose of: (a) increasing speed, memory, and power of computers; (b) teaching them to think like humans; (c) making them easier to use; and (d) finding practical applications for the existing technology.

Artificial Intelligence

It may seem that there is no place to go. After all, computers are now inexpensive and readily available to almost anyone in the U.S. who wants to use one. Computers can calculate many times faster than humans; computerized robots can work longer hours; and data banks can remember much more data than the human mind.

Most experts think that the next breakthrough will be **artificial intelligence (AI)**—the ability of machines to "think" and "reason" like humans, which in turn, the futurists predict, will change the way we use computers. Uses for these thinking machines will be found that were never before thought possible.

What it will take to accomplish this technological leap is more computer speed, more power, and more memory than ever before. These factors will be essential to accommodate the sophisticated programming that AI requires.

Although research in artificial intelligence started in the mid-1950s, it is still in its early stages of development. Progress is slow. Specifically, the areas of artificial intelligence that are being pursued are: (a) expert systems; (b) advanced robotics; (c) natural-language processing; (d) voice synthesis; (e) voice recognition; and (f) computer vision.

Expert Systems **Expert systems** (discussed in the InfoModule on page 309) are those software programs that store the knowledge of a human expert and then are used as consultants in particular fields, e.g., in medicine to help doctors diagnose illnesses or service/repair engineers determine equipment malfunctioning (Figure 18–1). Most of these systems do not come close to replacing human experts and are not considered by most AI experts to be truly artificial intelligence.

Robotics **Robotics** is the area of study dealing with the design, construction, and operation of robots. Robots are still used mainly for simple, repetitious tasks on factory assembly lines. However, they have become sophisticated enough for important and dangerous jobs, such as bomb disposal, ocean exploration, outer-space probes, coal mining excavation, and cleanup of a chemical or nuclear accident.

Areas of AI

- Expert systems
- Advanced robotics
- Natural language processing
- Voice recognition
- Voice synthesis
- Computer vision

FIGURE 18–1
Honeywell service people who maintain industrial and computer equipment use expert systems. The conversational programs are important for diagnostics, professional assistance, emergency management, and other uses. (Courtesy of Honeywell, Inc.)

Denning Mobile Robotics in Woburn, Massachusetts, makes robots that function as prison guards. These four-foot tall robots detect human movement through sensors. If a prisoner is detected in an unauthorized area, the robot alerts authorities and tells the prisoner to return to the cell.

MIT, Stanford University, and Carnegie-Mellon University are among several institutions and private companies that are heavily involved in robotics research. They are: (a) making robots "intelligent" by using the latest in AI research, i.e., giving them the ability to make decisions; (b) giving them highly sensitive tactile capabilities; (c) providing them with a capacity to "see" in great detail; and (d) designing them with dependable stabilizing systems.

Nolan Bushnell, now a designer of personal robots, believes that in just a few years we'll all have robots in our homes to do practical tasks. He believes we'll have robot pets, which might even look like the furry live ones, that are smarter than the real version. Bushnell says that these "robot rovers" won't shed, cause allergies, or need to be walked at 6 o'clock in the morning. They will take on all forms and be adaptable for work, fantasy, or fun. Sound outrageous? Bushnell's new company, Axlon, is already making computerized furry animal toys.

More progress must be made, however, before robots can be relied on to serve your household. The tasks involved in carrying out commands to vacuum the carpets or cook dinner demand more interpretation, decision making, and logic than the robot that sprays paint on objects moving on the assembly line. Most personal robots are not yet sophisticated enough for household tasks; they are more for amusement.

Raj Reddy, director of the Robotics Institute at Carnegie-Mellon University, oversees research projects for making computers with human-like attributes. He is working on a device with a sense of "smell" and designed another that can grasp a delicate object. Reddy and his colleagues are also working on robots with complex vision that will let them maneuver safely over unfamiliar terrain.

To create effective mobile robots, Eugene Fichter, an engineering professor at Oregon State University, and his colleagues look for walking robot designs by watching, studying, and filming spiders and their movements over difficult terrains. The movements will be digitized and computer analyzed to see if their motions can be adapted to the much heavier robot machines.

Future Robots

- Brains
- Complex sense of touch
- Complex sense of vision
- Stability when maneuvering

Natural Language Processing Finding ways to communicate with the computer as one would with a colleague depends not only on the right hardware and immense primary storage, it also demands sophisticated software in the form of a natural language processor.

Natural language processing is the ability of the computer to understand and translate natural, everyday language. Researchers have been trying for more than forty years to make machines that recognize and process natural language, but they have had only limited success.

Programs demonstrating some of these capabilities exist today, such as the one by Lotus Development Corporation, that permits users to operate a Lotus 1-2-3 spreadsheet through regular English commands. Not surprisingly, it's called HAL (Human Access Language). Among other things, it can compress what would ordinarily be a seven-step query to the program into a one-phrase English query.

Future systems using language-processing software will be able to understand input in the form of any human language—English, Chinese, or others—and perhaps translate it into any other.

Voice Recognition Most systems with **voice recognition** capability recognize only a few words. The computer must be "trained" to recognize the user's voice; then it accepts data or instructions by having commands spoken into the computer's microphone. However, the speaker must pause after each word.

There are other difficulties: (a) many words sound like other words; (b) different people pronounce the same word differently; (c) one word can have multiple meanings; and (d) the tone in which something is said, such as a sarcastic remark, carries more meaning than the actual words do.

Any programming that improves upon these limiting factors will have to be able to interpret *all* the characteristics that make up conversation, such as inflections, sentence structures, and speeds.

ROBOTS ON THE FRONT LINE

Scientists are perfecting a new breed of giant robots that can walk, climb stairs, "see" where they're going and what they're doing, and "hear" the sounds around them. They have been designed to operate in areas that are too hazardous or inaccessible for humans to work in, such as places with high radiation levels.

Price tags on these complex robots are high, ranging from just under $100,000 to well over $1 million. The devices not only move around and send signals back to their operators, but also lift and manipulate objects; take measurements of temperature, humidity and radiation; and, with some models, even wash themselves to get rid of debris and contaminants.

The Savannah River Walking Robot, built by Odetics, looks like something out of a science-fiction movie. The 700-pound machine maneuvers about on six legs. A sensing and stabilizing system is built into the unit that allows its legs to adapt to walking on all sorts of uneven surfaces. The robot "insect" works with a telescoping arm that has a 5½-foot reach and an ability to lift up to fifty pounds. These versatile robots can maneuver in hazardous environments doing tasks too dangerous for humans.

The Surveyor, designed and constructed by Advanced Resource Development, moves on tracks like those on an army tank. Weighing 380 pounds and powered by seven 12-volt batteries, the Surveyor can move through water and over loosely packed surfaces while carrying two people. It is operated from a computer-based control station that can function as far as 1,000 feet away. The human operator sees what the robot is doing through a 3-D camera that allows for depth perception and by a second camera that can pan across the area or zoom in close. The operator directs the robot's actions.

TSR-700, developed by 21st Century Corporation, is powered by a small gasoline engine and moves on four wheels. Its hydraulic arm can lift up to 110 pounds, even when it is fully extended to its eight-foot reach. For its operator's vision, it relies on two camera "eyes," a wide-angle color camera for the big picture, and a black and white camera that attaches to the arm and shows close-up details. Commands to the machine are encoded, and there is constant automatic monitoring to ensure that it responds to only coded instructions.

Although scientists from the Soviet Union examined all these robots when they were looking for machinery to inspect and clean up the site of the 1986 nuclear meltdown in Chernobyl, they eventually settled on three robots made in West Germany. The largest was a 30-ton shovel loader, equipped with a camera, and capable of lifting two and one-half tons.

The time seems near when all sorts of giant, remote-controlled robots will be nipping at the landscape like grazing dinosaurs.

Kurzweil's VoiceWriter and IBM's Talkwriter are devices to transform human speech into printed text.

Voice recognition capability may ultimately be the method for giving computers instructions or robots commands. Computers that can recognize and react properly to the human voice will make computers and other machines accessible to people who can't enter data or text in traditional ways.

Voice Synthesis Machines that "talk" to you—have the capability of **voice synthesis**—are not new. They respond to an inquiry in a simulated human voice. You may have heard the Coca-Cola vending machine say, "Thank you," or used a computerized bank teller that told your account balance in a human-like voice, or witnessed the talking cash registers in supermarkets.

A typical audio-response system speaks fewer than 200 words and is limited in its ability to combine them into sentences. As sophisticated as these devices now seem, they are primitive compared to what inventors visualize. The machines that Apple Computer, Inc., is working on will speak while doing other tasks. They will read numbers aloud as they are entered into an electronic spreadsheet or repeat words as children type them.

Computer Vision Scientists hope to develop computers that will process and interpret light waves just as the human brain does. Such a system would use scanning devices to sense and interpret graphics or text-character shapes. This computer would then "read" text in almost every written language.

Josephson Junction

The **Josephson junction**, developed by Brian Josephson of the University of Cambridge, is a very fast, electronic switch. Its key feature is that it

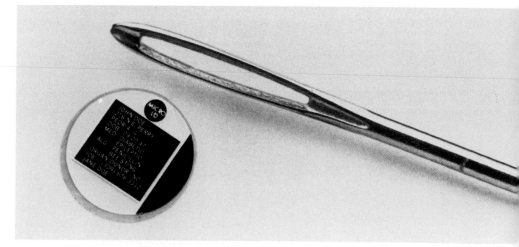

Advances in storage techniques offer small children who could get lost, senior citizens who live alone, or men and women who jog, swim, or hike a new way to carry personal identification. This microdot, which can be applied to a tooth, is a tiny disk that contains hundreds of characters of personal or medical information. In an emergency, the microdot can be read in the mouth or easily removed and read. (Courtesy of Micro I/D, Inc.)

works at low temperatures—nearly absolute zero—where there is little resistance to electricity. This lack of resistance means that on and off switching operations can occur about 1,000 times faster than with silicon transistors. The technology has been perfected slowly, but in 1986, Hypres, Inc., revealed the world's first commercial system using the junctions. One of the earlier problems in developing the technology was that the chips had to be immersed in liquid helium to achieve the low temperatures needed for superconductivity. However, Hypres found that it could simply spray liquid helium on just the corner where all the logic circuits are located, rather than immerse the circuitry totally.

Parallel Processing

Although progress is slow in the search for significantly increased computer speed and power, one technique looks promising—**parallel processing**. This technology links many processors allowing them to process volumes of data simultaneously.

Since von Neumann revealed his principles of computer design in 1945, all stored-program computers have been serial computers, i.e., they access and execute only one instruction at a time. However, a computer using parallel processing accesses several instructions at once and works on them at the same time using multiple CPUs (Figure 18–2). Parallel processing differs from multiprocessing. In multiprocessing, several programs can run at the same time, but each on a separate processor. Parallel processing assigns different portions of a single program to various processors. When programs run concurrently, parts of different programs share the same processor.

Cray Research and Control Data are among the companies working on parallel-processing computers. Floating Point Systems, Inc., a maker of scientific supercomputers, announced its T-series supercomputers with parallel processing. Thinking Machines Corporation's version is called the Connection Machine 2; it holds 64,000 silicon chip processors to simulate the brain's 40 million processing cells. The Cray-2, released in 1986, uses this technology to some degree. It is believed that someday, by using many millions of processors, all communicating with each other, the computer will come close to simulating human thinking processes.

Although these complex computers are being built now, it will be some time before they are perfected and widely used. Those people who do use them will have to spend a lot of time developing new programs and new ways to use the many processors.

Chips

Some experts think that the secret to the next generation of computers lies in new chip designs to increase speed, power, and memory. Since the first silicon chip was produced, improvements in chip technology have occurred at a tremendous pace, and each improvement squeezed more circuitry into smaller spaces.

FIGURE 18–2
Parallel versus serial processing

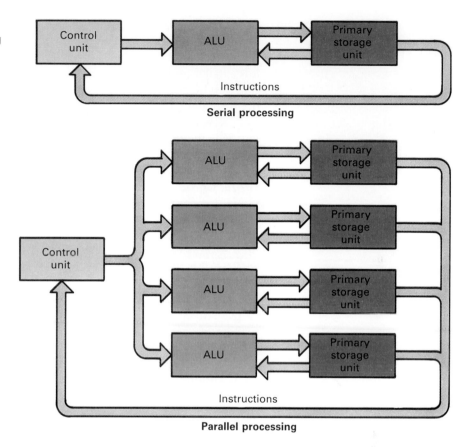

Building so many circuits and packing them so densely on a chip has brought its own set of problems, though. First, tremendous heat is generated when the chip is in use—enough to actually burn out the chip. Thus, large computers require special cooling systems, and even microcomputers need built-in fans to cool them.

Second, the circuits on these tiny chips are so small that the slightest particle of a foreign substance left on the circuit during its manufacture (a bit of dust, for example) ruins the chip.

Third, faulty connections are a major problem. Several chips are placed on a ceramic or metal cartridge with tiny gold wires connecting the chip to pins on the cartridge. In turn, the cartridge is connected to a circuit board. It is here that the faulty connections can occur.

Fourth, because circuits are packed so tightly on chips, sometimes there is "crosstalk," a condition where one circuit picks up signals from another nearby circuit.

Much of the research and experimentation is aimed at finding remedies for these problems. Some of the solutions being considered are

1. Making the features (circuitry) even smaller
2. Making larger chips—superchips
3. Using other substances as a semiconductor material in the chips
4. Growing chip circuitry—biochips

New Chip Ideas

- Smaller features
- Superchips
- New superconducting materials
- Biochips

Smaller Features The circuits on a chip are called its features. The amount of etched-in circuitry on a chip and how closely it is packed determines the chip's speed and power. There can be more circuitry on a chip if it is smaller and tightly packed. The smaller the features, the more densely they can be packed. Some scientists are experimenting with ways to make them smaller, i.e., decrease the width of the features.

Researchers at Sub-Micron Structures Laboratory at MIT are exploring with methods to create features one-tenth of a micron wide (so thin that a human hair would cover 500 of them).

Larger Chips Since the first chip was made, scientists have been building miniature chips to save space and make computers smaller. They have refined the process down to the point now that a chip is less than one-third of an inch square and is very densely packed with circuitry. It seems the only way to get any more circuitry on the chips is to make the features smaller, the chip larger, or both.

Why would scientists want to make a large chip? It appears to be backtracking in technology. But it is actually more difficult to build large chips because making the chip larger increases the flaw rate. In any chip-making process, the most minute manufacturing flaw—a speck of dust or flake of skin—renders the entire chip useless. Even with the sterile labs, called "clean rooms," in which they are made, a large percentage of the chips are unusable (Figure 18–3). Therefore, making a larger chip means creating a greater chance of contamination.

Several U.S. companies, however, including TRW and Motorola, are experimenting with **superchips**—larger chips with smaller features—with support from a $1 billion Defense Department program called VHSIC (Very High Speed Integrated Circuits). This kind of chip will be essential

FIGURE 18–3
Sterile environments called "clean rooms" are necessary in the production of silicon chips to prevent specks of dirt, hair, and other small debris from contaminating the tiny circuits. (Paul Chesley/Photographers Aspen)

where data from various sensors must be processed almost instantaneously, i.e., in real-time processing. The Defense Department plans to use these powerful chips in complex weapons systems they are designing. For example, they would be used for space-based computers that may some day control antimissile weapons.

TRW's new superchip will perform the work of more than 10,000 ordinary chips. The goal is to make a chip that has smaller features but which is larger overall and which has more circuitry. Their product is a 1.4-inch square, paper-thin chip, which has not gone into mass production yet and may not be available commercially until some time in the 1990s.

New Superconducting Materials   Although silicon is the foundation for current chip technology, scientists continue looking for materials to replace silicon as the film of conducting material to use in chips. They are looking for a material that offers conductivity at the speed of light and is also feasible to produce. It seems that there just might be substances better than silicon for conductivity.

One compound under consideration, **gallium arsenide**, is made by combining arsenic and gallium. It is the material of which the next Cray supercomputer, Cray-3, chips will be made. Although not perfected, gallium-arsenide elements have been used for over ten years on a small scale in applications where silicon is too slow, such as for transistors and small circuits in high-frequency microwave radio and satellite communication systems and for some satellite-dish antennas and radar detectors. In the future, gallium arsenide will probably compete with silicon in data-processing and optoelectronics applications.

Implementation of the gallium-arsenide chip, however, will be gradual because its components are expensive to acquire and manufacture, and because the technology of developing chips from it is behind silicon technology by a few years.

Other material being considered as superconductors are semiconducting oxides, basically ceramics, which are made from inexpensive elements, such as calcium and lutetium. The ceramic oxides can become superconductors at high temperatures meaning that they would not have to be cooled. They are also inexpensively and easily manufactured. These oxides could be used as a thin coating that would form the foundation of computer circuits instead of silicon. The main property of these ceramic superconductors is the fact that they can conduct electricity with no power lost due to resistance.

Finally, another discovery that mixed methane and hydrogen in a simple and inexpensive process produced a thin, synthetic diamond coating that could be used on chips as the base for circuitry. The Soviets discovered this technique over ten years ago, but it is just now being applied in the U.S.

Biochips   Most of the above innovations are merely improvements on current technologies. Many experts think chips with circuits made from living matter, **biochips**, and the molecular computer will be the technology that breaks through to the fifth generation of computers and artificial intelligence.

Some scientists are using biomolecular technology to develop the biochip. They think that eventually they will be able to grow tiny circuits from the proteins and enzymes of living material. The circuits would use oxygen and send signals similar to those sent and received by the human brain.

Of course, the molecular computer has not been built yet, but the model for it is the human brain. Could these chips, because they are living, also be connected to the cells (neurons) in the brain to replace damaged cells? Scientists are looking at implanted biochips as a possible way to restore sight to blind people.

Communication Technology

Telecommunication has sometimes been called the backbone of the Information Age. It was the largest growth area in high tech during the past few years and is expected to continue to grow.

Because of the demand for this technology, futurists predict these trends:

1. There will be more use of telecommunication and information networks.
2. Eventually all communication will be digital transmission.
3. The number of communication satellites in orbit will continue to increase.
4. There will be more use of fiber optics as it becomes cheaper and a phasing out of wire cable in phone systems.
5. Gallium arsenide will be used not only in computers, but also in telecommunication networks because it can handle both electronic and light signals.
6. The number of electronic funds transfer (EFT) transactions in banking and other business applications will increase.
7. Videotext applications, the use of computers and phones for two-way communication to order goods or services, will increase in the U.S.
8. The type of telephone in use today will merge with the home computer and other communication technology into a new device for communication.

Optoelectronics

Optoelectronics, the combination of electronics and optics, may eventually become the basis of information technology. By uniting the electron with the photon (a particle of light), greater efficiency is possible in communication and in data processing than electronics alone can achieve.

This technology has been used mainly for communication so far. Fiber optics, the communication channel for the photon, will continue to be improved because this type of channel has the tremendous benefits of speed and clarity of the signal.

Optical communication networks are already in place around the country. According to some scientists, when this technology is perfected, a single fiber may someday be able to handle all the world's telephone calls.

Scientists in the physics department of Heriot-Watt University in Edinburgh, Scotland, are conducting research to bring optics technology inside the computer. This will be done with circuits that process data with laser beams instead of electronics. Optical computers would use chips that combine electronic data processing with photonic switching and transmission.

In addition, Bell Labs has built the first optical counterpart of the transistor and brought us just a little closer to the day of the optical computer. This computer would be able to operate 1,000 times faster than an electronic one.

Software Innovations

Software development has always lagged behind hardware technology. Very powerful computers already exist, but they are not always used to their potential simply because the software doesn't yet exist for them. There are several areas in which software engineers and developers are working, and changes should be expected in the coming few years.

The tiny fibers of transparent glass in fiber optics cables transmit data at the speed of light. The beam of light sent through these fibers can be turned on or off at about one billion times per second. The cables are replacing traditional telephone lines and are used to connect computers in telecommunications systems. (Courtesy of United Telecommications)

The Information Age has made advances to help the physically challenged possible. Here, a VersaBraille™ II information center lets the blind user word process documents by touching a braille keyboard; the entry is indicated on the braille display. This system also communicates with other computer systems and printers. (Courtesy of Telesensory Systems, Inc.)

☐ They plan to make software more versatile and easier to use. Many programs are very difficult to use, and some require extensive study of the documentation. Future software will be easier to install in the computer and will need fewer commands to use. For the very sophisticated programs, the program itself will teach the user the skills needed to operate it.

☐ They want to make more application software available. Designers are reluctant to create software for a new machine that may not stay in the marketplace. Some supercomputers mentioned earlier do not yet have software that takes advantage of their power. When the Compaq 80386 microcomputer entered the marketplace in 1986, software developers had not had enough time to design programs for it. Although users could run the IBM PC software on it, little was available that challenged its high speed and ability to complete several tasks at once.

☐ Another aim is to expand programming in natural languages.

☐ Developers are working to find ways to mathematically prove programs correct.

☐ Finally, they want to produce programs that can write other programs.

THE INTERNATIONAL SCENE

Several countries are racing for the lead in high-tech development. It is generally agreed that the country or countries that lead in the development of the most sophisticated computers and have control over the information

HIGHLIGHT

MUSICAL CREATIVITY OR COMPUTERIZED THEFT?

If you create a distinctive sound, should you own it? The question being asked in relation to digital samples is, "Is it legal to sample an artist's works and use them without permission?"

A few years ago, such a question would have been unimaginable. With digital recording and sampling techniques, recording engineers can now record a particular vocal or instrumental sound from a performance or an existing recording and implant it into another one in all sorts of variations. For example, Eddie Van Halen's guitar "licks" or Phil Collins's distinctive drum sounds could be isolated by digital sampling, excerpted from the original recording without the artist's permission, and used in the creation of a new work.

This is yet another situation in which technology is expanding more quickly than the law can cover it. Copyright protects the sequence of notes in a song, but the law has nothing to say about the ownership to and property rights of particular notes of musical sounds. However, since digital sampling is becoming so commonplace, performers and the American Federation of Musicians are eager to assert their case against what many see as outright theft. Some producers and engineers argue that sampling existing recordings is both a creative and a time-saving technique that harms no one.

Ultimately, the courts will have to decide.

revolution and the electronics industry will have the economic and political edge on the rest of the world.

Several factors determine who leads in computer technology. Countries that are already in the lead can set goals to keep that lead. Another factor is the national commitment to that technology; much depends on the level of financial support government and private industry are willing to put into research.

The United States has always dominated advanced computer technologies. Until 1983, all the world's supercomputers were American made. The U.S. has also been the leader in the innovation and design of microprocessors. When Japan announced its $300 million Fifth Generation Project in 1982, the U.S. became concerned about losing its foothold in the computer industry. Private industry and the U.S. Defense Department provided huge funds for research in new computer architectures, software, and artificial intelligence.

Japan's ambitious Fifth Generation Project was a ten-year plan to develop a new computer, using a type of parallel processing and artificial intelligence, that would be radically different from then-current super-computers. Japan's goal is to build a faster, intelligent computer.

Always the world leader in printers (with Epson and NEC), Japan is also at the front line in robotics, owning two-thirds of the world's robots. Its factories are the most automated in the world. Japan excels at manufacturing and leads in the development of gallium arsenide.

Although the scientists in the U.S. brought forth the modern electronics age with the invention of the transistor, Japan put it to best use in consumer products. Japan's strength lies in its efficient manufacturing rather than in its innovation and design. The country is the leader in computer chip production and sales, but South Korea and Taiwan are closely behind.

West European companies lead in some areas of semiconductor technology. For example, West Germany was the first supplier of a line of components for transmitting data, voice, and video over the same communication channels.

Holland has the leadership in erasable optical storage technology. France has been the top user of videotext, and both Great Britain and France are moving ahead in artificial intelligence research.

The U.S.S.R. launched a fifth-generation project, START, with plans to build a massive parallel computer. Some think that because of its scientists' traditional strength in mathematics and logic, the Soviet Union can make significant progress.

In 1987, the Soviets announced the completion of a supercomputer they say surpasses the capabilities of the fewer than 200 supercomputers operating in the rest of the world. The Soviet supercomputer, described by the Moscow Institute of Precise Machines and Computer Technology, contains sixteen processors, uses the parallel-processing approach, and performs ten billion operations per second. A comparison to the Cray-2, often considered to be the world's fastest supercomputer, shows that the Cray-2 has only four processors and performs 1.2 billion calculations per second. The Cray-3, under construction, has specifications similar to the Soviet supercomputer.

Before this development, it was generally agreed that the U.S.S.R. had been about ten years behind other high-tech countries in most areas of electronics and in software (a little less behind in robotics, a little more behind in office automation). They have not been innovators in electronics, but followers. The same is true of Bulgaria, Czechoslovakia, Hungary, Poland, Romania, and East Germany.

China has about 100 computer companies. They are making a serious attempt to upgrade their 400,000 factories with automation. Personal computers already are playing a big role in education and industry. Because China buys as many personal computers as it can get, many American companies are moving into the Chinese market. Both IBM and Apple have set up Chinese subsidiaries. The Chinese buy a lot of Apple computers, but they also buy Apple imitations made in Taiwan and Japan.

While the U.S. still maintains the lead in the computer industry, which is the largest segment of the electronics industry, Japan is a formidable opponent in the race.

SOCIETY'S RESPONSE TO THE INFORMATION REVOLUTION

Because the Information Age is still in its infancy, it is not easy to predict all of the effects it will have on our way of life. There has been unprecedented progress in medical research and diagnosis, education, sea and space exploration, and in the relief of humans from dangerous and dull jobs. We have instant communication with the rest of the world. Computers have challenged and surpassed us at some intellectual games and technical skills, such as chess, mathematical computations, and some assembly-line work. Most of us view this technology as a contribution and a benefit to society, not as a threat.

Here are observations some forecasters are making about the changes in store for our society over the next few years:

☐ Efforts will be made to find more practical uses of the technology that has already been developed through routine scientific inquiry. The number of advances made during the last twenty to forty years is overwhelming. In fact, they still exceed our ability to adapt to them. Some technologies that have been in existence for several years are just now being put to use. MIT's Media Laboratory is doing just that. Researchers there buy off-the-shelf equipment and program it for new uses in music, film, theater, and broadcasting. They are looking at new ways to apply the computer to the home, classroom, and office.

☐ We will continue to move from a "brawn to brains" society as the Information Age progresses. Factories will become more automated, adding to our fears of unemployment. The nature of our work life and leisure time will change.

☐ Education will have to continue training students in computer-assisted services, rather than teaching them physical or industrial skills. Traditional jobs will change or disappear, just as the office typing pool has. We can hope and plan for more interesting and challenging jobs to emerge to replace the ones lost.

☐ There will be an increase in the number of people telecommuting. These changes will have significant effects on day-care centers, public transportation, and office and parking-lot design, as well as on many other institutions.

☐ Shopping at home, home banking, and EFT in general will increase and move us a little closer toward a "cashless society."

☐ The issues of computer crime, privacy, health and safety, and computer ethics will continue as major ethical and social concerns for at least the next few years. These issues are not going to be resolved quickly. No major technology is ever introduced into a society without causing waves.

☐ In many ways, the economies of nations have always been connected, and computers will help make the long-talked-about global village a distinct possibility. Because of computer and communication technology, worldwide communication (and the tightening of social bonds that comes from it) is immediate.

☐ Thinking machines are a long way off, but the concern of what they might do has been with us since the birth of science fiction.

If, indeed, computers can be made that will program, repair, and reproduce themselves, there will be upheavals in law, ethics, sociology, and all the sciences that deal with social relationships. At present, fears of "computers taking over" seem groundless. However, as computers gain more autonomy of operation and become more versatile, they can become a social menace in the wrong hands.

No one can really say what the future holds, but it is fairly certain that just as society has adapted in the past, it will continue to assimilate new technologies, trying to keep in balance the potential good they can bring and the potential problems.

SUMMARY

Artificial intelligence will probably be the breakthrough to the fifth-generation of computer technology. Scientists are still requiring more power, speed, and memory for computers so that artificial intelligence software can be developed.

Expert systems, advanced robotics, voice synthesis, natural language processing, voice recognition, and computer vision are areas of artificial intelligence that researchers are trying to improve.

More expert systems are being designed. Robots will become more sophisticated with human-like qualities. Ways to communicate with the computer are being refined and made easier. Computer vision will be improved with the ability to process and interpret light waves just as the human brain does.

Ways to improve computer power, speed, and memory might include the use of the Josephson junction, parallel processing, and new kinds of chips.

New kinds of chips being researched are superchips, biochips, chips made with smaller features, and chips made with gallium arsenide and other superconducting materials instead of silicon.

Some experts say that the largest growth area in high technology in the last few years has been and will remain telecommunication. Optoelectronics is a relatively new technology, but it has made fiber-optics communication networks a reality. In the future, it will make optical switching and data transmission inside the computer possible.

The United States and Japan are the key participants in the ongoing race for computer and information technology leadership.

Key Terms

artificial intelligence (AI) (p. 519)	gallium arsenide (p. 527)	natural language processing (p. 521)
biochip (p. 527)	Josephson junction (p. 523)	optoelectronics (p. 528)
expert system (p. 519)		

parallel processing (p. 524)

robotics (p. 519)

superchip (p. 526)

voice recognition (p. 521)

voice synthesis (p. 523)

Review Questions

1. What do some people think will be the breakthrough that will propel computer technology into a fifth generation?

2. _____ is the ability of machines to think and reason in ways similar to humans.

3. What are some of the areas in which research is being conducted to give machines "intelligence"?

4. What is the kind of software physicians can consult for advice to help them diagnose illnesses?

5. A sense of touch and sight are capabilities that will be important to _____ of the future.

6. How are some scientists involved in robotics research trying to improve robots?

7. Robots are currently used for mainly what kinds of tasks?

8. Why does a personal robot doing household tasks need to be more complex than a robot in the factory that welds pieces of metal?

9. How does one scientist's observations of spiders relate to the study of robots?

10. Describe natural language processing.

11. Why do computers have trouble recognizing voice input?

12. Which capability might ultimately be used to give robots and computers instructions or commands?

13. True or False: A machine with voice synthesis means that a user can give it instructions by voice command.

14. Why do scientists consider the Josephson junction for use in computers?

15. A computer using parallel processing is faster because _____.

16. Name four possible solutions relating to acquiring faster and better chips.

17. Why would making the circuits smaller increase chip power?

18. True or False: Software development has always lagged behind hardware development.

19. What are some trends in software development?

20. What are the "features" of a chip?

21. Describe some of the problems of packing so many circuits on a chip.

22. Why will the implementation of gallium arsenide chips be a gradual process?

23. What are some of the changes or trends forecast for communication technology?

24. What is the significance of being the world leader in the information and electronics industries?

25. Describe some of the major forecasts of changes and trends for our society as a result of the Information Age.

INFOMODULE
Artificial Intelligence

HISTORY

Giving machines **artificial intelligence (AI)**, the capabilities to do things that are human-like and to exhibit intelligence, is sometimes a controversial concept. Computers have traditionally been used to process data at phenomenal speed, control other machines and devices, and serve as tools for design and development.

Serious speculation about whether machines could think started in the 1950s, not too long after the digital computer was invented. Alan Turing, Europe's leading computer scientist, spent much of his life pondering this question.

Turing believed that "artificial" machines could probably be made to "think" since "natural" machines—humans—could. He worked for several years with John von Neumann and, in 1947, designed a machine that he thought simulated thinking. It performed a single move in a chess game, and to Turing this was proof that the machine was capable of deductive reasoning. Von Neumann, on the other hand, didn't believe that computers would ever duplicate human thinking.

Since then, artificial intelligence has been a subject for exploration and debate at major universities.

John McCarthy, who coined the phrase "artificial intelligence," Marvin Minsky, and Alan Newell are considered the founders of artificial intelligence as a field of study. Minsky and McCarthy established the first AI lab at the Massachusetts Institute of Technology (MIT) in 1957. McCarthy went on to Stanford University to start one there in 1963, and later a third at Carnegie-Mellon University.

Early attempts at artificial intelligence were tested on such games as chess and checkers. Scientists thought that if computers could play intellectual games, a major step would have been made toward artificial intelligence. If a machine could learn and understand a set of rules, they reasoned, then it could probably play games as well as humans. Arthur Samuel, at Stanford University, designed a checker game in which the computer would have to make the best move out of thousands possible.

Expert systems, considered one of the most practical applications resulting from AI research so far, began evolving in the late '70s.

Even though some segments of the computer industry have had slumps, the interest in expert systems has been growing. The ultimate goal of AI research today is not simply to satisfy scientific curiosity, but also to make computers that will help us by coming up with practical applications. Research is directed toward creating technically and economically feasible applications. As a result, more commercial products such as expert systems, advanced robotics, computer vision, and voice-recognition software, are being produced.

A computer with artificial intelligence will use common sense, judgment, intuition, and make logic inferences—qualities that are now unique to humans. Computer scientists are attempting to build software and computers that can make decisions, learn from their own mistakes, solve problems, and program themselves. The task of developing computers and software to reproduce and imitate the complex circuitry of the brain is an ambitious project.

PROBLEMS

One problem contributing to the slow progress in artificial intelligence is that people cannot agree on a definition. More accurately, the definition seems to be changing. What was once revolutionary for a computer is now not so extraordinary.

Raymond Kurzweil, a contributor to the field of AI, points out that the first checker and chess games that computers played were considered to be applications of artificial intelligence at the time. Today, there are inexpensive, pocket-sized machines that can play better chess than those first ponderous devices, but now we do not consider them examples of artificial intelligence.

Computers have no innate intelligence, and anything even resembling intelligence must be programmed by humans. As AI develops, the computer will acquire other abilities that are similar to human thinking. At what point are we going to call this artificial intelligence?

There are other questions: Can a computer possess consciousness, self-awareness, and creativity?

Computers can imitate thought processes such as those necessary to carry out some complex tasks very logically. They can manipulate symbols (data) extremely fast and possess great memories. But do they have intelligence? Hurbert Dreyfus, professor of philosophy at the University of California at Berkeley, remarked that a computer is still no more than a mechanized idiot savant, i.e., a dumb machine that exhibits a remarkable skill in a limited area.

What "intelligence" computers do have is their ability to recognize patterns and solve problems using programmed logic. They cannot reason, but can only make educated guesses; they cannot generalize. Sometimes solutions are based on the human attribute called common sense, which may not always be logical.

Another problem is that even if we define artificial intelligence as "the ability of computers to think and reason like the human mind; the ability to use common sense, intuition, judgment and evaluation," scientists have not determined exactly *how* the mind does all this. Human intelligence is not entirely understood, and scientists are just scratching the surface in the quest to discover how humans get ideas and how they think.

PROGRESS

Researchers are busy studying the neural networks (memory), with the brain as their model for artificial intelligence computers. By unlocking the secrets of how the mind works, they hope to be able to duplicate those workings in a machine.

Scientific exploration can come from two directions. First, the scientists who are examining the "hardware" of memory are trying to chart the network of nerve cells (neurons) and how they are related to each other. They know the network consists of about 40 billion neural-processing units that can store about 100 trillion bits of information, compared to a computer's mere billions. Even so, very little is known about how the neurons communicate with each other.

Marvin Minsky at MIT thinks that discovering how the billions of brain cells work together to help people think and remember will be a step toward learning how to join billions of computer circuits. Minsky says that if a person is like a machine, then once you get a wiring diagram of how the person works, you can make copies. He envisions the mind as many different machines—maybe 100 different computers inside the brain.

Leon Cooper of Brown University, a Nobel Prize winner in physics in 1972, also analyzes the neural networks of the brain, trying to determine how to create a thinking machine. There are those, however, who doubt that humans are merely machines. John von Neumann believed that the mind was more than a machine and that we would not be able to design systems that would operate exactly like it.

From the second direction in AI research, some researchers are studying the "software" of memory, i.e., the different kinds of memory, how it is organized, and how emotions affect it.

There are two schools of thought among AI theorists about the progress of artificial intelligence technology. One group believes that we already have the basic technology for making machines intelligent. According to this group, to make any machine equal or superior to human intelligence, we just make them faster and cram them with huge amounts of information. Herbert Simon of Carnegie-Mellon thinks we already have the technology—the parallel computer, which is faster and more powerful than the human brain.

Another group believes that technology is not yet advanced enough to allow artificial intelligence to develop. It is not, they say, merely a matter of making a bigger and faster computer, because the mind is more complex than that. Real AI will probably require a scientific breakthrough into the nature of thought processes.

Some bizarre research comes out of the search for the thinking computer. Hans Moravec, senior research scientist at Carnegie-Mellon's Mobile Robot Laboratory envisions a "robot immortality for Everyman." He suggests that once we learn how to make copies of our mental processes and to transfer these programs into robotic bodies, we could survive for perhaps centuries. This brings up not only social, but ethical, moral, and religious questions.

LANGUAGES

Because AI programs call for the creation and analysis of text information, John McCarthy created the **LISP** (LISt Processing) language in the late 1950s for this purpose. It is a programming language designed to handle data strings more efficiently than other languages.

More recently, another language, **PROLOG** (PROgramming LOGic), was designed in France and refined in England to write programs for expert systems. The characteristics that make this language appropriate are its type of logic, the mechanism that implements the program, and its ability for developing search techniques.

The C programming language is also being used in the development of AI systems.

Some think that if artificial-intelligence machines are ever possible, they exist far in the future. Still others say we are almost there. There are claims that programs with human-like intuition are being developed; and there are demonstrations of creative examples of what a computer can do. It is generally agreed that computers can solve problems using rules that have already been discovered. But can it make a new rule, a new discovery? Herbert Simon thinks so. He has written programs that can develop new theories by imitating some of the same mental processes used by humans to formulate rules in the past. These types of developments lead us closer to making an intelligent machine.

When will we know if computers have reached the point of human-like intelligence? Alan Turing's test was basically this: If it has convinced you it can think, then it can.

When asked how we would know when we have created a consciousness, Marvin Minsky replied, "If you can't tell, you didn't."

The debate goes on.

KEY TERMS

artificial intelligence   PROLOG (p. 539)
(AI) (p. 537)
LISP (p. 539)

QUESTIONS

1. What does the phrase "artificial intelligence" imply with regard to computers?
2. For what application was early artificial intelligence first tested?
3. What are some of the practical commercial applications of AI?
4. Name two AI programming languages.
5. Why does the definition of artificial intelligence seem to change?

Glossary

Absolute cell reference A method of copying in a spreadsheet where the exact formula is copied using the same cell references.

Acoustic modem Also called an acoustic coupler; a type of modem with two rubber cups in which the standard telephone receiver is placed to send and receive data.

Active cell The cell in a spreadsheet that is currently being used for data entry or data manipulation. Usually indicated by the cursor position.

Ada A programming language developed for the U.S. Department of Defense for use in military applications. Ada includes powerful control and data structures and a specialized set of commands that allow it to directly control hardware devices.

Adding The process of entering new records to an existing file or data base.

Address bus The electrical pathway used to transmit the storage locations for data or instructions.

Algorithm A finite set of step-by-step instructions for the purpose of solving a problem.

All-in-one integrated package An integrated application package that combines the features of several application programs into a single program.

Analog computer A type of computer that recognizes data as a continuous measurement of a physical property (e.g., voltage, pressure, speed) as opposed to counting discrete signals.

Analog data transmission The transmission of data in a continuous wave form.

Animation A feature of some graphics packages that rapidly displays drawings that are slightly different, thereby simulating motion.

Application The job or task that the user wants the computer to perform.

Application generator A type of fourth-generation language that allows the user to enter data and specify how the data are to be manipulated and output.

Application package See *application software.*

Application software Software that interfaces between the user and the system software to allow the user to perform specific tasks.

Arithmetic and logic unit (ALU) The part of the central processing unit (CPU) that performs all mathematical and logical functions.

Artificial intelligence (AI) The ability of computers to perform human-like thinking and reasoning.

Aspect ratio In a graphics program, the relationship between the height and width of an object. The aspect ratio may be altered by the user to change the shape of an object.

Assembler A language-translator program that translates assembly-language code into machine-language code.

Assembly language A low-level language that uses mnemonic codes instead of 1s and 0s.

Asynchronous transmission A method of data transmission in which characters are sent one at a time over a communication channel. Each character is surrounded by a start and stop bit that controls the transfer of that character.

Attributes The set of characteristics that are used to describe a data-entry field or to describe how the output will appear. These are often set by the user to fit a particular situation.

Audit trail A documentation of all activity in a file. This activity includes what was done, what was affected, when it was done, and by whom.

Autoanswer A feature of a communication package that will automatically answer calls from other computers. A computer with this feature can operate a bulletin board and receive electronic mail without the user being present at the computer.

Automated office An office environment that combines traditional office procedures, computers, and communication technology.

Automatic dialing A feature of a communication package that allows previously stored numbers to be accessed and automatically dialed to access another computer.

Automatic dimensioning A graphics feature that allows a user to change the dimensions of an object by entering the desired size.

Automatic message transfer A feature in a communication package that automatically dials a computer at a preset time and leaves a message on that computer.

Automatic page numbering An application-software feature that automatically places the consecutive page number on each page.

Automatic spillover A spreadsheet option in which a cell label is allowed to continue, or "spill over," into the next cell.

Back-end processor A special-purpose computer that handles the storage and retrieval of data from memory.

Background integration The placing of utility programs in memory to make them available to the user while using other software packages.

Backup file A duplicate copy of a file.

Band printer A line-at-a-time impact printer similar to the chain printer, but uses a band containing characters instead of a chain.

Bandwidth A characteristic of a communication channel that determines the rate, or speed, at which data can be transmitted over the channel.

Bar code A series of thick and thin black bars and spaces of various widths that represent data. Seen on many consumer products.

Bar graph A type of graph that uses a fixed scale to compare data in simple and compound relationships. The data may be represented as either a vertical or horizontal bar.

BASIC (Beginners' All-purpose Symbolic Instruction Code) A high-level language developed at Dartmouth College as an easy to learn and use language for beginning programmers.

Batch processing A method of data processing where data are processed periodically without user intervention during processing.

Baud rate The number of times per second that a transmitted signal changes (modulates or demodulates).

Binary system The base 2 numbering system, uses the digits 0 and 1. Computer data can be represented by this numbering system.

Biochip A newer technology for designing integrated circuits by using living protein and enzymes to grow circuits; exists in theory only.

Bit A binary digit. The smallest piece of data that can be recognized and used by the computer.

Block editing A word-processor feature that allows the user to edit large portions of text as a unit.

Blocked tape A storage technique used where records are grouped together on tape. This provides more storage and faster access by reducing the number of interrecord gaps.

Blocking factor The number of records stored between a pair of interblock gaps.

Break signal In a communication program, a feature in which a signal is sent to stop the current operation between two communicating computers without disconnecting the communication link between them.

Broad-band channel A communication channel, such as microwaves or fiber optics, that transmits data at rates as high as several megabits per second.

Bubble memory A type of nonvolatile memory where data are represented by the presence or absence of magnetized areas (bubbles) formed on a thin piece of garnet.

Buffer A temporary holding place for data; may be part of the CPU or may be part of an input or output device.

Built-in functions A function that is contained within an application program that will automatically perform a mathematical or logic function without the user manually entering a formula.

Bulletin-board system (BBS) An electronic equivalent of a conventional bulletin board. A BBS is used as part of a communication network where users can post messages, read messages posted by other users, communicate with the system operator, and upload or download programs.

Bus An electrical path for data flow from point to point in a circuit.

Bus network A computer network arrangement where each device is connected to a single communication cable by an interface. Each device can communicate directly with every other device.

Business and analytical program A type of graphics program that is capable of extracting numerical data and presenting it in the form of a graph or chart. Often a separate program, but may be integrated into another application program.

Byte A group of eight bits.

C A programming language that uses English-like statements. Uses sophisticated control and data structures, which make it a very concise, powerful language.

Card reader A device that translates the holes in a punched card into machine-readable code.

Cartridge tape A form of magnetic tape similar to cassette tape but with a much greater storage density. Used mainly with large computer systems.

Cassette tape A form of magnetic tape, about one-fourth inch wide; generally used for secondary storage with microcomputers.

Cathode-ray tube (CRT) A type of display that uses an electron beam to illuminate a phosphor-coated screen to form characters.

Cell A data-entry point in a spreadsheet defined by its row and column coordinates.

Centering A feature in application software that automatically places a word or words in the center of a defined space, such as a spreadsheet cell or document page.

Central processing unit (CPU) The name given to the processing unit of the computer which contains the arithmetic and logic unit (ALU), control unit, and primary storage unit.

Chain printer A line-at-a-time impact printer that uses a rotating chain containing all the characters.

Character enhancement A feature in application software that allows the user to alter the text style, such as by boldfacing or italicizing.

Chief programmer team A group of specialized personnel involved in designing and developing a computer program.

Child A data element at a level below the parent in a data-base structure.

Chip Another term for microchip. See *integrated circuit*.

COBOL (Common Business-Oriented Language) A high-level language used in business information processing. It was specifically designed to manipulate large data files.

Coding The process of writing the computer program instructions in a particular programming language.

Column In a spreadsheet, the alphabetic ordering from left to right, that along with the numeric row designation, locates the position of a cell.

Command-driven See *command-orientation*.

Command-orientation The attribute of a software program that requires a command be entered from rote memory or by consulting a manual. Choices are not presented to the user on the display screen.

Command mode A mode of operation in which application program commands can be selected.

Common carrier A company licensed and regulated by federal or state government to carry the data communication property of others at a regulated rate.

Communication channel The medium, or pathway, through which data are transmitted between devices. This pathway may be wire cable, microwave, or fiber optics.

Communication package An application package that allows the exchange of data between computers.

Communication parameters The basic parameters required in order for devices to communicate with each other. Four essential parameters are required for communication to take place: baud rate; the number of bits used to create each character; the number of stop bits; and the type of parity checking used.

Compatibility The ability of software and hardware from one computer system to work with that of another computer system.

Compiler A language-translator program that translates a whole high-level language program at once into machine language before it is executed.

Computer A device that can accept data, perform certain functions on that data, and present the results of those operations.

Computer-aided design (CAD) The integration of computers and graphics to aid in the design and drafting processes.

Computer-aided instruction (CAI) A method of teaching through the use of interactive dialogue between a computer and its user.

Computer-aided manufacturing (CAM) The use of computers to control machines in the manufacturing process.

Computer crime A crime that involves the use of computers and software.

Computer ethics A set of codes or rules governing the conduct of individuals and corporations in the use of computers; the accepted standard of behavior when dealing with computers and the information they contain.

Computer-integrated manufacturing (CIM) The linking and integration of manufacturing and all other aspects of a company by computers.

Computer literacy General knowledge of what

computers are, who uses them, how they are used, their functions, and their impact on society.

Computer network A system of two or more computers linked by data-communication channels.

Computer numerical control (CNC) The controlling of milling or cutting operations by a computer.

Computer operator The person responsible for starting and running computer equipment.

Computer output microform (COM) Hard copy in the form of photographic images recorded on microfilm or microfiche.

Computer service technician The person who installs and repairs computer equipment.

Concentration The process of connecting and serving more devices on a communication channel than the channel was designed to handle.

Concentrator A hardware device, often a minicomputer, that controls the process of concentration.

Concurrent operating system An operating system that allows one CPU to switch between two programs as instructions are received at a speed that makes it appear that both programs are executing simultaneously.

Contention A method for determining device access to a communication channel. With this method each device checks the channel to see if it is free before sending data. Once a device begins transmission, it maintains sole control of the channel until it completes its transmission.

Control bus The electrical pathway for all timing and controlling functions.

Control panel In an electronic spreadsheet, it is that area that displays information about the current file and the command or activity being performed.

Control programs The computer programs in an operating system that manage the computer's hardware and its resources, such as CPU time, primary storage, and input and output devices.

Control unit That part of the central processing unit that controls the sequence of events necessary to execute an instruction.

Converting The process of changing the data storage format of one file so that it may be used by another program with a different data storage format.

Coordinate In a spreadsheet, the intersection of a row and column used to define a cell's position in a worksheet.

Copy (1) The process of making a duplicate file from an existing file. (2) The process of duplicating text or graphics on the screen for placement elsewhere while leaving the original text or graphics intact.

Copyright Act of 1976 A law, which actually went into effect in 1978, that specifically lists computer programs among the works protected from the moment of creation against illegal copying.

Cursor A special character that indicates the user's present position on the computer display screen or acts as a pointer to focus attention to a particular point on the screen.

Cut and paste A feature in an application software package that cuts (erases) part or all of an object or text and places it in a buffer. The object or text may be pasted (inserted) at a later time.

Daisy-wheel printer A type of printer that uses a print wheel resembling a daisy. At the end of each ''petal'' is a fully formed character.

Data Numbers, letters, characters, or combinations thereof, that are capable of being entered and processed by a computer. Raw facts before processing.

Data base A collection of related files stored together in a logical manner.

Data-base administrator The person or persons in charge of designing, implementing, and maintaining the data base.

Data-base management system (DBMS) The software that allows data to be readily stored in, maintained, manipulated, and retrieved from a data base. It is the interface between programs, users, and the data in the data base.

Data-base query language A fourth-generation language that is used in conjunction with a relational data base. Acts as an interface between a user and a DBMS and helps users to easily access data without the use of complex programming code.

Data-base service An on-line computer service in which users may access large data bases of information. Like information services, these are subscriber services, but they contain information on more specialized topics.

Data bus The electrical pathway on which program data are transferred.

Data communication The process of electronically sending data from one point to another.

Data dictionary Documentation that details the type, structure, and intended use of data within a system.

Data-entry operator The person who enters data into a computer using a keyboard and video display terminal.

Data-flow diagram A type of diagram that shows the logical flow of data through a system.

Data manager An application package that allows the user to manage (manipulate, store, retrieve, display, and print) data. A data manager may be a file-management system or a data-base management system.

Data manipulation   Altering data that enters or exits the computer.

Data processing   The process of transforming data into useful information by the computer. Sometimes referred to as information processing.

Data stealing   A computer crime in which data gathered for a legitimate use are used in an unauthorized manner.

Data-transfer mode   In a communication package, the operational mode in which actual data transfer takes place between communicating devices.

Debugging   The process of finding and correcting a programming error.

Decimal system   The base 10 numbering system using the digits 0 through 9.

Decision support system (DSS)   An extension of an MIS that allows the manager to interact with the computer to help make "what if" type decisions. A DSS has stronger analytical capabilities than an MIS and is generally more user-friendly.

Decision table   An analysis tool that prescribes a course of action to be taken based on certain conditions and rules.

Decode   The step in the instruction cycle where the instruction is decoded and sent to the ALU along with any necessary data.

Dedicated processor   A special-purpose computer that's been modified to perform a specific function.

Dedicated word-processing system   A computer system designed mainly for the purpose of word processing.

Default setting   In application software, a parameter that is automatically entered unless changed by the user.

Delete   An application-software feature that allows existing text, data, fields, records, or files to be removed.

Demand report   A report usually used by middle- and top-level managers, issued on request, that contains data and some analysis.

Demodulation   The process of converting an analog signal to a digital signal.

Density   Refers to the amount of data that can be stored in a given area of a storage medium. The higher the density, the more data are stored.

Design program   A graphics program that is used as a designing tool to create and alter the image of an object. A computerized drafting table.

Desktop microcomputer   Another name for a microcomputer; so called because it fits on the top of a desk.

Desktop publishing   A concept that combines the use of a microcomputer with graphics-oriented, page-composition software and high-quality laser printers.

Digital computer   A high-speed, programmable electronic device that stores, processes, and retrieves data by counting discrete signals as opposed to measuring a continuous signal.

Digital data transmission   The transmission of data as distinct pulses, or on/off electrical states.

Digitizer   An input device that uses a tablet on which a special stylus is moved to provide data entry or indicate position. Also called a graphics tablet.

Direct access   A method of storing and accessing data directly. This method allows for faster access to the data than sequential or indexed-sequential methods.

Direct conversion   The process in which the old system is dismantled immediately as the new system is put into place.

Directory storage   A feature of some communication packages that allows the user to store the parameters required to set up communication between two computers. The user can recall this information from the directory instead of reentering it.

Disk operating system (DOS)   An operating system for microcomputers in which all or part resides on a disk and must be loaded into the computer; the set of programs that controls and supervises the microcomputer's hardware.

Disk pack   A removable, hard-disk storage device containing multiple hard disks in a plastic case; provides increased storage capabilities for large computer systems.

Distributed data processing (DDP)   The concept of dispersing computers, devices, software, and data connected through communication channels into areas where they are used; linked as a common system to process data at different locations.

Distributed processing   See *distributed data processing (DDP)*.

Documentation   (1) The written or graphic record of the steps involved in developing or maintaining an information system. (2) Written or graphic descriptions detailing the purpose and the operation of the software.

Document-oriented   A method of word processing where the entire document is loaded at once from secondary storage into primary storage.

Dot-matrix printer   A type of impact printer that uses a print head containing pins, usually 9 to 24, that produce characters by printing patterns of dots.

Downloading The process of receiving data from a computer and storing them on media located at the user's computer.

Draft-quality print Lowest quality print; characters are smaller than standard-quality print and are formed using a minimum number of dots; suitable for rough drafts. Also called compressed print.

Drag A feature of a graphics package that allows the user to move (drag) an object around the drawing area.

Drill A method of instruction in which the student memorizes ideas through repeated questioning.

Drum printer A line-at-a-time impact printer that uses a rotating drum of 80 to 132 print positions with each print position containing a complete set of characters.

Dumb terminal A stand-alone keyboard and display screen that can send or receive data, but cannot process that data.

Editing The process by which typographical errors, incorrect values, or erroneous formulas are corrected in an application program.

Electrically erasable programmable read-only memory (EEPROM) A type of memory that can be erased and reprogrammed electrically without removing the chip from the circuit board.

Electronic blackboard A pressure-sensitive chalkboard that digitizes and displays whatever is written on it on a monitor.

Electronic calendar An electronic scheduling system used for the same purpose as a standard paper calendar or appointment book would be.

Electronic eavesdropping Illegal tapping into communication lines that are used by computers to send and receive data.

Electronic funds transfer (EFT) The method of data communication that involves the transfer of money between accounts over a communication channel.

Electronic mail Refers to any mail or messages transmitted electronically by computers using communication channels.

Electronic spreadsheet An application package that displays, manipulates, and prints data in a row and column format. A computerized version of the paper spreadsheet.

Electronic teleconferencing A method of communicating using computers connected through a telephone system. Each user or group of users participates in the conference by keying in their conversations.

Electronic work monitoring A process of measuring worker productivity with the use of computers.

Embedded microprocessor A preprogrammed microprocessor used to control the functions of a device other than a computer.

Encoding system A system where alphanumeric characters are represented by patterns of 1s and 0s so that they can be recognized and used by a computer. The American Standard Code for Information Interchange (ASCII) and Extended Binary Coded Decimal Interchange Code (EBCDIC) are the two most widely used encoding systems.

Encryption A data-coding scheme that codes data into unintelligible characters so it cannot be read or used by unauthorized persons.

End effector The "hands" of the robot, which can be designed for a variety of tasks.

Entity In computer-aided design, an object (line, circle, point, etc.) drawn on the screen.

Erasable programmable read-only memory (EPROM) A type of memory that can be erased by removing it from the circuit and exposing the chip to ultraviolet light. It can then be reprogrammed.

Ergonomics The science of designing the workplace for the comfort and safety of the worker.

Exception report A report generated when a situation deviates from the norm; usually used by middle-level managers.

Exchange mode A mode in an application package; when new text is entered, it takes the place, or overwrites, any existing text occupying that same space.

Execution cycle The cycle where the instruction is executed by the ALU.

Expert system A type of computer software package that specializes in one area or application to help humans make a decision or solve a problem. Acts as a consultant, or expert, to the user.

Express warranty A claim, either written or verbal, about a product.

External direct-connect modem A type of modem that is external to the computer and connected directly to the telephone line. This type of modem reduces distortion and allows for faster data transmission than the acoustic type.

Facsimile A form of electronic mail that copies and sends text and graphics over long distances.

Feasibility study A preliminary study to determine if an information system should be developed. Looks at available technology, costs versus benefits, and likelihood of user acceptance.

Fetch The step in the instruction cycle where the instruction is located in memory and sent to the control unit.

Fiber optics   A type of data-communication channel; data are transmitted and received as digital pulses of light.

Field   Each data item contained in a record.

Fifth-generation computers   A phrase referring to the next generation of computers, which will incorporate artificial intelligence.

File   A collection of similar groups of data (records) that fall under one name or heading.

File-locking   A file protection procedure that allows only one user to access a file at a time.

File-management system   An application program that can manage (manipulate, store, retrieve, and print) data in separate files. In this system only one file may be accessed at one time.

File-transfer protocol   A set of rules for the transfer of data. Communicating devices must use the same protocol to make the transfer of data possible.

First-generation computers   Computers developed and used before 1960 and which employed vacuum tube technology.

Fixed disk   A hard-disk storage system of one or more nonremovable hard disks protected in a permanently sealed case.

Fixed-length record   A record in which its data length is set to a specific number of characters. Any unused spaces are stored as blank spaces in the records.

Flat-panel display   A type of display that does not use a picture tube to display characters. Types include liquid-crystal display (LCD) and gas plasma.

Floppy diskette   A flexible, mylar magnetic diskette commonly used with microcomputers on which data are magnetically stored.

Floppy-diskette drive   The device used to transfer to and from a floppy diskette.

Flowchart   A programming design tool comprised of standardized symbols; graphically shows the components of a system or steps in solving a problem.

Footer   Text that appears at the bottom of the page, often the page number.

Formatting   (1) The setting of parameters such as margins or tabs that control the appearance of text or the setting of attributes to describe how data are to be displayed. (2) The term used to describe the preparing of a disk or diskette for use.

Formula   A mathematical or logical equation from which data values are calculated.

FORTRAN (FORmula TRANslator)   A high-level language designed to solve complex numerical problems.

Fourth-generation computers   Those computers developed and in use from 1971 to the present which make use of large-scale integration (LSI).

Fourth-generation language   A class of programming language in which the user needs very little programming knowledge to write computer instructions. Examples are data-base query languages, report generators, and application generators.

Freedom of Information Act of 1970   A law passed in 1970 which allows citizens to find out which federal agencies are collecting and storing data about them and to secure copies of the records.

Front-end processor   A special-purpose computer that controls the input and output functions of the main computer.

Full-duplex mode   A method of transferring data over a communication channel in which data can be transmitted and received at the same time. A full-duplex device can transmit and receive data at the same time.

Gallium arsenide   A material used for making semiconductors to replace silicon because it allows faster transmission times, uses less power, is more radiation resistant, and can process both light and electronic digital data on one chip.

Gantt chart   A bar chart that depicts the timing of completion of a series of tasks.

Gateway service   A service where computer time is bought from many information and commercial data-base services at wholesale rates and sold to its subscribers at a retail rate. A gateway service provides the user with the convenience of being able to access many services through one central communication line.

General-purpose computer   A computer capable of performing a variety of tasks. The computer can be put to different uses by changing the software.

Generalized application package   An application package that can be applied to a variety of tasks.

Gigabyte   Approximately one billion bytes; used in reference to storage capabilities.

Glossary   A word-processor feature that allows abbreviations to be typed instead of longer words or phrases. As the abbreviation is being typed, the full word or phrase appears on the screen.

Grammar checker   A software program that locates grammar and punctuation errors in a document.

Graphics   Representation of data in the form of charts, graphs, or other pictorials.

Graphics package   An application program that allows the user to create, edit, display, and print graphic images. May be a separate software program or integrated into another software program.

Grid   A pattern of horizontal and vertical lines (sometimes just the dots representing the intersection of these lines) that are used to provide the user with a visual aid to help enter or find data at specific coordinate positions on the screen.

Half-duplex mode A method of transferring data over a communication channel in which data can be transmitted in only one direction at a time. A half-duplex mode device can transmit or receive but not at the same time.

Handheld computer A portable computer, slightly larger than a pocket calculator that can be held in one hand.

Handshaking The process of sending prearranged signals specifying the protocol to be followed when transmitting or receiving data.

Hard copy A form of relatively stable and permanent output. For example, paper or computer output microform.

Hard disk A hard metallic disk used for magnetically storing data. Because of its rigid construction, it can be produced with higher storage densities allowing more data to be stored; data can be accessed faster than with a floppy diskette.

Hard-disk drive The device used to transfer data to and from a hard disk.

Hardware The physical components of a computer system, such as the computer itself, input devices, and output devices.

Head crash The term describing the occurrence when the read/write head of a hard disk drive comes in contact with the hard disk, resulting in severe damage to the head, disk, or both.

Header Text that appears at the top of the page, often a title.

Help window A feature in many application programs that can be accessed to provide the user with information about commands or procedures.

Heuristic programming A programming technique of expert systems that attempts to emulate human intuition, judgment, and common sense.

Hexadecimal system The base 16 numbering system using the digits 0 through 9 and the letters A through F.

Hierarchical data-base structure A type of database structure in which the data elements are organized in a parent-child relationship, where each parent can have many children, but each child can have only one parent.

High-level language A programming language that uses instructions that closely resemble human language and mathematical notation. BASIC and Pascal are examples.

High-resolution graphics A method of creating graphic images by turning the pixels that make up the screen display on or off.

HIPO (hierarchy plus input, processing, output) chart A type of chart where each module's input, output, and processing needs are outlined.

Hyphenation A word-processor feature that determines how a word will be hyphenated. There are three basic types: hard hyphen; soft hyphen; and nonbreaking hyphen.

IBM PC compatible A computer similar in design to an IBM PC, capable of using some or most of the same software.

Impact printer A type of printer that produces characters by using a hammer or pins to strike an ink ribbon against a sheet of paper.

Implied warranty A warranty on goods sold that implies that the goods are reasonably fit and of average quality.

Indexed-sequential access A method of storing and accessing data; has the advantages of both direct and sequential access.

Industrial espionage A computer crime in which a computer is used to steal trade secrets such as design or marketing plans from a company.

Inference engine The program in an expert system that uses ''if-then,'' or situation-action, logic rules and applies them to solve a problem.

Information The result of processing data by a computer into a form usable by people.

Information service An on-line computer service in which users can access large data bases of general-interest information. Information services are usually offered for a fee and require a password to gain entry.

Information system A computer system in which data are processed to become information.

Information system manager The person who plans and oversees all the information resources in an organization.

Ink-jet printer A type of nonimpact printer that forms characters on paper by spraying ink through an electrical field that arranges the ink particles in the form of characters.

Input (1) The process of entering and translating data into a machine-readable form that the computer can use. (2) The data before processing takes place.

Input device A peripheral device through which data are entered and transformed into machine-readable form, such as a keyboard or a mouse.

Input line   The place in a spreadsheet where data are typed before actually being entered into the program. The input line often allows the user to edit the data before it is entered.

Insert   A feature in application software that allows text to be entered into an existing file.

Insert mode   A mode in an application package where adding new text results in all text to the right being moved over to make room for the new text.

Instruction cycle   The fetch and decode steps in the process of performing an instruction.

Instruction set   The group of instructions that define the basic operations of the computer, i.e., the arithmetic, logical, storage, and retrieval functions.

Integrated circuit (IC)   A single, complete, electronic semiconductor circuit contained on a piece of silicon. Also called a microchip or chip.

Integrated family of programs   A group of independent application packages that share the same data and use common commands and functions.

Integrated operating environment   A program called a window manager, or integrator, that allows several different application packages to work concurrently and share data.

Integrated software   Application software packages that can share the same data.

Interactive program   A program that allows the user to interact with the computer during processing.

Interblock gap (IBG)   The blank section of tape that separates groups of records. It provides a space for the tape to attain the proper speed for reading or writing.

Interface   The connection between two or more devices such as the CPU and a peripheral device.

Internal direct-connect modem   Similar in function to the external direct-connect modem, but this modem has all the circuitry on one circuit board that fits into an expansion slot inside the computer.

Interpreter   A language-translator program that translates a high-level language program into machine code one line at a time. Each line is executed after it is translated.

Interrecord gap (IRG)   The section of magnetic tape between individual records that allows the tape to attain proper speed for reading or writing.

Joining   Also called merging; the process of combining records from two or more tables in a relational data-base management system.

Josephson junction   An electronic switching device operated at extremely low temperatures; much faster than a transistor and consumes less power.

Joystick   An input device that uses a lever to control cursor movement.

Jumping   A cursor movement method in a spreadsheet where the user may go directly to any designated cell.

Justification   A feature in application software that allows the user to move text flush to the right or left margins.

Kermit protocol   A type of protocol used on large-system computers for sending and receiving nontext files.

Keyboard   An input device, similar to a typewriter keyboard, that contains letters, numbers, special-character keys, keys that control cursor movement, and keys that can be programmed for other uses.

Key field   A field in a record that contains data that uniquely identifies that record in a file.

Keyword menu   A menu display in which the entire command or alternative action selection is listed.

Knowledge base   In an expert system, the collection of facts and the rules by which the facts relate.

Knowledge engineer   A person involved in the gathering of facts, rules, and knowledge for the knowledge base of an expert system.

Label   An alphanumeric designator that describes the contents of an area or device, such as a title or heading for a report generated by an application program, the text contents of a cell in a spreadsheet, or the contents of a diskette, among others.

Language-translator program   A program that translates a programming language into machine code for execution by the computer.

Laptop computer   A portable computer, usually small enough to fit in a briefcase. Named so because it is small enough to fit in a person's lap.

Large-scale integration (LSI)   The process of putting several thousand complete circuits on a single chip.

Laser printer   A nonimpact printer that produces images on paper by directing a laser beam onto a drum, leaving a negative charge in the form of a character to which positively charged toner powder will stick. The toner powder is transferred to paper as it rolls by the drum and is bonded to the paper by hot rollers.

Lasso   The process of identifying a graphic element that is to be manipulated by pointing directly to that object. Only the object itself, not the background, is chosen.

Layout form   A form used to detail computer screens and hard-copy reports before they are being implemented.

Letter-quality print   Print of fully formed characters, similar to typewriter print.

Light pen   A light-sensitive input device that when touched to the screen detects the presence or absence of light; used to select an entry or indicate position.

Line graph   A type of graph that represents data as a series of connected points on the graph; used to show trends and to emphasize movement and direction of change over a period of time.

Line printer   A printer with a print mechanism capable of printing an entire line at a time. Also called line-at-a-time printer.

LISP (LISt Processing)   A programming language created in the 1950s for writing artificial intelligence programs.

Local-area network (LAN)   A type of computer network where two or more computers of the same or different sizes are directly linked within a small well-defined area, such as a room, building, or closely placed buildings.

Log-on sequence   A series of keystrokes, account numbers, and passwords needed to access a computer or information service.

Logic error   A type of computer program error that is caused by improperly coding either individual statements or sequences. It will not stop program execution, but will produce inaccurate results.

Logic function   A function where numbers or conditions are compared—greater than, less than, equal to, not equal to, greater than or equal to, and less than or equal to.

Low-level language   A programming language, such as machine language or assembly; requires the programmer to have detailed knowledge of the internal workings of the computer.

Low-level manager   A manager who is involved with the day-to-day operational aspects of a business and mainly directs personnel to implement the tactical decisions of middle-level managers.

Machine language   A programming language that the computer uses; based on electronic states represented by the binary number system of 1s and 0s.

Macro   A file in some application programs that contains a series of previously recorded keystrokes or commands that can be executed with one or two keystrokes. A macro is used to increase the speed and efficiency of making repeated entries.

Magnetic core memory   Small magnetic cores (doughnut-shaped metal rings) with wires through them; cores can be magnetized in different directions to represent data. Preceded semiconductor memory.

Magnetic disk   A mylar (floppy diskette) or metallic (hard disk) platter on which electronic data can be stored. Suitable for both direct-access or sequential-access storage and retrieval of data.

Magnetic-ink character recognition (MICR)   A source data input technique in which data are represented by magnetic ink characters that can be read either by special machines directly into the computer or by humans.

Magnetic strips   The thin bands of magnetically encoded data found on the backs of many credit cards and automatic banking cards.

Magnetic tape   Iron-oxide coated strip of mylar used to magnetically store data; a sequential storage medium.

Mail merge   The process of combining two documents into one. For example, a form letter can be merged with a file containing names and addresses to personalize the letter.

Mainframe computer   A large-scale computer with processing capabilities greater than a minicomputer but less than a supercomputer.

Management information system (MIS)   A system that supplies managers with information to aid them in their decision-making responsibilities.

Manager   A person responsible for using available resources to achieve an organizational goal.

Manufacturing automation protocol (MAP)   A communication link, developed by General Motors, to allow different types of computers to communicate with each other.

Margin settings   A parameter that specifies the blank spaces around the left, right, top, and bottom of a document.

Matching   The comparing of data in one computer data base to another computer data base for a specific purpose. Used by some government agencies to detect discrepancies that might indicate fraud.

Megabyte   1,048,576 bytes.

Menu   In application software, a screen listing of commands, actions, or other alternatives from which the user may select. The menu selection may perform an action or bring up another menu. The menu presents the choices to the user from that particular point in the program.

Menu-driven   See *menu-orientation.*

Menu-orientation   The attribute of a software program that gives the user a list (menu) of choices on the screen to choose from. These choices may be in the form of commands or directions for input.

Message characters The start and stop bits of asynchronous transmission, and the synchronizing characters in synchronous transmission that signal when data are being sent and when the transmission is finished.

Microchip See *integrated circuit*.

Microcomputer A small computer with processing capabilities less than a minicomputer. Sometimes called a personal computer.

Microcomputer system The microcomputer and its associated peripheral hardware devices and software.

Microprocessor A single chip that contains both the arithmetic and logic unit (ALU), and the control unit; may also contain the primary storage unit.

Micro-to-mainframe link A method of connecting a microcomputer to a mainframe computer to enable the microcomputer user to share data and computing power of the larger system.

Micro-to-micro link A method of connecting microcomputers directly to one another so that they can share data. Allows computers using incompatible data formats to share data.

Microwave A type of data-communication channel; data are transmitted through the air as analog signals for reception by satellites or microwave transmitting stations.

Middle-level manager A manager who is generally concerned with short-term, tactical decisions and divides his or her time on planning, organizing, directing, and controlling.

Minicomputer A computer in the large-scale category but having less processing capabilities than a mainframe computer.

MIPS Millions of instructions per second. A measure of computer processing speed.

Mirror A graphics feature that allows a mirror image of an object to appear as the user draws the original.

Mixed cell reference A method of copying a formula in a spreadsheet where the formula is the same and each cell reference must be specified as either absolute or relative.

Mnemonics Alphabetic abbreviations used as memory aids.

Modelname An identifying name given to a spreadsheet file. Another term for file name.

Modem Acronym for modulator-demodulator. The device that converts signals from analog to digital form and from digital to analog form.

Modula–2 A version of Pascal with improvements in modularity, input and output, and file-handling capabilities.

Modulation The process of converting a digital signal to an analog signal.

Module A group of related processing instructions. Part of a larger program.

Monitor A television-like device used to display data.

Motherboard The name given to the main circuit board of a microcomputer; contains the microprocessor, memory chips, and chips that handle input, output, and storage.

Mouse A small input device that controls the position of the cursor on the screen. Two types are used: the electromechanical mouse, which uses an enclosed sphere on its underside rolled along a flat surface; and the optical mouse, which uses light beams to mark its position on a special tablet of grid lines.

Multiplexer The hardware device that performs the multiplexing process.

Multiplexing The process of combining the transmission from more than one device, character by character, into a single data stream and can be sent over a single communication channel.

Multipoint channel configuration A type of communication channel configuration where three or more devices are connected together and share the same communication channel.

Multiprocessing A method of processing using more than one central processing unit where more than one set of instructions (or programs) can be executed at a time.

Multiprocessing operating system An operating system that allows a multiple CPU computer to execute more than one program at a time.

Multiuser data manager A data manager that can be accessed by more than one user at a time.

Multiuser microcomputer system A microcomputer system to which more than one person has access from separate computer terminals.

Narrow-band channel A communication channel, such as a telegraph line, that transmits data at 40 to 100 bits per second.

Nassi-Shneiderman chart A structured flowchart, developed by Isaac Nassi and Ben Shneiderman, that uses various shaped boxes to represent the sequence, selection, and repetition control structures to illustrate the processing steps of a program.

Natural language processing The ability of a computer to understand and translate a natural language, such as English, to commands to perform a specific operation.

Near-letter quality print   Print made from dots rather than fully formed characters; approaches the appearance of letter-quality print.

Near-typeset quality print   Print similar in quality to that produced by commercial typesetting equipment; produced by laser printers.

Network data-base structure   A type of data-base structure in which each parent can have more than one child, and also each child may have more than one parent.

Node   In a computer network system, each computer or device.

Nonimpact printer   A type of printer that produces characters without physically striking the paper.

Nonprocedural language   A programming language that describes the task to be accomplished without specifying how.

Null modem   A cable that eliminates the need for a modem when transferring data between two computers located near each other.

Octal system   The base 8 numbering system using the digits 0 through 7.

Off-line   (1) Refers to an operation or a device in which data are not directly transferred to or from a computer. (2) Refers to the condition when no communication link is established.

One-letter menu   A type of on-screen menu in which only the first letter of each selection is listed.

On-line   (1) Refers to an operation or a device in which data are directly transferred to or from a computer. (2) Refers to the condition when a computer is linked to and communicating with another computer.

Operating system (OS)   A set of programs that controls and supervises a computer system's hardware and provides services to programmers and users.

Optical-bar recognition (OBR)   A data input method that reads and interprets bar codes.

Optical card   A small card that stores data on a strip of special material similar to a magnetic strip. However, the data on an optical card are encoded by a laser rather than magnetically as with the magnetic strip.

Optical-character recognition (OCR)   The most sophisticated form of optical recognition; recognizes letters, numbers, and other optical character sets by their shapes in much the same way as the human eye does.

Optical laser disk   A type of storage medium on which data are stored and read by a laser. Optical laser disks have much higher data densities than their magnetic disk counterparts.

Optical-mark recognition (OMR)   A data input method in which a series of pen or pencil marks on a special form are scanned and their position is translated into machine-readable code. For example, computer-scored test answer sheets.

Optical tape   A storage medium similar in appearance to magnetic tape, but data are stored by optical-laser techniques.

Optoelectronics   The combination of both electronic and optical technology for data processing and communication applications.

Outliner   A word-processor feature that helps the user to organize ideas by representing them as headings or subheadings that can be rearranged in a logical pattern.

Output   (1) The process of translating machine-readable code into a form readable by humans or other machines. (2) The result of data processing.

Output device   A peripheral device that translates machine-readable codes into a form that can be used by humans or another machine.

Pacing   In communications, the feature that allows the user to designate the length of time between sending data. Often used when two communicating devices send and receive data at different rates.

Page break   An application-software parameter that controls the number of lines to a page. After the number of lines is reached, additional text will be automatically placed on the next page.

Page-oriented   A method of word processing where only one page of a document is loaded from secondary storage into primary storage. Pages are swapped between secondary storage and primary storage.

Painting and drawing program   A microcomputer graphics program that allows the user to "paint" an image by using an input device, such as a mouse, as the brush. The user may also draw, fill shapes, and change color and texture.

Pan   A feature of a graphics package that moves the entire graphic content on the screen from side-to-side, allowing the user to create and view images beyond the width of the computer screen.

Parallel conversion   The process of converting from an old system to a new system by running the new system simultaneously with the old system to allow for direct comparison.

Parallel interface   A type of interface that transmits data one byte at a time.

Parallel processing   A data-processing method in which a computer accesses several instructions from the same program at once and works on them at the same time using multiple CPUs. Much faster than traditional serial processing techniques.

Parent Also called the root; the top or main level of data in a data-base structure.

Pascal A high-level language originally designed to teach structured-programming concepts. Suited for both file processing and mathematical applications.

Password An alphanumeric code that restricts access to protected data only to those with knowledge of the correct password.

Peripheral device Any hardware item that is attached to the main unit of the computer, such as an input or output device or a secondary-storage device.

Personal computer A microcomputer that is used by and under the control of one person.

PERT Program Evaluation Review Technique. A diagram that shows the relationship between each project task in addition to the timing of the events.

Phased conversion The process of implementing only part of the new system at one time.

Picture library A predrawn collection of shapes or objects a user can select from to place in a drawing.

Pie graph A type of graph that uses a circle (pie) divided into segments to show the relationship of data to the whole.

Pilot conversion The process of converting from an old system by installing the entire new system, but using it in only part of the organization.

Piracy The illegal copying of copyrighted computer programs.

Pixel The smallest part of a display screen that can be individually controlled.

Plotter An output device especially designed to produce hard copy of graphics.

Point-of-sale (POS) terminal A device that reads data at the source of a transaction and immediately translates them into usable information.

Point-to-point channel configuration A type of communication channel configuration that directly connects a computer to a single device giving them sole use of the channel.

Polling A method of determining which device needs to access the communication channel. The main computer checks, or polls, each device on the channel one at a time to see if it has any data to send. Only one device can use the channel at a time.

Port A socket on a computer where a peripheral device can be connected.

Portable computer A microcomputer, but one small enough to be easily carried from place-to-place.

Predictive report A report used to predict or spot trends. Usually used by top-level managers. The report contains an in-depth analysis of the data.

Presentation graphics Graphics suitable for a formal presentation.

Prewritten application package A software application package written by a person or group; ready to use and made available for users to purchase.

Primary storage unit Also known as primary memory; the internal storage unit of the computer.

Printer An output device that produces hard copy, usually consisting of text but may contain graphics.

Printing The process of producing hard-copy output.

Privacy As related to computer data, the right of control over one's personal data.

Privacy Act of 1974 Established that the federal government has no right to keep secret files about any citizen; allows individuals to find out what data about them have been collected, how they are used, among other provisions.

Procedural language A programming language that specifies how a task is accomplished.

Process control The process of monitoring and controlling an operation.

Processing The steps the computer takes to convert data into information.

Program A series of instructions that tells the computer what to do.

Program development process The process of developing a computer program; consists of the following steps: (a) defining the problem; (b) designing the algorithm; (c) coding the program; (d) testing and debugging the program; (e) implementing the program and training the users; and (f) maintaining and updating the program. Documentation is maintained throughout all six steps.

Program flowchart A flowchart that graphically shows the processing steps of a computer program.

Programmable controller A computer-controlled unit consisting of a microprocessor, input and output modules, and a power supply, used to monitor and control machinery and processes.

Programmable read-only memory (PROM) A type of memory that can be programmed only once and then cannot be further altered.

Program maintenance The process of correcting errors that are discovered in a program after it has been installed.

Programmer The person who writes the instructions, or code, that tell the computer what to do.

Programming language A set of written symbols that instruct the computer to perform specific tasks.

Projecting In a relational data-base management

system, the process in which a subset of the larger table is created with only the needed rows and columns.

Project management team An assembled group of users, analysts, designers, programmers, and other specialists; led by a project manager.

PROLOG (PROgramming LOgic) A programming language created for writing programs for expert systems.

Prompt line A line that appears when using a software package that asks, or prompts, the user for a response. It may be posed as a question or be a listing of choices.

Protocol A set of rules and procedures for transmitting and receiving data so different devices can communicate with one another.

Prototype A smaller version of the proposed system, used to test the basic operation and suitability of the system.

Pseudocode A type of code that uses English-like phrases to describe the processing steps of a program or module.

Public domain program A computer program that is not protected by copyright law; available for public use. Also called freeware.

Punched card A rigid paper card that uses patterns of punched holes to represent data.

Query-by-example A query language style in which the user inputs the query conditions in the desired fields.

Random-access memory (RAM) A type of memory into which data and programs can be written and from which data and programs can be read. Data stored in RAM are erased when the computer's power is shut off.

Range of cells In a spreadsheet, a method of selecting specific cells by identifying the upper-left cell and the lower-right cell. Permits large blocks of cells to be manipulated together.

Read-only memory (ROM) A type of memory, the contents of which are entered during manufacturing. Contents can only be read; they are permanent and cannot be changed.

Read/write head The electromechanical component of the tape drive that performs the actual writing or reading of data on or from magnetic tape.

Reading The process of retrieving data from primary storage or from a secondary storage medium.

Ready/entry mode A mode of operation where a spreadsheet program indicates it is ready to receive information. When a character is entered, the program automatically switches to the entry mode.

Real-time operating system An operating system that allows the computer to respond to input immediately, or as soon as required.

Real-time processing A method of processing where the results are provided fast enough to control or modify a process or provide immediate answers to queries.

Record A collection of related data items. The data items are particular to that record, but fall under the general heading of the file name.

Reduce and expand In a graphics package, the process of changing the size of an object. The object may either be reduced or enlarged.

Reel-to-reel tape A form of magnetic tape usually one-half inch wide, wound on reels. Typically used with large computer systems for providing large amounts of secondary storage at a comparatively modest cost.

Register A temporary holding place for data or instructions that are to be worked on immediately; part of the CPU.

Relational data-base structure A type of database structure in which data do not rely on parent-child relationships. Data are grouped in tables, and relationships are structured as they are needed.

Relative cell reference A method of copying a formula in a spreadsheet where the formula is the same but the cells referenced in that formula are different.

Removable cartridge A hard-disk storage system that utilizes a cartridge containing one or more hard disks; cartridge can be removed from the hard-disk drive and replaced with another cartridge at any time.

Repetition control structure Also called looping; a programming control structure that allows a series of instructions to be executed more than once without having to be recoded.

Report generator A type of fourth-generation language that allows data to be extracted from a data base and formatted into a report.

Resolution The quality of the monitor's screen, measured by the number of pixels the screen contains.

Ring network A computer network arrangement where each computer or device is connected in a closed loop by a single communication channel. Communication flows through each device in the ring between the source and destination of the data.

Robot A reprogrammable machine that can be instructed to do a variety of tasks; often used to perform dangerous or boring tasks.

Robotics   The area of study dealing with the design, construction, and operation of robots.

Rotate   A feature of a graphics package that allows the user to turn (rotate) an object on the screen.

Row   In a spreadsheet, the numeric ordering from top to bottom, that along with the alphabetic column designation, locates the position of a cell.

RPG (Report Program Generator)   A programming language designed for producing reports and processing files.

Run-time error   An error that causes a program to stop executing.

Salami slicing   A type of computer crime; data manipulation in which a small amount of money is skimmed from many accounts and put into one central account.

Scatter graph   A type of graph in which two sets of data points are plotted; used to show the correlation, if any, between the data.

Scheduled report   A report issued at regular intervals containing data rather than analysis. Usually used by low- and middle-level managers.

Schema   The conceptual or logical design that shows the relationship among data elements in a data base.

Screen form   A layout form created for the purpose of defining the position of data fields and providing an entry point for the data in a data manager.

Scroll   A feature that allows movement of the edit window to create or view text that is outside the display screen. Scrolling can take place horizontally or vertically.

Search and replace   An application-software feature that allows the user to look for a word or phrase in a file. When the word or phrase is found, the user may be prompted as to whether or not it is to be replaced, or it may be automatically replaced, depending on the option selected.

Searching   The process of locating and retrieving data stored in a file.

Second-generation computers   Computers developed and used from 1959-1965, which used transistors to control internal operations.

Secondary storage   Refers to computer memory external to the computer that is typically used for long-term storage or large quantities of data or programs.

Sectors   A pie-shaped division of each magnetic-disk track which further identifies the storage location of data.

Select   The process of identifying a graphic element to be manipulated by drawing a rectangle around that image. The object, background area, and any other objects contained in the rectangle will be selected.

Selecting   The process of retrieving only certain records in a table in a relational data-base management system.

Selection control structure   A programming control structure that selects a processing option based on the result of the decision criteria.

Semiconductor memory   A memory type in which electronic circuits are "etched" onto silicon wafers.

Sequence control structure   A programming control structure that executes statements in order, one after another.

Sequential access   A method of storing and accessing data in a row, or one after another. To access a record, all preceding records must be read first.

Serial interface   A type of interface that transmits data one bit at a time.

Service program   An operating system program that provides a service, such as a utility or language-translator program to the user.

Shareware   Software programs available to the public; the authors sometimes request a donation if you use their programs.

Shell   In an expert system, a general-purpose inference engine and a skeleton of the knowledge base into which users can add their own special data.

Simplex mode   A method of transferring data over a communication channel in which data can be transmitted in only one direction. Simplex mode devices can transmit or receive but not both.

Simulation   A method of creating computerized models of "real-life" situations; also a method of computer instruction.

Single-program operating system   A type of operating system that allows only one program to execute at a time.

Slide show   In a graphics program, a feature that allows individual graphics files to appear on the screen in a predetermined order for a predetermined amount of time, similar to a slide projector and slides.

Soft copy   A form of volatile output, usually a screen display.

Software   The instructions that direct the operations of a computer.

Sorting   The process of arranging data in numeric or alphabetic sequence. This may be done either in ascending or descending order.

Source data entry   The data-entry process wherein data generated at a source are entered directly into a computer in machine-readable form.

Specialized application package An application package that is developed for a specific use; for example, a payroll package.

Specialized common carrier A type of common carrier that offers only a limited number of services and usually services only a limited area.

Special-purpose computer A computer that is dedicated (modified for one job) to a specific task or application.

Spelling checker Also called a dictionary; a word-processor program that locates misspelled words or words not in its dictionary.

Spreadsheet A paper form, divided into rows and columns, that can be used to keep track of and manipulate numeric data.

Spreadsheet analysis The process by which new values may be entered and the spreadsheet recalculated to view the results.

Standard-quality print Print made from dots but of lower quality than near-letter quality print; suitable for most informal applications.

Star network A computer network arrangement where each device is connected to one centralized computer. All communications must be routed through the central host computer.

Status line May be one or more lines, located at the top or bottom of the display screen, that provides information about the current file or operation in progress.

Structure chart A design aid in which the purpose of a module, the relationship to other modules, and the overall program logic are shown.

Structured programming A method of writing computer programs that emphasizes the systematic design, development, and management of the software-development process. This type of programming increases programmer productivity, improves the quality of the programs, and makes them easier to read.

Structured query language A data-base query language style that uses commands in a structured format to set the query conditions.

Structured walk-through A procedure in which the analyst discusses or "walks through" the design of the computer program with members of the chief programmer team.

Subschema A subset of a schema that defines the relationship among data elements within a specified portion of a data base.

Superchip Larger than many chips and with significantly more circuitry; designed for increased processing capabilities.

Supercomputer The most powerful type of com-

puter; used primarily by government agencies or organizations that process vast quantities of data.

Superimpose A graphics feature that allows the user to place one object over another without erasing either one.

Supermicrocomputer A high-performance microcomputer that contains greater processing capabilities than a standard desktop microcomputer.

Supervisor program Also called monitor, executive, or kernel; the main control program in an operating system.

Synchronous transmission A method of data transmission in which blocks of characters are sent in timed sequences. The block of characters is marked by special synchronizing characters. It is much faster than asynchronous transmission.

Syntax The rules by which a programming language is governed.

Syntax error A type of error that occurs when the rules of the programming language are violated when coding a computer program.

System The combination of people, devices, and methods interrelated for the purpose of achieving a common goal. These devices and methods often involve computers and software.

System analysis The process of analyzing an information system to ascertain whether or not it meets the user's current or projected needs.

System analyst A person who works with a user to determine his or her data processing needs.

System clock The portion of the control unit that sends out electrical pulses which are used to synchronize all tasks in the CPU; instrumental in determining speed of a processor.

System design The process of detailing the physical layout of a system, such as describing the hardware, software, and operating procedures. This may also include modifying the logical design of the proposed system.

System designer A person who modifies an old system or designs a new one based on the user's information needs.

System development The process of creating a system from the physical descriptions detailed in the system design.

System flowchart A type of chart used to graphically illustrate the physical requirements of a system, such as hardware devices and storage media needed to implement the logical design.

System implementation The process of testing the new system, converting from an old system to the new one, and training the users on the new system.

System librarian A person who compiles and maintains documentation for use by other personnel.

System life cycle The life span of an information system. The life cycle consists of: (a) system analysis; (b) system design; (c) system development; (d) system implementation; and (e) system maintenance.

System maintenance The ongoing process of monitoring and evaluating a system.

System operator (sysop) In an electronic network, a person in charge of operating a bulletin board system.

System resident device A device, such as a disk or tape, on which control and service programs are stored when not being used by the computer.

System software The programs that direct and control the operations of a computer system. An operating system is an example of system software.

Tab setting An application-software feature that sets indentions in a file, and aligns columns and decimal numbers.

Tactile sensing Refers to the sense of touch possessed by robots.

Tape drive An input/output device using a read/write head to read data from magnetic tape and write data on magnetic tape.

Telecommunication Also called teleprocessing; the process of using communication facilities, such as the telephone system or microwave relays, to send data to and from devices.

Telecommuting A method of working where a person uses a computer and a communication channel to link with a remote office computer. With a personal computer (or terminal) connected to the company's computer, the off-site employee can communicate with the office.

Telemarketing A marketing technique that uses the telephone lines and computers to reach potential markets, and manage accounts—often through prerecorded messages.

Template A screen form created in an application program that contains only those entries that do not change. A template may be used as an input form as well as an output form.

Terminal The combination of a monitor and a keyboard used to view output and to enter and check input; does not contain a processing unit. Also called a workstation.

Text editing The process of changing, adding, deleting, or otherwise altering text after it has been entered into a document.

Text graphics The method of creating a graphic image, such as a shape or line, with alphanumeric and other special characters.

Thermal-transfer printer A type of nonimpact printer that uses heat to transfer ink to paper to form the characters.

Thesaurus A software program that provides alternative words (synonyms) for a given word in a document.

Third-generation computers Computers developed and used from 1965-1971, which first used integrated circuits (ICs).

Time bomb A method of sabotaging a computer program so that it will destroy itself after a predetermined time or action occurs.

Time sharing A technique that allows more than one person access to the same computer at the same time.

Time-sharing operating system An operating system that allows more than one user to access a single computer system on a timed basis.

Time stealing A computer crime in which time on the computer is used without proper authorization, thus stealing time.

Titles (1) A feature in a graphics package that allows the user to enter text information, such as a title, to the drawing. (2) A feature in a spreadsheet package that freezes row and column titles so they remain stationary as the spreadsheet is scrolled.

Top-down design A structured-programming design concept that starts with the major functions and divides them into subfunctions until the problem has been divided as much as possible.

Top-level manager A manager who is involved in making long-range, strategic decisions. Most of a top-level manager's time is spent on planning and organizing.

Topology The method in which a computer or device is connected in a computer network.

Touch pad An input device that uses a pressure sensitive pad to record data input where the pad is touched.

Touch screen An input device that allows the user to enter data or show position by "touching" the screen with a finger or other object.

Trackball An input device that uses the movement of a hard sphere rotated by hand to control cursor movement.

Tracks The concentric circles of a magnetic disk where data are stored. Used by the computer to identify where data are stored.

Transaction processing A method of on-line processing in which data are processed, and files are updated immediately.

Transcriptive data entry The process of data entry wherein data generated at the source are written on a form that must be later transcribed to another medium that can be read and interpreted by a computer.

Transferring   The process of sharing a data file created in one application program with the file in another application program without having to convert the file.

Transistor   A semiconductor device that controls the flow of electricity.

Trap door   A special password created by the developer of a program; allows access to the program but its existence remains undocumented.

Tree network   A computer network arrangement where devices are linked in a tree-like manner through branches.

Tutorial   A method of computerized instruction where an idea is presented, then the understanding of that idea is tested. The computer may then explain incorrect answers.

Undo   A feature in application software that allows the user to cancel the action of the previous instruction.

Uniprocessing   A method of processing using only one central processing unit.

Updating   The process in which existing data in a file or data base can be changed in a record.

Uploading   The process of reading data from a user's disk and sending it to another computer.

User   A person or group of people who use a computer system.

User-friendly   A relative term generally meaning that a particular computer or software package is easy to learn and use.

User group   A formal or informal organization of users organized for the purpose of problem solving or exchanging software or hardware information.

User-written application package   An application package that was designed and written by the intended user for a specific need.

Utility program   A program that performs common or routine functions on the computer for the user such as preparing a disk for use and saving or copying a program.

Vacuum tubes   Devices, from which most of the air has been removed, that are used to control the flow of electricity; the main component in first-generation computers.

Validating   The process of checking data for appropriateness and accuracy as it is entered.

Validation   A method of checking data accuracy by programming a computer to accept only a certain range or kind of data entry.

Value-added carrier   A type of carrier that specializes in leasing services from common carriers in which extra or added services are provided.

Values   Any number or formula that is used to represent data in a program.

Variable-length record   A record in which spaces are allotted only to actual data. This eliminates the storage of empty spaces.

Verification   A method of checking data accuracy by comparing it against a known source.

Very large-scale integration (VLSI)   The process of putting several hundred thousand complete circuits on a single chip.

Videotext   An interactive computer information service that can transmit monochrome text as well as colors and graphics. A service in which computers and phones are used for two-way communication to order goods and services.

Virtual-machine (VM) operating system   An operating system that can run several operating systems at a time. Allows each workstation or terminal to choose the operating system applicable to its particular task.

Virtual memory   A computer storage scheme in which data are automatically swapped in and out of primary storage as they are needed, giving the appearance of expanded primary storage.

Virtual-storage operating system   An operating system that makes use of a secondary-storage device as an extension of primary storage.

Visual table of contents   A structure chart in which each module is numbered for easy reference.

Voice-band channel   A communication channel, such as a telephone line, that transmits data at 110 to 9600 bits per second.

Voice mail   A form of electronic mail that sends messages in the form of a computerized human voice.

Voice recognition   The capability of a computer to accept input in the form of the spoken word.

Voice synthesis   The capability of a computer to respond in a simulated human voice.

Volatile   In computers, refers to the loss of data from RAM when power is shut off.

Wide-area network   A computer network where the computers are geographically dispersed.

Window   A separate, defined area on the computer screen that can be used to display data, menus, or another software package.

Wire cable   A type of data communication channel; includes telegraph lines, telephone lines, and coaxial cables.

Word   The number of adjacent bits that can be stored and manipulated by the computer as a unit.

Word processing   The activity of entering, viewing, storing, retrieving, editing, rearranging, and printing text material using a computer and a word processor.

Word-processing system   The combination of hardware and software used when performing computerized word processing.

Word processor   An application package that creates, edits, manipulates, and prints text. Generally used for writing documents such as letters and reports.

Wordwrap   A word processor feature that automatically continues a sentence on the next line without the user pressing the return key at the end of that line. Any words that extend past the right margin are moved down to the next line.

Worksheet   The blank spreadsheet form used for entering and organizing numeric data. A paper form in a noncomputerized spreadsheet and the screen form in an electronic spreadsheet.

Workstation   See *terminal*.

Writing   The process of entering data into primary storage or placing data onto a storage medium.

Xmodem protocol   A public-domain, data-transfer protocol used with microcomputers to send and receive nontext files.

XON/XOFF protocol   A type of protocol that enables the software to control the transmitting of data. An XOFF signal instructs the transmitting computer to stop sending data. The XON signal instructs the computer to begin sending data.

Zoom   A feature of graphics packages that allows the user to enlarge a specified area of a drawing for viewing or to pull back and view the entire scene.

Index

Boldfaced page numbers indicate definitions.
Italicized page numbers indicate illustrations.

WE VALUE YOUR OPINION—PLEASE SHARE IT WITH US

Merrill Publishing and our authors are most interested in your reactions to this textbook. Did it serve you well in the course? If it did, what aspects of the text were most helpful? If not, what didn't you like about it? Your comments will help us to write and develop better textbooks. We value your opinions and thank you for your help.

Text Title _____ Edition _____

Author(s) _____ _____

Your Name (optional) _____

Address _____ _____ _____ _____ ____

City _____ State _____ Zip _____

School _____ _____

Course Title _____ _____

Instructor's Name _____ _____ _____

Your Major _____ _____

Your Class Rank _____ Freshman _____ Sophomore _____ Junior _____ Senior

_____ Graduate Student

Were you required to take this course? _____ Required _____ Elective

Length of Course? _____ Quarter _____ Semester

1. Overall, how does this text compare to other texts you've used?

_____ Superior _____ Better Than Most _____ Average _____ Poor

2. Please rate the text in the following areas:

	Superior	Better Than Most	Average	Poor
Author's Writing Style	_____	_____	_____	_____
Readability	_____	_____	_____	_____
Organization	_____	_____	_____	_____
Accuracy	_____	_____	_____	_____
Layout and Design	_____	_____	_____	_____
Illustrations/Photos/Tables	_____	_____	_____	_____
Examples	_____	_____	_____	_____
Problems/Exercises	_____	_____	_____	_____
Topic Selection	_____	_____	_____	_____
Currentness of Coverage	_____	_____	_____	_____
Explanation of Difficult Concepts	_____	_____	_____	_____
Match-up with Course Coverage	_____	_____	_____	_____
Applications to Real Life	_____	_____	_____	_____

3. Circle those chapters you especially liked:
   1 2 3 4 5 6 7 8 9 10 11 12 13 14 15 16 17 18 19 20
   What was your favorite chapter? _____
   Comments:

4. Circle those chapters you liked least:
   1 2 3 4 5 6 7 8 9 10 11 12 13 14 15 16 17 18 19 20
   What was your least favorite chapter? _____
   Comments:

5. List any chapters your instructor did not assign. _____

6. What topics did your instructor discuss that were not covered in the text?_____

_____

7. Were you required to buy this book? _____ Yes _____ No

   Did you buy this book new or used? _____ New _____ Used

   If used, how much did you pay? _____

   Do you plan to keep or sell this book? _____ Keep _____ Sell

   If you plan to sell the book, how much do you expect to receive? _____

   Should the instructor continue to assign this book? _____ Yes _____ No

8. Please list any other learning materials you purchased to help you in this course (e.g., study guide, lab manual).

_____

9. What did you like most about this text? _____

_____

10. What did you like least about this text? _____

_____

11. General comments:

May we quote you in our advertising? _____ Yes _____ No

Please mail to: Boyd Lane
                  College Division, Research Department
                  Box 508
                  1300 Alum Creek Drive
                  Columbus, Ohio 43216

Thank you!